The Lonergan Reader

EDITED BY MARK D. MORELLI AND ELIZABETH A. MORELLI

Bernard Lonergan's work is both original and comprehensive. It can be grasped only by working one's way slowly and carefully through his major writings. In order to make Lonergan's unique contribution to philosophy and theology accessible to students and teachers, the editors of *The Lonergan Reader* have brought together in a single volume selections that represent the depth and breadth of his thought. The full range of Lonergan's basic philosophical positions, the key transitional moments in the development of his thought, and the main elements of his innovative theological method are thoroughly represented.

The Lonergan Reader includes an abridgment of Lonergan's massive foundational work, *Insight,* and extensive selections from his last major work, *Method in Theology.* In addition, the collection contains the complete texts of several articles that expanded and transformed his original positions, as well as a broad range of shorter selections. The volume not only highlights Lonergan's essential philosophical writings, but also reveals the larger cultural and theological dimensions of his work.

MARK D. MORELLI is a professor in the Department of Philosophy at Loyola Marymount University. He is author of *Philosophy's Place in Culture: A Model.* ELIZABETH A. MORELLI is an associate professor in the Department of Philosophy, Loyola Marymount University. She is the author of *Anxiety: A Study of the Affectivity of Moral Consciousness.* The Morellis edited the first edition of Bernard Lonergan's *Understanding and Being* and collaborated on the more recent augmented and revised edition.

D1601373

Classical culture cannot be jettisoned without being replaced; and what replaces it cannot but run counter to classical expectations. There is bound to be formed a solid right that is determined to live in a world that no longer exists. There is bound to be formed a scattered left, captivated by now this, now that new development, exploring now this and now that new possibility. But what will count is a perhaps not numerous center, big enough to be at home in both the old and the new, painstaking enough to work out one by one the transitions to be made, strong enough to refuse half measures and insist on complete solutions even though it has to wait.

– Lonergan, 'Dimensions of Meaning'

The Lonergan Reader

Edited by Mark D. Morelli
and Elizabeth A. Morelli

B
29
.L592x
1997
West

•A15048 824447

UNIVERSITY OF TORONTO PRESS
Toronto Buffalo London

© University of Toronto Press Incorporated 1997
Toronto Buffalo London

Printed in Canada

ISBN 0-8020-4251-1 (cloth)
ISBN 0-8020-7648-3 (paper)

Printed on acid-free paper

Lonergan Studies

Canadian Cataloguing in Publication Data

Lonergan, Bernard J.F. (Bernard Joseph Francis),
  1904–1984
  The Lonergan reader

(Lonergan studies)
Includes bibliographical references and index.
ISBN 0-8020-4251-1 (bound)   ISBN 0-8020-7648-3 (pbk.)

1. Critical realism.   2. Knowledge, Theory of.
3. Theology – History – 20th century.   4. Catholic Church.
I. Morelli, Mark Denis, 1948–   .   II. Morelli,
Elizabeth Aileen, 1948–   .   III. Title.   IV. Series.

BX891.L642 1997   191   C96-931483-3

The editors acknowledge with gratitude permission to reprint portions of
Doctrinal Pluralism from Marquette University Press and permission to
reprint all other selections in this volume from the Bernard Lonergan Estate
and the Lonergan Research Institute, Regis College, University of Toronto.

University of Toronto Press acknowledges the financial assistance to its
publishing program of the Canada Council and the Ontario Arts Council.

Contents

Contents

THE LONERGAN READER

Introduction

The view of human life and culture developed by Bernard Lonergan, widely regarded as one of the most significant thinkers of the twentieth century, can be grasped thoroughly only by working one's way carefully through his major works. Lonergan himself suggested that the 'self-appropriation' he promotes throughout his writings 'occurs slowly, and, usually, only through a struggle with some such book as *Insight*,' his enormous study of human understanding.[1] Still, one may obtain from a volume of selections a broad familiarity with Lonergan's aims, basic positions, and major achievements, and an appreciation of his contribution to the solution of long-standing and more recent philosophical, theological, and cultural problems. The reader of this volume will be introduced to some of Lonergan's most central ideas: his scientific worldview of emergent probability, which is neither Aristotelian nor mechanist determinist, neither Darwinian nor indeterminist; his solution to the problem of objectivity in knowing and his grounding of objectivity in authentic subjectivity; his analysis of bias and sociocultural decline; his account of human consciousness as polymorphic; his analysis of history in terms of stages in the development of human meaning; and his proposal of a new method for theology, consisting of eight functional specialties, grounded in the self-transcending subject. In short, the reader will be introduced to Lonergan's 'critical realism,' to a standpoint which Lonergan described as 'at once methodical, critical, and comprehensive.'[2]

1 *Method in Theology*, 7 n. 2.
2 *Insight*, 6.

Bernard Lonergan: A Biographical Sketch

> To learn thoroughly is a vast undertaking that calls for relentless perse-
> verance. To strike out on a new line and become more than a week-end
> celebrity calls for years in which one's living is more or less constantly
> absorbed in the effort to understand ...[3]

Bernard Lonergan was born in Buckingham, Quebec, on December 17,
1904. Buckingham, a mill town on the Lièvre River, was predominantly French-speaking despite its very British name. Bernard's father,
Gerald, was trained in engineering and worked as a surveyor, map-
ping Canada's western provinces. His mother, Josephine Wood, was
the daughter of a millwright in Buckingham. Bernard enjoyed winter
sports and river rafting in the summer with his two younger brothers.
He read his first book, *Treasure Island*, at the age of six. As a child he
attended St Michael's, a local school run by the Christian Brothers,
whom Lonergan later credited with placing rigorous academic
demands on the students.

At the age of thirteen, Lonergan went off to Loyola College, a Jesuit
high school and junior college in Montreal. In later years he recalled
his first impression of his teachers: 'The Jesuits were the best-educated
people I had met.'[4] He complained, however, of Loyola's lax academic
standards in comparison with his elementary school. In his first year at
Loyola he completed the equivalent of three years of high school
instruction. In his second year he fell ill with a life-threatening infec-
tion, missing a half year of courses, but he was able to pass his year-
end exams. Lonergan later remarked that while he was at Loyola, he
had a notion of what understanding was and 'acquired great respect
for intelligence.'[5]

In the summer of 1922, at age seventeen, Lonergan entered the Jesuit
novitiate at Guelph, Ontario. He did not consider his original decision
to join the Jesuits to be remarkable: 'I went out to the Sault to make a
retreat, an election, and I decided on the street-car on the way out.'[6] Of
more interest to him, when he looked back over his life, was the fact

---

3 Ibid., 210.
4 P. Lambert, C. Tansey, and C. Going, eds., *Caring about Meaning: Patterns in the Life of
  Bernard Lonergan* (Montreal: Thomas More Institute, 1982), 135.
5 Ibid., 142.
6 Ibid., 131.

that he persevered in his religious vocation. The next four years at Guelph were spent in strictly regulated spiritual training and studying the classics in Greek and Latin, mathematics, English, French, and elocution, which entailed writing and delivering sermons in Latin and Greek.

The normal course of Jesuit training included the novitiate and juniorate years, followed by formal study of philosophy, a period of spiritual formation and work called 'regency,' and then formal study of theology. Lonergan followed the normal course. In 1926, his novitiate and juniorate completed, Lonergan was sent to study philosophy at Heythrop College, Oxford, which had just been founded for the Jesuits of England. Lonergan described the state of philosophy there as predominantly Suarezian. All of the textbooks were of German origin. He was to remark that he had to unlearn this type of philosophical training. It was during his time at Heythrop that Lonergan predicted that 'the theory of knowledge is what is going to interest me most of all.'[7] During this time, too, he developed a strong interest in John Henry Newman's *Grammar of Assent*: 'I was looking for someone who had some common sense, and knew what he was talking about. And what was Newman talking about? About judgment as assent; and real apprehension and notional apprehension, notional assent and real assent. He was answering the liberal view that all judgments are more or less probable but nothing is certain. And he could give examples.'[8] While at Heythrop he wrote essays for the student journal, the *Blandyke Papers*, which reflected his early interest in cognitional theory. These included 'The Form of Mathematical Inference,' 'The Syllogism,' and 'True Judgment and Science.' But Lonergan did not concentrate solely on philosophy. He also pursued a degree at the University of London – in 1930 he was awarded a BA in Greek, Latin, French, and mathematics – and he developed a special fondness for the writings of Lewis Carroll and G.K. Chesterton.

For his regency Lonergan was sent to Loyola College, Montreal, where he taught from 1930 to 1933. He apparently experienced a crisis in his religious vocation at this time owing to a number of strains, in particular the imposition by his superior of an extra year of teaching duty: 'I had regarded myself as one condemned to sacrifice his real

7 Cited by F.E. Crowe in *Lonergan* (Collegeville, MN: The Liturgical Press, 1972), 14.
8 *Caring*, 14; see also 46.

interests.'[9] In addition to his normal responsibilities, Lonergan found
time to continue his private studies. He devoted his free time to reading St Augustine and Plato's early dialogues. He was especially influenced by *Plato's Doctrine of Ideas*, by J.A. Stewart. Lonergan reflected in
1973, 'From Stewart I learned that Plato was a methodologist, that his
ideas were what the scientist seeks to discover.'[10] After his study of
Plato, he proceeded to read St Thomas's *Summa*, and he 'began to suspect that St Thomas was not nearly as bad as he was painted.'[11] He was
also influenced by Christopher Dawson's *The Age of the Gods*, which
introduced him to the anthropological, as distinct from the classicist,
notion of culture.

   In 1933, Lonergan was heartened by his superior's decision to send
him to the Gregorian University in Rome for his formal theological
studies. His letters at the time reflect his love of Italy and its people:
'Am still breathless with enthusiasm for Rome ... Italians the soul of
naturalness.'[12] In the first years of his theological studies, Lonergan
was increasingly exposed to the thought of St Thomas, yet his primary
concern was with issues in the philosophy of culture and history and
politico-economic theory. He read both Hegel and Marx during the
thirties, and the former had a lasting impact on his thought. His writings of this period reveal his deep concern with historical development
and the socio-economic condition. His paper 'Pantôn Anakephalaiôsis'
('The Restoration of All Things'), dated 1935, explores the issue of
human solidarity across time. Lonergan was to remark in his epilogue
to *Insight* that he had spent 'years reaching up to the mind of Aquinas,'
but it would be a mistake to assume that he was originally a Thomist.[13]
'My philosophical development was from Newman to Augustine,
from Augustine to Plato, and then I was introduced to Thomism
through a Greek, Stephanos Stephanou, who had his philosophic formation under Maréchal. It was in talking to him that I came first to
understand St Thomas, and see that there was something there.'[14]

   On July 25, 1936, Lonergan was ordained to the priesthood in Rome.
He finished his basic theology in 1937 and spent the following year in

9 Cited by Crowe in *Lonergan*, 17.
10 Bernard Lonergan, '*Insight* Revisited,' *A Second Collection*, 264.
11 Cited by Crowe in *Lonergan*, 40.
12 Ibid., 20.
13 *Insight*, 769.
14 *Understanding and Being*, 350.

Amiens for his 'tertianship,' a year devoted to spiritual reflection and development. He returned to the Gregorian in 1938 to write his doctoral dissertation in theology, but he had no definite topic in mind. After discussions with his director, Charles Boyer, he decided to write 'A History of St Thomas's Thought on Operative Grace,' a study of the development of St Thomas's notions of grace and human freedom. His completed dissertation consisted of six sections and was published as a series of four articles in *Theological Studies* (1941, 1942).

Lonergan then moved to Montreal and served as professor of theology at the Collège de l'Immaculée-Conception from 1940 to 1946. Pursuing his early interest in economics, he wrote the initial version of 'An Essay in Circulation Analysis' in 1944. The following year, Lonergan began working towards *Insight* with a lecture series entitled 'Thought and Reality,' which he delivered at the newly founded Thomas More Institute in Montreal: 'It seemed clear that I had a marketable product not only because of the notable perseverance of the class but also from the interest that lit up their faces and from such more palpable incidents as a girl marching in at the beginning of class, giving my desk a resounding whack with her hand, and saying, "I've got it." Those that have struggled with *Insight* will know what she meant.'[15]

Lonergan, however, undertook to write a historical treatise on St Thomas's cognitional theory before tackling the *Insight* project. He investigated the procession of the inner word (*verbum*) in the context of trinitarian theology, the internal dynamism of the human mind in light of the life of God in its internal dynamism. This study of *verbum* in Aquinas appeared as a series of five articles in *Theological Studies* (1946, 1947, 1949).

In 1947 Lonergan moved to Toronto to assume the post of professor of theology at Regis College. It was during his years at Regis College that the massive work *Insight* was written: 'I worked at *Insight* from 1949 to 1953. During the first three years my intention was an exploration of methods generally in preparation for a study of the method of theology. But in 1952 it became clear that I was due to start teaching at the Gregorian University in Rome in 1953, so I changed my plan and decided to round off what I had done and publish it.'[16] By the fall of 1952, Lonergan had completed chapters 1 to

15 Lonergan, '*Insight* Revisited,' 268.
16 Ibid.

13; the task of 'rounding off' consisted of writing seven more chapters by the next summer.

Lonergan returned to Rome and was professor of theology at the Gregorian from 1953 to 1965. During this period he worked on the thorny issue of the starting point and method of theology and the issue of the analytic and the synthetic approaches in theological studies. He took up the question of the role of history in theological method in light of the nineteenth-century German Historical School. At the Gregorian he taught graduate courses on theological method, and two undergraduate courses alternately for ten years, one on the Trinity and the other on the Incarnate Word. His lectures were delivered in Latin to large audiences of students from around the world: 'They were about six hundred and fifty strong and between them, not individually but distributively, they seemed to read everything. It was quite a challenge.'[17] To meet this challenge Lonergan read the works of those thinkers currently in vogue, primarily the existential phenomenologists. He remarked of this time: 'I was moving into the European atmosphere in which phenomenology was dominant.'[18] His series of lectures on existentialism, delivered at Boston College in 1957, exhibit his familiarity with Husserl, Heidegger, and the existentialists, and his high regard at that time for the work of Karl Jaspers. After 1954, Lonergan traveled to North America every summer to give institutes and lectures on his book *Insight* and on issues related to method in theology. Some highlights of this very productive period are his lectures on *Insight*, given at Saint Mary's University, Halifax, in 1958; his 'Philosophy of Education' lectures given in Cincinnati in 1959; and two major Latin treatises written in Rome, *De Deo Trino* (1957, 1961, 1964) and *De Verbo Incarnato* (1960, 1961, 1964).

In 1965, Lonergan returned to Canada for a sabbatical but had to undergo an operation for lung cancer. His recuperation took months. But that same year Lonergan made his breakthrough in theological method, which resulted in his model of eight functional specialties. He remained in Toronto as research professor at Regis College and devoted the next five years to developing this fundamental conception of theological method. The fruit of this creative effort, *Method in Theology*, was completed in 1971 and published in 1972. Lonergan gave a

17 Ibid., 276.
18 *Caring*, 105.

week-long institute on *Method in Theology* at Milltown Park, Dublin, in the summer of 1971, and lectures on this new work at the University of San Francisco in 1972.

In 1975, Lonergan moved from Regis to Boston College, where he was Visiting Distinguished Professor of Theology until 1983. He continued to expand on ideas he had developed in *Insight* and *Method in Theology*. He wrote on the historico-religious triad of progress, decline rooted in bias, and recovery, and on the need for both healing and creating in history. Lonergan's central interest during this period was to continue his work in economics. As he wrote in 'Healing and Creating in History,' 'When the system that is needed for our collective survival does not exist, then it is futile to excoriate what does exist while blissfully ignoring the task of constructing a technically viable economic system that can be put in its place.'[19] While at Boston College he developed and taught a course entitled 'Macro-economics and the Dialectic of History.' In 1983 he became ill and was unable to teach. He retired to the Jesuit infirmary in Pickering, Ontario, where he welcomed friends and students for brief discussions. Bernard Lonergan died on November 26, 1984.

Lonergan had written to his Jesuit superior in 1935, 'I know more luminously than anything else that I have nothing I have not received.'[20] This early remark clearly reveals a humility that was to characterize Lonergan for the rest of his life. But this genuine humility did not stop many people and organizations from recognizing the significance of his accomplishments. Lonergan was made Companion of the Order of Canada in 1970; the Catholic Theological Society of America presented him with the John Courtney Murray Award in 1972; he was made a Corresponding Fellow of the British Academy in 1975; and he was awarded nineteen honorary doctorates.[21] He was honored with a *Festschrift* on the occasion of his sixtieth birthday and by a symposium at Marquette University on the occasion of his seventy-fifth. Finally, two international congresses dedicated to the exploration of his thought have been held, at Saint Leo College in Florida in 1970 and at Santa Clara University in 1984.

This sketch provides the reader with a general idea of Lonergan's

19 Lonergan, *A Third Collection*, 108.
20 Cited by Crowe in *Lonergan*, 5.
21 Richard M. Liddy, *Transforming Light: Intellectual Conversion in the Early Lonergan* (Collegeville, MN: The Liturgical Press, 1993), 211–12.

intellectual roots, his professional involvements, and the chronology of
his major achievements, but such a listing of simple facts fails to convey the impression Lonergan might have made upon those who
attended his lectures and institutes and knew him personally. The
reader may be interested, then, in a few of our impressions, based on
our acquaintance with him.

Lonergan enjoyed a good joke and could tell one, but he was not a
conversationalist. He was not given to repartee either in ordinary conversation or in the question sessions which commonly followed his lectures at institutes and workshops. In general, he displayed a modesty
approaching shyness. He once described himself to us as 'a secondary
functions man.' By this he meant that the appropriate comment or
response to a question often would occur to him hours after the conversation had ended. In formal question sessions it was not uncom-
mon for Lonergan to respond to a long-drawn-out question with a
simple 'Yes' or 'No.' He did not suffer fools gladly. But he was always
generous in his responses to serious inquirers. At his lectures and in
discussions, one could witness the sheer joy Lonergan took in understanding. Seeing this for the first time, one might have suspected that
Lonergan had recalled a private joke; eventually it became apparent
that this was a genuine expression of the joy Lonergan felt in reaching
and communicating an insight.

Students of an innovative thinker hope to hear their mentor comment on every issue in which they take an interest and on each new
issue as it gains currency. In our experience, Lonergan was reluctant
to meet this expectation. He would not present himself as an authority
in any but the few areas in which he felt himself to have expertise.
Despite his deep and broad learning, he deferred readily and gra-
ciously to the expertise of other thinkers, both in public forums and in
private conversation. He would not speculate about issues he had not
thoroughly investigated for himself, but would direct attention to
those who had done the required research and invite his listeners to
read those thinkers' writings and draw their own conclusions. Only
rarely would Lonergan criticize other thinkers in discussion, prefer-
ring instead to emphasize those elements in their writings in which he
found some truth and to ignore what he regarded as mistaken. Of
those thinkers in whose work he found a deliberate and methodical
procedure he was especially generous with his praise, however much
he might have disagreed with their conclusions.

In Lonergan's writings and published interviews, there is no evidence of romanticism, moral idealism, or elitism. He was very down-to-earth, which was also evident in our conversations with him. Our discussions touched upon topics ranging from the philosophical and recondite to the mundane, and he spoke knowledgeably and with interest about current political events and recent technological innovations. He impressed us as a highly practical intellectual whose deep and broad learning was complemented by good common sense.

Lonergan's Place in Culture

Fortunately, I don't think I come under any single label.[22]

Any introduction to a major thinker should place that thinker in the current scheme of intellectual endeavors. With Bernard Lonergan, as with other comprehensive and innovative thinkers, this is not a simple matter of situating his work within the boundaries of a familiar field of study or department of inquiry. The originality of a powerful mind may reside precisely in raising the kinds of questions the steady pursuit of which weakens and breaks down traditional divisions and separations. These questions may bring about a radically different conception of the unity and organization of cultural pursuits. The very originality and comprehensiveness of Lonergan's work make it difficult to situate his writing within familiar categories of intellectual endeavor. Nevertheless, since Lonergan's comprehensive view and language have yet to penetrate our culture, we have no choice but to employ more familiar classifications – at least initially. Let us begin, then, with the labels that are commonly applied to Lonergan, briefly weigh their adequacy, and finally attempt to make the transition from the prevailing climate of opinion and its familiar language to Lonergan's quite different viewpoint and way of expressing things. In this way, the reader's desire to know where Lonergan stands, and what sorts of expectations to bring to the reading of the selections in this volume, may be satisfied by a recourse to Lonergan's own words and concepts to describe his project and cultural position.

Lonergan has been variously described. To some he is a theologian. To others he is a philosopher. To still others he is best described by the

22 *Caring,* 219.

less common but familiar name, methodologist. In certain respects, as F.E. Crowe has suggested, each of these labels may be applied to him.[23] In other respects, the title 'methodologist' suits him best, because its ties to traditional disciplines are fairly loose, while 'philosopher' and 'theologian' are perhaps too narrow and even misleading. Evidence may be found in Lonergan's life and works to support the use of all three descriptions.

Those who regard Lonergan as a theologian point to the following facts: he was a Jesuit priest; his doctoral dissertation was on operative grace; he was employed as Professor of Dogmatic Theology and taught many theological courses; he prepared for his students' use Latin notes and theological treatises, on the Incarnate Word, the consciousness of Christ, and the Trinity; he wrote theological articles on marriage, the Assumption, and Christology; he had a perduring concern to provide a new method for Catholic theology; and his model of progress–decline–redemption is found throughout his works.

Others who see Lonergan as a philosopher highlight different aspects of his work: his intense interest in cognitional theory in his student days; the obvious philosophical focus of *Insight: A Study of Human Understanding*, and Lonergan's explicit comparison in the introduction to *Insight* of his own strategy with that employed by Hume in his *Treatise of Human Nature*; his explicit and crucial reliance upon *Insight*'s conclusions in subsequent works, including his *Method in Theology*; his analysis of the existential subject; and his work in the area of meaning and the development of consciousness.

Still others characterize Lonergan as a methodologist. They point to his persistent concern with, and use of, methodical procedures and heuristic structures, to his own description of *Insight* as his 'book of methods'; to the apparent consistency of this methodological concern with the amount of attention he gives to historical method in works published after *Insight*; to the very title *Method in Theology* and his deliberate intention to let theologians determine for themselves the validity of his proposed foundational categories; and, finally, to the fact that after the publication of his proposed method for a renewed theology, instead of applying that method to theological questions and issues, he resurrected the project in macroeconomics, to which he had devoted a good deal of time during the 1930s and early 1940s. This last

23 Crowe, *Lonergan*, 128 ff.

piece of evidence further complicates the matter. Some may wish to say of Lonergan that he was an economist by avocation. It is clear, though, that the economic work, as interesting and important as it was to Lonergan, took second place to his other intellectual pursuits.

There is ample evidence, therefore, to support the view that Lonergan's primary concerns were questions and issues normally associated with philosophy, theology, and methodology. One might expect, then, that his works would receive the attention of philosophers, theologians, and those educated in what currently goes by the name of methodology. But, strangely, this is not generally the case. Anglo-American philosophers, with their emphasis on linguistic and conceptual analysis, have tended to dismiss Lonergan's philosophy because it gives primacy to the performance of mental acts and relegates the method of linguistic analysis to an auxiliary status.[24] If Lonergan's rejection of the traditional subject-object dichotomy, and his attention to the data of consciousness in the manner of phenomenological analysis, pose no problem for Continental philosophers, his critical realist account of objectivity continues to puzzle them.[25] Again, in *Method in Theology*, in which Lonergan proposes a collaborative theological method composed of eight functional specializations, his treatments of strictly theological issues serve predominantly as illustrations. This has left some theologians somewhat perplexed and dissatisfied.[26] Furthermore, efforts to introduce Lonergan's methodology into Germany have been hindered by the presumption that 'method' can mean only the method of Descartes, leading one of Lonergan's students to coin the term 'meta-method' to distinguish Lonergan's conception of method from the concerns and practices of an ahistorical, disembodied, detached Cartesian mind.[27] Elsewhere, the currency of commonsense notions of method as a recipe, a repeatable technique generating

---

24 Lonergan discusses the basic contentions of linguistic analysis briefly in *Method in Theology*, 254–7. See also Lonergan's comments in 1982 on analytic philosophy's dominance in England, in *Caring*, 218. As Hugo Meynell notes, Lonergan's 'appeal ... to mental acts and processes, as opposed to language, would generally be taken by contemporary philosophers to be a retrograde step.' See his 'Philosophy after Philosophy,' in Thomas J. Farrell and Paul A. Soukup, eds., *Communication and Lonergan: Common Ground for Forging the New Age* (Kansas City: Sheed and Ward, 1993), 149.
25 *Method in Theology*, 262 ff., on Jaspers and the problem of objective self-knowledge.
26 See, for example, Karl Rahner's remarks in 'Some Critical Thoughts on Functional Specialties in Theology,' in Philip McShane, ed., *Foundations of Theology: Papers from the International Lonergan Congress 1970* (Dublin: Gill and Macmillan, 1971), 194–6.
27 Lonergan comments on his reception in Germany in *Caring*, 13, 114–15, 217.

predetermined results, makes method appear irrelevant to the clarification of the complexities involved in concrete human living and its guidance.[28] Lastly, conventional critiques of method, as a manipulative procedure associated with a dominative natural science insensitive to human freedom, make it appear most unappealing as a topic for serious reflection.[29]

If Lonergan is justly described as a philosopher, a theologian, and a methodologist, why do philosophers and theologians apparently fail to find the philosophy and theology they expect in his writings, and why do those familiar with method in its current meanings apparently find it difficult to conceive of method in Lonergan's sense? The answer to both questions is to be found in Lonergan's unique meaning for the word 'methodologist' and his unique conception of method.[30] When asked a few years before his death if he liked to be described as a methodologist, Lonergan answered that he did, although he added without hesitation, 'but what most people understand by method is a recipe.'[31] Lonergan strongly rejected this common notion of method: 'Method can be thought of as a set of recipes that can be observed by a blockhead yet lead infallibly to astounding discoveries. Such a notion of method I consider sheer illusion.'[32] If his readers were able to get beyond this exclusive and narrow conception of method and the corresponding conception of methodology, they might discover that Lonergan's methodological work is basic in nature. Carrying it out forces a significant shift in the way the disciplines of philosophy and theology are conceived and practiced. Late in life Lonergan expressed the view that it would take at least one hundred years for the fruits of his work to permeate the culture.[33]

Let us now turn from preliminary considerations of the difficulty of placing Lonergan in the contemporary cultural scene to a brief survey of his vision of the situation in which he lived; his understanding of the demands to be met by the thinker who aims to live at the level of the

---

28 *Caring*, 220.
29 On the intrusion into the natural sciences of the extra-scientific opinions of scientists, and of mechanist determinism in particular, see *Method in Theology*, 248–9, 317.
30 David Tracy describes Lonergan's notion of method as 'entirely original' in 'Bernard Lonergan and the Return of Ancient Practice,' in Fred Lawrence, ed., *Lonergan Workshop* (Atlanta: Scholars Press, 1990), 10:319–31.
31 *Caring*, 220.
32 *Philosophy of God*, 48.
33 *Caring*, 175.

times; the strategy which he undertook to meet those demands; and the outcome of that strategy. In the process, a sufficient number of terms will be introduced to make possible a summary account in Lonergan's own words of his place in contemporary culture, which may be of real assistance to the reader who openly seeks to explore the perspectives revealed in this volume.

Reflection on the development of a thinker easily dissolves into mere speculation if it is not carried out methodically and thoroughly. As Lonergan put it, referring to efforts made to understand the various stages of his thought, such reflection can be 'a little bit of creative history,' which might hinder rather than assist in understanding his mature thought.[34] In the brief presentation to follow, then, we will make no attempt to trace the stages of Lonergan's intellectual development but will focus on his finished products.

Lonergan saw the twentieth century as marked by an unexpected, bitter, and widespread disillusionment. For the proximate sources of this disillusionment he points to the clash between the ideal of progress and the experiences of the Great Depression, two world wars, the rise of ideologies with their high-minded incoherence, conflicts rooted in competing group egoisms, the emergence and realization of totalitarian ambitions, and the insidious spread of simple-minded opportunism and violence. The remote source for this disillusionment, though, he locates in a prolonged cultural crisis and its related disarray and conflict within the domains of philosophical and theological practice. The framework of meanings and values by which we had informed and guided our common way of life has all but collapsed in the face of technological, economic, political, and intellectual upheavals and transformations. These meanings and values have yet to be replaced, and the failure to replace them has created a vacuum of meaning and value. The situation is rendered desperate, Lonergan believed, when its increasing absurdity, unintelligibility, and irrationality come to be regarded not as 'mere proof of aberration' but as 'evidence in favor of error.' Then the 'social surd,' as Lonergan names this unintelligible sociocultural context, expands as we assume the attitude of the 'realist': 'The dictates of intelligence and reasonableness are found irrelevant to concrete living. The facts have to be faced; and facing them means the adjustment of theory to practice. But every adjust-

34 *Caring*, 72–3.

ment makes the incidental sins of the past into the commonly accepted
rule of the present; the social surd expands; and its expansion
demands further adjustment.'[35]

Our century, in Lonergan's view, is merely the most recent moment
in a cycle of decline in which our self-understanding and our understanding of our common situation have become ever less comprehensive, and our capacity to respond to the challenges posed by this
situation has become more and more restricted. In this cycle of decline
our horizons contract, our language is devalued, our questions are
brushed aside, and our experiences become a flow of alienating absurdities. Moreover, these 'facts' about ourselves descend like an iron curtain and cut us off from the realization of our potentialities; they
provide ready-made justifications for the views of those who would see
us as little more than animals in a habitat; and we confirm their estima-
tion of us because we adhere to decadent routines and cavalierly disregard the role played by meanings and values in the conduct of our lives.

At the root of this crisis is a crisis in our knowledge of ourselves. We
formerly understood ourselves, or thought that we understood ourselves, in terms of a specific set of meanings and values, but their inadequacy has been revealed by modern technological, economic, social,
political, and intellectual developments. Reflection on the experience
of these transformations has sparked the realization of our embedded-
ness in history, of our historicity. The collapse of classical culture coincides with the realization that we are constituted by our situations, and
that we constitute ourselves and our situations. In the aftermath of
these developments and this realization, we are newly empowered but
radically disoriented. The previously authoritative meanings and values by which we defined ourselves and guided our living have lost
their aura of prestige, but a new set of meanings and values and a new
self-understanding have not emerged to replace them. This disorientation is felt at the level of everyday living no less than at the level of
philosophical and theological endeavor. But, in Lonergan's view, the
confusion that dominates philosophical and theological inquiry is
especially ominous. It is there that normative foundations for collaborative intellectual practice and moral living are formulated and explicitly mediated to the culture at large. It is there that the criteria by which
we distinguish progress from decline are ascertained and articulated.

35 *Insight*, 712.

Lonergan conceives a cultural matrix using the analogy of an organic whole. If one part becomes distorted and ceases to perform its function, the whole becomes distorted. Meanwhile, the hard-headed realism which aims to fill the resulting vacuum lifts to prominence a set of 'false facts' about ourselves and our potentialities. It ridicules serious intellectual endeavor as ivory-tower theorizing, hinders or even blocks the required renewal of the pursuit of self-knowledge and the renovation of philosophy and theology that might flow from it, and postpones indefinitely the regeneration of the cultural matrix.[36]

According to Lonergan, the prevailing demand of our time is the demand for an adequate, up-to-date answer to the question, What is man? To respond to this demand at the level of the times is, first, to conceive a strategy by which the pursuit of self-knowledge might be revived; and, second, to carry out that renewed quest with expectations framed, not by the outmoded classical ideal of static, abstract definitions and principles, but by an ideal of foundations that are intrinsically open to change and capable of surviving intact the most radical shifts of meaning and value. The foundations must be dynamic and flexible in themselves, resistant to all ideologies, and ever capable of giving the lie to the 'false facts' of the practical realist. They must be the source of short- and long-lived definitions and principles, the source of their revision, and the basic motivation for discarding and replacing them when they are legitimately discarded and replaced. In brief, the foundation to be grasped is the concrete, existing subject who engenders cultures and maintains them for a time or perhaps for millennia, but who eventually finds the matrix constituted by its own activities insufficient to accommodate its own creative thrust towards greater self-expression and fulfillment and more complete self-transcendence. Moreover, the needed foundation must carry within itself criteria of knowledge, objectivity, truth, reality, and values which are transcultural, perhaps not in their explicit acknowledgment but at least in their implicit employment. Finally, this pursuit of transcultural normative foundations, if it is truly to be a break with the abstract apprehension and account of humanity, must be simultaneously an effort to account for the variety of existing and past cultures and for the multitude of personal, social, and cultural aberrations and distortions which, at any given moment in human his-

---

36 *Insight*, 254 ff.; on the paradoxical category of the 'false fact,' see *Understanding and Being*, 236.

tory, mix with progressive expressions and manifestations of the thrust towards self-transcendence.

The strategy conceived and adopted by Lonergan to revive the pursuit of self-knowledge is what he names 'self-appropriation.' It is by self-appropriation that the obstruction set up by unbridled practicality is to be outflanked. In the first instance, self-appropriation is a shift of orientation: instead of being poured out on objects, we attend to ourselves as establishing relations to objects. Self-appropriation shifts our attention from the objects that are present to us through our operations to the events given in our presence to ourselves in our dealings with objects. It is not only a shift of attention from objects generally to our own flow of conscious events but also a shift of attention from the subject-as-object to the subject-as-subject. The subject-as-subject is the one who establishes by his or her own activities his or her relations to objects, including other subjects. The subject-as-object is the perceptible human being behaving and acting in the shared, public world. The activities of the subject-as-subject are not perceptible behaviors or 'external acts.' Rather, they are consciously experienced activities or what Lonergan calls 'interior operations.' Self-appropriation, in the first instance, is a shift of attention from objects, including the subject-as-object, to the subject-as-subject and the realm of interiority.[37]

But there are many interior operations, and Edmund Husserl, for example, complained that, upon turning to the subject-as-subject, he felt himself adrift on an infinite sea. But Lonergan's strategy is more deliberately planned. Whereas Husserl felt himself adrift, Lonergan anticipates and seeks out dynamic structures of operations. Once the realist obstruction is outflanked, a sequence of questions can be addressed to the previously obscured field of interior events. What am I doing when I'm knowing? Why is doing that called knowing? What do I know when I do that? What am I doing when I'm valuing? What ought I to do in light of the knowledge I've now acquired of my knowing and my valuing?

Self-appropriation is first and foremost a process of taking possession of oneself as a knower and a doer. Our knowing and deciding are of the greatest strategic importance in the effort to uncover a transcultural foundation. Our present disorientation, when distilled by analysis, is

---

37 On the presence of the subject to itself, see *Collection*, 208–11 and *Understanding and Being*, 15–17.

revealed to be at root a confusion about what counts as knowledge, what constitutes objectivity, what is meant by reality, and what is truly good. The meanings given to these notions by a culture, whether explicitly known or merely operative in cultural performance, are a culture's most basic constituents. Previously authoritative accounts of knowledge, objectivity, reality, and the truly good have fallen prey to scientific revolutions and the suspicions of a historically conscious age. Lonergan's strategy was to seek in the very performance of cognitive and moral operations the criteria of objectivity, truth, reality, and value that are always at work, quietly and subtly, prior to their deliberate formulation and even in our philosophizing about them. If these criteria are brought to light and adequately articulated, we will have equipped ourselves with a fundamental account of the notions informing and guiding the creation of the specific categories of meaning and value which inform and guide human ways of life. Such an account, Lonergan claims, is immune to radical revision, since any effort to revise it must employ either implicitly or explicitly the criteria described in the account. Self-appropriation, then, is the effort to give an account of the invariant dynamic structure of conscious intentionality with its immanent criteria of objectivity, truth, reality, and value. But, still more importantly, it is taking reflective possession of oneself as constituted fundamentally by operative, preconceptual, prelinguistic criteria of knowledge, objectivity, truth, reality, and value.[38]

Self-appropriation is radically different from the Cartesian strategy of cutting oneself off from external objects in order to find oneself in the internal remainder. Self-appropriation is not disengagement from the world of objects but development of an understanding of oneself in the widest possible range of cognitive and moral engagements. The criteria immanent in interior operations cannot be discovered unless the interior operations occur. Accordingly, Lonergan deliberately provides opportunities in *Insight* for his readers to catch themselves in the act of performing cognitional operations – to experience themselves questioning, imagining, having insights, reflecting on the correctness

---

38 David Tracy suggests an analogy between the role of self-appropriation in Lonergan's thought and the place of 'spiritual exercises' in ancient philosophy, and he suggests that 'the habitual belief of modern Western philosophers and even theologians that theory should be separate from practices' may account for their apparent hesitancy to place Lonergan firmly in either of those disciplines. See Tracy's 'Bernard Lonergan and the Return of Ancient Practice,' 325–6.

of their insights, and making judgments. Lonergan's subsequent accounts of deliberation, evaluation, and decision presuppose his readers' concomitant advertence to their concrete experience of performing these moral operations.

Self-appropriation is a strategy for meeting the demands of our times at the level of our times. The reflective self-possession Lonergan promotes is that of a truly contemporary self, a self experienced in thinking along with the most advanced intellectual endeavors of our day. While appropriation of a less developed self may be preferred to mere self-ignorance, only appropriation of a self at the level of its times equips one with the self-knowledge required to deal intelligently, reasonably, and effectively with the problems of one's times at the level at which they must be treated. Lonergan's invitation to self-appropriation, then, is also an invitation to self-development.

Finally, self-appropriation is self-criticism and self-correction. To seek to take possession of oneself as intelligent and reasonable, free and responsible, is also to discover one's lack of openness, oversights, unreasonableness, irresponsibility, and incompleteness of development. Appropriation of the immanent criteria of objectivity, truth, reality, and value, therefore, involves ongoing self-correction within one's historical community. Accordingly, Lonergan's positive account of the invariant dynamic structure of conscious intentionality is complemented by an account of the principal devices of the flight from understanding – of psychological, individual, group, and general bias. But this dialectical account serves to reveal a deeper dimension to the crisis we are facing. Lonergan's analysis of bias clearly exhibits, in a variety of contexts, the deeper, theological issue posed by our incapacity for sustained development, our moral impotence, and the insurmountable resistance of the problem of liberation to all humanly generated solutions. The enlightenment afforded by self-knowledge cannot reverse by itself the cumulative process of decline: 'A civilization in decline digs its own grave with a relentless consistency. It cannot be argued out of its self-destructive ways, for argument has a theoretical major premise, theoretical premises are asked to conform to matters of fact, and the facts in the situation produced by decline more and more are the absurdities that proceed from inattention, oversight, unreasonableness and irresponsibility.'[39] There is a need as well for religious eman-

39 *Method in Theology*, 55.

cipation if we are to transcend ourselves 'to the point, not merely of justice, but of self-sacrificing love.'[40]

Lonergan's project of self-development in which his readers are invited to join, unfolds as a methodological study. If one is to rise to the level of one's times intellectually, then one must involve oneself in the outstanding and successful intellectual endeavors of one's time, attend to oneself in that engagement, and formulate for oneself the normative dynamic structure of interior operations constitutive of that engagement. To carry out this self-appropriative involvement, in Lonergan's terms, is to engage in methodology, to study methods. Lonergan's methodological studies result in accounts of classical, statistical, genetic, and dialectical methods. Each of these accounts sheds light on the fundamental method of the human mind of which these methods are specifications. On the basis of these studies Lonergan formulated a general definition of method: 'A method is a normative pattern of recurrent and related operations yielding cumulative and progressive results. There is a method, then, where there are distinct operations, where each operation is related to the others, where the set of relations forms a pattern, where the pattern is described as the right way of doing the job, where operations in accord with the pattern may be repeated indefinitely, and where the fruits of such repetition are, not repetitious, but cumulative and progressive.'[41]

A method, in Lonergan's sense, differs significantly from a technique or a recipe. To employ a technique or recipe is virtually to dispense with intelligence, reasonableness, and responsibility. But to employ a method is to engage in a deliberate and responsible exercise of intelligence and reasonableness. To employ a technique is to know beforehand the result of its application. To employ a method is to seek knowledge of what won't be known until the method has been employed successfully. Similarly, a method differs from a logical procedure as interior operations and their dynamic relations differ from the terms, propositions, and relations among terms and propositions that interior operations generate and eventually revise. For Lonergan, logic is static, whereas method is dynamic.

The outcome of Lonergan's pursuit of dynamic foundations by way of a self-appropriative study of methods is formulated concisely in his

40 Ibid.
41 Ibid., 4.

notion of 'transcendental method.' The invariant dynamic structure of conscious intentionality is a four-level structure of successively sublating sets of operations. Lonergan designates each level by its most prominent operation: the level of experience, the level of understanding, the level of judgment, the level of decision. The transition from level to level is occasioned by an operator. We move from experiencing to understanding by asking questions; we move from understanding to judgment by asking critical questions; we move from judgment to decision and action by asking questions of the general form, Is it worthwhile? The criteria of knowledge, objectivity, truth, reality, and value are immanent in the operators; they are contained in the questions we raise. In the concrete emergence of wonder, doubt, and conscience to which our questions give articulate expression, we experience these immanent criteria. Lonergan formulated the operative criteria in four transcendental precepts: Be attentive; Be intelligent; Be reasonable; Be responsible. The four-level structure with its immanent criteria is the foundational heuristic structure that is specified in the exercise of all special methods and is spontaneously employed in everyday practical and social living. One may expect, moreover, that this same trancendental method will underpin and penetrate any specific method developed in the future.

To abide by the transcendental precepts in one's living is to transcend oneself, approach authenticity, and promote human progress. To disregard or violate the precepts is to refuse to transcend oneself, to be unauthentic, and to become an agent of decline. But the simplicity of these formulas may be deceiving. Lonergan finds in us an incapacity for sustained development, a moral impotence, and a need for emancipation. Even if one grasps the dynamic foundations which underpin, maintain, transform, and outlast cultural contexts one cannot overcome this incapacity solely by one's own efforts. The principle of progress may have been ascertained; the principle of decline may have been identified; but the question persists regarding the route to recovery and redemption. Lonergan's entire effort to meet the demands of his time at the level of his time is contained within the triad he uses to describe the structure of history: progress–decline–redemption.

There is, then, a second phase to Lonergan's methodological work, which incorporates our need for redemption and the redemptive role of religion. He has exposed the groundwork for a new conceptuality to replace the conceptuality which underpinned classical culture and for a way of understanding ourselves which displaces reactionary practical realism. But if the new conceptuality is to take hold, if it is to inform and guide our common way of life, if decline is to be reversed, the human sciences and human studies, philosophy, and theology must be appropriately anchored by the new foundations. Lonergan's methodological studies in *Insight* served to reorient philosophy. But the reorientation and renewal of theology, which has suffered the greatest damage with the collapse of classical culture and the rise of historical consciousness, and whose task it is to mediate a religious message of redemption within our culture, remains to be accomplished. Until that reorientation is accomplished the human sciences and human studies will be deprived of a fully concrete understanding of the subject-as-object. Lonergan's post-*Insight* reflections on the central categories of human studies – meaning, the good, and history – and his eventual proposal of a new method for theology, based on transcendental method, constitute the second phase of a single methodological project, a prolongation of his effort to anchor modern culture to its transcultural base in the self-transcending subject.

Where, then, does Lonergan fit in the existing scheme of intellectual endeavors? In his article 'Dimensions of Meaning,' Lonergan wrote: 'I have been attempting to persuade you that meaning is an important part of human living. I wish now to add that reflection on meaning and the consequent control of meaning are still more important. For if social and cultural changes are, at root, changes in the meanings that are grasped and accepted, changes in the control of meaning mark off the great epochs in human history.'[42] Lonergan goes on to describe the breakdown of the classical control of meaning in the face of the modern shift from the deductive to the empirical, from the abstract to the concrete, and the consequent plight of contemporary Western humanity:

> In brief, the classical mediation of meaning has broken down. It is being replaced by a modern mediation of meaning that interprets our dreams and our symbols, that thematizes our wan smiles and limp gestures, that analyzes our minds and charts our souls, that takes the whole of human history for its kingdom to compare and relate languages and literatures, art forms and religions, family arrangements and customary morals, political, legal, educational, economic systems, sciences, philosophies,

42 *Collection*, 235.

theologies, and histories. Now books pour forth annually by the thousands; our libraries need ever more space. But the vast modern effort to understand meaning in all its manifestations has not been matched by a comparable effort in judging meaning. The effort to understand is the common task of unnumbered scientists and scholars. But judging and deciding are left to the individual, and he finds his plight desperate. There is far too much to be learnt before he could begin to judge. Yet judge he must and decide he must if he is to exist.[43]

It is Lonergan's view, then, that we are in the midst of an epochal shift in the control of meaning, a shift which has not yet reached its term. The classical conceptuality, which assigned meanings to the basic notions of knowledge, objectivity, truth, reality, and goodness, cannot accommodate and comprehend the emerging multiplicity of endeavors and the still more numerous and diverse revelations which flow from them and threaten to immerse us. Reliance upon clear-cut definitions of the human soul and human nature, upon supposedly self-evident first principles and certain knowledge of things through their causes, and upon rigorous manipulation of static abstractions by logic no longer suffices. But no new controls are in place. So long as the issue of controls remains unresolved, the private disorientation and desperation of the individual will persist and continue to crystallize in the public field of human affairs. We need a new conceptuality, an articulation of the basic guiding notions, in light of which we can render judgments confidently and critically, make decisions freely and responsibly, promote progress, and resist decline.[44]

The required conceptuality must complete the transition, already in progress, from the metaphysical notion of the soul to the concrete subject; from abstract human nature to historicity; from self-evident, static first principles to dynamic operations; from logical to methodical control of meaning. We believe that the reader of this volume will discover that the task Lonergan set himself was to effect the completion, at the

43 Collection, 244.
44 In Caring, on page 8, Lonergan describes his Method in Theology as providing a new conceptuality or begrifflichkeit. On page 119 he discusses F.E. Crowe's comparison of his achievement with those of Aristotle and Bacon and characterizes it as both 'a different organon and a different style of organon.' See F.E. Crowe, The Lonergan Enterprise (Cambridge, MA: Cowley Publications, 1980); and Method in Theology: An Organon for Our Time (Milwaukee: Marquette University Press, 1980).

level of thought, of this transition, and to articulate a new mode of controlling meaning proportionate to the demands of our age.

In 'Natural Right and Historical Mindedness,' an article written near the end of his life, the character of Lonergan's project as an effort to complete the transposition from classical to modern controls of meaning is illustrated with stark clarity. Lonergan also describes in it the ideal of enlightenment appropriate to this epochal moment in our history: 'As always enlightenment is a matter of the ancient precept, Know thyself. But in the contemporary context, it aims to be such self-awareness, such self-understanding, such self-knowledge, as to grasp the similarities and the differences of common sense, science, and history, to grasp the foundations of these three in interiority which also founds natural right and, beyond all knowledge of knowledge, to give also knowledge of affectivity in its threefold manifestation of love in the family, loyalty in the community, and faith in God.'[45]

However, besides the need for enlightenment, there is the need for liberation and emancipation. For Lonergan, emancipation is not the Enlightenment project of 'replacing traditional backwardness by the rule of pure reason.' It is a radical, threefold shift of orientation:

> Again, as always, emancipation has its root in self-transcendence. But in the contemporary context it is such self-transcendence as includes an intellectual, a moral, and an affective conversion. As intellectual, this conversion draws a sharp distinction between the world of immediacy and the world mediated by meaning, between the criteria appropriate to operations in the former and, on the other hand, the criteria appropriate to operations in the latter. Next, as moral, it acknowledges a distinction between satisfactions and values, and it is committed to values even where they conflict with satisfactions. Finally, as affective, it is commitment to love in the home, loyalty in the community, faith in the destiny of man.[46]

As the very nature of self-appropriation implies, Lonergan's ultimate account of the dynamically operative foundation he uncovered, and its ongoing emancipation by conversion, is presented neither as a theory to be believed on his authority nor as a system to be judged on

45 *A Third Collection*, 179.
46 Ibid.

the basis of its logical consistency and coherence. Rather, it is an interior description or objectification of the subject-as-subject to be critically questioned and reflectively verified in oneself. In a series of lectures on *Insight* shortly after its publication he said to his audience: 'Your interest may quite legitimately be to find out what Lonergan thinks and what Lonergan says, but I am not offering you that, or what anyone else thinks or says, as a basis. If a person is to be a philosopher, his thinking as a whole cannot depend upon someone or something else. There has to be a basis within himself; he must have resources of his own to which he can appeal in the last resort.'[47]

The foundation towards which Lonergan guides us, as he says in his introduction to *Insight*, 'is not the transcendental ego of Fichtean speculation, nor the abstract pattern of relations verifiable in Tom and Dick and Harry, but the personally appropriated structure of one's own experiencing, one's own intelligent inquiry and insights, one's own critical reflection and judging and deciding.'[48] This structure is the immanent ground for the guidance and criticism of human thought and living, a foundation upon which a comprehensive, yet dynamically open, viewpoint may be constructed. A concrete, rather than a merely conceptual, apprehension of this invariant dynamic structure requires a serious engagement by the reader in the task of self-appropriation.

The Selections

We have imposed upon ourselves several guidelines in making selections for this volume. First, we have limited our materials to works offered by Lonergan for publication or prepared by others for publication with Lonergan's approval. Second, from this collection of works we have excluded from consideration for the present volume those works written for highly specialized audiences. As a result, this volume does not contain selections from Lonergan's Latin theological treatises or from his historical studies of Aquinas's thought. Finally, in making our selections we have attempted to balance the interests of the educated reader with the needs of teachers and students of philosophy, theology, and interdisciplinary studies. We have assembled

47 *Understanding and Being*, 35.
48 *Insight*, 13.

selections representative of Lonergan's major concerns, central ideas, and basic positions. But, in doing so, we have tried to make allowance for the scholar's interest in the relations of Lonergan's problematic to his ultimate conclusions, of his emerging ideas to one another, of his methodological, philosophical, and theological positions to the cultural and historical contexts out of which they emerged and to which they are responses.

Our selections are organized into four parts. Each part is composed of various selections. When appropriate, selections are divided into smaller excerpts. Part 1 is devoted almost entirely to selections from *Insight: A Study of Human Understanding* (1953). There are just two exceptions: excerpts from an unpublished preface to *Insight* and Lonergan's first series of lectures on that work. *Insight* is a fundamental philosophical work. Highly complex in its structure, it is eight hundred pages in length and provides essential background to understanding Lonergan's subsequent lectures and writings. Lonergan himself described *Insight* as more a 'program' than an 'argument.' Our choice of selections from *Insight* is an attempt to represent accurately the unfolding program without obscuring significant steps in a very lengthy argument, and to make available to a wider audience a basic understanding of this foundational work.

Part 2 consists of selections from lectures and writings completed after *Insight* but before the publication of *Method in Theology* in 1972. These selections represent an extension of positions established in *Insight* and contain Lonergan's further explorations of the notions of culture, meaning, value, and history on the way to his proposing a method for a renewed Catholic theology. No deliberate attempt has been made to represent developmental stages in the emergence of Lonergan's views on these topics; nevertheless, one who reads Parts 1 and 2 in sequence will discern an overall shift of focus from methodological issues surrounding the natural sciences, with which *Insight* dealt at length and in detail, to those surrounding human science and human studies.

Part 3 is devoted to selections from *Method in Theology*. The greater portion of these selections is taken from Part 1 of that work, in which Lonergan provides the background needed for understanding his account of theological method as a collaborative process of mediation between a cultural matrix and the role and significance of religion in that matrix. The remaining selections are taken from Part 2, in which each of the eight functional specialties is discussed separately. In making selections from this more specialized second half of *Method in Theology*, our aim is primarily to represent the foundations Lonergan proposes for the guidance of a methodical theology.

Part 4 consists of selections from works produced after the completion of *Method in Theology* in 1971. They are representative of Lonergan's deepening methodological reflections on issues bearing directly upon creative and healing intervention in the course of human affairs. These reflections followed his public proposal for a renovation of theological practice.

For each selection we have provided a brief introduction which is meant to give the reader a foretaste of the contents. For Parts 1 and 3, each of which consists of selections from a single work, we have also provided general introductions. At the end of each selection, whenever appropriate, we have appended a list of related selections for the reader who wishes to pursue specific ideas.

All references to Lonergan's works and to the works of others in these selections which are not enclosed in square brackets are Lonergan's own. When reference is made by Lonergan to a portion of his works which is wholly or partly contained in this volume, we have indicated its location in square brackets, e.g., [1.V.2–5 in this reader], indicating Part 1, Selection V, sections 2–5 in this volume.

We wish to express our appreciation and gratitude to the many Lonergan scholars who responded so thoroughly and helpfully to a questionnaire we distributed when *The Lonergan Reader* was at an early stage of planning. We regret that we have not been able to incorporate all of the recommended selections into the final product. But it is our hope and expectation that this volume will prove sufficient for their needs. We are also grateful to F.E. Crowe, R.M. Doran, and R.C. Croken of the Lonergan Research Institute for their expert advice and friendly cooperation. We wish to acknowledge Loyola Marymount University, Los Angeles, which provided grant support for the early stages of this project. Finally, we wish to thank the editors and readers of the University of Toronto Press for their indispensable guidance and assistance.

PART ONE

Insight: A Study of Human Understanding

Selections

Introduction to *Insight*

Insight was written between 1949 and 1953, and was published for the first time in 1957. Looking back on *Insight* Lonergan in 1972 wrote of that four-year period: 'During the first three years my intention was an exploration of methods generally in preparation for a study of the method of theology. But in 1952 it became clear that I was due to start teaching at the Gregorian University in Rome in 1953, so I changed my plan and decided to round off what I had done and publish it under the title, *Insight: A Study of Human Understanding*.'[1]

Insight was part of a larger project which came to virtual completion in Lonergan's last major published work, *Method in Theology*, in 1972. Despite the twenty-year hiatus, the two works may be viewed as bracketing a single, prolonged effort in the spirit of the program initiated by Pope Leo XIII in his encyclical *Aeterni Patris: Vetera novis augere et perficere* (Augment and complete the old with the new). By the old was meant the thought of Aquinas and the tradition he initiated; by the new was meant the many developments since the time of Aquinas, of which Aquinas naturally knew nothing, and which had yet to be appropriated by Catholic philosophy and theology and reconciled intellectually with Christianity. Lonergan's effort, begun in *Insight* and pursued to *Method in Theology* and beyond, pertained not to the *vetera* but to the *nova*. Prior to the writing of *Insight* Lonergan had completed two major historical studies of the *vetera*, of Aquinas's thought on operative grace and his views on understanding and the inner word. In the epilogue to *Insight* Lonergan wrote: 'After spending years reaching up to the mind of Aquinas, I came to a twofold conclusion. On the one hand, that reaching had changed me profoundly. On the other hand, that change was the essential benefit. For not only did it make me

---

1 *A Second Collection*, 268.

capable of grasping what, in the light of my conclusions, the *vetera* really were, but also it opened challenging vistas on what the *nova* could be.'[2]

With *Insight*, then, Lonergan initiated a prolonged effort to meet the demands of our age, just as Aquinas had struggled to meet the demands of an earlier age. Lonergan shared with Aquinas the broad objective of reconciling in some manner the Catholic faith with its cultural matrix. But as the demands of the twentieth century differ significantly from those of the thirteenth, so Lonergan's specific strategy in *Insight*, as well as the techniques he employs to achieve his designated aims, differ significantly from those of Aquinas. Not only have the components of the cultural matrix of Christianity undergone radical change and expansion, but the nature and complexity of the change pose a serious challenge to the very ideal of synthesis which guided Aquinas in his efforts. Thus Lonergan speaks, in the epilogue to *Insight*, of the Leonine program and of importing Aquinas's 'compelling genius to the problems of this later day,' but not of importing Aquinas's assumptions, categories, method, or ideal of synthesis.[3]

The following three selections are accounts of the aims and content of *Insight* in Lonergan's own words. The first selection is taken from the original preface, which accompanied the manuscript of Insight to the publisher in 1954. A short time after the manuscript was submitted, Lonergan met with the publisher and discussed at length his reasons for writing *Insight* and his hopes for the book. The publisher encouraged Lonergan to incorporate into the preface what he had expressed during their discussion. The second selection is taken from the new and quite different preface which actually accompanied *Insight* into print. The third and final introductory selection is taken from Lonergan's introduction to *Insight*.

Lonergan was fond of military metaphors, and use of a military metaphor here may serve to illuminate the differing emphases in these three presentations of the aims and content of *Insight*. In the original preface Lonergan offers a vision of the new cultural situation, characterizes the basic problem as a crisis of human self-knowledge, and emphasizes the programmatic nature of *Insight* as an attempt to rise to the level of our times in order to meet effectively the demands of our times. It describes the overall aims of the campaign. The published preface, in contrast, stands to the original preface as a set of strategic objectives stands to the aim of an entire campaign. The crisis of self-knowledge is to be met by insight into insight and insight into oversight, by unfolding the

2 *Insight*, 769.
3 Ibid., 770.

philosophic implications of insight into insight, by transposing the acquired self-knowledge to the practical sphere of human affairs. Finally, the introduction brings to light the tactics Lonergan employs in *Insight* to achieve his strategic objectives. His leading question about knowledge regards facts, not mere possibilities. Instances of insight from mathematics and science are chosen for their illustrative value in bringing to light the nature and significance of insight. The reader is asked to attend to his or her own intellectual performance and is invited to take possession of it. The presentation is structured with the incremental nature of personal development in mind. The book is written pedagogically, in an invitatory style, from a 'moving viewpoint.' The introduction contains the 'slogan' of the book: 'Thoroughly understand what it is to understand, and not only will you understand the broad lines of all there is to be understood but also you will possess a fixed base, an invariant pattern, opening upon all further developments of understanding.'

The three introductory selections, then, pertain to Lonergan's overall aim, his strategy in pursuing that aim, and his tactics in carrying out that strategy. But one theme in particular is repeated in all three selections, which pertains as much to the aims the careful reader should bring to *Insight* as to those of its writer: the theme of self-appropriation, of the appropriation of one's own rational self-consciousness. The reader may also find the last selection in Part 1 of this volume, on the nature and value of self-appropriation, a helpful preparation for tackling selections from the main body of *Insight*.

These extracts are taken from 'The Original Preface of *Insight*,' 3–7, and *Insight*, 3, 4, 5, 7–9, 11–14, 17–18, 20, 22–3.

1 The Original Preface

Rational self-consciousness is a peak above the clouds. Intelligent and reasonable, responsible and free, scientific and metaphysical, it stands above romantic spontaneity and the psychological depths, historical determinism and social engineering, the disconcerted existential subject and the undeciphered symbols of the artist and modernist.

Yet if man can scale the summit of his inner being, also he can fail to advert to the possibility of the ascent or, again, he can begin the climb only to lose his way. If then he knows himself as in fact he is, he can know no more than that he has been cast into the world to be afflicted with questions he does not answer and with aspirations he does not fulfil. For it is the paradox of man that what he is by nature is so much less than what he can become; and it is the tragedy of man that the truth, which portrays him as actually he is, can descend like an iron curtain to frustrate what he would and might be.

Facts, it is said, are stubborn things. But there is a sense in which, I believe, it is true to say that the facts about man can be outflanked. For a change in man, a development of potentialities that are no less real because, like all potentialities they are latent, not only is itself a fact but also can be a permanent source of new facts that cumulatively alter the complexion of the old.

So it is that the present work is a program rather than an argument. It begins not by assuming premises but by presuming readers. It advances not by deducing conclusions from the truths of a religious faith or from the principles of a philosophy but by issuing to readers an invitation, ever more precise and more detailed, to apprehend, to appropriate, to envisage in all its consequences, the inner focus of their own intelligence and reasonableness. That focus, it will be claimed, is insight. But to apprehend the focus is to gain insight into insight, to pierce the outer verbal and conceptual exhibitions of mathematics, of science, and of common sense, and to penetrate to the inner dynamism of intelligent inquiry and critical reflection. To appropriate the focus is both to know and to know what it is to know one's own intelligence, one's own reasonableness, one's own essential and restrictedly effective freedom. To envisage the focus in the full range of its implications is to discover for oneself what is meant by being, by objectivity, by metaphysics, by ethics, by God, and by evil.

Frankly, even as a program, even as a sketch that offers only to indicate the detailed map that is needed, the present work may be reproached for excessive ambition. But if I may borrow a phrase from Ortega y Gasset, one has to strive to mount to the level of one's time. The twentieth century has been described as the end of the Renaissance. Some four centuries ago there was projected a new world: new nations had arisen in new political constellations; a new art was matched with the promise of a new science; and new philosophies were disseminated through a new education. That new world has been realized, but the ideas that fostered its genesis have been discredited by its maturity. What was so new has become so old. To have been educated is no longer a matter of speaking Latin and writing Greek. Modern art would puzzle Raffaello, as modern technology would astound da Vinci. The new nations are not in Europe, and the issues of modern politics seem transcribed from the pages of *Utopia*. Einstein has revised momentously the thought of Galileo, and Heisenberg has contended that good Laplace, like Homer, nods. The novel outlook that is transforming the natural sciences cannot but affect profoundly the methods that were transferred with so sedulous a fidelity from the natural to the human sciences. Not even Renaissance ridicule of the Middle Ages has been able to prevent a rebirth of interest in logic. Not even the Enlightenment's insistence on the autonomy of man has been able to prevent the recurrence of theological themes under the guise of existentialist philosophy.

So it is that a new world has been bequeathed us and yet we, the heirs of the Renaissance, have been denied its spirit of bold confidence, of venturous assurance. For we know too much in too many fields, we have witnessed too much suffering in too many unexpected quarters, to purchase confidence by an easy exuberance of feeling or to accept words of assurance without answers to our questions. Nor was the basic question missed, when the late Prof. Ernst Cassirer, towards the end of a long and highly productive career, endeavored to communicate within a brief compass some of the main conclusions of his vast erudition and ever penetrating thought. Just what is man? Answers, he remarked, have been worked out by theologians and scientists, by politicians and sociologists, by biologists and psychologists, by ethnologists and economists. But not only do the many answers not agree, not only is there lacking some generally accepted principle that would select one and reject the others, but even within specialized fields there seems to be no method that can confront basic issues without succumbing to individual temperament and personal evaluations.

In the midst of this widespread disorientation, man's problem of self-knowledge ceases to be simply the individual concern inculcated by the ancient sage. It takes on the dimensions of a social crisis. It can be read as the historical issue of the twentieth century. If in that balance human intelligence and reasonableness, human responsibility and freedom, are to prevail, then they must be summoned from the dim and confused realm of latent factors and they must burst forth in the full flower of self-awareness and self-possession.

If such is the urgency of personal appropriation of rational self-consciousness, the difficulty of achievement should not discourage attempts at making a beginning. If the extent and the complexity of modern knowledge preclude the possibility in our time both of the

uomo universale of the Renaissance and of the medieval writer of a
Summa, at least the collaboration of many contains a promise of success, where the unaided individual would have to despair.

Still a collaboration has its conditions. It supposes a common vision
of a common goal. It supposes at least a tentative idea that would unify
and coordinate separate efforts in different fields. It supposes a central
nucleus that somehow could retain its identity yet undergo all the
modifications and enrichments that could be poured into its capacious
frame from specialized investigations.

It is with the conditions, preliminary to an effective collaboration,
that the present work is concerned. For in the measure that potential
collaborators move towards a personal appropriation of their rational
self-consciousness, in the same measure they will begin to attain the
needed vision of the common goal. In the measure that they discover
in themselves the structure of developing intelligence, in the same
measure they will share a tentative idea that can unify and coordinate
separate efforts in different fields. In the measure that they reach the
invariants of intellectual development, in the same measure they will
possess a central nucleus that retains its identity through all the possible developments of human intelligence.

Prof. Cassirer has told us that, from the viewpoint of a phenomenology of human culture, the explanatory definition of man is *animal
symbolicum* rather than *animal rationale*. But in the measure that men
appropriate their rational self-consciousness, not only do they reestablish the *animal rationale* but also they break through the phenomenological veil. For, as will be argued, they can reach a universal viewpoint from which individual temperament can be discounted, personal
evaluations can be criticized, and the many and disparate reports on
man, emanating from experts in various fields, can be welded into a
single view.

But if I believe that man's self-awareness and self-possession can
add a further, overarching component to Prof. Cassirer's portrayal of
man, it is not to be overlooked that a possibility is claimed and not an
achievement. I could not convey my meaning without venturing into
many fields, into mathematics and physics, into the subtleties of common sense and depth psychology, into the processes of history, the
intricacies of interpretation, the dialectic of the philosophies, and the
possibility of transcendent knowledge. I would not wish anyone to
entertain the fanciful nonsense that I can speak with authority or even

competence in so many fields. I do not expect many experts to recognize their science in the formulations that suit my purpose. Yet, perhaps, I may hope that there will be some that share my preoccupations and interests, that will divine what I am endeavoring to say and will proceed to say it more adequately, that will grasp how my ignorance and oversights can be remedied without completely invalidating the fundamental structures that make possible a common vision of a common goal. Finally, if in any measure that hope is realized, the relative isolation of my efforts will have ended and the preliminary conditions will begin to be fulfilled for the collaboration I would merely initiate ...

2 Preface

In the ideal detective story the reader is given all the clues yet fails to spot the criminal. He may advert to each clue as it arises. He needs no further clues to solve the mystery. Yet he can remain in the dark for the simple reason that reaching the solution is not the mere apprehension of any clue, not the mere memory of all, but a quite distinct activity of organizing intelligence that places the full set of clues in a unique explanatory perspective.

By insight, then, is meant not any act of attention or advertence or memory but the supervening act of understanding. It is not any recondite intuition but the familiar event that occurs easily and frequently in the moderately intelligent, rarely and with difficulty only in the very stupid. In itself it is so simple and obvious that it seems to merit the little attention that commonly it receives. At the same time, its function in cognitional activity is so central that to grasp it in its conditions, its working, and its results is to confer a basic yet startling unity on the whole field of human inquiry and human opinion ...

The aim of the work is to convey an insight into insight. Mathematicians seek insight into sets of elements. Scientists seek insight into ranges of phenomena. Men of common sense seek insight into concrete situations and practical affairs. But our concern is to reach the act of organizing intelligence that brings within a single perspective the insights of mathematicians, scientists, and men of common sense ...

Further, while all acts of understanding have a certain family likeness, a full and balanced view is to be reached only by combining in a single account the evidence obtained from different fields of intelligent activity. Thus, the precise nature of the act of understanding is to be seen most clearly in mathematical examples; the dynamic context in which understanding occurs can be studied to best advantage in an investigation of scientific methods; the disturbance of that dynamic context by alien concerns is thrust upon one's attention by the manner in which various measures of common nonsense blend with common sense.

However, insight is not only a mental activity but also a constituent factor in human knowledge. It follows that insight into insight is in some sense a knowledge of knowledge. Indeed, it is a knowledge of knowledge that seems extremely relevant to a whole series of basic problems in philosophy ...

Besides insights there are oversights. Besides the dynamic context of detached and disinterested inquiry in which insights emerge with a notable frequency, there are the contrary dynamic contexts of the flight from understanding in which oversights occur regularly and one might almost say systematically. Hence, if insight into insight is not to be an oversight of oversights, it must include an insight into the principal devices of the flight from understanding ...

The present work, then, may be said to operate on three levels: it is a study of human understanding; it unfolds the philosophic implications of understanding; it is a campaign against the flight from understanding. These three levels are solidary. Without the first there would be no base for the second and no precise meaning for the third. Without the second the first could not get beyond elementary statements, and there could be no punch to the third. Without the third the second would be regarded as incredible, and the first would be neglected ...

There remains the question, What practical good can come of this book? The answer is more forthright than might be expected, for insight is the source not only of theoretical knowledge but also of all its practical applications, and indeed of all intelligent activity. Insight into insight, then, will reveal what activity is intelligent, and insight into oversights will reveal what activity is unintelligent. But to be practical is to do the intelligent thing, and to be unpractical is to keep blundering about. It follows that insight into both insight and oversight is the very key to practicality.

Thus, insight into insight brings to light the cumulative process of progress. For concrete situations give rise to insights which issue into policies and courses of action. Action transforms the existing situation to give rise to further insights, better policies, more effective courses of action. It follows that if insight occurs, it keeps recurring; and at each recurrence knowledge develops, action increases its scope, and situations improve.

Similarly, insight into oversight reveals the cumulative process of decline. For the flight from understanding blocks the insights that concrete situations demand. There follow unintelligent policies and inept courses of action. The situation deteriorates to demand still further insights, and as they are blocked, policies become more unintelligent and action more inept. What is worse, the deteriorating situation seems to provide the uncritical, biased mind with factual evidence in which the bias is claimed to be verified. So in ever increasing measure intelligence comes to be regarded as irrelevant to practical living. Human activity settles down to a decadent routine, and initiative becomes the privilege of violence.

Unfortunately, as insight and oversight commonly are mated, so also are progress and decline. We reinforce our love of truth with a practicality that is equivalent to an obscurantism. We correct old evils with a passion that mars the new good. We are not pure. We compromise. We hope to muddle through. But the very advance of knowledge brings a power over nature and over men too vast and terrifying to be entrusted to the good intentions of unconsciously biased minds. We have to learn to distinguish sharply between progress and decline, learn to encourage progress without putting a premium upon decline, learn to remove the tumor of the flight from understanding without destroying the organs of intelligence.

No problem is at once more delicate and more profound, more practical and perhaps more pressing. How, indeed, is a mind to become conscious of its own bias when that bias springs from a communal flight from understanding and is supported by the whole texture of a civilization? How can new strength and vigor be imparted to the detached and disinterested desire to understand without the reinforcement acting as an added bias? How can human intelligence hope to deal with the unintelligible yet objective situations which the flight from understanding creates and expands and sustains? At least we can make a beginning by asking what precisely it is to understand, what are the dynamics of the flow of consciousness that favors insight, what are the interferences that favor oversight, what, finally, do the answers to such questions imply for the guidance of human thought and action.

3 Introduction

The aim of the present work may be bracketed by a series of disjunctions. In the first place, the question is not whether knowledge exists but what precisely is its nature. Secondly, while the content of the known cannot be disregarded, still it is to be treated only in the schematic and incomplete fashion needed to provide a discriminant or determinant of cognitive acts. Thirdly, the aim is not to set forth a list of the abstract properties of human knowledge but to assist the reader in effecting a personal appropriation of the concrete dynamic structure immanent and recurrently operative in his own cognitional activities. Fourthly, such an appropriation can occur only gradually, and so there will be offered, not a sudden account of the whole of the structure, but a slow assembly of its elements, relations, alternatives, and implications. Fifthly, the order of the assembly is governed, not by abstract considerations of logical or metaphysical priority, but by concrete motives of pedagogical efficacy.

The program, then, is both concrete and practical, and the motives for undertaking its execution reside, not in the realm of easy generalities, but in the difficult domain of matters of fact. If at the end of the course the reader will be convinced of those facts, much will be achieved; but at the present moment all I can do is to clarify my intentions by stating my beliefs.

I ask, accordingly, about the nature rather than about the existence of knowledge because in each of us there exist two different kinds of knowledge. They are juxtaposed in Cartesian dualism with its rational *Cogito, ergo sum* and with its unquestioning extroversion to substantial extension. They are separated and alienated in the subsequent rationalist and empiricist philosophies. They are brought together again to cancel each other in Kantian criticism. If these statements approximate the facts, then the question of human knowledge is not whether it exists but what precisely are its two diverse forms and what are the relations between them. If that is the relevant question, then any departure from it is, in the same measure, the misfortune of missing the point. But whether or not that is the relevant question can be settled only by undertaking an arduous exploratory journey through the many fields in which men succeed in knowing or attempt the task but fail.

Secondly, an account of knowing cannot disregard its content, and its content is so extensive that it mocks encyclopedias and overflows libraries; its content is so difficult that a man does well devoting his life to mastering some part of it; yet even so, its content is incomplete and subject to further additions, inadequate and subject to repeated future revisions. Does it not follow that the proposed exploratory journey is not merely arduous but impossible? Certainly it would be impossible, at least for the writer, if an acquaintance with the whole range of knowledge were a requisite in the present inquiry. But in fact our primary concern is not the known but the knowing. The known is extensive, but the knowing is a recurrent structure that can be investigated sufficiently in a series of strategically chosen instances. The known is difficult to master, but in our day competent specialists have labored to select for serious readers and to present to them in an adequate fashion the basic components of the various departments of knowledge. Finally, the known is incomplete and subject to revision, but our concern is the knower that will be the source of the future additions and revisions.

It will not be amiss to add a few corollaries, for nothing disorientates a reader more than a failure to state clearly what a book is not about. Basically, then, this is not a book on mathematics, nor a book on science, nor a book on common sense, nor a book on metaphysics; indeed, in a sense, it is not even a book about knowledge. On a first level, the book contains sentences on mathematics, on science, on common sense, on metaphysics. On a second level, the meaning of all these sentences, their intention and significance, are to be grasped only by going beyond the scraps of mathematics or science or common sense or metaphysics to the dynamic cognitional structure that is exemplified in knowing them. On a third level, the dynamic cognitional structure to be reached is not the transcendental ego of Fichtean speculation, nor the abstract pattern of relations verifiable in Tom and Dick and Harry, but the personally appropriated structure of one's own experiencing, one's own intelligent inquiry and insights, one's own critical reflection and judging and deciding. The crucial issue is an experimental issue, and the experiment will be performed not publicly but privately. It will consist in one's own rational self-consciousness clearly and distinctly taking possession of itself as rational self-consciousness. Up to that decisive achievement all leads. From it all follows. No one else, no matter what his knowledge or his eloquence, no matter what his logical rigor or his persuasiveness, can do it for you. But though the act is private, both its antecedents and its consequents have their public manifestation. There can be long series of marks on paper that communicate an invitation to know oneself in the tension of the duality of one's own knowing; and among such series of marks with an invitatory meaning the present book would wish to be numbered. Nor need it remain a secret whether such invitations are helpful or, when helpful, accepted. Winter twilight cannot be mistaken for the summer noonday sun.

In the third place, then, more than all else the aim of the book is to issue an invitation to a personal, decisive act. But the very nature of the act demands that it be understood in itself and in its implications. What on earth is meant by rational self-consciousness? What is meant by inviting it to take possession of itself? Why is such self-possession said to be so decisive and momentous? The questions are perfectly legitimate, but the answer cannot be brief.

However, it is not the answer itself that counts so much as the manner in which it is read. For the answer cannot but be written in words; the words cannot but proceed from definitions and correlations, analyses and inferences; yet the whole point of the present answer would be missed if a reader insisted on concluding that I must be engaged in setting forth lists of abstract properties of human knowing. The present work is not to be read as though it described some distant region of the globe which the reader never visited, or some strange and mystical experience which the reader never shared. It is an account of knowledge. Though I cannot recall to each reader his personal experiences, he can do so for himself and thereby pluck my general phrases from the dim world of thought to set them in the pulsing flow of life. Again, in such fields as mathematics and natural science it is possible to delineate with some accuracy the precise content of a precise insight; but the point of the delineation is not to provide the reader with a stream of words that he can repeat to others or with a set of terms and relations from which he can proceed to draw inferences and prove conclusions. On the contrary, the point here, as elsewhere, is appropriation; the point is to discover, to identify, to become familiar with, the activities of one's own intelligence; the point is to become able to discriminate with ease and from personal conviction between one's purely intellectual activities and the manifold of other, 'existential' concerns that invade and mix and blend with the operations of intellect to render it ambivalent and its pronouncements ambiguous ...

There is now to be explained the fourth disjunction, for the labor of self-appropriation cannot occur at a single leap. Essentially, it is a development of the subject and in the subject, and like all development it can be solid and fruitful only by being painstaking and slow.

Now it would be absurd to offer to aid a process of development and yet write as though the whole development were already an accomplished fact. A teacher of geometry may be convinced that the whole of Euclid is contained in the theory of the n-dimensional manifold of any curvature. But he does not conclude that Euclid is to be omitted from the elementary program and that his pupils should begin from the tensor calculus. For even though Euclid is a particular case, still it is the particular case that alone gives access to the general case. And even though Euclidean propositions call for qualification when the more general context is reached, still an effective teacher does not distract his pupils with qualifications they will understand only vaguely, when it is his business to herd them as best he can across the *pons asinorum*.

In similar fashion this book is written, not from above downwards, but from below upwards. Any coherent set of statements can be divided into definitions, postulates, and conclusions. But it does not follow that between the covers of a single book there must be a single coherent set of statements. For the single book may be written from a moving viewpoint, and then it will contain, not a single set of coherent statements, but a sequence of related sets of coherent statements. Moreover, as is clear, a book designed to aid a development must be written from a moving viewpoint. It cannot begin by presupposing that a reader can assimilate at a stroke what can be attained only at the term of a prolonged and arduous effort. On the contrary, it must begin from a minimal viewpoint and a minimal context; it will exploit that minimum to raise a further question that enlarges the viewpoint and the context; it will proceed with the enlarged viewpoint and context only as long as is necessary to raise still deeper issues that again transform the basis and the terms of reference of the inquiry; and clearly, this device can be repeated not merely once or twice but as often as may be required to reach the universal viewpoint and the completely concrete context that embraces every aspect of reality ...

In the fifth place – to turn to the final disjunction – the order in which the moving viewpoint assembles the elements for an appropriation of one's own intellectual and rational self-consciousness is governed, not by considerations of logical or metaphysical priority, but by considerations of pedagogical efficacy ...

To conclude, our aim regards (1) not the fact of knowledge but a discrimination between two facts of knowledge, (2) not the details of the known but the structure of the knowing, (3) not the knowing as an object characterized by catalogues of abstract properties but the appropriation of one's own intellectual and rational self-consciousness, (4) not a sudden leap to appropriation but a slow and painstaking development, and (5) not a development indicated by appealing either to the logic of the as yet unknown goal or to a presupposed and as yet unexplained ontologically structured metaphysics, but a development that can begin in any sufficiently cultured consciousness, that expands in virtue of the dynamic tendencies of that consciousness itself, and that heads through an understanding of all understanding to a basic understanding of all that can be understood.

The last phrase has the ring of a slogan, and happily enough it sums up the positive content of this work. *Thoroughly understand what it is to understand, and not only will you understand the broad lines of all there is to be understood but also you will possess a fixed base, an invariant pattern, opening upon all further developments of understanding.*

For the appropriation of one's own rational self-consciousness, which has been so stressed in this introduction, is not an end in itself but rather a beginning. It is a necessary beginning, for unless one breaks the duality in one's knowing, one doubts that understanding correctly is knowing. Under the pressure of that doubt, either one will sink into the bog of a knowing that is without understanding, or else one will cling to understanding but sacrifice knowing on the altar of an immanentism, an idealism, a relativism. From the horns of that dilemma one escapes only through the discovery – and one has not made it yet if one has no clear memory of its startling strangeness – that there are two quite different realisms, that there is an incoherent realism, half animal and half human, that poses as a halfway house between materialism and idealism, and on the other hand that there is an intelligent and reasonable realism between which and materialism the halfway house is idealism.

The beginning, then, not only is self-knowledge and self-appropriation but also a criterion of the real. If to convince oneself that knowing is understanding, one ascertains that knowing mathematics is understanding and knowing science is understanding and the knowledge of common sense is understanding, one ends up not only with a detailed account of understanding but also with a plan of what there is to be known. The many sciences lose their isolation from one another; the chasm between science and common sense is bridged; the structure of the universe proportionate to man's intellect is revealed; and as that revealed structure provides an object for a metaphysics, so the initial self-criticism provides a method for explaining how metaphysical and antimetaphysical affirmations arise, for selecting those that are correct, and for eliminating those that patently spring from a lack of accurate self-knowledge. Further, as a metaphysics is derived from the known structure of one's knowing, so an ethics results from knowledge of the compound structure of one's knowing and doing; and as the metaphysics, so too the ethics prolongs the initial self-criticism into an explanation of the origin of all ethical positions and into a criterion for passing judgment on each of them. Nor is this all. Still further questions press upon one. They might be ignored if knowing were not understanding or if understanding were compatible with the obscurantism that arbitrarily brushes questions aside. But knowing is understanding, and understanding is incompatible with the obscurantism that arbitrarily brushes questions aside. The issue of transcendent knowledge has to be faced. Can man know more than the intelligibility immanent in the world of possible experience? If he can, how can he conceive it? If he can conceive it, how can he affirm it? If he can affirm it, how can he reconcile that affirmation with the evil that tortures too many human bodies, darkens too many human minds, hardens too many human hearts?

Related selections: 1.XVII on self-appropriation and the aims of *Insight*.

II

The Act of Insight

The first five chapters of *Insight* are explorations of the nature and role of the act of insight in mathematics and empirical natural science. In these chapters Lonergan invites his readers to 'pierce the outer verbal and conceptual exhibitions' of their intellectual endeavors and to gain an insight into the act of insight. The purpose behind Lonergan's treatment of these disciplines is primarily illustrative. Nevertheless, these opening chapters presuppose considerable familiarity on the part of the reader with the procedures involved in mathematics and empirical science. After the publication of *Insight*, when the difficulties encountered by its readers became apparent, Lonergan reiterated his illustrative aim and advised readers daunted by scientific examples of insight and the associated use of mathematics to move directly to the later chapters on common sense and the role of insight in ordinary social and practical life. This advice, though, was qualified by his insistence on the importance of first studying the analysis of the elements of the act of insight in *Insight*'s opening chapter, upon which so many basic positions developed later on depend. That analysis draws on instances of insight in mathematics, but the illustrations are accessible to readers with ordinary familiarity with the discipline. Lonergan employs mathematical examples in his opening analysis because in mathematics the content and context of insights are clearly and precisely defined and the existence of intellectual operations underlying and generating concepts and expressions is most easily exhibited.

The present selection, from Chapter 1 and the beginning of Chapter 2 of *Insight*, opens with an account of a historic instance of insight and draws out the main features of the act. Lonergan details the nature of definition, the patterned set of concepts resulting from insight. He defines and relates the question, the image, concepts, and different kinds of definition. On the basis of his account of the cognitional elements surrounding insight, he goes on to explain how insights accumulate and give rise to higher viewpoints. In the fourth and fifth parts of this selection Lonergan introduces the related and centrally significant notions of inverse insight and the empirical residue. The occurrence of inverse insight plays a central role in the development of science, and the existence of an empirical residue from which insight abstracts underlies the very possibility of scientific generalization and collaboration. The final part is Lonergan's introduction to the third chapter of *Insight* which is on heuristic structures of empirical method. In it he compares and contrasts mathematical and scientific insights and highlights key features of his basic account of this central event in human knowing.

These extracts are taken from *Insight*, 27–45, 46–7; 49–54, 54–5; 57–9.

In the midst of that vast and profound stirring of human minds which we name the Renaissance, Descartes was convinced that too many people felt it beneath them to direct their efforts to apparently trifling problems. Again and again in his *Regulae ad directionem ingenii*, he reverts to this theme. Intellectual mastery of mathematics, of the departments of science, of philosophy is the fruit of a slow and steady accumulation of little insights. Great problems are solved by being broken down into little problems. The strokes of genius are but the outcome of a continuous habit of inquiry that grasps clearly and distinctly all that is involved in the simple things that anyone can understand.

I thought it well to begin by recalling this conviction of a famous mathematician and philosopher, for our first task will be to attain familiarity with what is meant by insight, and the only way to achieve this end is, it seems, to attend very closely to a series of instances all of which are rather remarkable for their banality.

1 A Dramatic Instance

Our first illustrative instance of insight will be the story of Archimedes rushing naked from the baths of Syracuse with the cryptic cry 'Eureka!' King Hiero, it seems, had had a votive crown fashioned by a smith of rare skill and doubtful honesty. He wished to know whether or not baser metals had been added to the gold. Archimedes was set the problem and in the bath had hit upon the solution. Weigh the crown in water! Implicit in this directive were the principles of displacement and of specific gravity.

With those principles of hydrostatics we are not directly concerned. For our objective is an insight into insight. Archimedes had his insight by thinking about the crown; we shall have ours by thinking about Archimedes. What we have to grasp is that insight (1) comes as a release to the tension of inquiry, (2) comes suddenly and unexpectedly, (3) is a function not of outer circumstances but of inner conditions, (4) pivots between the concrete and the abstract, and (5) passes into the habitual texture of one's mind.[1]

First, then, insight comes as a release to the tension of inquiry. This feature is dramatized in the story by Archimedes' peculiarly uninhibited exultation. But the point I would make does not lie in this outburst of delight but in the antecedent desire and effort that it betrays. For if the typical scientist's satisfaction in success is more sedate, his earnestness in inquiry can still exceed that of Archimedes. Deep within us all, emergent when the noise of other appetites is stilled, there is a drive to know, to understand, to see why, to discover the reason, to find the cause, to explain. Just what is wanted has many names. In what precisely it consists is a matter of dispute. But the fact of inquiry is beyond all doubt. It can absorb a man. It can keep him for hours, day after day, year after year, in the narrow prison of his study or his laboratory. It can send him on dangerous voyages of exploration. It can withdraw him from other interests, other pursuits, other pleasures, other achievements. It can fill his waking thoughts, hide from him the world of ordinary affairs, invade the very fabric of his dreams. It can demand endless sacrifices that are made without regret though there is only the hope, never a certain promise, of success. What better symbol could one find for this obscure, exigent, imperious drive, than a man, naked, running, excitedly crying, 'I've got it'?

Secondly, insight comes suddenly and unexpectedly. It did not occur when Archimedes was in the mood and posture that a sculptor would select to portray 'The Thinker.' It came in a flash, on a trivial occasion, in a moment of relaxation. Once more there is dramatized a universal aspect of insight. For it is reached, in the last analysis, not by learning rules, not by following precepts, not by studying any

---

1 A profusion of instances of insight is offered by E.D. Hutchinson in three articles originally published in *Psychiatry* and reprinted in *A Study of Interpersonal Relations*, ed. P. Mullahy (New York: Hermitage Press, 1949).

methodology. Discovery is a new beginning. It is the origin of new rules that supplement or even supplant the old. Genius is creative. It is genius precisely because it disregards established routines, because it originates the novelties that will be the routines of the future. Were there rules for discovery, then discoveries would be mere conclusions. Were there precepts for genius, then men of genius would be hacks. Indeed, what is true of discovery also holds for the transmission of discoveries by teaching. For a teacher cannot undertake to make a pupil understand. All he can do is present the sensible elements in the issue in a suggestive order and with a proper distribution of emphasis. It is up to the pupils themselves to reach understanding, and they do so in varying measures of ease and rapidity. Some get the point before the teacher can finish his exposition. Others just manage to keep pace with him. Others see the light only when they go over the matter by themselves. Some, finally, never catch on at all; for a while they follow the classes, but sooner or later they drop by the way.

Thirdly, insight is a function, not of outer circumstances, but of inner conditions. Many frequented the baths of Syracuse without coming to grasp the principles of hydrostatics. But who bathed there without feeling the water, or without finding it hot or cold or tepid? There is, then, a strange difference between insight and sensation. Unless one is deaf, one cannot avoid hearing. Unless one is blind, one has only to open one's eyes to see. The occurrence and the content of sensation stand in some immediate correlation with outer circumstance. But with insight internal conditions are paramount. Thus, insight depends upon native endowment, and so with fair accuracy one can say that insight is the act that occurs frequently in the intelligent and rarely in the stupid. Again, insight depends upon a habitual orientation, upon a perpetual alertness ever asking the little question, Why? Finally, insight depends on the accurate presentation of definite problems. Had Hiero not put his problem to Archimedes, had Archimedes not thought earnestly, perhaps desperately, upon it, the baths of Syracuse would have been no more famous than any others.

Fourthly, insight pivots between the concrete and the abstract. Archimedes' problem was concrete. He had to settle whether a particular crown was made of pure gold. Archimedes' solution was concrete. It was to weigh the crown in water. Yet if we ask what was the point to that procedure, we have to have recourse to the abstract formulations of the principles of displacement and of specific gravity. Without that point, weighing the crown in water would be mere eccentricity. Once the point is grasped, King Hiero and his golden crown become minor historical details of no scientific importance. Again the story dramatizes a universal aspect of insight. For if insights arise from concrete problems, if they reveal their value in concrete applications, nonetheless they possess a significance greater than their origins and a relevance wider than their original applications. Because insights arise with reference to the concrete, geometers use diagrams, mathematicians need pen and paper, teachers need blackboards, pupils have to perform experiments for themselves, doctors have to see their patients, troubleshooters have to travel to the spot, people with a mechanical bent take things apart to see how they work. But because the significance and relevance of insight goes beyond any concrete problem or application, men formulate abstract sciences with their numbers and symbols, their technical terms and formulae, their definitions, postulates, and deductions. Thus by its very nature insight is the mediator, the hinge, the pivot. It is insight *into* the concrete world of sense and imagination. Yet what is known by insight, what insight adds to sensible and imagined presentations, finds its adequate expression only in the abstract and recondite formulations of the sciences.

Fifthly, insight passes into the habitual texture of one's mind. Before Archimedes could solve his problem, he needed an instant of inspiration. But he needed no further inspiration when he went to offer the king his solution. Once one has understood, one has crossed a divide. What a moment ago was an insoluble problem now becomes incredibly simple and obvious. Moreover, it tends to remain simple and obvious. However laborious the first occurrence of an insight may be, subsequent repetitions occur almost at will. This, too, is a universal characteristic of insight, and indeed it constitutes the possibility of learning. For we can learn inasmuch as we can add insight to insight, inasmuch as the new does not extrude the old but complements and combines with it. Inversely, inasmuch as the subject to be learnt involves the acquisition of a whole series of insights, the process of learning is marked by an initial period of darkness in which one gropes about insecurely, in which one cannot see where one is going, in which one cannot grasp what all the fuss is about; and only gradually, as one begins to catch on, does the initial darkness yield to a subsequent period of increasing light, confidence, interest, absorption. Then the infinitesimal calculus or theoretical physics or the issues of philosophy cease to be the mysterious and foggy realms they had seemed. Imperceptibly we shift from the helpless infancy of the beginner to the modest self-confidence of the advanced student. Eventually we become capable of taking over the teacher's role and complaining of the remarkable obtuseness of pupils that fail to see what, of course, is perfectly simple and obvious to those that understand.

2 Definition

As every schoolboy knows, a circle is a locus of coplanar points equidistant from a center. What every schoolboy does not know is the difference between repeating that definition as a parrot might and uttering it intelligently. So, with a sidelong bow to Descartes's insistence on the importance of understanding very simple things, let us inquire into the genesis of the definition of the circle.

2.1 The Clue

Imagine a cartwheel with its bulky hub, its stout spokes, its solid rim.

Ask a question. Why is it round?

Limit the question. What is wanted is the immanent reason or ground of the roundness of the wheel. Hence a correct answer will not introduce new data such as carts, carting, transportation, wheelwrights, or their tools. It will refer simply to the wheel.

Consider a suggestion. The wheel is round because its spokes are equal. Clearly, that will not do. The spokes could be equal yet sunk unequally into the hub and rim. Again, the rim could be flat between successive spokes.

Still, we have a clue. Let the hub decrease to a point; let the rim and spokes thin out into lines; then, if there were an infinity of spokes and all were exactly equal, the rim would have to be perfectly round; inversely, were any of the spokes unequal, the rim could not avoid bumps or dents. Hence we can say that the wheel necessarily is round inasmuch as the distance from the center of the hub to the outside of the rim is always the same.

A number of observations are now in order. The foregoing brings us close enough to the definition of the circle. But our purpose is to attain insight, not into the circle, but into the act illustrated by insight into the circle.

The first observation, then, is that points and lines cannot be imagined. One can imagine an extremely small dot. But no matter how small a dot may be, still it has magnitude. To reach a point, all magnitude must vanish, and with all magnitude there vanishes the dot as well. One can imagine an extremely fine thread. But no matter how fine a thread may be, still it has breadth and depth as well as length. Remove from the image all breadth and depth, and there vanishes all length as well.

2.2   Concepts

The second observation is that points and lines are concepts.

Just as imagination is the playground of our desires and our fears, so conception is the playground of our intelligence. Just as imagination can create objects never seen or heard or felt, so too conception can create objects that cannot even be imagined. How? By supposing. The imagined dot has magnitude as well as position, but the geometer says, 'Let us suppose it has only position.' The imagined line has breadth as well as length, but the geometer says, 'Let us suppose it has only length.'

Still, there is method in this madness. Our images and especially our dreams seem very random affairs, yet psychologists offer to explain them. Similarly, the suppositions underlying concepts may appear very fanciful, yet they too can be explained. Why did we require the hub to decrease to a point and the spokes and rim to mere lines? Because we had a clue – the equality of the spokes – and we were pushing it for all it was worth. As long as the hub had any magnitude, the spokes could be sunk into it unequally. As long as the spokes had any thickness, the wheel could be flat at their ends. So we supposed a point without magnitude and lines without thickness, to obtain a curve that would be perfectly, necessarily round.

Note, then, two properties of concepts. In the first place, they are constituted by the mere activity of supposing, thinking, considering, formulating, defining. They may or may not be more than that. But if they are more, then they are not merely concepts. And if they are no more than supposed or considered or thought about, still that is enough to constitute them as concepts. In the second place, concepts do not occur at random; they emerge in thinking, supposing, considering, defining, formulating; and that many-named activity occurs, not at random, but in conjunction with an act of insight.

2.3   The Image

The third observation is that the image is necessary for the insight.

Points and lines cannot be imagined. But neither can necessity or impossibility be imagined. Yet in approaching the definition of the circle there occurred some apprehension of necessity and of impossibility. As we remarked, if all the radii are equal the curve must be perfectly round, and if any radii are unequal the curve cannot avoid bumps or dents.

Further, the necessity in question was not necessity in general but a necessity of roundness resulting from these equal radii. Similarly, the impossibility in question was not impossibility in the abstract but an impossibility of roundness resulting from these unequal radii. Eliminate the image of the center, the radii, the curve, and by the same stroke there vanishes all grasp of necessary or of impossible roundness.

But it is that grasp that constitutes the insight. It is the occurrence of that grasp that makes the difference between repeating the definition of a circle as a parrot might and uttering it intelligently, uttering it with the ability to make up a new definition for oneself.

It follows that the image is necessary for the insight. Inversely, it follows that the insight is the act of catching on to a connection between imagined equal radii and, on the other hand, a curve that is bound to look perfectly round.

2.4   The Question

The fourth observation adverts to the question.

There is the question as expressed in words. Why is the wheel round?

Behind the words there may be conceptual acts of meaning, such as 'wheel,' 'round,' etc.

Behind these concepts there may be insights in which one grasps how to use such words as 'wheel,' 'round,' etc.

But what we are trying to get at is something different. Where does the 'Why?' come from? What does it reveal or represent? Already we had occasion to speak of the psychological tension that had its release in the joy of discovery. It is that tension, that drive, that desire to understand, that constitutes the primordial 'Why?' Name it what you please – alertness of mind, intellectual curiosity, the spirit of inquiry, active intelligence, the drive to know. Under any name, it remains the same, and is, I trust, very familiar to you.

This primordial drive, then, is the pure question. It is prior to any insights, any concepts, any words; for insights, concepts, words, have to do with answers, and before we look for answers we want them; such wanting is the pure question.

On the other hand, though the pure question is prior to insights, concepts, and words, it presupposes experiences and images. Just as insight is into the concretely given or imagined, so the pure question is about the concretely given or imagined. It is the wonder which Aristotle claimed to be the beginning of all science and philosophy. But no one just wonders. We wonder about something.

2.5   Genesis

A fifth observation distinguishes moments in the genesis of a definition.

When an animal has nothing to do it goes to sleep. When a man has nothing to do he may ask questions. The first moment is an awakening to one's intelligence. It is release from the dominance of biological drive and from the routines of everyday living. It is the effective emergence of wonder, of the desire to understand.

The second moment is the hint, the suggestion, the clue. Insight has begun. We have got hold of something. There is a chance that we are on the right track. Let's see.

The third moment is the process. Imagination has been released from other cares. It is free to cooperate with intellectual effort, and its cooperation consists in endeavoring to run parallel to intelligent suppositions, while at the same time restraining supposition within some limits of approximation to the imaginable field.

The fourth moment is achievement. By their cooperation, by successive adjustments, question and insight, image and concept, present a solid front. The answer is a patterned set of concepts. The image strains to approximate to the concepts. The concepts, by added conceptual determinations, can express their differences from the merely approximate image. The pivot between images and concepts is the insight. And setting the standard which insight, images, and concepts must meet is the question, the desire to know, that could have kept the process in motion by further queries had its requirements not been satisfied.

2.6   Nominal and Explanatory Definition

A sixth observation distinguishes different kinds of definition. As Euclid defined a straight line as a line lying evenly between its extremes, so he might have defined a circle as a perfectly round plane curve. As the former definition, so also the latter would serve to determine unequivocally the proper use of the names 'straight line,' 'circle.' But in fact Euclid's definition of the circle does more than reveal the proper use of the name 'circle.' It includes the affirmation that in any circle all radii are exactly equal; and were that affirmation not included in the definition, then it would have had to be added as a postulate.

To view the same matter from another angle, Euclid did postulate that all right angles are equal. Let us name the sum of two adjacent right angles a straight angle. Then, if all right angles are equal, necessarily all straight angles will be equal. Inversely, if all straight angles are equal, all right angles must be equal. Now, if straight lines are really straight, if they never bend in any direction, must not all straight angles be equal? Could not the postulate of the equality of straight angles be included in the definition of the straight line, as the postulate of the equality of radii is included in the definition of the circle?

At any rate, there is a difference between nominal and explanatory definitions. Nominal definitions merely tell us about the correct usage of names. Explanatory definitions also include something further that, were it not included in the definition, would have to be added as a postulate.

What constitutes the difference? It is not that explanatory definitions suppose an insight while nominal definitions do not. For a language is an enormously complicated tool with an almost endless variety of parts that admit a far greater number of significant combinations. If insight is needed to see how other tools are to be used properly and effectively, insight is similarly needed to use a language properly and effectively.

Still, this yields, I think, the answer to our question. Both nominal and explanatory definitions suppose insights. But a nominal definition supposes no more than an insight into the proper use of language. An explanatory definition, on the other hand, supposes a further insight

into the objects to which language refers. The name 'circle' is defined
as a perfectly round plane curve, as the name 'straight line' is defined
as a line lying evenly between its extremes. But when one goes on to
affirm that all radii in a circle are equal or that all right angles are
equal, one no longer is talking merely of names. One is making assertions about the objects which names denote.

2.7   *Primitive Terms*

A seventh observation adds a note on the old puzzle of primitive
terms.

Every definition presupposes other terms. If these can be defined,
their definitions will presuppose still other terms. But one cannot
regress to infinity. Hence, either definition is based on undefined terms
or else terms are defined in a circle so that each virtually defines itself.

Fortunately, we are under no necessity of accepting the argument's
supposition. Definitions do not occur in a private vacuum of their own.
They emerge in solidarity with experiences, images, questions, and
insights. It is true enough that every definition involves several terms,
but it is also true that no insight can be expressed by a single term, and
it is not true that every insight presupposes previous insights.

Let us say, then, that for every basic insight there is a circle of terms
and relations, such that the terms fix the relations, the relations fix the
terms, and the insight fixes both. If one grasps the necessary and sufficient conditions for the perfect roundness of this imagined plane
curve, then one grasps not only the circle but also the point, the line,
the circumference, the radii, the plane, and equality. All the concepts
tumble out together, because all are needed to express adequately a
single insight. All are coherent, for coherence basically means that all
hang together from a single insight.

Again, there can be a set of basic insights. Such is the set underlying
Euclidean geometry. Because the set of insights is coherent, they generate a set of coherent definitions. Because different objects of definition
are composed of similar elements, such terms as point, line, surface,
angle keep recurring in distinct definitions. Thus, Euclid begins his
exposition from a set of images, a set of insights, and a set of definitions; some of his definitions are merely nominal; some are explanatory; some are derived partly from nominally and partly from
explanatorily defined terms.

2.8   Implicit Definition

A final observation introduces the notion of implicit definition.

D. Hilbert has worked out foundations of geometry that satisfy con-temporary logicians. One of his important devices is known as implicit definition. Thus, the meaning of both point and straight line is fixed by the relation that two and only two points determine a straight line.

In terms of the foregoing analysis, one may say that implicit defini-tion consists in explanatory definition without nominal definition. It consists in explanatory definition, for the relation that two points determine a straight line is a postulational element such as the equality of all radii in a circle. It omits nominal definition, for one cannot restrict Hilbert's point to the Euclidean meaning of position without magnitude. An ordered pair of numbers satisfies Hilbert's implicit def-inition of a point, for two such pairs determine a straight line. Simi-larly, a first-degree equation satisfies Hilbert's implicit definition of a straight line, for such an equation is determined by two ordered pairs of numbers.

The significance of implicit definition is its complete generality. The omission of nominal definitions is the omission of a restriction to the objects which, in the first instance, one happens to be thinking about. The exclusive use of explanatory or postulational elements concen-trates attention upon the set of relationships in which the whole scien-tific significance is contained.

3   Higher Viewpoints

The next significant step to be taken in working out the nature of insight is to analyze development. Single insights occur either in isolation or in related fields. In the latter case, they combine, cluster, coalesce, into the mastery of a subject; they ground sets of definitions, postulates, deduc-tions; they admit applications to enormous ranges of instances. But the matter does not end there. Still further insights arise. The shortcomings of the previous position become recognized. New definitions and pos-tulates are devised. A new and larger field of deductions is set up. Broader and more accurate applications become possible. Such a com-plex shift in the whole structure of insights, definitions, postulates, deductions, and applications may be referred to very briefly as the emergence of a higher viewpoint. Our question is, Just what happens?

Taking our clue from Descartes's insistence on understanding simple things, we select as our pilot instance the transition from arithmetic to elementary algebra. Moreover, to guard against possible misinterpretations, let us say that by arithmetic is meant a subject studied in grade school and that by elementary algebra is meant a subject studied in high school.

3.1   Positive Integers

A first step is to offer some definition of the positive integers 1, 2, 3, 4 ...

Let us suppose an indefinite multitude of instances of 'one.' They may be anything anyone pleases, from sheep to instances of the act of counting or ordering.

Further, let us suppose as too familiar to be defined the notions of 'one,' 'plus,' and 'equals.'

Then, there is an infinite series of definitions for the infinite series of positive integers, and it may be indicated symbolically by the following:

$$1 + 1 = 2$$
$$2 + 1 = 3$$
$$3 + 1 = 4$$
etc., etc., etc. ...

This symbolic indication may be interpreted in any of a variety of manners. It means one plus one equals two, or two is one more than one, or the second is the next after the first, or even the relations between classes of groups each with one, or two, or three, etc., members. As the acute reader will see, the one important element in the above series of definitions, is the etc., etc., etc. ... Without it the positive integers cannot be defined; for they are an indefinitely great multitude, and it is only insofar as some such gesture as etc., etc., etc., is really significant that an infinite series of definitions can occur. What, then, does the etc., etc., mean? It means that an insight should have occurred. If one has had the relevant insight, if one has caught on, if one sees how the defining can go on indefinitely, no more need be said. If one has not caught on, then the poor teacher has to labor in his apostolate of the obvious. For in defining the positive integers there is no alternative to insight.

Incidentally, it may not be amiss to recall what already has been remarked, namely, that a single insight is expressed in many concepts. In the present instance a single insight grounds an infinity of concepts.

3.2 *Addition Tables*

A second step will consist in making somewhat more precise the familiar notion of equality. Let us say that when equals are added to equals, the results are equal; that one is equal to one; and that, therefore, an infinite series of additional tables can be constructed.

The table for adding two is constructed by adding one to each side of the equations that define the positive integers. Thus,

From the table $2 + 1 = 3$
Adding one $2 + 1 + 1 = 3 + 1$
Hence from the table $2 + 2 = 4$.

In like manner the whole table for adding two can be constructed. From this table, once it is constructed, there can be constructed a table for adding three. From that table it will be possible to construct a table for adding four. Etc., etc., etc., which again means that an insight should have occurred.

Thus, from the definitions of the positive integers and the postulate about adding equals to equals, there follows an indefinitely great deductive expansion.

3.3 *The Homogeneous Expansion*

A third step will be to venture into a homogeneous expansion. The familiar notion of addition is to be complemented by such further notions as multiplication, powers, subtraction, division, and roots. This development, however, is to be homogeneous, and by that is meant that no change is to be involved in the notions already employed.

Thus, multiplication is to mean adding a number to itself so many times, so that five by three will mean the addition of three fives. Similarly, powers are to mean that a number is multiplied by itself so many times, so that five to the third will mean five multiplied by five with the result multiplied again by five. On the other hand, subtraction, division, and roots will mean the inverse operations that bring one back to the starting point.

By a few insights, that need not be indicated, it will be seen that tables for multiplication and for powers can be constructed from the addition tables. Similarly, tables for subtraction, division, and roots can be constructed from the tables for addition, multiplication, and powers.

The homogeneous expansion constitutes a vast extension of the initial deductive expansion. It consists in introducing new operations. Its characteristic is that the new operations involve no modification of the old.

3.4   The Need of a Higher Viewpoint

A fourth step will be the discovery of the need of a higher viewpoint. This arises when the inverse operations are allowed full generality, when they are not restricted to bringing one back to one's starting point. Then, subtraction reveals the possibility of negative numbers, division reveals the possibility of fractions, roots reveal the possibility of surds. Further, there arise questions about the meaning of operations. What is multiplication when one multiplies negative numbers or fractions or surds? What is subtraction when one subtracts a negative number? Etc., etc., etc. Indeed, even the meaning of 'one' and of 'equals' becomes confused, for there are recurring decimals, and it can be shown that point nine recurring is equal to one.[2]

3.5   Formulation of the Higher Viewpoint

A fifth step will be to formulate a higher viewpoint.

Distinguish (1) rules, (2) operations, and (3) numbers.

Let numbers be defined implicitly by operations, so that the result of any operation will be a number, and any number can be the result of an operation.

Let operations be defined implicitly by rules, so that what is done in accord with rules is an operation.

2 Let $x = 0.9$
   then $10x = 9.9$
   hence $9x = 9.0$
   and so $x = 1.0$

The trick will be to obtain the rules that fix the operations which fix the numbers.

The emergence of the higher viewpoint is the performance of this trick. It consists in an insight that (1) arises upon the operations performed according to the old rules, and (2) is expressed in the formulation of the new rules.

Let me explain. From the image of a cartwheel we proceeded by insight to the definition of the circle. But while the cartwheel was imagined, the circle consists of a point and a line, neither of which can be imagined. Between the cartwheel and the circle there is an approximation, but only an approximation. Now the transition from arithmetic to elementary algebra is the same sort of thing. For an image of the cartwheel one substitutes the image of what may be named 'doing arithmetic'; it is a large, dynamic, virtual image that includes writing down, adding, multiplying, subtracting, and dividing numbers in accord with the precepts of the homogeneous expansion. Not all of this image will be present at once, but any part of it can be present, and when one is on the alert any part that happens to be relevant will pop into view. In this large and virtual image, then, there is to be grasped a new set of rules governing operations. The new rules will not be exactly the same as the old rules. They will be more symmetrical. They will be more exact. They will be more general. In brief, they will differ from the old much as the highly exact and symmetrical circle differs from the cartwheel.

What are the new rules? At school the rules for fractions were generalized; rules for signs were introduced; rules for equations and for indices were worked out. Their effect was to redefine the notions of addition, multiplication, powers, subtraction, division, and roots; and the effect of the redefinitions of the operations was that numbers were generated not merely by addition but by any of the operations.

3.6 Successive Higher Viewpoints

The reader familiar with group theory will be aware that the definition of operations by rules, and of numbers – or more generally symbols – by operations is a procedure that penetrates deeply into the nature of mathematics. But there is a further aspect to the matter, and it has to do with the gradual development by which one advances through intermediate stages from elementary to higher mathematics. The logical analyst can leap from the positive integers to group theory, but one cannot learn mathematics in that simple fashion. On the contrary, one has to perform, over and over, the same type of transition as occurs in advancing from arithmetic to elementary algebra.

At each stage of the process there exists a set of rules that govern operations which result in numbers. To each stage there corresponds a symbolic image of doing arithmetic, doing algebra, doing calculus. In each successive image there is the potentiality of grasping by insight a higher set of rules that will govern the operations and by them elicit the numbers or symbols of the next stage. Only insofar as a man makes his slow progress up that escalator does he become a technically competent mathematician. Without it he may acquire a rough idea of what mathematics is about, but he will never be a master, perfectly aware of the precise meaning and the exact implications of every symbol and operation.

3.7   *The Significance of Symbolism*

The analysis also reveals the importance of an apt symbolism.

There is no doubt that, though symbols are signs chosen by convention, still some choices are highly fruitful while others are not. It is easy enough to take the square root of 1764. It is another matter to take the square root of MDCCLXIV. The development of the calculus is easily designated in using Leibniz's symbol dy/dx for the differential coefficient; Newton's symbol, on the other hand, can be used only in a few cases, and what is worse, it does not suggest the theorems that can be established.

Why is this so? It is because mathematical operations are not merely the logical expansion of conceptual premises. Image and question, insight and concepts, all combine. The function of the symbolism is to supply the relevant image, and the symbolism is apt inasmuch as its immanent patterns as well as the dynamic patterns of its manipulation run parallel to the rules and operations that have been grasped by insight and formulated in concepts.

The benefits of this parallelism are manifold. In the first place, the symbolism itself takes over a notable part of the solution of problems, for the symbols, complemented by habits that have become automatic, dictate what has to be done. Thus, a mathematician will work at a problem up to a point and then announce that the rest is mere routine.

In the second place, the symbolism constitutes a heuristic technique: the mathematician is not content to seek his unknowns; he names them; he assigns them symbols; he writes down in equations all their properties; he knows how many equations he will need; and when he has reached that number he can say that the rest of the solution is automatic.

In the third place, the symbolism offers clues, hints, suggestions. Just as the definition of the circle was approached from the clue of the equality of the spokes, so generally insights do not come to us in their full stature: we begin from little hints, from suspicions, from possibilities; we try them out; if they lead nowhere, we drop them; if they promise success, we push them for all they are worth. But this can be done only if we chance upon the hints, the clues, the possibilities; and the effect of the apt symbolism is to reduce, if not entirely eliminate, this element of chance. Here, of course, the classical example is analytic geometry. To solve a problem by Euclidean methods, one has to stumble upon the correct construction. To solve a problem analytically, one has only to manipulate the symbols.

In the fourth place, there is the highly significant notion of invariance. An apt symbolism will endow the pattern of a mathematical expression with the totality of its meaning. Whether or not one uses the Latin, Greek, or Hebrew alphabet is a matter of no importance. The mathematical meaning of an expression resides in the distinction between constants and variables, and in the signs or collocations that dictate operations of combining, multiplying, summing, differentiating, integrating, and so forth. It follows that, as long as the symbolic pattern of a mathematical expression is unchanged, its mathematical meaning is unchanged. Further, it follows that if a symbolic pattern is unchanged by any substitutions of a determinate group, then the mathematical meaning of the pattern is independent of the meaning of the substitutions.

In the fifth place, as has already been mentioned, the symbolism appropriate to any stage of mathematical development provides the image in which may be grasped by insight the rules for the next stage.

4 Inverse Insight

Besides direct insights, their clustering, and higher viewpoints, there exists the small but significant class of inverse insights. As direct, so also inverse insights presuppose a positive object that is presented by sense or represented by imagination. But while direct insight meets the spontaneous effort of intelligence to understand, inverse insight responds to a more subtle and critical attitude that distinguishes different degrees or levels or kinds of intelligibility. While direct insight grasps the point, or sees the solution, or comes to know the reason, inverse insight apprehends that in some fashion the point is that there is no point, or that the solution is to deny a solution, or that the reason is that the rationality of the real admits distinctions and qualifications. Finally, while the conceptual formulation of direct insight affirms a positive intelligibility though it may deny expected empirical elements, the conceptual formulation of an inverse insight affirms empirical elements only to deny an expected intelligibility.

Since the last phrase is crucial, let us attempt to elaborate it. By intelligibility is meant the content of a direct insight. It is the component that is absent from our knowledge when we do not understand, and added to our knowledge inasmuch as we are understanding in the simple and straightforward manner described in the earlier sections of this chapter. Now such an intelligibility may be already reached or it may be merely expected. To deny intelligibility already reached is not the result of inverse insight; it is merely the correction of a previous direct insight, the acknowledgment of its shortcomings, the recognition that it leaves problems unsolved. But to deny an expected intelligibility is to run counter to the spontaneous anticipations of human intelligence; it is to find fault not with answers but with questions. In a demonstrative science it is to prove that a question of a given type cannot be answered. In an empirical science it is to put forward a successful hypothesis or theory that assumes that certain questions mistakenly are supposed to require an answer. Finally, the occurrence of an inverse insight is not established by the mere presence of negative concepts: thus, 'not-red,' 'position without magnitude,' 'nonoccurrence' exclude respectively 'red,' 'magnitude,' 'occurrence'; but the latter terms refer to empirical components in our knowledge and not to the possibilities and necessities, the unifications and relations, that constitute the intelligibility known in direct insight.

While the general notion of inverse insight is fairly simple and obvious, I have been at some pains in presenting its characteristics because it is not too easy to set forth illustrations to the satisfaction of different groups of readers. Moreover, communication and discussion take place through concepts, but all insight lies behind the conceptual scene. Hence, while there is always the danger that a reader will attend to the concepts rather than the underlying insight, this danger is augmented considerably when the point to be grasped by insight is merely that there is no point. To make matters worse, inverse insights occur only in the context of far larger developments of human thought. A statement of their content has to call upon the later systems that positively exploited their negative contribution. The very success of such later systems tends to engender a routine that eliminates the more spontaneous anticipations of intelligence, and then, to establish a key feature of an inverse insight, it may be necessary to appeal to the often ambiguous witness of history. In the midst of such complexity it very easily can happen that a reader's spontaneous expectation of an intelligibility to be reached should outweigh mere verbal admonitions to the contrary, and when that occurs illustrations of inverse insight can become very obscure indeed. Accordingly, while there is nothing difficult about the examples to follow, I have thought it wise to indulge in a preliminary elucidation of the obvious ...

For a third example we turn to empirical science and consider the surprising part of Newton's first law of motion, namely, that a body continues in its existing state of uniform motion in a straight line unless that state is changed by external force.

In this statement and its context it is not too difficult to discern the three characteristics of the formulation of an inverse insight. For there is the positive object: a body continues to move at a uniform rate in a straight line. There is a negation: the continuance of the constant velocity depends not on the action of external force but on the absence of such action; for only as long as there is no acceleration does the velocity remain constant; and the moment the sum of the external forces differs from zero, there arises an acceleration. Finally, this negation of external force runs counter to the spontaneous anticipations of human intelligence, for spontaneously one thinks of uniform motion not as of a state like rest but as of a change that requires an external cause.

However, some readers may wish to refine on the issue. They will agree that the necessity of an external cause had been stressed by the Aristotelian theory of celestial movements, of projectiles, and of motion in a vacuum. But they will add that the Aristotelian view had been contradicted at least from the time of John Philoponus. On this contrary view projectiles were kept in motion not by any external force but by some internal principle or power or property or quality or other immanent ground. Finally, they will ask whether it is quite certain that Newton did not appeal to some innate power of matter to account for the continuance of inertial states.

Now clearly, Newtonian exegesis is not our present business. All we have to say is that inverse insight is not illustrated when explanation by external force is replaced by explanation in terms of some immanent power or property. For in that case there is merely the correction of an earlier direct insight by a later direct insight, and while the spontaneous anticipations of human intelligence are blocked in one direction, they are given an outlet in another.

Still, for purposes of illustration it may be permissible to block this second outlet without reopening the first. No doubt, when an external mover or force is denied, one may spontaneously think that there must be some innate quality that provides the real explanation. But while the assertion of an external mover or force can be tested experimentally, the assertion of some innate quality, of some *vis materiae insita* [force resident in matter], can hardly be regarded as a scientific statement. If one affirms that, when acceleration is zero, then the sum of the relevant external forces is also zero, one's affirmation admits the ordinary tests. But if one goes on to add that the innate qualities of matter render the action of external forces superfluous, one is very likely to be reminded that scientists do not appeal to occult causes.

Now if this remonstrance is regarded as peremptory, we arrive at an example of inverse insight. There is the positive object of inquiry: bodies continue in their existing states of uniform motion. There is the negation: the continuance of uniform motion is not to be explained by any appeal to external forces. Finally, this negation is regarded as definitive for science, for science refuses to extrapolate from known laws to ulterior explanations in terms of vague qualities, properties, powers, and the like ...

In conclusion, let us recall a point already mentioned. An inverse insight finds its expression only in some concomitant positive context. So the defect of intelligibility in constant velocity has been formulated in a whole series of different contexts. In the context of Eleatic philosophy, Zeno's paradoxes led to a denial of the fact of motion. In the context of his philosophy of being, Aristotle pronounced motion real yet regarded it as an incomplete entity, an infracategorial object. In the context of mathematical mechanics, Newton asserted a principle of inertia. In the context of Clerk Maxwell's equations for the electro-magnetic field, Lorentz worked out the conditions under which the equations would remain invariant under inertial transformations; Fitzgerald explained Lorentz's success by supposing that bodies contracted along the direction of motion; Einstein found a no less general explanation in problems of synchronization and raised the issue to the methodological level of the transformation properties of the mathematical expression of physical principles and laws; finally, Minkowski systematized Einstein's position by introducing the four-dimensional manifold. No doubt, it would be a mistake to suppose that the same inverse insight was operative from Zeno to special relativity. But throughout there is a denial of intelligibility to local motion, and while the successive contexts differ notably in content and in value, at least they point in the same direction, and they illustrate the dependence of inverse insight on concomitant direct insights.

5   The Empirical Residue

If inverse insights are relatively rare, they are far from being unimportant. Not only do they eliminate mistaken questions but also they seem regularly to be connected with ideas or principles or methods or techniques of quite exceptional significance. From the oddities of the mathematical continuum through the notions of correlation and limit there arises the brilliance of continuous functions and of the infinitesimal calculus. Similarly, the lack of intelligibility in constant velocity is linked with scientific achievements of the first order: the principle of inertia made it possible to conceive dynamics not as a theory of motions but as an enormously more compact and more powerful theory of accelerations; and the invariance of physical principles and laws under inertial transformations not only is an extremely neat idea but also has kept revealing its fruitfulness for the past fifty years.

To explore this significance, then, let us introduce the notion of an empirical residue that (1) consists in positive empirical data, (2) is to be denied any immanent intelligibility of its own, and (3) is connected with some compensating higher intelligibility of notable importance. In clarification of the first characteristic one may note that, inasmuch as a vacuum is merely an absence of data, it cannot be part of the empirical residue. In clarification of the second it is to be remembered that a denial of immanent intelligibility is not a denial of experience or description. Not only are elements in the empirical residue given positively but also they are pointed out, conceived, named, considered, discussed, and affirmed or denied. But though they are no less given than color or sound or heat, though they may be thought about no less accurately and talked about no less fluently, still they are not objects of any direct insight, and so they cannot be explained by transverse waves or longitudinal waves or molecular motion or any other theoretical construction that might be thought more apposite. Finally, in clarification of the third characteristic it is to be noted that inverse insight and the empirical residue are not exact correlatives. For inverse insight was not characterized by a connection with ideas, principles, methods, or techniques of exceptional significance. Again, the empirical residue has not been characterized by the spontaneity of the questions for intelligence that are to be met by a denial of intelligibility.

This difference not only makes the empirical residue a broader category than inverse insight but also renders a discussion of it more difficult. For a great part of the difficulty in discovering the further positive aspects of experience that are to be denied intelligibility is that no one supposes them to possess intelligibility.

Thus, particular places and particular times pertain to the empirical residue. They are positive aspects of experience. Each differs from every other. But because no one ever asks why one place is not another or why one time is not another, people are apt to be puzzled when the question is put, to imagine that something different from such obvious foolishness must be meant, and to experience a variety of fictitious difficulties before arriving at the simple conclusion that (1) particular places and particular times differ as a matter of fact, and (2) there is no immanent intelligibility to be grasped by direct insight into that fact.

For example, one will begin by saying that obviously the position A differs from the position B because of the distance AB that separates them. But take three equidistant positions: A, B, C. Why are the distances AB, BC, CA different? One would be in a vicious circle if one doubled back and explained the difference of the distances by the difference of the positions. One cannot say that the distances differ in length for they are equal in length. But one may say that the distances differ because the directions differ. Still, why do the directions differ? And why are equal and parallel distances different distances? Now perhaps it will be urged that we are going too far, that some difference must be acknowledged as primitive, that everything cannot be explained. Quite so, but there is a corollary to be added. For what is primitive is not the content of some primitive insight but the content of some primitive experience to which no insight corresponds. Were it the content of some primitive insight, there would not be the conspicuous absence of a clearheaded explanation. But because the difference of particular places and the difference of particular times are given prior to any questioning and prior to any insight, because these given differences cannot be matched by any insights that explain why places differ and times differ, there has to be introduced the category of the empirical residue.

However, one may not surrender yet. For particular places and particular times can be united by reference frames; the frames can be employed to distinguish and designate every place and every time; and evidently such constructions are eminently intelligent and eminently intelligible. Now, no doubt, reference frames are objects of direct insight, but what is grasped by that insight is an ordering of differences that are not explained by the order but merely presupposed. So it is that different geometries grasped by different insights offer different intelligible orders for the differences in place or time that all equally presuppose and, quite correctly, none attempt to explain.

There is a further aspect to the matter. Because the differences of particular places and particular times involve no immanent intelligibility of their own, they do not involve any modification in the intelligibility of anything else. It is not mere difference of place but something different in the places that gives rise to different observations or different experimental results in different places. Similarly, it is not mere difference in time but something different at the time that gives rise to different observations and different experimental results at different times. Moreover, were that not so, every place and every time would have its own physics, its own chemistry, its own biology; and since a science cannot be worked out instantaneously in a single place, there would be no physics, no chemistry, and no biology. Conversely, because the differences of particular places and particular times pertain to the empirical residue, there exists the powerful technique of scientific collaboration. Scientists of every place and every time can pool their results in a common fund, and there is no discrimination against any result merely because of the place or merely because of the time of its origin.

Even more fundamental than scientific collaboration is scientific generalization. When chemists have mastered all of the elements, their isotopes, and their compounds, they may forget to be grateful that they do not have to discover different explanations for each of the hydrogen atoms which, it seems, make up about fifty-five per cent of the matter of our universe. But at least the fact that such a myriad of explanations is not needed is very relevant to our purpose. Every chemical element and every compound differs from every other kind of element or compound, and all the differences have to be explained. Every hydrogen atom differs from every other hydrogen atom, and no explanation is needed. Clearly, we have to do with another aspect of the empirical residue, and no less clearly, this aspect is coupled with the most powerful of all scientific techniques, generalization.

However, this issue has been booted about by philosophers ever since the Platonists explained the universality of mathematical and scientific knowledge by postulating eternal and immutable Forms or Ideas only to find themselves embarrassed by the fact that a single, eternal, immutable One could hardly ground the universal statement that one and one are two or, again, that a single, eternal, immutable Triangle would not suffice for theorems on triangles similar in all respects. So there arose, it seems, the philosophic problem of merely numerical difference, and connected with it there have been formulated cognitional theories based on a doctrine of abstraction. Accordingly, we are constrained to say something on these issues, and lest we appear to be attempting to dilute water, we shall do so as briefly as possible.

The assertion, then, of merely numerical difference involves two elements. On the theoretical side it is the claim that, when any set of data has been explained completely, another set of data similar in all respects would not call for a different explanation. On the factual side it is the claim that, when any set of data has been explained completely, only an exhaustive tour of inspection could establish that there does not exist another set of data similar in all respects.

The basis of the theoretical contention is that, just as the same act of understanding is repeated when the same set of data is apprehended a second time, so also the same act of understanding is repeated when one apprehends a second set of data that is similar to a first in all respects. Thus, the physicist offers different explanations for 'red' and 'blue'; he offers different explanations for different shades of 'red'; and he would discern no sense in the proposal that he should try to find as many different explanations as there are different instances of exactly the same shade of exactly the same color.

The factual contention is more complex. It is not an assertion that there exist different sets of data similar in all respects. It is not a denial of unique instances, that is, of instances that are to be explained in a manner in which no other instance in the universe is to be explained. It is not even a denial that every individual in the universe is a unique instance. On the contrary, the relevant fact lies in the nature of the explanations that are applicable to our universe. It is to the effect that all such explanations are made up of general or universal elements and that, while these general or universal elements may be combined in such a manner that every individual is explained by a different combination of elements, still such a combination is an explanation of a singular combination of common properties and not an explanation of individuality. For if the individuality of the individual were explained, it would be meaningless to suppose that some other individual might be understood in exactly the same fashion. On the other hand, because the individuality of the individual is not explained, it is only an exhaustive tour of inspection that can settle whether or not there exists another individual similar in all respects. Hence, even if there were reached a single comprehensive theory of evolution that explained and explained differently every instance of life on this planet, still in strict logic we should have to inspect all other planets before we could be absolutely certain that in fact there did not exist another instance of evolution similar in all respects.

In brief, individuals differ, but the ultimate difference in our universe is a matter of fact to which there corresponds nothing to be grasped by direct insight. Moreover, as scientific collaboration rests on the empirically residual difference of particular places and of particular times, so scientific generalization rests on the empirically residual difference between individuals of the same class ...

Properly, then, abstraction is not a matter of apprehending a sensible or imaginative gestalt; it is not a matter of employing common names just as it is not a matter of using other tools; finally, it is not even a matter of attending to one question at a time and meanwhile holding other questions in abeyance. Properly, to abstract is to grasp the essential and to disregard the incidental, to see what is significant and set aside the irrelevant, to recognize the important as important and the negligible as negligible. Moreover, when it is asked what is essential or significant or important and what is incidental, irrelevant, negligible, the answer must be twofold. For abstraction is the selectivity of intelligence, and intelligence may be considered either in some given stage of development or at the term of development when some science or group of sciences has been mastered completely.

Hence, relative to any given insight or cluster of insights the essential, significant, important consists (1) in the set of aspects in the data necessary for the occurrence of the insight or insights, or (2) in the set of related concepts necessary for the expression of the insight or insights. On the other hand the incidental, irrelevant, negligible consists (1) in other concomitant aspects of the data that do not fall under the insight or insights, or (2) in the set of concepts that correspond to the merely concomitant aspects of the data. Again, relative to the full development of a science or group of allied sciences, the essential, significant, important consists (1) in the aspects of the data that are necessary for the occurrence of all insights in the appropriate range, or (2) in the set of related concepts that express all the insights of the science or sciences. On the other hand, the incidental, irrelevant, negligible consists in the empirical residue that, since it possesses no immanent intelligibility of its own, is left over without explanation even when a science or group of sciences reaches full development.

Finally, to conclude this chapter on the elements of insight, let us indicate briefly what is essential, significant, important in its contents and, on the other hand, what is incidental, irrelevant, negligible. What alone is essential is insight into insight. Hence the incidental includes (1) the particular insights chosen as examples, (2) the formulation of these insights, and (3) the images evoked by the formulation. It follows that for the story of Archimedes the reader will profitably substitute some less resounding yet more helpful experience of his own. Instead of the definition of the circle he can take any other intelligently performed act of defining and ask why the performance is, not safe, not accurate, not the accepted terminology, but a creative stroke of insight ...

6   Mathematical and Scientific Insights Compared

6.1   *Similarities*

Galileo's determination of the law of falling bodies not only is a model of scientific procedure but also offers the attraction of possessing many notable similarities to the already examined process from the image of a cartwheel to the definition of the circle.

In the first place, the inquiry was restricted to the immanent intelligibility of a free fall. Just as we ruled out of consideration the purpose of cartwheels, the materials from which they are made, the wheelwrights that make them, and the tools that wheelwrights use, so also Galileo was uninterested in the final cause of falling, he drew no distinction between the different materials that fall, he made no effort to determine what agencies produce a fall.

Secondly, just as we started from a clue – the equality of the spokes – so too Galileo supposed that some correlation was to be found between the measurable aspects of falling bodies. Indeed, he began by showing the error in the ancient Aristotelian correlation that bodies fell according to their weight. Then he turned his attention to two measurable aspects immanent in every fall: the body traverses a determinate distance; it does so in a determinate interval of time. By a series of experiments he provided himself with the requisite data and obtained the desired measurements. Then he discovered that the measurements would satisfy a general rule: the distance traversed is proportional to the time squared. It is a correlation that has been verified directly and indirectly for over four centuries.

Thirdly, once we had defined the circle we found ourselves in a realm of the nonimaginable, of the merely supposed. Strangely, something similar happens when one formulates the law of falling bodies. It holds in a vacuum, and to realize a perfect vacuum is impossible. What can be established experimentally is that the more closely one approximates to the conditions of a vacuum, the more accurate the law of constant acceleration is found to be.

6.2 Dissimilarities

But besides similarities there also are differences, and these are perhaps more instructive. In reaching the definition of the circle, it was sufficient to take as our starting point the mere image of a cartwheel. There was no need for fieldwork. But to reach the law of falling bodies Galileo had to experiment. Climbing the tower of Pisa and constructing inclined planes were an essential part of his job, for he was out to understand, not how bodies are imagined to fall, but how in fact they fall.

Secondly, the data that give rise to insight into roundness are continuous, but the data that give rise to insight into the law of falling bodies are discontinuous. One can imagine the whole cartwheel or a whole loop of very fine wire. But no matter how many experiments one makes on falling bodies, all one can obtain is a series of separate points plotted on a distance-time graph. No doubt, it is possible to join the plotted points by a smooth curve, but the curve represents, not data that are known, but a presumption of what understanding will grasp.

Thirdly, the insight into the image of the wheel grasps necessity and impossibility: if the radii are equal, the curve must be round; if the radii drawn from the center are unequal, the curve cannot be round. But the insight into the discontinuous series of points on the graph consists in a grasp, not of necessity or impossibility, but simply of possibility. The simplest smooth curve could represent the law of falling bodies, but any of a vast range of more elaborate curves could equally well pass through all the known points.

Fourthly, once one catches on to the law of the circle, the insight and consequent definition exert a backward influence upon imagination. The geometer imagines dots but thinks of points; he imagines fine threads but thinks of lines. The thinking is exact and precise, and imagination does its best to keep pace. In like manner the empirical investigator will tend to endow his images with the closest possible approximation to the laws he conceives. But while his imagination will do its best, while his perceptions will be profoundly influenced by the habits of his imagination, nonetheless the data that are available for the ideal observer make no effort towards such conformity. They go their own way with their unanalyzed multiplicity and their refractoriness to measurements that are more than approximate.

Fifthly, as we have seen, higher viewpoints in mathematics are reached inasmuch as initial images yield insights, insights yield definitions and postulates, definitions and postulates guide symbolic operations, and symbolic operations provide a more general image in which the insights of the higher viewpoint are emergent. Now in empirical method there is a similar circle, but it follows a slightly different route. The operations that follow upon the formulation of laws are not merely symbolic. For the formulation expresses a grasp of possibility. It is a hypothesis. It provides a basis for deductions and calculations no less than mathematical premises do. But it also provides a basis for further observations and experiments. It is such observation and experimentation, directed by a hypothesis, that sooner or later turns attention to data that initially were overlooked or neglected; it is attention to such further data that forces the revision of initial viewpoints and effects the development of empirical science.

The circuit, then, of mathematical development may be named immanent: it moves from images through insights and conceptions to the production of symbolic images whence higher insights arise. But the circuit of scientific development includes action upon external things: it moves from observation and experiment to tabulations and graphs, from these to insights and formulations, from formulations to forecasts, from forecasts to operations, in which it obtains fresh evidence either for the confirmation or for the revision of existing views.

Related selections: 1.IV.1 on common sense as intellectual; 1.IV.2 on scotosis; 1.V.1 on practical insights; 1.VIII.2 on reflective insight.

III

The Complementarity of Classical and Statistical Investigations

Insight may be viewed as an exploration of the role of insight in four different types of inquiry and the consequent definition of four methods. They are the classical and statistical methods of empirical science, the dialectical method of philosophy, and the genetic method employed to understand development. After exposing the key elements of the act of insight in Chapter 1, Lonergan devotes Chapters 2 through 5 of the book to the study of insight in the context of natural scientific inquiry in order 'to capture the essential dynamism of human intelligence.'[1]

The present selection, from Chapters 2 and 4 of *Insight*, begins with Lonergan's account of the heuristic structures of classical and statistical method. 'Heuristic' is from the Greek, *heurisko*, meaning 'I find.' So is the word 'eureka,' meaning 'I have found it.' A heuristic is a principle of discovering. A heuristic structure is a way of ordering means to an end when the end is knowledge and the knowledge is not yet acquired. All methodical investigations employ heuristic structures. The discussion of classical and statistical heuristic structures is followed by a brief summary of the complementarity of the types of *knowing* characteristic of classical and statistical science. Lonergan then elaborates the complementarity from the viewpoint of what is to be *known* by these two methods. His aim in this part is 'to determine the immanent design or order characteristic of a universe in which both classical and statistical laws obtain.'[2] The features of such a universe are worked out in his account of the worldview of emergent probability. The notion of a 'scheme of recurrence,' with its probabilities of emergence and survival, is a key to understanding Lonergan's world-

1 *Insight*, 57.
2 Ibid., 139.

view of emergent probability. Late in life Lonergan described the account of emergent probability as 'my transposition of Darwin.'[3] Lonergan's account of heuristic structures is expanded later, as the moving viewpoint of *Insight* develops, by his treatments of dialectical method and genetic method.

These extracts are taken from *Insight*, 60–3, 67–9; 76–8, 79–81; 137–8; 140–51.

1 Classical Heuristic Structures

1.1 'Nature'

In every empirical inquiry there are knowns and unknowns. But the knowns are apprehended whether or not one understands: they are the data of sense. The unknowns, on the other hand, are what one will grasp by insight and formulate in conceptions and suppositions.

Accordingly, let us bestow a name upon the unknown. Rather, let us advert to the fact that already it has been named. For what is to be known by understanding these data is called their *nature*. Just as in algebra the unknown number is x until one finds out what the number is, so too in empirical inquiry the unknown to be reached by insight is named 'the nature of ...' Once Galileo discovered his law, he knew that the nature of a free fall was a constant acceleration. But before he discovered the law, from the mere fact that he inquired, he knew that a free fall possessed a nature, though he did not know what that nature was.

The first step in the generalization is, then, that just as the mathematician begins by saying, 'Let the required number be x,' so too the empirical inquirer begins by saying, 'Let the unknown be the nature of ...'

1.2 Classification and Correlation

Next, similars are similarly understood.

Hence, because individuality pertains to the empirical residue, one knows at once that the 'nature of ...' will be universal, that when one understands these data, then one will understand similar data in exactly the same fashion.

Accordingly, just as the mathematician follows up his naming of the

3 *Caring*, 212.

unknown as x by writing down properties of x, so too the empirical inquirer follows up his declaration that he seeks the 'nature of ...' by noting that that 'nature of ...' must be the same for all similar sets of data.

But similarities are of two kinds.

There are the similarities of things in their relations to us. Thus, they may be similar in color or shape, similar in the sounds they emit, similar in taste or odor, similar in the tactile qualities of the hot and cold, wet and dry, heavy and light, rough and smooth, hard and soft.

There also are the similarities of things in their relations to one another. Thus, they may be found together or apart. They may increase or decrease concomitantly. They may have similar antecedents or consequents. They may be similar in their proportions to one another, and such proportions may form series of relationships, such as exist between the elements in the periodic table of chemistry or between the successive forms of life in the theory of evolution.

Now sensible similarities, which occur in the relations of things to our senses, may be known before the 'nature of ...' has been discovered. They form the basis of preliminary classifications. They specify the 'nature of ...,' so that one states that one is seeking the nature of color, the nature of heat, the nature of change, the nature of life.

On the other hand, similarities that reside in the relations of things to one another are the proximate materials of insight into nature. Hence the empirical inquirer, to emphasize this fact, will say that his objective is not merely the 'nature of ...' but more precisely the unspecified correlation to be specified, the undetermined function to be determined.

The second step in the generalization is, then, that just as the mathematician states that he seeks an x which has such and such properties, so too the empirical inquirer states that he seeks a 'nature of ...,' where the nature antecedently is specified by a classification based on sensible similarity and consequently will be known when some indeterminate function is determined.

The reader will observe that Galileo differed from his Aristotelian opponents by taking this second step. The Aristotelians were content to talk about the nature of light, the nature of heat, etc. Galileo inaugurated modern science by insisting that the nature of weight was not enough; from sensible similarity, which resides in the relations of things to our senses, one must proceed to relations that hold directly between things themselves.

1.3 Differential Equations

Now the correlations and functions that relate things directly to one another are determined empirically by measuring, plotting measurements on graphs, and grasping in the scattered points the possibility of a smooth curve, a law, a formulation. But our present concern is with the antecedent heuristic clues. Accordingly, we recall that, besides individuality, the continuum also pertains to the empirical residue, and as well, that just as the universal is reached by abstracting from the individual, so also the techniques of the infinitesimal calculus deal with the intelligibility reached by abstracting from the noncountable infinity of the continuum.

The third step, then, in our generalization is the observation that, where the mathematician says, 'Let x be the required number,' the empirical inquirer can say, 'Let some indeterminate function $f(x, y, z, ...) = 0$ be the required function.' Further, just as the mathematician reaches x by making statements about it, so too the empirical inquirer can move towards the determination of his indeterminate function by writing down differential equations which it must satisfy ...

1.4 Summary

Our concern has been the methodical genesis of insight. Scientists achieve understanding, but they do so only at the end of an inquiry. Moreover, their inquiry is methodical, and method consists in ordering means to achieve an end. But how can means be ordered to an end when the end is knowledge and the knowledge is not yet acquired? The answer to this puzzle is the heuristic structure. Name the unknown. Work out its properties. Use the properties to direct, order, guide the inquiry.

In prescientific thought what is to be known inasmuch as understanding is achieved is named the 'nature of ...' Because similars are understood similarly, the 'nature of ...' is expected to be the same for all similar data, and so it is specified as the nature of light, the nature of heat, and so forth, by constructing classifications based on sensible similarity.

Scientific thought involves a more exact anticipation. What is to be known inasmuch as data are understood is some correlation or function that states universally the relations of things not to our senses but to one another. Hence the scientific anticipation is of some unspecified correlation to be specified, some indeterminate function to be determined; and now the task of specifying or determining is carried out by measuring, by tabulating measurements, by reaching an insight into the tabulated measurements, and by expressing that insight through some general correlation or function that, if verified, will define a limit on which converge the relations between all subsequent appropriate measurements.

This basic anticipation and procedure may be enriched in two further manners. First, functions are solutions of differential equations; but in many cases relevant differential equations can be deduced from very general considerations. Hence the scientist may anticipate that the function which is the object of his inquiry will be one of the solutions of the relevant differential equations. Secondly, the functions that become known in the measure that understanding is achieved are, both in origin and in application, independent of the differences of particular places and particular times. In such a science as physics this anticipation of independence becomes formulated as the invariance of principles and laws under groups of transformations, and different grounds are invoked to determine which group of transformations is to leave the mathematical expression of laws unchanged in form. So a direct insight into the significance of measurements yields the anticipations of general relativity; an inverse insight into the insignificance of constant velocity yields the anticipations of special relativity; and a restriction of this inverse insight to the context of Newtonian dynamics yields the anticipations that sometimes are named Newtonian relativity.

Such in brief are the anticipations constitutive of classical heuristic structure. The structure is named classical because it is restricted to insights of a type most easily identified by mentioning the names of Galileo, Newton, Clerk Maxwell, and Einstein. It is named heuristic because it anticipates insights of that type, and while prescinding from their as yet unknown contents, works out their general properties to give methodical guidance to investigations. It is named a structure because, though operative, it is not known explicitly until oversight of insight gives way to insight into insight.

In particular one should observe that classical heuristic structure has no suppositions except the minimal suppositions that insights of a certain type occur and that inquiry aiming at such insights may be not haphazard but methodical. Further, advertence to classical heuristic structure has no additional suppositions except the possibility of an insight that grasps the set of relations linking methodical inquiry with anticipated insights, data, similarities in data, measurements, curve fitting, indeterminate functions, differential equations, the principle of inertia, special relativity, and general relativity. If there has been communicated some grasp of such diverse objects within the unity of a single view, then there has been communicated an insight into the genesis of insight. No doubt, that is a very small thing. An insight is no more than an act of understanding. It may prove to be true or false, or to hold some intermediate position of greater or less probability. Still, it is solely the communication of that act of understanding that has been our aim, and if the reader has been concerned with anything else, he has done all that is necessary to miss the little we have had to offer in the present context.

2 Statistical Heuristic Structures

2.1 Elementary Contrasts

Classical and statistical investigations exhibit marked differences that provide a convenient starting point for the present section.

In the first place, while classical investigation heads towards the determination of functions and their systematization, statistical investigation clings to concrete situations. Hence, while classical conclusions are concerned with what would be if other things were equal, statistical conclusions directly regard such aggregates of events as the sequences of occasions on which a coin is tossed or dice are cast, the sequences of situations created by the mobility of molecules in a gas, the sequences of generations in which babies are born, the young marry, and the old die.

Secondly, statistical inquiry attends not to theoretical processes but to palpable results. As Galileo sought the intelligibility immanent in a free fall, so Clerk Maxwell sought the intelligibility immanent in the electromagnetic field. But in a statistical investigation such theoretical analyses and constructions are set aside. The movement of dice observes perfectly the laws of mechanics, but the laws of mechanics are not premises in the determination of the probability of casting a 'seven.' Doctors commonly succeed in diagnosing the causes of death, but such causes are not studied in fixing death rates. The statistical scientist seems content to define events and areas, to count the instances of each defined class within the defined area, and to offer some general but rather vague view of things as a whole.

Thirdly, statistical science is empirical, but it does not endeavor to measure and correlate the spatial, temporal, and other variables that so fascinate classical investigators. Its attention is directed to *frequencies* that are straightforward numerical answers to the straightforward question, How often? Such frequencies may be *ideal* or *actual*, but while it is true that the ideal frequency or probability raises debatable issues, at least the *actual frequency* is a transparent report not of what should or might or will happen but of what in fact did happen. Such actual frequencies are *absolute* when they assign the actual number of events of a given kind within a given area during a given interval of time. However, since different areas commonly are not comparable, it is customary to proceed from absolute actual frequencies either to *rates*, say, per thousand of population or, when classes of events are alternative possibilities, to *relative actual frequencies* which are sets of proper fractions, say $p/n, q/n, r/n, \ldots$ where $n = p + q + r + \ldots$

Fourthly, behind the foregoing rather superficial differences there is a profound difference in the mentality of classical and statistical inquirers. Had astronomers been content to regard the wandering of the planets as a merely random affair, the planetary system never would have been discovered. Had Joule been content to disregard small differences, the mechanical equivalent of heat would have remained unknown. But statistical inquirers make it their business to distinguish in their tables of frequencies between significant and merely random differences. Hence, while they go to great pains to arrive at exact numbers, they do not seem to attempt the obvious next step of exact explanation. As long as differences in frequency oscillate about some average, they are esteemed of no account; only when the average itself changes, is intellectual curiosity aroused and further inquiry deemed relevant.

2.2   The Inverse Insight

The existence of this radical difference in mentality demands an explanation, and the obvious explanation is the occurrence of something like an inverse insight. For an inverse insight has three characteristics: it supposes a positive object of inquiry; it denies intelligibility to the object; and the denial runs counter to spontaneous anticipations of intelligence. But the differences named random are matters of fact: they occur in frequencies determined by counting the events in a given class in a given area during a given interval of time. Further, random differences are denied intelligibility, for, though statistical inquirers hardly would use such an expression, at least their deeds seem a sufficient witness to their thought. When differences are not random, further inquiry is in order; but when differences are random, not only is no inquiry attempted but also the very attempt would be pronounced silly. Finally, this denial of intelligibility is in open conflict with the anticipations of classical investigation. For classical precept and example tirelessly inculcate the lesson that no difference is to be simply neglected; and while one may doubt that this classical attitude is more spontaneous than its opposite, at least one can speak of a devaluated inverse insight that divides classical and statistical anticipations ...

First, statistical inquiry is concerned with coincidental aggregates of events. For it is not concerned with the intelligibly grouped events of systematic process: there are no statistics on the phases of the moon or on the transit of Venus, and there are no random differences in ordinary astronomical tables. Again, it is not concerned with events taken singly. For each single event amounts to just one more or less in tables of frequencies, and in general a difference of one more or one less may be regarded as random. Further, it is possible to discern random differences in some groups of events in which each event is determinate and deducible and no event is random. It remains, then, that the object of statistical inquiry is the coincidental aggregate of events, that is, the aggregate of events that has some unity by spatial juxtaposition or by temporal succession or by both but lacks unity on the level of insight and of intelligible relation. In other words, statistical inquiry is concerned with nonsystematic process.

Secondly, statistical inquiry investigates what classical inquiry neglects. For even if one grants that classical inquiry leads to the laws that explain every event, it remains that classical science rarely bothers to explain the single events of nonsystematic process, and still less does it offer any technique for the orderly study of groups of such events. Moreover, there are excellent reasons for this neglect. The deduction of each of the events of a nonsystematic process begins by demanding more abundant and more exact information than there is to be had. It proceeds through a sequence of stages determined by the coincidences of a random situation. It has to postulate unlimited time to be able to assert the possibility of completing the deduction. It would end up with a result that lacks generality, for, while the result would hold for an exactly similar nonsystematic process, it commonly would not provide a safe basis for an approximation to the course of another nonsystematic process with a slightly different basic situation. Finally, it would be preposterous to attempt to deduce the course of events for every nonsystematic process. Not only would the foregoing difficulties have to be surmounted an enormous number of times, but this Herculean labor would seem to be to no purpose. How could non-systematic processes be classified? How could one list in an orderly fashion the totality of situations of all nonsystematic processes? Yet without such a classification and such a list, how could one identify given situations with situations contained in the extremely long deductions of the extremely large set of nonsystematic processes?

Thirdly, statistical inquiry finds an intelligibility in what classical inquiry neglects. So far we have been concerned to stress the defect of intelligibility in nonsystematic process. But a mere defect in intelligibility is not the basis of a scientific method. There is needed a complementary direct insight that turns the tables on the defect. Just as scientific generalization exploits the fact that individuality pertains to an empirical residue, just as the real numbers, the theory of continuous functions, and the infinitesimal calculus exploit the defect of intelligibility in the continuum, just as scientific collaboration is possible because particular places and particular times pertain to the empirical residue, just as the principle of inertia and the basic postulate of special relativity rest on an empirically residual aspect of constant velocity, so also statistical science is the positive advance of intelligence through the gap in intelligibility in coincidental aggregates of events.

Accordingly, besides the devaluated inverse insight that has been our concern hitherto, there is to be acknowledged in statistical science another basic moment that is positive and creative. Aristotle was quite aware of what we have named nonsystematic process, for he contended that the whole course of terrestrial events was just a series of accidents. But to this devaluated inverse insight he failed to add the further creative moment. Instead of discovering statistical method, he attempted to account for the manifest continuity of the terrestrial series of accidents by invoking the continuous influence of the continuously rotating celestial spheres.

Fourthly, it is this further intelligibility that is denied when random differences are affirmed. For if the statistical investigator deals with nonsystematic processes, he does not find the intelligibility of systematic process either in the differences he pronounces significant or in the differences he pronounces random. Again, to discover the intelligibility that statistical science finds in nonsystematic process, we must look to the differences pronounced significant. It follows that differences in frequencies of events are random when they lack not only the intelligibility of systematic process but also the intelligibility of nonsystematic process.

3   The Complementarity of Classical and Statistical Investigations

We have been considering the complementarity of classical and statistical investigations as forms of knowing. We have found such complementarity to exist at each of the stages or components of the process of inquiry. There is the classical heuristic anticipation of the systematic; there is the complementary statistical heuristic anticipation of the nonsystematic. Next, to determine either a classical or a statistical law is to prepare the way for the determination of further laws of either type; for both classical and statistical laws pertain to a single complementary field, and to know either is to effect a mental separation between types of data that have been accounted for and types that still remain to be explained. Thirdly, there is a complementarity of formulations: the experiential and pure conjugates of classical laws can be verified only in events; the events occur only if other things are equal; and the failure to specify the other things amounts to an unconscious acknowledgment of the nonsystematic aggregate of patterns of diverging series of conditions; inversely, as conjugates are verified only in events, so events are defined only by conjugates, and statistical laws of events can possess scientific significance only in the measure that they employ definitions generated by classical procedures. Fourthly, there is a complementarity in modes of abstraction: classical laws regard the systematic in abstraction from the nonsystematic, the relations of things to one another in abstraction from their relations to our senses; but statistical laws consider the systematic as setting bounds to the nonsystematic, and they are confined to the observable events that include a relation to our senses. Fifthly, the two types of law are complementary in their verification: exact and complete knowledge of classical laws cannot successfully invade the field of statistical laws; and statistical investigations are confronted with regular recurrences that admit explanations of the classical type. Finally, there is complementarity in the aspects of data explained by the different types of laws: data as similar are explained on classical lines; but their numbers and their distributions become intelligible only by some synthesis of statistical considerations.

4 Complementarity in the Known

Just as the first part of this chapter was devoted to exhibiting the complementarity of classical and of statistical investigations from the viewpoint of knowing, so now the second part is to be directed to the determination of the corresponding complementarity from the viewpoint of what is to be known. For knowing and known, if they are not an identity, at least stand in some correspondence, and as the known is reached only through knowing, structural features of the one are bound to be reflected in the other. Aristotle's world view stemmed from his distinction between the necessary laws of the heavenly bodies and the contingent laws of things on this earth. Mechanist determinism had its scientific basis in the Galilean concept of explanation as the reduction of secondary to primary qualities. In similar fashion some parallel implication cannot be avoided by any fully conscious methodology, and so, if we are not to play the ostrich, we must face the question, What world view is involved by our affirmation of both classical and statistical laws? ...

We shall begin from the problem of showing how both classical and statistical laws can coalesce into a single unified intelligibility commensurate with the universe of our experience. Against this problem we shall set our clue, namely, the scheme of recurrence. On the one hand, the world of our experience is full of continuities, oscillations, rhythms, routines, alternations, circulations, regularities. On the other hand, the scheme of recurrence not only squares with this broad fact but also is related intimately both to classical and to statistical laws. For the notion of the scheme emerges in the very formulation of the canons of empirical method. Abstractly, the scheme itself is a combination of classical laws. Concretely, schemes begin, continue, and cease to function in accord with statistical probabilities. Such is our clue, our incipient insight. To develop it we shall consider (1) the notion of a conditioned series of schemes of recurrence, (2) the probability of a single scheme, (3) the emergent probability of a series of schemes, and (4) the consequent characteristics of a world order.

4.1 Schemes of Recurrence

The notion of the scheme of recurrence arose when it was noted that the diverging series of positive conditions for an event might coil around in a circle. In that case, a series of events A, B, C, ... would be so related that the fulfilment of the conditions for each would be the occurrence of the others. Schematically, then, the scheme might be represented by the series of conditionals: If A occurs, B will occur; if B occurs, C will occur; if C occurs, ... A will recur. Such a circular arrangement may involve any number of terms, the possibility of alternative routes, and in general any degree of complexity.

Two instances of greater complexity may be noted. On the one hand, a scheme might consist of a set of almost complete circular arrangements of which none could function alone yet all would function if conjoined in an interdependent combination. On the other hand, schemes might be complemented by defensive circles, so that if some event F tended to upset the scheme, there would be some such sequence of conditions as 'If F occurs, then G occurs; if G occurs, then H occurs; if H occurs, then F is eliminated.'

In illustration of schemes of recurrence the reader may think of the planetary system, of the circulation of water over the surface of the earth, of the nitrogen cycle familiar to biologists, of the routines of animal life, of the repetitive economic rhythms of production and exchange. In illustration of schemes with defensive circles, one may advert to generalized equilibria. Just as a chain reaction is a cumulative series of changes terminating in an explosive difference, so a generalized equilibrium is such a combination of defensive circles that any change within a limited range is offset by opposite changes that tend to restore the initial situation. Thus, health in a plant or animal is a generalized equilibrium; again, the balance of various forms of plant and animal life within an environment is a generalized equilibrium; again, economic process was conceived by the older economists as a generalized equilibrium.

However, we are concerned, not with single schemes, but with a conditioned series of schemes. Let us say that the schemes P, Q, R, ...

form a conditioned series if all prior members of the series must be functioning actually for any later member to become a concrete possibility. Then the scheme P can function though neither Q nor R exists; the scheme Q can function though R does not yet exist; but Q cannot function unless P is already functioning; and R cannot function unless Q is already functioning.

Thus, by way of a simple illustration, one may advert to the dietary schemes of animals. All carnivorous animals cannot live off other carnivorous animals. Hence a carnivorous dietary scheme supposes another, herbivorous dietary scheme, but inversely, there could be herbivorous animals without any carnivorous animals. Again, plants cannot in general live off animals; the scheme of their nourishment involves chemical processes; and that scheme can function apart from the existence of any animals. Finally, chemical cycles are not independent of physical laws, yet inversely, the laws of physics can be combined into schemes of recurrence that are independent of chemical processes.

Such in briefest outline is the notion of the conditioned series of schemes of recurrence ...

4.2   *The Probability of Schemes*

Our outline of the notion of a conditioned series of schemes of recurrence supposes that one can attribute a probability to the emergence and to the survival of a scheme of recurrence. However, our account of probability has been in terms of the frequency, not of schemes, but of events. Have schemes any probability? If they have, is there a distinct probability for their emergence and another for their survival? Such questions must be met.

Consider a set of events of the types $A, B, C, ...$ and a world situation in which they possess respectively the probabilities $p, q, r, ...$ Then by a general rule of probability theory, the probability of the occurrence of all the events in the set will be the product $pqr ...$ of their respective probabilities.

Now let us add a further assumption. Let us suppose that the set of events $A, B, C, ...$ satisfies a conditioned scheme of recurrence, say K, in a world situation in which the scheme K is not functioning, but in virtue of the fulfilment of prior conditions could begin to function. Then, if A were to occur, B would occur. If B were to occur, C would occur. If

C were to occur, ... A would occur. In brief, if any of the events in the set were to occur, then, other things being equal, the rest of the events in the set would follow.

In this case we may suppose that the probabilities of the single events are respectively the same as before, but we cannot suppose that the probability of the combination of all events in the set is the same as before. As is easily to be seen, the concrete possibility of a scheme beginning to function shifts the probability of the combination from the product pqr ... to the sum $p + q + r + $ ... For in virtue of the scheme, it now is true that A and B and C and ... will occur, if either A or B or C or ... occurs; and by a general rule of probability theory, the probability of a set of alternatives is equal to the sum of the probabilities of the alternatives.

Now a sum of a set of proper fractions $p, q, r,$ ... is always greater than the product of the same fractions. But a probability is a proper fraction. It follows that, when the prior conditions for the functioning of a scheme of recurrence are satisfied, then the probability of the combination of events constitutive of the scheme leaps from a product of fractions to a sum of fractions.

There exists, then, a probability of emergence for a scheme of recurrence. That probability consists in the sum of the respective probabilities of all the events included in the scheme, and it arises as soon as the prior conditions for the functioning of the scheme are satisfied.

There also exists a probability for the survival of schemes that have begun to function. For, of itself, a scheme tends to assure its own perpetuity. The positive conditions for the occurrence of its component events reside in the occurrence of those events. Even negative conditions, within limited ranges, can be provided for by the development of defensive circles. Nonetheless, the perpetuity of a scheme is not necessary. Just as classical laws are subject to the proviso 'other things being equal,' so also are the schemes constituted by combinations of classical laws; and whether or not other things will continue to be equal is a question that admits an answer only in terms of statistical laws. Accordingly, the probability of the survival of a scheme of recurrence is the probability of the nonoccurrence of any of the events that would disrupt the scheme.

4.3   Emergent Probability

There have been formulated the notion of a conditioned series of schemes of recurrence and, as well, the general sense in which one can speak of the probability of the emergence and the survival of single schemes. From these considerations there now comes to light the notion of an emergent probability. For the actual functioning of earlier schemes in the series fulfils the conditions for the possibility of the functioning of later schemes. As such conditions are fulfilled, the probability of the combination of the component events in a scheme jumps from a product of a set of proper fractions to the sum of those proper fractions. But what is probable, sooner or later occurs. When it occurs, a probability of emergence is replaced by a probability of survival; and as long as the scheme survives, it is in its turn fulfilling conditions for the possibility of still later schemes in the series.

Such is the general notion of emergent probability. It results from the combination of the conditioned series of schemes with their respective probabilities of emergence and survival. While by itself it is extremely jejune, it possesses rather remarkable potentialities of explanation. These must now be indicated in outline, and so we attempt brief considerations of the significance for emergent probability of spatial distribution, absolute numbers, long intervals of time, selection, stability, and development.

The notion of a conditioned series of schemes involves spatial concentrations. For each later set of schemes becomes possible in the places where earlier schemes are already functioning. Accordingly, the most elementary schemes, which are earliest in the series, can occur anywhere in the initial distribution of materials. But the second batch can occur only where the first have in fact occurred, the third can occur only where the second have in fact occurred, and so on. Moreover, since the realization of the schemes is in accord with the probabilities, which may be low, one cannot expect all possibilities to be actuated. Hence elementary schemes will not be as frequent as they could be, to narrow the possible basis for schemes at the second remove. These will not be as frequent as they could be, to narrow again the possible basis for schemes at the third remove, and so forth. It follows that, however widespread the realization of elementary schemes, there will be a succession of constrictions of the volumes of space in which later schemes can be found. Similarly, it follows that the points, so to speak, of greatest and least constriction occur where the probabilities of emergence of the next set of schemes are respectively the lowest and the highest. Finally, it follows that, since the latest schemes in the series have the greatest number of conditions to be fulfilled, their occurrence will be limited to a relatively small number of places.

Secondly, there is the significance of absolute numbers. For large numbers offset low probabilities. What occurs once on a million occasions is to be expected a million times on a million million occasions. Now the minimum probability pertains to the latest schemes in the series, for their emergence supposes the emergence of all earlier schemes. It follows that the lower the probability of the last schemes of the conditioned series, the greater must be the initial absolute numbers in which elementary schemes can be realized. In brief, the size of a universe is inversely proportionate to the probability of its ultimate schemes of recurrence.

Thirdly, there is the significance of long intervals of time. No matter how great the universe and how widespread the functioning of elementary schemes, there is an increasing concentration of the spatial volumes in which later schemes can be realized. Sooner or later the initial benefit of large numbers is lost by the successive narrowing of the basis for further developments. But at this point long intervals of time become significant. Just as a million million simultaneous possibilities yield a million probable realizations whose probability is one in a million, so also a million million successive possibilities yield a million probable realizations under the same expectation.

Fourthly, there is a selective significance attached to the distinction between probabilities of emergence and probabilities of survival. If both are low, the occurrence of the scheme will be both rare and fleeting. If both are high, the occurrences will be both common and enduring. If the probability of emergence is low and that of survival is high, the scheme is to be expected to be rare but enduring. Finally, in the opposite case, the expectation is that the scheme will be common but fleeting.

Fifthly, this selectivity has its significance for stability. The functioning of later schemes depends upon the functioning of earlier schemes, so that if the earlier collapse, then the later will collapse as well. It follows that the line of maximum stability would be of common and enduring schemes, while the line of minimum stability would be of rare and fleeting schemes.

Sixthly, no less than stability, the possibility of development must be considered. Unfortunately, these two can conflict. Schemes with high probabilities of survival tend to imprison materials in their own routines. They provide a highly stable basis for later schemes, but they also tend to prevent later schemes from emerging. A solution to this problem would be for the earlier, conditioning schemes to have a high probability of emergence but a low probability of survival. They would form a floating population on which later schemes could successively depend. Because their probability of survival was low, they would readily surrender materials to give later schemes the opportunity to emerge. Because their probability of emergence was high, they would readily be available to fulfil the conditions for the functioning of later schemes.

Needless to say, the foregoing considerations are extremely rudimentary. They are limited to the emergent probability of any conditioned series of schemes of recurrence. They make no effort towards developing that notion in the direction of its application to the conditions of the emergence and survival of modes of living. However, while absolutely such a fuller exposition would be desirable, still it has no place in a merely generic account of world order. For the premise of a generic account is, not the content of the natural sciences, but the possibility and validity of their assumptions and method.

The point we are endeavoring to make, within the limits of our narrow premise, is that the notion of emergent probability is explanatory. Intelligent inquiry aims at insight. But classical laws alone offer no insight into numbers, distributions, concentrations, time intervals, selectivity, uncertain stability, or development. On the contrary, they abstract from the instance, the place, the time, and the concrete conditions of actual functioning. Again, statistical laws, as a mere aggregate, affirm in various cases the ideal frequency of the occurrence of events. They make no pretence of explaining why there are so many kinds of events, or why each kind has the frequency attributed to it. To reach explanation on this level, it is necessary to effect the concrete synthesis of classical laws into a conditioned series of schemes of recurrence, to establish that such schemes, as combinations of events, acquire first a probability of emergence and then a probability of survival through the realization of the conditioned series, and finally to grasp that, if such a series of schemes is being realized in accord with probabilities, then there is available a general principle that promises answers to questions about the reason for numbers and distributions, concentrations and time intervals, selectivity and uncertain stability, development and breakdowns. To work out the answers pertains to the natural sciences. To grasp that emergent probability is an explanatory idea is to know what is meant when our objective was characterized as a generic, relatively invariant, and incomplete account of the immanent intelligibility, the order, the design of the universe of our experience.

4.4   Consequences of Emergent Probability

There remains the task of working out the generic properties of a world process in which the order or design is constituted by emergent probability. This we shall attempt in two main steps. First, we shall summarize the essentials of the notion of emergent probability. Secondly, we shall enumerate the consequences of that notion to be verified in world process.

The essentials of the notion of emergent probability may be indicated in the following series of assertions.

(1) An event is what is to be known by answering yes to such questions as, Did it happen? Is it occurring? Will it occur?

(2) World process is a spatiotemporal manifold of events. In other words, there are many events, and each has its place and time.

(3) Events are of kinds. Not every event is a new species, else there could be neither classical nor statistical laws.

(4) Events are recurrent. There are many events of each kind, and all are not at the same time.

(5) There are regularly recurrent events. This regularity is understood inasmuch as combinations of classical laws yield schemes of recurrence. Schemes are circular relationships between events of kinds, such that if the events occur once in virtue of the circular relationships, then, other things being equal, they keep on recurring indefinitely.

(6) Schemes can be arranged in a conditioned series, such that the earlier can function without the emergence of the later, but the later cannot emerge or function unless the earlier already are functioning.

(7) Combinations of events possess a probability, and that probability jumps, first when a scheme becomes concretely possible in virtue of the fulfilment of its prior conditions, and secondly when the scheme begins actually to function.

(8) The actual frequencies of events of each kind in each place and at each time do not diverge systematically from their probabilities. However, actual frequencies may diverge nonsystematically from proba-

bilities, and that nonsystematic divergence is chance. Accordingly, probability and chance are distinct and are not to be confused.

(9) Emergent probability is the successive realization in accord with successive schedules of probability of a conditioned series of schemes of recurrence.

The consequent properties of a world process in which the design is emergent probability run as follows:

(1) There is a succession of world situations. Each is characterized (*a*) by the schemes of recurrence actually functioning, (*b*) by the further schemes that now have become concretely possible, and (*c*) by the current schedule of probabilities of survival for existing schemes and of probabilities of emergence for concretely possible schemes.

(2) World process is open. It is a succession of probable realizations of possibilities. Hence it does not run along the iron rails laid down by determinists, nor on the other hand is it a nonintelligible morass of merely chance events.

(3) World process is increasingly systematic. For it is the successive realization of a conditioned series of schemes of recurrence, and the further the series of schemes is realized, the greater the systematization to which events are subjected.

(4) The increasingly systematic character of world process can be assured. No matter how slight the probability of the realization of the most developed and most conditioned schemes, the emergence of those schemes can be assured by sufficiently increasing absolute numbers and sufficiently prolonging intervals of time. For actual frequencies do not diverge systematically from probabilities; but the greater the numbers and the longer the time intervals, the clearer the need for a systematic intervention to prevent the probable from occurring.

(5) The significance of the initial or basic world situation is limited to the possibilities it contains and to the probabilities it assigns its possibilities. By the initial world situation is meant the situation that is first in time; by the basic world situation is meant the partial prolongation through time of initial conditions, such as arises, for instance, in certain contemporary hypotheses of continuous creation.

In either case, what is significant resides in possibilities and their probabilities, for in all its stages world process is the probable realization of possibilities. While the determinist would desire full information, exact to the *n*th decimal place, on his initial or basic situation, the advocate of emergent probability is quite satisfied with any initial situation in which the most elementary schemes can emerge and probably will emerge in sufficient numbers to sustain the subsequent structure.

(6) World process admits enormous differentiation. It envisages the totality of possibilities defined by classical laws. It realizes these possibilities in accord with its successive schedules of probabilities. And given sufficient numbers and sufficient time, even slight probabilities become assured.

(7) World process admits breakdowns. For no scheme has more than a probability of survival, so that there is for every scheme some probability of a breakdown; and since earlier schemes condition later schemes, a breakdown of the former entails the breakdown of the latter.

(8) World process includes blind alleys. For schemes with a high probability of survival have some probability of emergence. Insofar as they emerge, they tend to bind within their routines the materials for the possibility of later schemes, and so to block the way to full development.

(9) The later a scheme is in the conditioned series, the narrower is its distribution. For actual realization is less frequent than its concrete possibility; and each later set of schemes is concretely possible only where earlier, conditioning schemes are functioning.

(10) The narrower the basis for the emergence of each later set of schemes, the greater the need to invoke long intervals of time. For in this case the alternative of large numbers is excluded.

(11) The greater the probabilities of blind alleys and breakdowns, the greater must be the initial absolute numbers if the realization of the whole series of schemes is to be assured. For in this case the device of long time intervals might not be efficacious. Blind alleys with their inert routines could last for extremely long periods, and when they suffered breakdown, they might result in another blind alley. Again, a situation which led to some development only to suffer breakdown might merely repeat this process more frequently in a longer interval of time. On the other hand, the effect of large initial numbers is to assure at least one situation in which the whole series of schemes will win through.

(12) The foregoing properties of world process are generic. They assume that there are laws of the classical type, but they do not assume the determinate content of any particular classical law. They assume that classical laws can be combined into the circular relationships of

schemes, but they do not venture to analyze the structure of any scheme whatever. They assume that there are statistical laws, but there is no assumption of the determinate content of any statistical law.

Moreover, these properties are relatively invariant. They rest on the scientist's necessary presupposition that there are classical and statistical laws to be determined. But they in no way prejudge the determination of those laws nor the manner in which they are to be combined to yield schemes of recurrence and their successive probabilities. It follows that the foregoing properties of world process cannot be upset by any amount of scientific work in the determination of classical or statistical laws.

Again, these properties are explanatory of world process. They reveal an order, a design, an intelligibility. For they account in generic fashion for numbers and time intervals, for distributions and concentrations, for blind alleys and breakdowns, for enormous differentiation, for increasing systematization, for stability without necessity, for assurance without determinism, for development without chance.

Finally, the intelligibility offered by the explanation is immanent in world process. It exhibits the inner design of world process as an emergent probability, and from that design it concludes to the outstanding generic features of the same process. Accordingly, since empirical method aims at such an immanent intelligibility, emergent probability is a view of world order within the limits of empirical method. As we began by inviting the reader to grasp the intelligibility immanent in the image of a cartwheel, so now we are inviting him to perform again the same kind of act. The only difference is that, for the image of the cartwheel, he now must substitute the main features of the universe of our experience.

Related selections: 1.V 2 on the notion of dialectic; 1.XI on dialectical method; 1.XII.1 on the finality of the universe; 1.XII.3 on genetic method; 3.VI.2–3 on historical method; 1.XV.3 on critical method; 1.II.4–5 on inverse insight and the empirical residue.

Common Sense and Its Subject

The centrality of the act of insight to the methodical investigations of mathematicians and natural scientists has already been exposed. But insight plays an equally central role in ordinary social and practical living. Lonergan turns now to a consideration of the spontaneous intellectual development of common sense. Lonergan's usage of 'common sense' is in line with his overall aim of bringing to light the nature and role of insight and its surrounding context of preconceptual operations. By 'common sense' he means especially the ordinary, spontaneous mode of intellectual activity and development, rather than the stock of ideas and practices generated, maintained, and occasionally transformed by that activity.

In the first part of this selection, from Chapter 6 of *Insight*, Lonergan compares and contrasts common sense with logic and science as regards their modes of learning, reasoning, and expression, their planes of reality or worlds, and their ideals and aspirations. While Lonergan views common sense and science as ultimately complementary types of intelligent activity, men and women of common sense still remain in the familiar world of 'the relations of things to us,' whereas the scientist seeks understanding of 'the relations of things to one another.' The scientist as such is engaged primarily in knowing, but men and women of common sense are concerned with social and practical living. Commonsense and scientific activity are differently orientated.

In the second part, Lonergan explores the subjective field of human consciousness and identifies four 'patterns of experience.' Human consciousness is polymorphic; it assumes a variety of dynamic shapes. It is variously biological, esthetic, intellectual, dramatic, and practical. In ordinary human living the stream of consciousness is patterned primarily by dramatic and practical concerns. The discussion concludes with analyses of the dramatic artistry of

human living, the conscious and preconscious conditions for successful performance, and the relation of the refusal of insight – blindspots – to dramatic bias.
Here Lonergan describes the aberration of understanding that he names *scotosis*. When Lonergan turns to the objective field of common sense – the field of
human affairs and relationships – the account of the dramatic component in
everyday living will be complemented by that of commonsense practicality.

These extracts are taken from *Insight*, 196–204; 204–20.

1   Common Sense as Intellectual

The light and drive of intelligent inquiry unfolds methodically in
mathematics and empirical science. In the human child it is a secret
wonder that, once the mystery of language has been unraveled, rushes
forth in a cascade of questions. Far too soon the questions get out of
hand, and weary adults are driven to ever more frequent use of the
blanket 'My dear, you cannot understand that yet.' The child would
understand everything at once. It does not suspect that there is a strategy in the accumulation of insights, that the answers to many questions depend on answers to still other questions, that often enough
advertence to these other questions arises only from the insight that to
meet interesting questions one has to begin from quite uninteresting
ones. There is, then, common to all men the very spirit of inquiry that
constitutes the scientific attitude. But in its native state it is untutored.
Our intellectual careers begin to bud in the incessant What? and Why?
of childhood. They flower only if we are willing, or constrained, to
learn how to learn. They bring forth fruit only after the discovery that,
if we really would master the answers, we somehow have to find them
out ourselves.

Just as there is spontaneous inquiry, so too there is a spontaneous
accumulation of related insights. For questions are not an aggregate of
isolated monads. Insofar as any question is followed by an insight,
one has only to act, or to talk, or perhaps merely to think, on the basis
of that insight, for its incompleteness to come to light and thereby generate a further question. Insofar as the further question is in turn met
by the gratifying response of a further insight, once more the same
process will reveal another aspect of incompleteness, to give rise to
still further questions and still further insights. Such is the spontaneous process of learning. It is an accumulation of insights in which each

successive act complements the accuracy and covers over the deficiency of those that went before. Just as the mathematician advances from images through insights and formulations to symbols that stimulate further insights, just as the scientist advances from data through insights and formulations to experiments that stimulate further insights, so too the spontaneous and self-correcting process of learning is a circuit in which insights reveal their shortcomings by putting forth deeds or words or thoughts, and through that revelation prompt the further questions that lead to complementary insights.

Such learning is not without teaching. For teaching is the communication of insight. It throws out the clues, the pointed hints, that lead to insight. It cajoles attention to drive away the distracting images that stand in insight's way. It puts the further questions that reveal the need of further insights to modify and complement the acquired store. It has grasped the strategy of developing intelligence, and so begins from the simple to advance to the more complex. Deliberately and explicitly, all this is done by professional teachers that know their job. But the point we would make is that it also is done, though unconsciously and implicitly, by parents with their offspring and by equals among themselves. Talking is a basic human art. By it each communicates to others what he knows, and at the same time provokes the contradictions that direct his attention to what he has overlooked. Again, far more impressive than talking is doing. Deeds excite our admiration and stir us to emulation. We watch to see how things are done. We experiment to see if we can do them ourselves. We watch again to discover the oversights that led to our failures. In this fashion the discoveries and inventions of individuals pass into the possession of many, to be checked against their experience, to undergo the scrutiny of their further questions, to be modified by their improvements. By the same token, the spontaneous collaboration of individuals is also the communal development of intelligence in the family, the tribe, the nation, the race. Not only are men born with a native drive to inquire and understand; they are born into a community that possesses a common fund of tested answers, and from that fund each may draw his variable share, measured by his capacity, his interests, and his energy. Not only does the self-correcting process of learning unfold within the private consciousness of the individual; for by speech, and still more by example, there is effected a sustained communication that at once disseminates and tests and improves every advance, to make the achievement of each successive generation the starting point of the next.

From spontaneous inquiry, the spontaneous accumulation of related insights, and the spontaneous collaboration of communication, we have worked towards the notion of common sense as an intellectual development. Naturally enough, there will arise the question of the precise inventory of this public store. How does it define its terms? What are its postulates? What are the conclusions it infers from the premises? But if the question is obvious enough, the answer is more difficult. For the answer rests on one of those queer insights that merely grasps the false supposition of the question. Definitions, postulates, and inferences are the formulation of general knowledge. They regard, not the particular but the universal, not the concrete but the abstract. Common sense, unlike the sciences, is a specialization of intelligence in the particular and the concrete. It is common without being general, for it consists in a set of insights that remains incomplete until there is added at least one further insight into the situation in hand; and once that situation has passed, the added insight is no longer relevant, so that common sense at once reverts to its normal state of incompleteness. Thus, common sense may seem to argue from analogy, but its analogies defy logical formulation. The analogy that the logician can examine is merely an instance of the heuristic premise that similars are similarly understood. It can yield a valid argument only if the two concrete situations exhibit no significant dissimilarity. But common sense, because it does not have to be articulate, can operate directly from its accumulated insights. In correspondence with the similarities of the situation, it can appeal to an incomplete set of insights. In correspondence with the significant difference of situations, it can add the different insights relevant to each. Again, common sense may seem to generalize. But a generalization proposed by common sense has quite a different meaning from a generalization proposed by science. The scientific generalization aims to offer a premise from which correct deductions can be drawn. But the generalizations issued by common sense are not meant to be premises for deductions. Rather they would communicate pointers that ordinarily it is well to bear in mind. Proverbs are older far than principles, and like rules of grammar they do not lose their validity because of their numerous exceptions. For they aim to express, not the scientist's rounded set of insights that either holds in every instance or in none at all, but the incomplete set of insights which is called upon in every concrete instance but becomes proximately relevant only after a good look around has resulted in the needed additional insights. Look before you leap!

Not only does common sense differ from logic and from science in the meaning it attaches to analogies and generalizations. In all its utterances it operates from a distinctive viewpoint and pursues an ideal of its own. The heuristic assumptions of science anticipate the determination of natures that always act in the same fashion under similar circumstances, and as well the determination of ideal norms of probability from which events diverge only in a nonsystematic manner. Though the scientist is aware that he will reach these determinations only through a series of approximations, still he also knows that even approximate determinations must have the logical properties of abstract truth. Terms, then, must be defined unambiguously, and they must always be employed exactly in that unambiguous meaning. Postulates must be stated; their presuppositions must be examined; their implications must be explored. Automatically there results a technical language and a formal mode of speech. Not only is one compelled to say what one means and to mean what one says, but the correspondence that obtains between saying and meaning has the exact simplicity of such primitive utterances as 'This is a cat.'

Common sense, on the other hand, never aspires to universally valid knowledge, and it never attempts exhaustive communication. Its concern is the concrete and particular. Its function is to master each situation as it arises. Its procedure is to reach an incomplete set of insights that is to be completed only by adding on each occasion the further insights that scrutiny of the occasion reveals. It would be an error for common sense to attempt to formulate its incomplete set of insights in definitions and postulates and to work out their presuppositions and implications. For the incomplete set is not the understanding either of any concrete situation or of any general truth. Equally, it would be an error for common sense to attempt a systematic formulation of its completed set of insights in some particular case; for every systematic formulation envisages the universal, and every concrete situation is particular.

It follows that common sense has no use for a technical language and no tendency towards a formal mode of speech. It agrees that one must say what one means and mean what one says. But its correspondence between saying and meaning is at once subtle and fluid. As the proverb has it, a wink is as good as a nod. For common sense not merely says what it means; it says it to someone; it begins by exploring the other fellow's intelligence; it advances by determining what further insights have to be communicated to him; it undertakes the communication, not as an exercise in formal logic, but as a work of art; and it has at its disposal not merely all the resources of language but also the support of modulated tone and changing volume, the eloquence of facial expression, the emphasis of gestures, the effectiveness of pauses, the suggestiveness of questions, the significance of omissions. It follows that the only interpreter of commonsense utterances is common sense. For the relation between saying and meaning is the relation between sensible presentations and intellectual grasp, and if that relation can be as simple and exact as in the statement 'This is a cat,' it can also take on all the delicacy and subtlety, all the rapidity and effectiveness, with which one incarnate intelligence can communicate its grasp to another by grasping what the other has yet to grasp and what act or sound or sign would make him grasp it. Such a procedure, clearly, is logical, if by 'logical' you mean 'intelligent and reasonable.' With equal clearness, such a procedure is not logical, if by 'logical' you mean conformity to a set of general rules valid in every instance of a defined range; for no set of general rules can keep pace with the resourcefulness of intelligence in its adaptations to the possibilities and exigencies of concrete tasks of self-communication.

Just as the elliptical utterances of common sense have a deeper ground than many logicians and practically all controversialists have managed to reach, so too the plane of reality envisaged by commonsense meaning is quite distinct from the plane that the sciences explore. It has been said that the advance of science is from description to explanation, from things as related to our senses, through measurements, to things as related to one another. It is clear that common sense is not concerned with the relations of things to one another, and that it does not employ the technical terms that scientists invent to express those relations. Still, this obvious difference provides no premise for the inference that the object of scientific description is the same as the object of commonsense communication. It is true enough that both types of utterance deal with things as related to our senses. But also it is true that they do so from different viewpoints and with different ends. Scientific description is the work of a trained scientific observer.

It satisfies the logician's demand for complete articulateness and exhaustive statement. It reveals the imprint of the scientist's anticipation of attainment of the pure conjugates that express the relations of things to one another. For, though scientific description deals with things as related to our senses, it does so with an ulterior purpose and under the guidance of a method that strains towards its realization.

Common sense, on the other hand, has no theoretical inclinations. It remains completely in the familiar world of things for us. The further questions by which it accumulates insights are bounded by the interests and concerns of human living, by the successful performance of daily tasks, by the discovery of immediate solutions that will work. Indeed, the supreme canon of common sense is the restriction of further questions to the realm of the concrete and particular, the immediate and practical. To advance in common sense is to restrain the omnivorous drive of inquiring intelligence and to brush aside as irrelevant, if not silly, any question whose answer would not make an immediately palpable difference. Just as the scientist rises in stern protest against the introduction into his field of metaphysical questions that do not satisfy his canon of selection, so the man of common sense (and nothing else) is ever on his guard against all theory, ever blandly asking the proponent of ideas what difference they would make, and if the answer is less vivid and less rapid than an advertisement, then solely concerned with thinking up an excuse for getting rid of the fellow. After all, men of common sense are busy. They have the world's work to do.

Still, how can the world's work be done either intelligently or efficiently, if it is done by men of common sense that never bother their heads a minute about scientific method? That question can be answered, I think, if we begin from another. Why is it that scientists need scientific method? Why must such intelligent men be encumbered with the paraphernalia of laboratories and the dull books of specialized libraries? Why should they be trained in observation and logic? Why should they be tied down by abstruse technical terms and abstract reasoning? Clearly it is because their inquiry moves off from the familiar to the unfamiliar, from the obvious to the recondite. They have to attend to things as related to us, in the manner that leads to things as related to one another. When they reach the universal relations of things to one another, they are straining beyond the native range of insight into sensible presentations, and they need the crutches of method to fix their gaze on things as neither sensibly given nor concrete nor particular.

Common sense, on the other hand, has no such aspirations. It clings to the immediate and practical, the concrete and particular. It remains within the familiar world of things for us. Rockets and space platforms are superfluous if you intend to remain on this earth. So also is scientific method superfluous in the performance of the tasks of common sense. Like the sciences, it is an accumulation of related insights into the data of experience. Like the sciences, it is the fruit of a vast collaboration. Like the sciences, it has been tested by its practical results. Still, there is a profound difference. For the sciences have theoretical aspirations, and common sense has none. The sciences would speak precisely and with universal validity, but common sense would speak only to persons and only about the concrete and particular. The sciences need methods to reach their abstract and universal objects; but scientists need common sense to apply methods properly in executing the concrete tasks of particular investigations, just as logicians need common sense if they are to grasp what is meant in each concrete act of human utterance. It has been argued that there exists a complementarity between classical and statistical investigations; perhaps it now is evident that the whole of science, with logic thrown in, is a development of intelligence that is complementary to the development named common sense. Rational choice is not between science and common sense; it is a choice of both, of science to master the universal, and of common sense to deal with the particular.

There remain to be mentioned the differentiations of common sense. Far more than the sciences, common sense is divided into specialized departments. For every difference of geography, for every difference of occupation, for every difference of social arrangements, there is an appropriate variation of common sense. At a given place, in a given job, among a given group of people, a man can be at intelligent ease in every situation in which he is called upon to speak or act. He always knows just what is up, just the right thing to say, just what needs to be done, just how to go about it. His experience has taken him through the cycle of eventualities that occur in his milieu. His intelligence has ever been alert. He has made his mistakes, and from them he has learnt not to make them twice. He has developed the acumen that notices movements away from the familiar routine, the poise that sizes them up before embarking on a course of action, the resourcefulness that hits upon the response that meets the new issue. He is an embodiment of the ideal of common sense, yet his achievement is relevant only to its environment. Put him among others in another place or at another job, and until they become familiar, until he has accumulated a fresh set of insights, he cannot avoid hesitancy and awkwardness. Once more he must learn his way about, catch on to the tricks of a new trade, discern in little signs the changing moods of those with whom he deals. Such, then, is the specialization of common sense. At once, it adapts individuals in every walk of life to the work they have chosen or the lot that has befallen them, and no less, it generates all those minute differences of viewpoint and mentality that separate men and women, old and young, town and country, until in the limit one reaches the cumulative differences and mutual incomprehension of different strata of society, different nations, different civilizations, and different epochs of human history.

We have been endeavoring to conceive the intellectual component in common sense. Our effort began from spontaneous questions, spontaneous accumulations of insights, spontaneous collaboration in testing and improving them. Next, there was formulated the central notion of an habitual but incomplete set of insights that was completed with appropriate variations in each concrete set of circumstances that called for speech or action. It was shown that such an intellectual development not only aimed at mastering the concrete and particular but also achieved its aim in a concrete and particular manner that contrasted with the general rules of logic and the general methods of science, yet provided a necessary complement both for the concrete use of general techniques and the concrete application of general conclusions. Finally, attention was drawn to the differentiations of common sense which multiply, not by theoretical differences as do the departments of science, but by the empirical differences of place and time, circumstance and environment.

2   The Subjective Field of Common Sense

If there is a parallel between a scientific and a commonsense accumulation of insights, there also exists a difference. Where the scientist seeks the relations of things to one another, common sense is concerned with the relations of things to us. Where the scientist's correlations serve to define the things that he relates to one another, common sense not merely relates objects to a subject but also constitutes relations of the subject to objects. Where the scientist is primarily engaged in knowing, common sense cannot develop without changing the subjective term in the object-to-subject relations that it knows.

There is, then, a subtle ambiguity in the apparently evident statement that common sense relates things to us. For who are we? Do we not change? Is not the acquisition of common sense itself a change in us? Clearly, an account of common sense cannot be adequate without an investigation of its subjective field. To this end we propose in the present section to introduce the notion of patterns of experience, to distinguish biological, aesthetic, intellectual, and dramatic patterns, to contrast the patterns of consciousness with the unconscious patterns of neural process, and finally, to indicate the connection between a flight from insight and, on the other hand, repression, inhibition, slips of the tongue, dreams, [and] screening memories ...

2.1 Patterns of Experience

The notion of the pattern of experience may best be approached by remarking how abstract it is to speak of a sensation. No doubt, we are all familiar with acts of seeing, hearing, touching, tasting, smelling. Still, such acts never occur in isolation both from one another and from all other events. On the contrary, they have a bodily basis; they are functionally related to bodily movements; and they occur in some dynamic context that somehow unifies a manifold of sensed contents and of acts of sensing.

Thus, without eyes, there is no seeing; and when I would see with my eyes, I open them, turn my head, approach, focus my gaze. Without ears, there is no hearing; and to escape noise, I must move beyond its range or else build myself soundproof walls. Without a palate, there is no tasting; and when I would taste, there are involved movements of the body and arms, of hands and fingers, of lips and tongue and jaws. Sensation has a bodily basis, and functionally it is linked to bodily movements.

Nor is this all. Both the sensations and the bodily movements are subject to an organizing control. Besides the systematic links between senses and sense organs, there is, immanent in experience, a factor variously named conation, interest, attention, purpose. We speak of consciousness as a stream, but the stream involves not only the temporal succession of different contents but also direction, striving, effort. Moreover, this direction of the stream is variable. Thales was so intent upon the stars that he did not see the well into which he tumbled. The milkmaid was so indifferent to the stars that she could not overlook the well. Still, Thales could have seen the well, for he was not blind; and perhaps the milkmaid could have been interested in the stars, for she was human.

There are, then, different dynamic patterns of experience, nor is it difficult for us to say just what we mean by such a pattern. As conceived, it is the formulation of an insight; but all insight arises from sensitive or imaginative presentations, and in the present case the relevant presentations are simply the various elements in the experience that is organized by the pattern.

2.2   The Biological Pattern of Experience

A plant draws its sustenance from its environment by remaining in a single place and by performing a slowly varying set of routines in interaction with a slowly varying set of things. In contrast, the effective environment of a carnivorous animal is a floating population of other animals that move over a range of places and are more or less well equipped to deceive or elude their pursuers. Both plant and animal are alive, for in both aggregates of events insight discerns an intelligible unity that commonly is formulated in terms of biological drive or purpose. But plants adapt slowly, animals rapidly, to changing situations; and if we endeavor to understand the sudden twists and turns both of fleeing quarry and pursuing beast of prey, we ascribe to them a flow of experience not unlike our own. Outer senses are the heralds of biological opportunities and dangers. Memory is the file of supplementary information. Imagination is the projection of courses of action. Conation and emotion are the pent-up pressure of elemental purposiveness. Finally, the complex sequence of delicately coordinated bodily movements is at once the consequence of striving and a cause of the continuous shift of sensible presentations.

In such an illustration insight grasps the biological pattern of experience. By such a pattern is not meant the visible or imaginative focus of attention offered by the characteristic shape and appearance of an animal. Nor again is the pattern reached by grasping that spatially and temporally distinct data all belong to a single living thing, for plants no less than animals are alive, and as yet we have not satisfied ourselves upon the validity of the notion of the thing. Rather, the pattern is a set of intelligible relations that link together sequences of sensations, memories, images, conations, emotions, and bodily movements; and to name the pattern biological is simply to affirm that the sequences converge upon terminal activities of intussusception or reproduction, or, when negative in scope, self-preservation. Accordingly, the notion of the pattern takes us beyond behaviorism, inasmuch as attention is not confined to external data; it takes us beyond a narrow positivism, inasmuch as the canon of relevance leads us to acknowledge that there is a content to insight; but it observes the canon of parsimony by adding no more than a set of intelligible relations to elements of experience.

A more informative characterization of the biological pattern of experience is to be obtained by comparing animals and plants. For conscious living is only a part of the animal's total living. As in the plant, so in the animal there go forward immanent vital processes without the benefit of any conscious control. The formation and nutrition of organic structures and of their skeletal supports, the distribution and neural control of muscles, the physics of the vascular system, the chemistry of digestion, the metabolism of the cell, all are sequences of events that fit into intelligible patterns of biological significance. Yet it is only when their functioning is disturbed that they enter into consciousness. Indeed, not only is a large part of animal living nonconscious, but the conscious part itself is intermittent. Animals sleep. It is as though the full-time business of living called forth consciousness as a part-time employee, occasionally to meet problems of malfunctioning, but regularly to deal rapidly, effectively, and economically with the external situations in which sustenance is to be won and into which offspring are to be born.

Thus extroversion is a basic characteristic of the biological pattern of experience. The bodily basis of the senses in sense organs, the functional correlation of sensations with the positions and movements of the organs, the imaginative, conative, emotive consequences of sensible presentations, and the resulting local movements of the body, all indicate that elementary experience is concerned, not with the immanent aspects of living, but with its external conditions and opportunities. Within the full pattern of living, there is a partial, intermittent, extroverted pattern of conscious living.

It is this extroversion of function that underpins the confrontational element of consciousness itself. Conation, emotion, and bodily movement are a response to stimulus; but the stimulus is over against the response; it is a presentation through sense and memory and imagination of what is responded to, of what is to be dealt with. The stimulating elements are the elementary object; the responding elements are the elementary subject. When the object fails to stimulate, the subject is indifferent; and when nonconscious vital process has no need of outer objects, the subject dozes and falls asleep.

2.3 The Aesthetic Pattern of Experience

There exists in man an exuberance above and beyond the biological account books of purposeful pleasure and pain. Conscious living is itself a joy that reveals its spontaneous authenticity in the untiring play of children, in the strenuous games of youth, in the exhilaration of sunlit morning air, in the sweep of a broad perspective, in the swing of a melody. Such delight is not, perhaps, exclusively human, for kittens play and snakes are charmed. But neither is it merely biological. One can well suspect that health and exercise are not the dominant motive in the world of sport; and it seems a little narrow to claim that good meals and fair women are the only instances of the aesthetic. Rather, one is led to acknowledge that experience can occur for the sake of experiencing, that it can slip beyond the confines of serious-minded biological purpose, and that this very liberation is a spontaneous, self-justifying joy.

Moreover, just as the mathematician grasps intelligible forms in schematic images, just as the scientist seeks intelligible systems that cover the data of his field, so too the artist exercises his intelligence in discovering ever novel forms that unify and relate the contents and acts of aesthetic experience.[1] Still, sense does not escape one master merely to fall into the clutches of another. Art is a twofold freedom. As it liberates experience from the drag of biological purposiveness, so it liberates intelligence from the wearying constraints of mathematical proofs, scientific verifications, and commonsense factualness. For the validation of the artistic idea is the artistic deed. The artist establishes his insights, not by proof or verification, but by skilfully embodying

1 Insight in musical composition is described by Susanne K. Langer, *Feeling and Form: A Theory of Art Developed from 'Philosophy in a New Key'* (New York: Charles Scribner's Sons, 1953), 120–32.

them in colors and shapes, in sounds and movements, in the unfolding situations and actions of fiction. To the spontaneous joy of conscious living there is added the spontaneous joy of free intellectual creation.

The aesthetic and artistic also are symbolic. Free experience and free creation are prone to justify themselves by an ulterior purpose or significance. Art then becomes symbolic, but what is symbolized is obscure. It is an expression of the human subject outside the limits of adequate intellectual formulation or appraisal. It seeks to mean, to convey, to impart, something that is to be reached, not through science or philosophy, but through a participation, and in some fashion a re-enactment of the artist's inspiration and intention. Prescientific and prephilosophic, it may strain for truth and value without defining them. Post-biological, it may reflect the psychological depths, yet by that very fact it will go beyond them.

Indeed, the very obscurity of art is in a sense its most generic meaning. Prior to the neatly formulated questions of systematizing intelligence, there is the deep-set wonder in which all questions have their source and ground. As an expression of the subject, art would show forth that wonder in its elemental sweep. Again, as a twofold liberation of sense and of intelligence, art would exhibit the reality of the primary object for that wonder. For the animals, safely sheathed in biological routines, are not questions to themselves. But man's artistry testifies to his freedom. As he can do, so he can be what he pleases. What is he to be? Why? Art may offer attractive or repellent answers to these questions, but in its subtler forms it is content to communicate any of the moods in which such questions arise, to convey any of the tones in which they may be answered or ignored.

2.4   *The Intellectual Pattern of Experience*

The aesthetic liberation and the free artistic control of the flow of sensations and images, of emotions and bodily movements, not merely break the bonds of biological drive but also generate in experience a flexibility that makes it a ready tool for the spirit of inquiry. To the liveliness of youth, study is hard. But in the seasoned mathematician, sensitive process easily contracts to an unruffled sequence of symbolic notations and schematic images. In the trained observer, outer sense forgets its primitive biological functions to take on a selective alertness that keeps pace with the refinements of elaborate and subtle classifications. In the theorist intent upon a problem, even the subconscious goes to work to yield at unexpected moments the suggestive images of clues and missing links, of patterns and perspectives, that evoke the desiderated insight and the delighted cry 'Eureka!' In reflection, there arises a passionless calm. Memory ferrets out instances that would run counter to the prospective judgment. Imagination anticipates the shape of possibilities that would prove the judgment wrong. So deep is the penetration, so firm the dominance, so strange the transformation of sensitive spontaneity, that memories and anticipations rise above the threshold of consciousness only if they possess at least a plausible relevance to the decision to be made. For the stream of sensitive experience is a chameleon; and as its pattern can be biological or artistic, so too it can become the automatic instrument, or rather the vitally adaptive collaborator, of the spirit of inquiry.

No doubt, the frequency, intensity, duration, and purity of the intellectual pattern of experience are subject to great variation. For they depend upon native aptitude, upon training, upon age and development, upon external circumstance, upon the chance that confronts one with problems and that supplies at least the intermittent opportunity to work towards their solution. To be talented is to find that one's experience slips easily into the intellectual pattern, that one's sensitive spontaneity responds quickly and precisely to the exigencies of mind. Insights come readily. Exact formulation follows promptly. Outer sense pounces upon significant detail. Memory tosses out immediately the contrary instance. Imagination devises at once the contrary possibility. Still, even with talent, knowledge makes a slow, if not a bloody entrance. To learn thoroughly is a vast undertaking that calls for relentless perseverance. To strike out on a new line and become more than a weekend celebrity calls for years in which one's living is more or less constantly absorbed in the effort to understand, in which one's understanding gradually works round and up a spiral of viewpoints with each complementing its predecessor and only the last embracing the whole field to be mastered.

2.5 The Dramatic Pattern of Experience

If now we turn to ordinary human living, it is plain that we have to do with neither the biological nor the artistic nor the intellectual pattern of experience. Still, there is a stream of consciousness, and the stream involves not only succession but also direction. Conspicuous in this direction is a concern to get things done. But behind palpable activities, there are motives and purposes; and in them it is not difficult to discern an artistic, or more precisely, a dramatic component.

For human desires are not simply the biological impulses of hunger for eating and of sex for mating. Indeed, man is an animal for whom mere animality is indecent. It is true enough that eating and drinking are biological performances. But in man they are dignified by their spatial and psychological separation from the farm, the abattoir, the kitchen; they are ornamented by the elaborate equipment of the dining room, by the table manners imposed upon children, by the deportment of adult convention. Again, clothes are not a simple-minded matter of keeping warm. They are the colored plumes of birds as well as the furs of animals. They disguise as well as cover and adorn, for man's sensible and sensing body must not appear to be merely a biological unit. Sex, finally, is manifestly biological yet not merely so. On this point man can be so insistent that, within the context of human living, sex becomes a great mystery, shrouded in the delicacy of indirect speech, enveloped in an aura of romantic idealism, enshrined in the sanctity of the home.

Not only, then, is man capable of aesthetic liberation and artistic creativity, but his first work of art is his own living. The fair, the beautiful, the admirable is embodied by man in his own body and actions before it is given a still freer realization in painting and sculpture, in music and poetry. Style is the man before it appears in the artistic product. Still, if the style of living is more fundamental, it is also more constrained. For man's own body and actions cannot be treated as the painter treats his uncomplaining oils and the poet his verbal materials. As in the animal, so also in man, there exist the exigencies of underlying materials, and the pattern of experience has to meet these exigencies by granting them psychic representation and conscious integration. The biological cannot be ignored, and yet in man it can be transformed. The transformation varies with the locality, the period, the social milieu; but the occurrence of the variations only serves to reveal the existence of the variable. Men will claim that they work because they must live; but it is plain that they work so hard because they must make their living dignified. To lack that dignity is to suffer embarrassment, shame, degradation; it is to invite amusement, laughter, ridicule. Inversely, to grant free rein to man's impulse for artistically manifested dignity is to set so-called hardheaded industrialists and financiers to the task of stimulating artistic imagination with advertisements and of meeting its demands with the raw materials of the earth and with the technology of an age of science.

Such artistry is dramatic. It is in the presence of others, and the others too are also actors in the primordial drama that the theatre only imitates. If aesthetic values, realized in one's own living, yield one the satisfaction of good performance, still it is well to have the objectivity of that satisfaction confirmed by the admiration of others; it is better to be united with others by winning their approval; it is best to be bound to them by deserving and obtaining their respect and even their affection. For man is a social animal. He is born in one family only to found another of his own. His artistry and his knowledge accumulate over the centuries because he imitates and learns from others. The execution of his practical schemes requires the collaboration of others. Still, the network of man's social relationships has not the fixity of organization of the hive or the anthill; nor again is it primarily the product of pure intelligence devising blueprints for human behavior. Its ground is aesthetic liberation and artistic creativity, where the artistry is limited by biological exigence, inspired by example and emulation, confirmed by admiration and approval, sustained by respect and affection.

The characters in this drama of living are molded by the drama itself. As other insights emerge and accumulate, so too do the insights that govern the imaginative projects of dramatic living. As other insights are corrected through the trial and error that give rise to further questions and yield still further complementary insights, so too does each individual discover and develop the possible roles he might play, and under the pressure of artistic and affective criteria, work out his own selection and adaptation. Out of the plasticity and exuberance of childhood through the discipline and the play of education there gradually is formed the character of the man. It is a process in which rational consciousness with its reflection and criticism, its deliberation and choice, exerts a decisive influence. Still, there is no deliberation or choice about becoming stamped with some character; there is no deliberation about the fact that our past behavior determines our present habitual attitudes; nor is there any appreciable effect from our present good resolutions upon our future spontaneity. Before there can be reflection or criticism, evaluation or deliberation, our imaginations and intelligence must collaborate in representing the projected course of action that is to be submitted to reflection and criticism, to evaluation and decision. Already in the prior collaboration of imagination and intelligence, the dramatic pattern is operative, outlining how we might behave before others and charging the outline with an artistic transformation of a more elementary aggressivity and affectivity. Ordinary living is not ordinary drama. It is not learning a role and developing in oneself the feelings appropriate to its performance. It is not the prior task of assembling materials and through insight imposing upon them an artistic pattern. For in ordinary living there are not first the materials and then the pattern, nor first the role and then the feelings. On the contrary, the materials that emerge in consciousness are already patterned, and the pattern is already charged emotionally and conatively.

2.6   Elements in the Dramatic Subject

The first condition of drama is the possibility of acting it out, of the subordination of neural process to psychic determinations. Now in the animals this subordination can reach a high degree of complexity to ensure large differentiations of response to nuanced differences of stimuli. Nonetheless, this complexity, so far from being an optional acquisition, seems rather to be a natural endowment and to leave the animal with a relatively small capacity for learning new ways and for mastering other than native skills. In contrast, man's bodily movements are, as it were, initially detached from the conative, sensitive, and emotive elements that direct and release them; and the initial plasticity and indeterminacy ground the later variety. Were the pianist's arms, hands, and fingers locked from birth in natural routines of biological stimulus and response, they never could learn to respond quickly and accurately to the sight of a musical score. To take another illustration, the production of sound is a complicated set of correlated oscillations and movements; but the wailing and gurgling of infants develop through the prattle of children into articulate speech, and this vocal activity can be complemented with the visual and manual activities of reading and writing; the whole structure rests upon conventional signs, yet the endlessly complex correlations that are involved between the psychic and the neural have become automatic and spontaneous in a language that one knows.

Inverse to the control of the psychic over the neural are the demands of neural patterns and processes for psychic representation and conscious integration. Just as an appropriate schematic image specifies and leads to a corresponding insight, so patterns of change in the optic nerve and the cerebrum specify and lead to corresponding acts of seeing. What is true of sight is also true of the other outer senses, and though the matter is far from fully explored, one may presume that memory and imagination, conation and emotion, pleasure and pain, all have their counterparts in corresponding neural processes and originate from their specific demands.

It would be a mistake, however, to suppose that such demands are unconditional. Perceiving is a function not only of position relative to an object, of the intensity of the light, of the healthiness of eyes, but also of interest, anticipation, and activity. Besides the demands of neural processes, there also is the pattern of experience in which their demands are met; and as the elements that enter consciousness are already within a pattern, there must be exercised some preconscious selection and arrangement. Already we have noticed, in treating the intellectual pattern of experience, how the detached spirit of inquiry cuts off the interference of emotion and conation, how it penetrates observation with the abstruse classifications of science, how it puts the unconscious to work to have it bring forth the suggestions, the clues, the perspectives, that emerge at unexpected moments to release insight and call forth a delighted 'Eureka!' In similar fashion, the dramatic pattern of experience penetrates below the surface of consciousness to exercise its own domination and control, and to effect, prior to conscious discrimination, its own selections and arrangements. Nor is this aspect of the dramatic pattern either surprising or novel: there cannot be selection and arrangement without rejection and exclusion, and the function that excludes elements from emerging in consciousness is now familiar as Freud's censor.

Since, then, the demands of neural patterns and processes are subject to control and selection, they are better named demand functions. They call for some psychic representation and some conscious integration, but their specific requirements can be met in a variety of different manners. In the biological pattern of experience, where both unconscious vital process and conscious striving pursue the same end, there is, indeed, little room for diversification of psychic contents. But aesthetic liberation, artistic creativity, and the constant shifting of the dramatic setting open up vast potentialities. All the world's a stage, and not only does each in his time play many parts but also the many parts vary with changes of locality, period, and social milieu. Still, there are limits to this versatility and flexibility. The demand functions of neural patterns and processes constitute the exigence of the organism for its conscious complement; and to violate that exigence is to invite the anguish of abnormality.

2.7   Dramatic Bias

Just as insight can be desired, so too it can be unwanted. Besides the love of light, there can be a love of darkness. If prepossessions and prejudices notoriously vitiate theoretical investigations, much more easily can elementary passions bias understanding in practical and personal matters. Nor has such a bias merely some single and isolated effect. To exclude an insight is also to exclude the further questions that would arise from it, and the complementary insights that would carry it towards a rounded and balanced viewpoint. To lack that fuller view results in behavior that generates misunderstanding both in ourselves and in others. To suffer such incomprehension favors a withdrawal from the outer drama of human living into the inner drama of fantasy. This introversion, which overcomes the extroversion native to the biological pattern of experience, generates a differentiation of the persona that appears before others and the more intimate ego that in the daydream is at once the main actor and the sole spectator. Finally, the incomprehension, isolation, and duality rob the development of one's common sense of some part, greater or less, of the corrections and the assurance that result from learning accurately the tested insights of others and from submitting one's own insights to the criticism based on others' experience and development.

2.7.1   Scotosis

Let us name such an aberration of understanding a scotosis, and let us call the resultant blind spot a scotoma. Fundamentally, the scotosis is an unconscious process. It arises, not in conscious acts, but in the censorship that governs the emergence of psychic contents. Nonetheless, the whole process is not hidden from us, for the merely spontaneous exclusion of unwanted insights is not equal to the total range of eventualities. Contrary insights do emerge. But they may be accepted as correct, only to suffer the eclipse that the bias brings about by excluding the relevant further questions. Again, they may be rejected as incorrect, as mere bright ideas without a solid foundation in fact; and this rejection tends to be connected with rationalization of the scotosis and with an effort to accumulate evidence in its favor. Again, consideration of the contrary insight may not reach the level of reflective and critical consciousness; it may occur only to be brushed aside in an emotional reaction of distaste, pride, dread, horror, revulsion. Again, there are the inverse phenomena. Insights that expand the scotosis can appear to lack plausibility; they will be subjected to scrutiny; and as the subject shifts to and from his sounder viewpoint, they will oscillate wildly between an appearance of nonsense and an appearance of truth. Thus, in a variety of manners, the scotosis can remain fundamentally unconscious yet suffer the attacks and crises that generate in the mind a mist of obscurity and bewilderment, of suspicion and reassurance, of doubt and rationalization, of insecurity and disquiet.

2.7.2   Repression

Nor is it only the mind that is troubled. The scotosis is an aberration, not only of the understanding, but also of the censorship. Just as wanting an insight penetrates below the surface to bring forth schematic images that give rise to the insight, so not wanting an insight has the opposite effect of repressing from consciousness a scheme that would suggest the insight. Now this aberration of the censorship is inverse to it. Primarily, the censorship is constructive; it selects and arranges materials that emerge in consciousness in a perspective that gives rise to an insight; this positive activity has by implication a negative aspect, for other materials are left behind, and other perspectives are not brought to light; still, this negative aspect of positive activity does not introduce any arrangement or perspective into the unconscious demand functions of neural patterns and processes. In contrast, the aberration of the censorship is primarily repressive; its positive activity is to prevent the emergence into consciousness of perspectives that would give rise to unwanted insights; it introduces, so to speak, the exclusion of arrangements into the field of the unconscious; it dictates the manner in which neural demand functions are not to be met; and the negative aspect of its positive activity is the admission to consciousness of any materials in any other arrangement or perspective. Finally, both the censorship and its aberration differ from conscious advertence to a possible mode of behavior and conscious refusal to behave in that fashion. For the censorship and its aberration are operative prior to conscious advertence, and they regard directly not how we are to behave but what we are to understand. A refusal to behave in a given manner is not a refusal to understand; so far from preventing conscious advertence, the refusal intensifies it and makes its recurrence more likely; and, finally, while it is true that conscious refusal is connected with a cessation of the conscious advertence, still this connection rests, not on an obnubilation of intelligence, but on a shift of effort, interest, preoccupation. Accordingly, we are led to restrict the name 'repression' to the exercise of the aberrant censorship that is engaged in preventing insight.

2.7.3 Inhibition

The effect of the repression is an inhibition imposed upon neural demand functions. However, if we distinguish between demands for images and demands for affects, it becomes clear that the inhibition will not block both in the same fashion. For insights arise, not from the experience of affects, but rather from imaginative presentations. Hence, to prevent insights, repression will have to inhibit demands for images. On the other hand, it need inhibit demands for affects only if they are coupled with the undesired images. Accordingly, the repression will not inhibit a demand for affects if that demand becomes detached from its apprehensive component, slips along some association path, and attaches itself to some other apprehensive component. Inversely, when there emerges into consciousness an affect coupled with an incongruous object, then one can investigate association paths, argue from the incongruous to the initial object of the affect, and conclude that this combination of initial object and affect had been inhibited by a repression. Nor is this conclusion to be rejected as preposterous because the discovered combination of image and affect is utterly alien to conscious behavior. For the combination was inhibited precisely because it was alien. Insights are unwanted, not because they confirm our current viewpoints and behavior, but because they lead to their correction and revision. Inasmuch as the scotosis grounds the conscious affective attitudes of the persona performing before others, it also involves the repression of opposite combinations of neural demand functions; and these demands will emerge into consciousness with the affect detached from its initial object and attached to some associated and more or less incongruous object. Again, inasmuch as the scotosis grounds the conscious affective attitudes of the ego performing in his own private theatre, it also involves the repression of opposite combinations of neural demand functions; and in like manner these demands make their way into consciousness with the affect detached from its initial object and attached to some other more or less incongruous object. In a systematization of Jung's terminology, the conscious ego is matched with an inverse nonconscious shadow, and the conscious persona is matched with an inverse nonconscious anima. Thus the persona of the dispassionate intellectual is coupled with a sentimental anima, and an ego with a message for mankind is linked to a diffident shadow.

2.7.4 Performance

Apprehension and affect are for operations, but as one would expect, the complex consequences of the scotosis tend to defeat the efforts of the dramatic actor to offer a smooth performance. To speak fluently or to play a musical instrument, one has to be able to confine attention to higher-level controls and to leave the infinite details of the execution to acquired habit. But the division of conscious living between the two patterns of the ego and persona can hamper attention to the higher-level controls and allow the sentiments of the ego or shadow to slip into the performance of the persona. Thus, a friend of mine who had been out of town asked me how my work was getting on. I answered with a dreaded didactic monologue on the connection between insight and depth psychology. His laudatory comment ended with the remark, 'Certainly, while I have been away, you have not been wasting my time.'

Besides the waking performance of the dramatic actor, there is also the strange succession of fragmentary scenes that emerge in sleep. Then experience is not dominated by a pattern. Not only are there lacking the critical reflection and deliberate choosing that make waking consciousness reasonable, but also the preconscious activity of the censor, selecting and arranging neural demands, is carried out in a half-hearted and perfunctory manner. This relaxation of the censorship, however, not only accounts for the defective pattern of experience in dreamland but also explains the preponderant influence of the other determinant of conscious contents, namely, the neural demand functions. Claims ignored during the day become effective in sleep. The objects and affects of the persona and of the ego make an overt appearance, and with them mingle the covert affects of the shadow and the anima attached to their incongruous objects.

The basic meaning of the dream is its function. In the animal, consciousness functions as a higher technique for the effective prosecution of biological ends. In man, not only does it fulfil this purpose but also it provides the center for the operations of the self-constituting dramatic actor. Sleep is the negation of consciousness. It is the opportunity needed by unconscious vital process to offset without interference the wear and tear suffered by nerves during the busy day. Within this function of sleep lies the function of the dream. Not only have nerves their physical and chemical basis but also they contain dynamic patterns that can be restored to an easy equilibrium only through the offices of psychic representations and interplay. Besides restoring the organism, sleep has to knit up the raveled sleeve of care, and it does so by adding dreams, in which are met ignored claims of neural demand functions.

Functionally, then, the dream is a psychic flexibility that matches and complements the flexibility of neural demands. If consciousness is to yield to the preoccupations of the intellectual or of the dramatic actor, it cannot be simply a function of neural patterns and processes. Inversely, if neural demands ignored by consciousness are to be met without violating the liberation of the artistic, intellectual, or dramatic pattern of experience, then they find their opportunity in the dream.

There is a further aspect to this twofold flexibility. The liberation of consciousness is founded on a control of apprehensions; as has been seen, the censorship selects and arranges materials for insight, or in its aberration excludes the arrangements that would yield insight. Inversely, the imperious neural demands are not for apprehensive psychic contents but for the conations and emotions that are far more closely linked with activity; thus, while we imagine much as we please, our feelings are quite another matter. Accordingly, since the dream is the psychic safety valve for ignored neural demands, and since the imperious neural demands are affective rather than apprehensive, the dream will appear as a wish fulfilment. This statement, of course, must not be taken in the sense that the unconscious has wishes which are fulfilled in dreams, for wishing is a conscious activity. Nor again does it mean that the wishes fulfilled in dreams are those of the conscious subject, for inverse to the ego is the shadow and inverse to the persona is the anima. The accurate statement is that dreams are determined by neural demands for conscious affects, and the affects in question may be characteristic not only of the ego or the persona but also of the shadow or the anima. However, as has been seen, if the affects emergent in the dream are characteristic of the shadow or the anima, they emerge disassociated from their initial objects and attached to some incongruous object; and in this fact there now may easily be discerned a functional significance. The affects of the shadow and anima are alien to the conscious performer; were they to emerge into consciousness with their proper objects, not only would they interfere with his sleep but also they would violate his aesthetic liberation. The disguise of the dream is essential to its function of securing a balance between neural demands and psychic events while preserving the integrity of the conscious stream of experience.

Hence, to penetrate to the latent content of the dream is to bring to light a secret that, so to speak, has purposely been hidden. To equip an animal with intelligence constitutes not only the possibility of culture and of science but also the possibility of every abomination that has occurred in the course of human history. To affirm the latter human potentiality in abstract terms is somewhat unpleasant. To proceed syllogistically from the universal to the particular is distasteful. To assert that potentialities inherent in human nature exist in one's acquaintances, one's relatives, one's parents, oneself, is logical enough yet outrageous. Yet far more vivid than the utterance of such truths is their apprehension through insights into images that are affectively charged. In his waking hours man may preclude the occurrence of such insights. Even if his unconscious patterns and processes have been so stimulated as to demand them, the demand can be met in a dream in which the disassociation of the affect from its proper object respects the immanent direction of the stream of consciousness.

A similar functional significance may be found in the formation of screening memories. Of our childhood we are apt to remember only a few vivid scenes, and when these are submitted to scrutiny and investigation, they are likely to prove mere fictions. Freud has divined such false memories to be screens. Behind them are actions which later understanding would view in a fashion unsuspected by the child that performed them. If the memory of such actions is not to enter consciousness, it has to be repressed; if it is repressed, it undergoes the dis-association and recombination that result from inhibition. In this fashion there is formed the false and screening memory that enables the dramatic actor to play his present role with all the more conviction because he does not believe his past to differ too strikingly from his present.

Related selections: 2.I on the significance of art for ordinary living; 1.IV.3–5 for an expanded account of bias; 1.VI.2–3, 1.XI.1, 1.XII.2,4, 1.XIII.2, and 2.XIV, where Lonergan unfolds the far-reaching implications of the polymorphism of consciousness.

V

Common Sense as Object

Common sense, considered as a mode of intellectual development, pursues insights into the relations of things to us. In the preceding selection Lonergan distinguished the biological, esthetic, intellectual, and dramatic patterns of the variable stream of human consciousness. He now turns to a consideration of the commonsense subject as practical, as making and doing, as engendering and maintaining enormous structures of technology, economics, politics, and culture. Commonsense practicality leads to the separation of humanity from nature and establishes a series of new dimensions in the network of human relationships. Here Lonergan is concerned primarily with the role played by the act of understanding or insight in human affairs, in the collaborative effort to promote progress and to offset the decline of civilization. Reasonable judgment and responsible choice are also highly significant conscious acts, but the treatment of their nature and roles is postponed to later chapters of *Insight*. The aim at the present stage is to show the indispensability of the notion of insight to an adequate view of the vicissitudes of the historical course of human affairs.

In the first part of this selection from Chapter 7 of *Insight*, Lonergan identifies the scheme of recurrence which constitutes technological, economic, and political advance: *situation – insight – communication – persuasion – agreement – decision – action – new situation – insight* ... He notes the similarities and differences between schemes of human events and schemes in nature. In the next part Lonergan introduces the notion of a dialectical social process rooted in the tension between intersubjective spontaneity and practical common sense in human community. The progress or decline of a community depends on successful adaptation of human spontaneity to the demands of practical intelligence. In the subsequent parts Lonergan turns to the issue of bias and adds to

his account of the psychological bias of the dramatic subject accounts of the
bias of the individual and of the group, and of the general bias to which all
men and women of common sense are prone. Lonergan is especially concerned
with the manner in which refusal of insight disrupts the scheme of recurrence
constitutive of human progress and leads to what he calls 'the longer cycle of
decline,' the succession of ever less comprehensive syntheses which constitutes the cumulative disintegration of a civilization. In the final sections of his
discussion of general bias Lonergan argues that reversal of decline is beyond
the capacities of common sense. An appeal to a higher principle, a higher viewpoint, named 'cosmopolis' by Lonergan, seems to be required if decline is to be
reversed. Lonergan's account of the higher, cosmopolitan viewpoint, however,
is not his last word on the problem of decline. As the moving viewpoint of
Insight continues to expand, Lonergan will eventually take the position that the
problem of decline is resistant to all humanly generated solutions, and he will
point beyond higher viewpoints in the mind to the need for a religious integration and transformation of concrete human living.

These extracts are taken from *Insight*, 234–7; 242–67.

1   The Dynamic Structure

As in the fields of physics, chemistry, and biology, so in the field of
human events and relationships there are classical and statistical laws
that combine concretely in cumulating sets of schemes of recurrence.
For the advent of man does not abrogate the rule of emergent probability. Human actions are recurrent; their recurrence is regular; and the
regularity is the functioning of a scheme, of a patterned set of relations
that yields conclusions of the type: If an X occurs, then an X will recur.
Children are born only to grow, mature, and beget children of their
own. Inventions outlive their inventors and the memory of their origins. Capital is capital because its utility lies not in itself but in the acceleration it imparts to the stream of useful things. The political machinery
of agreement and decision is the permanent yet self-adapting source of
an indefinite series of agreements and decisions. Clearly, schemes
of recurrence exist and function. No less clearly, their functioning is
not inevitable. A population can decline, dwindle, vanish. A vast technological expansion, robbed of its technicians, would become a monu-
ment more intricate but no more useful than the pyramids. An
economy can falter, though resources and capital equipment abound,

though skill cries for its opportunity and desire for skill's product, though labor asks for work and industry is eager to employ it; then one can prime the pumps and make X occur; but because the schemes are not functioning properly, X fails to recur. As the economy, so too the polity can fall apart. In a revolution violence goes unchecked; laws lose their meaning; governments issue unheeded decrees; until from sheer weariness with disorder men are ready to accept any authority that can assert itself effectively. Yet a revolution is merely a passing stroke of paralysis in the state. There are deeper ills that show themselves in the long-sustained decline of nations, and in the limit in the disintegration and decay of whole civilizations. Schemes that once flourished lose their efficacy and cease to function; in an ever more rapid succession, as crises multiply and remedies have less effect, new schemes are introduced; feverish effort is followed by listlessness; the situation becomes regarded as hopeless; in a twilight of straitened but gracious living men await the catalytic trifle that will reveal to a surprised world the end of a once brilliant day.

Still, if human affairs fall under the dominion of emergent probability, they do so in their own way. A planetary system results from the conjunction of the abstract laws of mechanics with a suitable concrete set of mass-velocities. In parallel fashion there are human schemes that emerge and function automatically once there occurs an appropriate conjunction of abstract laws and concrete circumstances. But as human intelligence develops, there is a significant change of roles. Less and less importance attaches to the probabilities of appropriate constellations of circumstances. More and more importance attaches to the probabilities of the occurrence of insight, communication, persuasion, agreement, decision. Man does not have to wait for his environment to make him. His dramatic living needs only the clues and the opportunities to originate and maintain its own setting. The advance of technology, the formation of capital, the development of the economy, the evolution of the state are not only intelligible but also intelligent. Because they are intelligible, they can be understood as are the workings of emergent probability in the fields of physics, chemistry, and biology. But because they also are increasingly intelligent, increasingly the fruit of insight and decision, the analogy of merely natural process becomes less and less relevant. What possesses a high probability in one country or period or civilization may possess no probability in another; and the ground of the difference may lie only slightly in outward and palpable material factors and almost entirely in the set of insights that are accessible, persuasive, and potentially operative in the community. Just as in the individual the stream of consciousness normally selects its own course out of the range of neurally determined alternatives, so too in the group commonly accessible insights, disseminated by communication and persuasion, modify and adjust mentalities to determine the course of history out of the alternatives offered by emergent probability.

Such is the high significance of practical common sense, and it will not be amiss, I believe, to pause and make certain that we are not misconceiving it. For the practical common sense of a group, like all common sense, is an incomplete set of insights that is ever to be completed differently in each concrete situation. Its adaptation is too continuous and rapid for it ever to stand fixed in some set of definitions, postulates, and deductions; even were it outfitted, like David in Saul's armor, with such a logical panoply, it could be validated neither in any abstract realm of relations of things to one another nor in all members of any class of concrete situations. As its adaptation is continuous, so its growth is as secret as the germination, the division, the differentiation of cells in seed and shoot and plant. Only ideal republics spring in full stature from the mind of man; the civil communities that exist and function know only a story of their origins, only an outline of their development, only an estimate of their present complexion. For the practical common sense operative in a community does not exist entire in the mind of any one man. It is parceled out among many, to provide each with an understanding of his role and task, to make every cobbler an expert at his last, and no one an expert in another's field. So it is that to understand the working of even a static social structure, one must inquire from many men in many walks of life, and as best one can, discover the functional unity that organically binds together the endlessly varied pieces of an enormous jigsaw puzzle.

2 The Dialectic of Community

The name 'dialectic' has been employed in a variety of meanings. In Plato, it denoted the art of philosophic dialogue and was contrasted with eristic. In Aristotle, it referred to an effort to discover clues to the truth by reviewing and scrutinizing the opinions of others. For the schoolmen, it became the application of logical rules to public disputation. Hegel employed the word to refer to his triadic process from the concept of being to the Absolute Idea. Marx inverted Hegel and so conceived as dialectical a nonmechanical materialist process. Summarily, then, dialectic denotes a combination of the concrete, the dynamic, and the contradictory; but this combination may be found in a dialogue, in the history of philosophic opinions, or in historical process generally.

For the sake of greater precision, let us say that a dialectic is a concrete unfolding of linked but opposed principles of change. Thus there will be a dialectic if (1) there is an aggregate of events of a determinate character, (2) the events may be traced to either or both of two principles, (3) the principles are opposed yet bound together, and (4) they are modified by the changes that successively result from them. For example, the dramatic bias described above[1] was dialectical. The contents and affects emerging into consciousness provide the requisite aggregate of events of a determinate kind; these events originate from two principles, namely, neural demand functions and the exercise of the constructive or repressive censorship; the two principles are linked as patterned and patterning; they are opposed inasmuch as the censorship not only constructs but also represses, and again inasmuch as a misguided censorship results in neglected neural demands forcing their way into consciousness; finally, change is cumulative, for the orientation of the censorship at any time and the neural demands to be met both depend on the past history of the stream of consciousness.

Now as there is a dialectic of the dramatic subject, so also there is a larger dialectic of community. Social events can be traced to the two principles of human intersubjectivity and practical common sense. The two principles are linked, for the spontaneous, intersubjective individual strives to understand and wants to behave intelligently; and inversely, intelligence would have nothing to put in order were there not the desires and fears, labors and satisfactions, of individuals. Again, these linked principles are opposed, for it is their opposition that accounts for the tension of community. Finally, these linked and opposed principles are modified by the changes that result from them; the development of common sense consists in the further questions and insights that arise from the situations produced by previous operations of practical common sense; and the alternations of social tranquility and social crisis mark successive stages in the adaptation of

1 [See 1.IV.2 in this reader.]

human spontaneity and sensibility to the demands of developing intelligence.

In two manners this dialectic of community differs from the dialectic of the dramatic subject. First, there is a difference in extent, for the dialectic of community regards the history of human relationships, while the inner dialectic of the subject regards the biography of an individual. Secondly, there is a difference in the level of activity, for the dialectic of community is concerned with the interplay of more or less conscious intelligence and more or less conscious spontaneity in an aggregate of individuals, while the dialectic of the subject is concerned with the entry of neural demands into consciousness. Accordingly, one might say that a single dialectic of community is related to a manifold of individual sets of neural demand functions through a manifold of individual dialectics. In this relationship the dialectic of community holds the dominant position, for it gives rise to the situations that stimulate neural demands, and it molds the orientation of intelligence that preconsciously exercises the censorship. Still, as is clear, one must not suppose this dominance to be absolute, for both covertly and overtly neural demands conspire with an obnubilation of intelligence, and what happens in isolated individuals tends to bring them together and so to provide a focal point from which aberrant social attitudes originate.

This raises the basic question of a bias in common sense. Four distinct aspects call for attention. There is the already mentioned bias arising from the psychological depths, and commonly it is marked by its sexual overtones. There also are the individual bias of egoism, the group bias with its class conflicts, and a general bias that tends to set common sense against science and philosophy. On these three something must now be said.

3   Individual Bias

There is a rather notable obscurity in the meaning of the terms 'egoism' and 'altruism.' When a carnivorous animal stalks and kills its prey, it is not properly egoistic; for it is simply following its instincts, and in general for animals to follow their instincts is for them to secure the biological ends of individual and specific survival. By parity of reasoning, when a female animal fosters its young, it too is following its instincts; though it contributes to a general biological end, still it does so rather by the scheming of nature than by altruism in its proper sense. Finally, if animal spontaneity is neither egoistic nor altruistic, it seems to follow that the same must be said of human spontaneity; men are led by their intersubjectivity both to satisfy their own appetites and to help others in the attainment of their satisfactions; but neither type of activity is necessarily either egoistic or altruistic.

There is a further aspect to the matter. In his *Ethics* Aristotle asked whether a good friend loved himself. His answer was that while true friendship excluded self-love in the popular sense, nonetheless it demanded self-love in a higher sense; for a man loves himself if he wants for himself the finest things in the world, namely, virtue and wisdom; and without virtue and wisdom a man can be a true friend neither to himself nor to anyone else. Accordingly, as Aristotle's answer suggests, when one turns from the realm of spontaneity to that of intelligence and reasonableness, one does not find that egoism and altruism provide ultimate categories. For intelligence and reasonableness with their implications automatically assume the ultimate position; and from their detached viewpoint there is set up a social order in which, as in the animal kingdom, both taking care of oneself and contributing to the well-being of others have their legitimate place and necessary function.

Nonetheless, it remains that there is a sense in which egoism is always wrong and altruism its proper corrective. For man does not live exclusively either on the level of intersubjectivity or on the level of detached intelligence. On the contrary, his living is a dialectical resultant springing from those opposed but linked principles; and in the tension of that union of opposites, the root of egoism is readily to be discerned. For intelligence is a principle of universalization and of ultimate synthesis; it understands similars in the same manner; and it gives rise to further questions on each issue until all relevant data are understood. On the other hand, spontaneity is concerned with the present, the immediate, the palpable; intersubjectivity radiates from the self as from a center, and its efficacy diminishes rapidly with distance in place or time. Egoism is neither mere spontaneity nor pure intelligence but an interference of spontaneity with the development of intelligence. With remarkable acumen one solves one's own problems. With startling modesty one does not venture to raise the relevant further questions, Can one's solution be generalized? Is it compatible with the social order that exists? Is it compatible with any social order that proximately or even remotely is possible?

The precise nature of egoistic interference with intellectual process calls for attention. It is not to be thought that the egoist is devoid of the disinterestedness and detachment of intelligent inquiry. More than many others, he has developed a capacity to face issues squarely and to think them through. The cool schemer, the shrewd calculator, the hardheaded self-seeker are very far from indulging in mere wishful thinking. Without the detachment of intelligence, they cannot invent and implement stratagems that work. Without the disinterestedness of intelligence, they cannot raise and meet every further question that is relevant within their restricted terms of reference. Nor can one say that egoism consists in making intelligence the instrument of more elementary desires and fears. For as long as the egoist is engaged upon his problems, the immanent norms of intelligent inquiry overrule any interference from desire or fear; and while the egoist refuses to put the still further questions that would lead to a profound modification of his solution, still that refusal does not make intelligence an instrument but merely brushes it aside.

Egoism, then, is an incomplete development of intelligence. It rises above a merely inherited mentality. It has the boldness to strike out and think for itself. But it fails to pivot from the initial and preliminary motivation provided by desires and fears to the self-abnegation involved in allowing complete free play to intelligent inquiry. Its inquiry is reinforced by spontaneous desires and fears; by the same stroke it is restrained from a consideration of any broader field.

Necessarily, such an incompleteness of development is an exclusion of correct understanding. Just as in the sciences intelligence begins from hypotheses that prove insufficient and advances to further hypotheses that successively prove more and more satisfactory, so too in practical living it is through the cumulative process of further questions and further insights that an adequate understanding is reached. As in the sciences, so also in practical living, individuality pertains to the empirical residue, so that there is not one course of action that is intelligent when I am concerned and quite a different course when anyone else is involved. What is sauce for the goose is sauce for the gander. But egoistic emancipation rests on a rejection of merely proverbial wisdom yet fails to attain the development of personal intelligence that would reestablish the old sayings.

Thus, the golden rule is to do to others as you would have them do to you. One may object that common sense is never complete until the concrete situation is reached, and that no two concrete situations are identical. Still, it does not follow that the golden rule is that there is no golden rule. For the old rule did not advocate identical behavior in significantly different situations; on the contrary, it contended that the mere interchange of individual roles would not by itself constitute a significant difference in concrete situations.

Nor is the egoist totally unaware of his self-deception. Even in the bias and scotosis of the dramatic subject, which operates preconsciously, there is a measure of self-suspicion and disquiet. In the egoist there are additional grounds for an uneasy conscience, for it is not by sheer inadvertence but also by a conscious self-orientation that he devotes his energies to sizing up the social order, ferreting out its weak points and its loopholes, and discovering devices that give access to its rewards while evading its demands for proportionate contributions. As has been insisted already, egoism is not spontaneous, self-regarding appetite. Though it may result automatically from an incomplete development of intelligence, it does not automatically remain in that position. There have to be overcome both the drive of intelligence to raise the relevant further questions that upset egoistic solutions and, as well, the spontaneous demands of intersubjectivity, which, if they lack the breadth of a purely intellectual viewpoint with its golden rule, at least are commonly broader in their regard for others than is intelligent selfishness. Hence it is that, however much the egoist may appreciate the efforts of philosophers to assure him that intelligence is instrumental, he will be aware that, in his cool calculations, intelligence is boss and that, in his refusal to consider further questions, intelligence is not made into a servant but merely ruled out of court. Again, however much he may reassure himself by praising the pragmatists, still he suffers from the realization that the pragmatic success of his scheming falls short of a justification; for prior to the criteria of truth invented by philosophers, there is the dynamic criterion of the further question immanent in intelligence itself. The egoist's uneasy conscience is his awareness of his sin against the light. Operative within him there is the eros of the mind, the desire and drive to understand; he knows its value, for he gives it free rein where his own interests are concerned; yet he also repudiates its mastery, for he will not grant serious consideration to its further relevant questions.

4   Group Bias

As individual bias, so also group bias rests on an interference with the development of practical common sense. But while individual bias has to overcome normal intersubjective feeling, group bias finds itself supported by such feeling. Again, while individual bias leads to attitudes that conflict with ordinary common sense, group bias operates in the very genesis of commonsense views.

Basically, social groups are defined implicitly by the pattern of relations of a social order, and they are constituted by the realization of those dynamic relations. In its technological aspect the social order generates the distinctions between scientists and engineers, technicians and workers, skilled and unskilled labor. In its economic aspect it differentiates the formation of capital from the production of consumer goods and services, distinguishes income groups by offering proportionate rewards to contributions, and organizes contributors in hierarchies of employees, foremen, supervisors, superintendents, managers, and directors. In its political aspect it distinguishes legislative, judicial, diplomatic, and executive functions with their myriad ramifications, and it works out some system in which the various offices are to be filled and the tasks performed.

However, in the dialectic of community there is the operation not only of practical common sense but also of human intersubjectivity. If human intelligence takes the lead in developments, still its products do not function smoothly until there is effected a suitable adaptation of sensitive spontaneity. In a school, a regiment, a factory, a trade, a profession, a prison, there develops an ethos that at once subtly and flexibly provides concrete premises and norms for practical decisions. For in human affairs the decisive factor is what one can expect of the other fellow. Such expectations rest on recognized codes of behavior; they appeal to past performance, acquired habit, reputation; they attain a maximum of precision and reliability among those frequently brought together, engaged in similar work, guided by similar motives, sharing the same prosperity or adversity. Among strangers we are at a loss what to say or do. The social order not only gathers men together in functional groups but also consolidates its gains and expedites its operations by turning to its own ends the vast resources of human imagination and emotion, sentiment and confidence, familiarity and loyalty.

However, this formation of social groups, specifically adapted to the smooth attainment of social ends, merely tends to replace one inertial force with another. Human sensitivity is not human intelligence, and if sensitivity can be adapted to implement easily and readily one set of intelligent dictates, it has to undergo a fresh adaptation before it will cease resisting a second set of more intelligent dictates. Now social progress is a succession of changes. Each new idea gradually modifies the social situation to call forth further new ideas and bring about still further modifications. Moreover, the new ideas are practical; they are applicable to concrete situations; they occur to those engaged in the situations to which they are to be applied. However, while the practical common sense of a community may be a single whole, its parts reside separately in the minds of members of social groups, and its development occurs as each group intelligently responds to the succession of situations with which it immediately deals. Were all the responses made by pure intelligences, continuous progress might be inevitable. In fact, the responses are made by intelligences that are coupled with the ethos and the interests of groups, and while intelligence heads for change, group spontaneity does not regard all changes in the same cold light of the general good of society. Just as the individual egoist puts further questions up to a point, but desists before reaching conclusions incompatible with his egoism, so also the group is prone to have a blind spot for the insights that reveal its well-being to be excessive or its usefulness at an end.

Thus group bias leads to a bias in the generative principle of a developing social order. At a first approximation, one thinks of the course of social change as a succession of insights, courses of action, changed situations, and fresh insights. At each turn of the wheel, one has to distinguish between fresh insights that are mere bright ideas of no practical moment and, on the other hand, the fresh insights that squarely meet the demands of the concrete situation. Group bias, however, calls for a further distinction. Truly practical insights have to be divided into operative and inoperative; both satisfy the criteria of practical intelligence; but the operative insights alone go into effect for they alone either meet with no group resistance or else find favor with groups powerful enough to overcome what resistance there is.

The bias of development involves a distortion. The advantage of one group commonly is disadvantageous to another, and so some part of the energies of all groups is diverted to the supererogatory activity of devising and implementing offensive and defensive mechanisms. Groups differ in their possession of native talent, opportunities, initiative, and resources; those in favored circumstances find success the key to still further success; those unable to make operative the new ideas that are to their advantage fall behind in the process of social development. Society becomes stratified; its flower is far in advance of average attainment; its roots appear to be the survival of the rude achievement of a forgotten age. Classes become distinguished, not merely by social function, but also by social success; and the new differentiation finds expression not only in conceptual labels but also in deep feelings of frustration, resentment, bitterness, and hatred.

Moreover, the course of development has been twisted. The social order that has been realized does not correspond to any coherently developed set of practical ideas. It represents the fraction of practical ideas that were made operative by their conjunction with power, the mutilated remnants of once excellent schemes that issued from the mill of compromise, the otiose structures that equip groups for their offensive and defensive activities. Again, ideas are general, but the stratification of society has blocked their realization in their proper generality. Ideas possess retinues of complementary ideas that add further adjustments and improvements; but these needed complements were submitted to the sifting of group interests and to the alterations of compromise.

Still, this process of aberration creates the principles for its own reversal. When a concrete situation first yields a new idea and demands its realization, it is unlikely that the idea will occur to anyone outside the group specialized in dealing with situations of that type. But when some ideas of a coherent set have been realized, or when they are realized in a partial manner, or when their realization does not attain its proper generality, or when it is not complemented with a needed retinue of improvements and adjustments, then there is no need to call upon experts and specialists to discover whether anything has gone wrong, nor even to hit upon a roughly accurate account of what can be done. The sins of group bias may be secret and almost unconscious. But what originally was a neglected possibility, in time becomes a grotesquely distorted reality. Few may grasp the initial possibilities; but the ultimate concrete distortions are exposed to the inspection of the multitude. Nor has the bias of social development revealed the ideas that were neglected without also supplying the power that will realize them. For the bias generates unsuccessful as well as successful classes; and the sentiments of the unsuccessful can be crystallized into militant force by the crusading of a reformer or a revolutionary.

The ensuing conflict admits a variety of forms. The dominant groups may be reactionary or progressive or any mixture of the two. Insofar as they are reactionary, they are out to block any correction of the effects of group bias, and they employ for this purpose whatever power they possess in whatever manner they deem appropriate and effective. On the other hand, insofar as they are progressive, they make it their aim both to correct existing distortions and to find the means that will prevent their future recurrence. Now to a great extent the attitude of the dominant groups determines the attitude of the depressed groups. Reactionaries are opposed by revolutionaries. Progressives are met by liberals. In the former case the situation heads towards violence. In the latter case there is a general agreement about ends with disagreement about the pace of change and the mode and measure of its execution.

5   General Bias and the Longer Cycle of Decline

To err is human, and common sense is very human. Besides the bias of the dramatic subject, of the individual egoist, of the member of a given class or nation, there is a further bias to which all men are prone. For men are rational animals, but a full development of their animality is both more common and more rapid than a full development of their intelligence and reasonableness. A traditional view credits children of seven years of age with the attainment of an elementary reasonableness. The law regards as a minor anyone under twenty-one years of age. Experts in the field of public entertainment address themselves to a mental age of about twelve years. Still more modest is the scientific attitude that places man's attainment of knowledge in an indefinitely removed future. Nor is personal experience apt to be reassuring. If everyone has some acquaintance with the spirit of inquiry and reflection, few think of making it the effective center of their lives; and of that few, still fewer make sufficient progress to be able to withstand other attractions and persevere in their high purpose.

The lag of intellectual development, its difficulty, and its apparently meager returns bear in an especial manner on common sense. It is concerned with the concrete and particular. It entertains no aspirations

about reaching abstract and universal laws. It easily is led to rationalize its limitations by engendering a conviction that other forms of
human knowledge are useless or doubtfully valid. Every specialist
runs the risk of turning his specialty into a bias by failing to recognize
and appreciate the significance of other fields. Common sense almost
invariably makes that mistake; for it is incapable of analyzing itself,
incapable of making the discovery that it too is a specialized development of human knowledge, incapable of coming to grasp that its pecu-
liar danger is to extend its legitimate concern for the concrete and the
immediately practical into disregard of larger issues and indifference
to long-term results.

5.1   The Longer Cycle

This general bias of common sense combines with group bias to
account for certain features of the distorted dialectic of community. As
has been noted, at each turn of the wheel of insight, proposal, action,
new situation, and fresh insight, the tendency of group bias is to
exclude some fruitful ideas and to mutilate others by compromise.
Now fruitful ideas are of several kinds. They may lead to technical and
material improvements, to adjustments of economic arrangements, or
to modifications of political structure. As one might expect, technical
and material improvements are less subject to the veto of dominant
groups than are changes in economic and political institutions. Again,
when we shift to the second phase of the distorted dialectic, the reso-
nant demands of the unsuccessful are for material well-being; and
when the clamor goes up for economic or political change, such change
is apt to be viewed simply as a necessary means for attaining more palpably beneficial ends.

Accordingly, there arises a distinction between the shorter cycle, due
to group bias, and the longer cycle, originated by the general bias of
common sense. The shorter cycle turns upon ideas that are neglected
by dominant groups only to be championed later by depressed groups.
The longer cycle is characterized by the neglect of ideas to which all
groups are rendered indifferent by the general bias of common sense.
Still, this account of the longer cycle is mainly negative; to grasp its
nature and its implications, we must turn to fundamental notions.

Generically, the course of human history is in accord with emergent
probability; it is the cumulative realization of concretely possible

schemes of recurrence in accord with successive schedules of probabilities. The specific difference of human history is that among the probable possibilities is a sequence of operative insights by which men grasp possible schemes of recurrence and take the initiative in bringing about the material and social conditions that make these schemes concretely possible, probable, and actual. In this fashion man becomes for man the executor of the emergent probability of human affairs. Instead of being developed by his environment, man turns to transforming his environment in his own self-development. He remains under emergent probability, inasmuch as his insights and decisions remain probable realizations of concrete possibilities, and inasmuch as earlier insights and decisions determine later possibilities and probabilities of insight and decision. Still, this subjection to emergent probability differs from the subjection of electrons or of evolving species. For in the first place, insight is an anticipation of possible schemes, and decision brings about the concrete conditions of their functioning instead of merely waiting for such conditions to happen; moreover, the greater man's development, the greater his dominion over circumstances, and so the greater his capacity to realize possible schemes by deciding to realize their conditions. But there is also a second and profounder difference. For man can discover emergent probability; he can work out the manner in which prior insights and decisions determine the possibilities and probabilities of later insights and decisions; he can guide his present decisions in the light of their influence on future insights and decisions; finally, this control of the emergent probability of the future can be exercised not only by the individual in choosing his career and in forming his character, not only by adults in educating the younger generation, but also by mankind in its consciousness of its responsibility to the future of mankind. Just as technical, economic, and political development gives man a dominion over nature, so also the advance of knowledge creates and demands a human contribution to the control of human history.

So far from granting common sense a hegemony in practical affairs, the foregoing analysis leads to the strange conclusion that common sense has to aim at being subordinated to a human science that is concerned, to adapt a phrase from Marx, not only with knowing history but also with directing it. For common sense is unequal to the task of thinking on the level of history. It stands above the scotosis of the dramatic subject, above the egoism of the individual, above the bias of

dominant and of depressed but militant groups that realize only the
ideas they see to be to their immediate advantage. But the general bias
of common sense prevents it from being effective in realizing ideas,
however appropriate and reasonable, that suppose a long view or that
set up higher integrations or that involve the solution of intricate and
disputed issues. The challenge of history is for man progressively
to restrict the realm of chance or fate or destiny and progressively to
enlarge the realm of conscious grasp and deliberate choice. Common
sense accepts the challenge, but it does so only partially. It needs to be
guided but it is incompetent to choose its guide. It becomes involved in
incoherent enterprises. It is subjected to disasters that no one expects,
that remain unexplained even after their occurrence, that can be
explained only on the level of scientific or philosophic thought, that
even when explained can be prevented from recurring only by subor-
dinating common sense to a higher specialization of human intelligence.

This is not the whole story. The general bias of common sense
involves sins of refusal as well as of mere omission. Its complacent
practicality easily twists to the view that, as insistent desires and con-
tracting fears necessitate and justify the realization of ideas, so ideas
without that warrant are a matter of indifference. The long view, the
higher integration, the disputed theoretical issue fall outside the realm
of the practical; it may or may not be too bad that they do; but there is
no use worrying about the matter; nothing can be done about it;
indeed, what could be done about it probably would not be done. Now
I am far from suggesting that such practical realism cannot adduce
impressive arguments in its favor. Like the characters in Damon Run-
yon's stories, politicians and statesmen are confined to doing what
they can. Nonetheless, if we are to understand the implications of the
longer cycle, we must work out the consequences of such apparently
hardheaded practicality and realism.

5.2   Implications of the Longer Cycle

Already we have explained the nature of the succession of higher
viewpoints that characterize the development of mathematics and of
empirical science. Now we must attend to the inverse phenomenon, in
which each successive viewpoint is less comprehensive than its predecessor. In each stage of the historical process, the facts are the social sit-

uation produced by the practical intelligence of the previous situation. Again, in each stage practical intelligence is engaged in grasping the concrete intelligibility and the immediate potentialities immanent in the facts. Finally, at each stage of the process, the general bias of common sense involves the disregard of timely and fruitful ideas; and this disregard not only excludes their implementation but also deprives subsequent stages both of the further ideas to which they would give rise and of the correction that they and their retinue would bring to the ideas that are implemented. Such is the basic scheme, and it has three consequences.

In the first place, the social situation deteriorates cumulatively. For just as progress consists in a realization of some ideas that leads to the realization of others until a whole coherent set is concretely operative, so the repeated exclusion of timely and fruitful ideas involves a cumulative departure from coherence. The objective social situation possesses the intelligibility put into it by those that brought it about. But what is put in, less and less is some part of a coherent whole that will ask for its completion, and more and more it is some arbitrary fragment that can be rounded off only by giving up the attempt to complete the other arbitrary fragments that have preceded or will follow it. In this fashion social functions and enterprises begin to conflict; some atrophy and others grow like tumors; the objective situation becomes penetrated with anomalies; it loses its power to suggest new ideas and, once they are implemented, to respond with still further and better suggestions. The dynamic of progress is replaced by sluggishness and then by stagnation. In the limit, the only discernible intelligibility in the objective facts is an equilibrium of economic pressures and a balance of national powers.

The second consequence is the mounting irrelevance of detached and disinterested intelligence. Culture retreats into an ivory tower. Religion becomes an inward affair of the heart. Philosophy glitters like a gem with endless facets and no practical purpose. For man cannot serve two masters. If one is to be true to intellectual detachment and disinterestedness, to what can be intelligently grasped and reasonably affirmed, then one seems constrained to acknowledge that the busy world of practical affairs offers little scope to one's vocation. Intelligence can easily link culture, religion, philosophy to the realm of concrete living only if the latter is intelligible. But concrete living has become the function of a complex variable; like the real component of such a function, its intelligibility is only part of the whole. Already we have spoken of an empirical residue from which understanding always abstracts; but the general bias of common sense generates an increasingly significant residue that (1) is immanent in the social facts, (2) is not intelligible, yet (3) cannot be abstracted from if one is to consider the facts as in fact they are.

Let us name this residue the social surd.

The third consequence is the surrender of detached and disinterested intelligence. There is the minor surrender on the level of common sense. It is an incomplete surrender, for common sense always finds a profoundly satisfying escape from the grim realities of daily living by turning to men of culture, to representatives of religion, to spokesmen for philosophy. Still, the business of common sense is daily life. Its reality has to be faced. The insights that accumulate have to be exactly in tune with the reality to be confronted and in some measure controlled. The fragmentary and incoherent intelligibility of the objective situation sets the standard to which commonsense intelligence must conform. Nor is this conformity merely passive. Intelligence is dynamic. Just as the biased intelligence of the psychoneurotic sets up an ingenious, plausible, self-adapting resistance to the efforts of the analyst, so men of practical common sense become warped by the situation in which they live, and regard as starry-eyed idealism and silly unpracticality any proposal that would lay the axe to the root of the social surd.

Besides this minor surrender on the level of common sense, there is the major surrender on the speculative level. The function of human intelligence, it is claimed, is not to set up independent norms that make thought irrelevant to fact, but to study the data as they are, to grasp the intelligibility that is immanent in them, to acknowledge as principle or norm only what can be reached by generalization from the data. There follow the need and the development of a new culture, a new religion, a new philosophy; and the new differs radically from the old. The new is not apriorist, wishful thinking. It is empirical, scientific, realistic. It takes its stand on things as they are. In brief, its many excellences cover its single defect. For its rejection of the normative significance of detached and disinterested intelligence makes it radically uncritical. It possesses no standpoint from which it can distinguish between social achievement and the social surd. It fails to grasp that an excellent method for the study of electrons is bound to prove naive and inept in the study of man. For the data on man are largely the product of man's own thinking; and the subordination of human science to the data on man is the subordination of human science to the biased intelligence of those that produce the data. From this critical incapacity there follow the insecurity and the instability of the new culture, religion, philosophy. Each new arrival has to keep bolstering its convictions by attacking and denouncing its predecessors. Nor is there any lack of new arrivals, for in the cumulative deterioration of the social situation there is a continuous expansion of the surd, and so there is an increasing demand for further contractions of the claims of intelligence, for further dropping of old principles and norms, for closer conformity to an ever growing manmade incoherence immanent in manmade facts.

It is in this major surrender of intellectual detachment that the succession of ever less comprehensive viewpoints comes to light. The development of our Western civilization, from the schools founded by Charlemagne to the universities of today, has witnessed an extraordinary flowering of human intelligence in every department of its activity. But this course of human progress has not been along a smooth and mounting curve. It has taken place through the oscillations of the shorter cycle, in which social groups become factions, in which nations go to war, in which the hegemony passes from one center to another to leave its former holders with proud memories and impotent dreams. No less does it exhibit the successive lower viewpoints of the longer cycle. The medieval synthesis through the conflict of church and state shattered into the several religions of the reformation. The wars of religion provided the evidence that man has to live not by revelation but by reason. The disagreement of reason's representatives made it clear that, while each must follow the dictates of reason as he sees them, he also must practice the virtue of tolerance to the equally reasonable views and actions of others. The helplessness of tolerance to provide coherent solutions to social problems called forth the totalitarian, who takes the narrow and complacent practicality of common sense and elevates it to the role of a complete and exclusive viewpoint. On the totalitarian view every type of intellectual independence, whether personal, cultural, scientific, philosophic, or religious, has no better basis than nonconscious myth. The time has come for the conscious myth that will secure man's total subordination to the requirements of reality. Reality is the economic development, the military equipment, and the political dominance of the all-inclusive state. Its ends justify all means. Its means include not merely every technique of indoctrination and propaganda, every tactic of economic and diplomatic pressure, every device for breaking down the moral conscience and exploiting the secret affects of civilized man, but also the terrorism of a political police, of prisons and torture, of concentration camps, of transported or extirpated minorities, and of total war. The succession of less comprehensive viewpoints has been a succession of adaptations of theory to practice. In the limit, practice becomes a theoretically unified whole, and theory is reduced to the status of a myth that lingers on to represent the frustrated aspirations of detached and disinterested intelligence.

5.3   Alternatives of the Longer Cycle

What is the subsequent course of the longer cycle generated by the general bias of common sense? Insofar as the bias remains effective, there would seem to be only one answer. The totalitarian has uncovered a secret of power. To defeat him is not to eliminate a permanent temptation to try once more his methods. Those not subjected to the temptation by their ambitions or their needs will be subjected to it by their fears of danger and by their insistence on self-protection. So in an uneasy peace, in the unbroken tension of a prolonged emergency, one totalitarianism calls forth another. On an earth made small by a vast human population, by limited natural resources, by rapid and easy communications, by extraordinary powers of destruction, there will arise sooner or later the moment when the unstable equilibrium will seem threatened and the gamble of war will appear the lesser risk to some of the parties involved. If the war is indecisive, the basic situation is unchanged. If it is totally destructive, the longer cycle has come to its end. If there results a single world empire, then it inherits both the objective stagnation of the social surd and the warped mentality of totalitarian practicality; but it cannot whip up the feverish energy of fear or of ambition; it has no enemy to fight; it has no intelligible goal to attain.

Common sense, on the other hand, has no use for any theoretical integration, even for the totalitarian integration of commonsense practicality. It will desert the new empire for the individual or group interests that it understands. This centrifugal tendency will be augmented by the prepossessions and prejudices, the resentments and hatreds, that have been accumulating over the ages; for every reform, every revolution, every lower viewpoint overstates both the case in its own favor and the case against those it would supersede; from each generation to the next there are transmitted not only sound ideas but also incomplete ideas, mutilated ideas, enthusiasms, passions, bitter memories, and terrifying bogies. In this fashion the objective social surd will be matched by a disunity of minds all warped but each in its private way. The most difficult of enterprises will have to be undertaken under the most adverse circumstances, and under the present hypothesis that the general bias of common sense remains effective, one cannot but expect the great crises that end in complete disintegration and decay.

Still, on the assumption of emergent probability, nothing is inevitable. Indeed, the essential logic of the distorted dialectic is a reversal. For dialectic rests on the concrete unity of opposed principles; the dominance of either principle results in a distortion, and the distortion both weakens the dominance and strengthens the opposed principle to restore an equilibrium. Why, then, is it that the longer cycle is so long? Why is the havoc it wreaks so deep, so extensive, so complete? The obvious answer is the difficulty of the lesson that the longer cycle has to teach. Nor are we quite without hints or clues on the nature of that lesson. On the contrary, there is a convergence of evidence for the assertion that the longer cycle is to be met, not by any idea or set of ideas on the level of technology, economics, or politics, but only by the attainment of a higher viewpoint in man's understanding and making of man.

In the first place, the general bias of common sense cannot be corrected by common sense, for the bias is abstruse and general, and common sense deals with the particular. In the second place, man can discover how present insights and decisions influence through emergent probability the occurrence of future insights and decisions; as he can make this discovery, so he can use it, not only in shaping individual biographies and educating children in the image of their parents and of the state authorities, but also in the vastly more ambitious task of directing and in some measure controlling his future history. In the third place, the longer cycle of Western civilization has been drawing attention repeatedly to the notion of a practical theory of history. It was conceived in one manner or another by Vico in his *Scienza nuova*, by Hegel, and by Marx. It has exercised a conspicuous influence on events through the liberal doctrine of automatic progress, through the Marxian doctrine of class war, through the myths of nationalist totalitarianism. In the fourth place, a remedy has to be on the level of the disease; but the disease is a succession of lower viewpoints that heads towards an ultimate nihilism; and so the remedy has to be the attainment of a higher viewpoint.

As there is evidence for the necessity of a higher viewpoint, so also there is some evidence on its nature. Inquiry and insight are facts that underlie mathematics, empirical science, and common sense. The refusal of insight is a fact that accounts for individual and group egoism, for the psychoneuroses, and for the ruin of nations and civilizations. The needed higher viewpoint is the discovery, the logical expansion, and the recognition of the principle that intelligence contains its own immanent norms and that these norms are equipped with sanctions which man does not have to invent or impose. Even in the sphere of practice, the last word does not lie with common sense and its panoply of technology, economy, and polity; for unless common sense can learn to overcome its bias by acknowledging and submitting to a higher principle, unless common sense can be taught to resist its perpetual temptation to adopt the easy, obvious, practical compromise, then one must expect the succession of ever less comprehensive viewpoints, and in the limit the destruction of all that has been achieved.

5.4   Reversal of the Longer Cycle

What is the higher principle? Since we have not as yet discussed such notions as truth and error, right and wrong, human science and philosophy, culture and religion, our immediate answer can be no more than a series of notes.

In the first place, there is such a thing as progress, and its principle is liberty. There is progress, because practical intelligence grasps ideas in data, guides activity by the ideas, and reaches fuller and more accurate ideas through the situations produced by the activity. The principle of progress is liberty, for the ideas occur to the man on the spot, their only satisfactory expression is their implementation, their only adequate correction is the emergence of further insights; on the other hand, one might as well declare openly that all new ideas are taboo, as require that they be examined, evaluated, and approved by some hierarchy of officials and bureaucrats; for members of this hierarchy possess authority and power in inverse ratio to their familiarity with the concrete situations in which the new ideas emerge; they never know whether or not the new idea will work; much less can they divine how it might be corrected or developed; and since the one thing they dread is making a mistake, they devote their energies to paper work and postpone decisions.

However, while there is progress and while its principle is liberty, there also is decline and its principle is bias. There is the minor principle of group bias, which tends to generate its own corrective. There is the major principle of general bias, and though it too generates its own corrective, it does so only by confronting human intelligence with the alternative of adopting a higher viewpoint or perishing. To ignore the fact of decline was the error of the old liberal views of automatic progress. The far more confusing error of Marx was to lump together both progress and the two principles of decline under the impressive name of dialectical materialism, to grasp that the minor principle of decline would correct itself more rapidly through class war, and then to leap gaily to the sweeping conclusion that class war would accelerate progress. What in fact was accelerated was major decline, which in Russia and Germany leaped to fairly thorough brands of totalitarianism. The basic service of the higher viewpoint will be a liberation from confusion through clear distinctions. Progress is not to be confused with decline; the corrective mechanism of the minor principle of decline is not to be thought capable of meeting the issues set by the major principle.

Secondly, as there are sciences of nature, so also there is a science of man. As the sciences of nature are empirical, so also the science of man is empirical; for science is the resultant of an accumulation of related insights, and scientific insights grasp ideas that are immanent not in what is imagined but in what is given. If the sciences of nature can be led astray by the blunder that the objective is, not the verified, but the 'out there,' so also can the human sciences; but while this blunder in physics yields no more than the ineptitude of Galileo's primary qualities and Newton's true motion, it leads zealous practitioners of scientific method in the human field to rule out of court a major portion of the data and so deny the empirical principle. Durkheimian sociology and behaviorist psychology may have excuses for barring the data of consciousness, for there exist notable difficulties in determining such data; but the business of the scientist is not to allege difficulties as excuses but to overcome them, and neither objectivity in the sense of verification nor the principle of empiricism can be advanced as reasons for ignoring the data of consciousness. Further, as mathematics has to deal not only with direct intelligibilities but also with such inverse instances as primes, surds, imaginaries, continua, and infinities, as the physicist has to employ not only the classical procedures and techniques that deal with the systematic but also the statistical procedures and techniques that take into account the nonsystematic, so also human science has to be critical. It can afford to drop the nineteenth-century scientific outlook of mechanist determinism in favor of an emergent probability. It can profit by the distinction between the intelligible emergent probability of prehuman process and the intelligent emergent probability that arises in the measure that man succeeds in understanding himself and in implementing that understanding. Finally, it can be of inestimable value in aiding man to understand himself and in guiding him in the implementation of that understanding, if, and only if, it can learn to distinguish between progress and decline, between the liberty that generates progress and the bias that generates decline. In other words, human science cannot be merely empirical; it has to be critical; to reach a critical standpoint, it has to be normative. This is a tall order for human science as hitherto it has existed. But people looking for easy tasks had best renounce any ambition to be scientists; and if mathematicians and physicists can surmount their surds, the human scientist can learn to master his.

5.5   Culture and Reversal

In the third place, there is culture. The dramatic subject, as practical, originates and develops capital and technology, the economy and the state. By his intelligence he progresses, and by his bias he declines. Still, this whole unfolding of practicality constitutes no more than the setting and the incidents of the drama. Delight and suffering, laughter and tears, joy and sorrow, aspiration and frustration, achievement and failure, wit and humor stand, not within practicality but above it. Man can pause and with a smile or a forced grin ask what the drama, what he himself is about. His culture is his capacity to ask, to reflect, to reach an answer that at once satisfies his intelligence and speaks to his heart.

Now if men are to meet the challenge set by major decline and its longer cycle, it will be through their culture that they do so. Were man a pure intelligence, the products of philosophy and human science would be enough to sway him. But as the dialectic in the individual and in society reveals, man is a compound-in-tension of intelligence and intersubjectivity, and it is only through the parallel compound of a culture that his tendencies to aberration can be offset proximately and effectively.

The difficulty is, of course, that human aberration makes an uncritical culture its captive. Mario Praz in *The Romantic Agony* has found that depth psychology throws an unpleasantly penetrating light upon romanticism. Nor is the ooze of abnormality anything more than a secondary symptom, for the expanding social surd of the longer cycle is not matched by a succession of less comprehensive viewpoints, without the services of a parallel series of cultural transformations. Opinions and attitudes that once were the oddity of a minority gradually spread through society to become the platitudes of politicians and journalists, the assumptions of legislators and educators, the uncontroverted nucleus of the common sense of a people. Eventually, they too become antiquated; they are regarded as the obstinacy of an old guard that will not learn; their influence is restricted to backwaters immune to the renewing force of the main current of human thought and feeling. Change succeeds change. Indiscriminately, each of the new arrivals rests upon the good it brings, upon the opposite defects of the old, and upon a closer harmony with the fact of the social surd. In the limit, culture ceases to be an independent factor that passes a detached yet effective judgment upon capital formation and technology, upon economy and polity. To justify its existence, it had to become more and more practical, more and more a factor within the technological, economic, political process, more and more a tool that served palpably useful ends. The actors in the drama of living become stagehands; the setting is magnificent; the lighting superb; the costumes gorgeous; but there is no play.

Clearly, by becoming practical, culture renounces its one essential function, and by that renunciation condemns practicality to ruin. The general bias of common sense has to be counterbalanced by a representative of detached intelligence that both appreciates and criticizes, that identifies the good neither with the new nor with the old, that, above all else, neither will be forced into an ivory tower of ineffectualness by the social surd nor, on the other hand, will capitulate to its absurdity.

Marx looked forward to a classless society and to the withering of the state. But as long as there will be practical intelligence, there will be technology and capital, economy and polity. There will be a division of labor and a differentiation of functions. There will be the adaptation of human intersubjectivity to that division and differentiation. There will be common decisions to be reached and to be implemented. Practical intelligence necessitates classes and states, and no dialectic can promise their permanent disappearance. What is both unnecessary and disastrous is the exaltation of the practical, the supremacy of the state, the cult of the class. What is necessary is a cosmopolis that is neither class nor state, that stands above all their claims, that cuts them down to size, that is founded on the native detachment and disinterestedness of every intelligence, that commands man's first allegiance, that implements itself primarily through that allegiance, that is too universal to be bribed, too impalpable to be forced, too effective to be ignored.

5.6   Cosmopolis

Still, what is cosmopolis? Like every other object of human intelligence, it is in the first instance an X, what is to be known when one understands. Like every other X, it possesses some known properties and aspects that lead to its fuller determination. For the present, we must be content to indicate a few of these aspects and to leave until later the task of reaching conclusions.

First, cosmopolis is not a police force. Before such a force can be organized, equipped, and applied, there is needed a notable measure of agreement among a preponderant group of men. In other words, ideas have to come first, and at best force is instrumental. In the practical order of the economy and polity, it is possible, often enough, to perform the juggling act of using some ideas to ground the use of force in favor of others, and then using the other ideas to ground the use of force in favor of the first. The trouble with this procedure is that there is always another juggler that believes himself expert enough to play the same game the other way by using the malcontents held down by the first use of force to upset the second set of ideas and, as well, using malcontents held down by the second use of force to upset the first set of ideas. Accordingly, if ideas are not to be merely a façade, if the reality is not to be merely a balance of power, then the use of force can be no more than residual and incidental. But cosmopolis is not concerned with the residual and incidental. It is concerned with the fundamental issue of the historical process. Its business is to prevent practicality from being shortsightedly practical and so destroying itself. The notion that cosmopolis employs a police force is just an instance of the short-sighted practicality that cosmopolis has to correct. However, I am not saying that there should not be a United Nations or a world government; I am not saying that such political entities should not have a police force; I am saying that such political entities are not what is meant by cosmopolis. Cosmopolis is above all politics. So far from being rendered superfluous by a successful world government, it would be all the more obviously needed to offset the tendencies of that and any other government to be shortsightedly practical.

Secondly, cosmopolis is concerned to make operative the timely and fruitful ideas that otherwise are inoperative. So far from employing power or pressure or force, it has to witness to the possibility of ideas being operative without such backing. Unless it can provide that witness, then it is useless. For at the root of the general bias of common sense and at the permanent source of the longer cycle of decline, there stands the notion that only ideas backed by some sort of force can be operative. The business of cosmopolis is to make operative the ideas that, in the light of the general bias of common sense, are inoperative. In other words, its business is to break the vicious circle of an illusion: men will not venture on ideas that they grant to be correct, because they hold that such ideas will not work unless sustained by desires or fears; and inversely, men hold that such ideas will not work, because they will not venture on them and so have no empirical evidence that such ideas can work and would work.

Thirdly, cosmopolis is not a busybody. It is supremely practical by ignoring what is thought to be really practical. It does not waste its time and energy condemning the individual egoism that is in revolt against society and already condemned by society. It is not excited by group egoism, which in the short run generates the principles that involve its reversal. But it is very determined to prevent dominant groups from deluding mankind by the rationalization of their sins; if the sins of dominant groups are bad enough, still the erection of their sinning into universal principles is indefinitely worse; it is the univer-salization of the sin by rationalization that contributes to the longer cycle of decline; it is the rationalization that cosmopolis has to ridicule, explode, destroy. Again, cosmopolis is little interested in the shifts of power between classes and nations; it is quite aware that the dialectic sooner or later upsets the shortsighted calculations of dominant groups; and it is quite free from the nonsense that the rising star of another class or nation is going to put a different human nature in the saddle. However, while shifts of power in themselves are incidental, they commonly are accompanied by another phenomenon of quite a different character. There is the creation of myths. The old regime is depicted as monstrous; the new envisages itself as the immaculate embodiment of ideal human aspiration. Catchwords that carried the new group to power assume the status of unquestionable verities. On the bandwagon of the new vision of truth there ride the adventurers in ideas that otherwise could not attain a hearing. Inversely, ideas that merit attention are ignored unless they put on the trappings of the current fashion, unless they pretend to result from alien but commonly acceptable premises, unless they disclaim implications that are true but unwanted. It is the business of cosmopolis to prevent the formation of the screening memories by which an ascent to power hides its nastiness; it is its business to prevent the falsification of history with which the new group overstates its case; it is its business to satirize the catchwords and the claptrap and thereby to prevent the notions they express from coalescing with passions and resentments to engender obsessive nonsense for future generations; it is its business to encourage and support those that would speak the simple truth though simple truth has gone out of fashion. Unless cosmopolis undertakes this essential task, it fails in its mission. One shift of power is followed by another, and if the myths of the first survive, the myths of the second will take their stand on earlier nonsense to bring forth worse nonsense still.

Fourthly, as cosmopolis has to protect the future against the rationalization of abuses and the creation of myths, so it itself must be purged of the rationalizations and myths that became part of the human heritage before it came on the scene. If the analyst suffers from a scotoma, he will communicate it to the analysand; similarly, if cosmopolis itself suffers from the general bias of common sense in any of its manifestations, then the blind will be leading the blind and both will head for a ditch. There is needed, then, a critique of history before there can be any intelligent direction of history. There is needed an exploration of the movements, the changes, the epochs of a civilization's genesis, development, and vicissitudes. The opinions and attitudes of the present have to be traced to their origins, and the origins have to be criticized in the light of dialectic. The liberal believer in automatic progress could praise all that survives; the Marxist could denounce all that was and praise all that would be; but anyone that recognizes the existence both of intelligence and of bias, both of progress and of decline, has to be critical, and his criticism will rest on the dialectic that simply affirms the presuppositions of possible criticism.

Perhaps enough has been said on the properties and aspects of our X named cosmopolis for a synthetic view to be attempted. It is not a group denouncing other groups; it is not a superstate ruling states; it is not an organization that enrolls members, nor an academy that endorses opinions, nor a court that administers a legal code. It is a withdrawal from practicality to save practicality. It is a dimension of consciousness, a heightened grasp of historical origins, a discovery of historical responsibilities. It is not something altogether new, for the Marxist has been busy activating the class consciousness of the masses, and before him the liberal had succeeded in indoctrinating men with the notion of progress. Still, it possesses its novelty, for it is not *simpliste*. It does not leap from a fact of development to a belief in automatic progress nor from a fact of abuse to an expectation of an apocalyptic utopia reached through an accelerated decline. It is the higher synthesis of the liberal thesis and the Marxist antithesis. It comes to minds prepared for it by these earlier views, for they have taught man to think historically. It comes at a time when the totalitarian fact and threat have refuted the liberals and discredited the Marxists. It stands on a basic analysis of the compound-in-tension that is man; it confronts problems of which men are aware; it invites the vast potentialities and pent-up energies of our time to contribute to their solution by developing an art and a literature, a theatre and a broadcasting, a journalism and a history, a school and a university, a personal depth and a public opinion, that through appreciation and criticism give men of common sense the opportunity and help they need and desire to correct the general bias of their common sense.

Finally, it would be unfair not to stress the chief characteristic of cosmopolis. It is not easy. It is not a dissemination of sweetness and light, where sweetness means sweet to me, and light means light to me. Were that so, cosmopolis would be superfluous. Every scotosis puts forth a plausible, ingenious, adaptive, untiring resistance. The general bias of common sense is no exception. It is by moving with that bias rather than against it, by differing from it slightly rather than opposing it thoroughly, that one has the best prospect of selling books and newspapers, entertainment and education. Moreover, this is only the superficial difficulty. Beneath it lies the almost insoluble problem of settling clearly and exactly what the general bias is. It is not a culture but only a compromise that results from taking the highest common factor of an aggregate of cultures. It is not a compromise that will check and reverse the longer cycle of decline. Nor is it unbiased intelligence that yields a welter of conflicting opinions. Cosmopolis is not Babel, yet how can we break from Babel? This is the problem. So far from solving it in this chapter, we do not hope to reach a full solution in this volume. But, at least, two allies can be acknowledged. On the one hand, there is common sense, and in its judgments, which as yet have not been treated, common sense tends to be profoundly sane. On the other hand, there is dialectical analysis; the refusal of insight betrays itself; the Babel of our day is the cumulative product of a series of refusals to understand; and dialectical analysis can discover and expose both the series of past refusals and the tactics of contemporary resistance to enlightenment.

Related selections: 1.XI and 3.VII.3–4 for further application of the notion of dialectic; 1.XVI on the problem of evil and the limitations of cosmopolis; 1.XII.4 on human development; 1.XIII.2 on the appropriation of truth; 1.XIV.2 on the problem of liberation; 1.XVI.1 on the problem of evil; 3.II.2 on the structure of the human good; 4.II on the dialectic of authority; 4.III.1 on social alienation; 4.IV on healing and creating in history.

Things and Bodies

The notion of a thing involves a new type of insight. Classical method seeks insight into law and system. Statistical method relies on an inverse insight which rests upon a lack of system. Both methods of inquiry consider the data of experience from an abstract viewpoint to determine relations among things and events. Insight into things is insight into data in their concrete individuality and in the totality of their aspects.

In the first part of this selection from Chapter 8 of *Insight* Lonergan presents his technical notion of the thing as a unity, identity, whole in data. The notion of the thing is 'the basic synthetic construct of scientific thought and development.'[1] Things, in this technical meaning, are distinguished, not from people, but from 'bodies.' Human beings are also things in this technical sense. In the second part, he contrasts things with bodies. Things are grasped by insight, but bodies, which are commonly mistaken for things, are confronted experientially in a non-conceptual 'knowing.' Here Lonergan introduces his idea of the 'already out there now real.' Things and bodies, Lonergan argues, are commonly confused, and the confusion is rooted in the failure to make a critical distinction between two types of knowing. Elementary knowing involves neither questioning nor insight but is constituted completely on the level of experiential operations. Fully human knowing includes but goes beyond elementary knowing. It is a complex process of questioning, insight, formulation, and verification. The critical distinction between the two types of knowing is a key constituent of Lonergan's philosophical position. So too is the corresponding distinction between being and the 'already out there now real.' The duality in knowing is highlighted in the introduction to *Insight*, given

---

1 *Insight*, 273.

important underpinnings in his account of the polymorphism of consciousness, makes its first vivid appearance in his discussion of things, and is established as the preeminent critical tool in his dialectical analyses of persistent
disputes about objectivity and reality. The need for the critical distinction of
two types of knowing is most clearly illustrated by our confusion of bodies
with things.

These extracts are taken from *Insight*, 270–1, 272–4; 275–9; 293.

1   The General Notion of the Thing

Since the notion of a thing involves a new type of insight, we had best
begin by recalling the main features of the old and now familiar type.
It rested upon the presence or absence of laws governing the relations
between data. Thus, experiential conjugates were reached by grasping
the correlation between such terms as 'red as seen' and 'seeing red,' or
'heat as felt' and 'feeling heat.' Similarly, explanatory conjugates were
reached by grasping the higher and more remote correlations that link
and implicitly define, say, masses or the electromagnetic field vectors.
On the other hand, probabilities were reached by arguing from the
absence of system in the relations between data.

This attention to law and system led to a consideration of data, not
in the totality of their concrete aspects, but only from some abstractive
viewpoint. To employ an experiential conjugate is to prescind from all
aspects of data except some single quality such as 'red' or 'hot.' To
employ an explanatory conjugate is to turn attention away from all
directly perceptible aspects and direct it to a nonimaginable term that
can be reached only through a series of correlations of correlations of
correlations. To speak of a probability is to suppose a process of reasoning that rests, not directly on what is given, nor positively on what
can be understood in the given, but indirectly and negatively on what
follows from a lack of system in the given.

Now the notion of a thing is grounded in an insight that grasps, not
relations between data, but a unity, identity, whole in data; and this
unity is grasped, not by considering data from any abstractive viewpoint, but by taking them in their concrete individuality and in the
totality of their aspects. For if the reader will turn his mind to any
object he names a thing, he will find that object to be a unity to which
belongs every aspect of every datum within the unity. Thus, the dog

Fido is a unity, and to Fido is ascribed a totality of data whether of color or shape, sound or odor, feeling or movement. Moreover, from this grasp of unity in a concrete totality of data there follow the various characteristics of things.

Thus, things are conceived as extended in space, permanent in time, and yet subject to change. They are extended in space, inasmuch as spatially distinct data pertain to the unity at any given instant. They are permanent in time, inasmuch as temporally distinct data pertain to the same unity. They are subject to change, inasmuch as there is some difference between the aggregate of data at one instant and the aggregate of data on the same unity at another instant.

Again, things possess properties and are subject to laws and to probabilities. For the very data that, taken concretely, are understood as pertaining to a single thing may also be taken abstractly and so may lead to a grasp of experiential conjugates, explanatory conjugates, and probabilities. Because the data are the same, there results an obvious relation between the insights and between the consequent concepts. This relation is expressed by saying that the conjugates are properties of the thing and that the probabilities regard the occurrence of changes in the thing ...

Again, without the notion of the thing there can be no notion of change. For a change is not just a newly observed datum, nor the substitution of one datum for another, nor the creation of a datum that previously did not exist. Moreover, there are no changes in the realm of abstractions, for every abstraction is eternally whatever it is defined to be. If there is change, there has to be a concrete unity of concrete data extending over some interval of time, there has to be some difference between the data at the beginning and at the end of the interval, and this difference can be only partial, for otherwise there would occur not a change but an annihilation and a new creation.

As the notion of the thing is necessary for the notion of change, so also is it necessary for the continuity of scientific thought and development. For scientific development involves a succession of explanatory systems. Each of such systems serves to define implicitly a set of conjugate terms that through a series of correlations of correlations can be linked with concrete data. Still, this succession of systems with their implications does not suffice to constitute scientific thought. For the systems have to be discovered in data and verified in data; they cannot be discovered and verified in any data whatever; neither can they be discovered and verified in the data which they themselves select, for then a number of incompatible systems would be equally verifiable for each would satisfy equally well the data it selected. Accordingly, scientific thought needs, not only explanatory systems, but also descriptions that determine the data which explanations must satisfy. Moreover, scientific thought needs the notion of the thing, which has as its properties both experiential and explanatory conjugates, which remains identical whether it is described or explained, which by its identity demands a coherent explanation or set of explanations that is verifiable in the easily ascertainable data of the thing as described.

Thus the thing is the basic synthetic construct of scientific thought and development. It embraces in a concrete unity a totality of spatially and temporally distinct data. It possesses as its qualities and properties the experiential conjugates that can be determined by observation. It is subject to change and variation inasmuch as its data at one time differ from its data at another. Through observations of qualities, things are classified by their sensible similarities. Through measurements of changes, there are reached classical laws and statistical frequencies. Such laws and frequencies are subject to revision, and the revision is effected by showing that the earlier view does not satisfy completely the data on the thing as described. Finally, not only experiential conjugates, explanatory conjugates, and probabilities of events are verifiable; the construct of the thing is itself verifiable; for the ancient list of four elements – earth, water, fire, and air – has been rejected, and the new list of the periodic table has been established on the scientific ground of hypothesis and verification; both the old list and the new are lists of kinds of things.

Further, things are said to exist. Earlier we distinguished between questions that admit the simple answers yes and no, and questions that do not. It is meaningless to answer either yes or no to the question, What is a thing? On the other hand, that answer is quite appropriate when one asks whether there are any things. Now existence may be defined as what is known inasmuch as an affirmative answer is given to the question, Are there things? Accordingly, existence stands to the thing as event or occurrence stands to the conjugate. For the existence of the thing is known by verifying the notion of the thing, as the occurrence is known by verifying the conjugate. Moreover, general knowledge of things, like knowledge of conjugates, is reached by classical procedures, but general knowledge of existence, like knowledge of occurrence, is obtained through statistical laws. Thus, the definitions of chemical elements and compounds are of the classical type, but predictions of successful analysis or synthesis in nature or in the laboratory have to be based on probabilities ...

2 Bodies

The name 'thing' has been employed in a very precise meaning. It denotes a unity, identity, whole; initially it is grasped in data as individual; inasmuch as it unifies spatially and temporally distinct data, it is extended and permanent; inasmuch as the data it unifies also are understood through laws, conjugates become its properties, and probabilities govern its changes; finally, things exist, and only particulars exist, though the particularity, and indeed the reality, of things themselves give rise to disconcerting problems.

Now there may be men that employ the name 'body' in exactly the same meaning as we have assigned to the name 'thing.' But men are not pure intelligences. They are animals; they live largely under the influence of their intersubjectivity; they are guided by a common sense that does not bother to ask nice questions on the meaning of familiar names. Accordingly, it would not be rash to suspect that their usage of the name 'thing' does not quite coincide with the account we have given; and it is to follow up this suspicion that in the present section we turn our attention to the notion of a body or, rather, of a 'body,' where the quotation marks denote some divergence from the notion to be reached by intelligence and reasonableness.

To begin from a clear-cut instance in which there is no need to suppose either intelligence or reasonableness, let us consider a kitten. It is awake, and its stream of consciousness flows in the biological pattern. Such consciousness is a higher technique for attaining biological ends. It may be described as orientated toward such ends and as anticipating means to the ends. Moreover, the means lie in external situations, and so the anticipation is extroverted. The kitten's consciousness is directed outwards towards possible opportunities to satisfy appetites. This extroversion is spatial: as it is by the spatial maneuvers of moving its head and limbs that the kitten deals with means to its end, so the means also must be spatial, for otherwise spatial maneuvers would be inept and useless. The extroversion is also temporal: present data are distinct from the memories that enrich them; they are no less distinct from the imagined courses of future action to which they lead. Finally, the extroversion is concerned with the 'real': a realistic painting of a saucer of milk might attract a kitten's attention, make it investigate, sniff, perhaps try to lap; but it could not lead to lapping, and still less to feeling replete; for the kitten, painted milk is not real. Let us now characterize a 'body' as an 'already out there now real.' 'Already' refers to the orientation and dynamic anticipation of biological consciousness; such consciousness does not create but finds its environment; it finds it as already constituted, already offering opportunities, already issuing challenges. 'Out' refers to the extroversion of a consciousness that is aware, not of its own ground, but of objects distinct from itself. 'There' and 'now' indicate the spatial and temporal determinations of extroverted consciousness. 'Real,' finally, is a subdivision within the field of the 'already out there now': part of that is mere appearance; but part is real; and its reality consists in its relevance to biological success or failure, pleasure or pain.

As the reader will have surmised, the terms 'body,' 'already,' 'out,' 'there,' 'now,' 'real' stand for concepts uttered by an intelligence that is grasping, not intelligent procedure, but a merely biological and nonintelligent response to stimulus. In other words, the point to the preceding paragraphs is not to suggest that a kitten can understand and describe its spontaneity but, on the contrary, to indicate through human concepts the elements in a nonconceptual 'knowing.'

Again, as the reader once more will have surmised, our interest in kittens is rather limited. For the point we wish to make is that not a few men mean by 'thing' or 'body,' not simply an intelligible unity grasped in data as individual, but also an 'already out there now real' which is as accessible to human animals as to kittens. When Galileo pronounced secondary qualities to be merely subjective, he meant that they were not 'already out there now real.' When the decadent Aristotelians and, generally, people that rely on good common sense insist that secondary qualities obviously are objective, they mean that they are 'already out there now real.' When Descartes maintained that material substance must be identical with spatial extension, his material substance was the 'already out there now real.' When Kant argued that primary and secondary qualities are merely phenomenal, he meant that for him the reality of the 'already out there now real' was mere appearance. Our own position, as contained in the canon of parsimony, was that the real is the verified; it is what is to be known by the knowing constituted by experience and inquiry, insight and hypothesis, reflection and verification. Our present point is that, besides knowing in that rather complex sense, there is also 'knowing' in the elementary sense in which kittens know the 'reality' of milk.

It is not difficult to set forth the differences between the two types of knowing. The elementary type is constituted completely on the level of experience; neither questions for intelligence nor questions for reflection have any part in its genesis; and as questions do not give rise to it, neither can they undo it; essentially it is unquestionable. On the other hand, in fully human knowing experience supplies no more than materials for questions; questions are essential to its genesis; through questions for intelligence it moves to accumulations of related insights which are expressed or formulated in concepts, suppositions, definitions, postulates, hypotheses, theories; through questions for reflection it attains a further component, which hitherto has been referred to as verification and presently will have to be examined more closely in a series of chapters on judgment, its suppositions, and its implications.

Both types of knowing possess their validity. One cannot claim that one is concerned with mere appearance while the other is concerned with reality. For elementary knowing vindicates its validity by the survival, not to mention the evolution, of animal species. On the other hand, any attempt to dispute the validity of fully human knowing involves the use of that knowing, and so, if the attempt is not to be frustrated by its own assumptions, it must presuppose that validity.

The problem set by the two types of knowing is, then, not a problem of elimination but a problem of critical distinction. For the difficulty lies, not in either type of knowing by itself, but in the confusion that arises when one shifts unconsciously from one type to the other. Animals have no epistemological problems. Neither do scientists, as long as they stick to their task of observing, forming hypotheses, and verifying. The perennial source of nonsense is that, after the scientist has verified his hypothesis, he is likely to go a little further and tell the layman what, approximately, scientific reality looks like! Already we have attacked the unverifiable image; but now we can see the origin of the strange urge to foist upon mankind unverifiable images. For both the scientist and the layman, besides being intelligent and reasonable, also are animals. To them as animals, a verified hypothesis is just a jumble of words or symbols. What they want is an elementary knowing of the 'really real,' if not through sense, at least by imagination.

As is apparent, we are back at the notion of dialectic. There are two types of knowing. Each is modified by its own development. They are opposed, for one arises through intelligent and reasonable questions and answers, and the other does not. They are linked together in man, who at once is an animal, intelligent, and reasonable. Unless they are distinguished sharply by a critical theory of knowledge, they become confused to generate aberrations that afflict not only scientific thought but far more conspicuously the thought of philosophers. Further development of this point must be left to the chapter on the method of metaphysics,[2] but perhaps enough has been said to justify the following conclusions.

(1) By a thing is meant an intelligible concrete unity. As differentiated by experiential conjugates and commonsense expectations, it is a thing for us, a thing as described. As differentiated by explanatory conjugates and scientifically determined probabilities, it is a thing itself, a thing as explained.

(2) The notion of thing satisfies the canon of parsimony. For it adds to data only what is grasped by intelligence and reasonably is affirmed. Indeed, not only does it satisfy the canon of parsimony but it seems necessary to scientific thought, both because it is presupposed by the necessary notion of change, and because the scientist has to possess a construct that combines both descriptive and explanatory knowledge.

(3) By a 'body' is meant primarily a focal point of extroverted biological anticipation and attention. It is an 'already out there now real,' where these terms have their meaning fixed solely by elements within sensitive experience and so without any use of intelligent and reasonable questions and answers.

(4) By a 'body' is meant secondarily any confusion or mixture of elements taken both from the notion of a thing and from the notion of a 'body' in its primary meaning ...

3 Summary

The basic difficulty is from the side of the subject. He is involved in a dialectical tension, and he can be made aware of the fact only after he has grasped what is meant and what is not meant by inquiry, insight, and conception as opposed to sensible data and schematic images.

2 [1.XI in this reader.]

Accordingly, our first task was to clarify the nature of insight, and to it we devoted our first five chapters.[3] On that foundation we constructed, first, a pure theory of common sense, and secondly, an account of its dialectical involvement. Only then could we hope to distinguish effectively between things and 'bodies,' between the intelligible unities to be grasped when one is within the intellectual pattern of experience and, on the other hand, the highly convincing instances of the 'already out there now real' that are unquestioned and unquestionable not only for animals but also for the general bias of common sense.

If that distinction has been drawn effectively, still it does not follow that the reader will always find it convincing. For the distinction is a work of intelligence operating in the intellectual pattern of experience. No one can hope to live exclusively in that pattern. As soon as anyone moves from that pattern to the dramatic pattern of his intercourse with others or the practical pattern of his daily tasks, things as intelligible unities once more will take on for him the appearance of unreal speculation, while 'bodies' or instances of the 'already out there now real' will resume the ascendancy that they acquired without opposition in his infancy. Accordingly, the attainment of a critical position means not merely that one distinguishes clearly between things and 'bodies' but also that one distinguishes between the different patterns of one's own experience and refuses to commit oneself intellectually unless one is operating within the intellectual pattern of experience. Inversely, it is the failure to reach the full critical position that accounts for the endless variety of philosophic positions so rightly lamented by Kant; and it is by a dialectical analysis, based on the full critical position, that one can hope to set up a philosophy of philosophies in the fully reflective manner that at least imperfectly was initiated by Hegel and still is demanded by modern needs. But clearly enough, these points can be developed only after we have answered questions on the nature of rational consciousness, of critical reflection, of judgment, of the notions of being and objectivity.

Related selections: 1.IV.2, 1.X.4, 1.XI.1, and 2.III.2 on the duality in human knowing; 2.IV.1 on a later, related distinction between the world of immediacy and the world mediated by meaning; 1.XII.4 on the human being as a type of thing.

---

3 [1.II–III in this reader.]

Judgment

Up to this point in *Insight* Lonergan has been concerned with insight, with the act of understanding. As the earlier selections on common sense and bias make abundantly clear, one of the many properties of human understanding is that it is prone to incompleteness, inadequacy, and error. Insights into our experience, Lonergan often repeated, are a dime a dozen. They are to be considered merely bright ideas until such time as they are subjected to rational reflection and judgment. Besides the type of question that sets the stage for direct insight into the data of our experience – What is it? – there is a second type of question raised about the idea grasped by direct insights – Is it so? This second type of question sets the stage for reflective judgment on the correctness of direct insights.

In the first part of this selection from Chapters 9 and 10 of *Insight* Lonergan pulls together the threads of the preceding investigations, distinguishes and relates three levels of cognitional process, and exposes the nature and role of judgment as the final increment in the complex process of human knowing. Cognitional process begins in experiencing, moves on to understanding, and culminates in judging: human knowing is experiencing–understanding–judging. In the second part Lonergan locates the link between the reflective question and the act of judgment in a new type of insight, reflective insight. He distinguishes between a grasp of the 'formally unconditioned,' which has no conditions whatever, and a grasp of the 'virtually unconditioned,' which has conditions but whose conditions are fulfilled. This analysis of reflective insight, in which we grasp the sufficiency of evidence for a judgment, was regarded by Lonergan as one of his most important contributions to cognitional theory. In the third part, Lonergan illustrates reflective insight as a grasp of the virtually unconditioned by analyzing a single concrete judgment of fact.

In the final selection Lonergan asks on what grounds we are able to pronounce insights into concrete situations correct or incorrect, and his answer is given in terms of the grasp of the virtually unconditioned.

These extracts are taken from *Insight*, 296–303, 305–12.

1   The Notion of Judgment

A first determination of the notion of judgment is reached by relating it to propositions.

For present purposes it will suffice to distinguish (1) utterance, (2) sentence, and (3) proposition, in the following summary manner.

If you say, 'The king is dead,' and I say, 'The king is dead,' then there are two utterances but only one sentence.

If you say, 'Der König ist tot,' and I say, 'The king is dead,' then there are two utterances and two sentences but only one proposition.

Similarly, if you write in decimal notation, '2 + 2 = 4,' and I write in binary notation, '10 + 10 = 100,' again there are two utterances and two sentences but only one proposition.

Further, it will be supposed that utterances may be spoken, written, or merely imagined, and that the imagining may be visual, auditory, or motor; again, grammarians distinguish declarative, interrogative, optative, and exclamatory sentences, but of these only the declarative corresponds to the proposition.

Now with regard to propositions there are two distinct mental attitudes: one may merely consider them, or one may agree or disagree with them. Thus, what I write I also affirm; but what you are reading you may neither affirm nor deny but merely consider.

A proposition, then, may be simply an object of thought, the content of an act of conceiving, defining, thinking, supposing, considering.

But a proposition also may be the content of an act of judging; and then it is the content of an affirming or denying, an agreeing or disagreeing, an assenting or dissenting.

A second determination of the notion of judgment is reached by relating it to questions.

Questions fall into two main classes. There are questions for reflection, and they may be met by answering yes or no. There are questions for intelligence, and they may not be met by answering yes or no.

Thus, one may ask, 'Is there a logarithm of the square root of minus one?' This is a question for reflection. It is answered correctly by saying 'Yes.' On the other hand, though it would be a mistake to answer 'No,' still that answer would make sense. But if one asks, 'What is the logarithm of the square root of minus one?' there is no sense in answering either yes or no. The question is not for reflection but for intelligence. The only appropriate answer is to show that the square root of minus one results from raising a given base to a certain power.

Our second determination of the notion of judgment is, then, that judging is answering yes or no to a question for reflection.

A third determination of the notion of judgment is that it involves a personal commitment. As de la Rochefoucauld remarked, 'Everyone complains of his memory but no one of his judgment.' One is ready to confess to a poor memory because one believes that memory is not within one's power. One is not ready to confess to poor judgment because the question for reflection can be answered not only by yes or no but also by 'I don't know'; it can be answered assertorically or modally, with certitude or only probability; finally, the question as presented can be dismissed, distinctions introduced, and new questions substituted. The variety of possible answers makes full allowance for the misfortunes and shortcomings of the person answering, and by the same stroke it closes the door on possible excuses for mistakes. A judgment is the responsibility of the one that judges. It is a personal commitment.

However, just what a person is, or what responsibility is, or why the person is responsible for his judgments are further questions that cannot be considered as yet. We now observe the fact and leave explanation to more appropriate occasions.

On the basis of the foregoing determinations we next attempt to relate judgment to the general structure of our cognitional process. We distinguish a direct and an introspective process, and in both of these we distinguish three levels: a level of presentations, a level of intelligence, and a level of reflection.

Hitherto, our inquiry has centered on the level of intelligence. It consists in acts of inquiry, understanding, and formulation. Thus, the question, What is it? leads to a grasp and formulation of an intelligible unity-identity-whole in data as individual. The question, Why? leads to a grasp and formulation of a law, a correlation, a system. The question, How often? leads to a grasp and formulation of an ideal frequency from which actual frequencies nonsystematically diverge.

Our account of the classical and statistical phases of empirical method, of the notion of the thing, of explanatory abstraction and system has been concerned with the level of intelligence in cognitional process.

However, this level of intelligence presupposes and complements another level. Inquiry presupposes elements in knowledge about which inquiry is made. Understanding presupposes presentations to be understood. Formulation expresses not only what is grasped by understanding but also what is essential to the understanding in the understood. This prior level was described in the chapter on common sense. It is the level of presentations. Its defining characteristic is the fact that it is presupposed and complemented by the level of intelligence, that it supplies, as it were, the raw materials on which intelligence operates, that, in a word, it is empirical, given indeed but merely given, open to understanding and formulation but by itself not understood and in itself ineffable.

Thirdly, the level of intelligence, besides presupposing and complementing an initial level, is itself presupposed and complemented by a further level of reflection.

The formulations of understanding yield concepts, definitions, objects of thought, suppositions, considerations. But man demands more. Every answer to a question for intelligence raises a further question for reflection. There is an ulterior motive to conceiving and defining, thinking and considering, forming suppositions, hypotheses, theories, systems. That motive appears when such activities are followed by the question, Is it so? We conceive in order to judge. As questions for intelligence, What? and Why? and How often? stand to insights and formulations, so questions for reflection stand to a further kind of insight and to judgment. It is on this third level that there emerge the notions of truth and falsity, of certitude and the probability that is not a frequency but a quality of judgment. It is within this third level that there is involved the personal commitment that makes one responsible for one's judgments. It is from this third level that come utterances to express one's affirming or denying, assenting or dissenting, agreeing or disagreeing.

It will be useful to represent schematically the three levels of cognitional process.

I. Data. Perceptual Images. Free Images. Utterances.

II. Questions for Intelligence. Insights. Formulations.
III. Questions for Reflection. Reflection. Judgment.

The second level presupposes and complements the first. The third level presupposes and complements the second. The exception lies in free images and utterances, which commonly are under the influence of the higher levels before they provide a basis for inquiry and reflection. Further, by questions for intelligence and reflection are not meant utterances or even conceptual formulations; by the question is meant the attitude of the inquiring mind that effects the transition from the first level to the second, and again the attitude of the critical mind that effects the transition from the second level to the third. Finally, the scheme is anticipatory inasmuch as the nature of reflection comes up for discussion only in the next chapter.

Now, as has been remarked, the three levels of the cognitional process operate in two modes. Data include data of sense and data of consciousness. Data of sense include colors, shapes, sounds, odors, tastes, the hard and soft, rough and smooth, hot and cold, wet and dry, and so forth. The direct mode of cognitional process begins from data of sense, advances through insights and formulations to reach reflection and judgment. Thus, empirical science pertains to the direct mode of cognitional process. On the other hand, the data of consciousness consist of acts of seeing, hearing, tasting, smelling, touching, perceiving, imagining, inquiring, understanding, formulating, reflecting, judging, and so forth. As data, such acts are experienced; but as experienced, they are not described, distinguished, compared, related, defined, for all such activities are the work of inquiry, insight, and formulation. Finally, such formulations are, of themselves, just hypotheses; they may be accurate or inaccurate, correct or mistaken; and to pronounce upon them is the work of reflection and judgment. Thus the three levels of the direct mode of cognitional process provide the data for the introspective mode; and as the direct mode, so also the introspective unfolds on the three levels: an initial level of data, a second level of understanding and formulation, and a third level of reflection and judgment.

The foregoing offers an analysis of cognitional process. A whole is divided into different levels; on each level different kinds of operation are distinguished and related; each level is related to the others; and two modes of the whole process are contrasted. But analysis prepares the way for synthesis. Accordingly, we have now to ask how the various elements come together to constitute knowing. As yet, we are unprepared to answer the Kantian question that regards the constitution of the relation of knowing subject and known object. Our concern is the more elementary question of the unification of the contents of several acts into a single known content.

To this the general answer has already been indicated. Contents of different acts come together inasmuch as the earlier are incomplete without the later while the later have nothing to complete without the earlier. Questions for intelligence presuppose something to be understood, and that something is supplied by the initial level. Understanding grasps in given or imagined presentations an intelligible form emergent in the presentations. Conception formulates the grasped idea along with what is essential to the idea in the presentations. Reflection asks whether such understanding and formulation are correct. Judgment answers that they are or are not.

The cognitional process is thus a cumulative process: later steps presuppose earlier contributions and add to them. However, not all additions have the same significance. Some are merely provisional, as are free images. Some put together in a new mode the contributions of previous acts; thus, abstract formulation puts generally what insight grasps in a particular presentation. Finally, some constitute, as it were, the addition of new dimensions in the construction of the full cognitional content; and it is this addition of a new dimension that forms the basis of the distinction between the three levels of presentation, intelligence, and reflection.

From this viewpoint one may distinguish between the proper and the borrowed content of judgment.

The proper content of a judgment is its specific contribution to cognitional process. This consists in the answers yes or no.

The borrowed content of a judgment is twofold. There is the direct borrowed content that is found in the question to which one answers yes or no; and there is the indirect borrowed content that emerges in the reflective act linking question and answer, that claims the yes or no to be true and, indeed, either certainly or only probably true.

Thus, the direct borrowed content of the judgment, I am writing, is the question, Am I writing? The proper content of that judgment is the answer, Yes, I am. The indirect borrowed content of the same judgment is the implicit meaning 'It certainly is true that I am writing.'

Again, from the same viewpoint, the judgment may be described as the total increment in cognitional process.

Every element in that process is at least a partial increment. It makes some contribution to knowing. But the judgment is the last act in the series that begins from presentations and advances through understanding and formulation ultimately to reach reflection and affirmation or denial. Thus, the proper content of judgment, the yes or no, is the final partial increment in the process. But this proper content is meaningless apart from the question it answers. With the question it forms an integrated whole. But the question takes over a formulation from the level of intelligence, and that formulation draws upon both insight and presentation. It follows that the judgment as a whole is a total increment in cognitional process, that it brings to a close one whole step in the development of knowledge.

Finally, there is the contextual aspect of judgment. Though single judgments bring single steps in inquiries to their conclusion, still the single steps are related to one another in a highly complex fashion.

The most general aspects of cognitional context are represented by logic and dialectic. Logic is the effort of knowledge to attain the coherence and organization proper to any stage of its development. Dialectic, on the other hand, rests on the breakdown of efforts to attain coherence and organization at a given stage, and consists in bringing to birth a new stage in which logic again will endeavor to attain coherence and organization.

From the viewpoint of the logical ideal, every term has one and only one precise meaning, every relation of every term to every other term is set down in an unequivocal proposition, the totality of propositions is neatly divided into primitive and derived, the derived may all be obtained by the rules of inference from a minimum number of primitive propositions, no proposition contradicts any other, and finally the employment of the principle of excluded middle does not introduce undefined or false suppositions, as does the question, Have you or have you not stopped beating your wife?

Now the pursuit of the logical ideal, so far from favoring a static immobility, serves to reveal the inadequacy of any intermediate stage in the development of knowledge. The more deeply it probes, the more effectively it forces the cognitional process to undergo a radical revision of its terms and postulates and so to pursue the logical ideal from a new base of operations. However, such revision has its limits, for there is no revision of revisers themselves. They are subject to the general conditions of beginning from presentations, advancing through insights and formulations, to terminate with reflections and judgments. Their insights are acts of grasping concrete unities, systematic regularities, or ideal frequencies. Their judgments are personal commitments to a yes or no; both answers cannot be given to the same question; and under ideal conditions either one of the two answers has to be given. The simple fact of the uniformity of nature in revisers provides both logic and dialectic with an immutable ultimacy.

Within the general schemes of logic and dialectic, the contextual aspect of judgment appears in three manners.

There is the relation of the present to the past. Thus, past judgments remain with us. They form a habitual orientation, present and operative, but only from behind the scenes. They govern the direction of attention, evaluate insights, guide formulations, and influence the acceptance or rejection of new judgments. Previous insights remain with us. They facilitate the occurrence of fresh insights, exert their influence on new formulations, provide presuppositions that underlie new judgments whether in the same or in connected or in merely analogous fields of inquiry. Hence, when a new judgment is made, there is within us a habitual context of insights and other judgments, and it stands ready to elucidate the judgment just made, to complement it, to balance it, to draw distinctions, to add qualifications, to provide defence, to offer evidence or proof, to attempt persuasion.

Secondly, there are the relations within the present. Existing judgments may be found to conflict, and so they release the dialectical process. Again, though they do not conflict, they may not be completely independent of each other, and so they stimulate the logical effort for organized coherence.

Thirdly, there are the relations of the present to the future. The questions we answer are few compared to the questions that await an answer. Knowing is a dynamic structure. If each judgment is a total increment consisting of many parts, still it is only a minute contribution towards the whole of knowledge. But further, our knowing is dynamic in another sense. It is irretrievably habitual. For we can make but one judgment at a time, and one judgment cannot bring all we know into the full light of actual knowing. A judgment may be very comprehensive and so bear witness to the depth and breadth of our perspectives. It may be very concrete and so reveal our grasp of nuance and detail. But it cannot be both comprehensive and concrete. All we know is somehow with us; it is present and operative within our knowing; but it lurks behind the scenes, and it reveals itself only in the exactitude with which each minor increment to our knowing is effected. The business of the human mind in this life seems to be, not contemplation of what we know, but relentless devotion to the task of adding increments to a merely habitual knowledge.

2   The General Form of Reflective Insight

To grasp evidence as sufficient for a prospective judgment is to grasp the prospective judgment as virtually unconditioned.

Distinguish, then, between the formally and the virtually unconditioned. The formally unconditioned has no conditions whatever. The virtually unconditioned has conditions indeed, but they are fulfilled.

Accordingly, a virtually unconditioned involves three elements, namely, (1) a conditioned, (2) a link between the conditioned and its conditions, and (3) the fulfilment of the conditions. Hence a prospective judgment will be virtually unconditioned if (1) it is the conditioned, (2) its conditions are known, and (3) the conditions are fulfilled. By the mere fact that a question for reflection has been put, the prospective judgment is a conditioned: it stands in need of evidence sufficient for reasonable pronouncement. The function of reflective understanding is to meet the question for reflection by transforming the prospective judgment from the status of a conditioned to the status of a virtually unconditioned; and reflective understanding effects this transformation by grasping the conditions of the conditioned and their fulfilment.

Such is the general scheme, and we proceed to illustrate it from the form of deductive inference. Where A and B each stand for one or more propositions, the deductive form is

If A, then B
But A
Therefore B.

For instance

If X is material and alive, X is mortal

But men are material and alive
Therefore, men are mortal.

Now the conclusion is a conditioned, for an argument is needed to support it. The major premise links this conditioned to its conditions, for it affirms 'If A, then B.' The minor premise presents the fulfilment of the conditions, for it affirms the antecedent A. The function, then, of the form of deductive inference is to exhibit a conclusion as virtually unconditioned. Reflective insight grasps the pattern, and by rational compulsion there follows the judgment.

However, deductive inference cannot be the basic case of judgment, for it presupposes other judgments to be true. For that reason we have said that the form of deductive inference is merely a clear illustration of what is meant by grasping a prospective judgment as virtually unconditioned. Far more general than the form of deductive inference is the form of reflective insight itself. If there is to be a deduction, the link between the conditioned and its conditions must be a judgment, and the fulfilment of the conditions must be a further judgment. But judgments are the final products of cognitional process. Before the link between conditioned and conditions appears in the act of judgment, it existed in a more rudimentary state within cognitional process itself. Before the fulfilment of conditions appears in another act of judgment, it too was present in a more rudimentary state within cognitional process. The remarkable fact about reflective insight is that it can make use of those more rudimentary elements in cognitional process to reach the virtually unconditioned. Let us now see how this is done in various cases.

3   Concrete Judgments of Fact

Suppose a man to return from work to his tidy home and to find the windows smashed, smoke in the air, and water on the floor. Suppose him to make the extremely restrained judgment of fact 'Something happened.' The question is, not whether he was right, but how he reached his affirmation.

The conditioned will be the judgment that something happened.

The fulfilling conditions will be two sets of data: the remembered data of his home as he left it in the morning; the present data of his home as he finds it in the evening. Observe that the fulfilling conditions are found on the level of presentations. They are not judgments, as is the minor premise of syllogisms. They involve no questions for intelligence nor insights nor concepts. They lie simply on the level of past and present experience, of the occurrence of acts of seeing and smelling.

The link between the conditioned and the fulfilling conditions is a structure immanent and operative within cognitional process. It is not a judgment. It is not a formulated set of concepts, such as a definition. It is simply a way of doing things, a procedure within the cognitional field.

The general form of all such structures and procedures has already been outlined in terms of the three levels of presentations, intelligence, and reflection. Specializations of the general form may be exemplified by the classical and statistical phases of empirical method, by the notion of the thing, and by the differences between description and explanation. However, such accounts of the general form and its specializations pertain to introspective analysis. Prior to such an investigation and formulation, the structures and procedures exist and operate; nor, in general, do they operate any better because the analysis has been effected.

Now in the particular instance under consideration, the weary worker not only experiences present data and recalls different data but by direct insights he refers both sets of data to the same set of things, which he calls his home. The direct insight, however, fulfils a double function. Not merely are two fields of individual data referred to one identical set of things but a second level of cognitional process is added to a first. The two together contain a specific structure of that process, which we may name the notion of knowing change. Just as knowing a thing consists in grasping an intelligible unity-identity-whole in individual data, so knowing change consists in grasping the same identity or identities at different times in different individual data. If the same thing exhibits different individual data at different times, it has changed. If there occurs a change, something has happened. But these are statements. If they are affirmed, they are judgments. But prior to being either statements or judgments, they exist as unanalyzed structures or procedures immanent and operative within cognitional process. It is such a structure that links the conditioned with the fulfilling conditions in the concrete judgment of fact.

The three elements have been assembled. On the level of presentations there are two sets of data. On the level of intelligence there is an insight referring both sets to the same things. When both levels are taken together, there is involved the notion of knowing change. Reflective understanding grasps all three as a virtually unconditioned to ground the judgment 'Something happened.'

While our illustrative instance was as simple as it could be, still it provides the model for the analysis of more complex instances of the concrete judgment of fact. The fulfilling conditions may be any combination of data from the memories of a long life, and their acquisition may have involved exceptional powers of observation. The cognitional structure may suppose the cumulative development of understanding exemplified by the man of experience, the specialist, the expert. Both complex data and a complex structure may combine to yield a virtually unconditioned that introspective analysis could hardly hope to reproduce accurately and convincingly. But the general nature of the concrete judgment of fact would remain the same as in the simple case we considered.

However, the reader is probably asking how we know whether the insights that constitute the pivot of such structures are themselves correct. To this point we have now to turn.

4 Insights into Concrete Situations

Direct and introspective insights arise in response to an inquiring attitude. There are data to be understood; inquiry seeks understanding; and the insight arises as the relevant understanding. But a mere bright idea is one thing, and a correct idea is another. How do we distinguish between the two?

The question is asked, not in its full generality, but with respect to concrete situations that diverge from our expectations and by that divergence set us a problem. Thus, to retain our former illustration, the man on returning home might have said, 'There has been a fire.' Since there no longer was any fire, that judgment would suppose an insight that put two and two together. Our question is on what grounds such an insight could be pronounced correct.

First, then, observe that insights not only arise in answer to questions but also are followed by further questions. Observe, moreover, that such further questions are of two kinds. They may stick to the initial issue, or they may go on to raise distinct issues. 'What started the fire?' 'Where is my wife?' Observe, thirdly, that the transition to distinct issues may result from very different reasons; it may be because different interests supervene to draw attention elsewhere; but it may also be because the initial issue is exhausted, because about it there are no further questions to be asked.

Let us now distinguish between vulnerable and invulnerable insights. Insights are vulnerable when there are further questions to be asked on the same issue. For the further questions lead to further insights that certainly complement the initial insight, that to a greater or less extent modify its expression and implications, that perhaps lead to an entirely new slant on the issue. But when there are no further questions, the insight is invulnerable. For it is only through further questions that there arise the further insights that complement, modify, or revise the initial approach and explanation.

Now this reveals a law immanent and operative in cognitional process. Prior to our conceptual distinction between correct and mistaken insights, there is an operational distinction between invulnerable and vulnerable insights. When an insight meets the issue squarely, when it hits the bull's eye, when it settles the matter, there are no further questions to be asked, and so there are no further insights to challenge the initial position. But when the issue is not met squarely, there are further questions that would reveal the unsatisfactoriness of the insight and would evoke the further insights that put a new light on the matter.

Such, then, is the basic element in our solution. The link between the conditioned and its conditions is a law immanent and operative in cognitional process. The conditioned is the prospective judgment 'This or that direct or introspective insight is correct.' The immanent law of cognitional process may be formulated from our analysis: Such an insight is correct if there are no further pertinent questions.

At once it follows that the conditions for the prospective judgment are fulfilled when there are no further pertinent questions.

Note that it is not enough to say that the conditions are fulfilled when no further questions occur to me. The mere absence of further questions in my mind can have other causes. My intellectual curiosity may be stifled by other interests. My eagerness to satisfy other drives may refuse the further questions a chance to emerge. To pass judgment in that case is to be rash, to leap before one looks.

As there is rash judgment, so also there is mere indecision. As the mere absence of further questions in my mind is not enough, so it is too much to demand that the very possibility of further questions has to be excluded. If in fact there are no further questions, then in fact the insight is invulnerable; if in fact the insight is invulnerable, then in fact the judgment approving it will be correct.

But how is one to strike this happy balance between rashness and indecision? How is one to know when it is reached? Were there some simple formula or recipe in answer to such questions, then men of good judgment could be produced at will and indefinitely. All we can attempt is an analysis of the main factors in the problem and an outline of the general nature of their solution.

In the first place, then, one has to give the further questions a chance to arise. The seed of intellectual curiosity has to grow into a rugged tree to hold its own against the desires and fears, conations and appetites, drives and interests, that inhabit the heart of man. Moreover, every insight has its retinue of presuppositions, implications, and applications. One has to take the steps needed for that retinue to come to light. The presuppositions and implications of a given insight have to knit coherently with the presuppositions and implications of other insights. Its possibilities of concrete application have to enter into the field of operations and undergo the test of success or failure. I do not mean, of course, that concrete living is to pursue this logical and operational expansion in the explicit, deliberate, and elaborate manner of the scientific investigator. But I do mean that something equivalent is to be sought by intellectual alertness, by taking one's time, by talking things over, by putting viewpoints to the test of action.

In the second place, the prior issue is to be noted. Behind the theory of correct insights, there is a theory of correct problems. It was to dodge this prior issue that we supposed a concrete situation that diverges from our expectations and by that divergence defines a problem. In other words, there has been postulated an inquirer that understands the background of the situation and so knows what is to be expected; there also has been postulated a problem that exists, that is accurately defined by the divergence of the situation from current expectations, that in turn provides a definition of the pertinence of any further questions.

Now this amounts to saying that good judgment about any insight has to rest on the previous acquisition of a large number of other, connected, and correct insights. But before attempting to break this vicious circle, let us assure ourselves of the fact of its existence. Children ask endless questions; we have no doubt about their intellectual curiosity;

but so far from crediting them with good judgment, we do not suppose them to reach the age of reason before their seventh year. Young men and women have the alertness of mind that justifies their crowding into schools and universities, but the law doubts the soundness of their judgment and regards them as minors, while Aristotle denied they had enough experience to study ethics with profit. Nor is there merely the initial difficulty of acquisition, but as well there is the subsequent necessity of keeping in touch. The man that returns to a field of commerce or industry, to a profession or a milieu, in which once he was completely at home may try to carry on from where he left off. But unless from mistakes and minor ineptitudes he learns to be more wary, he is merely inviting blunders and disaster. Good judgment about concrete insights presupposes the prior acquisition of an organized set of complementary insights.

In the third place, then, there is the process of learning. It is the gradual acquisition and accumulation of insights bearing on a single domain. During that process one's own judgment is in abeyance. It is being developed and formed but it has not yet reached the maturity needed for its independent exercise. For the gradual acquisition and accumulation of insights are not merely a matter of advancing in direct or introspective understanding. At the same time, intellectual curiosity is asserting itself against other desires. At the same time, the logical retinues of presuppositions and implications of each insight are being expanded, either to conflict and provoke further questions or else to mesh into coherence. At the same time, operational possibilities are envisaged, to be tested in thought experiments, to be contrasted with actual practice, to be executed in ventures that gradually increase in moment and scope to enlighten us by failures and to generate confidence through success.

So it is the process of learning that breaks the vicious circle. Judgment on the correctness of insights supposes the prior acquisition of a large number of correct insights. But the prior insights are not correct because we judge them to be correct. They occur within a self-correcting process in which the shortcomings of each insight provoke further questions to yield complementary insights. Moreover, this self-correcting process tends to a limit. We become familiar with concrete situations; we know what to expect; when the unexpected occurs, we can spot just what happened and why, and what can be done to favor or to prevent such a recurrence; or, if the unexpected is quite novel, we know enough to recommence the process of learning, and we can recognize when, once more, that self-correcting process reaches its limit in familiarity with the concrete situation and in easy mastery of it.

In the fourth place, rashness and indecision commonly have a basis in temperament. Apart from occasional outbursts, that we view as out of character, the rash man nearly always is quite sure, and the indecisive man regularly is unable to make up his mind. In such cases it is not enough to point out that learning is a self-correcting process that tends to a limit or that, while the limit is not marked with a label, still its attainment is revealed by a habitual ability to know just what is up. For unless a special effort is made to cope with temperament itself, the rash man continues to presume too quickly that he has nothing more to learn, and the indecisive man continues to suspect that deeper depths of shadowy possibilities threaten to invalidate what he knows quite well.

Finally, we note that we leave to another occasion a discussion of the philosophic opinions that no one ever can be certain. Our immediate purpose is to explain the facts. Human judgments and refusals to judge oscillate about a central mean. If the precise locus of that divide can hardly be defined, at least there are many points on which even the rash would not venture to pronounce and many others on which even the indecisive would not doubt. What, then, is the general form of such certitude of ignorance and such certitude of knowledge?

Our answer is in terms of the virtually unconditioned. There occurs a reflective insight in which at once one grasps (1) a conditioned, the prospective judgment that a given direct or introspective insight is correct, (2) a link between the conditioned and its conditions, and this on introspective analysis proves to be that an insight is correct if it is invulnerable and it is invulnerable if there are no further pertinent questions, and (3) the fulfilment of the conditions, namely, that the given insight does put an end to further pertinent questioning and that this occurs in a mind that is alert, familiar with the concrete situation, and intellectually master of it.

Related selections: 1.IV.2 on the first, experiential level of consciousness; 1.II.2 on the role played by images in the emergence of insight; 1.III.1–3 on scientific understanding; 1.IV.1 on the development of commonsense understanding; 1.XV.2 on the relation of judgment to arguments for God's existence.

Self-Affirmation of the Knower

Lonergan's preceding investigations of mathematical, natural scientific, and commonsense knowing have brought to light the three-level structure of cognitional process. Knowing, as it actually occurs in mathematics, natural science, and common sense, is an ordered set of related operations of experiencing, understanding, and judging. But Lonergan's aim in *Insight* is not merely to expose the nature of cognitional process in the variety of human endeavors, but to invite us to take possession of ourselves as knowers. Widespread neglect of the facts about human knowing has resulted in a confusion of complex human knowing with 'knowing' in the elementary sense as confrontation with the 'already out there now real.' This confusion of human knowing with elementary extroversion, Lonergan points out in his introduction to *Insight*, leads us to doubt that understanding correctly, which differs greatly from experiential confrontation, is knowing. In the presence of such doubt we may cling to the confrontational view, and then understanding correctly is regarded as irrelevant to knowing; or we may insist on the importance of understanding, acknowledge its radical difference from experiential confrontation, but retain an ideal of knowing as confrontation with the 'already out there now real,' and conclude that knowledge is unattainable.

In the present selection, taken from the pivotal Chapter 11 of *Insight*, Lonergan invites us to appeal to our own experience of experience, understanding, and judgment; to understand that experience; to ask ourselves the reflective question, Is it so?, about that understanding; and to grasp the sufficiency of the evidence for the judgment of fact, 'I am a knower.' With this affirmation, Lonergan argues, we take an essential step in the ongoing appropriation of ourselves as empirically, intelligently, and rationally conscious subjects. As he puts it in the introduction, we take possession of 'a fixed base, an invariant pattern, opening upon all further developments of understanding.' Or, as he puts it in the following selection, in coming to know ourselves as knowers we take possession of an 'unrevisable ground.' Every attempt to undermine, refute, or revise Lonergan's account of human knowing, if it is intelligent and reasonable, serves only to provide still more evidence for judging the account correct. Cognitional self-appropriation is appropriation of the 'unrevisable reviser.'

In subsequent chapters of *Insight*, this breakthrough to self-affirmation will be consolidated by explorations of its implications for accounts of objectivity, being, and truth. Further, the human subject is not just a knower but also an actor and doer in the field of human affairs. The invitation to cognitional self-appropriation in the first half of *Insight* will be broadened in the second half as the moving viewpoint of *Insight* expands. Eventually, Lonergan will invite us to appropriate ourselves as rationally self-conscious, as not only knowing but also as deliberating, deciding, and acting.

In the first five parts of this selection Lonergan exposes his notion of consciousness and then, in the personal style of a meditation, evokes the evidence for the judgment of self-affirmation. In the last three parts he argues that the knowledge achieved through cognitional analysis in self-affirmation surpasses the knowledge gained by empirical science. When we know our own knowing, we know something that, in a significant respect, is not subject to revision.

This extract is taken from *Insight*, 343–60.

It is time to turn from theory to practice. Judgment has been analyzed. Its grounds in reflective understanding have been explored. Clearly the next question is whether correct judgments occur, and the answer to it is the act of making one.

Since our study has been of cognitional process, the judgment we are best prepared to make is the self-affirmation of an instance of such a process as cognitional. By the 'self' is meant a concrete and intelligible unity–identity–whole. By 'self-affirmation' is meant that the self both affirms and is affirmed. By 'self-affirmation of the knower' is meant that the self as affirmed is characterized by such occurrences as sensing, perceiving, imagining, inquiring, understanding, formulating, reflecting, grasping the unconditioned, and affirming.

The affirmation to be made is a judgment of fact. It is not that I exist necessarily, but merely that in fact I do. It is not that I am of necessity a knower, but merely that in fact I am. It is not that an individual performing the listed acts really does know, but merely that I perform them and that by 'knowing' I mean no more than such performance.

As all judgment, self-affirmation rests upon a grasp of the unconditioned. The unconditioned is the combination of (1) a conditioned, (2) a link between the conditioned and its conditions, and (3) the fulfilment of the conditions. The relevant conditioned is the statement 'I am a knower.' The link between the conditioned and its conditions may be cast in the proposition 'I am a knower, if I am a concrete and intelligible unity-identity-whole, characterized by acts of sensing, perceiving, imagining, inquiring, understanding, formulating, reflecting, grasping the unconditioned, and judging.' The fulfilment of the conditions is given in consciousness.

The conditioned offers no difficulty. It is merely the expression of what is to be affirmed. Similarly, the link offers no difficulty; the link itself is a statement of meaning; and the conditions which it lists have become familiar in the course of this investigation. The problematic element, then, lies in the fulfilment of the conditions, and we proceed to indicate what is meant and not meant by consciousness and by the fulfilment of conditions.

1   The Notion of Consciousness

First, consciousness is not to be thought of as some sort of inward look. People are apt to think of knowing by imagining a man taking a look at something, and further, they are apt to think of consciousness by imagining themselves looking into themselves. Not merely do they indulge in such imaginative opinions but also they are likely to justify them by argument. Knowing, they will say, is knowing something; it is being confronted by an object; it is the strange, mysterious, irreducible presence of one thing to another. Hence, though knowing is not exclusively a matter of ocular vision, still it is radically that sort of thing. It is gazing, intuiting, contemplating. Whatever words you care to employ, consciousness is a knowing, and so it is some sort of inward looking.

Now, while consciousness is a factor in knowing, and while knowing is an activity to which a problem of objectivity is annexed, still it is one thing to give an account of the activity, and it is something else to tackle the problem of objectivity. For the present we are concerned simply with an account of the activity, and so we have defined the knower, not by saying that he knows something, but solely by saying that he performs certain kinds of acts. In like manner, we have not asked whether the knower knows himself; we ask solely whether he can perform the act of self-affirmation. Hence, while some of our readers may possess the rather remarkable power of looking into themselves and intuiting things quite clearly and distinctly, we shall not base our case upon their success. For after all, there may well exist other readers that, like the writer, find looking into themselves rather unrewarding.

Secondly, by consciousness we shall mean that there is an awareness immanent in cognitional acts. Already a distinction has been drawn between act and content: for instance, between seeing and color, hearing and sound, imagining and image, insight and idea. To affirm consciousness is to affirm that cognitional process is not merely a procession of contents but also a succession of acts. It is to affirm that the acts differ radically from such unconscious acts as the metabolism of one's cells, the maintenance of one's organs, the multitudinous biological processes that one learns about through the study of contemporary medical science. Both kinds of acts occur, but the biological occur outside consciousness, and the cognitional occur within consciousness. Seeing is not merely a response to the stimulus of color and shape; it is a response that consists in becoming aware of color and shape. Hearing is not merely a response to the stimulus of sound; it is a response that consists in becoming aware of sound. As color differs from sound, so seeing differs from hearing. Still seeing and hearing have a common feature, for in both occurrences there is not merely content but also conscious act.

By the conscious act is not meant a deliberate act; we are conscious of acts without debating whether we will perform them. By the conscious act is not meant an act to which one attends; consciousness can be heightened by shifting attention from the content to the act, but consciousness is not constituted by that shift of attention, for it is a quality immanent in acts of certain kinds, and without it the acts would be as unconscious as the growth of one's beard. By the conscious act is not meant that the act is somehow isolated for inspection, nor that one grasps its function in cognitional process, nor that one can assign it a name, nor that one can distinguish it from other acts, nor that one is certain of its occurrence.

Does, then, 'conscious act' mean no more than 'cognitional act'? A distinction has to be drawn. First, I do not think that only cognitional acts are conscious. Secondly, there are those that would define 'seeing' as 'awareness of color' and then proceed to argue that in seeing one was aware of color but of nothing else whatever, that 'awareness of color' occurs but that a concomitant 'awareness of awareness' is a fiction. This, I think, does not accurately reflect the facts. If seeing is an awareness of nothing but color and hearing is an awareness of nothing but sound, why are both named 'awareness'? Is it because there is some similarity between color and sound? Or is it that color and sound are disparate, yet with respect to both there are acts that are similar? In the latter case, what is the similarity? Is it that both acts are occurrences, as metabolism is an occurrence? Or is it that both acts are conscious? One may quarrel with the phrase 'awareness of awareness,' particularly if one imagines awareness to be a looking and finds it preposterous to talk about looking at a look. But one cannot deny that, within the cognitional act as it occurs, there is a factor or element or component over and above its content, and that this factor is what differentiates cognitional acts from unconscious occurrences.

2   Empirical, Intelligent, and Rational Consciousness

By consciousness is meant an awareness immanent in cognitional acts. But such acts differ in kind, and so the awareness differs in kind with the acts. There is an empirical consciousness characteristic of sensing, perceiving, imagining. As the content of these acts is merely presented or represented, so the awareness immanent in the acts is the mere givenness of the acts. But there is an intelligent consciousness characteristic of inquiry, insight, and formulation. On this level cognitional process not merely strives for and reaches the intelligible, but in doing so it exhibits its intelligence; it operates intelligently. The awareness is present but it is the awareness of intelligence, of what strives to understand, of what is satisfied by understanding, of what formulates the understood, not as a schoolboy repeating by rote a definition, but as one that defines because he grasps why that definition hits things off. Finally, on the third level of reflection, grasp of the unconditioned, and judgment, there is rational consciousness. It is the emergence and the effective operation of a single law of utmost generality, the law of sufficient reason, where the sufficient reason is the unconditioned. It emerges as a demand for the unconditioned and a refusal to assent unreservedly on any lesser ground. It advances to grasp of the uncon-

ditioned. It terminates in the rational compulsion by which grasp of
the unconditioned commands assent.

Empirical consciousness needs, perhaps, no further comment, for by
it we illustrated the difference between conscious and unconscious
acts. Intelligent and rational consciousness, on the other hand, may be
clarified by a contrast. In their different manners both common sense
and positive science view the material world as subject to intelligible
patterns and as governed by some law of causality. To confine our
attention to what man knows best, namely, his own artifacts, there is
discernible in them an intelligible design, and their existence has its
ground in the labor of production. But before the design is realized in
things, it was invented by intelligence; before the sequence of productive operations was undertaken, it was affirmed as worth while for
some sufficient or apparently sufficient reason. In the thing there is the
intelligible design, but in the inventor there was not only the intelligibility on the side of the object but also intelligent consciousness on the
side of the subject. In the thing there is the groundedness that consists
in its existence being accounted for by a sequence of operations, but in
the entrepreneur there was not only the groundedness of his judgment
in the reasons that led to it but also the rational consciousness that
required reasons to reach judgment.

Intelligence and intelligibility are the obverse and reverse of the second level of knowing: intelligence looks for intelligible patterns in presentations and representations; it grasps such patterns in its moments of
insight; it exploits such grasp in its formulations and in further operations equally guided by insights. In like manner, reasonableness and
groundedness are the obverse and reverse of the third level of knowing.
Reasonableness is reflection inasmuch as it seeks groundedness for
objects of thought; reasonableness discovers groundedness in its reflective grasp of the unconditioned; reasonableness exploits groundedness
when it affirms objects because they are grounded. In man's artifacts
there are the reverse elements of the intelligibility and groundedness,
but there are not the obverse elements of intelligence and reasonableness. The obverse elements pertain to cognitional process on its second
and third levels; they do not pertain to the contents emergent on those
levels, to the idea or concept, to the unconditioned or affirmed; on the
contrary, they characterize the acts with which those contents are coupled, and so they are specific differentiations of the awareness of
consciousness. Clear and distinct conception not only reveals the

intelligibility of the object but also manifests the intelligence of the subject. Exact and balanced judgment not only affirms things as they are but also testifies to the dominance of reasonableness in the subject.

Still, it may be asked, 'Am I really conscious of intelligence and reasonableness?' The question, I think, is misleading. It suggests that there is a type of knowing in which intelligence and reasonableness come up for inspection. But what is asserted is not that you can uncover intelligence by introspection, as you can point to Calcutta on a map. The assertion is that you have conscious states and conscious acts that are intelligent and reasonable. Intelligent and rational consciousness denote characters of cognitional process, and the characters they denote pertain not to the contents but to the proceeding. It is repugnant to me to place astrology and astronomy, alchemy and chemistry, legend and history, hypothesis and fact, on exactly the same footing. I am not content with theories, however brilliantly coherent, but insist on raising the further question, Are they true? What is that repugnance, that discontent, that insistence? They are just so many variations on the more basic expression that I am rationally conscious, that I demand sufficient reason, that I find it in the unconditioned, that I assent unreservedly to nothing less, that such demanding, finding, self-committing occur, not like the growth of my hair, but within a field of consciousness or awareness.

Again, if at moments I can slip into a lotus land in which mere presentations and representations are juxtaposed or successive, still that is not my normal state. The Humean world of mere impressions comes to me as a puzzle to be pieced together. I want to understand, to grasp intelligible unities and relations, to know what's up and where I stand. Praise of the scientific spirit that inquires, that masters, that controls, is not without an echo, a deep resonance within me, for in my more modest way I too inquire and catch on, see the thing to do and see that it is properly done. But what are these but variations on the more basic expression that I am intelligently conscious, that the awareness characteristic of cognitional acts on the second level is an active contributing to the intelligibility of its products? When I listen to the story of Archimedes and when I read the recital of a mystical experience, there is a marked difference. What a mystic experiences I do not know. But though I never enjoyed so remarkable an insight as Archimedes, still I do know what it is to miss the point and to get the point, not to have a clue and then to catch on, to see things in a new light, to grasp how they hang together, to come to know why, the reason, the explanation, the cause. After Archimedes shouted, 'I've got it,' he might well be puzzled by the question whether he was conscious of an insight. Still, there can be no doubt that he was conscious of an increment of knowledge, an increment that he had wanted very much. Did he want the king's favor? Did he want to enhance his reputation? Perhaps, but at a deeper and more spontaneous level, he wanted to know how to do something; he wanted to solve a problem; he wanted to understand; his consciousness was on the second level where it seeks the intelligible and follows up partial insights with further questions until there comes the final crowning insight that ends questioning and satisfies intelligent consciousness.

3   The Unity of Consciousness

In the fourth place, there are unities of consciousness. Besides cognitional contents there are cognitional acts; different kinds of acts have different kinds of awareness: empirical, intelligent, rational. But the contents cumulate into unities: what is perceived is what is inquired about; what is inquired about is what is understood; what is understood is what is formulated; what is formulated is what is reflected on; what is reflected on is what is grasped as unconditioned; what is grasped as unconditioned is what is affirmed. Now just as there are unities on the side of the object, so there are unities on the side of the subject. Conscious acts are not so many isolated, random atoms of knowing, but many acts coalesce into a single knowing. Not only is there a similarity between my seeing and your hearing, inasmuch as both acts are conscious; there also is an identity involved when my seeing and my hearing or your seeing and your hearing are compared. Moreover, this identity extends all along the line. Not only is the percept inquired about, understood, formulated, reflected on, grasped as unconditioned, and affirmed, but also there is an identity involved in perceiving, inquiring, understanding, formulating, reflecting, grasping the unconditioned, and affirming. Indeed, consciousness is much more obviously of this unity in diverse acts than of the diverse acts, for it is within the unity that the acts are found and distinguished, and it is to the unity that we appeal when we talk about a single field of consciousness and draw a distinction between conscious acts occurring within the field and unconscious acts occurring outside it.

One might go further and argue that, were the unity of consciousness not given, then it would have to be postulated. For many contents on diverse levels cumulate into a single known. But how can that occur? How can images be derived from sensations? How can inquiry be about percepts? How can insight be into images? How can definition draw upon both images and the ideas grasped in insight? How can reflecting be about formulations? How can the grasp of the unconditioned be obtained by combining the conditioned that is thought and the fulfilment that is sensed? How can each judgment emerge in a context of other judgments that determine its meaning, complement it, qualify it, defend it, so that it is but a single increment within a far vaster knowing? I cannot inquire into your experience or reflect on your thoughts. But if there were no 'I,' how could there be a 'my experience' with respect to which a 'my inquiry' occurred, or 'my thoughts' with respect to which 'my reflection' occurred? If there were not one consciousness, at once empirical, intelligent, and rational, how could rational judgment proceed from an unconditioned grasped in the combination of thought and sensible experience?

4   The Unity as Given

Still, if the unity of consciousness would have to be postulated on the hypothesis that it were not given, it remains that it is given. By this, of course, I do not mean that it is the object of some inward look. What is meant is that a single agent is involved in many acts, that it is an abstraction to speak of the acts as conscious, that, concretely, consciousness pertains to the acting agent. Seeing and hearing differ inasmuch as one is an awareness of color and the other an awareness of sound. Seeing and hearing are similar inasmuch as each is an awareness. But the similarity between my seeing and your hearing is an abstract indication of consciousness, which, as it is given, is primarily an identity uniting my seeing and my hearing or your seeing and your hearing.

We have been engaged in determining what precisely is meant by consciousness. We have contended that it is not some inward look but a quality of cognitional acts, a quality that differs on the different levels of cognitional process, a quality that concretely is the identity immanent in the diversity and the multiplicity of the process. However, one cannot insist too strongly that such an account of consciousness is not itself consciousness. The account supposes consciousness as its data for inquiry, for insight, for formulation, for reflection, for grasp of the unconditioned, for judgment. But giving the account is the formulating and the judging, while the account itself is what is formulated and affirmed. Consciousness as given is neither formulated nor affirmed. Consciousness is given independently of its being formulated or affirmed. To formulate it does not make one more conscious, for the effect of formulation is to add to one's concepts. To affirm it does not make one more conscious, for the effect of affirmation is to add to one's judgments. Finally, as consciousness is not increased by affirming it, so it is not diminished by denying it, for the effect of denying it is to add to the list of one's judgments and not to subtract from the grounds on which judgments may be based.

This remark brings us to our second topic. We proposed to say what was meant and not meant by consciousness. We also proposed to say what was meant and not meant by the experiential fulfilment of conditions for the affirmation of the conditioned. By such experiential fulfilment, then, one does not mean the conditioned, nor the link between the conditioned and its conditions, nor the conditions as formulated, let alone as affirmed. One does mean that the conditions which are formulated also are to be found in a more rudimentary state within cognitional process. Just as inquiry brings about the advance from the perceived and not understood to the perceived and understood, so there is a reverse shift by which one moves from the perceived and understood to the merely perceived. It is this reverse shift that commonly is meant by verification. If from a more general theory I obtain the formula $PV = 64$, then I can infer that when P is 2, 4, 8, 16, 32, V will have theoretically the values 32, 16, 8, 4, 2. By setting up suitable apparatus and securing appropriate conditions defined by the theory, I can advance from theoretical inference to an experimental check. The results of the experiment may be expressed in a series of propositions, such as the statement that, when P was approximately 2, V was approximately 32; but such a series of statements, however accurate, is not what was given by the experiment. The statements represent judgments of fact; the judgments rest on grasping the unconditioned; the grasp rests on formulations and visual experiences. The experiment gives neither statements nor judgments nor reflective understanding nor formulations but only visual experiences. The experiment gives not visual experiences as described but visual experiences on the level of merely seeing. That P is 2 when the needle on a dial stands at a certain place is a judgment. That V is 32 when certain dimensions of an object coincide with certain dimensions of a measuring rod is another judgment. All that is seen is the needle in a position on the dial or the dimensions of an object standing in coincidence with numbered units on a rod. Nor is it this description that is seen, but only what is so described. In brief, verification is an appropriate pattern of acts of checking; acts of checking are reversals from formulations of what would be perceived to the corresponding but more rudimentary cognitional contents of acts of perceiving or sensing. In the formulation there always are elements derived from inquiry, insight, conceiving. But in virtue of the checking one can say that the formulation is not pure theory, that it is not merely supposed or merely postulated or merely inferred, that its sensible component is given.

Now just as there is reversal to what is given sensibly, so there is reversal to what is given consciously. Just as the former reversal is away from the understood as understood, the formulated as formulated, the affirmed as affirmed, and to the merely sensed, so also the latter reversal is from the understood, formulated, affirmed as such, to the merely given. Hence in the self-affirmation of the knower the conditioned is the statement 'I am a knower.' The link between the conditioned and its conditions is cast in the proposition 'I am a knower if I am a unity performing certain kinds of acts.' The conditions as formulated are the unity-identity-whole to be grasped in data as individual and the kinds of acts to be grasped in data as similar. But the fulfilment of the conditions in consciousness is to be had by reverting from such formulations to the more rudimentary state of the formulated, where there is no formulation but merely experience.

5   Self-Affirmation

From preliminary clarifications, we turn to the issue. 'Am I a knower?' Each has to ask the question of himself. But anyone who asks it is rationally conscious. For the question is a question for reflection, a question to be met with a yes or no; and asking the question does not mean repeating the words but entering the dynamic state in which dissatisfaction with mere theory manifests itself in a demand for fact, for what is so. Further, the question is not any question. If I ask it, I know what it means. What do I mean by 'I'? The answer is difficult to formulate, but strangely, in some obscure fashion, I know very well what it means without formulation, and by that obscure yet familiar awareness, I find fault with various formulations of what is meant by 'I.' In other words, 'I' has a rudimentary meaning from consciousness, and it envisages neither the multiplicity nor the diversity of contents and conscious acts but rather the unity that goes along with them. But if 'I' has some such rudimentary meaning from consciousness, then consciousness supplies the fulfilment of one element in the conditions for affirming that I am a knower. Does consciousness supply the fulfilment for the other conditions? Do I see, or am I blind? Do I hear, or am I deaf? Do I try to understand, or is the distinction between intelligence and stupidity no more applicable to me than to a stone? Have I any experience of insight, or is the story of Archimedes as strange to me as the account of Plotinus's vision of the One? Do I conceive, think, consider, suppose, define, formulate, or is my talking like the talking of a parrot? I reflect, for I ask whether I am a knower. Do I grasp the unconditioned, if not in other instances, then in this one? If I grasped the unconditioned, would I not be under the rational compulsion of affirming that I am a knower, and so either affirm it or else find some loophole, some weakness, some incoherence, in this account of the genesis of self-affirmation? As each has to ask these questions of himself, so too he has to answer them for himself. But the fact of the asking and the possibility of the answering are themselves the sufficient reason for the affirmative answer.

6   Self-Affirmation as Immanent Law

The foregoing account of self-affirmation stresses its positive aspect. It is a judgment of fact, and so it rests heavily upon the experiential component in knowing. Still, it is a singular type of judgment for it possesses a variety of overtones. I might not be, yet if I am, I am. I might be other than I am, yet in fact I am what I am. The contingent, if you suppose it as a fact, becomes conditionally necessary, and this piece of elementary logic places the merely factual self-affirmation in a context of necessity.

Am I a knower? The answer yes is coherent, for if I am a knower, I can know that fact. But the answer no is incoherent, for if I am not a knower, how could the question be raised and answered by me? No less, the hedging answer 'I do not know' is incoherent. For if I know that I do not know, then I am a knower; and if I do not know that I do not know, then I should not answer.

Am I a knower? If I am not, then I know nothing. My only course is silence. My only course is not the excused and explained silence of the sceptic, but the complete silence of the animal that offers neither excuse nor explanation for its complacent absorption in merely sensitive routines. For if I know nothing, I do not know excuses for not knowing. If I know nothing, then I cannot know the explanation of my ignorance.

It is this conditional necessity of contingent fact that involves the talking sceptic in contradiction. If enthusiasm for the achievement of Freud were to lead me to affirm that all thought and affirmation is just a byproduct of the libido, then since I have admitted no exceptions, this very assertion of mine would have to be mere assertion from a suspect source. If second thoughts lead me to acknowledge an exception, they lead me to acknowledge the necessary presuppositions of the exception. By the time that list has been drawn up and accepted, I am no longer a sceptic.

Still, the Aristotelian prescription of getting the sceptic to talk derives its efficacy not only from the conditional necessity of contingent fact but also from the nature, the natural spontaneities and natural inevitabilities, that go with that fact. Why is it that the talking sceptic does not talk gibberish? Why is it that one can count on his being nonplussed by self-contradiction? It is because he is conscious, empirically, intelligently, and rationally. It is because he has no choice in the matter. It is because extreme ingenuity is needed for him not to betray his real nature. It is because, were his ingenuity successful, the only result would be that he had revealed himself an idiot and lost all claim to be heard.

This aspect of the matter deserves further attention. Cognitional process does not lie outside the realm of natural law. Not merely do I possess the power to elicit certain types of acts when certain conditions are fulfilled, but also with statistical regularity the conditions are fulfilled and the acts occur. I cannot escape sensations, percepts, images. All three keep occurring during my waking hours, and the images often continue during my sleep. No doubt, I can exercise a selective control over what I sense, perceive, imagine. But the choice I cannot make effective is to sense nothing, perceive nothing, imagine nothing. Not only are the contents of these acts imposed upon me, but also consciousness in some degree is inseparable from the acts. Nor is that consciousness merely an aggregate of isolated atoms; it is a unity.

If I cannot escape presentations and representations, neither can I be content with them. Spontaneously I fall victim to the wonder that Aristotle named the beginning of all science and philosophy. I try to understand. I enter, without questioning, the dynamic state that is revealed in questions for intelligence. Theoretically there is a disjunction between 'being intelligent' and 'not being intelligent.' But the theoretical disjunction is not a practical choice for me. I can deprecate intelligence; I can ridicule its aspirations; I can reduce its use to a minimum; but it does not follow that I can eliminate it. I can question everything else, but to question questioning is self-destructive. I might call upon intelligence for the conception of a plan to escape intelligence, but the effort to escape would only reveal my present involvement, and strangely enough, I would want to go about the business intelligently, and I would want to claim that escaping was the intelligent thing to do.

As I cannot be content with the cinematographic flow of presentations and representations, so I cannot be content with inquiry, understanding, and formulation. I may say I want not the quarry but the chase, but I am careful to restrict my chasing to fields where the quarry lies. If, above all, I want to understand, still I want to understand the facts. Inevitably, the achievement of understanding, however stupendous, only gives rise to the further question, Is it so? Inevitably, the progress of understanding is interrupted by the check of judgment. Intelligence may be a thoroughbred exulting in the race; but there is a rider on its back; and without the rider the best of horses is a poor bet. The insistence that modern science envisages an indefinite future of repeated revisions does not imply an indifference to fact. On the contrary, it is fact that will force the revisions, that will toss into the wastebasket the brilliant theories of previous understanding, that will make each new theory better because it is closer to the facts. But what is fact? What is that clear, precise, definitive, irrevocable, dominant something that we name fact? The question is too large to be settled here. Each philosophy has its own view on what fact is and its consequent theory on the precise nature of our knowledge of fact. All that can be attempted now is to state what we happen to mean by knowing fact.

Clearly, then, fact is concrete as is sense or consciousness. Again, fact is intelligible: if it is independent of all doubtful theory, it is not independent of the modest insight and formulation necessary to give it its precision and its accuracy. Finally, fact is virtually unconditioned: it might not have been; it might have been other than it is; but as things stand, it possesses conditional necessity, and nothing can possibly alter it now. Fact, then, combines the concreteness of experience, the determinateness of accurate intelligence, and the absoluteness of rational judgment. It is the natural objective of human cognitional process. It is the anticipated unity to which sensation, perception, imagination, inquiry, insight, formulation, reflection, grasp of the unconditioned, and judgment make their several, complementary contributions. When Newton knew that the water in his bucket was rotating, he knew a fact, though he thought that he knew absolute space. When quantum mechanics and relativity posit the unimaginable in a four-dimensional manifold, they bring to light the not too surprising fact that scientific intelligence and verifying judgment go beyond the realm of imagination to the realm of fact. Just what that realm is, as has been said, is a difficult and complicated problem. Our present concern is that we are committed to it. We are committed, not by knowing what it is and that it is worth while, but by an inability to avoid experience, by the subtle conquest in us of the eros that would understand, by the inevitable aftermath of that sweet adventure when a rationality identical with us demands the absolute, refuses unreserved assent to less than the unconditioned, and when that is attained, imposes upon us a commitment in which we bow to an immanent Anankê.

Confronted with the standard of the unconditioned, the sceptic despairs. Set before it, the products of human understanding are ashamed. Great are the achievements of modern science; by far are they to be preferred to earlier guesswork; yet rational consciousness finds that they approximate indeed to the unconditioned but do not attain it; and so it assigns them the modest status of probability. Still, if rational consciousness can criticize the achievement of science, it cannot criticize itself. The critical spirit can weigh all else in the balance, only on condition that it does not criticize itself. It is a self-assertive spontaneity that demands sufficient reason for all else but offers no justification for its demanding. It arises, fact-like, to generate knowledge of fact, to push the cognitional process from the conditioned structures of intelligence to unreserved affirmation of the unconditioned. It occurs. It will recur whenever the conditions for reflection are fulfilled. With statistical regularity those conditions keep being fulfilled. Nor is that all, for I am involved, engaged, committed. The disjunction between rationality and nonrationality is an abstract alternative but not a concrete choice. Rationality is my very dignity, and so closely to it do I cling that I would want the best of reasons for abandoning it. Indeed, I am so much one with my reasonableness that, when I lapse from its high standards, I am compelled either to repent my folly or to rationalize it.

Self-affirmation has been considered as a concrete judgment of fact. The contradiction of self-negation has been indicated. Behind that contradiction there have been discerned natural inevitabilities and spontaneities that constitute the possibility of knowing, not by demonstrating that one can know, but pragmatically by engaging one in the process. Nor in the last resort can one reach a deeper foundation than that pragmatic engagement. Even to seek it involves a vicious circle; for if one seeks such a foundation, one employs one's cognitional process; and the foundation to be reached will be no more secure or solid than the inquiry utilized to reach it. As I might not be, as I might be other than I am, so my knowing might not be and it might be other than it is. The ultimate basis of our knowing is not necessity but contingent fact, and the fact is established, not prior to our engagement in knowing, but simultaneously with it. The sceptic, then, is not involved in a conflict with absolute necessity. He might not be; he might not be a knower. Contradiction arises when he utilizes cognitional process to deny it.

7   Description and Explanation

There is a further aspect to the matter. Is the self-affirmation that has been outlined descriptive of the thing-for-us or explanatory of the thing-itself? We have spoken of natural inevitabilities and spontaneities. But did we speak of these as they are themselves or as they are for us?

Unfortunately, there is a prior question. The distinction that was drawn earlier between description and explanation was couched in terms that sufficed to cover the difference in the fields of positive science. But human science contains an element not to be found in other departments. Both the study of man and the study of nature begin from inquiry and insight into sensible data. Both the study of man and the study of nature can advance from the descriptive relations of the object to the inquirer, to the explanatory relations that obtain immediately between objects. Just as the physicist measures, correlates measurements, and implicitly defines correlatives by the correlations, so too the student of human nature can forsake the literary approach, to determine economic, political, sociological, cultural, historical correlations. But the study of man also enjoys through consciousness an immediate access to man, and this access can be used in two manners.

The initial use is descriptive. In this fashion we began from an account of an event named insight. We pointed out that it was satisfying, that it came unexpectedly, that its emergence was conditioned more by a dynamic inner state of inquiry than by external circumstance, that while the first emergence was difficult, repeated occurrence was easy and spontaneous, that single acts of insight accumulate into clusters bearing on a single topic, that such clusters may remain without exact formulation, or may be worked out into a systematic doctrine. Naturally enough, this general description of insight was presupposed and utilized when we came to examine it more closely; and this closer examination was in turn presupposed in our account of explanatory abstraction and explanatory system and in our study of empirical method. Moreover, since data, percepts, and images are prior to inquiry, insight, and formulation, and since all definition is subsequent to inquiry and insight, it was necessary to define data, percepts, and images as the materials presupposed and complemented by inquiry and insight, and further, it was necessary to distinguish between them by contrasting the formulations of empirical science with those of mathematics and the formulations of both of these with the formulations of common sense. Finally, the analysis of judgment and the account of reflective understanding consisted in relating these acts to each other, and to the formulations of understanding, and to the fulfilment provided by experience.

As the reader will discern, the initial procedure of description gradually yielded to definition by relation; and the defining relations obtained immediately between different kinds of cognitional state or act. But definition by this type of relation is explanatory, and so descriptive procedure was superseded by explanatory.

There are, then, two types of description and two types of explanation. If the inquirer starts from the data of sense, he begins by describing but goes on to explain. Again, if he starts from the data of consciousness, he begins by describing and goes on to explain. Still, there is an important difference between the two types of explaining.

For explanation on the basis of sense can reduce the element of hypothesis to a minimum but it cannot eliminate it entirely. But explanation on the basis of consciousness can escape entirely the merely supposed, the merely postulated, the merely inferred.

First, explanation on the basis of sense can reduce hypothesis to a minimum. This, of course, is the point of the principle of relevance. Galileo's law of falling bodies does not merely suppose or postulate distance or time or the measurements of either. It does not merely suppose or postulate the correlation between distance and time; for there is some relation between the two inasmuch as a falling body falls farther in a longer time; and the actual measurements ground a numerical determination of that relation. Moreover, what holds for the law of falling bodies holds for the other laws of mechanics. If one pleases, one may contend that the use of inquiry, insight, formulation, and consequent generalization is mere supposition or mere postulation; but at least it is not the type of mere supposition that the empirical scientist systematically avoids or that he seriously fears will be eliminated in some more intelligent method of inquiry to be devised and accepted in the future. To reach the element of mere supposition that makes any system of mechanics subject to future revision, one must shift attention from single laws to the set of primitive terms and relations which the system employs in formulating all its laws. In other words, one has to distinguish between, say, mass as defined by correlations between masses and, on the other hand, mass as enjoying the position of an ultimate mechanical concept. Any future system of mechanics will have to satisfy the data that now are covered by the notion of mass. But it is not necessary that every future system of mechanics will have to satisfy the same data by employing our concept of mass. Further developments might lead to the introduction of a different set of ultimate concepts, to a consequent reformulation of all laws, and so to a dethronement of the notion of mass from its present position as an ultimate of mechanical system. Hence, while empirical method can reduce the hypothetical to a minimum, it cannot eliminate it entirely. Its concepts as concepts are not hypothetical, for they are defined implicitly by empirically established correlations. Nonetheless, its concepts as systematically significant, as ultimate or derived, as preferred to other concepts that might be empirically reached, do involve an element of mere supposition. For the selection of certain concepts as ultimate occurs in the work of systematization, and that work is provisional. At any time a system is accepted because it provides the simplest account of all the known facts. But at the same time it is acknowledged that there may be unknown yet relevant facts, that they might give rise to further questions that would lead to further insights, and that the further insights might involve a radical revision of the accepted system.

Secondly, explanation on the basis of consciousness can escape this limitation. I do not mean, of course, that such explanation is not to be reached through the series of revisions involved in the self-correcting process of learning. Nor do I mean that, once explanation is reached, there remains no possibility of the minor revisions that leave basic lines intact but attain a greater exactitude and a greater fulness of detail. Again, I am not contending here and now that human nature and so human knowledge are immutable, that there could not arise a new nature and a new knowledge to which present theory would not be applicable. What is excluded is the radical revision that involves a shift in the fundamental terms and relations of the explanatory account of the human knowledge underlying existing common sense, mathematics and empirical science.

8   The Impossibility of Revision

The impossibility of such revision appears from the very notion of revision. A revision appeals to data. It contends that previous theory does not satisfactorily account for all the data. It claims to have reached complementary insights that lead to more accurate statements. It shows that these new statements either are unconditioned or more closely approximate to the unconditioned than previous statements. Now, if in fact revision is as described, then it presupposes that cognitional process falls on the three levels of presentation, intelligence, and reflection; it presupposes that insights are cumulative and complementary; it presupposes that they head towards a limit described by the adjective 'satisfactory'; it presupposes a reflective grasp of the unconditioned or of what approximates to the unconditioned. Clearly, revision cannot revise its own presuppositions. A reviser cannot appeal to data to deny data, to his new insights to deny insights, to his new formulation to deny formulation, to his reflective grasp to deny reflective grasp.

The same point may be put in another manner. Popular relativism is prone to argue that empirical science is the most reliable form of human knowledge; but empirical science is subject to indefinite revision; therefore, all human knowledge is equally subject to indefinite revision. Now such argument is necessarily fallacious. One must definitively know invariant features of human knowledge before one can assert that empirical science is subject to indefinite revision; and if one definitively knows invariant features of human knowledge, then one knows what is not subject to revision. Moreover, as is obvious, such knowledge surpasses empirical science at least in the respect that it is not subject to revision.

Related selections: 1.I and 1.VII for especially pertinent background to Lonergan's treatment of self-affirmation; 3.I on transcendental method; 4.VII on degrees of self-transcendence; 1.XVII on self-appropriation.

IX

The Notion of Being

The three-level process of human knowing unfolds, Lonergan has argued, as we ask and answer questions for intelligence and for reflection, as we seek insights into our experience and, beyond that, seek to grasp the sufficiency of the evidence for judgment on the correctness of our insights. But these questions, Lonergan holds, are expressions and formulations of a primordial wonder motivating all mathematical, scientific, and commonsense pursuits of knowledge. That primordial wonder, prior to and giving rise to all our questions, is also the source of our notion of being. If we know, what we know is being; when we wish to know, what we wish to know is being.

In the present selection from Chapter 12 of *Insight* Lonergan provides a definition of being. The definition offered is a second-order definition. A first-order definition would be the complete set of answers to the complete set of questions, the formulation in concepts of a knowledge of everything about everything. Because we do not know everything about everything, the definition of being must be of the second order: Being is the objective of the pure desire to know. Lonergan proceeds, then, to analyze the pure desire to know, our dynamic orientation towards being, in order to shed light on the notion of being at work in all human inquiries and investigations. In the course of the analysis Lonergan gives the term 'notion' a precise, technical meaning. A notion is an intelligent and reasonable desire. The pure desire to know, Lonergan argues, is an unrestricted, spontaneous, all-pervasive notion of being, and the core of meaning.

This extract is taken from *Insight*, 372–83.

1   A Definition

Being, then, is the objective of the pure desire to know.

By the desire to know is meant the dynamic orientation manifested in questions for intelligence and for reflection. It is not the verbal utterance of questions. It is not the conceptual formulation of questions. It is not any insight or thought. It is not any reflective grasp or judgment. It is the prior and enveloping drive that carries cognitional process from sense and imagination to understanding, from understanding to judgment, from judgment to the complete context of correct judgments that is named knowledge. The desire to know, then, is simply the inquiring and critical spirit of man. By moving him to seek understanding, it prevents him from being content with the mere flow of outer and inner experience. By demanding adequate understanding, it involves man in the self-correcting process of learning in which further questions yield complementary insights. By moving man to reflect, to seek the unconditioned, to grant unqualified assent only to the unconditioned, it prevents him from being content with hearsay and legend, with unverified hypotheses and untested theories. Finally, by raising still further questions for intelligence and reflection, it excludes complacent inertia; for if the questions go unanswered, man cannot be complacent; and if answers are sought, man is not inert.

Because it differs radically from other desire, this desire has been named pure. It is to be known, not by the misleading analogy of other desire, but by giving free rein to intelligent and rational consciousness. It is, indeed, impalpable, but also it is powerful. It pulls man out of the solid routine of perception and conation, instinct and habit, doing and enjoying. It holds him with the fascination of problems. It engages him in the quest of solutions. It makes him aloof to what is not established. It compels assent to the unconditioned. It is the cool shrewdness of common sense, the disinterestedness of science, the detachment of philosophy. It is the absorption of investigation, the joy of discovery, the assurance of judgment, the modesty of limited knowledge. It is the relentless serenity, the unhurried determination, the imperturbable drive of question following appositely on question in the genesis of truth.

This pure desire has an objective. It is a desire to know. As mere desire, it is for the satisfaction of acts of knowing, for the satisfaction of understanding, of understanding fully, of understanding correctly. But as pure desire, as cool, disinterested, detached, it is not for cognitional acts and the satisfaction they give their subject, but for cognitional contents, for what is to be known. The satisfaction of mistaken understanding, provided one does not know it as mistaken, can equal the satisfaction of correct understanding. Yet the pure desire scorns the former and prizes the latter; it prizes it, then, as dissimilar to the former; it prizes it not because it yields satisfaction but because its content is correct.

The objective of the pure desire is the content of knowing rather than the act. Still, the desire is not itself a knowing, and so its range is not the same as the range of knowing. Initially in each individual, the pure desire is a dynamic orientation to a totally unknown. As knowledge develops, the objective becomes less and less unknown, more and more known. At any time the objective includes both all that is known and all that remains unknown, for it is the goal of the immanent dynamism of cognitional process, and that dynamism both underlies actual attainment and heads beyond it with ever further questions.

What is this objective? Is it limited or unlimited? Is it one or many? Is it material or ideal? Is it phenomenal or real? Is it an immanent content or a transcendent object? Is it a realm of experience, or of thought, or of essences, or of existents? Answers to these and to any other questions have but a single source. They cannot be had without the functioning of the pure desire. They cannot be had from the pure desire alone. They are to be had inasmuch as the pure desire initiates and sustains cognitional process. Thus, if it is true that A is, that A is one, and that there is only A, then the objective of the pure desire is one. But if it is true that A is, that B is, that A is not B, then the objective is many. Which, you ask, is true? The fact that you ask, results from the pure desire. But to reach the answer, desiring is not enough; answers come only from inquiring and reflecting.

Now our definition was that being is the objective of the pure desire to know. Being, then, is (1) all that is known, and (2) all that remains to be known. Again, since a complete increment of knowing occurs only in judgment, being is what is to be known by the totality of true judgments. What, one may ask, is that totality? It is the complete set of answers to the complete set of questions. What the answers are remains to be seen. What the questions are awaits their emergence. Meaningless or incoherent or illegitimate questions may be possible, but how they are to be defined is a further question. The affirmation in hand is that there exists a pure desire to know, an inquiring and critical spirit, that follows up questions with further questions, that heads for some objective which has been named being.

Our definition of being, then, is of the second order. Other definitions determine what is meant. But this definition is more remote for it assigns, not what is meant by being, but how that meaning is to be determined. It asserts that if you know, then you know being; it asserts that if you wish to know, then you wish to know being; but it does not settle whether you know or what you know, whether your wish will be fulfilled or what you will know when it is fulfilled.

Still, though our definition is of the second order, it is not simply indeterminate. For neither the desire to know nor knowing itself is indeterminate. Inasmuch as knowing is determinate, we could say that being is what is to be known by true judgments. Inasmuch as the desire to know ever goes beyond actual knowledge, we could say that being is what is to be known by the totality of true judgments. Hence being has at least one characteristic: it is all-inclusive. Apart from being there is nothing. Again, being is completely concrete and completely universal. It is completely concrete: over and above the being of any thing, there is nothing more of that thing. It is completely universal: apart from the realm of being, there is simply nothing.

2 An Unrestricted Notion

One may wonder just how all-inclusive being is. That wonder may be formulated in a variety of manners. But no matter how it is formulated, no matter whether it can be formulated, it can serve only to show how all-inclusive being is. For the wonder is inquiry. It is the desire to know. Anything it can discover or invent, by that very fact is included in the notion of being. Hence the effort to establish that being is not all-inclusive must be self-defeating; for at the root of all that can be affirmed, at the root of all that can be conceived, is the pure desire to know; and it is the pure desire, underlying all judgment and formulation, underlying all questioning and all desire to question, that defines its all-inclusive objective.

Nonetheless, it may not be amiss to illustrate this principle concretely. It will be said that there is much we do not know. No doubt, our ignorance is great, but we know that fact by raising questions that we do not answer; and being is defined not only by the answers we give but also by the questions we ask. Next, it will be said that there is much it would be futile for us to try to learn. No doubt, the proximately fruitful field of inquiry is restricted. But we know that fact by distinguishing between the questions we can hope soon to answer and those that as yet we are not prepared to tackle; and being is defined, not only by the questions we can hope to answer, but also by the questions whose answer we have to postpone.

Thirdly, it will be objected by many that they have no desire to know everything about everything. But how do they know that they do not already know everything about everything? It is because so many questions can be asked. Why do they not effectively will to know everything about everything? Because it is so troublesome to reach even a few answers that they are completely disheartened by the prospect of answering all the questions they could ask.

The attack may be made from the opposite flank. The trouble is that the definition of being is too inclusive. Questions can be meaningless, illusory, incoherent, illegitimate. Trying to answer them does not lead to knowledge of anything. Now, no doubt, there are mistaken questions that lead nowhere. But mistaken questions are formulated questions. Being has been defined, not as the objective of formulated questions, but as the objective of the pure desire to know. Just as that desire is prior to any answer, and it itself is not an answer, so too it is prior to any formulated question, and it itself is not a formulation. Moreover, just as the pure desire is the intelligent and rational basis from which we discern between correct and incorrect answers, so also it is the intelligent and rational basis from which we discern between valid and mistaken questions. In brief, the pure desire to know, whose objective is being, is the source not only of answers but also of their criteria, and not only of questions but also of the grounds on which they are screened. For it is intelligent inquiry and reasonable reflection that just as much yield the right questions as the right answers.

More fundamental misgivings may arise. If one pleases, one may define being as what is to be known through the totality of true judgments. But is being really that? Might it not be something entirely different? The questions arise. They may be valid or mistaken. If they are mistaken, they are to be ignored. If they are valid, then our misgivings are without foundation. For the being that might be totally different turns out to be exactly what we are talking about. If we ask whether it might be, we ask; and the being we are talking about is whatever we ask about.

Again, might there not be an unknowable? If the question is invalid, it is to be ignored. If the question is valid, the answer may be yes or no. But the answer 'yes' would be incoherent, for then one would be knowing that the unknowable is; and the answer 'no' would leave everything knowable and within the range of being.

Other doubts may arise, but instead of chasing after them one by one, it will be better to revert to our initial theorem. Every doubt that the pure desire is unrestricted serves only to prove that it is unrestricted. If you ask whether X might not lie beyond its range, the fact that you ask proves that X lies within its range. Or else, if the question is meaningless, incoherent, illusory, illegitimate, then X turns out to be the mere nothing that results from aberration in cognitional process.

Not only, then, is judgment absolute, not only does it rest upon a grasp of the unconditioned, not only does reflection set the dichotomy 'Is it or is it not?' But at the root of cognitional process there is a cool, detached, disinterested desire to know, and its range is unrestricted. Being is the anything and everything that is the objective of that desire.

3 A Spontaneous Notion

If we have explained what we mean by being, we must now ask what the notion of being is.

In the first place, a distinction has to be drawn between the spontaneously operative notion and, on the other hand, theoretical accounts of its genesis and content. The spontaneously operative notion is invariant; it is common to all men; it functions in the same manner no matter what theoretical account of it a man may come to accept. On the other hand, theoretical accounts of the content and genesis of the notion are numerous; they vary with philosophic contexts, with the completeness of a thinker's observations, with the thoroughness of his analysis. First, we shall give our account of the spontaneously operative notion, and then we shall add a few notes on other theoretical accounts of it.

On the supposition of our analysis of cognitional process, it is easy enough to conclude that the spontaneously operative notion of being has to be placed in the pure desire to know. For, first of all, men are apt to agree that things are, whether or not we know them, and moreover that there are many things that are known only incompletely or even not at all. The notion of being, then, extends beyond the known. Secondly, being is known in judgment. It is in judgment that we affirm or deny, and until we are ready to affirm or deny, we do not yet know whether or not any X happens to be. Still, though being is known only in judging, the notion of being is prior to judging. For prior to any judgment there is reflection, and reflection is formulated in the question, Is it? That question supposes some notion of being, and strangely enough, it is prior to each instance of our knowing being. Not only, then, does the notion of being extend beyond the known but also it is prior to the final component of knowing when being is actually known. Thirdly, there are objects of thought. I can think of a horse, and no less I can think of a centaur. I can think of the best available scientific opinion on any subject, and no less I can think of all the previous opinions that in their day were the best available on the same subject. In one sense, they are all equivalent, for as long as one is merely thinking, merely considering, merely supposing, one deals merely with the conditioned, and it makes no difference whether or not its conditions are fulfilled. Thinking, then, prescinds from existing. But if it prescinds from existing, does it not prescind from being? And if it prescinds from being, is not all thinking about nothing? The trouble with this argument is that thinking also prescinds from not existing. If I think of a centaur or of phlogiston, I prescind from the fact that they do not exist; hence, if prescinding from existing is prescinding from being, prescinding from nonexistence is prescinding from not being; if prescinding from being proves that I am thinking of nothing, then prescinding from not being proves that I am thinking of something.

Now this type of consideration has led many thinkers to suppose that being is one thing and existing is another, that horses and centaurs, electrons and phlogiston equally are, but horses and electrons exist while centaurs and phlogiston do not exist. Still, that conclusion does not satisfy the facts, for apart from the oddity of asserting that the nonexistent is, there is the oversight of the dynamism of cognitional process. In a sense, thinking prescinds from existing and not existing, for it is not thinking but judging that determines whether or not anything exists. In another sense, thinking does not prescind from existing and not existing, for thinking is purposive; we think to get our concepts straight; we wish to get our concepts straight that we may be able to judge; so far from prescinding from existing and not existing, thinking is for the purpose of determining whether or not what is thought does exist.

It follows that the notion of being goes beyond the merely thought, for we ask whether or not the merely thought exists. No less, it follows that the notion of being is prior to thinking, for were it not, then think-

ing could not be for the purpose of judging, for the purpose of determining whether or not the merely thought exists. The notion of being,
then, is prior to conception and goes beyond it; and it is prior to judgment and goes beyond it. That notion must be the immanent, dynamic
orientation of cognitional process. It must be the detached and unrestricted desire to know as operative in cognitional process. Desiring to
know is desiring to know being; but it is merely the desire and not yet
the knowing. Thinking is thinking being; it is not thinking nothing; but
thinking being is not yet knowing it. Judging is a complete increment
in knowing; if correct, it is a knowing of being; but it is not yet knowing being, for that is attained only through the totality of correct judgments.

Still, how can an orientation or a desire be named a notion? A fetal
eye is orientated towards seeing; but a fetal eye does not see, and it has
no notion of seeing; a notion arises only insofar as understanding discerns future function in present structure. Hunger is orientated
towards food and eating; it is a desire; it lies within empirical consciousness; but a notion arises only insofar as the orientation of hunger
is understood. Purposive human action is orientated towards some
end or product; cognitional elements provide the rule and guide of
such action; but the cognitional elements are prior to the action; they
are constituted, not by the action itself, but by the planning that precedes it.

It remains that none of these instances is exactly parallel to the relation between the desire to know and cognitional process. For the desire
to know is not unconscious, as is the fetal eye, nor empirically conscious, as is hunger, nor a consequence of intellectual knowledge, as
are deliberation and choice. The desire to know is conscious intelligently and rationally; it is inquiring intelligence and reflecting reasonableness. Simply as desire, it is orientation, without as yet involving
any cognitional content or notion. Still, intelligence as obverse looks
for the intelligible as reverse. Reasonableness as obverse looks for the
grounded as reverse. More fundamentally, the looking for, the desiring, the inquiring-and-reflecting is an obverse that intelligently and
rationally heads for an unrestricted objective named being. Were that
heading unconscious, there would be an orientation towards being but
there would be no desire to know being and no notion of being. Were
that heading empirically conscious, there would be an orientation
towards being and a felt desire to know being, but there would be no

notion of being. In fact, the heading is intelligent and rational, and so there is not only an orientation towards being, not only a pure desire to know being, but also a notion of being.

Let us try to catch this notion, this intention of being, in the act. We speak of abstraction, and commonly we mean a direction of attention to some aspects of the given with a concomitant neglect of other aspects. The geometer considers the circle as a plane figure obeying a certain rule; he disregards the size, the color, the inexactitude, of the figure he draws or imagines; still more does he disregard other and more loosely connected aspects of the given. But that is not all. He disregards all other questions in geometry, all other departments of mathematics, all other fields of science, all other human occupations to which he could turn his hand. He considers only the circle. He abstracts from everything else. He does so intelligently, for though the objective of his desire is unrestricted, still he can move towards it only by concentrating on one element at a time. Again, as intelligence abstracts, so reflection prescinds. If I am to judge whether or not this is a typewriter, I have to prescind from all that is not relevant to that issue. I have to know all that is relevant. If I were a relativist, I would have to know the universe to know all that is relevant to that single judgment. Even though I am not a relativist, even though I find that many conditioned propositions become virtually unconditioned on the fulfillment of a manageable number of conditions, still this restriction of the relevant is accompanied by an acknowledgment of a universe of irrelevances.

Finally, as intelligence concentrates on the significant to abstract from all else, as reflection concentrates on the relevant to prescind from all else, so further questions and further issues arise neither as a surprise nor as a new beginning. The abstracting and the prescinding were provisional; they were only moments in a larger process. Nor is that larger process merely the object of introspective analysis. Immanent within it and operative of it lies an intelligent and rational consciousness that unrestrictedly intends a correspondingly unrestricted objective named being, or the all, or everything about everything, or the concrete universe. Just as the notion of the intelligible is involved in the actual functioning of intelligence, just as the notion of the grounded is involved in the actual functioning of reasonableness, so the notion of being is involved in the unrestricted drive of inquiring intelligence and reflecting reasonableness.

4   An All-Pervasive Notion

Hence it is that the notion of being is all-pervasive: it underpins all cognitional contents; it penetrates them all; it constitutes them as cognitional.

It underpins all cognitional contents. Without the pure desire to know, sensitive living would remain in its routine of perception and conation, instinct and habit, emotion and action. What breaks that circuit and releases intellectual activity is the wonder Aristotle described as the beginning of all science and philosophy. But that wonder is intelligent inquiry. It selects data for insight, and by that selecting it underpins even the empirical component in our knowing. Still more obviously, all ideas and all concepts are responses to the desire to understand, and all judgments are responses to the demand for the unconditioned.

Secondly, the notion of being penetrates all cognitional contents. It is the supreme heuristic notion. Prior to every content, it is the notion of the to-be-known through that content. As each content emerges, the 'to-be-known through that content' passes without residue into the 'known through that content.' Some blank in universal anticipation is filled in, not merely to end that element of anticipation, but also to make the filler a part of the anticipated. Hence, prior to all answers, the notion of being is the notion of the totality to be known through all answers. But once all answers are reached, the notion of being becomes the notion of the totality known through all answers.

Thirdly, the notion of being constitutes all contents as cognitional. Experiencing is only the first level of knowing: it presents the matter to be known. Understanding is only the second level of knowing: it defines the matter to be known. Knowing reaches a complete increment only with judgment, only when the merely experienced has been thought and the merely thought has been affirmed. But the increment of knowing is always completed in the same fashion. Experience is a kaleidoscopic flow. Objects of thought are as various as the inventiveness of human intelligence. But the contribution of judgment to our knowing is ever a mere yes or no, a mere 'is' or 'is not.' Experience is for inquiring into being. Intelligence is for thinking out being. But by judgment being is known, and in judgment what is known is known as being. Hence knowing is knowing being, yet the known is never mere being, just as judgment is never a mere yes apart from any question that 'yes' answers.

5   The Core of Meaning

As the notion of being underpins all contents and penetrates them and constitutes them as cognitional, so also it is the core of meaning.

For present purposes it will suffice to distinguish (1) sources of meaning, (2) acts of meaning, (3) terms of meaning, and (4) the core of meaning.

Any element of knowledge may serve as a source of meaning. Hence, sources of meaning include data and images, ideas and concepts, the grasp of the unconditioned and judgment, and no less, the detached and unrestricted desire to know.

Acts of meaning are of three kinds. They are (1) formal, (2) full, (3) instrumental. The formal act of meaning is an act of conceiving, thinking, considering, defining, supposing, formulating. The full act of meaning is an act of judging. The instrumental act of meaning is the implementation of a formal or of a full act by the use of words or symbols in a spoken, written, or merely imagined utterance.

Terms of meaning are what is meant. They are formal or full. Formal terms of meaning are what is conceived, thought, considered, defined, supposed, formulated. Full terms of meaning are what is affirmed or denied.

Now the all-inclusive term of meaning is being, for apart from being there is nothing. Inversely, the core of all acts of meaning is the intention of being.

Thus, any given judgment pertains to a context of judgments, and it is from the context that the meaning of the given judgment is determined. But why is the meaning of the given judgment a function of a context of other judgments? Because any judgment is but an increment in a whole named knowledge; because the meaning of the judgment is but an element in the determination of the universal intention of being.

Again, judgments may be true or false. The true judgment affirms what is and denies what is not. In the true judgment there is harmony between what is intended and what is meant. But in the false judgment there is conflict between intention and meaning. The false judgment as a judgment intends being; it intends to affirm what is and to deny what is not. But the false judgment as false is a failure to carry out its intention as a judgment. It affirms what is not and denies what is. It means not what is but only what would be, were it not false but true; again, in its negative form, it means, not what is not, but what would not be, were it not false but true.

Perhaps it is this internal conflict that has led some to the conclusion that a false judgment is meaningless. But such a conclusion seems astoundingly false. Were the false judgment meaningless, there would be nothing to be false. The false judgment is false precisely because it means a state of affairs that is the opposite of the state one intends to affirm, namely, the state that truly is.

On the level of conception there is a similar but less conspicuous contrast between meaning and its core, which is the intention of being. Horses and unicorns, electrons and phlogiston may be equally valid as formal terms of meaning. One can suppose them, or consider them, or define them, and that is all that is required of the formal term of meaning. Still, horses and electrons seem preferable as formal terms to unicorns and phlogiston. Absolutely, one can think of the latter, but there is something idle, something superfluous, something futile, about such thinking. The reason for this is that thinking is a moment in the unfolding of the pure desire to know; though the thought as thought is merely a formal term of meaning, though the unicorn is just as valid a formal term as is the horse, still we do not merely think. Our thinking is purposive. It is a tentative determination of the all-inclusive notion of being. It not merely thinks the object of thought but also anticipates the object of judgment. It not merely means the formal term of meaning but also looks ahead to the full term. Because the unicorn and phlogiston are known to be unsuccessful determinations of being, they are formal terms in which the core of meaning, the intention of being, has become uninterested.

Finally, in view of the prevalence of empiricist theories of meaning, a few words may be added on instrumental acts. Ordinary instrumental acts, such as spoken or written words or symbols, offer no special interest. But the empiricist emphasizes ostensive acts, such as demonstrative pronouns and adjectives and, of course, gestures. The reason for this emphasis may be readily grasped if one distinguishes between the function of gestures in any theory of meaning and the function gestures acquire in virtue of empiricist affirmations. In any theory of meaning an ostensive act is an instrumental act of meaning; it presupposes formal or full acts of meaning, inasmuch as one knows what one means; and it refers to formal or full terms of meaning, inasmuch as all meaning refers to a meant. Again, in any theory of meaning the ostensive act is operative inasmuch as it succeeds in drawing another's attention to a sensible source of meaning, so that by drawing on that source, by understanding, and by reflecting, he may reach the appropriate formal or full term of meaning that is meant. But in empiricist opinion the ostensive act has a third function; for the empiricist identifies the valid field of full terms of meaning (that is, the universe of being) with the range of sensible presentations; hence, for the empiricist, the ostensive act indicates not merely a source of meaning but also a full term of meaning. Whether or not this empiricist modification of the general theory of meaning is correct will depend on the question whether or not the set of propositions that enunciate empiricism is to be pronounced true or false.

Related selections: 1.XI.2–3 on method in metaphysics; 1.XIII.1,3 on truth; 1.XV.1 on the immanent source of transcendence; 2.II on openness; 3.I.2 on the transcendental mode of intending; 1.XI.5 on empiricism.

X

The Notion of Objectivity

In this selection from Chapter 13 of *Insight* Lonergan presents the notion of objectivity that he finds presupposed and utilized by both common sense and science. It is a minimal notion. Objectivity in any particular instance will be an achievement of the knowing subject. Further, the objectivity of Lonergan's own account of objectivity must be settled, Lonergan insists, by our own understanding and judgment of his account. As human knowing is a compound of three levels of operation constituted by the unfolding desire to know, so objectivity has three partial aspects corresponding to the three levels of cognitional process: an absolute aspect supplied on the level of judgment; a normative aspect supplied on the level of understanding; and an experiential aspect supplied on the level of experience. These three elements together, Lonergan claims, constitute human objectivity; no single aspect by itself is human objectivity. The principal notion of objectivity, Lonergan maintains, is contained in a patterned context of judgments. Lonergan is concerned here, as he is throughout the first half of *Insight*, with the facts about human knowing. Accordingly, his account of the notion of objectivity responds to the question of fact – What is objectivity? – rather than to the question of possibility – Can objectivity be achieved?

This extract is taken from *Insight*, 399–409.

Human knowing is cyclic and cumulative. It is cyclic inasmuch as cognitional process advances from experience through inquiry and reflection to judgment, only to revert to experience and recommence its ascent to another judgment. It is cumulative, not only in memory's store of experiences and understanding's clustering of insights, but also in the coalescence of judgments into the context named knowledge or mentality.

This complexity of our knowing involves a parallel complexity in our notion of objectivity. Principally the notion of objectivity is contained within a patterned context of judgments which serve as implicit definitions of the terms 'object,' 'subject.' But besides this principal and complete notion, there also are partial aspects or components emergent within cognitional process. Thus, there is an experiential aspect of objectivity proper to sense and empirical consciousness. There is a normative aspect that is contained in the contrast between the detached and unrestricted desire to know and, on the other hand, merely subjective desires and fears. Finally, there is an absolute aspect that is contained in single judgments considered by themselves inasmuch as each rests on a grasp of the unconditioned and is posited without reservation.

1   The Principal Notion

Principally, the notion of objectivity is contained in a patterned context of judgments. For one may define as object any $A, B, C, D, ...$ where, in turn, $A, B, C, D, ...$ are defined by the correctness of the set of judgments

A is; B is; C is; D is; ...
A is neither B nor C nor D nor ...
B is neither C nor D nor ...
C is neither D nor ...

Again, one may define a subject as any object, say A, where it is true that A affirms himself as a knower in the sense explained in the chapter on self-affirmation.

The bare essentials of this notion of objectivity are reached if we add to the judgments already discussed – I am a knower, This is a typewriter – the further judgment that I am not this typewriter. An indefinite number of further objects may be added by making the additional appropriate positive and negative judgments. Finally, insofar as one can intelligently grasp and reasonably affirm the existence of other knowers besides oneself, one can add to the list the objects that also are subjects.

The properties of the principal notion of objectivity have now to be noted. First, as has already been remarked, the notion resides in a context of judgments; without a plurality of judgments that satisfy a definite pattern, the notion does not emerge. Secondly, there follows an immediate corollary: the principal notion of objectivity, as defined, is not contained in any single judgment, and still less in any experiential or normative factor that occurs in cognitional process prior to judgment. Thirdly, the validity of the principal notion of objectivity is the same as the validity of the set of judgments that contain it; if the judgments are correct, then it is correct that there are objects and subjects in the sense defined, for the sense defined is simply the correctness of the appropriate pattern of judgments.

Fourthly, to turn to certain broader aspects of the principal notion, judgments in the appropriate pattern commonly are made and commonly are regarded as correct. It follows that commonly people will know objects and subjects and that commonly they will be surprised that any doubt should be entertained about the matter. On the other hand, it does not follow that people will commonly be able to give a lucid account of their knowledge of objects and subjects. For the lucid account employs the somewhat recondite art of implicit definition, and at the same time people are apt to jump to the conclusion that so evident a matter as the existence of objects and subjects must rest on something as obvious and conspicuous as the experiential aspect of objectivity. Hence, on the one hand, they will say that the typewriter is an object because they see it or feel it; on the other hand, however, they will admit they would not consider the typewriter an object if they knew it to be true either that there was no typewriter at all or that what they named a typewriter was identical with everything else.

Fifthly, the principal notion of objectivity is closely related to the notion of being. Being is what is to be known through the totality of correct judgments. Objectivity in its principal sense is what is known through any set of judgments satisfying a determinate pattern. In brief, there is objectivity if there are distinct beings, some of which both know themselves and know others as others. Moreover, the notion of being explains why objectivity in its principal sense is to be reached only through a pattern of judgments. For the notion of being becomes determinate only insofar as judgments are made; prior to judgment, one can think of being but one cannot know it; and any single judgment is but a minute increment in the process towards knowing it.

Again, being is divided from within; apart from being there is nothing; it follows that there cannot be a subject that stands outside being and looks at it; the subject has to be before he can look; and once he is, then he is not outside being but either the whole of it or some part. If he is the whole of it, then he is the sole object. If he is only a part, then he has to begin by knowing a multiplicity of parts (*A* is; *B* is; *A* is not *B*) and add that one part knows others ('I' am *A*).

Sixthly, the principal notion of objectivity solves the problem of transcendence. How does the knower get beyond himself to a known? The question is, we suggest, misleading. It supposes the knower to know himself and asks how he can know anything else. Our answer involves two elements. On the one hand, we contend that, while the knower may experience himself or think about himself without judging, still he cannot know himself until he makes the correct affirmation, 'I am,' and then he knows himself as being and as object. On the other hand, we contend that other judgments are equally possible and reasonable, so that through experience, inquiry, and reflection there arises knowledge of other objects both as beings and as being other than the knower. Hence we place transcendence, not in going beyond a known knower, but in heading for being within which there are positive differences and, among such differences, the difference between object and subject. Inasmuch as such judgments occur, there are in fact objectivity and transcendence; and whether or not such judgments are correct is a distinct question to be resolved along the lines reached in the analysis of judgment.

2   Absolute Objectivity

Besides the principal notion of objectivity, there also are the partial aspects of experiential, normative, and absolute objectivity. It will be convenient to begin from the last of the three.

The ground of absolute objectivity is the virtually unconditioned that is grasped by reflective understanding and posited in judgment. The formally unconditioned, which has no conditions at all, stands outside the interlocked field of conditioning and conditioned terms; it is intrinsically absolute. The virtually unconditioned stands within that field; it has conditions; it itself is among the conditions of other instances of the conditioned; still its conditions are fulfilled; it is a de facto absolute.

Because the content of the judgment is an absolute, it is withdrawn from relativity to the subject that utters it, the place in which he utters it, the time at which he utters it. Caesar's crossing of the Rubicon was a contingent event occurring at a particular place and time. But a true affirmation of that event is an eternal, immutable, definitive validity. For if it is true that he did cross, then no one whatever at any place or time can truly deny that he did.

Hence it is in virtue of absolute objectivity that our knowing acquires what has been named its publicity. For the same reason that the unconditioned is withdrawn from relativity to its source, it also is accessible not only to the knower that utters it but also to any other knower.

Again, it is the absolute objectivity of the unconditioned that is formulated in the logical principles of identity and contradiction. The principle of identity is the immutable and definitive validity of the true. The principle of contradiction is the exclusiveness of that validity. It is, and what is opposed to it is not.

Further, absolute objectivity pertains to single judgments as single. As has been argued, the principal notion of objectivity is constituted only by a suitable constellation of judgments. But each judgment in such a constellation is an absolute, and moreover, it is an absolute in virtue of its own affirmation of the unconditioned. The validity of the principal notion is a derived validity resting on the set of absolutes it involves. But the absolute aspect of objectivity has its ground in the single judgment to which it pertains. It is quite compatible with the affirmation that there is but one being, that there is no object except the affirming subject; accordingly, the absolute aspect of objectivity does not imply any subject-object relation; it constitutes the entry of our knowing into the realm of being, but by itself it does not suffice to posit, distinguish, and relate beings. However, this insufficiency arises, not from some defect of absolute objectivity, nor because the posited beings, their distinction, and their relations are not all unconditioned, but because several judgments are needed to posit, to distinguish, and to relate.

It is important not to confuse the absolute objectivity of any correct judgment with the invariance proper to the expression of universal judgments. Both universal and particular judgments, if correct, are absolutely objective. But the former are expressed invariantly because the expression is independent of variations in spatiotemporal reference frames, while the latter are expressed relatively because their expression does not enjoy such independence. However, the variation of the expression presupposes and reveals the absolute objectivity of what is expressed. Because 'I am here now' has absolute objectivity, there is an identical truth to be repeated only by employing the different words, 'He was there then.'

Again, absolute objectivity has no implications of an absolute space or of an absolute time. If it is true that space is, then what is absolute is the truth and not the space. Whether the space is absolute or relative is a further question. If it is true that space consists of an infinite set of immovable and empty places, then space is absolute. If it is true that space is not such a set, then space is relative. Which is correct? At least the issue cannot be settled by appealing to the fact that a true judgment posits an unconditioned.

Further, as Zeno argued, to affirm that something or other is does not imply that it is within space. If it did, one could ask whether or not the space (within which it is) is. If space is not, it is nothing, and to affirm things within nothing is meaningless. If, however, it is, then since 'to be' is 'to be within space,' the question recurs; if 'X is' means 'X is within space,' it would seem to follow that 'space is' means that 'space is within space'; the second space cannot be identical with the first, else it would not contain it; and if it is distinct, then it can be only by being within a further space, and so on indefinitely.

The same argument holds for being within time. If 'to be' is 'to be at some time,' then either there is time or there is not. If there is not, then 'to be at some time' is really a mere 'to be.' If there is time, then it has to be at some time, and that at some time, and so forth to infinity.

Interpretations of being or of absolute objectivity in terms of space and time are mere intrusions of imagination. Absolute objectivity is simply a property of the unconditioned; and the unconditioned, as such, says nothing about space or time. If one's imagination makes the use of the preposition 'within' imperative, then one may say that every judgment is within a context of other judgments and that every unconditioned is within a universe of being. Then 'space is' by being within the universe of being, and 'time is' by being within the universe of being, where 'to be within the universe of being' is 'to be unconditioned along with other instances of the unconditioned.'

3 Normative Objectivity

The second of the partial aspects of objectivity is the normative. It is objectivity as opposed to the subjectivity of wishful thinking, of rash or excessively cautious judgments, of allowing joy or sadness, hope or fear, love or detestation, to interfere with the proper march of cognitional process.

The ground of normative objectivity lies in the unfolding of the unrestricted, detached, disinterested desire to know. Because it is unrestricted, it opposes the obscurantism that hides truth or blocks access to it in whole or in part. Because it is detached, it is opposed to the inhibitions of cognitional process that arise from other human desires and drives. Because it is disinterested, it is opposed to the well-meaning but disastrous reinforcement that other desires lend cognitional process only to twist its orientation into the narrow confines of their limited range.

Normative objectivity is constituted by the immanent exigence of the pure desire in the pursuit of its unrestricted objective. A dynamic orientation defines its objective. No less, it defines the means towards attaining its objective. Not only does the pure desire head for the universe of being, but also it does so by desiring to understand and by desiring to grasp the understood as unconditioned. Hence, to be objective, in the normative sense of the term, is to give free rein to the pure desire, to its questions for intelligence, and to its questions for reflection. Further, it is to distinguish between questions for intelligence that admit proximate solutions and other questions of the same type that, at present, cannot be solved. Similarly, it is to distinguish between sound questions and, on the other hand, questions that are meaningless or incoherent or illegitimate. For the pure desire not only desires; it desires intelligently and reasonably; it desires to understand because it is intelligent, and it desires to grasp the unconditioned because it desires to be reasonable.

Upon the normative exigences of the pure desire rests the validity of all logics and all methods. A logic or method is not an ultimate that can be established only by a hullabaloo of starry-eyed praise for Medieval Philosophy or for Modern Science, along with an insecure resentment of everything else. Logic and method are intelligent and rational; their grounds are not belief nor propaganda nor the pragmatic utility of atom bombs and nylon stockings; their grounds are the inner exigence of the pure desire to know. They are to be accepted insofar as they succeed in formulating that dynamic exigence; and they are to be revised insofar as they fail.

In various manners this dependence has already been noted. Thus, the logical principles of identity and contradiction result from the unconditioned and the compulsion it exercises upon our reasonableness. The principle of excluded middle possesses ultimate but not immediate validity: it possesses ultimate validity because, if a judgment occurs, it must be either an affirmation or a denial; it does not possess immediate validity, for with respect to each proposition, rational consciousness is presented with the three alternatives of affirmation, of negation, and of seeking a better understanding and so a more adequate formulation of the issue. Again, the procedures of empirical method in its classical and statistical phases have been accounted for by the pure desire's movement towards understanding, towards an understanding that regards not only things as related to us by our senses but also things as related functionally among themselves, towards an understanding that presupposes data to admit systematization in the classical phase and in other respects to be nonsystematic and so necessitate a statistical phase. Finally, precepts regarding judgment can be derived from the general requirement of the unconditioned and from the special circumstances of different kinds of judgments, which may be primitive or derived, theoretical or concrete, descriptive or explanatory, certain or probable.

4 Experiential Objectivity

The third partial aspect of objectivity is the experiential. It is the given as given. It is the field of materials about which one inquires, in which one finds the fulfillment of conditions for the unconditioned, to which cognitional process repeatedly returns to generate the series of inquiries and reflections that yield the contextual manifold of judgments.

Further, the given is unquestionable and indubitable. What is constituted by answering questions can be upset by other questions. But the given is constituted apart from questioning; it remains the same no matter what the result of questioning may be; it is unquestionable in the sense that it lies outside the cognitional levels constituted by questioning and answering. In the same fashion the given is indubitable. What can be doubted is the answer to a question for reflection; it is a yes or a no. But the given is not the answer to any question; it is prior to questioning and independent of any answers.

Again, the given is residual and, of itself, diffuse. It is possible to select elements in the given and to indicate them clearly and precisely. But the selection and indication are the work of insight and formulation, and the given is the residue that remains when one subtracts from the indicated (1) the instrumental act of meaning by which one indicates, (2) the concepts expressed by that instrumental act, (3) the insights on which the concepts rest. Hence, since the given is just the residue, since it can be selected and indicated only through intellectual activities, of itself it is diffuse; the field of the given contains differences, but insofar as they simply lie in the field, the differences are unassigned.

Again, the field of the given is equally valid in all its parts but differently significant in different parts.

It is equally valid in all its parts in the sense that there is no screening prior to inquiry. Screening is the fruit of inquiry. It takes place once inquiry has begun.

It is differently significant in different parts in the sense that some parts are significant for some departments of knowledge and other parts for other departments. The physicist has to disregard what he merely imagines, merely dreams, merely derives from his personal equation. The psychologist has to explain imagination, dreaming, and personal equations. Hence, once inquiry begins, the first step is the screening that selects the relevant field of the given.

We are employing the name 'given' in an extremely broad sense. It includes not only the veridical deliverances of outer sense but also images, dreams, illusions, hallucinations, personal equations, subjective bias, and so forth. No doubt, a more restricted use of the term would be desirable if we were speaking from the limited viewpoint of natural science. But we are working at a general theory of objectivity, and so we have to acknowledge as given not only the materials into which natural science inquires but also the materials into which the psychologist or methodologist or cultural historian inquires.

There is a profounder reason. Our account of the given is extrinsic. It involves no description of the stream of sensitive consciousness. It involves no theory of that stream. It discusses neither the contribution of the empirically conscious subject nor the contribution of other 'outside' agents. It simply notes that reflection and judgment presuppose understanding, that inquiry and understanding presuppose materials for inquiry and something to be understood. Such presupposed materials will be unquestionable and indubitable, for they are not constituted by answering questions. They will be residual and diffuse, for they are what is left over once the fruits of inquiry and reflection are subtracted from cognitional contents.

Now such unquestionable and indubitable, residual and diffuse materials for inquiry and reflection must be regarded as equally valid in all their parts. Were they all invalid, there could be neither inquiry nor reflection, and so no reasonable pronouncement that they are invalid. Were some valid and others invalid, there would have to be a reasonably affirmed principle of selection; but such a principle can be grasped and reasonably affirmed only after inquiry has begun. Prior to inquiry there can be no intelligent discrimination and no reasonable rejection.

There is still a deeper reason. Why is the given to be defined extrinsically? Because all objectivity rests upon the unrestricted, detached, disinterested desire to know. It is that desire that sets up the canons of normative objectivity. It is that desire that gives rise to the absolute objectivity implicit in judgment. It is that desire that yields the constellation of judgments that implicitly define the principal notion of distinct objects in the universe of being, some of which know others. Experiential objectivity has to rest on the same basis, and so the given is defined, not by appealing to sensitive process, but by the pure desire regarding the flow of empirical consciousness as the materials for its operation.

5 Characteristics of the Notion

An account has been given of a principal notion of objectivity and of its three partial aspects: the experiential, the normative, and the absolute. However, there also exists subjectivity, and the reader may be inclined to find in the present section a full confirmation of a suspicion that he has for some time entertained, namely, that we have failed to place our finger on what really is objective, that we are confusing with the objective either in part or in whole what really is subjective. To deal with this problem will call for a further and rather complex investigation, but before we go on to it, let us note the more general characteristics of the notion of objectivity that has just been outlined.

First of all, despite its complexity, it can be the notion of objectivity that common sense presupposes and utilizes. The principal notion is implicit within a suitable pattern of judgments; it arises automatically when the judgments that happen to be made fall within such a pattern. The absolute aspect is implicit in judgment for, as we have argued at length, judgment affirms the unconditioned that reflective understanding grasps. The normative aspect is not any set of rules that has to be invented; it results from the intelligent inquiry and the reflective reasonableness that are the unfolding of the pure desire to know. Finally, the experiential aspect, while it may appear to do violence to commonsense expectations, is fully in accord with scientific practice, which claims to be an extension and refinement of common sense.

Secondly, the notion of objectivity that has been outlined is a minimal notion. There arises the question, What is objectivity? If the answer is to be intelligent and reasonable, then the pure desire and its normative exigences must be respected. Moreover, there must be materials into which intelligence inquires and on which reasonableness reflects. Further, if there is a definitive answer, the unconditioned and so the absolute will be attained. Finally, if the question and answer have a point, there will be other judgments which, if they occur in an appropriate pattern, will yield the principal notion.

Thirdly, our notion of objectivity begs no questions. Just as our notion of being does not decide between empiricism and rationalism, positivism and idealism, existentialism and realism, but leaves that decision to the content of correct judgments that are made, so also our notion of objectivity is equally open. If judgments occur in the appropriate pattern, then it involves a plurality of knowing subjects and known objects. If in effect there is only one true judgment, say, the affirmation of the Hegelian Absolute Idea, our notion of objectivity undergoes no formal modification. If true judgments are never reached, there arises the relativist position that acknowledges only experiential and normative objectivity. Only on the supposition that inquiry and reflection, intelligence and reasonableness have nothing to do with objectivity, is our notion invalidated. But in that case there does not arise the question, What is objectivity?

Related selections: 1.VII on judgment; 1.VIII on self-affirmation; 2.VII.1–3 on relevance of an unresolved problem of objectivity to neglect of the subject; 3.VIII.4 on the objectivity of theological categories.

Method in Metaphysics

Human knowing is a three-level structure of empirical, intellectual, and rational operations. Being is the objective of the pure desire to know that moves us from experience to questioning, from questioning to insight, from insight to formulation, from formulated understanding to critical reflection, from critical reflection to reflective insight, and from reflective insight to judgment. Objectivity, finally, is a compound of the experiential, normative, and absolute aspects that parallel the three levels of our knowing. This is Lonergan's position. But the history of philosophy is a record of conflicting and disparate accounts of knowledge, being, and objectivity. As Lonergan points out in his introduction to *Insight*, a cognitional theory that attends to the facts about knowing will discover the requirement of distinguishing two facts about knowing. There is complex human knowing as experiencing–understanding–judging motivated by the pure desire to know, and there is elementary knowing as experiential confrontation. This persistent duality of orientation, Lonergan argues in this selection from Chapter 14 of *Insight*, is at the root of our confusion about knowing, self-knowledge, being, and objectivity. Similarly, the historical failure to provide a clear and precise account of this persistent duality underlies philosophic difference.

In this selection on the method of philosophy, Lonergan locates the source of philosophic difference in the polymorphism of human consciousness, in the variable patterning of the stream of human consciousness, and the reason for the intractability of philosophic disputes in the general failure to recognize this polymorphism. He distinguishes the 'basic positions' on knowing, self-knowledge, being, and objectivity, based on an accurate cognitional theory, from the 'basic counterpositions' rooted in the confusion of experiential confrontation with complex human knowing. This distinction supplies the key categories for Lonergan's dialectical critique of opposing philosophic views. Lonergan proceeds then to define metaphysics. But as his definition of being is of the second order, so he defines metaphysics as 'the conception, affirmation, and implementation of the integral heuristic structure' of being proportionate to human knowing.[1] As classical and statistical methods are specific heuristic structures of empirical inquiry, so the three-level structure of complex human knowing that is specified by those methods and spontaneously operative in common sense may be named the 'integral heuristic structure' of being proportionate to our knowing. The full articulation of this structure in all its complexity, Lonergan argues, will be the ordered set of all heuristic notions. In the third part of this selection Lonergan describes the methodological directives that should guide the promotion and practice of metaphysics so conceived. At this point in *Insight*, with the critical groundwork in place, Lonergan provides illustrative dialectical analyses of other philosophic methods. The first illustration included here is a sketch for a dialectical critique of the method of universal doubt prescribed by René Descartes. The second is a sketch for a dialectical critique of empiricism.

The extracts in this section are taken from *Insight*, 410–15; 421–6; 433–6; 437–40, 441.

1 The Underlying Problem

It is not difficult to set antitheses against the conclusions of the preceding three chapters. Against the objectivity that is based on intelligent inquiry and critical reflection, there stands the unquestioning orientation of extroverted biological consciousness and its uncritical survival not only in dramatic and practical living but also in much of philosophic thought. Against the concrete universe of being, of all that can be intelligently grasped and reasonably affirmed, there stands in a prior completeness the world of sense, in which the 'real' and the 'apparent' are subdivisions within a vitally anticipated 'already out there now.' Against the self-affirmation of a consciousness that at once is empirical, intellectual, and rational, there stands the native bewilderment of the existential subject, revolted by mere animality, unsure of his way through the maze of philosophies, trying to live without a known purpose, suffering despite an unmotivated will, threatened

1 *Insight*, 416.

with inevitable death and, before death, with disease and even insanity.

The peculiarity of these antitheses is not to be overlooked. They are not mere conflicting propositions. They are not pure logical alternatives, of which one is simply true and the other is utterly false. But in each case both the thesis and the antithesis have their ground in the concrete unity-in-tension that is man. For human consciousness is polymorphic. The pattern in which it flows may be biological, aesthetic, artistic, dramatic, practical, intellectual, or mystical. These patterns alternate; they blend or mix; they can interfere, conflict, lose their way, break down. The intellectual pattern of experience is supposed and expressed by our account of self-affirmation, of being, and of objectivity. But no man is born in that pattern; no one reaches it easily; no one remains in it permanently; and when some other pattern is dominant, then the self of our self-affirmation seems quite different from one's actual self, the universe of being seems as unreal as Plato's noetic heaven, and objectivity spontaneously becomes a matter of meeting persons and dealing with things that are 'really out there.'

Not merely are the antitheses based on the polymorphic fact of a protean consciousness, but initially there is the bewildering fact without the clear antitheses. To reach that sharp formulation, it was necessary for us to begin from insight, to study its functioning in mathematics, in empirical science, and in common sense, to turn to reflective understanding and judgment, and throughout to avoid involvement in obviously pressing problems on the nature of knowledge, of reality, and of the relation between them. Even in unfolding the process that ends in self-affirmation, we were unprepared to say whether affirming the self was knowing the self. Affirming the self became knowing the self inasmuch as knowing being was seen to be affirming it; and knowing being became objective knowing through a grasp of the nature of experiential, normative, absolute, and the consequent principal objectivity.

If a clear and sharp formulation of the antitheses occurs only at the end of a long and difficult inquiry, still that inquiry today is prepared and supported in a manner unattainable in earlier centuries. The development of mathematics, the maturity of some branches of empirical science, the investigations of depth psychology, the interest in historical theory, the epistemological problems raised by Descartes, by Hume, and by Kant, the concentration of modern philosophy upon

cognitional analysis, all serve to facilitate and to illumine an investigation of the mind of man. But if it is possible for later ages to reap the
harvest of earlier sowing, still before that sowing and during it there
was no harvest to be reaped.

It is not too surprising, then, that the philosophies have been many,
contradictory, and disparate. For surprise merely expresses the mistaken assumption that the task of philosophy lies in the observation or
utterance of some simple entity by some simple mind. In fact, the mind
is polymorphic; it has to master its own manifold before it can determine what utterance is, or what is uttered, or what is the relation
between the two; and when it does so, it finds its own complexity at
the root of antithetical solutions. From the welter of conflicting philosophic definitions and from the babel of endless philosophic arguments, it has been concluded that the object of philosophy either does
not exist or cannot be attained. But this conclusion disregards two
facts. On the one hand, the philosophers have been men of exceptional
acumen and profundity. On the other hand, the many, contradictory,
disparate philosophies can all be contributions to the clarification of
some basic but polymorphic fact; because the fact is basic, its implications range over the universe; but because it is polymorphic, its alternative forms ground diverse sets of implications.

Such is the view to be developed in the present account of the
method of philosophy. As in our remarks on mathematics, on empirical science, and on common sense, so also here, the one object of our
inquiry is the nature and fact of insight. Philosophers and philosophies
engage our attention inasmuch as they are instances and products of
inquiring intelligence and reflecting reasonableness. It is from this
viewpoint that there emerges a unity not only of origin but also of goal
in their activities; and this twofold unity is the ground for finding in
any given philosophy a significance that can extend beyond the philosopher's horizon and, even in a manner he did not expect, pertain to the
permanent development of the human mind.

The possibility of contradictory contributions to a single goal is, in
its main lines, already familiar to the reader. Besides the direct insights
that grasp the systematic, there are also the inverse insights that deal
with the nonsystematic. As both types of insight are needed by the
mathematician, the empirical scientist, the depth psychologist, and the
theorist of history, so also both types are needed by the philosopher.
Moreover, inasmuch as the philosopher employs both direct and

inverse insights in his survey and estimate of the philosophic process, his mind and grasp become the single goal in which contradictory contributions attain their complex unity. Finally, the heuristic structure of that unity admits determination through the principle that positions invite development and counterpositions invite reversal. This principle we now must explain.

First, in any philosophy it is possible to distinguish between its cognitional theory and, on the other hand, its pronouncements on metaphysical, ethical, and theological issues. Let us name the cognitional theory the basis, and the other pronouncements the expansion.

Secondly, there are two aspects to the basis. On the one hand, cognitional theory is determined by an appeal to the data of consciousness and to the historical development of human knowledge. On the other hand, the formulation of cognitional theory cannot be complete unless some stand is taken on basic issues in philosophy.

Thirdly, the inevitable philosophic component immanent in the formulation of cognitional theory will be either a basic position or else a basic counterposition.

It will be a basic position (1) if the real is the concrete universe of being and not a subdivision of the 'already out there now'; (2) if the subject becomes known when it affirms itself intelligently and reasonably and so is not known yet in any prior 'existential' state; and (3) if objectivity is conceived as a consequence of intelligent inquiry and critical reflection, and not as a property of vital anticipation, extroversion, and satisfaction.

On the other hand, it will be a basic counterposition if it contradicts one or more of the basic positions.

Fourthly, any philosophic pronouncement on any epistemological, metaphysical, ethical, or theological issue will be named a position if it is coherent with the basic positions on the real, on knowing, and on objectivity; and it will be named a counterposition if it is coherent with one or more of the basic counterpositions.

Fifthly, all counterpositions invite reversal. For any lack of coherence prompts the intelligent and reasonable inquirer to introduce coherence. But counterpositions, though coherent with one another, though the insertion of their symbolic equivalents into an electronic computer would not lead to a breakdown, nonetheless are incoherent with the activities of grasping them intelligently and affirming them reasonably. For these activities contain the basic positions; and the basic positions are incoherent with any counterposition. One can grasp and accept, propose and defend a counterposition; but that activity commits one to grasping and accepting one's grasping and accepting; and that commitment involves a grasp and acceptance of the basic positions. The only coherent way to maintain a counterposition is that of the animal; for animals not only do not speak but also do not offer excuses for their silence.

Sixthly, all positions invite development. For they are coherent not only with one another but also with the activities of inquiring intelligence and reflective reasonableness; because these activities are coherent with existing attainment, their exercise is possible; because existing attainment is incomplete, further development is invited.

A simple example will clarify the meaning of the foregoing abstract statements. Let us say that Cartesian dualism contains both a basic position and a basic counterposition. The basic position is the *cogito, ergo sum*, and as Descartes did not endow it with the clarity and precision that are to be desired, its further development is invited by such questions as, What is the self? What is thinking? What is being? What are the relations between them? On the other hand, the basic counterposition is the affirmation of the *res extensa*; it is real as a subdivision of the 'already out there now'; its objectivity is a matter of extroversion; knowing it is not a matter of inquiry and reflection. This counterposition invites reversal, not merely in virtue of its conjunction with the other component in Cartesian thought, but even when posited by itself in anyone's thought. Thus, Hobbes overcame Cartesian dualism by granting reality to the *res cogitans* only if it were another instance of the *res extensa*, another instance of matter in motion. Hume overcame Hobbes by reducing all instances of the 'already out there now real' to manifolds of impressions linked by mere habits and beliefs. The intelligence and reasonableness of Hume's criticizing were obviously quite different from the knowledge he so successfully criticized. Might one not identify knowledge with the criticizing activity rather than the criticized materials? If so, Cartesian dualism is eliminated by another route. One is back at the thinking subject, and at the term of this reversal one's philosophy is enriched not only by a stronger affirmation of the basic position but also by an explicit negation of the basic counterposition.

In the light of the dialectic, then, the historical series of philosophies would be regarded as a sequence of contributions to a single but complex goal. Significant discoveries, because they are not the prerogative of completely successful philosophers, are expressed either as positions or as counterpositions. But positions invite development, and so the sequence of discoveries expressed as positions should form a unified, cumulative structure that can be enriched by adding the discoveries initially expressed as counterpositions. On the other hand, since counterpositions invite reversal, a free unfolding of human thought should tend to separate the discovery from its author's bias in the measure that its presuppositions are examined and its implications tested.

However, the dialectic itself has a notable presupposition, for it supposes that cognitional theory exercises a fundamental influence in metaphysics, in ethics, and in theological pronouncements ...

2 A Definition of Metaphysics

Just as the notion of being underlies and penetrates and goes beyond all other notions, so also metaphysics is the department of human knowledge that underlies, penetrates, transforms, and unifies all other departments.

It underlies all other departments, for its principles are neither terms nor propositions, neither concepts nor judgments, but the detached and disinterested drive of the pure desire to know and its unfolding in the empirical, intellectual, and rational consciousness of the self-affirming subject. From the unfolding of that drive proceed all questions, all insights, all formulations, all reflections, all judgments; and so metaphysics underlies logic and mathematics, the various sciences and the myriad instances of common sense.

It penetrates all other departments. For other departments are constituted by the same principles as metaphysics. They are particular departments inasmuch as they are restricted to some particular viewpoint and field. Yet despite the restrictions that make them particular, all departments spring from a common source and seek a common compatibility and coherence, and in both these respects they are penetrated by metaphysics.

It transforms all other departments. For the consciousness of man is polymorphic, and it ever risks formulating its discoveries not as positions but as counterpositions. Common sense is subject to a dramatic bias, an egoistic bias, a group bias, and a general bias that disregards the complex theoretical issues in which it becomes involved and their long-term consequences from which it blindly suffers. Scientists are not just scientists but also men of common sense; they share its bias insofar as their specialty does not correct it; and insofar as their specialty runs counter to the bias of common sense, they find themselves divided and at a loss for a coherent view of the world. Metaphysics springs from the pure desire to know; it is free from the restrictions of particular viewpoints; it distinguishes positions from counterpositions in the whole of knowledge; it is a transforming principle that urges positions to fuller development and, by reversing counterpositions, liberates discoveries from the shackles in which at first they were formulated.

It unifies all other departments. For other departments meet particular ranges of questions, but it is the original, total question, and it moves to the total answer by transforming and putting together all other answers. Metaphysics, then, is the whole in knowledge but not the whole of knowledge. A whole is not without its parts, nor independent of them, nor identical with them. So it is that, while the principles of metaphysics are prior to all other knowledge, still the attainment of metaphysics is the keystone that rests upon the other parts and presses them together in the unity of a whole.

From the foregoing account, it would appear that metaphysics can exist in three stages or forms. In its first stage, it is latent. Empirical, intellectual, and rational consciousness are immanent and operative in all human knowing; from them spring both the various departments of knowledge and the attempts that are made to reverse counterpositions and to attain coherence and unity; but the common source of all knowledge is not grasped with sufficient clarity and precision; the dialectical principle of transformation is not a developed technique; and efforts at unification are haphazard and spasmodic. In its second stage, metaphysics is problematic. The need of a systematic effort for unification is felt; studies of the nature of knowledge abound; but these very studies are involved in the disarray of the positions and counterpositions that result from the polymorphic consciousness of man. In its third stage, metaphysics is explicit. Latent metaphysics, which always is operative, succeeds in conceiving itself, in working out its implications and techniques, and in affirming the conception, the implications, and the techniques.

What is this explicit metaphysics? It will simplify matters enormously if, in the present chapter, we prescind from the complicated and disputed question of the possibility of man's knowing what lies beyond the limits of human experience. Accordingly, we introduce the notion of proportionate being. In its full sweep, being is whatever is to be known by intelligent grasp and reasonable affirmation. But being that is proportionate to human knowing not only is to be understood and affirmed but also is to be experienced. So proportionate being may be defined as whatever is to be known by human experience, intelligent grasp, and reasonable affirmation.

Now let us say that explicit metaphysics is the conception, affirmation, and implementation of the integral heuristic structure of proportionate being. The meaning and implications of this statement have now to be explored.

First, what is meant by an integral heuristic structure? To begin by assembling the elements of the answer, conceptual contents may be primitive or derived; the derived are defined by appealing to the primitive; the primitive are fixed inasmuch as terms and relations proceed from a single understanding, with the relations settled by the terms and the terms settled by the relations. However, prior to the understanding that issues in answers, there are the questions that anticipate answers; and as has been seen, such anticipation may be employed systematically in the determination of answers that as yet are unknown; for while the content of a future cognitional act is unknown, the general characteristics of the act itself not only can be known but also can supply a premise that leads to the act. A heuristic notion, then, is the notion of an unknown content, and it is determined by anticipating the type of act through which the unknown would become known. A heuristic structure is an ordered set of heuristic notions. Finally, an integral heuristic structure is the ordered set of all heuristic notions.

In illustration, one may point to the definition of proportionate being. It is whatever is to be known by human experience, intelligent grasp, and reasonable affirmation. The definition does not assign the content of any experience, of any understanding, of any affirmation. Yet it does assign an ordered set of types of acts, and it implies that every proportionate being is to be known through such an ordered set. Accordingly, the definition is an instance of a heuristic structure; but it is not an instance of an integral heuristic structure, for it does not exhaust the resources of the human mind in anticipating what it is to know.

Secondly, if the integral heuristic structure of proportionate being were conceived, affirmed, and implemented, then latent metaphysics would become explicit. For latent metaphysics is the dynamic unity of empirical, intellectual, and rational consciousness as underlying, penetrating, transforming, and unifying the other departments of knowledge. But an integral heuristic structure of proportionate being would perform these offices in an explicit manner. As heuristic, it would underlie other knowledge. As the questions which other knowledge answers, it would penetrate other fields. As dialectical, it would transform these answers. As integral, it would contain in itself the order that binds other departments into a single intelligible whole.

Thirdly, such an explicit metaphysics would be progressive. For heuristic notions and structures are not discovered by some Platonic recall of a prior state of contemplative bliss. They result from the resourcefulness of human intelligence in operation. They are to be known only by an analysis of operations that have become familiar and are submitted to examination. Just as the other departments of knowledge advance by discovering new methods, so metaphysics advances by adding these discoveries to its account of the integral heuristic structure of proportionate being.

Fourthly, such an explicit metaphysics would be nuanced. It would be a whole of many parts, and different parts would possess varying degrees of clarity and precision, of evidence and inevitability. It follows that not all parts could be affirmed with the same confidence, that some could be regarded as certain, others as highly probable, others as recommended by the lack of alternatives, others as doubtful and in need of further confirmation.

Fifthly, such a metaphysics would be factual. Proportionate being is not the merely possible nor need it be absolutely necessary. It is what in fact is, and the science that views it as a whole can be content to ascertain what in fact is true. Moreover, the various empirical sciences and the myriad instances of common sense aim at no more than knowing what in fact is so; but metaphysics is their unification; as a principle, it precedes them; but as an attainment, it follows upon them, emerges from them, depends upon them; and so, like them, it too will be factual.

Sixthly, the dependence of such a metaphysics upon the sciences and upon common sense would be the dependence, neither of a conclusion on premises nor of an effect upon its cause, but of a generating, transforming, and unifying principle upon the materials that it generates, transforms, and unifies. Metaphysics does not undertake either to discover or to teach science; it does not undertake either to develop or to impart common sense; it does not pretend to know the universe of proportionate being independently of science and common sense; but it can and does take over the results of such distinct efforts, it works them into coherence by reversing their counterpositions, and it knits them into a unity by discerning in them the concrete prolongations of the integral heuristic structure which it itself is.

Seventhly, such a metaphysics, once it had surmounted its initial difficulties, would be stable. It would admit incidental modifications and improvements, but it could not undergo the revolutionary changes to which the empirical sciences are subject. For a science is open to revolutionary change inasmuch as it is possible to reach a higher viewpoint and consequently to alter the content of its primitive terms and relations. But it is possible to reach a higher viewpoint only within the framework of inquiring and critical intelligence; there is not, in human knowledge, any possible higher viewpoint that goes beyond that framework itself and replaces intelligent inquiry and critical reflection by some surrogate; and the viewpoint of metaphysics is constituted by nothing less than inquiring intelligence and critical reflection. Moreover, a higher viewpoint can alter the content of primitive terms and relations only if that content is some determinate object of thought or affirmation. The Aristotelian, the Galilean, the Newtonian, and the Einsteinian accounts of the free fall of heavy bodies are all open to revision, for all are determinate contents. On the other hand, a merely heuristic account is not open to revision. One cannot revise the heuristic notion that the nature of a free fall is what is to be known when the free fall is understood correctly; for it is that heuristic notion that is both antecedent to each determinate account and, as well, subsequent to each and the principle of the revision of each. Accordingly, since metaphysics is the integral heuristic structure of proportionate being, since it is a structure that is coincident with inquiring intelligence and critical reflection, metaphysics is not open to revolutionary change.

Eighthly, metaphysics primarily regards being as explained, but secondarily it includes being as described. Primarily, it regards being as explained, for it is a heuristic structure, and a heuristic structure looks to what is to be known when one understands. Secondarily, it includes being as described. For explanation is of things as related to one another; description is of things as related to us; and so, since we are things, the descriptive relations must be identical with some of the explanatory relations ...

Perhaps enough has been said to clarify what we mean by metaphysics. The detached and disinterested desire to know and its unfolding in inquiry and reflection not only constitute a notion of being but also impose a normative structure upon man's cognitional acts. Such a structure provides the relations by which unknown contents of the acts can be defined heuristically. This heuristic structure is immanent and operative in all human knowing, but initially it is latent, and the polymorphism of human consciousness makes it problematic as well. Nonetheless, it can be conceived, affirmed, and implemented, and from that implementation there follow a transformation and an integration of the sciences and of the myriad instances of common sense. But knowing is knowing being. So the integral heuristic structure of proportionate being, as determined by the sciences and common sense, is knowledge of the organizing structure of proportionate being. As has been said, such a metaphysics is progressive, nuanced, factual, formally dependent on cognitional theory and materially dependent on the sciences and on common sense, stable, and in its outlook explanatory.

There remains the clarification that results from a discussion of method, and to this we now turn our attention.

3   Method in Metaphysics

A method is a set of directives that serve to guide a process towards a result. The result at which we are aiming is the explicit metaphysics outlined in the previous section. It would consist in a symbolic indication of the total range of possible experience, in a set of acts of insight that unify such experience, and in a grasp of the virtually unconditioned issuing in a reasonable affirmation of the unified view.

This result can exist only in the empirical, intellectual, and rational consciousness of the self-affirming subject. Metaphysics, then, is not something in a book but something in a mind. Moreover, it is produced not by a book but only by the mind in which it is. Books can serve to supply the stimulus for a set of precise visual experiences, to issue through experiences an invitation to acts of insight, to lead through the insights to a grasp of the virtually unconditioned. But books cannot constitute the visual experiences, nor necessitate the insights, nor impose the attainment of the high moment of critical reflection that through the unconditioned reaches judgment. Further, the subject that is envisaged is not some general or transcendental or absolute subject; from the viewpoint of the writer it is any particular subject that can experience, can inquire intelligently, can reflect critically; but from the viewpoint of the reader the particular subject is the subject that he or she is. No one can understand for another or judge for another. Such acts are one's own and only one's own. Explicit metaphysics is a personal attainment.

Particular subjects are many. Their respective histories and attainments are diverse. Their outlooks on the universe are disparate. Yet despite their multiplicity, their diversity, their disparateness, they, as they actually are, constitute the starting point for the process that leads to explicit metaphysics. There is no use addressing minds that could be or should be but in fact are not, if one would encourage the genesis of explicit metaphysics in the minds that are. Just as metaphysics can exist only in a mind and can be produced only by the mind in which it is to be, so also metaphysics can begin only in minds that exist, and it can proceed only from their actual texture and complexion. Bluntly, the starting point of metaphysics is people as they are.

Between this starting point and the goal, there is the process. It is a process from latent through problematic to explicit metaphysics. People as they are cannot avoid experience, cannot put off their intelligence, cannot renounce their reasonableness. But they may never have adverted to these concrete and factual inevitabilities. They may be unable to distinguish between them sharply, or discern the immanent order that binds them together, or find in them the dynamic structure that has generated all their scientific knowledge and all their common sense, or acknowledge in that dynamic structure a normative principle that governs the outcome of all inquiry, or discover in themselves other equally dynamic structures that can interfere with the detached and disinterested unfolding of the pure desire to know, or conclude to the polymorphism of their subjectivity and the untoward effects it can have upon their efforts to reach a unified view of the universe of proportionate being.

The process, then, to explicit metaphysics is primarily a process to self-knowledge. It has to begin from the polymorphic subject in his native disorientation and bewilderment. It cannot appeal to what he knows, for as yet he has not learnt to distinguish sharply and effectively between the knowing men share with animals, the knowing that men alone possess, and the manifold blends and mixtures of the two that are the disorientation and ground the bewilderment of people as they are. Since an appeal to disorientated knowledge would only extend and confirm the disorientation, the appeal must be to the desire that is prior to knowledge, that generates knowledge, that can effect the correction of miscarriages in the cognitional process. Still, it cannot be taken for granted that the subject knows his own desire and its implications; were there such knowledge, the disorientation would be remedied already; and so the initial appeal is to the desire, not as known, but as existing and operative. The first directive, then, is to begin from interest, to excite it, to use its momentum to carry things along. In other words, the method of metaphysics primarily is pedagogical: it is headed towards an end that is unknown and as yet cannot be disclosed; from the viewpoint of the pupil, it proceeds by cajoling or forcing attention and not by explaining the intended goal and by inviting an intelligent and reasonable cooperation. So it was that without mentioning metaphysics, we studied the fact and the nature of insight in mathematics, in the empirical sciences, in common sense, in judgments on mathematics, on the empirical sciences, and on the myriad concrete and particular objects of common sense. So too we examined self-affirmation and the notions of being and of objectivity. So too we began to talk about the dialectic of philosophy. In the measure in which we have been successful, the reader will know what is meant by insight, what is meant by reasonableness, how both differ from the internal and external experience that they presuppose, how all three form a patterned orientation that differs from other orientations that commonly are more familiar and more frequent. In the measure that such self-knowledge has been reached, it is possible to leave pedagogy and to discuss method; and so we find ourselves discussing method.

A method, as was remarked, is a set of directives that guide a process to a result. But the result can exist only in a self-affirming subject, and the process can be produced only by the subject in which the result is to exist. It follows that the directives of the method must be issued by the self-affirming subject to himself. The initial pedagogical stage was to enable the subject to issue the proper directives; and the present discussion of method has to be the subject's own determination of the directives he is to issue.

The method, then, of metaphysics is dictated by the self-affirming subject in the light of his pedagogically acquired self-knowledge. For that self-knowledge is dynamic. It has revealed the source of disorientation and bewilderment. Spontaneously it moves towards the attainment of reorientation and integration.

The reorientation is to be effected in the field of common sense and of the sciences. On the one hand, these departments of the subject's knowledge and opinion are not to be liquidated. They are the products of experience, intelligence, and reflection, and it is only in the name of experience, intelligence, and reflection that self-knowledge issues any directives. As they are not to be liquidated, so they are not to be taken apart and reconstructed, for the only method for reaching valid scientific views is the method of science, and the only method for attaining common sense is the method common sense already employs. As metaphysicians neither teach science nor impart common sense, so they cannot revise or reconstruct either science or common sense. Still, this is not the whole story. For it would be excessively naive for the self-knowing subject to suppose that his scientific knowledge and his common sense are purely and simply the product of experience, intelligent inquiry, and critical reflection. The subject knows the polymorphism of his own consciousness; he knows how it generates a dramatic, an egoistic, a group, and a general bias in common sense; he knows how it intrudes into science confused notions on reality, on objectivity, and on knowledge. While, then, science and common sense are to be accepted, the acceptance is not to be uncritical. There are precise manners in which common sense can be expected to go wrong; there are definite issues on which science is prone to issue extrascientific opinions; and the reorientation demanded and effected by the self-knowledge of the subject is a steadily exerted pressure against the common nonsense that tries to pass for common sense and against the uncritical philosophy that pretends to be a scientific conclusion.

As the subject's advertence to the polymorphism of his consciousness leads to a transforming reorientation of his scientific opinions and his common sense, so his advertence both to his detached and disinterested desire to know and to the immanent structure of its unfolding leads to an integration of what is known and of what is to be known of the universe of proportionate being. It is in this integration that metaphysics becomes explicit; and to forestall misapprehension and misinterpretation, let us attempt to state as clearly as we can the nature of the transition from latent to explicit metaphysics.

First, then, in its general form, the transition is a deduction. It involves a major premise, a set of primary minor premises, and a set of secondary minor premises.

Secondly, the major premise is the isomorphism that obtains between the structure of knowing and the structure of the known. If the knowing consists of a related set of acts and the known is the related set of contents of these acts, then the pattern of the relations between the acts is similar in form to the pattern of the relations between the contents of the acts. This premise is analytic.

Thirdly, the set of primary minor premises consists of a series of affirmations of concrete and recurring structures in the knowing of the self-affirming subject. The simplest of these structures is that every instance of knowing proportionate being consists of a unification of experiencing, understanding, and judging. It follows from the isomorphism of knowing and known that every instance of known proportionate being is a parallel unification of a content of experience, a content of understanding, and a content of judgment.

Fourthly, the set of secondary minor premises is supplied by reorientated science and common sense. From the major and the primary minor premises there is obtained an integrating structure; but from the secondary minor premises there are obtained the materials to be integrated. Again, from the major and the primary minor premises there is obtained a well-defined and definitive set of questions to be answered; from the secondary minor premises there is obtained the fact of answers and their frequency.

Fifthly, this use of the above premises effects a transition from a latent to an explicit metaphysics. For in any case, cognitional activity operates within heuristic structures towards goals that are isomorphic with the structures. If this basic feature of cognitional activity is overlooked, metaphysics is latent. If this feature is noted, if the structures are determined, if the principle of isomorphism is grasped, then the latent metaphysics to which everyone subscribes without knowing he does so ceases to be latent and becomes explicit.

Sixthly, the method is not essential to obtaining the results. There is nothing to prevent an intelligent and reasonable man from beginning with the set of secondary minor premises, from discovering in them the structures that they cannot escape, and from generalizing from the totality of examined instances to the totality of possible instances. In fact, this has been the procedure of the Aristotelian and Thomist schools, and as will appear, their results largely anticipate our own.

Seventhly, however, there is much to be gained by employing the method. Aristotelian and Thomist thought has tended to be, down the centuries, a somewhat lonely island in an ocean of controversy. Because of the polymorphism of human consciousness, there are latent in science and common sense not only metaphysics but also the negation of metaphysics; and only the methodical reorientation of science and common sense puts an end, at least in principle, to this permanent source of confusion. Further, without the method it is impossible to assign with exactitude the objectives, the presuppositions, and the procedures of metaphysics; and this lack of exactitude may result in setting one's aim too low or too high, in resting one's case on alien or insecure foundations, in proceeding to one's goal through unnecessary detours.

Finally, the misconceptions in which metaphysics thus becomes involved may rob it of its validity and of its capacity for development; what should provide an integration for the science and the common sense of any age risks taking on the appearance of a mummy that would preserve for all time Greek science and medieval common sense.

To recapitulate, the goal of the method is the emergence of explicit metaphysics in the minds of particular men and women. It begins from them as they are, no matter what that may be. It involves a preliminary stage that can be methodical only in the sense in which a pedagogy is methodical; that is, the goal and the procedure are known and pursued explicitly by a teacher but not by the pupil. The preliminary stage ends when the subject reaches an intelligent and reasonable self-affirmation. Such self-affirmation is also self-knowledge. It makes explicit the pursuit of the goal that has been implicit in the pure desire to know. From that explicit pursuit there follow the directives, first, of reorientating one's scientific knowledge and one's common sense, and secondly, of integrating what one knows and can know of proportionate being through the known structures of one's cognitional activities.

4   Universal Doubt

In its simplest form the method of universal doubt is the precept 'Doubt everything that can be doubted.' Let us begin by attempting to determine the consequences of following out this precept, by applying rigorously its criterion of indubitability.

First, all concrete judgments of fact are to be excluded. For while they rest on invulnerable insights, still the invulnerability amounts to no more than the fact that further relevant questions do not arise. A criterion of indubitability is more exigent. It demands the impossibility of further relevant questions, and in concrete judgments of fact such impossibility neither exists nor is apprehended.

Secondly, both empirical science and common sense are excluded. For both aim at ascertaining what in fact is so, and neither succeeds in reaching the indubitable. No doubt, it would be silly to suppose that there are further relevant questions that would lead to the correction of the insights grounding bare statements of fact or elementary measurements. But that is beside the point, for the question is not what certainly is true or false but what indubitably is true or false; and indubitability requires not the fact but the impossibility of further relevant questions.

Thirdly, the meaning of all judgments becomes obscure and unsettled. For the meaning of a judgment can be clear and precise only if one can assign a clear and precise meaning to such terms as reality, knowledge, objectivity. A clear and precise meaning can be assigned to such terms only if one succeeds in clarifying the polymorphic consciousness of man. Such a clarification can be effected by a lengthy, difficult, and delicate inquiry into the facts of human cognitional activity. But if one excludes all concrete judgments of fact, one excludes the clarification, and so one is bound to regard the meaning of every judgment as obscure and unsettled.

Fourthly, all mere suppositions satisfy the criterion of indubitability. For the mere supposition excludes the question for reflection, and doubt becomes possible only after the question for reflection arises. Thus, if you suppose that *A* is *B*, and I ask whether *A* really is *B*, you are entitled to point out that you are merely supposing *A* to be *B*, and that my question tries to put an end to mere supposing. On the other hand, there is no possibility of doubting whether or not *A* is *B* until that question arises, and so all mere suppositions are indubitable. It follows that all analytic propositions are indubitable, inasmuch as they rest on rules of syntax and on definitions of terms, and all such rules and definitions are regarded as mere suppositions. On the other hand, analytic principles are not indubitable, for they require concrete judgments of fact in which occur the defined terms in their defined sense; and, as has been seen, all concrete judgments of fact are excluded by the criterion of indubitability.

Fifthly, the existential subject survives, for the existential subject is

the subject as prior to the question, Am I? The criterion of indubitability does not eliminate the experienced center of experiencing, the intelligent center of inquiry, insight, and formulations, the rational center
of critical reflection, scrutiny, hesitation, doubt, and frustration.
Indeed, the method of universal doubt presupposes the existence of
this center and imposes frustration upon it. One can argue that before I
can doubt, I must exist, but what does the conclusion mean? What is
the 'I'? What is existing? What is the meaning of affirming? All these
questions can be given answers that are correct in fact. But as long as
the criterion of indubitability remains in force, they cannot be given
any clear or precise answer, for that would suppose a clarification of
the polymorphism of human consciousness.

Sixthly, not even the criterion of indubitability is indubitable. It is
clear enough that one makes no mistake in accepting the indubitable. It
is not at all clear that one makes no mistake in rejecting everything that
in fact is true. But the criterion of indubitability excludes all concrete
judgments of fact, no matter how true and certain they may be. Therefore, the criterion of indubitability is not itself indubitable. It follows
that the frustrated existential subject practicing universal doubt cannot
console himself with the thought that there is anything rational about
his doubting.

Seventhly, every assignable reason for practicing universal doubt is
eliminated by a coherent exercise of the doubt. Thus, one might adopt
the method of universal doubt in the hope of being left with premises
for a deduction of the universe; but the exercise of the doubt removes
all premises and leaves only mere suppositions; moreover, even if it
left some premises, it would question the validity of the project of
deducing the universe, for it is not indubitable that the universe can be
deduced. Again, one might adopt the method of universal doubt
because one felt the disagreement of philosophers to reveal their
incompetence and to justify the use of a violent remedy; but the exercise of the doubt leaves nothing for philosophers to disagree about,
and as well it leaves open to suspicion the assumption that their disagreement stems from their incompetence; for it is conceivable that
philosophic process is dialectical, with positions inviting development
and counterpositions inviting reversal.

Eighthly, the method of universal doubt is a leap in the dark. If we
have been able to determine a list of precise consequences of universal
doubt, we also have presupposed our account of the structure of

human knowledge and of the polymorphism that besets it. But that account is not indubitable. At most, it is true as a matter of fact. Accordingly, to accept the criterion of indubitability is to deprive oneself of the means of ascertaining what precisely that criterion implies; and to accept a criterion without being able to determine its precise implications is to make a leap in the dark.

Ninthly, while the consequences of universal doubt will come to light in the long run, the proximate results of the method will be arbitrary and illusory. Proximate results will be arbitrary, for the exact implications of the method are unknown. Moreover, proximate results will be illusory, for doubting affects, not the underlying texture and fabric of the mind, but only the explicit judgments that issue from it. One can profess in all sincerity to doubt all that can be doubted, but one cannot abolish at a stroke the past development of one's mentality, one's accumulation of insights, one's prepossessions and prejudices, one's habitual orientation in life. So one will have little difficulty in seeing that the views of others are very far from being indubitable; at the same time, because the doubt is applied arbitrarily, one's own rooted convictions not merely will survive but also will be illuminated with the illusory splendor of having passed unscathed through an ordeal that the views of others could not stand. Accordingly, it will be only in the long run that the full implications of universal doubt will come to light, when the method has been applied by many persons with quite different initial convictions.

However, if I believe that universal doubt was practiced more successfully by Hume than by Descartes, and perhaps more successfully by the existentialists and some of the logical positivists than by Hume, I must also recall that my topic has been, not the concrete proposal entertained by Descartes, but the consequences of interpreting literally and applying rigorously the precept 'Doubt everything that can be doubted.' Clearly enough, the implications of that precept fail to reveal the profound originality and enduring significance of Descartes, for whom universal doubt was not a school of skepticism but a philosophic program that aimed to embrace the universe, to assign a clear and precise reason for everything, to exclude the influence of unacknowledged presuppositions. For that program we have only praise, but we also believe that it should be disassociated from the method of universal doubt, whether that method is interpreted rigorously or mitigated in a fashion that cannot avoid being arbitrary.

Finally, it should be noted that a rejection of universal doubt implies a rejection of the excessive commitment with which it burdens the philosophic enterprise. The only method to reach the conclusions of science is the method of science. The only method to reach the conclusions of common sense is the method of common sense. Universal doubt leads the philosopher to reject what he is not equipped to restore. But philosophers that do not practice universal doubt are not in that predicament, and it is only a mistaken argument from analogy that expects of them a validation of scientific or commonsense views.

5 Empiricism

A second method that offers to guide the subject issues the precept 'Observe the significant facts.' Unfortunately, what can be observed is merely a datum; significance accrues to data only through the occurrence of insights; correct insights can be reached only at the term of a prolonged investigation that ultimately reaches the point where no further relevant questions arise; and without the combination of data and correct insights that together form a virtually unconditioned, there are no facts. Such, I believe, is the truth of the matter, but it is an extremely paradoxical truth, and the labor of all the pages that precede can be regarded as a sustained effort both to clarify the nature of insight and judgment and to account for the confusion, so natural to man, between extroversion and objectivity. For man observes, understands, and judges, but he fancies that what he knows in judgment is not known in judgment and does not suppose an exercise of understanding but simply is attained by taking a good look at the 'real' that is 'already out there now.' Empiricism, then, is a bundle of blunders, and its history is their successive clarification.

In its sublimest form, the observation of significant facts occurs in St Augustine's contemplation of the eternal reasons. For years, as he tells us, St Augustine was unable to grasp that the real could be anything but a body. When with neo-Platonist aid he got beyond that view, his name for reality was *veritas*; and for him truth was to be known, not by looking out, nor yet by looking within, but rather by looking above, where in an immutable light men consult and contemplate the eternal reasons of things. It is disputed, of course, just how literally St Augustine intended this inspection of the eternal to be understood. Aquinas insisted that the uncreated light grounds the truth of our judgments, not because we see that light, but because our intellects are created participations of it. But if St Augustine's meaning is doubtful, there is less doubt about a group of nineteenth-century Catholics known as ontologists, who believed that the only way to meet Kant's claim that the unconditioned is, not a constitutive element in judgment, but a merely regulative ideal, was to issue under Augustinian auspices the counterclaim that the notion of being was an obscure intuition of God.

As there is an empiricism on the level of critical reflection, so there is an empiricism on the level of understanding. The Scotist theory of abstraction was outlined above, and as was said, its second step consists in intellect taking a look at a conceptual content produced in the intellect by the unconscious cooperation of the intellective and the imaginative powers of the soul. Moreover, such intellectual empiricism reaches far beyond the confines of the Scotist school. The objective universals of Platonist thought seem to owe their origin to the notion that, as the eye of the body looks upon colors and shapes, so there is a spiritual eye of the soul that looks at universals, or at least recalls them. Finally, the Aristotelian and Thomist traditions are not without their ambiguities. Though Aristotle acknowledged the fact of insight and Aquinas added to Aristotle a transposition of Augustinian thought on judgment and of neo-Platonist thought on participation and being, still Aristotle's physics probably is a study of 'bodies,' and until recently Thomist commentators have tended almost universally to ignore Aquinas's affirmation of insight and to take it for granted that, while Aquinas obviously differed from Scotus in the metaphysical analysis of cognitional process, still the psychological content of his doctrine was much the same as that of Scotus.

The conflict between objectivity as extroversion and intelligence as knowledge has provided a fundamental theme in the unfolding of modern philosophy. Cartesian dualism was the juxtaposition of the rational affirmation *Cogito, ergo sum* and of the 'already out there now real' stripped of its secondary qualities and of any substantiality distinct from spatial extension. While Spinoza and Malebranche attempted to swallow the dualism on the rationalist side, Hobbes reduced thinking to an unprivileged instance of matter in motion. The Cambridge Platonists endeavored to accept Hobbes's conception of the real as 'out there now' and yet to affirm God as supremely real because his omnipresence was the reality of space and his eternity was the reality of time. Berkeley sought the same end by a different route; he granted secondary qualities to be mere appearance, and concluded that primary qualities with still greater certainty were mere appearance; being then was being perceived, and so reality shifted from apparent 'bodies' to the cognitional order. Finally, Hume brought analysis to bear effectively on the issue; our knowing involves not only elements but also unities and relations; the elements consist in a manifold of unrelated sense impressions; the unities and relations have no better foundation than our mental habits and beliefs; whatever may be the practical utility of our knowledge, at least it cannot pretend to philosophic validity.

If it is merely confusion of thought that interprets objectivity in terms of extroversion, Kant's Copernican revolution was a half-hearted affair. He pronounced both primary and secondary qualities to be phenomena. He made absolute space and absolute time a priori forms of outer and inner sense. He regarded the things themselves of Newtonian thought to be unknowable. But he was unable to break cleanly from the basic conviction of animal extroversion that the 'real' is the 'already out there now.' Though unknowable, Newton's things themselves were somehow known to produce impressions on our senses and to appear. The category of reality was to be employed by understanding when there occurred some filling in the empty form of time. The category of substance was identified with the permanence of reality in time. However convinced Kant was that 'taking a look' could not be valid human knowing, he devoted his energies to showing how it could seem to be knowing and in what restricted sense it could be regarded as valid. Nor is the anomaly of his position surprising. If the schematism of the categories comes within striking distance of the virtually unconditioned, still Kant failed to see that the unconditioned is a constituent component in the genesis of judgment, and so he relegated it to the role of a regulative ideal of systematizing rationality. But once extroversion is questioned, it is only through man's reflective grasp of the unconditioned that the objectivity and validity of human knowing can be established. Kant rightly saw that animal knowing is not human knowing; but he failed to see what human knowing is. The combination of that truth and that failure is the essence of the principle of immanence that was to dominate subsequent thought.

Cartesian dualism had been a twofold realism, and both the realisms were correct; for the realism of the extroverted animal is no mistake, and the realism of rational affirmation is no mistake. The trouble was that, unless two distinct and disparate types of knowing were recognized, the two realisms were incompatible. For rational affirmation is not an instance of extroversion, and so it cannot be objective in the manner proper to the 'already out there now.' On the other hand, the flow of sensible contents and acts is neither intelligent nor reasonable, and so it cannot be knowledge of the type exhibited by science and philosophy. The attempt to fuse disparate forms of knowing into a single whole ended in the destruction of each by the other; and the destruction of both forms implied the rejection of both types of realism. The older materialism and sensism were discredited, but there was room for positivism and pragmatism to uphold the same viewpoint in a more cultured tone. German idealism swung through its magnificent arc of dazzling systems to come to terms with reality in relativism and neo-Kantian analysis. But if a century and a half have brought forth no solution, it would seem necessary to revert to the beginning and distinguish two radically distinct types of knowing in the polymorphic consciousness of man ...

In brief, empiricism as a method rests on an elementary confusion. What is obvious in knowing is, indeed, looking. Compared to looking, insight is obscure, and grasp of the unconditioned is doubly obscure. But empiricism amounts to the assumption that what is obvious in knowing is what knowing obviously is. That assumption is false, for if one would learn mathematics or science or philosophy or if one sought commonsense advice, then one would go to a man that is intelligent and reasonable rather than to a man that is stupid and silly.

Related selections: 1.VII.1 and 1VIII.2 on the structure of human knowing; 1.IX on the notion of being; 1.X on the notion of objectivity; 1.VI.2–3 on the duality in human knowing; 1.IV.2 on the polymorphism of consciousness; 1.XVI.1 on the dialectical problem in its full dimensions; 1.XVI.4 on the critique of beliefs; 3.VII.2 on intellectual conversion; 1.XVII.1 on the existential problem in self-appropriation.

XII

Development

Up to this point in *Insight* Lonergan has provided accounts of three methods of investigation: the classical and statistical methods of natural science, and the dialectical method of philosophy. In the present selection from Chapter 15 of *Insight* he introduces his account of a fourth, or genetic, method. While classical method, for example, attempts to reduce regular events to laws, genetic method seeks insight into sequences in which correlations and regularities change. The central element of this heuristic structure is the notion of development.

In the first part of this selection Lonergan affirms a parallelism between the open dynamism of the human mind and the dynamism of the universe. The universe 'is not at rest, not static, not fixed in the present, but in process, tension, fluid.'[1] The striving of human knowing is 'the intelligent and reasonable part of a universal striving towards being.'[2] Here Lonergan introduces his notion of the finality of the universe. In the second part Lonergan defines development as a linked sequence of dynamic higher integrations and outlines the principles of development. This discussion sheds additional light on Lonergan's claim, in his earlier treatment of the dialectic of community, that the problem of decline is to be met by some type of higher integration. In the third part Lonergan compares and contrasts genetic method, which is guided by the notion of development, with classical method, and he concludes that the technique of measurement so basic to physics and chemistry loses its efficacy when one turns to the study of development. In *Insight*, subsequent to this analysis, Lonergan illustrates the employment of genetic method in the study of the

1 *Insight*, 470.
2 *Insight*, 471.

development of the organism, in psychic and intellectual development, and in the interlocking of organic, psychic, and intellectual development in the development of a human being. The last part of this selection is Lonergan's account of human development with its inevitable tensions and conflicts. This discussion concludes with Lonergan's account of genuineness, the admission of the tension of development into consciousness, upon which continuous development depends. Developmental processes and the tensions associated with them make their appearance in *Insight* well before this explicit treatment. Genetic method is employed, without being discussed, in Lonergan's accounts of the development of mathematics, of natural science, and of common sense.

   These extracts are taken from *Insight* 470–1; 476–9; 484–8; 494–503.

1   Finality

Being has been conceived heuristically as the objective of the detached and disinterested desire to know, and more precisely as whatever is to be known by intelligent grasp and reasonable affirmation. This heuristic notion has been found to underlie all our knowing, to penetrate all conceptual contents, to go beyond them, to provide a core for all meaning. We have now to formulate a reciprocal notion of equal significance. For it is not only our notion of being that is heuristic, that heads for an objective that can be defined only in terms of the process of knowing it, but also the reality of proportionate being itself exhibits a similar incompleteness and a similar dynamic orientation towards a completeness that becomes determinate only in the process of completion.

   Just as intellectually patterned experience heads towards insights and judgments, so potency heads towards forms and acts. Just as cognitional activity mounts through accumulations of insights to higher viewpoints, so objective process involves the information and actuation of prime potency only to uncover a residue of coincidental manifolds and so mount through successive levels of higher systematization. Just as cognitional activity does not know in advance what being is and so has to define it heuristically as whatever is to be known by intelligent grasp and reasonable affirmation, so objective process is not the realization of some blueprint but the cumulation of a conditioned series of things and schemes of recurrence in accord with successive schedules of probabilities. Just as cognitional activity is the becoming known of being, so objective process is the becoming of proportionate being. Indeed, since cognitional activity is itself but a part of this universe, so its heading to being is but the particular instance in which universal striving towards being becomes conscious and intelligent and reasonable.

Such is the meaning we would attach to the name 'finality.' Accordingly, we do not mean by finality some expedient of a lazy intelligence attempting to make amends for the deficiencies in its account of efficient causality. Much less do we mean by finality some pull exerted by the future on the present. By finality we refer to a theorem of the same generality as the notion of being. This theorem affirms a parallelism between the dynamism of the mind and the dynamism of proportionate being. It affirms that the objective universe is not at rest, not static, not fixed in the present, but in process, in tension, fluid. As it regards present reality in its dynamic aspect, so it affirms this dynamism to be open. As what is to be known becomes determinate only through knowing, so what is to be becomes determinate only through its own becoming. But as present knowing is not just present knowing but also a moment in process towards fuller knowing, so also present reality is not just present reality but also a moment in process to fuller reality.

The objective ground of this open dynamism is potency. For potency is what is to be known by intellectually patterned experience of the empirical residue. But intellectually patterned experience is dynamic; it is experience under some heuristic structure that is derived from the detached and disinterested desire to know; it is experience dominated by that desire. And the dynamic orientation of such experience no less than the experience itself has its counterpart in proportionate being. Indeed, since cognitional activity is itself but a part of this universe, its striving to know being is but the intelligent and reasonable part of a universal striving towards being.

2   The Notion of Development

Because the notion of development is peculiarly subject to the distorting influence of counterpositions, our account of insight as activity made no attempt to discuss the nature of genetic method. This omission has now to be remedied, and perhaps the simplest procedure will be to begin by stating and illustrating the principles of development.

First, there is the already familiar principle of emergence. Otherwise coincidental manifolds of lower conjugate acts invite the higher integration effected by higher conjugate forms. Thus, in our account of explanatory genera chemical elements and compounds are higher integrations of otherwise coincidental manifolds of subatomic events; organisms are higher integrations of otherwise coincidental manifolds of chemical processes; sensitive consciousness is a higher integration of otherwise coincidental manifolds of changes in neural tissues; and accumulating insights are higher integrations of otherwise coincidental manifolds of images or of data.

Secondly, there is the principle of correspondence. Significantly different underlying manifolds require different higher integrations. Thus, the chemical elements differ by atomic numbers and atomic weights, and these differences are grounded in the underlying manifold. Different aggregates of aggregates of chemical processes involve different organisms. Neural events in the eye and in the ear call forth different conscious experiences. Different data lead to different theories. It is true, of course, that not every difference in the underlying manifold demands a different integration; the same kind of atom can have subatomic components at different energy levels; the same kind of organism admits differences of size, shape, weight; similarities of character and temperament are compatible, probably enough, with neural differences; and the same theory can be reached from different data. Accordingly, the principle of correspondence enjoys a measure of flexibility; within limits the same higher integration will systematize differing manifolds; the point to the principle is that these limits exist and that to transgress them is to eliminate the higher integration.

Thirdly, there is the principle of finality. The underlying manifold is an upwardly but indeterminately directed dynamism towards ever fuller realization of being. Any actual realization will pertain to some determinate genus and species, but this very determinacy is limitation, and every limitation is to finality a barrier to be transcended.

There follows at once a distinction between static and dynamic higher integrations. Every higher integration systematizes an otherwise coincidental manifold, but the systematization may be effected in two different manners. It is static when it dominates the lower manifold with complete success and thereby brings about a notable imperviousness to change. Thus, the inert gases lock coincidental manifolds of subatomic events in remarkably permanent routines. On the other hand, the higher integration is dynamic when it is not content to systematize the underlying manifold but keeps adding to it and modifying it until, by the principle of correspondence, the existing integration is eliminated and, by the principle of emergence, a new integration is introduced.

Fourthly, then, there is the principle of development itself. It is the linked sequence of dynamic higher integrations. An initial coincidental manifold is systematized and modified by a higher integration so as to call forth a second; the second leads to a third; the third to a fourth; and so on, until the possibilities of development along a given line are exhausted and the relative stability of maturity is reached.

Fifthly, the course of development is marked by an increasing explanatory differentiation. The initial integration in the initial manifold pertains to a determinate genus and species; still, exclusive attention to the data on the initial stage would yield little knowledge and less understanding of the relevant genus and species. What is to be known by understanding is what is yet to come, what may be present virtually or potentially but as yet is not present formally or actually. Accordingly, if one attends simply to the data on each successive stage of a development, one finds that the initial integration can be understood only in a generic fashion, that subsequent integrations are increasingly specific intelligibilities, that the specific intelligible differentiation of the ultimate stage attained is generated in the process from the initial stage. Thus, initial single cells of different organisms admit material differences, for example, in the number of chromosomes, but their functioning does not exhibit differences that are comparable to the later differences in functioning. Again, men of widely different temperament and character began, as infants, from instances of sensitive consciousness that not only were remarkably similar but also remarkably undifferentiated; there were sensations, but perceptiveness was undeveloped; there was nothing to remember, and powers of imagination were latent; affects were global affairs of elementary types; and skills were limited to wailing. Finally, intellectual development has its roots in the detached and disinterested desire to know; but the mere desire is not knowledge of anything; it will lead to highly differentiated structures that are masteries of logic, mathematics, natural science, common sense, philosophy, and human science; but these intelligible differentiations are yet to come, and they come only in and through the process of development.

Sixthly, the course of development is capable of a minor flexibility inasmuch as it can pursue the same ultimate goal along different routes. In other words, the initial manifold with its material differences, though it can evoke no more than the initial integration, nonetheless suffices to determine what the ultimate goal is to be. In virtue of this determination, the course of development can yield to circumstances and so follow any of a set of alternative linked sequences. Thus, a normal sea urchin can result from an embryo subjected to distorting pressures; psychic health can be due to untutored spontaneity or to the ministrations of the psychiatrist; the same science can be taught successfully in accord with different methods, and the same discovery can be made in different manners.

Seventhly, the course of development is capable of a major flexibility that consists in a shift or modification of the ultimate objective. In biology this is the familiar fact of adaptation; in depth psychology it may be illustrated by sublimation; in cognitional activity it appears in the manner in which inquirers, often enough, begin from one problem only to find themselves by the logic of issues forced to engage in the solution of another.

Major flexibility appears to conflict with minor flexibility, for the former involves a shift in the objective while the latter rests on the fixity of the objective. However, this difference is merely descriptive. In minor flexibility there is at work the determination of the development that rests on the initial manifold. This determination exhibits potency as the ground of limitation. But potency is also the ground of finality, and from this viewpoint it heads to ever fuller realizations. Moreover, a higher integration is characterized only partially by its systematization of an underlying manifold; on an adequate account, it is the emergence of a solution to the compound problem of systematizing a coincidental manifold in a given milieu or context; and this solution consists in a set of conjugate forms that are related not only to one another within the integration but also to other instances of the same type outside the integration.

In the light of the foregoing considerations, a development may be defined as a flexible, linked sequence of dynamic and increasingly differentiated higher integrations that meet the tension of successively transformed underlying manifolds through successive applications of the principles of correspondence and emergence ...

3   Genetic Method

As classical method anticipates an unspecified correlation to be specified, an indeterminate function to be determined, so genetic method
finds its heuristic notion in development. In the plant there is the single development of the organism; in the animal there is the twofold
development of the organism and the psyche; in man there is the threefold development of the organism, the psyche, and intelligence ...

But far more conspicuous than the parallel, there are the differences
between physics and, on the other hand, biology, psychology, and
intellectual theory. Regular physical events are apt to recur in some
single determinate scheme. But organic, psychic, and intellectual
events are recurrent, not in single schemes, but in flexible circles of
ranges of schemes. Nor is this all. There is the fact of development. In
the course of time the conjugate forms advance from generic indeterminacy towards a specific perfection. Concomitantly the flexible circle
of schemes of recurrence both shifts and expands. Operations that initially were impossible or extremely awkward and inefficient become
possible, spontaneous, economical, rapid, and effective. Masses and
electric charges, atoms and molecules, are statically systematic; their
performance is not a function of their age; there is not a different law of
gravitation for each succeeding century. In contrast, organic, psychic,
and intellectual development involves a succession of stages; and in
that succession the previously impossible becomes possible and the
previously awkward and difficult becomes a ready routine. The infant
can neither walk nor talk, and once we all were infants. Hence, where
the physicist or chemist is out to determine single sets of conjugate
forms and consequent schemes of recurrence, the biologist or psychologist or intellectual theorist is out to determine genetic sequences of
conjugate forms and consequent sequences of flexible circles of
schemes of recurrence ...

[T]here follows the outstanding difference between classical and
genetic method. Classical method is concerned to reduce regular
events to laws. Genetic method is concerned with sequences in which
correlations and regularities change. Accordingly, the principal object
of genetic method is to master the sequence itself, to understand the
development, and thereby to proceed from the correlations and regularities of one stage to those of the next. If a mathematical illustration is
helpful and not too much out of place, one might say that genetic

method is concerned with a sequence of operators that successively generate further functions from an initial function ...

[A]s the heuristic assumption of classical method is the indeterminate function to be determined, so the heuristic assumption of genetic method lies in the notion of development ...

The extraordinary success of the physical sciences naturally enough led investigators of the organism, the psyche, and intelligence to a servile rather than an intelligent adoption of the successful procedures. In physics and chemistry, measuring is a basic technique that takes inquiry from the relations of things to our senses to their relations to one another. But when one mounts to the higher integrations of the organism, the psyche, and intelligence, one finds that measuring loses both in significance and efficacy. It loses in significance, for the higher integration is, within limits, independent of the exact quantities of the lower manifold it systematizes. Moreover, the higher the integration, the greater the independence of lower quantities, so that the meaning of one's dreams is not a function of one's weight, and one's ability in mathematics does not vary with one's height. Besides this loss in significance, there is also a loss in efficacy. Classical method can select among the functions that solve differential equations by appealing to measurements and empirically established curves. What the differential equation is to classical method, the general notion of development is to genetic method. But while the differential equation is mathematical, the general notion of development is not. It follows that, while measurement is an efficacious technique for finding boundary conditions that restrict differential equations, it possesses no assignable efficacy when it comes to particularizing the general notion of development.

4 Human Development and Genuineness

It remains that a word be said on total development in man. Organic, psychic, and intellectual development are not three independent processes. They are interlocked, with the intellectual providing a higher integration of the psychic and the psychic providing a higher integration of the organic. Each level involves its own laws, its flexible circle of schemes of recurrence, its interlocked set of conjugate forms. Each set of forms stands in an emergent correspondence to otherwise coincidental manifolds on the lower levels. Hence a single human action can involve a series of components: physical, chemical, organic, neural, psychic, and intellectual; and the several components occur in accord with the laws and realized schemes of their appropriate levels. However, while physical and chemical laws are static, higher correlations pertain to systems on the move, and quite obviously there results the problem of formulating the heuristic structure of the investigation of this triply compounded development. What the existentialist discovers and talks about, what the ascetic attempts to achieve in himself, what the psychiatrist endeavors to foster in another, what the psychologist aims at understanding completely, the metaphysician outlines in heuristic categories.

First, then, at any stage of his development a man is an individual existing unity differentiated by physical, chemical, organic, psychic, and intellectual conjugates. The organic, psychic, and intellectual conjugate forms ground respective flexible circles of ranges of schemes of recurrence that are revealed in the man's spontaneous and effective behavior, in his bodily movements, in his dealings with persons and things, in the content of his speech and writing. Moreover, if one turns from outward behavior to inner experience, one finds that it shifts into quite different patterns as one engages in different types of activity; absorption in intellectual issues tends to eliminate sensitive emotions and conations, and inversely, mystical absorption tends to eliminate the flow of sensitive presentations and imaginative representations; again, aesthetic experience and the pattern of practical activity tend to be mutually exclusive; finally, while the dramatic pattern of one person dealing with other persons draws upon all one's resources, still it subdivides, like the successive coatings in an onion, into a series of zones from the ego or *moi intime* to the outer rind of the persona, so that one is aloof with strangers, courteous with acquaintances, at ease with one's friends, occasionally unbosoms oneself to intimates, keeps some matters entirely to oneself, and refuses even to face others.

Secondly, man develops. Whatever he is at present, he was not always so, and generally speaking he need not remain so. The flexible circles of ranges of schemes of recurrence shift and expand, for neural, psychic, and intellectual conjugates pertain to systems on the move. The functioning of the higher integration involves changes in the underlying manifold, and the changing manifold evokes a modified higher integration. There obtains the law of effect, for development occurs along the directions in which it succeeds. But there also obtains an anticipated law of effect on the psychic and intellectual levels. Thus, unless one asks the further questions, one remains with the insights one has already, and so intelligence does not develop; inversely, because one wants to develop, one can frequent the lectures and read the books that put the further questions and help one to learn. Again, one develops through functioning, and until one has developed, one's functioning has the lack of poise, of economy, of effectiveness, that betrays as yet undifferentiated potentialities. Unless one is encouraged out of shyness, timidity, pretended indifference, to zest and risk and doing, to humility and laughter, one will not develop but merely foster the objective grounds for one's feeling of inferiority. Rather, one will not develop along a certain more common line; one will seek and find less common fields in which to excel; and there one will be apt to over-compensate for deficiencies elsewhere.

Thirdly, there is a law of integration. The initiative of development may be organic, psychic, intellectual, or external, but the development remains fragmentary until the principle of correspondence between different levels is satisfied. Thus, the initiative may be organic, for the organism is an upwardly directed dynamism, seeking to be more fully, evoking its higher integration by calling forth psychic images and feelings. So man is prompted to waking and sleeping, to eating and drinking, to shade in the summer and the fireside in winter, to loving and begetting children and fending for them; and these psychic, sensitive, corporal activities in their turn call forth the family and technology, the economy and polity, morality and law. Again, the initiative may be psychic, for man's sensitivity not only reflects and integrates its biological basis but also is itself an entity, a value, a living and developing. Inter-subjectivity, companionship, play and artistry, the idle hours spent with those with whom one feels at home, the common purpose, labor, achievement, failure, disaster, the sharing of feeling in laughter and lamenting, all are human things, and in them man functions primarily in accord with the development of his perceptiveness, his emotional responses, his sentiments. Thirdly, the initiative may be intellectual; its source is a problem; one is out to understand, to judge, to decide, to choose. Finally, the initiative may spring from a change in one's material circumstances, in the perceptiveness or sentiments of another, in the discoveries of other minds and the decisions of other wills.

Still, the initiation of a development is one thing and its integrated completion is another. If one adapts to external change merely out of deference to material necessity or social pressure, the behavior of the outward persona is modified in a manner that, at best, is tolerated by the inner subject. Again, if one sincerely makes an excellent resolution about one's mode or style of behavior, the resolution is apt to remain sterile if the appropriate perceptiveness and feelings are not forthcoming and one does not know how to evoke them. Inversely, a development can begin in one's perceptiveness and feelings, yet it will remain frustrated if one fails to understand oneself, to plan the strategy, and to execute the tactics that secure congenial companionship or employment. Finally, the nonconscious neural basis can send up its signals that express a starved affectivity or other demands for fuller living, but the signals need an interpreter and the interpreter an intelligent and willing pupil.

The law of integration, then, is a declaration of what is meant by human development. Because man is a unity, his proper development is no more than initiated when a new scheme of recurrence is established in his outward behavior, in his thinking and willing, in his perceptiveness and feeling, in the organic and neural basis of his action. Generally speaking, such an initiation of development invites complementary adjustments and advances, and unless they are effected, either the initiated development recedes and atrophies in favor of the dynamic unity of the subject, or else that unity is sacrificed and deformed to make man a mere dumping ground for unrelated, unintegrated schemes of recurrence and modes of behavior.

Fourthly, there is a law of limitation and transcendence. It is a law of tension. On the one hand, development is in the subject and of the subject; on the other hand, it is from the subject as he is and towards the subject as he is to be. Finality has been conceived as the upwardly but not determinately directed dynamism of proportionate being. Its realization may be regular, but its regularity is not according to law, according to settled spontaneity, according to acquired habit, according to existing schemes of recurrence; on the contrary, it is a change in the law, the spontaneity, the habit, the scheme; it is the process of introducing and establishing a new law, spontaneity, habit, scheme. Its point of departure necessarily is the subject as he happens to be; but its direction is against his remaining as he is; and though its term will involve him in a fresh temptation to inertial repetition and recurrence, that term is to be approached only by breaking away from the inertia of his prior stage.

Now the tension that is inherent in the finality of proportionate being becomes in man a conscious tension. Present perceptiveness is to be enlarged, and the enlargement is not perceptible to present perceptiveness. Present desires and fears have to be transmuted, and the transmutation is not desirable to present desire but fearful to present fear. Moreover, as has been noted, the organism reaches its highest differentiation under the psychic integration of the animal, and the psyche reaches its highest differentiation under the intellectual integration in man. Because psychic development is so much more extensive and intricate in man than in other animals, it is involved in a more prolonged tension, and it is open to more acute and diversified crises.

There is a further and deeper aspect to the matter. Intellectual development rests upon the dominance of a detached and disinterested desire to know. It reveals to a man a universe of being in which he is but an item, and a universal order in which his desires and fears, his delight and anguish, are but infinitesimal components in the history of mankind. It invites man to become intelligent and reasonable not only in his knowing but also in his living, to guide his actions by referring them, not as an animal to a habitat, but as an intelligent being to the intelligible context of some universal order that is or is to be. Still, it is difficult for man, even in knowing, to be dominated simply by the pure desire, and it is far more difficult for him to permit that detachment and disinterestedness to dominate his whole way of life. For the self as perceiving and feeling, as enjoying and suffering, functions as an animal in an environment, as a self-attached and self-interested center within its own narrow world of stimuli and responses. But the same self as inquiring and reflecting, as conceiving intelligently and judging reasonably, is carried by its own higher spontaneity to quite a different mode of operation with the opposite attributes of detachment and disinterestedness. It is confronted with a universe of being in which it finds itself, not the center of reference, but an object coordinated with other objects and, with them, subordinated to some destiny to be discovered or invented, approved or disdained, accepted or repudiated.

Such, then, is the height of the tension of human consciousness. On the side of the object, it is the opposition between the world of sense of man the animal and, on the other hand, the universe of being to be known by intelligent grasp and reasonable affirmation. On the side of the subject, it is the opposition between a center in the world of sense operating self-centeredly and, on the other hand, an entry into an intelligibly ordered universe of being to which one can belong, and in which one can function, only through detachment and disinterestedness. Not only is the opposition complete but also it is ineluctable. As a man cannot divest himself of his animality, so he cannot put off the eros of his mind. To inquire and understand, to reflect and judge, to deliberate and choose are as much an exigence of human nature as waking and sleeping, eating and drinking, talking and loving. Nor is there any escape from the universe of being and its intelligible order by devising some particular type of metaphysics or countermetaphysics. For the universe of being is whatever is intelligently grasped and reasonably affirmed; by its definition it includes an intelligible order; and to set up as a philosopher of any school whatever, one has to claim to understand and pretend to be reasonable.

It is this heightened tension that in human development supplies the content of the compound, antithetical law of limitation and transcendence. All development is development inasmuch as it goes beyond the initial subject, but in man this 'going beyond' is anticipated immanently by the detachment and disinterestedness of the pure desire. Again, all development is development inasmuch as it possesses a point of departure, a concrete material to be transmuted, but in man this concrete material is permanent in the self-centered sensitive psyche content to orientate itself within its visible and palpable environment and to deal with it successfully. Nor are the pure desire and the sensitive psyche two things, one of them 'I' and the other 'It.' They are the unfolding on different levels of a single, individual unity, identity, whole. Both are 'I,' and neither is merely 'It.' If my intelligence is mine, so is my sexuality. If my reasonableness is mine, so are my dreams. If my intelligence and my reasonableness are to be thought more representative of me than my organic and psychic spontaneity, that is only in virtue of the higher integration that in fact my intelligence and reasonableness succeed in imposing on their underlying manifold, or proleptically, in virtue of the development in which the higher integration is to achieve a fuller measure of success. But no matter how full the success, the basic situation within the self is unchanged, for the perfection of the higher integration does not eliminate the integrated or modify the essential opposition between self-centeredness and detachment. The same 'I' on different and related levels of operation retains the opposed characters.

Fifthly, there is a law of genuineness. At first sight it is an obvious matter of simplicity and honesty, of perspicacity and sincerity. But a little probing brings to light a paradox. Insofar as development occurs nonconsciously, there is no relevance to genuineness, for simplicity and honesty, perspicacity and sincerity are qualities of conscious acts. On the other hand, one may argue, the more consciously a development occurs, the less the likelihood that it will be marked by genuineness, for when one speaks of a simple and honest soul, one is not thinking of a person given to deep and prolonged self-scrutiny. What, then, can genuineness be? It does not pertain to nonconscious development, and it seems to stand in conflict with any notable consciousness of development. Is it a property of some twilight development that is neither unconscious nor fully conscious? And if it is, how can there be a general law of genuineness? Such is the paradox.

To meet it, let us say that the requirement of genuineness is conditional and analogous. It is conditional, for it arises only inasmuch as development occurs through consciousness. It is analogous, for the requirement has a different content in different cases. The genuineness of which we think when we speak of a simple and honest soul is the happy fruit of a life in which illusion and pretense have had no place. But there is another genuineness that has to be won back through a self-scrutiny that expels illusion and pretense; and as this enterprise is difficult and its issue doubtful, we do not think of its successful outcome when we cast about for an obvious illustration of genuineness.

In the light of these distinctions, the law of genuineness can be put as follows. Every development involves a starting point in the subject as he is, a term in the subject as he is to be, and a process from the starting point to the term. However, inasmuch as a development is conscious, there is some apprehension of the starting point, the term, and the process. But such apprehensions may be correct or mistaken. If they are correct, the conscious and unconscious components of the development are operating from the same base along the same route to the same goal. If they are mistaken, the conscious and unconscious components, to a greater or less extent, are operating at cross-purposes. Such a conflict is inimical to the development, and so we have the conditional law of genuineness, namely, that if a development is conscious, then its success demands correct apprehensions of its starting point, its process, and its goal.

Further, besides being correct or mistaken, the apprehensions that make a development conscious may be minimal or more or less extensive. They are minimal when they involve little more than the succession of fragmentary and separate acts needed to carry out the successive steps of the development with advertence, intelligence, and reasonableness. They are more or less extensive when one begins to delve into the background, the context, the premises, the interrelations, of the minimal series of conscious acts, and to subsume this understanding of oneself under empirical laws and philosophic theories of development. Now, other things being equal, there is less likelihood of error in the minimal series alone than in the minimal series fitted out with its concrete background and its theoretical explanation; and for this reason we expect genuineness to be more common in the simple and honest soul innocent of introspection and depth psychology. But it very well may be that other things are not equal, that errors have become lodged in the habitual background whence spring our direct and reflective insights, that if we relied upon our virtual and implicit self-knowledge to provide us with concrete guidance through a conscious development, then the minimal series, so far from being probably correct, would be certainly mistaken. Accordingly, the law of genuineness not only is conditional but also is analogous; it becomes relevant insofar as development is conscious; and what it demands will be spontaneous in some cases and in others only obtained through more or less extensive self-scrutiny.

The necessity, then, of genuineness is the necessity of avoiding conflict between the unconscious and the conscious components of a development. But one moves to a deeper grasp of the issue when one asks why conflict should arise. For if one does not have to look far to find a reason, the reason is not without its profundity. As we have seen, all development involves a tension between limitation and transcendence. On the one hand, there is the subject as he is functioning more or less successfully in a flexible circle of ranges of schemes of recurrence. On the other hand, there is the subject as a higher system on the move. One and the same reality is both integrator and operator; but the operator is relentless in transforming the integrator. The integrator resides in successive levels of interrelated conjugate forms that are more familiar under the common name of acquired habits. But habits are inertial. The whole tendency of present perceptiveness, of present affectivity and aggressivity, of present ways of understanding and judging, deliberating and choosing, speaking and doing, is for

them to remain as they are. Against this solid and salutary conserva-
tism, however, there operate the same principles that gave rise to the
acquired habits and now persist in attempting to transform them.
Unconsciously operative is the finality that consists in the upwardly
but indeterminately directed dynamism of all proportionate being.
Consciously operative is the detached and disinterested desire raising
ever further questions. Among the topics for questioning are one's
own unconscious initiatives, their subsumption under the general
order intelligence discovers in the universe of being, their integration
in the fabric of one's habitual living. So there emerges into consciousness a concrete apprehension of an obviously practicable and proximate ideal self; but along with it there also emerges the tension
between limitation and transcendence; and it is no vague tension
between limitation in general and transcendence in general, but an
unwelcome invasion of consciousness by opposed apprehensions of
oneself as one concretely is and as one concretely is to be.

Genuineness is the admission of that tension into consciousness, and
so it is the necessary condition of the harmonious cooperation of the
conscious and unconscious components of development. It does not
brush questions aside, smother doubts, push problems down, escape
to activity, to chatter, to passive entertainment, to sleep, to narcotics. It
confronts issues, inspects them, studies their many aspects, works out
their various implications, contemplates their concrete consequences
in one's own life and in the lives of others. If it respects inertial tendencies as necessary conservative forces, it does not conclude that a defective routine is to be maintained because one has grown accustomed to
it. Though it fears the cold plunge into becoming other than one is, it
does not dodge the issue, nor pretend bravery, nor act out of bravado.
It is capable of assurance and confidence, not only in what has been
tried and found successful, but also in what is yet to be tried. It grows
weary with the perpetual renewal of further questions to be faced, it
longs for rest, it falters and it fails, but it knows its weakness and its
failures, and it does not try to rationalize them.

Such genuineness is ideal. It goes far beyond the native endowment
of detachment and disinterestedness that we possess in the pure desire
to know. For it presupposes the accumulations of direct, introspective,
and reflective insights that are needed to discriminate between issues.
Some are momentous, some important, some secondary, some minor,
some merely silly. Without due perspective and discrimination, the

exercise of genuineness, as described above, results only in the earnest person with a remarkable flair for concentrating on the wrong questions. Nor can perspective and discrimination be acquired without asking the significant questions. There is, then, a vicious circle to be broken, for we cannot become wise and discriminating without concentrating on the right questions, and we cannot select those questions unless we already are wise and discriminating.

Still, vicious circles are logical entities, and development is a series of emergent leaps from the logic of one position to the logic of the next. Higher system as on the move, as operator, is not to be deduced from precepts and maxims alone, nor from inner impulses alone, nor from external circumstances alone. It is a creative response that meets the requirements of all three in a concrete intelligible synthesis. Man is alive, sensitive, intelligent, reasonable. Nor is he an isolated monad. His development is a movement from the relative dependence of childhood to the relative autonomy of maturity. And as he develops, the content of the analogous requirement of genuineness-for-him shifts from the simple demand of the pure desire for detachment to an ever more intelligent, more wise, more self-reliant unfolding of that desire.

Finally, there is the sanction of genuineness. To fail in genuineness is not to escape but only to displace the tension between limitation and transcendence. Such a displacement is the root of the dialectical phenomena of scotosis in the individual, of the bias of common sense, of basic philosophical differences, and of their prolongation in natural and human science, in morals and religion, in educational theory and history.

Related selections: 1.II.3 on higher viewpoints; 1.III.1–2 on classical and statistical heuristic structures; 1.IV.1 on commonsense intellectual development; 1.IX.1 on the unrestricted notion of being; 1.IV.2, 1.V.2, 1.VI.2–3, and 1.XI.1 on aspects of the tension of development; 1.XIII.2 and 1.XVI.1 on the fundamental problem posed for human beings by the fact of development; 3.IV.3 on religious development.

XIII

Truth and Interpretation

In the present selection from Chapter 17 of *Insight* Lonergan pulls together conclusions drawn in earlier discussions of reflective insight, rational consciousness, objectivity, and the notion of being to provide an account of truth. Knowing is true by its relation to being, and truth is a relation of knowing to being. This relation has been a basic concern throughout the preceding chapters of *Insight*. Lonergan's investigations of the nature and role of insight in classical, statistical, philosophic, and genetic methods, and in ordinary living, aim to expose the key constituents of the relations of knowing to being. Especially significant for an understanding of the notion of truth is Lonergan's analysis of the third, or rational, level of knowing, on which reflective questioning, reflective insight, and judgment occur. Truth is 'the conformity or correspondence of the subject's affirmations and negations to what is and is not.'[1]

In the first part of the present selection Lonergan finds a proximate criterion of truth in reflective insight, the grasp of the virtually unconditioned to which he has already devoted an entire chapter. The greater portion of the discussion is given over to the remote criterion which Lonergan locates in the proper unfolding of the pure desire to know, the notion of being. The 'correspondence' of knowing and being is not to be conceived in terms of elementary knowing and experiential confrontation with the 'already out there now real,' but in terms of complex human knowing and its intelligent and reasonable judgments. In the second part Lonergan exposes the three dimensions of full appropriation of a truth. We make a truth our own cognitively by learning it, volitionally by willing to live consistently with our knowledge, and sensitively by the adaptation of our sensibility to the demands of our intelligence and rea-

1 *Insight*, 575.

sonableness. The solidarity of the three dimensions poses a problem: without the appropriation of truth, our wills cannot be positively good; but bad will makes truth unwelcome. In the final part, taken from a longer study of the truth of interpretation, Lonergan presents his notion of a universal viewpoint, of a 'ground from which one can proceed to the content and context of every meaning.'[2] That ground, Lonergan argues, is not found in the actual possession of the contents of the totality of developmentally and dialectically related viewpoints, but in the appropriation of the dynamic structure of cognitional activity in which the *potential totality* of viewpoints resides. A philosophy that succeeds in knowing human knowing will be capable of grounding a universal viewpoint from which an understanding of the content and context of any expression of meaning may be approached. This discussion concludes with Lonergan's consideration of the ability of his own philosophical position to ground a universal viewpoint.

The extracts in this section are taken from *Insight*, 573–5; 581–5; 587–91.

1   The Criterion of Truth

The proximate criterion of truth is reflective grasp of the virtually unconditioned. Because it proceeds by rational necessity from such a grasp, the act of judgment is an actuation of rational consciousness, and the content of judgment has the stamp of the absolute.

Essentially, then, because the content of judgment is unconditioned, it is independent of the judging subject. Essentially, again, rational consciousness is what issues in a product that is independent of itself. Such is the meaning of absolute objectivity, and from it there follows a public or common terrain through which different subjects can and do communicate and agree.

Concretely, however, while reflective understanding grasps the virtually unconditioned, it itself is conditioned by the occurrence of other cognitional acts; and while the content of the judgment is grasped as unconditioned, still that content either demands or rests on the contents of experiences, insights, and other judgments for its full clarification. This concrete inevitability of a context of other acts and a context of other contents is what necessitates the addition of a remote to a proximate criterion of truth.

2 Ibid., 590.

The remote criterion is the proper unfolding of the detached and disinterested desire to know. In negative terms this proper unfolding is
the absence of interference from other desires that inhibit or reinforce,
and in either case distort, the guidance given by the pure desire. A
more positive account of the matter, perhaps, will be suggested by
clarifying the differences between six terms: infallibility and certitude,
certainty and probability, ideal and actual frequency.

A frequency is a numerical ratio of occurrences to occasions. An
actual frequency is reached by counting both occurrences and occasions. An ideal frequency is a numerical ratio from which actual frequencies diverge but do not do so systematically. Finally, both actual
and ideal frequencies may be affirmed or denied, and the affirmation
or denial may be certain or probable. It follows that, while judgments
are occurrences with actual frequencies, while in principle their ideal
frequencies might be estimated or calculated, still the ideal frequency
of a judgment is one thing and its probability is another. For certain
judgments admit an ideal frequency no less than probable judgments;
and if the ideal frequency of the probable judgment were its probability, then the probability of affirming that ideal frequency would be
another ideal frequency, so that an infinite regress would result.

Accordingly, the probability of a judgment, like the certainty of a
judgment, is a property of its content. If that content coincides with
what is grasped as virtually unconditioned, then it is a certainty. But
what is grasped as virtually unconditioned may be that a given content
heads towards the virtually unconditioned, and then the content is a
probability. On this analysis, every judgment rests on a grasp of the
virtually unconditioned, and the probability of a probable judgment is
a certainty. But the content grasped as virtually unconditioned may be
coincident with the content of the judgment or, on the other hand,
merely with the approximation of that content towards an ideal content that would be virtually unconditioned.

However, there is a third sense of probability, that is reached by contrasting infallibility with a certitude that admits degrees. A subject
may grasp the virtually unconditioned and yet may ask whether that
fulfilment of the proximate criterion of truth has been vitiated by subjective bias. Then there arises the question of the remote criterion. The
subject becomes more or less secure or anxious about the genuineness
of his inquiry and reflection, and further inquiry and reflection will in
their turn be open to similar questioning. What is in doubt is the sub-

ject himself, and all his efforts to remove the doubt will proceed from the same suspected source.

One component in this situation may be the subject's flight from the personal commitment involved in judgment; another may be a temperamental inclination to anxiety; but the objective issue is the habitual and actual disinterestedness and detachment of the subject in his cognitional activities; and in resolving that issue further considerations come into play.

Thus, one may call upon the judgments of others to support one's own. Detachment and disinterestedness are independent of circumstances, but bias, unless it is general, tends to vary with circumstances. Hence certitudes may be strengthened by the agreement of others, and this strengthening will vary with the numbers of those that agree, the diversity of their circumstances, the consequent virtual elimination of individual and group bias, and the absence of any ground for suspecting general bias.

Again, there are judgments that express the conditions of possible truth or error, certainty and probability, detachment or distortion. To call them into question is to presuppose their validity. To suppose that they will be revised is to postulate a fictitious reviser and to strip the name 'revision' of its current meaning. In such cases the subject is confronted with limiting structures that carry their own guarantee. He may fail in his formulation of the less obvious limiting structures; he may expect others with greater penetration of mind and greater detachment of spirit to improve on the formulation at which he has arrived; but at least he has some grasp of the principle of limiting structures and so some firm foothold against the fear of general bias.

There are, then, degrees of certitude, and their ground lies behind the proximate criterion of the virtually unconditioned in the more obscure region of the remote criterion. Only if this obscure region were to become completely clarified, either in fact, or more radically as a matter of principle, would certitude reach the absolute of infallibility.

2   The Appropriation of Truth

To appropriate a truth is to make it one's own. The essential appropriation of truth is cognitional. However, our reasonableness demands consistency between what we know and what we do; and so there is a volitional appropriation of truth that consists in our willingness to live up to it, and a sensitive appropriation of truth that consists in an adaptation of our sensibility to the requirements of our knowledge and our decisions.

The essential appropriation of truth sets a threefold problem. First, there is the problem of learning, of gradually acquiring the accumulation of habitual insights that constitute a viewpoint, and eventually of moving from lower to ever higher viewpoints.

Secondly, there is the problem of identification. By insights one grasps unities and correlations; but besides the unity, there are the elements to be unified; and besides the correlation, there are the elements to be distinguished and related. Until one gets the insight, one has no clue (apart from the directions given by a teacher) for picking out accurately the elements that are to be unified or related. But once the insight is reached, one is able to find in one's own experience just what it is that falls under the insight's grasp and what lies outside it. However, ability is one thing, and performance is another. Identification is performance. Its effect is to make one possess the insight as one's own, to be assured in one's use of it, to be familiar with the range of its relevance. Aristotle remarked, I think, that if one understands, one can teach. But the understanding that enables one to teach adds identification to insight. By that addition one is able to select and arrange and indicate to others the combination of sensible elements that will give rise to the same insight in them. One is able to vary the elements at the demand of circumstances. One is able to put the questions that elicit from the pupil indications of his blind spots, and then to proceed afresh to the task of bringing him to the prior insights he must reach before he can master the present lesson.

Thirdly, there is the problem of orientation. Every discovery can be formulated either as a position or as a counterposition. But counterpositions both seem obvious and yet are destined to ultimate reversal. Inasmuch as we inquire intelligently and reflect critically, we operate under the drive of the detached and disinterested desire to know. But once we have reached the truth, we are prone to find it unreal, to shift from the realm of the intelligible and the unconditioned back into the realm of sense, to turn away from truth and being and settle down like good animals in our palpable environment. In the measure that we fail to orientate ourselves towards truth, we both distort what we know and restrict what we might know. We distort what we know by imposing upon it a mistaken notion of reality, a mistaken notion of objectivity, and a mistaken notion of knowledge. We restrict what we might know; for we can justify to ourselves and to others the labor spent in learning only by pointing to the palpable benefits it brings, and the demand satisfied by palpable benefits does not enjoy the unrestricted range of the detached and disinterested desire to know.

The reader will note that the three problems of cognitional appropriation run parallel to the three levels in our knowing. The problem of learning is met on the level of understanding and formulation. The problem of identification is met on the level of experience (where 'experience' is used broadly to denote not only sense experience but also intellectual and rational consciousness). The problem of orientation is met on the level of reflection and judgment when at last we grasp (1) that every issue closes when we can say definitively, 'It is so,' or 'It is not so,' (2) that the objective of knowing is being, (3) that, while being is a protean notion, still its content is determined by intelligent grasp and reasonable affirmation and, after affirmation, by nothing else.

We have cast our account of appropriation in terms of problems rather than in terms of results, and this purely dynamic viewpoint is of some importance. For it excludes all fetishism, all mistaking of means for ends. Clear definition, precise language, orderly arrangement, rigorous proof, and all the other paraphernalia of cognitional activity possess their value. They serve to mark clearly the successive stages of advance. They consolidate in masterly fashion what at any given moment appears to be attained solidly and more or less permanently. They provide magnificent expressions of the truth that is to be appropriated. But of their very nature they are static. They shed no light either on the pupil's task of coming to appropriate them or on the investigator's task of going beyond them to the appropriation of further truth. Yet it is precisely that twofold task that an account of appropriation should envisage. The well-formulated system becomes mine insofar as I understand it, insofar as I can identify its empirical elements in my experience, insofar as I grasp the unconditioned or the approximation to the unconditioned that grounds a reasonable affirmation of it, insofar as my orientation permits me to be content with that affirmation as the final increment in my knowledge of the system and does not drive me to seek in the 'already out there now' some imaginative representation of what, after all, it really means. Exactly the same procedure governs efforts to go beyond the well-formulated system and to generate the stresses and strains in knowledge that will lead it to its replacement by a more adequate account of reality.

It may be noted further that the three problems of appropriation are solidary. One cannot go far in understanding without turning to the problem of identification, and without understanding, one is unable to identify. Again, a mistaken orientation gives rise to pseudo problems, but in the limit pseudo problems bring about their own reversal and with it the correction of the mistaken orientation. Thus, contemporary physics finds itself compelled to say that it deals with the entities that satisfy certain types of equations, even though such entities and their processes defy our powers of imagination. Finally, unless one gives oneself to the effort to understand, one has no means of identifying in one's experience what precisely is meant by the proper orientation of the detached and disinterested desire towards the universe of truth and being.

In a somewhat looser fashion, cognitional appropriation of truth is solidary with volitional and with sensitive appropriation. Bad will makes truth unwelcome, and unwelcome truth tends to be overlooked. For the appropriation of truth even in the cognitional field makes demands upon the whole man; his consciousness has to slip into the intellectual pattern of experience, and it has to remain there with the minimum of distractions; his subconsciousness has to throw up the images that lead to insight; his desire to know has to be sufficiently dominant to keep ever further questions complementing and correcting previous insights; his observation and his memory have to contribute spontaneously to the presentation and the recall of relevant data, in which the fulfilment or nonfulfilment of the unconditioned is to be found. Bad will, however, either prevents one from initiating an inquiry or, if that cannot be avoided, from prosecuting it earnestly and effectively. For the collaboration of all our powers towards the grasping of truth, bad will substitutes their conspiracy to bring forth doubts about truth and evidence for error. Inversely, if the attainment of truth demands good will, still good will, as we shall see in the next chapter, is nothing but a willingness to follow the lead of intelligence and truth. So it is that man is boxed in: without the appropriation of truth, his will cannot be positively good; and without good will he cannot proceed to the attainment of truth. On this basic problem something has been said already in the account of genuineness as the operator of human intellectual development; and something more will be added in the chapters to follow.

Human intelligence and reasonableness function as the higher integration of the sensitive flow of percepts and images, emotions and feelings, attitudes and sentiments, words and deeds. It follows that, as the cognitional and volitional appropriations of truth are solidary with each other, so also they condition and are conditioned by adaptations of human sensibility. Here the basic problem is to discover the dynamic images that both correspond to intellectual contents, orientations, and determinations, yet also possess in the sensitive field the power to issue forth not only into words but also into deeds. On this problem we have touched in asserting the necessity of either mysteries or myths; and to it we shall return in attempting to analyze the structure of history. For the moment it must suffice to draw attention to the fact that, as intellectual development occurs through insights into sensible presentations and imaginative representations, so also the intelligent and reasonable control of human living can be effective only in the measure that it has at its disposal the symbols and signs by which it translates its directives to human sensibility. Finally, unless one can carry out in deeds what one knows and wills, then the willing already is a failure, and from failing will to bad will to unconcern for truth there are the easy and, unfortunately, familiar steps.

3   The Notion of a Universal Viewpoint

By a universal viewpoint will be meant a potential totality of genetically and dialectically ordered viewpoints. Our present concern will be to clarify this notion. Though we believe it to be relevant to the problem of scientific interpretation, its relevance is a further question that can be discussed only later.

First, then, the totality in question is potential. A universal viewpoint is not universal history. It is not a Hegelian dialectic that is complete apart from matters of fact. It is not a Kantian a priori that in itself is determinate and merely awaits imposition upon the raw materials of vicarious experience. It is simply a heuristic structure that contains virtually the various ranges of possible alternatives of interpretations; it can list its own contents only through the stimulus of documents and historical inquiries; it can select between alternatives and differentiate its generalities only by appealing to the accepted norms of historical investigation.

Secondly, the totality is of viewpoints. Hence it is concerned with the principal acts of meaning that lie in insights and judgments, and it reaches these principal acts by directing attention to the experience, the understanding, and the critical reflection of the interpreter. Accordingly, it differs radically from such disciplines as phonetics, comparative grammar, the principles of lexicography, or linguistic and stylistic analysis, for though they ultimately are concerned with meaning, their attention is centered directly upon expression. In contrast, the universal viewpoint is concerned with the interpreter's capacity to grasp meanings; it would open his mind to ideas that do not lie on the surface and to views that diverge enormously from his own; it would enable him to find clues where otherwise he might look but would fail to see; it would equip him with a capacity to transport his thinking to the level and texture of another culture in another epoch. There are the external sources of historical interpretation, and in the main they consist in spatially ordered marks on paper or parchment, papyrus or stone. But there are also sources of interpretation immanent in the historiographer himself, in his ability to distinguish and recombine elements in his own experience, in his ability to work backwards from contemporary to earlier accumulations of insights in human development, in his ability to envisage the protean possibilities of the notion of being, the core of all meaning, which varies in content with the experience, the insights, the judgments, and the habitual orientation of each individual.

Thirdly, the universal viewpoint is an ordered totality of viewpoints. It has its base in an adequate self-knowledge and in the consequent metaphysics. It has a retrospective expansion in the various genetic series of discoveries through which man could advance to his present knowledge. It has a dialectical expansion in the many formulations of discoveries due to the polymorphic consciousness of man, in the invitation issued by positions to further development, and in the implication in counterpositions of their own reversal. Finally, it can reach a concrete presentation of any formulation of any discovery through the identification in personal experience of the elements that, as confused or as distinguished and related, as related under this or that orientation of polymorphic consciousness, could combine to make the position or counterposition humanly convincing.

However, as the totality is potential, so also is the ordering of the viewpoints. The totality is a heuristic structure; its contents are sequences of unknowns; and the relations between the unknowns are determinate not specifically but only generically. Thus, there are genetic sequences, but the same discoveries can be made in different manners. There are dialectically opposed formulations with their contrasting invitations to further development and to reversal; but the dialectical oppositions are not simply the clear-cut identifications of the real either with being or with the 'already out there now,' of the objective either with the intelligent and reasonable or with elementary extroversion, of knowledge either with inquiry and critical reflection or with the look that is prior to all questions; on the contrary, such extremes tend to merge in the ambivalence of the aesthetic, the dramatic, and the practical patterns of experience, to give rise to questions that not only are unsolved but also inadequately conceived, to make their clearest appearance not in the field of knowledge but rather in the volitional tension between moral aspiration and practical living.

Not only is the ordering potential but also what is ordered is itself advancing from the generic to the specific, from the undifferentiated to the differentiated, from the awkward, the global, the spontaneous to the expert, the precise, the methodical. Our distinctions between mathematics, science, common sense, and philosophy are based upon the different manners in which insights can be accumulated. Since the manner in which insights are accumulated is simply a dynamic structure that can be utilized without conscious advertence, it is possible for us to ask whether primitives or children have any interest in mathematical, scientific, or philosophic questions. But even if interests were to be ascribed to primitives or to children, it would be necessary to add not merely that they were uncomplicated by the divisions and subdivisions of later thought but also that they mingled indiscriminately with the questions of common sense and tended both to distort and to be distorted by commonsense procedures.

Fourthly, the universal viewpoint is universal not by abstractness but by potential completeness. It attains its inclusiveness, not by stripping objects of their peculiarities, but by envisaging subjects in their necessities. There are no interpretations without interpreters. There are no interpreters without polymorphic unities of empirical, intelligent, and rational consciousness. There are no expressions to be interpreted without other similar unities of consciousness. Nor has the work of interpreting anything more than a material determinant in the spatially ordered set of marks in documents and monuments. If the interpreter assigns any meaning to the marks, then the experiential component in that meaning will be derived from his experience, the intellectual component will be derived from his intelligence, the rational component will be derived from his critical reflection on the critical reflection of another. Such are the underlying necessities, and from them springs the potential completeness that makes the universal viewpoint universal.

To approach the same issue from another angle, the core of meaning is the notion of being, and that notion is protean. Being is (or is thought to be) whatever is (or is thought to be) grasped intelligently and affirmed reasonably. There is, then, a universe of meanings, and its four dimensions are the full range of possible combinations (1) of experiences and lack of experience, (2) of insights and lack of insight, (3) of judgments and of failures to judge, and (4) of the various orientations of the polymorphic consciousness of man. Now in the measure that one grasps the structure of this protean notion of being, one possesses the base and ground from which one can proceed to the content and context of every meaning. In the measure that one explores human experience, human insights, human reflection, and human polymorphic consciousness, one becomes capable, when provided with the appropriate data, of approximating to the content and context of the meaning of any given expression.

Fifthly, since what we have named the universal viewpoint is simply a corollary of our own philosophic analysis, it will be objected that we are offering not a universal viewpoint but simply the viewpoint of our own philosophy.

To meet this charge, it will be well to begin by distinguishing a universal viewpoint and a universal language. Insofar as we employ names and epithets with laudatory or pejorative implications, such as 'real' and 'illusory,' 'position' and 'counterposition,' 'intelligence' and 'obtuseness,' 'mystery' and 'myth,' it is plain enough that we are not offering a universal language. For anyone that disagreed with our views would prefer a redistribution of the implicit praise and blame. Still, there would be in principle no difficulty in reaching a universal language, for any term that was offensive to anyone could be replaced by some arbitrary name or symbol that was free from all the associations of human imagination and human feeling.

On the other hand, we would contend that there is at least one particular philosophy that could ground a universal viewpoint. For there is a particular philosophy that would take its stand upon the dynamic structure of human cognitional activity, that would distinguish the various elements involved in that structure, that would be able to construct any philosophic position by postulating appropriate and plausible omissions and confusions of the elements, that would reach its own particular views by correcting all omissions and confusions. Now such a philosophy, though particular, would provide a base and ground for a universal viewpoint; for a universal viewpoint is the potential totality of all viewpoints; the potential totality of all viewpoints lies in the dynamic structure of cognitional activity; and the dynamic structure of cognitional activity is the basis of the particular philosophy in question.

Finally, we would argue that the particular philosophy we are offering also is the particular philosophy that can ground a universal viewpoint. By this we do not mean that our views will not be improved vastly by more accurate accounts of experience, of insight and its formulation, of reflection and judgment, and of the polymorphic consciousness of man. Rather our meaning is that such improvements will not involve any radical change in the philosophy, for the philosophy rests, not on the account of experience, of insight, of judgment, and of polymorphic consciousness, but on the defining pattern of relations that bring these four into a single dynamic structure. Again, it is the grasp of that structure that grounds the universal viewpoint since, once the structure is reached, the potential totality of viewpoints is reached. For more refined accounts of the elements in the structure modify, not the potential totality, but the accuracy and completeness with which one can proceed from the universal viewpoint to the reconstruction of particular contents and contexts of meaning.

Related selections: 1.VII.2 on reflective insight; 1.VIII.2 on rational consciousness; 1.IX on the notion of being; 1.X on objectivity; 1.VIII.8 on the unrevisability of the account of human knowing; 1.XV.3 on the continuity of transcendent knowledge with the universal viewpoint; 3.VI.2–3 on historical method; 1.XVII on self-appropriation.

The Problem of Liberation

In Chapter 18 of *Insight*, 'The Possibility of Ethics,' Lonergan develops a method of ethics parallel to his method of metaphysics. Both methods are based on his account of the integral heuristic structure of proportionate being. The method of ethics is developed in three stages. First, Lonergan outlines the general notion of the good and its structure, and the notions of will, value, and obligation. Next, he argues for the possibility of freedom in light of his worldview of emergent probability. Third, he treats the problems raised by human freedom and its limitations.

The first part of the present selection is a portion of Lonergan's larger discussion of the very possibility of freedom. Here Lonergan introduces his idea, which becomes increasingly significant in his post-*Insight* lectures and writings, of a fourth level of human consciousness. Beyond the levels of empirical, intelligent, and rational consciousness there is a 'final enlargement and transformation of consciousness' which Lonergan names rational self-consciousness. It is the level of decision. In this discussion decision is defined and related to other elements of rational self-consciousness. Special attention is given to how decision differs from judgment, and the freedom of the act of decision is affirmed. Decision is a response, not to a rational necessity, but to a rational exigence. But the ability to make a free decision is not the same as actually deciding freely. In the second part of this selection Lonergan draws a distinction between our essential freedom and our effective freedom. He outlines the common conditions of effective freedom – external circumstance, one's psychoneural state, the limitations of one's intellectual development, and one's antecedent willingness. Next, Lonergan addresses the grave restriction of effective freedom which is moral impotence. Moral impotence is the restriction of effective freedom that results from incomplete intellectual and volitional development. It is experienced as a heightening of the tension between limitation and transcendence and is reflected in the social sphere. Lonergan concludes with a summary of the nature and the significance of the problem of liberation, stating that 'essentially the problem lies in an incapacity for sustained development.' In Lonergan's view, the solution must lie in a higher integration of human living: 'only a still higher integration than any that so far has been considered can deal with the dialectical manifold immanent in human subjects and the human situation.'[1]

The extracts in this section are taken from *Insight*, 636–8; 643–7, 650–6.

1   The Decision

There remains to be considered the fourth element in our analysis. It is the decision, and one will do well to distinguish between the decision itself and its manifestation whether in execution, or in knowledge, or in expression of that knowledge. For the decision itself is an act of willing. It possesses the internal alternatives of either consenting or refusing. It may also possess external alternatives, when different courses of action are considered simultaneously, and then consent to one and refusal of the others constitute a choice.

The fundamental nature of decision is best revealed by comparing it with judgment. Decision, then, resembles judgment inasmuch as both select one member of a pair of contradictories; as judgment either affirms or denies, so decision either consents or refuses. Again, both decision and judgment are concerned with actuality; but judgment is concerned to complete one's knowledge of an actuality that already exists, while decision is concerned to confer actuality upon a course of action that otherwise will not exist. Finally, both decision and judgment are rational, for both deal with objects apprehended by insight, and both occur because of a reflective grasp of reasons.

However, there is a radical difference between the rationality of judgment and the rationality of decision. Judgment is an act of rational consciousness, but decision is an act of rational self-consciousness. The rationality of judgment emerges in the unfolding of the detached and disinterested desire to know in the process towards knowledge of the universe of being. But the rationality of decision emerges in the

1 *Insight*, 655.

demand of the rationally conscious subject for consistency between his knowing and his deciding and doing. Again, the rationality of judgment emerges if in fact a reasonable judgment occurs, but the rationality of decision emerges if in fact a reasonable decision occurs. Finally, the effective rationality of the subject of rational consciousness is radically negative, for then the subject is effectively rational if he does not allow other desire to interfere with the functioning of the pure desire to know; but the effective rationality of the subject of rational self-consciousness is radically positive, for then the subject is effectively rational only if his demand for consistency between knowing and doing is followed by his deciding and doing in a manner consistent with his knowing.

In other words, there is a succession of enlargements of consciousness, a succession of transformations of what consciousness means. Waking replaces dreaming. Intelligent inquiry emerges in waking to compound intelligent with empirical consciousness. Critical reflection follows understanding and formulation to add rational consciousness to intelligent and empirical consciousness. But the final enlargement and transformation of consciousness consists in the empirically, intelligently, and rationally conscious subject (1) demanding conformity of his doing to his knowing, and (2) acceding to that demand by deciding reasonably.

Again, a set of corollaries is to be noted. For, in the first place, it is now possible to explain why practical reflection lacks an internal term. If it were concerned simply with knowing what the proposed course of action is and what are the motives in its favor, it would be an activity of rational consciousness and would possess an internal term in certain judgments upon the object and the motives of the proposed action. But practical reflection is concerned with knowing only in order to guide doing. It is an activity that involves an enlarging transformation of consciousness. In that enlarged consciousness the term is not judgment but decision. Consequently, practical reflection does not come to an end once the object and motives of a proposed action are known; it comes to an end when one decides either in favor of the proposal or against it.

Secondly, the same enlarging transformation of consciousness illuminates both the meaning and the frequent inefficacy of obligation. It is possible for practical reflection to reach with certitude the conclusion that a proposed course of action is obligatory, that either I decide in favor of the proposal or else I surrender consistency between my knowing and my doing. Now in such instances it is apparent that the emergence of an obligation is the emergence of a rational necessity in rational consciousness. I cannot prevent questions for reflection from arising; once they arise, I cannot set aside the demand of my rationality that I assent if and only if I grasp the virtually unconditioned; and once I judge that I ought to act in a determinate manner, that I cannot both be reasonable and act otherwise, then my reasonableness is bound to the act by a link of necessity. Such is the meaning of obligation.

Yet the fact remains that I can fail to fulfil my known obligations, that the iron link of necessity can prove to be a wisp of straw. How can this be? How can necessity turn out to be contingence? The answer lies in the enlarging transformation of consciousness. The rationality that imposes an obligation is not conditioned internally by an act of will. The rationality that carries out an obligation is conditioned internally by the occurrence of a reasonable act of will. To repeat the point in other words, the rational subject as imposing an obligation upon himself is just a knower, and his rationality consists radically in not allowing other desire to interfere with the unfolding of the detached and disinterested desire to know. But the rational subject as carrying out an obligation is not just a knower but also a doer, and his rationality consists not merely in excluding interference with cognitional process but also in extending the rationality of his knowing into the field of doing. But that extension does not occur simply by knowing one's obligations. It occurs just inasmuch as one wills to meet one's obligations.

How then does necessity turn out to be contingence? Clearly, there is no change in the necessity itself, but there occurs a change in the context. Rational consciousness is being transformed into rational self-consciousness. What in the context of rational consciousness is a rational necessity, in the context of rational self-consciousness becomes a rational exigence. If a proposed action is obligatory, then one cannot be a rational knower and deny the obligation, and one cannot be a rational doer and not fulfil the obligation. But one can be a rational knower without an act of willing, and one cannot be a rational doer without an act of willing. It is the addition of the further constitutive requirement of an act of will that (1) marks the shift from rational consciousness to rational self-consciousness, and (2) changes what is rational necessity in the field of knowing into rational exigence in the larger field of both knowing and doing.

Thirdly, the same enlarging transformation throws light upon the difference between the acknowledgment of actuality in judgment and the bestowal of actuality by decision. As has been seen, both judgment and decision are concerned with actuality; but judgment merely acknowledges an actuality that already exists; while decision confers actuality upon a course of action that otherwise is merely possible ...

2 The Problem of Liberation

2.1 Essential and Effective Freedom

The difference between essential and effective freedom is the difference between a dynamic structure and its operational range. Man is free essentially inasmuch as possible courses of action are grasped by practical insight, motivated by reflection, and executed by decision. But man is free effectively to a greater or less extent inasmuch as this dynamic structure is open to grasping, motivating, and executing a broad or a narrow range of otherwise possible courses of action. Thus, one may be essentially but not effectively free to give up smoking.

A consideration of effective freedom is meaningless, unless essential freedom exists. Nonetheless, the negation of full effective freedom may appear a negation of essential freedom if the proper grounds of the latter are not grasped clearly and distinctly. Accordingly, it hardly will be amiss to recall briefly the main points that already have been made.

First, then, all formal intelligibility within the domain of proportionate being is contingent. It is not what of itself must be but merely what in fact happens to be. Hence, species are not realizations of static descriptive concepts but intelligible solutions to the concrete problems of generalized emergent probability and so subject to variation with variation of the problems. Again, natural laws are not to be determined by pure speculation but solely by an empirical method in which what is grasped by insight is mere hypothesis until confirmed by verification. Finally, the possible courses of action grasped by practical insight are merely possible until they are motivated by reflection and executed by decision.

Secondly, not only are possible courses of action contingent but also they constitute a manifold of alternatives. The sensitive flow of a man's percepts and images, feelings and conations offers an otherwise coincidental manifold for higher systematization. In fact, that higher systematization is effected in different manners, whether one considers the same individual at different times, or different individuals, or aggregates of individuals in different environments or different epochs or different cultures.

Thirdly, not only are possible courses of action a manifold, but man is aware of the alternatives. He does not suffer from the illusion that because a course of action is possible therefore it also is necessary. The possibilities that he grasps are submitted to reflective examination, and such examination commonly leads to a grasp of further possibilities. Nor does the examination come to an end out of its own resources but only through the intervention of the will's decision.

Fourthly, the will's decision is not determined by its antecedents. For the remote antecedents lie on the levels of physics, chemistry, biology, and sensitive psychology; and events on such lower levels determine merely the materials that admit a manifold of alternative higher systematizations. On the other hand, the proximate antecedents merely define and motivate the alternative higher systematizations; they present no more than a projected formal intelligibility, which, so far from necessitating its own actuality, can attain actuality only if the will decides in its favor.

Fifthly, the most obvious bit of evidence for the freedom of man's decisions lies in the possibility of inconsistency between human knowing and doing; for if such inconsistency is possible, then there cannot be any valid argument from determinate knowing to determinate willing and doing. However, one is not to mistake the obvious for the essential. Man is not free because he can be unreasonable in his choices. Rather the root of freedom lies in the contingence of the formal intelligibility of proportionate being. Because such intelligibility is contingent, it cannot guarantee its own existence or occurrence. Again, because it is contingent, it is not unique but a manifold of alternatives. Further, because it is contingent, it is known as merely possible, as in need of motivation, as needing motivation because it will exist or occur only if decision is forthcoming. Finally, because it is contingent, there cannot be valid motives for it that necessitate decision in its favor.

To put the point in another manner, any practical insight can be formulated in a proposition of the type 'Under such and such circumstances the intelligent thing to do is to make such and such a decision.' Let the totality of circumstances be denoted by P and the decision by Q. Then the content of the practical insight will be the inferential relation 'If P, then Q.' But such an inferential relation ceases to be a mere supposition about what might be or should be and becomes a true statement of what is, only when the act of will Q occurs. But any attempt to show that the act of will is necessitated by its proximate antecedents must suppose the truth of the inferential relation 'If P, then Q.' Therefore, it must suppose that the act of will is occurring. And so it is involved in a *petitio principii* or, if you prefer, in a simple appeal to the principle of identity, namely, If the act Q is occurring, then it must be occurring.

Sixthly, though the act of will is free, it is not arbitrary. A course of action is intelligent and intelligible if it is grasped by a practical insight. It is reasonable if it is motivated favorably by rational reflection. The act of will has the function of conferring actuality upon an intelligible, intelligent, and reasonable course of action; and what is intelligible, intelligent, and reasonable is not arbitrary.

Seventhly, the analysis is quite general. For while there is presupposed a sensitive flow that receives a higher integration, still intelligent grasp, reflection, and decision rise from the flow as content, and that content may be not representative but symbolic. Thus, one can make decisions about deciding by having the sensitive flow present the relevant words.

2.2   Conditions of Effective Freedom

Conditions of effective freedom may be listed under the four headings of (1) external circumstance, (2) the subject as sensitive, (3) the subject as intelligent, and (4) the subject as antecedently willing.

Everyone is familiar with the limitations placed upon effective freedom by external constraint. But just as the prisoner is not free to go and come as he pleases, so the Eskimo is not free to mount a camel or the desert nomad to go fishing in a kayak. Whatever one's external circumstances may be, they offer only a limited range of concretely possible alternatives and only limited resources for bringing about the enlargement of that range.

In the second place, there are the limitations that arise from one's psychoneural state. It is the proximate source of the otherwise coincidental manifold that receives its higher integration from intelligence and will. In the normal state, there is a spontaneous adaptation and adjustment between the orientations of intellectual and of psychoneural development. But even perfect adjustment does not dispense one from the necessity of acquiring sensitive skills and habits, and until they are acquired, one is not free to speak a foreign language or to play the violin merely by taking thought. Moreover, perfect adjustment may be lacking; scotosis can result in a conflict between the operators of intellectual and of psychoneural development; and then the sensitive subject is invaded by anxiety, by obsessions, and by other neurotic phenomena that restrict his capacity for effective deliberation and choice.

Thirdly, there are the limitations of intellectual development. Once one has understood, one can reproduce almost at will the act of understanding. But until one has understood, one has to struggle through the process of learning. Moreover, the greater one's accumulation of insights, the broader is the base from which one can move towards still further insights and, perhaps, the greater is the facility with which one can reach them. Now the same laws hold for the occurrence of practical insights as for insights generally, and so it is that the greater the development of one's practical intelligence, the greater the range of possible courses of action one can grasp and consider. Inversely, the less the development of one's practical intelligence, the less the range of possible courses of action that here and now will occur to one.

Fourthly, we have distinguished already between the conjugate potency 'will,' the conjugate form 'willingness,' and the conjugate act 'willing.' Will is the bare capacity to make decisions. Willingness is the state in which persuasion is not needed to bring one to a decision. Willing, finally, is the act of deciding.

Now the function of willingness runs parallel to the function of the habitual accumulation of insights. What one does not understand yet, one can learn; but learning takes time, and until that time is devoted to learning, otherwise possible courses of action are excluded. Similarly, when antecedent willingness is lacking, persuasion can be invoked; but persuasion takes time, and until that time is devoted to persuading oneself or to being persuaded by others, one remains closed to otherwise possible courses of action.

There is a further aspect to the matter. For genetically one mounts from empirical to intellectual consciousness, from intellectual to rational consciousness, and from rational consciousness to rational self-consciousness. As long as one is moving towards full self-possession, the detached and disinterested desire to know tends to be in control.

But once one is in the state of rational self-consciousness, then one's decisions are in control, for they set the objective of one's total activity and select the actions that are to lead to the goal. So it is that a person, caught as it were unawares, may be ready for any scheme or exploit but, on the second thoughts of rational self-consciousness, settles back into the narrow routine defined by his antecedent willingness. For unless one's antecedent willingness has the height and breadth and depth of the unrestricted desire to know, the emergence of rational self-consciousness involves the addition of a restriction upon one's effective freedom.

In brief, effective freedom itself has to be won. The key point is to reach a willingness to persuade oneself and to submit to the persuasion of others. For then one can be persuaded to a universal willingness; so one becomes antecedently willing to learn all there is to be learnt about willing and learning and about the enlargement of one's freedom from external constraints and psychoneural interferences. But to reach the universal willingness that matches the unrestricted desire to know is indeed a high achievement, for it consists not in the mere recognition of an ideal norm but in the adoption of an attitude towards the universe of being, not in the adoption of an affective attitude that would desire but not perform but in the adoption of an effective attitude in which performance matches aspiration.

Finally, if effective freedom is to be won, it is not to be won easily. Just as the pure desire to know is the possibility but not in itself the attainment of the scientist's settled habit of constant inquiry, so the potency 'will' is the possibility but not in itself the attainment of the genuine person's complete openness to reflection and to rational persuasion. Clearly, this confronts us with a paradox. How is one to be persuaded to genuineness and openness, when one is not yet open to persuasion? ...

2.3 Moral Impotence

To assert moral impotence is to assert that man's effective freedom is restricted, not in the superficial fashion that results from external circumstance or psychic abnormality, but in the profound fashion that follows from incomplete intellectual and volitional development. For when that development is incomplete, there are practical insights that could be had if a man took time out to acquire the necessary preparatory insights, and there are courses of action that would be chosen if a man took time out to persuade himself to willingness. There follows a gap between the proximate effective freedom he actually possesses and, on the other hand, the remote and hypothetical effective freedom that he would possess if certain conditions happened to be fulfilled. Now this gap measures one's moral impotence. For complete self-development is a long and difficult process. During that process one has to live and make decisions in the light of one's undeveloped intelligence and under the guidance of one's incomplete willingness. And the less developed one is, the less one appreciates the need of development and the less one is willing to take time out for one's intellectual and moral education.

Moreover, as the scotosis of the dramatic subject, so the moral impotence of the essentially free subject is neither grasped with perfect clarity nor totally unconscious. For if one were to represent a man's field of freedom as a circular area, then one would distinguish a luminous central region in which he was effectively free, a surrounding penumbra in which his uneasy conscience keeps suggesting that he could do better if only he would make up his mind, and finally an outer shadow to which he barely if ever adverts. Further, these areas are not fixed; as he develops, the penumbra penetrates into the shadow and the luminous area into the penumbra while, inversely, moral decline is a contraction of the luminous area and of the penumbra. Finally, this consciousness of moral impotence not only heightens the tension between limitation and transcendence but also can provide ambivalent materials for reflection; correctly interpreted, it brings home to man the fact that his living is a developing, that he is not to be discouraged by his failures, that rather he is to profit by them both as lessons on his personal weaknesses and as a stimulus to greater efforts; but the same data can also be regarded as evidence that there is no use trying, that moral codes ask the impossible, that one has to be content with oneself as one is.

This inner tension and its ambivalence are reflected and heightened in the social sphere. For rational self-consciousness demands consistency between knowing and doing not only in the individual but also in the common concerns of the group. To the ethics of the individual conscience there is added an ethical transformation of the home, of the technological expansion, of the economy, and of the polity. But just as individual intelligence and individual reasonableness lead to the individual decisions that may be right or wrong, so too common intelligence and common reasonableness lead to common decisions that may be right or wrong. Moreover, in both cases, decisions are right not because they are the pronouncements of the individual conscience, nor because they proceed from this or that type of social mechanism for reaching common decisions, but because they are in the concrete situation intelligent and reasonable. Again, in both cases, decisions are wrong, not because of their private or public origin, but because they diverge from the dictates of intelligence and reasonableness.

Now, as has been seen, common sense is subject to a threefold bias. Accordingly, we can expect that individual decisions will be likely to suffer from individual bias, that common decisions will be likely to suffer from the various types of group bias, and that all decisions will be likely to suffer from general bias. There will result conflicts between the individual and the group, between economic and national groups within the state, and between states. But far more significant than these relatively superficial and overt conflicts will be the underlying opposition that general bias sets up between the decisions that intelligence and reasonableness would demand and the actual decisions, individual and common, that are made. For this opposition is both profound and unnoticed. As individuals, so societies fail to distinguish sharply and accurately between positions and counterpositions. As individuals, so societies fail to reach the universal willingness that reflects and sustains the detachment and disinterestedness of the unrestricted desire to know. More or less automatically and unconsciously, each successive batch of possible and practical courses of action is screened to eliminate as unpractical whatever does not seem practical to an intelligence and a willingness that not only are developed imperfectly but also suffer from bias. But the social situation is the cumulative product of individual and group decisions, and as these decisions depart from the demands of intelligence and reasonableness, so the social situation becomes, like the complex number, a compound of the rational and irrational. Then if it is to be understood, it must be met by a parallel compound of direct and inverse insights, of direct insights that grasp its intelligibility and of inverse insights that grasp its lack of intelligibility. Nor is it enough to understand the situation; it must also be managed. Its intelligible components have to be encouraged towards fuller development; and its unintelligible components have to be hurried to their reversal.

Still, this is only the outer aspect of the problem. Just as the social situation with its objective surd proceeds from minds and wills that oscillate between the positions and the counterpositions, so too it constitutes the materials for their practical insights, the conditions to be taken into account in their reflection, the reality to be maintained and developed by their decisions. Just as there are philosophies that take their stand upon the positions and urge the development of the intelligible components in the situation and the reversal of the unintelligible components, so too there are counterphilosophies that take their stand upon the counterpositions, that welcome the unintelligible components in the situation as objective facts that provide the empirical proof of their views, that demand the further expansion of the objective surd, and that clamor for the complete elimination of the intelligible components that they regard as wicked survivals of antiquated attitudes. But philosophies and counterphilosophies are for the few. Like Mercutio, the average man imprecates a plague on both their houses. What he wants is peace and prosperity. By his own light he selects what he believes is the intelligent and reasonable but practical course of action; and as that practicality is the root of the trouble, the civilization drifts through successive less comprehensive syntheses to the sterility of the objectively unintelligible situation and to the coercion of economic pressures, political forces, and psychological conditioning.

Clearly, both the outward conditions and the inner mentality prevalent in social decline intensify to the point of desperation the tension, inherent in all development but conscious in man, between limitation and transcendence. One can agree with Christian praise of charity, with Kant's affirmation that the unqualified good is the good will, with existentialist exhortations to genuineness. But good will is never better than the intelligence and reasonableness that it implements. Indeed, when proposals and programs only putatively are intelligent and reasonable, then the good will that executes them so faithfully and energetically is engaged really in the systematic imposition of ever further evils on the already weary shoulders of mankind. And who will tell which proposals and programs truly are intelligent and reasonable, and which are not? For the only transition from the analytic proposition to the analytic principle is through concrete judgments of fact, and alas, the facts are ambivalent. The objective situation is all fact, but partly it is the product of intelligence and reasonableness, and partly it is the product of aberration from them. The whole of man is all fact, but it also is malleable, polymorphic fact. No doubt, a subtle and protracted analysis can bring to light the components in that polymorphic fact and proceed to a dialectical criticism of any proposal or program. But to whom does it bring the light? To how many? How clearly and how effectively? Are philosophers to be kings or kings to learn philosophy? Are they to rule in the name of wisdom subjects judged incapable of wisdom? Are all the members of our democracies to be philosophers? Is there to be a provisional dictatorship while they are learning philosophy?

2.4 The Problem of Liberation

The elements in the problem are basically simple. Man's intelligence, reasonableness, and willingness (1) proceed from a detached, disinterested, unrestricted desire to know, (2) are potentialities in process of development towards a full effective freedom, (3) supply the higher integration for otherwise coincidental manifolds on successively underlying psychic, organic, chemical, and physical levels, (4) stand in opposition and tension with sensitive and intersubjective attachment, interest, and exclusiveness, and (5) suffer from that tension a cumulative bias that increasingly distorts immanent development, its outward products, and the outer conditions under which the immanent development occurs.

Essentially the problem lies in an incapacity for sustained development. The tension divides and disorientates cognitional activity by the conflict of positions and counterpositions. This conflict issues into contrary views of the good, which in turn make good will appear misdirected, and misdirected will appear good. There follows the confounding of the social situation with the social surd to provide misleading inspiration for further insights, deceptive evidence for further judgments, and illusory causes to fascinate unwary wills.

The problem is radical, for it is a problem in the very dynamic structure of cognitional, volitional, and social activity. It is not a question of error on this or that general or particular issue. It is a question of orientation, approach, procedure, method. It affects concretely every issue, both general and particular, for it recurs with every use of the dynamic structure.

The problem is permanent. It vanishes if one supposes man's intelligence, reasonableness, and willingness not to be potentialities in process of development but already in possession of the insights that make learning superfluous, of the reasonableness that makes judgments correct, of the willingness that makes persuasion unnecessary. Again, it vanishes if one supposes the elimination of the tension and opposition between the detached, disinterested, unrestricted desire to know and, on the other hand, attached, interested, and narrow sensitivity and intersubjectivity. But in fact both development and tension pertain to the very nature of man, and as long as they exist the problem remains in full force.

The problem is independent of the underlying manifolds. No doubt, if the underlying manifolds were different, the higher cognitional and volitional integration would differ in its content. But such a change of content would leave the dynamic structure of the higher integration unmodified; and it is in the structure that the problem resides. It follows that neither physics nor chemistry nor biology nor sensitive psychology can bring forth devices that go to the root of the trouble.

The problem is not primarily social. It results in the social surd. It receives from the social surd its continuity, its aggravation, its cumulative character. But its root is elsewhere. Hence it is that a revolution can sweep away old evils and initiate a fresh effort; but the fresh effort will occur through the same dynamic structure as the old effort and lead to essentially the same results.

The problem is not to discover a correct philosophy, ethics, or human science. For such discoveries are quite compatible with the continued existence of the problem. The correct philosophy can be but one of many philosophies, the correct ethics one of many ethical systems, the correct human science an old or new view among many views. But precisely because they are correct, they will not appear correct to minds disorientated by the conflict between positions and counterpositions. Precisely because they are correct, they will not appear workable to wills with restricted ranges of effective freedom. Precisely because they are correct, they will be weak competitors for serious attention in the realm of practical affairs.

The problem is not met by setting up a benevolent despotism to enforce a correct philosophy, ethics, or human science. No doubt, if there is to be the appeal to force, then it is better that the force be directed by wisdom than by folly, by benevolence than by malevolence. But the appeal to force is a counsel of despair. So far from solving the problem, it regards the problem as insoluble. For if men are intelligent, reasonable, and willing, they do not have to be forced. Only in the measure that men are unintelligent, unreasonable, unwilling, does force enter into human affairs. Finally, if force can be used by the group against the wayward individual and by the larger group against the smaller, it does not follow that it can be used to correct the general bias of common sense. For the general bias of common sense is the bias of all men, and to a notable extent it consists in the notion that ideas are negligible unless they are reinforced by sensitive desires and fears. Is everyone to use force against everyone to convince everyone that force is beside the point?

The problem is real. In the present work it has been reached in the compendious fashion that operates through the integral heuristic structure of proportionate being and the consequent ethics. But the expeditiousness of the procedure must not be allowed to engender the mistake that the problem resides in some theoretical realm. On the contrary, its dimensions are the dimensions of human history, and the fourth, fifth, and sixth volumes of Arnold Toynbee's *Study of History* illustrate abundantly and rather relevantly the failure of self-determination, the schism in the body social, and the schism in the soul that follow from an incapacity for sustained development.

The solution has to be a still higher integration of human living. For the problem is radical and permanent; it is independent of the underlying physical, chemical, organic, and psychic manifolds; it is not met by revolutionary change, nor by human discovery, nor by the enforced implementation of discovery; it is as large as human living and human history. Further, the solution has to take people just as they are. If it is to be a solution and not a mere suppression of the problem, it has to acknowledge and respect and work through man's intelligence and reasonableness and freedom. It may eliminate neither development nor tension yet it must be able to replace incapacity by capacity for sustained development. Only a still higher integration can meet such requirements. For only a higher integration leaves underlying manifolds with their autonomy yet succeeds in introducing a higher systematization into their nonsystematic coincidences. And only a still higher integration than any that so far has been considered can deal with the dialectical manifold immanent in human subjects and the human situation.

There is needed, then, a further manifestation of finality, of the upwardly but indeterminately directed dynamism of generalized emergent probability. Earlier, in the chapter on common sense as object, it was concluded that a viewpoint higher than the viewpoint of common sense was needed; moreover, that X was given the name 'cosmopolis,' and some of its aspects and functions were indicated. But the subsequent argument has revealed that, besides higher viewpoints in the mind, there are higher integrations in the realm of being; and both the initial and subsequent argument have left it abundantly clear that the needed higher viewpoint is a concrete possibility only as a consequence of an actual higher integration.

Finally, whether the needed higher integration has emerged or is yet to emerge is a question of fact. Similarly, its nature is an object not for speculation but for empirical inquiry. Still, what can that empirical inquiry be? Since our metaphysics and ethics have been developed under a restriction to proportionate being, we have to raise the question of transcendent knowledge before we can attempt an investigation of the ulterior finality of man.

Related selections: 1.XI.2 on the integral heuristic structure of proportionate being; 1.IV.2 and 1.V.3–5 on the four biases and the longer cycle of decline; 1.XII.4 on the tension of human development; 1.XVI on the problem of liberation and the heuristic structure of the solution; 2.VII.4 on the notion of value and the fourth level of consciousness; 3.II.1 on judgments of value.

Knowledge of God

Lonergan describes the argument of *Insight* as unfolding in four stages. The first stage is an investigation of cognitional activity *as activity*, the second is a study of cognitional activity *as cognitional*. The third treats the general case of knowledge of proportionate being, distinguishes positional from counterpositional formulations of the discoveries of human intelligence, and puts in place the groundwork for a metaphysics of being proportionate to human knowing and a consequent ethics. In the fourth stage of the argument, to which the present selection from Chapter 19 of *Insight* belongs, Lonergan raises the issue of human knowledge of transcendent being and the question of God. The issue of transcendent knowledge is to be settled, not by 'the bland procedure of consigning transcendental issues to oblivion,'[1] but by an exercise of 'critical method,' which differs from other methods only in its subject matter. In his employment of critical method Lonergan extrapolates from the already familiar *notion*, or intelligent and rational anticipation, of being to the general features of the *idea* of being, of the content of an unrestricted act of understanding. He then proceeds to work out the implications of the concept of an unrestricted act of understanding and to formulate the notion of God. But the notion of God remains merely an object of thought until such time as the reflective question of existence is raised and answered. Lonergan next turns to the question of God's existence. The selection presented here does not reproduce Lonergan's argument in its full complexity but pertains to the starting point and the conclusion of his application of critical method.

In the first part of this selection, Lonergan locates an 'immanent source of transcendence' in the unrestricted desire to know. In the second part, he raises

---

1 *Insight*, 708.

the reflective question, Does God exist?, rejects every form of the much-disputed ontological argument, recalls the personal character of rational judgment, and presents and explains the premises of his own argument. In the concluding part Lonergan reflects on his procedure, asserts that the affirmation of God is 'not only continuous with all that has gone before but also its culmination,'[2] and concludes with a comparison of critical method with the four methods exposed earlier in *Insight*.

Lonergan's treatment of God's existence and nature in *Insight* met with some criticism at the Lonergan Congress of 1970. In a lectures series of 1972, on the philosophy of God and theology, Lonergan acknowledged an incongruity in his approach to the issue in *Insight*: 'while my cognitional theory was based on a long and methodical appeal to experience, in contrast my account of God's existence and attributes made no appeal to religious experience.'[3] In his later works, leading up to and including his *Method in Theology*, the manner of treatment shifts. In '*Insight* Revisited,' in 1973, Lonergan puts the matter this way: 'In *Method* the question of God is considered more important than the precise manner in which an answer is formulated, and our basic awareness of God comes to us not through our arguments or choices but primarily through God's gift of his love.'[4] While Lonergan never retracted his claim that critical method yields knowledge of God's existence, his later treatments introduce explicitly the religious horizon of the inquiring subject.

The extracts in this chapter are taken from *Insight*, 659–62; 692–9; 704–8.

1   The Immanent Source of Transcendence

The immanent source of transcendence in man is his detached, disinterested, unrestricted desire to know. As it is the origin of all his questions, it is the origin of the radical further questions that take him beyond the defined limits of particular issues. Nor is it solely the operator of his cognitional development. For its detachment and disinterestedness set it in opposition to his attached and interested sensitivity and intersubjectivity; and the knowledge it yields demands of his will the endeavor to develop in willingness and so make his doing consistent with his knowing.

Still, if this tension is too manifest for the existence of the pure desire

---

2 Ibid., 706.
3 *Philosophy of God*, 13.
4 *A Second Collection*, 277.

to be doubted, the claim that it is an unrestricted desire seems so extravagant as to cause misgivings even in those that already accept all its implications. Accordingly, it will be well to clarify once more this point before attempting to advance further in our inquiry.

The desire in question, then, is a desire to understand correctly. To affirm that the desire is unrestricted is not to affirm that man's understanding is unrestricted or that the correctness of his understanding is unrestricted. For the desire is prior to understanding, and it is compatible with not understanding. Were it not, the effort and process of inquiry would be impossible; for inquiry is a manifestation of a desire to understand, and it occurs before one does understand.

Secondly, to affirm that the desire is unrestricted is not to affirm that the attainment of understanding will be unrestricted. For the transition from the desire to the attainment has conditions that are distinct from desiring. It is to help fulfil such conditions that scientific and philosophic methods exist. Hence, to affirm an unrestricted desire to understand is to affirm the fulfilment of only one of many conditions for the attainment of unrestricted understanding. So far from stating that the other conditions will be fulfilled, it does not attempt to determine what the other conditions might be.

Thirdly, to affirm that the desire is unrestricted is not to affirm that, in a wisely ordered universe, the attainment of understanding ought to be unrestricted. Such an affirmation would follow from the premise 'In every wisely ordered universe desire for attainment entails exigence for attainment.' But the premise is obviously false: a desire to commit murder does not entail a duty to commit murder, and least of all does it do so in a wisely ordered universe. It may be contended, however, that the premise is correct when the desire is good, natural, spontaneous. But this contention has its own suppositions. In a universe of static horizontal strata, such as is envisaged by autonomous abstract physics, autonomous abstract chemistry, autonomous abstract biology, and so forth, the tendencies and desires natural and spontaneous on any level would have to be confined to that level; because they were confined to their own level, they could and would be fulfilled on their own level; and because they could and would be fulfilled on their own level, it would be true to claim that in a wisely regulated universe of static horizontal strata desire for attainment entailed exigence for attainment. It remains to be shown, however, that this universe corresponds to a set of abstract, unrelated sciences and so consists in a set of static horizontal strata. The fact seems to be that this universe is concrete and that logically unrelated sciences are related intelligently by a succession of higher viewpoints. Accordingly, besides the tendencies and desires confined to any given level, there are the tendencies and desires that go beyond any given level; they are the reality of finality conceived as an upwardly but indeterminately directed dynamism; and since this dynamism of finality attains its successive goals statistically, since probabilities decrease as attainment increases, the implication of unrestricted attainment in unrestricted desire is neither necessity nor exigence but, at most, negligible probability.

If one has to labor to clarify what the unrestricted desire is not, it is relatively simple to reveal what it is. Man wants to understand completely. As the desire to understand is the opposite of total obscurantism, so the unrestricted desire to understand is the opposite of any and every partial obscurantism no matter how slight. The rejection of total obscurantism is the demand that some questions, at least, are not to be met with an arbitrary exclamation, 'Let's forget it!' The rejection of any and every partial obscurantism is the demand that no question whatever is to be met arbitrarily, that every question is to be submitted to the process of intelligent grasp and critical reflection. Negatively, then, the unrestricted desire excludes the unintelligent and uncritical rejection of any question, and positively the unrestricted desire demands the intelligent and critical handling of every question.

Nor is the existence of this unrestricted desire doubtful. Neither centuries of inquiry nor enormous libraries of answers have revealed any tendency for the stream of further questions to diminish. Philosophies and counterphilosophies have been multiplied, but whether intellectualist or antiintellectualist, whether they proclaim the rule of reason or advocate thinking with the blood, they do not exclude any field of inquiry without first arguing that the effort is useless or enervating or misleading or illusory. And in this respect we may be confident that the future will resemble the past, for unless someone comes forth to speak in the name of stupidity and silliness, he will not be able to claim that some questions, specified or unspecified, are to be brushed aside though there is no reason whatever for doing so.

Analysis yields the same conclusion. For apart from being there is nothing. The proposition is analytic, for it cannot be denied without internal contradiction. If apart from being there were something, that something would be; and if that something were, it would be another instance of being and so not apart from being. Moreover, being is the objective of the detached and disinterested desire to know; for that desire grounds inquiry and reflection; inquiry leads to understanding, reflection leads to affirmation; and being is whatever can be grasped intelligently and affirmed reasonably. But being is unrestricted, for apart from it there is nothing. Therefore the objective of the detached and disinterested desire is unrestricted. But a desire with an unrestricted objective is an unrestricted desire, and so the desire to know is unrestricted.

Introspective reflection brings us once more to the same affirmation. For whatever may be true about the cognitional aspirations of others, might not my own be radically limited? Might not my desire to understand correctly suffer from some immanent and hidden restriction and bias, so that there could be real things that lay quite beyond its utmost horizon? Might not that be so? Yet if I ask the question, it is in virtue of my desire to know; and as the question itself reveals, my desire to know concerns itself with what lies quite beyond a suspected limited horizon. Even my desire seems unrestricted.

2 The Affirmation of God

Our knowledge of being is by intelligent grasp and reasonable affirmation. By asking what being is, we have been led to grasp and conceive what God is. Since it has been shown that being is the core of all meaning, it follows that our grasp and conception of the notion of God is the most meaningful of all possible objects of our thought. Still, every object of thought raises a further question; for once the activity of intelligent consciousness is completed, the activity of reflective consciousness begins. Is God then merely an object of thought? Or is God real? Is he an object of reasonable affirmation? Does he exist?

These four further questions are one and the same. For the real is being, and apart from being there is nothing. Being is not known without reasonable affirmation, and existence is the respect in which being is known precisely inasmuch as it is affirmed reasonably. Hence it is one and the same thing to say that God is real, that he is an object of reasonable affirmation, and that he exists.

Again, to affirm that God exists is not to ascribe to him the *Existenz* or the subtly drawn *Dasein* of existentialist thought. For such existence is the existence of man, not as intelligently grasped and reasonably affirmed, but as experiencing, inquiring, and reflecting, yet not obtaining any definitive answers to his questions about himself.

Further, while both the existence of any proportionate being and the existence of God are to be known through a rationally posited yes, it does not follow that both the existences are the same. For the meaning of the yes varies with the question that it answers. If one asks whether a contingent being exists, an affirmative answer means a contingent existence. But if one asks whether a self-explanatory being exists, an affirmative answer means a self-explanatory existence.

Again, in the self-knowledge of a self-explanatory being it would be one and the same thing for him to know what he is and whether he is. For his knowledge of what he is would consist in a grasp of the formally unconditioned, and as the grasp answers the question, What? so the unconditioned answers the question, Whether?

But it does not follow that the two questions have a single answer in our knowledge. For when we grasp what God is, our grasp is not an unrestricted act of understanding but a restricted understanding that extrapolates from itself to an unrestricted act and by asking ever further questions arrives at a list of attributes of the unrestricted act. Accordingly, what is grasped is not the unrestricted act but the extrapolation that proceeds from the properties of a restricted act to the properties of the unrestricted act. Hence, when the extrapolation is completed, there remains the further question whether the unrestricted act is just an object of thought or a reality.

It follows that all forms of the ontological argument are fallacious. For they argue from the conception of God to his existence. But our conceptions yield no more than analytic propositions. And, as has been seen, one can effect the transition from the analytic proposition to the analytic principle only inasmuch as the terms and relations of the proposition occur in concrete judgments of fact. Hence, while there is no difficulty in so conceiving God that the denial of his existence would be a contradiction in terms, still that conception yields no more than an analytic proposition; and the proposition in question can become an analytic principle only if we can affirm in a concrete judgment of fact that God does exist.

The Anselmian argument, then, is to be met by distinguishing the premise *Deus est quo maius cogitari nequit* [God is (the Being, the One) than which nothing greater can be conceived]. One grants that by appropriate definitions and syntactical rules it can be made into an analytic proposition. But one asks for the evidence that the terms as defined occur in concrete judgments of fact.

The Cartesian argument seems to be from the concept to the existence of a perfect being. This would be valid if conceiving were looking and looking were knowing. But that view involves the counterpositions; and when one shifts to the positions, one finds that conceptions become knowing only through reflective grasp of the unconditioned.

The Leibnizian argument is from the possibility to the actuality of God. As we have seen, God is either necessary or impossible. But he is not impossible, for the notion of God is not a contradiction in terms. Therefore, he exists necessarily. But the major is only an analytic proposition, and so the conclusion can be no more than an analytic proposition. Further, the reason offered for the minor calls for a distinction. If there is an omnipotent God, and if omnipotence consists in the power to produce whatever does not involve an internal contradiction, then the absence of internal contradiction proves possibility. But if one does not presuppose the existence of divine omnipotence, then the absence of internal contradiction proves no more than the coherence of an object of thought.

However, if the ontological argument is to be regarded as fallacious, it may seem that there is no possibility of affirming rationally the existence of God. For our distinction between analytic propositions and analytic principles is equivalent to the verification principle of the logical positivists. But there seems no possibility of verifying an unrestricted act of understanding either in our external or in our internal experience. And even if the experience were possible, still there would be needed the fact before the existence of God could be affirmed reasonably.

This objection, however, rests on an identification of the notions of verification and of experience. Yet clearly, if the law of falling bodies is verified, it is not experienced. All that is experienced is a large aggregate of contents of acts of observing. It is not experience but understanding that unifies the aggregate by referring them to a hypothetical law of falling bodies. It is not experience but critical reflection that asks whether the data correspond to the law and whether the correspondence suffices for an affirmation of the law. It is not experience but a reflective grasp of the fulfilment of the conditions for a probable affirmation that constitutes the only act of verifying that exists for the law of falling bodies; and similarly it is a reflective grasp of the unconditioned that grounds every other judgment.

Moreover, the point to the demand for a transition from analytic propositions to analytic judgments primarily is a distinction between different types of unconditioned, and only secondarily does it involve a resemblance to the verification principle. There is a virtually unconditioned that has its conditions fulfilled solely by acts of defining and postulating; such is the analytic proposition. To this virtually unconditioned there can accrue a further fulfilment inasmuch as what it defines and what it postulates also prove to be virtually unconditioned; such is the analytic principle. This further fulfilment arises in concrete judgments of fact, such as occur in the process of verification; and so our position resembles that of the logical positivists. But resemblance need not be identity. For unlike the logical positivists, we are completely disillusioned of the notion that knowing the real is somehow looking at what is already out there now. Unlike them, we have much to say about the unconditioned, and indeed it is in the unconditioned that we place the whole meaning and force of verification.

On the one hand, then, the ontological argument is to be rejected, for conception alone is an insufficient ground for judgment. On the other hand, what has to be added to mere conception is, not an experience of God, but a grasp of the unconditioned. Affirming is an intrinsically rational act; it proceeds with rational necessity from grasp of the unconditioned; and the unconditioned to be grasped is, not the formally unconditioned that God is and that unrestricted understanding grasps, but the virtually unconditioned that consists in inferring God's existence from premises that are true. There remains but one more preliminary. Already we have remarked, but again we must repeat, that proof is not some automatic process that results in a judgment, as taking an aspirin relieves a headache, or as turning on a switch sets the digital computer on its unerring way. All that can be set down in these pages is a set of signs. The signs can represent a relevant virtually unconditioned. But grasping it and making the consequent judgment is an immanent act of rational consciousness that each has to perform for himself and no one else can perform for him.

The existence of God, then, is known as the conclusion to an argument, and while such arguments are many, all of them, I believe, are included in the following general form.

If the real is completely intelligible, God exists. But the real is completely intelligible. Therefore, God exists.

To begin from the minor premise, one argues that being is completely intelligible, that the real is being, and that therefore the real is completely intelligible.

Now being is completely intelligible. For being is the objective of the detached, disinterested, unrestricted desire to know; this desire consists in intelligent inquiry and critical reflection; it results in partial knowledge inasmuch as intelligent inquiry yields understanding and critical reflection grasps understanding to be correct; but it reaches its objective, which is being, only when every intelligent question has been given an intelligent answer and that answer has been found to be correct. Being, then, is intelligible, for it is what is to be known by correct understanding; and it is completely intelligible, for being is known completely only when all intelligent questions are answered correctly.

Moreover, the real is being. For the real is what is meant by the name 'real.' But all that is meant is either a mere object of thought or else both an object of thought and an object of affirmation. The real is not merely an object of thought; and so it is both an object of thought and an object of affirmation. Nor is the real merely some of the objects of both thought and affirmation but all of them. And similarly, being is all that is to be known by intelligent grasp and reasonable affirmation.

If this coincidence of the real and being presupposes an acceptance of the positions and a rejection of the counterpositions, the reader will not expect at this stage of the argument any repetition of the basic points that have been made over and over again in the preceding pages of this work. To accept the positions is to accept one's own intelligence and reasonableness and to stand by that acceptance. To reject the counterpositions is to reject the interference of other desire with the proper functioning of the detached, disinterested, and unrestricted desire to know. Hence every counterposition leads to its own reversal; for it is involved in incoherence as soon as the claim is made that it is grasped intelligently and affirmed reasonably; and an intelligent and reasonable subject cannot avoid making that claim.

There remains the major premise, namely, If the real is completely intelligible, then God exists. The argument may be cast as follows.

If the real is completely intelligible, then complete intelligibility exists. If complete intelligibility exists, the idea of being exists. If the idea of being exists, then God exists. Therefore, if the real is completely intelligible, God exists.

Let us comment on each of the premises in turn.

First, if the real is completely intelligible, then complete intelligibility exists. For just as the real could not be intelligible if intelligibility were nonexistent, so the real could not be completely intelligible if complete intelligibility were nonexistent. In other words, to affirm the complete intelligibility of the real is to affirm the complete intelligibility of all that is to be affirmed. But one cannot affirm the complete intelligibility of all that is to be affirmed without affirming complete intelligibility. And to affirm complete intelligibility is to know its existence.

Secondly, if complete intelligibility exists, the idea of being exists. For intelligibility either is material or spiritual or abstract: it is material in the objects of physics, chemistry, biology, and sensitive psychology; it is spiritual when it is identical with understanding; and it is abstract in concepts of unities, laws, ideal frequencies, genetic operators, dialectical tensions and conflicts. But abstract intelligibility necessarily is incomplete, for it arises only in the self-expression of spiritual intelligibility. Again, spiritual intelligibility is incomplete as long as it can inquire. Finally, material intelligibility necessarily is incomplete, for it is contingent in its existence and in its occurrences, in its genera and species, in its classical and statistical laws, in its genetic operators and the actual course of its emergent probability; moreover, it includes a merely empirical residue of individuality, noncountable infinities, particular places and times, and for systematic knowledge a nonsystematic divergence. It follows that the only possibility of complete intelligibility lies in a spiritual intelligibility that cannot inquire because it understands everything about everything. And such unrestricted understanding is the idea of being.

Thirdly, if the idea of being exists, God exists. For if the idea of being exists, at least its primary component exists. But the primary component has been shown to possess all the attributes of God. Therefore, if the idea of being exists, God exists.

Such, then, is the argument. As a set of signs printed in a book, it can do no more than indicate the materials for a reflective grasp of the virtually unconditioned. To elicit such an act is the work that the reader has to perform for himself. Further, inasmuch as any reader has been impressed by the widely diffused contemporary view that the existence of God cannot be proved, he will be wondering just where the fallacy lies, just when the unjustified step was taken, in the foregoing endeavor to accomplish the reputedly impossible. Let us join him in his reflection.

Certainly, there would have to be some fallacy in the argument if it did not presuppose a complete break with the various currents of modern thought that insist on atheism or agnosticism. But such a complete break does exist in the rejection, root and branch, of the counter-positions and in a complete acceptance of the positions. Granted that the real is being, granted that being is known by intelligent grasp and reasonable affirmation, then God is a reality if he is a being, and he is a being if intelligent grasp conceives him and reasonableness affirms what intelligence conceives. Again, granted the exclusion of all obscurantism, intelligence is committed to the effort to conceive a notion of God; for if the real is being, then one must face the question, What is being? and as has been seen, the answer to that question includes the answer to the question, What is God? But the answer to a question for intelligence necessarily raises the corresponding question for reflection, and the exclusion of obscurantism once more commits us to an effort to answer. If the answer is negative, atheism is correct. If no answer is possible, agnosticism is correct. If the answer is affirmative, theism is correct. The only issue is to decide which of the three is the answer to be given by the unity of empirical, intelligent, and rational consciousness that I happen to be. Finally, if I am operating in the intellectual pattern of experience, if I am genuine in my acceptance of the domination of the detached, disinterested, unrestricted desire to inquire intelligently and reflect reasonably, then I have no just grounds for surprise if I find myself unable to deny either that there is a reality or that the real is being or that being is completely intelligible or that complete intelligibility is unrestricted understanding or that unrestricted understanding is God.

Still, a conclusion can contain no more than its premises. If at the start one does not know that God exists, at least that knowledge must emerge in the process if it is to be present at its end. Where, then, in the process does knowledge of God's existence make its implicit entry?

It is a fair question, but to answer it a distinction has to be drawn between (1) affirming a link between other existence and God's and (2) affirming the other existence that is linked to God's existence. The second element lies in the affirmation of some reality: it took place in the chapter on self-affirmation, and it was expanded to the universe of proportionate being in subsequent chapters. The first element is the process that identifies the real with being, then identifies being with complete intelligibility, and finally identifies complete intelligibility with the unrestricted act of understanding that possesses the properties of God and accounts for everything else. In this process the expansive moment is the first: for if the real is being, the real is the objective of an unrestricted desire to understand correctly; to be such an objective, the real has to be completely intelligible, for what is not intelligible is not the objective of a desire to understand, and what is not completely intelligible is the objective, not of an unrestricted desire to understand correctly, but of such a desire judiciously blended with an obscurantist refusal to understand. Once this expansive moment is achieved, the rest follows. The real cannot be completely intelligible if complete intelligibility is unreal. Nor can complete intelligibility be real if the unrestricted act of understanding is merely an object of thought. For the intelligibility of the merely conceived is not real; the intelligibility of material reality is dependent on a merely empirical residue, and so it is incomplete; the intelligibility of inquiring and developing intelligence is seeking its own completion and thereby proclaiming its incompleteness; and so the only possibility of an intelligibility that is at once complete and real is the unrestricted act of understanding.

Yet who are we to pretend to knowledge of every possibility? Might not there be some further alternative? Might not intelligibility be both real and complete in some quite different fashion that lies beyond the narrow confines of our comprehension? There might be, if we were ready to take refuge in the counterpositions or to give way to our tendencies to obscurantism. But the presupposition is that we are not. And if we are not, then the possible is possible being, being is intrinsically intelligible, and the intelligible either is identical with understanding or else related to it as something that could be understood. But intelligibility of the latter type is incomplete, for it is conditioned in its very intelligibility by its relation to something else. Nor is inquiring and developing understanding complete. So there remains only the unrestricted act of understanding. Nor is there any paradox in our claiming to envisage all possible alternatives; for if we can know that our attainment is extremely limited, we can do so because our knowledge springs from an unrestricted desire to understand correctly; and so it is one and the same unrestricted desire that both reveals to us the vastness of the range of possibilities and, by the same stroke, defines the basic conditions that every possibility must satisfy.

Finally, it may be objected that, for all we know, an unrestricted act of understanding may be a contradiction in terms. But at least an unrestricted desire to understand correctly is not a contradiction, for it is a fact. Nor has contradiction any other origin but the existence of different acts of understanding with respect to the same object. Nor does contradiction imply impossibility unless reality is completely intelligible. But the unrestricted act of understanding is a single act, so that contradiction cannot originate from it; and only because the unrestricted act grounds all that is and would ground all that could be, is it true that the contradictory cannot be.

3 Conclusion

Now if the notion and affirmation of God pertain to the positions, not in any incidental fashion, but as necessary answers to the inevitable questions about the idea of being and the identity of being with the real, it follows that the counterpositions, ever sustained by the polymorphism of human consciousness, will involve prephilosophic notions of the divine in the mythical, will generate counterphilosophic misconceptions, doubts, and denials, and will tend to corrupt even correct notions and affirmations if they are unsupported by an effective criticism of the influences that rise from the unconscious into human sensitivity and intersubjectivity and that invade the realm of truth at the demand of tribal, national, economic, and political necessity and utility.

If, then, the procedure of the present chapter in conceiving the nature and affirming the reality of God appears to be excessively laborious, complex, and difficult, it would be unfair to overlook the fact that our concern has been, not to select the easiest approach to the notion of God, not to offer the simplest proof of his existence, but so to advance from proportionate to transcendent being that the universal viewpoint, attained in the earlier stages of the argument, might be preserved as well as expanded. It is an old saying that *veritas est una et error multiplex*, but even truth changes its appearance as human understanding develops, and it is not a negligible advantage to be able to account from a single base not only for the changing face of truth, not only for the multiplicity of error, but also for the worst of enemies, the one in a man's own household, that so spontaneously and so naturally tends to adjust and color the truth one knows to the exigences of one's sociocultural milieu and to the hue of one's temperament ...

Because it is difficult to know what our knowing is, it also is difficult to know what our knowledge of God is. But just as our knowing is prior to an analysis of knowledge and far easier than it, so too our knowledge of God is both earlier and easier than any attempt to give it formal expression. For without any formulation of the notion of being, we use it whenever we inquire and understand, reflect and judge. Without any explicit repudiation of obscurantism, we ask questions and further questions in our search for the intelligible and unconditioned. But all that we know and can know about ourselves and about the world around us raises the same further question; for it is known to be just as a matter of fact through a reflective grasp of the virtually unconditioned; and the ubiquitous and incessant further question admits only one answer, namely, an intelligibility that formally is unconditioned. So it is that, just as all men understand what they mean by the 'nature of ...' though they are at a loss to say what they mean, similarly they all understand what they mean by God though they are at a loss when asked to explain so basic and familiar a notion. Again, just as every inquirer knows something when he knows that there is a nature to be known though he still has to discover what the nature is, similarly everyone knows something when he knows that there is a God even though he entertains no hope of ever reaching an unrestricted act of understanding and so knowing what God is. Again, just as the notion of nature can be misused by the gnostic and the magician yet, if used properly, provides the dynamic base on which the whole of scientific knowledge is erected, so too the notion of God can be corrupted by mythical consciousness and distorted by misplaced practicality yet, if used properly, it supplies the dynamic base on which rise not only the whole of intelligent and rational knowing but also the whole of intelligent and rational living. Finally, just as misuse of the notion of nature makes it ridiculous in the eyes of those most eager to know what is to be known by understanding, so too misconception and misuse of the notion of God lead to its rejection by the very men that are most insistent in denouncing obscurantism, in demanding judgments to rest on the unconditioned, and in calling for consistency between knowing and doing. But if one is eager to know what is to be known by understanding, one can ridicule the notion of nature only because one does not know what the name means; and if one is genuine in denouncing obscurantism and in demanding the unconditioned, either one already adores God without naming him or else one has not far to go to reach him ...

We have admitted the existence of a critical problem because man's unrestricted desire asks more questions than man's limited attainment can answer; we have contended that a solution to the problem must be piecemeal because questions of possibility are to be settled only by appealing to facts; and we have pointed out that the piecemeal solution becomes methodical in the measure that it executes a comprehensive and effective strategy in selecting the facts to which it successively appeals. Earlier elements in the strategy which we have been following already are familiar to the reader; but it remains to be shown that the fact that we can conceive God as the transcendent idea and affirm him as the transcendent reality of being not only is continuous with all that has gone before but also is its culmination.

Our subject has been the act of insight or understanding, and God is the unrestricted act of understanding, the eternal rapture glimpsed in every Archimedean cry of 'Eureka.' Understanding meets questions for intelligence and questions for reflection. The unrestricted act meets all at once; for it understands understanding and all the intelligibility based on it; and it understands its own understanding as unrestricted, invulnerable, true. What is known by true understanding is being, and the being known by unrestricted understanding's self-knowledge is primary being, self-explanatory, unconditioned, necessary, without any lack or defect. The good is the intelligible, and so the primary being also is the primary good. As intelligibility without intelligence would be defective, so also would truth without affirming, or the good without loving; but God is without defect, not because the act of understanding is complemented by further acts, but by a single act that at once is understanding and intelligible, truth and affirming, goodness and loving, being and omnipotence.

Our subject has been understanding in its genesis. It arises in intelligent and rational consciousness, but before it arises it is anticipated, and that anticipation is the spontaneous ground that, when reflectively enucleated, becomes the methods of science and the integral heuristic structure implemented in the metaphysics of proportionate being. But the fundamental anticipation is the detached, disinterested, unrestricted desire to understand correctly; the fundamental assumption is that the real is coincident with the grounded intelligibility to be known by correct understanding; the fundamental reflective enucleation of all intelligent and rational anticipation and assumption is to conceive the idea of being, and thereby the notion of God, and to affirm that the real is being, and thereby to affirm the reality of God.

Our subject has been the flight from understanding in the scotosis of the dramatic subject, in the threefold bias of common sense, in the murkiness of mythical consciousness, in the aberrations of the counter-philosophies. But it is not the spirit of inquiry that refuses to ask what being is, nor critical reflection that ignores the question whether being and only being is the real. It is not flight from understanding that forms the notion of an unrestricted act of understanding, nor the demand of rational consciousness for the unconditioned that draws back in alarm when there arises a demand for the formally unconditioned. It is by the positions that the notion of God is developed and the affirmation of God is sustained, and it is by the counterpositions that the issues are misconceived and confused.

Kant spoke of a transcendental illusion, and if what he meant has been shown to be a mistake, the expression survives to generate distrust. But it is not the detached and disinterested desire to understand correctly that can be named an illusion, for it is interference with that desire that is at the root of all error. Nor can the unrestricted desire be named a transcendental illusion, for there has to exist some illusion before it can be either immanental or transcendental. Nor can one say that the pure desire exists, that it is not illusory, yet in fact it is not unrestricted. After all, Kantians and positivists are not deluded but merely mistaken when they endeavor to restrict human inquiry within bounds that everyone naturally and spontaneously transcends.

What, then, is critical method? It is method with respect to the ultimate, method applied to the most basic issues. Now it has been seen that the method of the empirical sciences rests on the heuristic structure of man's desire and capacity to understand data correctly. In similar fashion the method of metaphysics consisted in integrating and implementing classical and statistical, genetic and dialectical methods. Critical method differs from other methods only in its subject matter. As they, so it takes its stand on the detached, disinterested, unrestricted desire to understand correctly. As they, so it grasps and affirms an object correlative to the desire. As they, so it insists both that general statements can be made about the object before it actually is understood and that such statements, though valid and true and useful, fall far short of what is to be known if understanding is attained. In brief, critical method neither is nor can be the bland procedure of consigning transcendental issues to oblivion. Just as scientific method does not repudiate the notion of nature but makes it explicit and pre-

cise as the indeterminate function to be determined, as the ideal frequency from which actual frequencies cannot diverge systematically,
as the genetic operator, as the dialectical tension and opposition
between the pure desire and human sensitivity, so critical method does
not repudiate the notion of God but formulates it as the unrestricted
act of understanding and works out its general attributes. Just as scientific method does not confuse knowledge of method with its fruits, so
critical method does not confuse our formulation of unrestricted
understanding with a claim that we understand everything about
everything. Just as the scientist is ready to abandon every scientific
hypothesis and theory without losing confidence in the correctness of
scientific method, so the metaphysician affirms the reality of what the
scientist seeks to know, and the critical thinker does not allow developments in the notion of God to generate any doubt that it is one and
the same being to which all men refer whether they are more or less
successful in conceiving him, whether correctly they affirm his existence or mistakenly they deny it.

Related selections: 1.IX on the notion of being; 1.XIII.3 on the notion of a universal viewpoint; 1.XII.4 on human development; 2.II, 2.VI, 2.VII.4, 3.IV.1–3, 3.VII.2,
and 3.VIII.3 pertaining to Lonergan's later emphasis on religious experience;
1.VII.2 on grasp of the virtually unconditioned; 3.IV.1 on the question of God;
3.IV.5 on the interior and theoretic modes in theology.

XVI

The Problem of Evil
and Its Solution

In the present selection from the final chapter of *Insight*, 'Special Transcendent Knowledge,' Lonergan brings to the fore a question which grows ever more urgent as his moving viewpoint methodically expands in its sweep. What is to be done about the concrete fact of evil? This fact has come to light repeatedly in a variety of ever more inclusive contexts. It surfaces in Lonergan's treatment of the subjective field of common sense and the scotosis of the dramatic subject. It arises again in his discussion of the dialectic of community, of the need for a higher synthesis of liberalism and socialism, of individual, group, and general bias, and the longer cycle of decline. It reemerges in his account of the problem underlying philosophic differences. It surfaces yet again in Lonergan's discussion of the solidarity of cognitional, volitional, and sensitive appropriations of the truth. Finally, in the analysis of the problem of liberation and the conditions of effective freedom, it takes on the dimensions of a radical and permanent problem, rooted in our 'incapacity for sustained development' and calling for a solution in a 'still higher integration of human living.'[1] What is required, Lonergan argues, is 'a further manifestation of finality, of the upwardly but indeterminately directed dynamism of generalized emergent probability.'[2] The final two chapters of *Insight* are devoted to uncovering the general characteristics of this higher integration. In the penultimate chapter, from which the preceding selection is taken, Lonergan raises the question of the existence of God and answers affirmatively. His final chapter, accordingly, opens with an appropriate specification of the question regarding the fact of evil and its solution: 'the question really is what God is or has been doing about the fact of evil.'[3]

1 *Insight*, 653, 655.
2 Ibid., 655–6.
3 Ibid., 709.

In the first part of the present selection Lonergan reviews the individual, social, and historical dimensions of the fact of evil, emphasizes its intractability in the face of humanly generated solutions, and exposes the need to add a theological dimension to the analysis of human history. In the second part he argues that the fact of evil comes to be regarded as a 'problem' only if we attempt to reconcile it with God's goodness; accordingly, to affirm a problem of evil is to imply the existence of a solution. In the third part Lonergan provides a heuristic outline of the cosmic and metaphysical aspects of the solution. He then proceeds to locate the required 'higher conjugate forms' constitutive of the higher integration of human living in a self-sacrificing love, in a confident hope, in a new and higher collaboration of men and women with one another and with God in faith, and in a harmonizing adaptation of human sensibility. This part concludes with a discussion of the heightened tension of human development that may be expected to result from the introduction into human history of the supernatural solution to the problem of evil. The final part is taken from a lengthy excursus on the nature of belief, which interrupts Lonergan's discussion of the heuristic structure of the solution in *Insight* just prior to his account of faith. Collaboration, among ourselves and with God, involves belief, but the gravest evils result from erroneous and mistaken beliefs. There is needed a critique of beliefs. In this discussion Lonergan first analyzes the general context of belief and makes a distinction, commonly overlooked, between immanently generated knowledge and belief. He proceeds to explain how mistaken beliefs arise and how they are eliminated. While Lonergan does not deny that a critique of beliefs may be efficacious, it remains that 'the basic problem lies not in mistaken beliefs but in the mistaken believer.'[4]

The extracts in this section are taken from *Insight*, 709–17, 718–22, 723–5, 725–8, 735–9, 740–3, 744–7, 747–50.

Knowledge is transcendent, in our present usage, inasmuch as it goes beyond the domain of proportionate being.

General transcendent knowledge is the knowledge of God that answers the basic questions raised by proportionate being, namely, what being is and whether being is the real.

Still, there is a fact of evil, and man is inclined to argue from that fact to a denial of the intelligence or the power or the goodness of God. Even though it is agreed that the evil of objects of aversion is, from an intellectualist viewpoint, a potential good, even though it is agreed that the evil of disorder is an absence of intelligibility that is to be understood only by the inverse insight that grasps its lack of intelligibility, there remains the concrete fact of evil and the practical problem of determining what one is to do about it.

Indeed, since God is the first agent of every event and emergence and development, the question really is what God is or has been doing about the fact of evil. The answer to that question we shall name special transcendent knowledge, and our discussion will fall under four main heads, namely, the fact of evil, the existence of a solution, the heuristic structure of the properties of the possible solutions, and the identification of the solution that exists.

To these main topics we are forced to add a lengthy excursus on the notion of belief. For among the evils that afflict man, none is graver than the erroneous beliefs which at once distort his mind and make systematic the aberrations of his conduct. Yet, despite its potentialities for evil, belief is inevitable in human collaboration, and the policy of believing nothing is as illusory as the Cartesian program of doubting everything that can be doubted. So we are compelled to determine just what is the necessity of belief, what precisely occurs when one believes, and what one can do to free oneself from false beliefs ...

1 The Problem

The cult of progress has suffered an eclipse, not because man does not develop, nor because development does not imply a revision of what has been, but because development does imply that perfection belongs not to the present but to the future. Had that implication of present shortcomings not been overlooked with such abandon, had the apostles of progress not mistaken their basic views for premature attainments of future perfection, then the disillusionment of the twentieth century could hardly have been at once so unexpected, so bitter, and so complete.

Yet as things are, in the aftermath of economic and political upheavals, amidst the fears of worse evils to come, the thesis of progress needs to be affirmed again. For the very structure of man's being is dynamic. His knowing and willing rest on inquiry, and inquiry is unrestricted. His knowing consists in understanding, and every act of understanding not only raises further questions but also opens the way to further answers. His good will is consistent with his knowledge, and as his knowledge develops, he can be persuaded effectively to an ever fuller willingness. His sensitivity and his intersubjectivity are, like his knowledge and willingness, systems on the move; if their adaptation to spiritual advance is slow, at least it tends to endure; and so the accepted manners and customs of an earlier time can become abominations, at once incredible and repulsive, to a later age.

But if the thesis of progress must be affirmed, it must be taken to imply, not only a contrast with the past, but also a contrast with its goal. An unrestricted desire to understand correctly heads towards an unrestricted act of understanding, towards God. A will that is good by its consistency with knowledge is headed towards an antecedent willingness that matches the desire to know both in its essential detachment from the sensitive subject and in its unrestricted commitment to complete intelligibility, to God. A sensitivity and an intersubjectivity that have their higher integration in knowing and willing are headed towards objects and activities that can be no more than symbols and signs of what they cannot comprehend or appreciate. The whole world of sense is to be, then, a token, a mystery, of God, for the desire of intelligence is for God, and the goodness of will is the love of God.

There is a further implication. As the thesis of progress never places man on the pinnacle of perfection, it ever asserts that his knowledge is incomplete, that his willingness is imperfect, that his sensitivity and intersubjectivity still need to be adapted. Knowledge comes by the apparently random process of discovery, and it is disseminated by the laborious process of teaching and learning, writing and reading. Willingness to live consistently with knowledge has to be acquired by persuading oneself or by being persuaded by others. Sensitivity and intersubjectivity need time to become at ease with new ways. So it is that the present is ever a pattern of lags. No one can postpone his living until he has learnt, until he has become willing, until his sensitivity has been adapted. To learn, to be persuaded, to become adapted, occur within living and through living. The living is ever now, but the knowledge to guide living, the willingness to follow knowledge, the sensitive adaptation that vigorously and joyously executes the will's decisions, these belong to the future, and when the future is present, there will be beyond it a further future with steeper demands.

Now, inasmuch as the courses of action that men choose reflect either their ignorance or their bad will or their ineffectual self-control, there results the social surd. Then, to understand his concrete situation, man has to invoke not only the direct insights that grasp intelligibility but also the inverse insights that acknowledge the absence of intelligibility. Still, this subtle procedure has to be discovered, taught, learnt. Until the discovery is made and disseminated and accepted, man tends to regard his situation as a homogeneous array of intelligible facts. The social surd, which should be discounted as mere proof of aberration, is regarded as evidence in favor of error. Man becomes a realist. The dictates of intelligence and reasonableness are found irrelevant to concrete living. The facts have to be faced, and facing them means the adjustment of theory to practice. But every adjustment makes the incidental sins of the past into the commonly accepted rule of the present; the social surd expands; and its expansion demands a further adjustment.

If this succession of ever less comprehensive syntheses can be deduced from man's failure to understand himself and his situation dialectically, if, historically, evidence for the failure and its consequences is forthcoming both in the distant and in the recent past, still it is far too general a theorem to unravel at a stroke the tangled skein of intelligibility and absurdity in concrete situations. Its generality has to be mediated by a vast accumulation of direct and inverse insights and by a long series of judgments of truth and of value, before any concrete judgments can be made. And on what Galahad shall we call to do the understanding and to make the judgments? For the social surd resides least of all in outer things and most of all in the minds and wills of men. Without an unbiased judge, the truth would not be reached; and if an unbiased judge were found, would the biased remainder of mankind acknowledge the rectitude of his decisions and effectively abide by them?

It was to this point that we were brought by our study of common sense and by its revelation of the scotosis of the dramatic subject and of the threefold bias of the practical subject. Then we appealed to a higher viewpoint, to an X named cosmopolis; and we indicated some of its features. But if the need of some cosmopolis makes manifest the inadequacy of common sense to deal with the issue, on a deeper level it makes manifest the inadequacy of man. For the possibility of a cosmopolis is conditioned by the possibility of a critical human science, and a critical human science is conditioned by the possibility of a correct and accepted philosophy.

However, as the intervening chapters have attempted to explain, and as the history of philosophy rather abundantly confirms, the polymorphism of human consciousness loses none of its ambivalence because men have turned to philosophy. On the contrary, the many philosophies are but the adequate expression of the inner polymorphic fact. For every human discovery can be formulated either as a position or as a counterposition. The positions invite development, and in the measure that they are developed they are expressed in many ways. Initially each may appear singly. Then it is joined with further antithetical questions. Then positions begin to coalesce, first in more numerous but lesser syntheses, later in fewer but more comprehensive unities. Besides the many expressions of the positions, there are the counterpositions, and they invite reversal. But the reversal that could come from a single penetrating stroke more commonly is delayed. The counterposition expands by the unfolding of its logical implications; it recognizes its fellows and unites with them in a common cause; together they foresee the impending danger of reversal, not in its root, but in some particular manifestation; and then they shift their ground and avoid the menaced attack. So the counterpositions multiply; they occupy a vast territory from high-minded incoherence to simple-minded opportunism and violence; and if the worst of the counterpositions has no truck with any position, if the most perfect expression of the positions happens to be free from any taint of the counterpositions, still philosophers are men, and the vast majority of them cling to some blend of both.

This conclusion may sound like scepticism. But certainly I would be the last to deny the possibility of working out a philosophy on the basis of the polymorphism of human consciousness and of the dialectical opposition between positions and counterpositions. After all, one does not deem impossible what one labors to achieve. Yet, if I fancy that I have made some contribution towards a philosophy of philosophies, I cannot dream so complex a transposition to end multiplicity; I cannot but suppose that those that will accept my conclusions also will endeavor to improve upon them, while those that disagree, if ever they cease to believe silence the more efficacious weapon, will labor manfully to reverse my views. Moreover, in the measure that this work and subsequent improvements upon it possess concrete and practical implications, in that measure not only human intelligence and reasonableness but also human will and the established routines of human sensitivity and intersubjectivity are involved. So the Babel of men's minds passes into the conflict of their wills, and the conflict of wills reaches for its panoply of image and emotion, sound and passion.

Now if philosophy speaks with so many voices that a correct philosophy must be too complicated to pierce the din, should one not appeal directly to men of good will? Indeed one should, provided one can find them. But there must be no illusions. One is not to define good will by its resemblance to one's own will, or even by its resemblance to the will one would like to possess but does not. Will is good by its conformity to intelligence. It is good in the measure that antecedently and without persuasion it matches the pure desire both in its detachment from the sensitive subject and in its incessant dedication to complete intelligibility. A will less good than that is less than genuine; it is ready for the obnubilation that takes flight from self-knowledge; it is inclined to the rationalization that makes out wrong to be right; it is infected with the renunciation that approves the good yet knows itself to be evil. In brief, as man's intelligence has to be developed, so also must his will. But progress in willingness is effected by persuasion, persuasion rests upon intelligent grasp and reasonable judgment, and so the failure of intellect to develop entails the failure of the will.

There is a deeper level to the problem. In an earlier paragraph it was concluded that the pure desire of the mind is a desire of God, that the goodness of man's will consists in a consuming love of God, that the world of sense is, more than all else, a mystery that signifies God as we know him and symbolizes the further depths that lie beyond our comprehension. There is a theological dimension that must be added to our detached analysis of the compounding of man's progress with man's decline. Bad will is not merely the inconsistency of rational self-consciousness; it also is sin against God. The hopeless tangle of the social surd, of the impotence of common sense, of the endlessly multiplied philosophies, is not merely a *cul-de-sac* for human progress; it also is a reign of sin, a despotism of darkness; and men are its slaves.

No doubt, men are free. Were they not free, there would be no question of their sinning. But their essential freedom is one thing, and their effective freedom is another. Their essential freedom lies in the dynamic structure of rational self-consciousness; it is a higher integration of lower manifolds that can be integrated in many different manners; each element in that higher integration appears, first, as a possible course of action revealed by insight, secondly, as a value to be weighed by reflection, and thirdly, as an actuality only if it is chosen. No single course of action is necessary. If insight grasps only one at a time, still the insight raises the further question that leads to reflection, and the reflection leads to the further insights that reveal the alternative possibilities of the concrete situation. Again, reflection can pronounce one course of action preferable to all others, but that pronouncement has its suppositions, and the suppositions are not all that necessarily is so, but at least in part merely what one chooses or has chosen to prefer. Finally, reflection never settles the issue; it can determine that a given course is valuable or pleasurable or useful; but only the decision makes the course actual; nor does the decision follow because the reflection ends, but the reflection ends because the decision is made. Because man determines himself, he is responsible; because the course of action determined upon and the process of determining are both contingent, man is free.

Effective freedom supposes essential freedom, as statistical law supposes classical law. Essential freedom is an intrinsic property of acts of a determinate class; but effective freedom regards the relative frequencies of different kinds of acts within the class. Essential freedom is concerned with the manner in which acts occur; but effective freedom asks what acts are to be expected to occur.

The reign of sin, then, is the expectation of sin. On a primary level, it is the priority of living to learning how to live, to acquiring the willingness to live rightly, to developing the adaptation that makes right living habitual. On a second level, it is man's awareness of his plight and his self-surrender to it; on each occasion, he could reflect and through reflection avoid sinning; but he cannot bear the burden of perpetual reflection; and long before that burden has mounted to the limit of physical impossibility, he chooses the easy way out. On both the primary and the second levels, there is the transposition of the inner issue into the outer social milieu; concrete situations become infected with the social surd; they are intractable without dialectical analysis; and the intractability is taken as evidence that only in an increasingly limited fashion can intelligence and reasonableness and good will have any real bearing upon the conduct of human affairs. Finally, dialectical analysis can transpose the issue, but it cannot do so effectively. It goes beyond common sense to a critical human science that supposes a correct and accepted philosophy; but a correct philosophy will be but one of many philosophies, and precisely because it is correct it will be too complicated to be commonly accessible and too alien to sinful man to be widely accepted.

2   The Existence of a Solution

There is a fact of evil. It is not an incidental waywardness that provides the exceptions to prove a rule of goodness. Rather it is a rule. If it is not a necessary but only a statistical rule, it is no less a fact, and indeed it is a worse fact. Were the rule necessary, it would exclude freedom; were freedom excluded, there would be no sin. But the rule is statistical; freedom remains essentially intact; and so effectively man's rational self-consciousness is frustrated with the burden of responsibility for sins it could avoid but does not.

But is there also a problem of evil? There can be a problem only if there is an intelligibility to be grasped. But what intelligibility and as well what lack of intelligibility there are in man's condition and situation have been grasped already. There are intelligible possibilities of intelligent and reasonable and good courses of action. There is the intelligibility of the frequencies with which they are and are not executed. There is the intelligibility of actual choices that are good. There is the surd of sin, and it is understood inasmuch as one grasps its lack of intelligibility. Nor are there further questions, as long as one directs one's attention to man; for while intelligence can grasp what man might do, it also grasps that man will not do it.

Nonetheless, there is a problem of evil, for besides man there also is God. The order of this universe in all its aspects and details has been shown to be the product of unrestricted understanding, of unlimited power, of complete goodness. Because God is omniscient, he knows man's plight. Because he is omnipotent, he can remedy it. Because he is good, he wills to do so. The fact of evil is not the whole story. It also is a problem. Because God exists, there is a further intelligibility to be grasped.

Certain remarks are in order. First of all, I have employed the name 'problem' in a technical sense, so that it is meaningless to speak of a problem for which no solution exists. But the argument does not depend upon the definition of terms. No matter how one cares to phrase it, the point seems to remain that evil is, not a mere fact, but a problem, only if one attempts to reconcile it with the goodness of God; and if God is good then there is not only a problem of evil but also a solution.

In the second place, since a solution exists, our account of man's moral impotence and of the limitations on his effective freedom cannot be the whole story. There is a further component in the actual universe that as yet has not been mentioned. Because it has not been mentioned, our statements on man's plight are true as far as they go, but they are not the whole truth. They are true hypothetically inasmuch as they tell what would be did the further component not exist; but they are not true absolutely, for they prescind from a further component that both exists and is relevant to the issue.

In the third place, because this book has been written from a moving viewpoint, we have mentioned first a problem and only later its solution. But it would be an anthropomorphic blunder to transfer this succession to God. There are no divine afterthoughts. The unrestricted act of understanding grasps the total range of possible world orders; each is a consequence and manifestation of divine intelligence and wisdom, of divine reality and truth, of divine goodness and love; since all are worthy of God, any can be chosen, and that choice will be intelligent and wise, good and loving. Moreover, as has been seen already, the good is potential or formal or actual; but the problem under consideration is potentially good, for it is the potency to the solution; the solution as a further order is formally good and as a possible object of choice is a value or actual good in prospect or in process or in its term. It follows that the problem and its solution are related both from the viewpoint of intelligence and from the viewpoint of the good; and so once more there appears the absurdity of thinking of the problem without its solution ...

3 The Heuristic Structure of the Solution

We have affirmed the existence both of a problem and of its solution within the intelligible unity of the actual order of the universe. But this implies the existence of a heuristic structure. For there is a heuristic structure whenever the object of an inquiry admits antecedent determinations; and the solution that we are seeking is an object of inquiry that satisfies the intelligible unity of the actual world order and that solves the problem defined above.

Now it would seem that this heuristic structure is worth investigating. For even when such a structure fails to determine a single answer, at least it offers a set of alternative answers; and then through an appeal to the facts it becomes possible to settle which of the alternatives is correct.

First, then, the solution will be one. For there is one God, one world order, and one problem that is both individual and social.

Secondly, the solution will be universally accessible and permanent. For the problem is not restricted to men of a particular class or of a particular time; and the solution has to meet the problem.

Thirdly, the solution will be a harmonious continuation of the actual order of this universe. For there are no divine afterthoughts.

Fourthly, the solution will not consist in the addition of central forms of a new genus or species. For the solution is to a human problem; the problem has to be solved for men, and it would merely be dodged by introducing a new genus or species.

Fifthly, the solution can consist in the introduction of new conjugate forms in man's intellect, will, and sensitivity. For such forms are habits. But man's intellect is an unrestricted potency, and so it can receive habits of any kind; man's will is good insofar as it follows intellect, and so it can receive habits that correspond to the habits received in intellect; finally, man's sensitivity is a lower manifold under the higher integration of intellectual and volitional acts, and so it can be adapted habitually to the acts that occur.

Sixthly, the solution will include the introduction of such conjugate forms. For the problem arises from the nature of development; because man's living is prior to learning and being persuaded, it is without the guidance of knowledge and without the direction of effective good will; as long as that priority remains, the problem remains. The solution, then, must reverse the priority, and it does so inasmuch as it provides intellect, will, and sensitivity with forms or habits that are operative throughout living.

Seventhly, the relevant conjugate forms will be in some sense transcendent or supernatural. For what arises from nature is the problem. The forms that solve the problem, then, do not arise from nature; they are not the result of accumulated insights, for such accumulation takes time, and the problem arises because man has to live during the interval in which insights are being accumulated. Moreover, the understanding man acquires in this fashion, the judgments that he forms, and the willingness that he obtains all suffer from the fourfold bias of the dramatic and practical subject and from the tendency of speculative thought to the counterpositions.

Eighthly, since the solution is a harmonious continuation of the actual order of the universe, and since that order involves the successive emergence of higher integrations that systematize the nonsystematic residues on lower levels, it follows that the relatively transcendent conjugate forms will constitute a new and higher integration of human activity and that that higher integration will solve the problem by controlling elements that otherwise are nonsystematic or irrational.

Ninthly, these higher conjugate forms will pertain not to static system but to system on the move. For they have their place in a harmonious continuation of the actual order of the universe, and in that order the lower static systems of physics and chemistry are succeeded by the higher dynamic systems of biology, sensitive psychology, and human intellectual activity. Moreover, the higher conjugate forms have to meet a problem that varies as man develops and declines, and so they too must be capable of some development and adaptation.

Tenthly, since higher integrations leave intact the natures and laws of the underlying manifold, and since man is intelligent and rational, free and responsible, it follows that the solution will come to men through their apprehension and with their consent.

Eleventhly, since the solution is a harmonious continuation of the actual order of the universe, and since that order is an emergent probability, it follows that the emergence of the solution and its propagation will be in accord with the probabilities. It is to be borne in mind, however, that emergent probability has the same meaning here as in the earlier chapters of this work; it does not denote any sort of efficient cause; it refers to the immanent intelligibility of the design or order in which things exist and events occur.

Twelfthly, the relevant probabilities are those that regard the occurrence of man's intelligent and rational apprehension of the solution and his free and responsible consent to it. But there are stages in human development when there is no probability that men will apprehend and consent to a universally accessible and permanent solution that meets the basic problem of human nature. Moreover, all human development has been seen to be compounded with decline, and so it fails to prepare men directly and positively to apprehend and consent to the solution. Accordingly, it seems necessary to distinguish between the realization of the full solution and, on the other hand, the emergent trend in which the full solution becomes effectively probable.

From the cosmic and metaphysical aspects of the solution, we now turn to a closer determination of the appropriate higher conjugate forms.

In the thirteenth place, then, the appropriate willingness will be some type or species of charity.

For good will follows intellect, and so it matches the detached, disinterested, unrestricted desire of intellect for complete understanding; but complete understanding is the unrestricted act that is God; and so the good that is willed by good will is God. Moreover, to will the good of a person is to love the person; but God is a person, for he is intelligent and free; and so good will is the love of God. Further, good will matches the detachment and disinterestedness of the pure desire to know, and so good will is a love of God that is prompted not by a hope of one's own advantage but simply by God's goodness.

Again, a man or woman knows that he or she is in love by making the discovery that all spontaneous and deliberate tendencies and actions regard the beloved. Now as the arm rises spontaneously to protect the head, so all the parts of each thing conspire to the good of the whole, and all things in all their operations proceed to the realization of the order of the universe. But the order of this universe is actual, and the orders of all other universes are possible, because of the completeness of the intelligibility, the power of the reality, and the perfection of the goodness and love of God. It follows that, apart from the surd of sin, the universe is in love with God; and good will is the opposite of the irrationality of sin; accordingly, the man of good will is in love with God.

Again, the actual order of the universe is a good and value chosen by God for the manifestation of the perfection of God. Moreover, it grounds the emergence, and includes the excellence, of every other good within the universe, so that to will any other good is to will the order of the universe. But good will follows intellect, and so, as intellect apprehends, so it wills, every other good because of the order of the universe, and the order of the universe because of God.

Again, the order of the universe includes all the good that all persons in the universe are or enjoy or possess. But to will the good of a person is to love the person; and so to will the order of the universe because of one's love of God is to love all persons in the universe because of one's love of God.

Again, the order of the universe is its intelligibility to be grasped by following the appropriate classical or statistical or genetic or dialectical method. Hence, to will the order of the universe is not to will the clock-work perfection of mechanist thought but the emergent probability of the universe that exists. It is not to demand that all things be perfect in their inception but to expect and will that they grow and develop. It is not to exclude from man's world the possibility of the social surd, nor to ignore it (for it is a fact), nor to mistake it for an intelligibility and so systematize and perpetuate it, but to acknowledge it as a problem and to embrace its solution.

Now the will can contribute to the solution of the problem of the social surd inasmuch as it adopts a dialectical attitude that parallels the dialectical method of intellect. The dialectical method of intellect consists in grasping that the social surd neither is intelligible nor is to be treated as intelligible. The corresponding dialectical attitude of will is to return good for evil. For it is only inasmuch as men are willing to meet evil with good, to love their enemies, to pray for those that persecute and calumniate them, that the social surd is a potential good. It follows that love of God above all and in all so embraces the order of the universe as to love all men with a self-sacrificing love ...

In the fourteenth place, besides the charity by which the will itself is made good, there will be the hope by which the will makes the intellect good.

For intellect functions properly inasmuch as the detached and disinterested desire to know is dominant in cognitional operations. Still, this desire is merely spontaneous. It is the root of intelligent and rational self-consciousness, and it operates prior to our insights, our judgments, and our decisions. Now if this desire is to be maintained in its purity, if it is not to suffer from the competition of the attached and interested desires of man's sensitivity and intersubjectivity, if it is not to be overruled by the will's connivance with rationalizations, then it must be aided, supported, reinforced by a deliberate decision and a habitual determination of the will itself.

Now such a decision and determination of the will can have as its object only the proper good of intellect. But the proper good of intellect is the attainment of the objective of the detached, disinterested, unrestricted desire to know; and the attainment of that objective is knowledge of God, who is at once the transcendent idea of being and the transcendent reality of being. It follows that, as intellect spontaneously desires knowledge of God, so the will deliberately desires attainment of that knowledge. Moreover, since the act of will is an act of rational self-consciousness, it will not be a mere repetition of the intellect's desire but also will take issue with conflicting tendencies and considerations. On the one hand, then, it will be a decision against man's despair, for the secret of the counterpositions is not the superficial confusion generated by the polymorphism of human consciousness but the deeper hopelessness that allows man's spirit to surrender the legitimate aspirations of the unrestricted desire and to seek comfort in the all too human ambitions of the Kantian and the positivist. On the other hand, it will be a decision against presumption no less than against despair. The objective of an unrestricted desire to understand correctly lies beyond the reach of empirical science, of common sense, of their unification in metaphysics, of the transcendent knowledge by which we know that God exists and that he is the unrestricted act of understanding. That objective is some attainment by knowledge of God who is the unrestricted act. The fulfilment of the conditions for that attainment lie not with man but with God, whose wisdom designed the order of the universe and whose goodness brings a solution to man's problem of evil. Now a desire that excludes both despair and presumption is a confident hope, and so the conjugate form of willingness that aids and supports and reinforces the pure desire is a confident hope that God will bring man's intellect to a knowledge, participation, possession of the unrestricted act of understanding ...

In the fifteenth place, there is to be considered the appropriate, relatively transcendent conjugate form that a realization of the solution to the problem of evil would involve in man's intellect. For if hope aids and supports the pure desire by striving for its goal, still hope is not knowledge but only an expectation of knowledge. It is not the knowledge that we hope for but the knowledge we possess that will supply the will's hope with its object and assurance and the will's charity with its motives. There is needed in the present a universally accessible and permanently effective manner of pulling men's minds out of the counterpositions, of fixing them in the positions, of securing for them certitude that God exists and that he has provided a solution which they are to acknowledge and to accept.

However, at first sight, this seems an impossibility within the limits of the problem. For the problem arises inasmuch as human knowledge bogs down in the counterpositions; and the solution has to be received by man not merely as intelligent and rational, free and responsible, but also as operating within a harmonious continuation of the present order of the universe. Not only is there demanded a leap from the counterpositions, but also it is expected that its occurrence will be probable not in a few cases but in a general and permanent fashion.

This argument, however, can be met with a distinction. For there are two ways in which men reach truth and certitude. If one asks a mathematician what is the logarithm of the square root of minus one, he will set down the relevant definitions and postulates and then proceed to deduce the answer. But if you ask a non-mathematician, he will turn and ask the mathematicians, and in the measure he is confident of their ability and sincerity he will have no doubt that the answer they give is correct. In both cases truth and certitude are attained, but in the first case it is generated immanently, while in the second case it is obtained through communication with those whom one knows to know. Now the argument outlined above goes to prove that there is no probability of men generally moving from the counterpositions to the positions by immanently generated knowledge. On the other hand, as far as the argument goes, it reveals no obstacles to the attainment of truth through the communication of reliable knowledge.

Still, one has only to notice the similarity between such communicated knowledge and belief to be aware that this proposal bristles with difficulties. For on the subject of belief the counterpositions have been both abundant and eloquent ...

In the sixteenth place, then, the solution in its cognitional aspect will consist in a new and higher collaboration of men in the pursuit of truth. For it has been seen that the solution meets a problem of error and sin through a higher integration that, though in some sense transcendent, nonetheless is a harmonious continuation of the actual order of the universe. Now in the actual order of the universe man's intellectual development occurs within a collaboration which men maintain by their truthfulness and accuracy, in which they participate by their beliefs, and to which they contribute by the addition of their immanently generated knowledge. Accordingly, because the solution is a harmonious continuation of the actual order, it too will be a collaboration that involves belief, truthfulness, accuracy, and immanently generated knowledge. Again, because the solution is a higher integration, it will be a new and higher collaboration. Finally, because the solution meets a problem of error and sin, the new and higher collaboration in the pursuit of truth will provide an antidote to the errors to which man is inclined.

In the seventeenth place, the new and higher collaboration will be, not simply a collaboration of men with one another, but basically man's cooperation with God in solving man's problem of evil. For if men could collaborate successfully in the pursuit of the truth that regards human living, there would be no problem, and so there would be no need of a solution. But the problem exists, and the existence of a solution is affirmed because of divine wisdom, divine goodness, and divine omnipotence. It follows that the new and higher collaboration is, not the work of man alone, but principally the work of God.

In the eighteenth place, man's entry into the new and higher collaboration and his participation of its fruits will be some species of faith.

By faith is meant the requisite conjugate form that the solution brings to man's intellect. By some species of faith is meant any of the conjugate forms that perfect intellect in any of the series of possible solutions within the reach of divine omnipotence.

Moreover, it can be shown that this faith will be a transcendent belief. For the solution is to be universally accessible, yet it is not to violate the probabilities of the actual order of the universe. But belief and only belief is universally accessible within a harmonious continuation of the existing order. Moreover, the relevant belief will be transcendent; for it makes a man a participant in the new and higher collaboration in which God is the initiator and the principal agent.

In the nineteenth place, with regard to faith three stages have to be distinguished. For it has been seen that the solution introduces into man's will a hope of knowledge of God that reinforces the pure desire to know. There is, then, a final stage when the attainment of knowledge supplants faith and realizes the object of hope. Moreover, it has been seen that the solution itself divides into two parts, with first an emergent trend, and only secondly its full realization. Accordingly, there will be an introductory faith and collaboration in the emergent trend towards the solution, and there will be a full faith and collaboration in the full realization of the solution.

In the twentieth place, because faith is a transcendent belief operative within a new and higher collaboration of man with God, the act of faith will be an assent of intellect to truths transmitted through the collaboration, and it will be motivated by man's reliance on the truthfulness of God. For, as a belief, the act of faith will be an assent of intellect to an object and because of a motive. As a belief within a new and higher collaboration, the object of faith will be the truths transmitted by the collaboration. Because it is a belief within a collaboration of man with God as initiator and principal agent, the motive of faith will be the omniscience, goodness, and omnipotence of God originating and preserving the collaboration.

In the twenty-first place, the act of faith as specified by its object will include an affirmation of man's spiritual nature, of his freedom, responsibility, and sinfulness, of God's existence and nature, and of the transcendent solution God provides for man's problem of evil. It will include the basic truths about man and about God, not because the ordinary collaboration of men cannot arrive at them, but because it invariably fails to reach unanimity upon them. It will include an announcement and an account of the solution because, as has been seen, though man cannot originate the solution nor preserve it, still he must be intelligent and reasonable in his acknowledgment of it and his acceptance of it.

In the twenty-second place, man will be intelligent and reasonable in his acknowledgment of the solution inasmuch as (1) he grasps the existence of the problem of evil and, in particular, of man's inability to cope with it, (2) he infers that divine wisdom must know many possible solutions, that divine omnipotence can effect any of them, and that divine goodness must have effected some one of them, (3) he recognizes that, in fact, there has been in human history, first an emergent trend, and later the full realization of a solution that possesses all the characteristics determined or to be determined in such a heuristic structure as the present.

In the twenty-third place, man will be intelligent and reasonable in his acceptance of the solution inasmuch as the foregoing judgments enable him to grasp as unconditioned the value of deciding to assent to the truths of the new and higher collaboration because of the initiating and preserving truthfulness of God. For from that grasp of the unconditioned there will follow with rational necessity a judgment on the value of deciding to assent, with free responsibility a decision to assent, and with conditioned natural necessity the act of assent itself.

In the twenty-fourth place, since the solution is a harmonious continuation of the actual order of the universe, man will not only acknowledge and accept the solution but also will collaborate with it. Accordingly, because the solution is for all men and universally accessible, there will be the collaboration that consists in making known to others the good news of the solution and its nature. Again, because the solution is permanent, there will be the collaboration that consists in transmitting it from each generation to the next. Again, because human expression is relative to its audience, there will be the collaboration that consists in recasting the expression of the solution into the equivalent expressions of different places, times, classes, and cultures. Again, because man can arrive at a universal viewpoint, there will be the collaboration that consists in conceiving and expressing the solution in terms of the universal viewpoint. Finally, because the solution regards man's problem of evil, there will be the collaboration that consists in grasping and formulating the manner in which the solution is relevant and effective in each of the successive situations of individuals, classes, national groups, and of men generally ...

In the twenty-seventh place, though the solution as a higher integration will be implemented principally in man's intellect and will through conjugate forms of faith and hope and charity, it must also penetrate to the sensitive level and envelop it. For, in the main, human consciousness flows in some blend of the dramatic and practical patterns of experience, and as the solution harmoniously continues the actual order of the universe, it can be successful only if it captures man's sensitivity and intersubjectivity. Moreover, as has been seen, all exercise of human intelligence presupposes a suitable flow of sensitive and imaginative presentations, and again, inasmuch as intelligence and reasonableness and will issue into human words matched with deeds, they need at their disposal images so charged with affects that they succeed both in guiding and in propelling action. Again, besides the image that is a sign of intelligible and rational contents and the image that is a psychic force, there is the image that symbolizes man's orientation into the known unknown; and since faith gives more truth than understanding comprehends, since hope reinforces the detached, disinterested, unrestricted desire to know, man's sensitivity needs symbols that unlock its transforming dynamism and bring it into harmony with the vast but impalpable pressures of the pure desire, of hope, and of self-sacrificing charity.

It follows that the solution will be not only a renovation of will that matches intellectual detachment and aspiration, not only a new and higher collaboration of intellects through faith in God, but also a mystery that is at once symbol of the uncomprehended and sign of what is grasped and psychic force that sweeps living human bodies, linked in charity, to the joyful, courageous, wholehearted, yet intelligently controlled performance of the tasks set by a world order in which the problem of evil is not suppressed but transcended.

Further, since mystery is a permanent need of man's sensitivity and intersubjectivity, while myth is an aberration not only of mystery but also of intellect and will, the mystery that is the solution as sensible must be not fiction but fact, not a story but history. It follows, then, that the emergent trend and the full realization of the solution must include the sensible data that are demanded by man's sensitive nature and that will command his attention, nourish his imagination, stimulate his intelligence and will, release his affectivity, control his aggressivity, and, as central features of the world of sense, intimate its finality, its yearning for God.

In the twenty-eighth place, the solution will be effective in the sense that it meets the problem of evil not by suppressing the consequences of man's waywardness but by introducing a new, higher integration that enables man, if he will, to rise above the consequences, to halt and reverse the sequence of ever less comprehensive syntheses in which theory keeps surrendering to practice, to provide a new and more solid base on which man's intellectual and social development can rise to heights undreamed of, and perpetually to overcome the objective surd of social situations by meeting abundant evil with a more generous good.

In the twenty-ninth place, the solution will have a nature and content and significance and power of its own. For if we have approached the solution through the problem of evil, and consequently have emphasized the aspects in which it is related to the problem, nonetheless the solution will be a new and higher integration, a new level on which human living develops and rejoices. However, many different solutions are possible to divine omnipotence, and a heuristic structure necessarily is confined to determining the generalities that are common to all solutions. Accordingly, for a specific account of the new and higher integration, of the content of its faith, of the object of its hope, of the intimacy of its charity, of the mystery of its transformed humanism, it is necessary to proceed from the heuristic structure of the solution to its identification in the facts of human living and human history.

In the thirtieth place, while every solution is transcendent in the sense that it involves a new and higher integration, while every solution is religious inasmuch as it is constituted by a faith and hope and love that look primarily to God, still in the measure that the higher integration goes beyond the minimal essentials of every solution, in that measure there will be revealed to faith truths that man never could discover for himself nor, even when he assented to them, could he understand them in an adequate fashion. For the greater the proper perfection and significance of the higher integration, the more it will lie beyond man's familiar range, and the more it will be grounded in the absolutely transcendent excellence of the unrestricted act of understanding.

Accordingly, if we specialize the general heuristic structure by adding further alternative hypotheses, we are led to distinguish between natural solutions, relatively supernatural[5] solutions, and absolutely supernatural solutions. All three types would have the common feature that they provide solutions to man's problem of evil. But the natural solutions would not offer to faith any truths that man could not discover for himself through the development of his own understanding; they would not offer to hope more than the natural immortality that can be deduced from the spirituality of the human soul, and the knowledge of God that is consequent upon the separation of the immortal soul from the mortal body; they would not offer to charity more than the perfection of a total, self-sacrificing love in a creature for his or her creator. In the relatively supernatural solutions, man's natural capacities cease to set a limiting rule; the object of faith includes truths that man could not reach through the development of his understanding; the object of hope is a knowledge of God beyond the appropriate attainment of an immortal soul; and charity is the more abundant response to a more indulgent beneficence. Still, all such solutions are only relatively supernatural, for though they go beyond the measure set by human nature, still there are other possible creatures more excellent than man for whom they would be natural solutions. Finally, there are the absolutely supernatural solutions. Conceived negatively, they are absolutely supernatural, because there is no possible creature for which they would be the natural solutions. Conceived positively, they are absolutely supernatural, because their sole ground

5 I should explain that I use the word 'supernatural' not in its current meaning, but as the English equivalent to the medieval theologians' *supernaturale*. It was a technical term that referred to the entitative disproportion between nature and grace, reason and faith, good will and charity, human esteem and merit before God.

and measure is the divine nature itself. Then faith includes objects beyond the natural reach of any finite understanding. Then hope is for a vision of God that exhausts the unrestricted desire of intelligence. Then charity is the transport, the ecstasy and unbounded intimacy that result from the communication of the absolute love that is God himself and alone can respond to the vision of God.

In the thirty-first place, if the solution which in fact is provided for man happens to be supernatural, and in particular if it happens to be absolutely supernatural, there will result a heightening of the tension that, as we have seen, arises whenever the limitations of lower levels are transcended. Moreover, when the higher integration is emergent in consciousness, not only is the tension itself conscious as an inner opposition and struggle but also it is objectified socially and culturally in the dialectical unfolding of human living and human history ...

The assent of faith is the starting point for an ever fuller understanding of its meaning, its implications, and its applications. The antecedent willingness of hope has to advance from a generic reinforcement of the pure desire to an adapted and specialized auxiliary ever ready to offset every interference either with intellect's unrestricted finality or with its essential detachment and disinterestedness. The antecedent willingness of charity has to mount from an affective to an effective determination to discover and to implement in all things the intelligibility of universal order that is God's concept and choice. Accordingly, even in those in whom the solution is realized, there are endless gradations in the measure in which it is realized, and by a necessary consequence there are endless degrees in which those that profess to know and embrace the solution can fail to bring forth the fruits it promises in their individual lives and in the human situations of which those lives are part.

But the point I would make is that in solutions of the supernatural type these difficulties are augmented. Even of natural solutions it would be probable that universal accessibility would not ensure universal acceptance, that intellectual collaboration would develop down the ages, that the faith and hope and charity of successive generations of members more commonly would hover about intermediate values than reach maxima of intensity and efficacy. Still, natural solutions would not exceed the bounds of humanism. Their faith would be not only believing to understand (*crede ut intelligas*) but also believing what man in this life eventually could understand. Their hope would reinforce the pure desire without introducing a displacement away from human concerns. Their charity would be a self-sacrificing love of God that bore no appearance of a contempt for human values. In contrast, the supernatural solution involves a transcendence of humanism, and the imperfect realization of the supernatural solution is apt to oscillate between an emphasis on the supernatural and an emphasis on the solution. Imperfect faith can insist on believing to the neglect of the understanding that makes faith an effective factor in human living and human history; and an even less perfect faith can endanger the general collaboration in its hurry to show forth its social and cultural fruits. Imperfect hope can so expect the New Jerusalem as to oppose any foretaste of intellectual bliss and union in this life; and an even less perfect hope can forget that a supernatural solution involves a real displacement of the center of human concerns. Imperfect charity lacks the resources needed to combine both true loving and the true transformation of loving. It can be absorbed in the union of the family, in the intersubjectivity of comrades in work and in adventure, in the common cause of fellows in nationality and in citizenship, in the common aspiration of associates in scientific, cultural, and humanitarian pursuits. On the other hand, it can withdraw from home and country, from human cares and human ambitions, from the clamor of the senses and the entanglement of the social surd, to fix its gaze upon the unseen ultimate, to respond to an impalpable presence, to grow inwardly to the stature of eternity. But imperfect charity, inasmuch as it is imperfect, will not realize at once the opposed facets of its perfection; if it is in the world, it ever risks being of the world; and if it withdraws from the world, the human basis of its ascent to God risks a contraction and an atrophy.

Moreover, the heightened tension which would result from a supernatural solution would not lack its objectification in the dialectical succession of human situations. Hitherto, the dialectic has been conceived to rest on a bipolar conjunction and opposition. Within each man there are both the attachment and interestedness of sensitivity and intersubjectivity and, on the other hand, the detachment and disinterestedness of the pure desire to know. From this conjunction of opposites there follow (1) the interference of the lower level with the unfolding of inquiry and reflection, of deliberation and decision, (2) the consequent unintelligibility of situations, and (3) the increasing irrelevance of intelligence and reasonableness to the real problem of human living.

But when this problem of evil is met by a supernatural solution, human perfection itself becomes a limit to be transcended, and then the dialectic is transformed from a bipolar to a tripolar conjunction and opposition. The humanist viewpoint loses its primacy, not by some extrinsicist invasion, but by submitting to its own immanent necessities. For if the humanist is to stand by the exigences of his own unrestricted desire, if he is to yield to the demands for openness set by every further question, then he will discover the limitations that imply man's incapacity for sustained development, he will acknowledge and consent to the one solution that exists, and if that solution is supernatural, his very humanism will lead beyond itself.

At the same time, because the supernatural solution is realized in accord with probability schedules, because it is accepted by some and rejected by others, because acceptance is no more than the base and beginning for further development, because the undeveloped is imperfect and the imperfection of the supernatural solution misses the higher synthesis of human living, there will be a humanism in revolt against the proffered supernatural solution. It will ignore the problem of evil; it will contest the fact of a solution; it will condemn mystery as myth; it will demand reason and exclude faith; it will repudiate hope and labor passionately to build the city of man with the hands of man; it will be ready to love God in song and dance, in human feasting and human sorrow, with human intelligence and human good will, but only so. For a time it may base its case upon the shortcomings of those that profess the solution but live it imperfectly or intermittently or not at all. But this incidental argument sooner or later will give place to its real basis. For it rests on man's proud content to be just a man, and its tragedy is that, on the present supposition of a supernatural solution, to be just a man is what man cannot be. If he would be truly a man, he would submit to the unrestricted desire and discover the problem of evil and affirm the existence of a solution and accept the solution that exists. But if he would be only a man, he has to be less. He has to forsake the openness of the pure desire; he has to take refuge in the counterpositions; he has to develop what counterphilosophies he can to save his dwindling humanism from further losses; and there will not be lacking men clear-sighted enough to grasp that the issue is between God and man, logical enough to grant that intelligence and reason are orientated towards God, ruthless enough to summon to their aid the dark forces of passion and of violence.

4 Belief

4.1 The General Context of Belief

The general context of belief is the collaboration of mankind in the advancement and the dissemination of knowledge. For if there is such a collaboration, then men not only contribute to a common fund of knowledge but also receive from it. But while they contribute in virtue of their own experience, understanding, and judgment, they receive not an immanently generated but a reliably communicated knowledge. That reception is belief, and our immediate concern is its general context.

Already the reader is familiar with the distinctions between empirical, intelligent, and rational consciousness, and the further enlargement that we have named rational self-consciousness. One is empirically conscious inasmuch as one is aware of data into which one can inquire. One is intelligently conscious inasmuch as one inquires, understands, formulates, and raises further questions for intelligence. One is rationally conscious inasmuch as one puts questions for reflection, grasps the unconditioned, and passes judgment. But one becomes rationally self-conscious inasmuch as one adverts to the self-affirming unity, grasps the different courses of action it can pursue, reflects upon their value, utility, or agreeableness, and proceeds to a free and responsible decision.

Now just as the pure desire to know, which is spontaneous, can be aided, supported, reinforced, by a free decision of the will in which one determines to be quite genuine in all one's investigations and judgments, so also the spontaneous procedures of the mind can be submitted to introspective analysis, formulated as methods, and reinforced by free decisions in which one wills to be faithful to methodological precepts.

But a fundamental methodological issue is whether each man should confine his assents to what he knows in virtue of his personal experience, his personal insights, and his personal grasp of the virtually unconditioned or, on the other hand, there can and should be a collaboration in the advancement and dissemination of knowledge.

In fact, the collaboration exists. Our senses are limited to an extremely narrow strip of space-time, and unless we are ready to rely on the senses of others, we must leave blank all other places and times or, as is more likely, fill them with our conjectures and then explain our conjectures with myths. Again, the personal contribution of any individual to the advance of human understanding is never large. We may be astounded by men of genius; but the way for their discoveries was prepared by many others in a long succession; and if they took enormous strides, commonly it was because the logic of their circumstances left them no opportunity to take shorter ones. But without collaboration each successive generation, instead of beginning where its predecessor left off, would have to begin at the very beginning and so could never advance beyond the most rudimentary of primitive levels.

Some collaboration, then, is inevitable. But once it begins, it spreads. Mathematicians expedite their calculations by having the recurrent parts of their work done once for all and then published in tables of various kinds. Again, the departments of mathematics multiply, and as it becomes obvious that no one can master all, it follows that each begins to rely on others for results obtained in branches in which he himself is not competent. What holds for mathematics also holds in a broader manner for the empirical sciences. Not only must each physicist and chemist rely on the reports of his predecessors and colleagues, not only are the further questions set by an objective and general process of advance rather than by the individual's desire to learn, but even the verification of each hypothesis really lies not in the confirmation that any one man's work can bring but rather in the cumulative evidence that is provided by the whole scientific tradition.

It is true, of course, that if the engineer suspects his tables, if the mathematician doubts the theorems propounded in a different branch, if the empirical scientist has reason to challenge accepted views, then it is not only possible but also highly laudable for them to labor to bring about a revision. But if this possibility and encouragement offer a necessary safeguard, they must not blind us to the actual facts. Engineers tend to feel their duty has been done when they learn how to use a slide rule, and no one would dream of imposing upon their intellectual consciences the obligation of working out independently the trigonometric functions and the logarithmic tables. When it is claimed that any engineer could have immanently generated knowledge of the correctness of his slide rule, it is not to be forgotten that all engineers merely believe slide rules to be correct and that none of them has any intention of seeking to establish the matter by carrying out for himself the endless computations that the slide rule so compactly summarizes.

When it is claimed that each scientist could repeat and check the results of any experiment, it is not to be forgotten that no scientist has any intention of repeating and checking all the experiments which his thinking presupposes. Nor is this all, for empirical science is a collective enterprise to so radical an extent that no scientist can have immanently generated knowledge of the evidence that really counts; for the evidence that really counts for any theory or hypothesis is the common testimony of all scientists that the implications of the theory or hypothesis have been verified in their separate and diverse investigations. In plainer language, the evidence that really counts is the evidence for a belief.

Because collaboration is a fact, because it is inevitable, because it spreads into a highly differentiated network of interdependent specialties, the mentality of any individual becomes a composite product in which it is impossible to separate immanently generated knowledge and belief. As was seen in the chapter on the notion of judgment, there stands in the habitual background of our minds a host of previous judgments and assents that serve to clarify and define, to explain and defend, to qualify and limit, the prospective judgment that one is about to make. But if this host is submitted to scrutiny, one finds that one's beliefs are no less operative than one's immanently generated knowledge; and if one pursues the examination, one is forced to the conclusion that, as no belief is independent of some items of immanently generated knowledge, so there are extraordinarily few items of immanently generated knowledge that are totally independent of beliefs. One does not simply know that England is an island. Neither does one merely believe it. Perhaps no one has immanently generated knowledge that general relativity is more accurate than Newtonian theory on the perihelion of Mercury. But it does not follow that for everyone it is purely a matter of belief. The development of the human mind is by the self-correcting process of learning, and in that process personal knowledge and belief practice an unrelenting symbiosis. The broadening of individual experience includes hearing the opinions and the convictions of others. The deepening of individual understanding includes the exploration of many viewpoints. The formation of individual judgment is a process of differentiation, clarification, and revision, in which the shock of contradictory judgments is as relevant as one's own observation and memory, one's own intelligent inquiry and critical reflection. So each of us advances from the nescience of infancy to the fixed mentality of old age, and however large and determinate the contributions of belief to the shaping of our minds, still every belief and all its implications have been submitted to the endlessly repeated, if unnoticed, test of fresh experiences, of further questions and new insights, of clarifying and qualifying revisions of judgment.

The general context of belief, then, is a sustained collaboration of many instances of rational self-consciousness in the attainment and the dissemination of knowledge. The alternative to the collaboration is a primitive ignorance. But the consequence of the collaboration is a symbiosis of knowledge and belief ...

4.2 The Critique of Beliefs

In principle, belief is possible because the criterion of truth is the unconditioned. In practice, belief is as intelligent and reasonable as is the collaboration of men in the advancement and in the dissemination of knowledge. In fact, if the collaboration in the field of natural science enjoys enormous prestige, it does not merit the same high praise in other fields. Mistaken beliefs exist, and the function of an analysis of belief is overlooked if it fails to explain how mistaken beliefs arise and how they are to be eliminated.

Fortunately, the present question raises no new issues. Already there has been carried through a general critique of error, and, as error in general, so mistaken beliefs have their roots in the scotosis of the dramatic subject, in the individual, group, and general bias of the practical subject, in the counterpositions of philosophy, and in their ethical implications and consequences. In belief as in personal thought and judgment, men go wrong when they have to understand and to judge either themselves or other things in relation to themselves. The serenity and surefootedness of the mathematician, the physicist, the chemist are not independent of the remoteness of these fields from human living. If in the past physicists and chemists have been prominent in propagating an erroneous mechanist determinism, still it was a single sweeping mistake, it had its origin in the polymorphism of human consciousness, and it has been corrected by the abstractness of relativity and the indeterminism of quantum mechanics. If Haeckel offers an instance of scientific fraudulence, it also is true that his deception was in the interest not of biology but of a materialist philosophy. On the other hand, when it comes to the study of life, of the psychological depths, of human institutions, of the history of nations, cultures, and religions, then diversity multiplies, differences become irreconcilable, and the name of science can be invoked with plausibility only by introducing methodological conventions that exclude from scientific consideration the heart of the matter. The life of man on earth lies under the shadow of a problem of evil; the evil invades his mind; and as it distorts his immanently generated knowledge, so also it distorts his beliefs.

If the determination of the origin of mistaken beliefs raises no new issues, neither does the problem of eliminating from one's own mind the rubbish that may have settled there in a lifelong symbiosis of personal inquiry and of believing. For learning one's errors is but a particular case of learning. It takes as its starting point and clue the discovery of some precise issue on which undoubtedly one was mistaken. It advances by inquiring into the sources that may have contributed to that error and, perhaps, contributed to other errors as well. It asks about the motives and the supporting judgments that, as they once confirmed one in that error, may still be holding one in others. It investigates the consequences of the view one now rejects, and it seeks to determine whether or not they too are to be rejected. The process is cumulative. The discovery of one error is exploited to lead to the discovery of others; and the discovery of the others provides a still larger base to proceed to the discovery of still more. Moreover, this cumulative process not only takes advantage of the mind's native process of learning, in which one insight leads on to other insights that open the way to still further insights, but it also exploits the insistence of rational consciousness on consistency; for just as our love of consistency, once we have made one mistake, leads us to make others, so the same love of consistency leads us to reject other mistakes when one is rejected, and at the same time it provides us with abundant clues for finding the others that are to be rejected.

If our general principles enable us to be brief both on the origin of mistaken beliefs and on the method of eliminating them, there is not to be overlooked the clarification that comes from contrast.

In the first place, the critique rests on a systematically formulated notion of belief. There exists a human collaboration in the pursuit and the dissemination of truth. It implies that in the mentality of any individual there exists in principle a distinction between his judgments, which rest on immanently generated knowledge, and his other assents, which owe their existence to his participation in the collaboration. Without some immanently generated knowledge, there would be no contributions to the collaboration. Without some beliefs, there would be no one that profited by the collaboration. It follows, further, that immanently generated knowledge and belief differ, not in their object or their modes, but in their motives and their origin. Thus, the same proposition, say $E = mc^2$, may be known by some and believed by others; it may be known or believed as more or less probable; but if it is known, the proposition itself is grasped as unconditioned; and if it is believed rationally, then the unconditioned that is grasped is the value of being willing to profit by the intellectual labors of others. Hence, because the object of belief is the same as the object of immanently generated knowledge, we have to disagree with all the views that attribute belief to the psychological depths or to desire or fear or to sentiment or to mere will. On the other hand, because even an intellectual collaboration is conditioned by decisions of the will, we also disagree with all the views that admit any belief to be simply a matter of cognitional activity.

In the second place, though there exists in principle a distinction between immanently generated knowledge and belief, it does not follow that there exist two compartments in anyone's mind and that he can retain what he knows and throw out what he believes. On the contrary, the external collaboration is matched by an internal symbiosis, and the counsel that one should drop all belief has the same ludicrous consequences as the Cartesian philosophic criterion of indubitability. For the counsel can be followed only if one has a quite inaccurate notion of the nature and the extent of belief; it leads to the rejection of all beliefs that, on erroneous suppositions, are taken to be beliefs; and so not only are true beliefs rejected, which is not an act of devotion to truth, but also there arises the absurd conviction that one's mistaken but covert beliefs must be named either science or sound common sense or philosophy.

No doubt there are mistaken beliefs. No doubt mistaken beliefs are to be eliminated. But the first step is to know what a belief is. It is to make the discovery, perhaps startling to many today, that a report over the radio of the latest scientific discovery adds, not to one's scientific knowledge, but to one's beliefs. The second step, no less necessary than the first, is to grasp the method to be followed in eliminating mistaken beliefs. For if one fails to hit upon the right method, one gets nowhere. The elimination of mistaken beliefs is not a matter of taking up a book and of believing the author when he proceeds to enumerate your mistaken beliefs; for that procedure adds to your beliefs; the addition varies with the author that you happen to read; it is extremely unlikely that he will hit off with any accuracy your personal list of mistaken beliefs; and it is not improbable that your mistaken beliefs will determine which author you prefer and so covertly govern your critique of belief by belief. Again, the elimination of mistaken beliefs is not a matter of attempting to assign explicitly the grounds for each of your beliefs and of rejecting those for which adequate explicit grounds are not available. For inquiry into the grounds of any belief soon brings to light that it depends on, say, ten other beliefs; each of the ten, in turn, will be found to depend on ten others; one's neglect of method now has one attempting to test at once one hundred and eleven beliefs, and they will be found not only to be linked together in an organic interdependence of mutual conditioning but also to raise still further considerations that partly are matters of immanently generated knowledge and partly matters of further belief. The simple fact is that a man cannot reconstruct his mind by the process of explicit analysis; for explicit analysis takes more time than the spontaneous procedures of the mind; it has taken each of us our lifetime to reach by spontaneous procedures the mentalities we now possess; and so if it were necessary for us to submit our mentalities to a total explicit analysis, it would also be necessary for us to have twofold lives, a life to live, and another, longer life in which to analyze the life that is lived.

In contrast, the method offered by our critique asks no one to believe that he subscribes to mistaken beliefs. Without undue optimism it expects people of even moderate intelligence to be able to discover for themselves at least one mistaken belief. Again, the proposed method does not offer anyone a putative list of his mistaken beliefs; it does not even offer a list of alternative lists, as the clothing industry offers a range of ready-made suits of different sizes. Rather it aims at the perfect fit, and so it is content to point out the far-reaching significance of the discovery of even one mistaken belief. For that discovery enables one to set in reverse the same spontaneous and cumulative process that gave rise to one's mistaken beliefs. So one secures at a stroke the procedure that is both economical and efficacious: it is economical, for it wastes no time examining beliefs that are true; and it is efficacious, for it begins from the conviction that one has made one bad mistake, and it proceeds along the structural lines of one's own mentality and through the spontaneous and cumulative operations of the mind that alone can deal successfully with concrete issues.

In the third place, though we claim the method to be efficacious against mistaken beliefs, we do not claim that it goes to the root of the problem. For the basic problem lies not in mistaken beliefs but in the mistaken believer. Far more than they, he is at fault. Until his fault is corrected, until his bias is attacked and extirpated, he will have little heart in applying an efficacious method, little zeal in prosecuting the lesser culprits, little rigor in pronouncing sentence upon them, little patience with the prospect of ferreting out and examining and condemning still further offenders. A critique of mistaken beliefs is a human contrivance, and a human contrivance cannot exorcize the problem of human evil. If man's will matched the detachment and the unrestricted devotion of the pure desire to know, the problem of evil would not arise. Inversely, as long as will fails to match the desire of intellect, intellect may devise its efficacious methods but the will fails to give them the cooperation they demand. Still, this pessimism is only hypothetical. It acknowledges a problem of evil, yet it prescinds from the existence of a solution. The solution does exist, and so no one can assure himself that its realization has not begun in him. And if in him that realization has begun, then his discovery and rejection of one mistaken belief can lead him on to the discovery and the rejection of as many more as the God of truth demands of him.

Related selections: 2.VII.3 on immanentism; 1.IV.2 on dramatic bias; 1.V.2–5 on individual, group, and general bias and the longer cycle of decline; 1.XI.1 on the problem underlying philosophic difference; 1.XIII.2 on appropriation of truth; 1.XIV.2 on the problem of liberation. 1.XII.2 and 4 on the principles of development and human development; 4.V.3 on the dialectic of history; 4.IV on healing in history; 3.IV.3 on dialectical religious development; 1.IV.1 on commonsense intellectual collaboration; 1.XI.4 on the method of universal doubt.

XVII

Self-Appropriation

In the summer of 1958, at Saint Mary's University in Halifax, Nova Scotia, Lonergan delivered his first series of lectures on *Insight*. These lectures were tape-recorded. In the 1970s an edition of the lectures was prepared under Lonergan's direction and, in 1980, the lectures were published under the title *Understanding and Being: An Introduction and Companion to 'Insight.'* A second edition, with editorial notes and additional material from the evening discussions, appeared in 1990 as a volume of the Collected Works. The lectures are Lonergan's own presentation of the main thrust of his major work and are very useful in their entirety to those seeking a deeper grasp of ideas presented in *Insight*. Especially noteworthy are Lonergan's decision to open the lecture series with an account of self-appropriation and his characterization of self-appropriation as the way to 'get around' what he describes as the 'Hegelian difficulty' – that any explicit ideal of knowledge is going to be abstract and will be found to be inadequate. In the first part of this selection, from the first lecture in the Halifax series, Lonergan emphasizes the personal, existential dimension of self-appropriation and connects it to issues raised by the historical development of the ideal of knowledge. He also introduces a distinction between three senses of presence and expresses his notion of consciousness in terms of self-presence. The second part, from the beginning of his second lecture, is a brief statement of the value of self-appropriation.

These extracts are taken from *Understanding and Being*, 3–21, 33–5.

1   Self-Appropriation

What is self-appropriation? *Insight* may be described as a set of exercises in which, it is hoped, one attains self-appropriation. The question naturally arises, What does that mean, and why go to all the trouble? Unfortunately, the question is so fundamental that to answer it is in a way more difficult than to attain self-appropriation.

You may have heard this story about Columbus. When he was hailed before the grandees of Spain for some misdemeanor or crime, he alleged in his defense the greatness of his exploit in discovering America. They said to him, 'Well, there was nothing wonderful about that. All you had to do was get in a boat and travel west, and you were bound to hit it sometime.' To make his point Columbus asked, 'Which one of you can make an egg stand on its end?' All of them thought about it, and some tried it, but none succeeded. 'Well, can you?' they demanded. Columbus took the egg, gave it a little tap, and it stood on its end. 'Well, that's easy!' they said. 'It's easy when you know how,' Columbus replied.

More generally, it is much simpler to do things than to explain what you are trying to do, what the method is that you are employing in doing it, and how that method will give you the results. In other words, the simple matter of attaining self-appropriation can be complicated by an enormous series of surrounding questions that are all more difficult than the actual feat of attaining self-appropriation. For that reason I do not start talking about the method of the book *Insight* until about chapter 14.[1] Prior to that there is a method, but it is pedagogical – the type of method employed by a teacher who does not explain to his pupils what he is trying to do but goes ahead and does it. He has a method, but they are being cajoled. They have their attention held, one thing is given them after another, and they get there. But if the teacher had to answer such questions as 'What are we trying to do?' and 'How are we going to get there?' he would never succeed in teaching anything. Questions about method and questions about the possibility of knowledge are much more difficult than the knowledge itself or the actual achievement. Still, because there is needed perhaps some framework for these lectures, I will begin by discussing self-appropriation.

1.1   The Pursuit of the Unknown

First, then, seeking knowledge is seeking an unknown. If we knew

1 [1.XI.3 in this reader.]

what we were looking for when we are seeking knowledge, we would not have to look for it, we would have it already. If you want a motorcar, you know exactly what you want, but when you want knowledge you cannot know what you want.

Now this seeking of knowledge is a special kind of tendency. Aristotle spoke about heavy bodies seeking the center of the earth. They had a natural appetite to fall, but it was an unconscious appetite. In us, when we are hungry we seek food, and when we are thirsty we seek drink, and in that there is a conscious tendency, a conscious feeling. It is not merely a tendency towards an object, it is a conscious tendency. But in seeking knowledge, not only do we tend towards it, not only do we do so consciously, but we also do so intelligently. Moreover, we do so critically; we examine what we have been given and wonder if it is right, and we test it and control it. Furthermore, one can seek knowledge quite deliberately; one can travel all the way from California to Halifax to follow a course of lectures and discussions. Seeking knowledge may be not only conscious, intelligent, and rational, but also deliberate. Scientists seek knowledge, aim at something, seek an unknown, and yet they go about it methodically. They have a series of well-defined steps which they take. This deliberate, methodical seeking of an unknown that you find in science is quite different from the deliberateness and method, for example, of a construction company putting up a new building. They have blueprints; they know exactly what they want all along the line. But when you're seeking knowledge you're seeking an unknown.

There is a combination, then, of knowledge and ignorance: knowledge, in the sense that knowledge is sought consciously, intelligently, rationally, deliberately, methodically; and ignorance, because if you already knew you would not have to bother seeking. This combination indicates the existence of an ideal, the pursuit of an ideal. Moreover, it is a built-in ideal; it is based upon innate tendencies. Aristotle's *Metaphysics* begins with the statement, 'All men naturally desire to know.'[2] He goes on to add, 'particularly with their eyes,' but the point is that there is a natural tendency, a natural desire to know.

The scholastics distinguished natural, acquired, and infused habits. Supernatural habits are said to be infused. Faith, hope, and charity do not come by nature, or by the efforts of nature, but by the grace of God.

---

2 Aristotle, *Metaphysics*, I, 1, 980a 21–6.

There are also acquired habits: you are not born knowing how to play the violin or with an innate tendency to typewrite so many words per minute; the habit has to be acquired. But besides infused and acquired habits there are also tendencies with which we start out and which we must have in order to start. If a child never asks questions, you cannot teach him. You class him as retarded or lower than retarded. There has to be something with which to start, and that is this tendency towards the ideal.

The pursuit of knowledge, then, is the pursuit of an unknown, and the possibility of that pursuit is the existence of an ideal.

1.2   The Development of the Ideal of Knowledge

My second point is that this ideal is not conceptually explicit. It becomes explicit only through the pursuit of knowledge. I will illustrate that first from science and then from philosophy.

1.2.1   In Science

It is well known that Pythagoras proved the theorem that the square of the hypotenuse is equal in area to the sum of the squares of the other two sides of a right-angled triangle. But the Pythagoreans also made another famous discovery, that of the harmonic ratios. The harmonic ratios are the reciprocals of an arithmetical progression: thus $1/2$, $1/4$, $1/6$, ... are harmonic ratios because 2, 4, 6, ... form an arithmetical progression. The Pythagoreans discovered that the fractions corresponded to the tension or the length of strings on a musical instrument, and that discovery was a knockout – there is a connection between mathematics and the sounds that are harmonious! They discovered not only that the mathematics was very interesting in itself, but also that it had a relation to what is listened to, the music: it accounted for the harmony in music. You can see how the Pythagoreans obtained from that the notion that the whole of reality is made up of numbers. The ideal that the universe is to be explained by numbers came as a generalization of this discovery – that, at least, is a fair guess about the origin of this Pythagorean doctrine.

The discovery of the relation between numbers and sensible phenomena was developed by Archimedes. He made the famous statement, 'Give me a place to stand, and I will lift the earth' – he discovered the law of the lever. He wrote a treatise on floating bodies in which elementary principles of hydrostatics are worked out in the same way as geometry was worked out by Euclid.

Then in the modern world Galileo put forward the ideal that what you are seeking in knowledge is the mathematization of nature, the expression of nature through numbers. He discovered the law of falling bodies: when bodies fall in a vacuum the distance traversed is proportional to the square of the time elapsed. Such is the mathematical formula for the free fall of a body. Kepler discovered his law of planetary motion, that the planets move in ellipses, that the sun is at one of the foci of the ellipse, that the area covered by the radius vector is a function of the time. There are two foci; the radius vector is the line from a focus to the perimeter; the planet moves around the perimeter; the moving radius vector sweeps over equal areas in equal times; and the square of the period (the time taken by the planet to complete a circuit) is proportional to the cube of its average distance from the sun. All of these further discoveries are analogous to the Pythagorean discovery of harmonic ratios: Archimedes' law relating displacement and buoyancy; Galileo's law of falling bodies; Kepler's three laws of planetary motion. In each case there was formulated a mathematical expression verifiable in concrete data.

An enormous further step was taken by Newton in his *Mathematical Principles of Natural Philosophy*. He went from particular laws, such as those of Galileo and Kepler, to system. In other words, just as Euclid posited a set of definitions, axioms, and postulates from which followed a series of theorems and problems, so Newton proposed not just particular laws but a whole system. Just as Euclid demonstrated his theorems, so Newton proved that if a body moves in a field of central force with some velocity v, then that body will move in a conic section. The geometry of conic sections was worked out by the Greeks; what Newton proved was that a body moving in a field of central force will move in a conic section. He did not merely establish a particular law, but from a set of axioms regarding laws of motion he deduced the movements of the planets. Kepler discovered the figure inductively by examining the data on the movements. Newton explained deductively why it had to be that figure, why it had to be an ellipse or some other conic section, after the fashion of Euclid deducing his theorems from his definitions and axioms.

I have illustrated the development of an ideal of knowledge. What is that ideal? It is the mathematization of nature. It starts from particular laws; it moves towards a system; and its great achievement was Newtonian system. It lasted for a few hundred years, but it had been on the basis of Euclidean geometry. Einstein moved it to another basis, a more general geometry, and quantum mechanics has taken us right out of the field of law and system. The fundamental ideal has become states and probabilities.

The ideal, then, not only develops; it changes. So one's ideal of knowledge, what one is seeking in knowledge, is something that is not conceptually explicit. It becomes explicit in the pursuit of knowledge.

This particular line of development starts from particular discoveries and moves to Newtonian system and beyond that to the system of relativity. When scientists still fail to obtain theories that satisfy all the data, they change the ideal itself from law and system to states and probabilities. They begin working towards a different ideal of what knowledge really would be if they reached it.

We may take another example, one that runs concomitantly. The scholastic definition of a science is 'certain knowledge of things through their causes.' Certain knowledge of things expresses common sense. If through certain knowledge of things – for example, I know this is a brush – I work out all the causes, I have moved into science. This notion of science has an implication. If you are seeking certain knowledge of things through their causes, you start out from the thing, and you work to the discovery of the causes. When you have the causes, you want to check; so you work back from the causes until you can construct things out of them. The scholastics called the first part of this movement resolution into the causes, *resolutio in causas*, analysis. The second part of the movement was *compositio ex causis*, synthesis. From the ideal of science as knowledge of things by their causes we get the two ideas of analysis and synthesis: movement from the things to the causes, and then movement from the causes back to the things.

Moreover, Aristotle had a very precise idea about things and an equally precise idea about causes. What is a thing? A thing falls under the predicaments: substance, quantity, quality, relation, action, passion, place, time, posture, habit. A thing is what fits under the ten predicaments. What are causes? There are four: end, agent, matter, and form. The end moves the agent, the agent moves the matter, and from the matter being moved arises the form, which is the end as realized.[3]

Now what took place? We had an ideal: science is knowledge of things through their causes. The ideal implied a double movement of analysis and synthesis – analysis to discover causes, and synthesis to move from causes to the things. What happened is that analysis and synthesis survived, but not the things and causes as understood by Aristotle.

This can be illustrated in two ways, first from Thomist Trinitarian theory and then from science.

Thomist Trinitarian theory is a clear instance of first an analytic movement and then a synthetic movement. In the New Testament what we are told regarding the Blessed Trinity is the mission of the Son and the mission of the Holy Ghost. After a series of Greek councils we arrive at three persons in one nature. There is nothing in the New Testament about persons or nature; these technical terms do not occur. Since the three persons are distinct, we find in the Cappadocian fathers the treatment of the properties of the distinct persons. Each person must have something proper to himself, otherwise he would be the same as the others. Further, both the Cappadocian fathers and Augustine had the idea that these properties must be relative. They cannot be something absolute, because God is simple; if these properties are to be reconciled with the simplicity of God, they have to be relative. Where do the relations come from? They come from the processions. Augustine explained the processions by a psychological analogy. He said they were something like the movement in the mind from understanding to conception, from judgment to willing. So first we have missions, then persons and nature, then properties, relations, processions.

What do we find in St Thomas's *Summa theologiae*, part 1, questions 27–43? Thomas does not start out from the missions; missions come at the end, in question 43. He is making the other movement, from causes to things, synthesis. He begins from a psychological analogy and moves to the processions, to the relations, to the persons, to the missions. The order of discovery is just the opposite of the order of

3 Aristotle, *Categories*, 4; *Physics*, II, 3, 194b 16 to 195a 26; *Metaphysics*, V, 2, 1013a 24 to 1013b 2.

doctrine. In doctrine you start from principles and draw all the conclusions, but in discovery you discover one conclusion after another and gradually you move on to your principles.

In Trinitarian theory, then, we have analysis and synthesis. We have the analytic movement up to St Thomas, and the synthetic movement in St Thomas's *Summa theologiae*. But we do not have things, and we do not have causes. God is not a thing in the sense of the Aristotelian predicaments, and the generation of the Son by the Father is not a matter of causality. The Son is not another God, and neither is the Holy Ghost. Things and causes vanish, but analysis and synthesis remain.

Now we may take a scientific illustration. There are over three hundred thousand compounds known to present-day chemistry, and those are not mixtures but compounds. Chemists explain all of these compounds by a periodic table of about one hundred elements. On the one hand, there is the composition of the compounds from the elements, sometimes in fact and sometimes just in theory (for compounds cannot always be synthesized). On the other hand, there is the analysis of the compounds into their elements. But these elements are not Aristotle's things. In a chemistry course you may be given an introductory definition of hydrogen – hydrogen is an odorless gas with various sensible properties – but you very soon forget that definition, and operate in terms of atomic weight, atomic number, and other properties implicit in the periodic table. The one hundred elements are defined by their relations to one another; they are not defined in terms of substance, quantity, quality, and so on, as these terms are taken in their ordinary meaning.

Thus we have what Whitehead called the bifurcation of nature.[4] Eddington distinguished two tables.[5] One of them was brown with a smooth surface on four solid legs and pretty hard to move around. The other was a pack of electrons that you could not even imagine. Which of the two tables is the real table? For the chemist the elements are atoms, and we do not see atoms; so he moves away from the field of things in the Aristotelian sense and from causes in the sense of end, agent, matter, and form. He thinks instead in terms of analysis and

---

4 Alfred North Whitehead, *The Concept of Nature* (Ann Arbor: University of Michigan Press, 1957), chap. 2.
5 Sir Arthur Eddington, *The Nature of the Physical World* (Cambridge: Cambridge University Press, 1928), xi–xv; also his *New Pathways in Science* (Cambridge: Cambridge University Press, 1947), 1.

synthesis. The ideal of knowledge, then, develops in the pursuit of knowledge. The ideal becomes explicit through the pursuit.

1.2.2   In Philosophy

Our first point was that seeking knowledge is seeking an unknown, and this implies an ideal, a set of tendencies. But this ideal is not explicit; it becomes explicit in the process of seeking knowledge. That becoming explicit involves a change in the ideal. In Newton science achieves law and system, and that ideal is pursued up to Einstein. But there follows a phase in which what is sought is not law and system but states and probabilities. Similarly and concomitantly, science starts off with an ideal in terms of things and causes, and moves to a practice that is a matter of analysis and synthesis.

The question arises, What is going to happen next? Scientists have moved from law and system to states and probabilities. Is there going to be another change, and if so what will it be? They have moved from things and causes to analysis and synthesis. Will there be another change, and if so what will that be? Above all, what on earth can the philosopher be aiming at? If he is seeking knowledge, he is seeking the implementation of some ideal. What can that ideal be?

The ideal of pure reason resulted from the transference from mathematics to philosophy of the ideal of a set of fundamental, analytic, self-evident, necessary, universal propositions from which, by deduction, we reach equally necessary and universal conclusions. Philosophy became the product of the movement of pure reason from self-evident principles to absolutely certain conclusions. That was one ideal, and it was implemented by Spinoza, Leibniz, and Wolff.

Kant's *Critique of Pure Reason* is a critique of that ideal. He is criticizing an ideal of knowledge, and introducing into philosophy the same type of movement as we find in the movement of scientific ideals. Briefly, Kant's criticism is that in mathematics pure reason can arrive at satisfactory results because it can construct concepts, that is, because it can represent, as he puts it, in a pure a priori intuition, the concept itself; but that cannot be done in philosophy, and therefore philosophy cannot successfully follow the method of pure reason.

There we have an ideal in philosophy, a deductivist ideal proceeding from analytic propositions to universal and necessary conclusions, and also a criticism of that ideal. In fact, the ideal of pure reason is the

Euclidean ideal. It is what in contemporary scholastic circles is called essentialism.

However, there is a more general theorem that might be put by a Hegelian, regarding the explicitation of ideals. It involves six terms: implicit, explicit, abstract, alien, mediation, reconciliation.

The transition from the implicit to the explicit may be illustrated by the ideal of temperance, as during the prohibition period. When you seek temperance, you are expressing a tendency towards the ideal. The ideal arouses a lot of enthusiasm. But that expression of man's capacity for the ideal is abstract; it does not express the whole of man's capacity and desire for the ideal. It does not deal with the whole concrete situation, and in that way it is an abstraction. Because it is an abstraction there is an opposition between the expressed, explicit ideal and the subject in whom the ideal is implicit. That opposition is alienation. The pursuit of temperance through prohibition gave rise to considerable alienation, and the laws of prohibition were repealed. While temperance is a fine ideal, still that particular means of bringing it about led to all sorts of abuses. The expression of the ideal, because it was just an abstraction, something inadequate to the subject in whom the ideal is implicit, was alien, and that alien aspect brings to light the opposition between the subject and the expression. Alienation mediates or draws forth from the subject a more adequate expression of his ideal. When that more adequate expression is thus mediated, we have reconciliation.

A Hegelian might argue that, since any expression of any ideal is bound to be abstract, it cannot be adequate to what is implicit in the subject. Law and system is one abstract expression; certain knowledge of things through their causes is another. Because they are abstract, these expressions really are alien. The more you use them, the more you will bring out the aspect of antithesis, alienation, opposition, and consequently you will call forth something else to correct it. So there is a movement from law and system to states and probabilities, from knowing things through their causes to analysis and synthesis. But analysis and synthesis, states and probabilities, are also abstract. In due course the inadequacy of those realizations will become apparent, and we will move on to something else.

Let us take another illustration from philosophy. In the nineteenth century there began to appear, and there may still exist, books on epistemology that took their starting point in the existence of knowledge.

Universal scepticism is self-contradictory; because it is contradictory, knowledge exists. But just knowing that knowledge exists is knowing something very abstract. What kind of knowledge exists? What is the knowledge that exists? If you express the knowledge that exists abstractly, what will follow? You will have a mere abstraction, and it will give rise to alienation. It will give rise, for example, to what has been called the Catholic ghetto. Catholics have held on to this idea of knowledge, while the rest of the world pays little attention to it. Merely to assert the existence of knowledge without saying as fully as you can just what knowledge is, is to utter an abstraction, which gives rise to alienation. No solution is reached until that alienation is changed into a means by which something else is brought forth which is at least less abstract. However, the Hegelian difficulty probed rather deeply; it attacked *any* explicit ideal of knowledge.

1.3   The Problem

Perhaps I have given enough illustrations to enable us to conclude that there exists a problem. What have we seen? The pursuit of knowledge is the pursuit of an unknown. It is not only a conscious pursuit but an intelligent, rational, deliberate, and methodical pursuit. The pursuit of building a house with the aid of a set of blueprints is clearly deliberate and methodical. But how do you proceed methodically and deliberately to the attainment of something that you do not know, something which, if known, would not have to be pursued? We have to acknowledge, then, the existence in man of something like a natural ideal that moves towards knowledge. Moreover, this ideal is not explicitly conceived by nature. While the tendency is innate, while it belongs to man by nature, while it is not something acquired like facility on the violin or the piano or the typewriter, still the exact goal of this tendency is not explicitly conceived by nature. Man has to work out his conception of this goal, and he does so insofar as he actually pursues knowledge. In the working out, this ideal becomes concrete or explicit in a series of different forms in the sciences and in philosophy.

And therefore there exists a problem, first, because the ideal of pure reason has been criticized: on the one hand by Kant for his reasons, and on the other hand by most contemporary scholastics in their objections to what they call essentialism. That ideal is wrong, but what is the right one? If it is not pure reason, then philosophy is not a movement from self-evident, universal, necessary principles to equally certain conclusions. What is it? What are we trying to do? Next, there is the Hegelian difficulty, that any explicit ideal will be an abstraction and will be found to be inadequate; another will arise, and the new one will suffer from the same inadequacy.

The problem exists not only theoretically but also concretely. You cannot take a single step without presupposing or implicitly invoking some ideal of knowledge, and in many of the exercises throughout these lectures we will be adverting to this fact, that in all one's questions, in all one's efforts to know, one is presupposing some ideal of knowledge, more or less unconsciously perhaps.

1.4   Self-Appropriation

The solution offered in *Insight* to this problem is self-appropriation. Self-appropriation is being introduced in terms of a problem. The ideal we seek in seeking the unknown, in trying to know, is conceptually implicit. There does not exist naturally, spontaneously, through the whole of history, a set of propositions, conceptions, and definitions that define the ideal of knowledge. But to say that conceptually it is implicit, that it is implicit with regard to statements, that these statements differ in different places and at different times – they are historically conditioned – is not to say that it is nonexistent. While the conception of the ideal is not by nature, still there is something by nature. The ideal of knowledge is myself as intelligent, as asking questions, as requiring intelligible answers. It is possible to get to these fundamental tendencies of which any conceived ideal is an expression, and if we can turn in upon these fundamental tendencies, then we are on the way to getting hold of matters of fact that are independent of the Hegelian objection. We are capable of getting hold of fundamental matters of fact in terms of which we can give a fairly definitive account of the cognitional ideal.

What you hear are words. If the words mean something, then there are concepts in the mind, acts of meaning. If you or I hold that the words means something that is true, then there is judgment. It is in judgments, concepts, and words that you make your goal in knowledge explicit. The trick in self-appropriation is to move one step backwards, to move into the subject as intelligent – asking questions; as having insights – being able to form concepts; as weighing the evidence – being able to judge. We want to move in there where the ideal is functionally operative prior to its being made explicit in judgments, concepts, and words. Moving in there is self-appropriation; moving in there is reaching what is prepredicative, preconceptual, pre-judicial. In what may resemble Heidegger's terminology, it is moving from ontology, which is the *logos*, the word about being, the judgment about being, to the ontic, which is what one is.

How do you move in there where the ideals are functionally operative in tendencies and achievements? What exactly happens when one is trying to achieve self-appropriation? Let us take the word 'presence.' It is an ambiguous word. First, you can say that the chairs are present in the room, but you cannot say that the chairs are present to the room or that the room is present to the chairs. The latter is a different, a second, sense of 'presence': being present to someone. It has a meaning with regard to animals. A dog walks along the street, sees another dog on the other side, and crosses over. The other dog is present to him, but not in the sense that the chairs are present in the room. Here we have presence to someone; I am present to you, and you are present to me; this presence is different from the presence of the chairs in the room. Moreover, there is a third meaning of 'presence': you could not be present to me unless I were somehow present to myself. If I were unconscious, you would not be present to me in the second sense. If you were unconscious, I would not be present to you in the second sense. So there is a third sense of presence: presence to oneself. To sum up: there is a merely material sense of presence – the chairs are present in the room; there is a second sense – one person is present to the other; there is a third sense – a person has to be somehow present to himself for others to be present to him. In self-appropriation it is the third presence that is of interest. You are there, and your being there to yourself is the type of presence with which we are concerned.

Now what on earth do you do to get that presence of yourself to yourself? Do you crane your neck around and look into yourself to see if you are there? First of all, that cannot be done. You cannot turn yourself inside out and take a look. In the second place, even if you could, it would be beside the point. Why is that? Because if you could, what you would arrive at would be, not the third type of presence, but only the second. You would be looking at yourself, you would have yourself 'out there' to be present to yourself. But we want the *you* that is present, to whom you would be present. What is important, in other words, is the looker, not the looked-at, even when the self is what is looked at. So it is not a matter of introspection in any spatial sense, in any sense of 'looking back into,' because what counts is not the presence of what is looked at, but the presence of the subject that looks, even when he is looking at himself.

That third presence is the fundamental presence. But simply as presence it is *empirical consciousness.* You can go a step higher, beyond empirical consciousness; you need not be just there. When you are teaching a class, for example, you can see from the looks on students' faces who is getting it and who is finding it rather dull. If it is clicking, if it means something to them, then there is not merely presence, empirical consciousness, but also *intelligent consciousness, intellectual consciousness.* They are catching on; they are understanding, or they are trying to understand; they are very puzzled or tense – intellectual consciousness. On this level, you are present to yourself as trying to understand, as saying 'I've got it!' and as conceiving and expressing. But beyond this second level, there is a third level on which you are present to yourself, *rational consciousness.* When you do understand, you think, 'After all, is that just another bright idea, or have I really got it properly?' On the level of rational consciousness, the level of reflection, the question is, Is it true or false? And when your judgments move on to action, you have, fourth, *rational self-consciousness.* Then your rational reflection is about yourself. It is conscience in the ordinary sense – 'Am I doing right or wrong?' – where rational reflection is concerned with your own action.

What, then, is this business of moving in on oneself, self-appropriation? It is not a matter of looking back into yourself, because it is not what you look at but the looking that counts. But it is not just the looking; it is not being entirely absorbed in the object; rather, it is adverting to the fact that, when you are absorbed in the object, you are also present to yourself. If you were not, it would not count. If there were no one there to see, there would be nothing present to the seer. That to whom other things are present, that which must be present to itself for other things to be present to it, is not merely there. He or she is intelligent, rational, rationally self-conscious.

So our concern in *Insight* is a series of exercises in which we move towards the functionally operative tendencies that ground the ideal of knowledge. The first part of *Insight* is primarily concerned with moving in there. In the second part we begin to draw conclusions, and that is where the arguable issues arise. But there is very little point to the argument unless one has been in there, because that is what we are trying to express, that is where the evidence lies, that is the point that has to be made.

The book *Insight* is therefore a series of exercises in self-appropriation, in reaching the factual, functionally operative tendencies that express themselves successively in the series of ideals found in the sciences and in philosophy and, for that matter, in theology (and that is why I am interested). In fact, chapters 1 to 8 are concerned with understanding understanding, insight into insight. In those eight chapters there is a series of insights presented, and the point is not having all the insights – you do not have to have them all – but to notice when you have them, to advert to them, to move into self-appropriation. Chapters 9 and 10 are concerned with understanding judgment, the next level. Chapter 11 is affirming *your* understanding and *your* judgment.

That, roughly, is the technical side of the problem.

1.5   The Existential Element

Now there is a joker in this business of self-appropriation. We do not start out with a clean slate as we move towards self-appropriation. We already have our ideals of what knowledge is, and we want to do self-appropriation according to the ideal that is already operative in us – not merely in terms of the spontaneous, natural ideal, but in terms of some explicit ideal. I do not suppose that any of you will want to do self-appropriation by way of measurements and experiments, but many would say that our results cannot be really scientific unless we do it that way. Perhaps some of you will think that the thing to do is to define our terms very clearly, establish our self-evident principles, and then proceed with deducing. And there can be other ideals besides these that govern one's procedure. Again, the results at which we arrive may not fit in with preexistent explicit ideals, and there will arise another conflict.

In other words, the business of self-appropriation is not a simple matter of moving in and finding the functionally operative tendencies that ground ideals. It is also a matter of pulling out the inadequate ideals that may be already existent and operative in us. There is a conflict, there is an existential element, there is a question of the subject, and it is a personal question that will not be the same for everyone. Everyone will have his own difficulties. There is an advantage, then, to having a seminar on the subject. It gives people a chance to talk these things out in the evening session, to talk them out with others. There is a set of concrete opportunities provided by the seminar that cannot be provided by any mere book. The more you talk with one another and throw things out, the more you probe, and the more you express yourself spontaneously, simply, and frankly, not holding back in fear of making mistakes, then the more quickly you arrive at the point where you get the thing cleared up.

This matter may be illustrated in another way. We are aiming at an explicit ideal of knowledge based upon self-appropriation. But you know the Latin tag, *Qualis quisque est, talis finis videtur ei,* the end seems to vary with each man. The kind of man one is determines what his ideals will be. The kind of ideal you have at the present time is a function of your past experience, your past study, your past teachers, your past courses in philosophy. Insofar as there is a struggle about agreeing with *Insight* or disagreeing with it, that struggle arises on a very fundamental existential level. It is akin to Heidegger's classification of men as authentic and inauthentic; in other words, there is a criticism of the subject. Something similar comes up in *Insight* – the existential problem.

The problem can be illustrated from scholastic thought. I believe that the fact of insight is explicitly and with complete universality acknowledged by Aristotle and determinative in Aristotle's thought. I believe the same is true of St Thomas. But in an article published in 1933 in *Gregorianum* by Fr Peter Hoenen on the knowledge of first principles, in which he was trying to draw attention to this matter, he reported that he could find only seven scholastics in the course of seven hundred years who adverted to the possibility.[6] Why is it, if I am right in saying that insight is fundamental in Aristotle and St Thomas, that in the course of seven hundred years only seven scholastics advert to the possibility, and only some of those accept it? It is this existential problem. It is the presence of a ready-made ideal of what knowledge must be, blocking self-appropriation.

The existential problem is a fundamental issue that arises in *Insight,*

---

6 Peter Hoenen, 'De origine primorum principiorum scientiae,' *Gregorianum* 14 (1933): 153–84.

and those who have read the book will probably know about it. I certainly know about it; I certainly have experienced it in myself, or I would not have written the book. But why is it that insight has been neglected? It is because, if you frankly acknowledge that intellect is intelligence, you discover that you have terrific problems in epistemology. It is much simpler to soft-pedal the fact that intellect is intelligence than to face out the solution to the epistemological problem. That, of course, is only my opinion on the matter, which I cannot force upon you; self-appropriation is something you do yourself.

1.6 Summary

So much, then, for the general question, What is self-appropriation, and why bother about it? We noted that this type of talk is really much more difficult than self-appropriation itself, because we are talking around the subject. To work out the theory of how to make the egg stand on its end is much harder than giving the egg a little tap, as Columbus did, and having it stand there. In general, questions of method, questions of the possibility of knowledge, are in the second remove, and they are much more difficult, much more abstract, much more complicated, than the business of doing it. However, to have a framework for our lectures and our evening discussions, we put down a series of points that give some idea of what self-appropriation is. But note: this is only a framework; it is not a premise from which we are going to draw conclusions; it is an invitation to self-appropriation. What are you trying to do, how do you move towards it, and why do you bother about it?

Our first point was that seeking knowledge is seeking an unknown. Our second point was that the movement to that unknown is the movement towards an ideal that is not conceptually explicit. It becomes conceptually explicit as an axiomatic system, as observation in an experiment, and in many other ways in the course of pursuing knowledge. Thirdly, we provided illustrations from science of the development of the ideal. There is the movement from Pythagoras, through Archimedes, Galileo, Kepler, Newton, and Einstein. In that movement the ideal of law and system is worked out fully. When it is deserted one moves on to an ideal of states and probabilities. There is the ideal of certain knowledge of things through their causes, which implies analysis and synthesis. Analysis and synthesis survive, while things and causes in the Aristotelian sense are not operative in that scientific knowledge. A chemist does not bother his head about matter or form or end, but talks about agents and reagents, and so on. In other words, the ideal assumes explicit forms historically.

Fourthly, the philosophic problem arises when the ideal of pure reason, as developed by Spinoza, Leibniz, and more systematically in schoolbook fashion by Wolff, is criticized by Kant. Kant's *Critique of Pure Reason* is a critique of a particular ideal of knowledge. But then, fifthly, there is the general Hegelian objection, that any explicitly formulated ideal is going to be abstract. Because it is abstract it is going to come into conflict with the source of the ideal, and it will be consequently a source of further discoveries that change that explicit formulation.

The answer to that Hegelian objection is not easy; you cannot put it into a formula. But our approach, our way to get around it, is to move in on the concrete subject, where the tendencies that are expressed in the ideal are functionally operative. That turning in is a matter of consciousness, and we have distinguished three senses of the word 'presence.' The chairs are present in the room. We are present to one another. We are all present to ourselves. And as present to ourselves we are not looking at ourselves, we are not objects, we are subjects. It is the present subject that counts, and that present subject is not only present but also intelligent, reasonable, and, when he makes decisions, self-conscious.

Finally, there is a joker in the problem, the existential element. There are already existent ideals, and there are those who want self-appropriation spontaneously and naturally. Spontaneously, naturally, your ideal of knowledge will govern your attempts at self-appropriation, and unless your ideal is perfectly correct before you start, it will prevent you from arriving. In other words, there is the need of some sort of a jump, a leap.

2 The Value of Self-Appropriation

We have been discussing self-appropriation, and we wish now to take the question further. But let us preface our lecture with some reflections on the value of the self-appropriation we discussed yesterday.

First of all, self-appropriation is advertence – advertence to oneself as experiencing, understanding, and judging. Secondly, it is understanding oneself as experiencing, understanding, and judging. Thirdly, it is affirming oneself as experiencing, understanding, and judging. The analysis of knowledge, then, yields the three elements: experience, understanding, judging.

In direct knowledge, the experienced is the sensible object of seeing, hearing, feeling, tasting, smelling, and movement. Understanding is with respect to that object; as St Thomas puts it, quoting Aristotle perpetually, phantasms, images, are to the understanding as colors are to sight ... Finally, in direct knowledge there is the third step, judging: Is it so?

Self-appropriation involves the same three steps, except that the experience is taken on the subjective side. We have spoken of the ambiguity of presence. For you to be present to me, I have to be already present to myself. Now I can be present to myself not merely as experiencing, as empirically conscious, but also as trying to understand, as actually understanding, as reflecting and about to judge, and as judging. The repetition of the same three steps with regard precisely to the levels of self-presence is what gives you self-appropriation, self-knowledge.

Consequently, we have a theory of knowledge that accounts for itself and thus solves a fundamental difficulty in theory of knowledge, the self-referential problem. People can work out a theory of knowledge and say what knowledge is, but the knowledge they describe may not be capable of providing that account of knowledge. The simplest case of this is Hume's theory of knowledge. Hume said that our knowledge consists in sense impressions which are put together by habit. Is that theory of knowledge a matter of sense impressions put together by habit? If it is, it is of no more value than the knowledge that Hume criticizes. In other words, there is the knowledge of the critic and the knowledge that he criticizes. If the knowledge that he criticizes is inadequate, where did he get his criticism? Is *it* knowledge? But in our account, we have exactly the same structure, the same type of acts occurring, in the knowledge as described and in the knowledge that does the describing or gives the account.

But why are we attempting self-appropriation? To use an expression borrowed from Kant ..., if one is to be a philosopher, one cannot be just a plaster cast of a man.[7] To deal with philosophical questions, one

---

7 Immanuel Kant, *Critique of Pure Reason*, A836/B864.

needs a point of reference, a basis that is one's own. Your interest may quite legitimately be to find out what Lonergan thinks and what Lonergan says, but I am not offering you that, or what anyone else thinks or says, as a basis. If a person is to be a philosopher, his thinking as a whole cannot depend upon someone or something else. There has to be a basis within himself; he must have resources of his own to which he can appeal in the last resort. Kant put the issue this way: knowledge is either a matter of principles or a matter of data.[8] Thus people can learn a science that is a matter of principles, or their learning can be simply a matter of data. They can quote Wolff, for example, to meet every possible occasion, but if you dispute any of Wolff's definitions they are at a loss – they do not know what to say. In that case, Kant says, what you have is a plaster cast of a man. The value of self-appropriation, I think, is that it provides one with an ultimate basis of reference in terms of which one can proceed to deal satisfactorily with other questions.

Related selections: 1.I on the aims of *Insight*; 1.VIII on self-affirmation; 1.XI.1,3 on the underlying problem and method in philosophy; 1.XIII.2 on the appropriation of truth; 2.III.3 on consciousness and self-knowledge; 2.VII.1 on the neglected subject; 4.I on static and dynamic viewpoints.

8 Ibid.

PART TWO

From *Insight* to *Method in Theology*

I

A Definition of Art

In 1959 Lonergan conducted an institute on the philosophy of education at Xavier University in Cincinnati. The lectures were tape-recorded. Transcription and editing for eventual publication were initiated by several of Lonergan's students, with his encouragement, in the late 1970s. In these lectures Lonergan addresses a broad range of topics of concern to educators. Among them is an extended discussion of the nature of art and its significance for human living. In the following selection Lonergan, inspired by Susanne K. Langer's theory of art, provides a detailed analysis of the definition of art as an objectification of a purely experiential pattern and reflects on the role of symbols in ordinary human living.

This extract is taken from *Topics in Education*, 211–22, 232.

I propose to reflect on a definition of art that I thought was helpful. It was worked out by Susanne Langer in her book, *Feeling and Form*.[1] She conceives art as an objectification of a purely experiential pattern. If we consider the words one by one, we will have some apprehension of what art is, and through art an apprehension of concrete living.

1 Pattern

First we will meditate on the word 'pattern.' Art is the objectification of a purely experiential *pattern*. One can think of an abstract pattern, such

1 Susanne K. Langer, *Feeling and Form: A Theory of Art* (New York: Charles Scribner's Sons, 1953).

as a musical score. It contains all the notes, but it is not the music. It has all the pattern of the music, but the pattern as in the musical score is existing differently from the way it exists when the music is being played. The pattern is being realized concretely only when the music is being played. Again, we can think of the pattern of indentations in a gramophone record. The pattern is there, but the pattern is in the world of sound only when the record is playing. That pattern when the record is playing or the score is played is in the concrete, in these tones; or, with painting, it is in these colors, with sculpture in these volumes, with the dance in these movements. The pattern is the set of internal relations between these tones, or between these colors, or between these volumes, or between these movements. Music is not a note simply by itself. In music a note is related to the other notes with which it is united in the work of art. What we have to attend to are the internal relations. There may be as well an external relation; the work of art may be representative; but that is not the point to attend to. What is to be attended to are the internal relations of the pattern. They are there whether or not the art is representative.

2   Experiential

I have been illustrating the notion of a concrete pattern of internal relations in a work of art. But first we want to think of an *experiential* pattern. The coming to consciousness in the dream of the morning is patterned. The difference between the dream of morning and the dream of night that is under the influence of digestive functions and organic disturbances is that there is more pattern to the dream of morning.[2] Consciousness is a selecting, an organizing. And being awake is more organized than the dream of the morning. Patterning is essential to consciousness. If one hears a tune or a melody, one can repeat it; but if one hears a series of street noises, one cannot reproduce them. The pattern in the tune or melody makes it more perceptible, something that consciousness can pick out and be conscious of, so to speak.

Similarly, verse makes words memorable. One can remember 'Thirty days has September, April, June, and November,' because there

2 [The distinction is made by Ludwig Binswanger in his essay 'Dream and Existence,' in *Being-in-the-World: Selected Papers of Ludwig Binswanger*, trans. Jacob Needleman (New York: Harper Torchbooks, 1963), 222–48.]

is a jingle in it, a pattern to it. And decoration makes a surface visible. We can see curtains better than we can the wall between them because there is a pattern on the curtains. So decoration makes a surface visible because it imposes on it a pattern. Spontaneous patterns, moreover, are organic; decorations and motifs are modeled on roots, trunks, branches, leaves, flowers; the curlicues in carpets have an organic swing to them.

What we experience is patterned because to be conscious of something involves a patterning of what is perceived and a pattern of the feelings that flow out of and are connected with the perceiving. The perceiving is not by itself, not without a pattern. Consciousness, basically and commonly, is undifferentiated, not in some specialized pattern such as the intellectual. But on the sensitive level it is patterned.

3 Pure Pattern

Now we have to add a further term. Art is the objectification of a *purely* experiential pattern. We have considered the word 'pattern' and the word 'experiential,' and now we have to attend to the word 'purely.' We do so in two ways: first, insofar as it modifies the term 'pattern,' and second, insofar as it modifies the term 'experiential.' We can say that it modifies both by a process of condensation.

When we speak of a *pure pattern* we mean the exclusion of alien patterns that instrumentalize experience.

First, our senses can be an apparatus for receiving and transmitting signals. At a red light the brake goes on, and at the green the car starts again. Then our senses are just an apparatus for connecting the lights with the movements of the car. Our sensitive living, in such a case, has become simply a sensory apparatus in a mechanical process. The pattern is not *purely* experiential; it is not the subject coming to life in his dream and in his awakening. It is not the sort of pattern that arises out of the subject. It is rather an instrumentalization of man's sensory power.

Secondly, one's senses can be at the service of scientific intelligence. Sensory experience will be patterned by conceptual classification, by genera and series of *differentiae*. A man who knows nothing of botany does not see a flower in the same way as a botanist does. Nor in looking at a bug does the ordinary person see all that the entomologist sees. The scientist will see all kinds of things that ordinary people will miss;

and he will see them because he is able to take the whole lot successively into view. The person who has no special knowledge of the
flower or the bug does not have the categories in which to organize the
sensitive experience. He may attend to various features; the scientist
may point them out to him one by one, and he may see them all; but he
soon will not know whether they are all different, and he will not be
able to repeat the series. His capacities for experiencing have not been
developed in the specialized way that makes sense an instrument of
scientific intelligence. Again, the geometer will geometrize his experience. Any type of subordination, of putting one's spontaneous consciousness at the disposal of intellect or of a mechanical society, is an
instrumentalization of experience. I do not say that there is anything
wrong with such instrumentalization, but just that this is not what we
want to think about when we think about art.

Thirdly, one's sensitive experience can be reshaped by a psychological or epistemological theory. One can have a notion of sense data and
a notion of objectivity which can make one try to apprehend according
to the dictates of the theory. In that fashion one can instrumentalize the
experiences one would have, eliminate the spontaneous experiences
one would have, or reshape them according to the dictates of the theory. For example, if someone holds that impressions are objective and
the patterning of impressions is subjective, one is introducing a philosophic motif and devaluating the pattern. But if one thinks that one
knows when one arrives at truth, then the difference between subjectivity and objectivity does not arise on the level of experience.

Fourthly, experience can be patterned by one's motives, and then
one will not have a pure pattern. If during the whole of one's life or a
large part of it one is thinking with regard to everything one senses
simply of 'what I can get out of it,' then one is putting one's sensitive
living at the disposal of a utilitarian motive. There are many ways,
then, in which one's sensitive living may be instrumentalized. And
when one speaks of a pure pattern of experience one intends to
exclude that instrumentalization.

4   Purely Experiential

Further, the pattern is purely *experiential*. It is of the seen as seen, of the
heard as heard, of the felt as felt. It is accompanied by a retinue of associations, affects, emotions, incipient tendencies that are part of one,

that arise spontaneously and naturally from the person. It *can* be didactic, a lesson can arise out of it, but the lesson must not be imposed from outside in the manner of didacticism, moralism, or social realism. The Russian art that attempts to inculcate communist doctrine is not purely experiential.

Moreover, besides the retinue of associations, affects, emotions, tendencies, there is also in the purely experiential pattern what in *Insight* I referred to as the operator. Just as on the intellectual level the operator is wonder, the pure desire to know, so on the sensitive level there is a corresponding operator. With it are associated feelings of awe, fascination, the uncanny. It is an openness to the world, to adventure, to greatness, to goodness, to majesty.

5 Release

So far I have been describing largely in terms of exclusion an experience that is purely patterned and purely experiential. More positively, we must note that it is also a release. This in fact is the point to be noted. When experience is in a purely experiential pattern, it is not curtailed, not fitted upon some Procrustean bed. It is allowed its full complement of feelings. Experience falls into its own proper pattern and takes its own line of expansion, development, organization, fulfilment. It is not dictated to by the world of science, the world of inquiry, the world of information, the world of theories about what experience should be, or by utilitarian motives. It *is*. It has its proper rhythm, just as breathing has. In breathing, exhaling occurs, and when it reaches its peak, it sets going the opposite movement of inhaling. A rhythm is a succession of opposite movements where each movement calls forth and makes necessary the other movement. Inhaling builds up tensions that are resolved by exhaling; and exhaling builds up tensions that are resolved by inhaling. Such rhythms can involve increasing variations and complexity. That increase in variation and complexity, like the build-up of a symphony, will be enclosed within a unity. There is what is called the inevitability of form. If you sing a single note, there are no implications as to what the next note must be; but if you sing four or five, the inevitability of form is taking over; there is only a limited number of notes you can go on to. The surprise that the master musician or composer causes is to go on always to further notes that would not occur to you, and yet retain the inevitability of form.

6 Elemental Meaning

Now the purely experiential pattern that is also a release has a meaning, but the meaning is elemental. What do I mean by an elemental meaning?

According to the Aristotelian axiom, sense in act is the sensible in act, and intellect in act is the intelligible in act. But a full theory of knowledge cannot be formulated simply on that basis. According to Aristotle, knowledge is rooted in an identity, an identity of the sensible and the sense in act, and of the intellect and the intelligible in act. But if knowledge is merely identity, you are never knowing anything. You have to go beyond that initial identity to reach a knowledge that is *of* something, to reach a meaning that means some 'meant.' This occurs through the pattern of true judgments.

But we are not doing epistemology now. My point now is that meaning has an initial stage, which is the Aristotelian identity, and a second stage when it moves on to a meant, and by elemental meaning I mean that first stage. When meaning is fully developed, we have distinctions between objects; but prior to the fuller development there is an elemental meaning. When meaning involves one in an ontology, it is about objects. But prior to the ontology there is the ontic of which Heidegger speaks; and that is another way of indicating what is meant by elemental meaning.

Let us try to say something more about elemental meaning. It is, first of all, a transformation of one's world. When experience slips into a purely experiential pattern, one is out of the ready-made world of one's everyday living. One's experience is not being instrumentalized to one's functions in society, to one's job, to one's task, to all the things one has to do. It is on its own. One's experience is a component in one's apprehension of reality. And this quite different type of experience that corresponds to the release of the purely experiential pattern is a transformation of the world. To put it another way, it is an opening of the horizon. Some people will say that art is an illusion, others that art reveals a fuller, profounder reality. But the artistic experience itself does not involve a discussion of the issue. What we can say is that it is opening a new horizon, it is presenting something that is other, different, novel, strange, new, remote, intimate – all the adjectives that are employed when one attempts to communicate the artistic experience.

When experience slips into a pattern that is purely experiential, one is transported, for example, from the space in which one stands and moves and looks, and into the space represented by the picture. The space represented in the picture is not just two-dimensional; you cannot move about in it, but it is the space into which consciousness has moved. Again, one moves from the time of sleeping and waking, working and resting, into the time of the music. One moves from the pressures and determinisms of home and office, economics and politics, to a more elementary apprehension of aspiration and limitation, of help from outside and hope. One moves from the language of conversation, the newspaper, television, from the technical use of words in a science or in philosophy, to the vocal tools that focus and mold and grow with one's consciousness.

Next, slipping into the purely experiential pattern is a transformation not only on the side of the object, but also on the side of the subject. The subject in act is the object in act on the level of elemental meaning. The subject is liberated from being a replaceable part adjusted to and integrated in a ready-made world. He is liberated from being a responsible inquirer in search of exact knowledge of some aspect of the universe. He is just himself – subject in act, emergent, ecstatic, standing out. He is his own originating freedom.

Now this elemental meaning, with the transformation it involves of the world and the subject, can be set within a conceptual field. It can be described and explained. But words and thoughts will not reproduce it, just as thermodynamic equations do not make us feel warmer or cooler. Art is another case of withdrawal for return. The mathematician goes off into his speculations, but returns to concrete reality, to the natural sciences. Similarly, the artist withdraws from the ready-made world, but that withdrawal has its significance. It is a withdrawal from practical living to explore possibilities of fuller living in a richer world. Just as the mathematician explores the possibilities of what physics can be, so the artist explores possibilities of what life, ordinary life, can be. There is an artistic element in all consciousness, in all living. Our settled modes have become humdrum, and we may think of all our life simply in terms of utilitarian categories. But in fact the life we are living is a product of artistic creation. We ourselves are products of artistic creation in our concrete living, and art is an exploration of potentiality.

7   Objectification

Art has been defined as the objectification of a purely experiential pattern. We have been speaking of the purely experiential pattern. But art is the *expression*, the *objectification*, of such a pattern. The purely experiential pattern is a mode of experience, but it is merely experience. It is within the cognitional order, an awareness; it is intentional, but it has not reached the full stage of intending. It is elemental meaning. That experience not only is unknown to other people, it is not fully known even to the one who does experience it. Within the one who is experiencing, the pattern of his experience in its complexity, its many-sidedness, is only implicit, folded up, veiled, unrevealed, unobjectified. The subject is aware of it, but has yet to get hold of it. He would behold, inspect, dissect, enjoy, repeat it; and to do that he has to objectify, unfold, make explicit, unveil, reveal.

This process of objectifying is analogous to the process from the act of understanding to the definition. The definition is the inner word, an expression, an unfolding of what one has got hold of in the insight. Similarly, the purely experiential pattern becomes objectified, expressed, in a work of art.

The process of objectifying introduces, so to speak, a psychic distance. No longer is one simply experiencing. Objectification involves a separation, a distinction, a detachment, between oneself and one's experience. One can experience emotions and feelings, but at that moment one is not artistic. Poetry, according to Wordsworth, is emotion recollected in tranquility. The phrase 'recollection in tranquility' expresses the psychic distance between the subject and his experience. And that separation is needed for the subject to express his experience.

Again, one can distinguish between art and symptomatic expression. When one feels intensely, one will reveal it in one's gestures, facial movements, tone of voice, pauses, and silences. All that revelation of experience is not art, but simply the symptoms of the experience itself. One moves to art when the actor, understanding how a person would feel, puts forth deliberately those symptoms. The necessity of the psychic distance explains why the artist, when he is perturbed, cannot work. Mozart complained that he could not compose when he was being troubled and harassed in various ways. Art is not simply spontaneous manifestation of feeling.

The process of expression or objectification involves not only psychic distance but also an idealization of the purely experiential pattern. Art is not autobiography; it is not going to confession or telling one's tale to a psychiatrist. It is grasping what is or seems significant, of moment, of concern, of import to man in the experience. In a sense, it is truer than the experience, leaner, more effective, more to the point. It grasps the central moment of the experience and unfolds ideally its proper implications, apart from the distortions, the interferences, the accidental intrusions that would arise in the concrete experience itself.

Art is the abstraction of a form, where the form becomes idealized by the abstraction. And the form is not conceptual. It is the pattern of internal relations that will be immanent in the colors, in the tones, in the spaces. The expression, the work, the what-is-done is isomorphic with the idealized pattern of experience. It may also be isomorphic with something else, and in that case the art is representative. If I draw a house, the work represents a house, but it also corresponds to a dynamic image in me. Otherwise I would not have been able to draw it. There is here a double correspondence: there is a similarity between the house I draw and something further, namely, the house itself, but there is also a similarity between the house I draw and the image in me that led to the drawing. If there is a similarity to something else, the art is representative. But whether or not there is the further similarity is not the point. The immediate point is the similarity between the pattern in the work and the pattern of free experience. The pattern, then, is not a conceptual pattern, and it cannot be conceptualized. It is intelligibility in a more concrete form than is got hold of on the conceptual level – just as, for example, the intelligibility of the simple harmonic oscillator or the planetary system is an intelligibility of a more concrete type than the intelligibility of a scientific synthesis. There are material conditions that must be fulfilled to have this concrete type of intelligibility. By contrast, the scientific synthesis will be true regardless of whether determinate material conditions are fulfilled or not.

Moreover, the conceptual is also reflective. The conceptual answers the questions, or is prepared to answer the questions, What do you mean? What is the evidence for what you mean? It is prepared to determine whether one is certain that the meaning is correct or only probable, and whether that probability is of importance or negligible. Anything that is conceptual is also at least incipiently reflective. But the expression of the artistic meaning not only is on a more concrete level than the conceptual, but also it is without the reflexivity of conceptual meaning. The symbolic meaning of the work of art is immediate. The work is an invitation to participate, to try it, to see it for oneself. It has its own criteria, but they are immanent to it, and they do not admit formulation. We have already seen an example of this in the inevitability of form.

8   Symbolic Meaning

With symbolic meaning we reach a fundamental point of importance in many ways. The symbolic is an objectifying, revealing, communicating consciousness. But it is not reflective, critical consciousness. Critical consciousness deals with classes, with univocal terms, with proofs; it follows the principles of excluded middle and of noncontradiction. But the symbol is concerned, not with the class but with the representative figure, not with univocity but with multiple meanings. The artist does not care how many different meanings one gives to his work or finds in it. The symbol does not give proofs, but reinforces its statement by repetition, variation, and all the arts of rhetoric. It is not a matter of excluded middle, but is rather overdetermined, as are dreams. Freud speaks of the overdetermination of the dream, of all sorts of reasons for one and the same symbol. The symbol has no means of saying 'is not,' of negating, and so it is not a matter of contradiction in the logical sense; rather it piles up positives which it overcomes. So St Paul says, Neither height nor depth nor principality nor power. He gives a long series of negations. Why does he negate all these things? Because he is on an immediate level of symbolic communication. He posits all these terms and then brushes them aside to communicate the completeness of his devotion to Christ. The symbolic does not move on some single level or track, dealing with one thing at a time. There is a condensation, an overexuberance, in the symbol. We see this in a particularly striking way in Shakespeare, where images come crowding in from all sides to express the same point.

Finally, if one apprehends what is meant by the symbolic and the artistic, one has an apprehension of the reality behind the abstraction 'figures of speech.' 'Figures of speech' is a reflective construction of grammarians who did not quite understand why people live and talk in the apparently irrational way that grammarians find that they do. But the real meaning of simile, metaphor, synecdoche, and the rest is the normal flow of symbolic consciousness. If you try to understand St Paul in terms of logical categories, you are constantly being baffled. But think of St Paul in terms of representative figures which are constantly returning, such as sin and death, life and resurrection – not in terms of univocity. How many different meanings, how the meanings constantly change! There are many meanings of *zôê* and *thanatos* in St Paul. His use of the symbolic is not a proof but a reinforcement. St Thomas asks the question, Is theology argumentative? and quotes St Paul, If one man rose from the dead, then we also rise.[3] But it is very difficult to find such syllogisms in St Paul. It is anything but the general rule. Normally he is using reinforcement; the properties of the normal artistry of everyday life come out in the symbol.

9 Ulterior Significance

So far we have been considering art analytically, and on the level of its proper nature and in a manner consonant with the theory of knowledge and the philosophy we have presented. We are concerned with the subject coming to be himself. What makes the difference between dreaming and being awake? When awake you are more yourself, you have more control over the patterning of your experience. The dream is a negation of the patterning of your experience. But that patterning is proper to experience, and the patterns imposed upon experience that instrumentalize it also falsify it. Just as to think that we have to be looking at an object instead of thinking of the identity in act of seeing and seen falsifies the experience, so instrumentalizing experience in various ways can remove us from the primal mode of being that is proper to man and that is the normal level of human living apart from the differentiations of consciousness.

Mircea Eliade, in a small book entitled *Images et symboles*,[4] points out that rationalism drew man's attention away from his symbols and the importance of symbols in his life. But, though man's attention was drawn away from symbols, and though man tried to live under the influence of rationalism as though he were a pure spirit, a pure reason, this did not eliminate the symbols in their concrete efficacy in human living, but simply led to a degradation and a vulgarization of the sym-

3 Thomas Aquinas, *Summa theologiae*, 1, q. 1, a. 8 c.
4 Mircea Elilade, *Images and Symbols: Studies in Religious Symbolism*, trans. Philip Mairet (New York: Sheed & Ward, 1961).

bol. Hera and Artemis and Aphrodite were replaced with the pinup girl, and 'Paradise Lost' by 'South Pacific.' But symbols remain necessary and constant in human experience whether we attend to them or not. Their importance in the whole of human living is exemplified, for example, by the saying, Let me write a nation's songs, and I care not who writes her laws. This points to the fundamental fact that it is on the artistic, symbolic level that we live.

Now questions are raised about art: Is what I said all there is to it, is that all it is? That question can be put in several ways. Part of the indictment against Socrates in Athens was that he held the moon to be just earth and the clouds just water. To think of the moon as just earth and the clouds as just water, of the mountains as thrown up by contractions in the earth's surface and of rivers as just part of the earth's circulatory system is to drop something away from reality, away from man's world of experience. Art, whether by an illusion or a fiction or a contrivance, *presents* the beauty, the splendor, the glory, the majesty, the 'plus' that is in things and that drops out when you say that the moon is just earth and the clouds are just water. It draws attention to the fact that the splendor of the world is a cipher, a revelation, an unveiling, the presence of one who is not seen, touched, grasped, put in a genus, distinguished by a difference, yet is *present*. St Augustine says in his *Confessions* that he sought in the stars, and it was not the stars; in the sun and the moon, and it was not the sun and the moon; in the earth, the trees, the shrubs, the mountains, the valleys, and it was none of these.[5] Art can be viewing this world and looking for the something more that this world reveals, and reveals, so to speak, in silent speech, reveals by a presence that cannot be defined or got hold of. In other words, there is to art an interpretative significance as a possibility. Not all art has it, but when art is without this ulterior significance, which is not formulated but lived, it becomes play, it is separating objects from the ready-made world by way of exuberance, like the exuberance of a child, or by way of a distraction. Or it becomes aestheticism, just the enjoyment of the pattern. Works of art then supply the materials for exercises in one's skill of appreciation. Or art becomes technique. The compelling form is there, but there is no sense of that ulterior *presence* ...

---

5 See Augustine, *Confessions*, trans. F. J. Sheed (London: Sheed and Ward, 1951), book 10, chap. 6, 170–1.

10   Conclusion

What I want to communicate in this talk about art is the notion that art is relevant to concrete living, that it is an exploration of the potentialities of concrete living. That exploration is extremely important in our age, when philosophers for at least two centuries, through doctrines on politics, economics, education, and through ever further doctrines, have been trying to remake man, and have done not a little to make human life unlivable. The great task that is demanded if we are to make it livable again is the re-creation of the liberty of the subject, the recognition of the freedom of consciousness. Normally, we think of freedom as freedom of the will, as something that happens within consciousness. But the freedom of the will is a control over the orientation of the flow of consciousness, and that flow is not determined either by environment, external objects, or by the neurobiological demands of the subject. It has its own free component. Art is a fundamental element in the freedom of consciousness itself. Thinking about art helps us think, too, about exploring the full freedom of our ways of feeling and perceiving.

Related selections: 1.IV.2 on the esthetic pattern of experience; 1.XIII.2 on sensitive appropriation of the truth; 1.XVI.2 on the adaptation of human sensibility; 2.IV.1 and 3.III on meaning.

Openness and Religious Experience

In this selection from a 1961 article Lonergan offers no more than a sketch of a philosophy of religious experience. He first outlines what he means by 'philosophy of ...' It is a basic set of terms and correlations and a basic orientation. He remarks that in *Insight* he provides such a philosophy with his account of the levels of conscious operation and the centrality of the pure desire to know. Lonergan then discusses openness as fact, achievement, and gift. The primordial fact of openness is our natural desire to know; the gift of openness is an effect of grace; and the achievement of openness is one's degree of self-appropriation and self-realization. He correlates the actual achievement with its basis in the fact and its condition in the gift. All three dimensions of openness are indicated by the term 'religious experience.' Religious experience takes on a foundational significance in Lonergan's proposed method for theology.

This extract is taken from *Collection*, 185–7.

1 Philosophy of Religious Experience

I should say that it [philosophy of religious experience] involves (1) a material component, viz., 'religious experience,' and (2) a formal component, viz., 'philosophy of ...'

In other words I should defend the existence of a discipline, viz., 'philosophy of ...,' which with minor adaptations to diverse materials may be extended into any of the particular departments such as (1) philosophy of nature, (2) philosophy of science, (3) philosophy of man, (4) philosophy of history, (5) philosophy of the state, (6) philosophy of education, (7) philosophy of spirit, (8) philosophy of religion, etc.

With respect to each and all of its particularizations, 'philosophy of ...' determines (1) basic terms, (2) basic correlations, (3) a basic orientation.

In illustration, I should say that my book, *Insight*, may be taken as a 'philosophy of ...' In it the basic terms are empirical, intellectual, and rational consciousness; and I should note that as levels of consciousness they are immediate in their content though mediated by reflection in their formulation.

The basic correlations are the relations of empirical to intellectual consciousness and of empirical and intellectual consciousness to rational consciousness. I note that these relations are isomorphic with the relations of potency, form, and act in the Aristotelian-Thomist tradition.

The basic orientation, finally, is the pure, detached, disinterested, and unrestricted desire to know. I should note that this desire, when it is functioning, is no less immediate than the levels of consciousness when they are functioning.

2   Openness as Fact, Achievement, and Gift

Openness as a fact is the pure desire to know. It is, when functioning, immediately given. It is referred to by Aristotle when he speaks of the wonder that is the beginning of all science and philosophy. It is referred to by Aquinas when he speaks of the natural desire to know God by his essence.

Openness as an achievement has two aspects. In its more fundamental aspect it regards the subject, the *noêsis* [(the act of) understanding], the *pensée pensante*. Here stages towards its acquisition are communicated or objectified in precepts, methods, criticism. Achievement itself arises when the actual orientation of consciousness coincides with the exigences of the pure, detached, disinterested, unrestricted desire to know.

But openness as achievement also has a consequent aspect that regards the object, the *noêma* [the understood (object)], the *pensée pensée*. For the pure desire to function fully, to dominate consciousness, there are needed not only precepts, methods, criticism, but also a formulated view of our knowledge and of the reality our knowledge can attain. Thus I should maintain that the crop of philosophies produced since the Enlightenment are not open to revealed truths because they possess no adequate account of truth.

I have spoken of openness as (1) fact and (2) achievement.

As fact, it is an intrinsic component in man's makeup. But as fact it does not consistently and completely dominate human consciousness.

It is a fact to which man has to advert, which he has to acknowledge and accept, whose implications for all his thinking and acting have to be worked out and successfully applied to actual thinking and actual acting.

Hence, besides openness as primordial fact, there also is openness as achievement. The history of religion, of science, of philosophy in all their vicissitudes is the history of such achievement.

But there is also openness as a gift, as an effect of divine grace.

Man's natural openness is complete. The pure desire is unrestricted. It inquires into everything, and asks everything about everything.

The correlative to the pure desire is 'being,' *omnia*, at once completely universal and completely concrete.

Nonetheless, there is a contrast, almost an antinomy, between the primordial fact and achievement, for the primordial fact is no more than a principle of possible achievement, a definition of the ultimate horizon that is to be reached only through successive enlargements of the actual horizon.

But such successive enlargements only too clearly lie under some law of decreasing returns. No one ever believed that the world would be converted by philosophy. In the language at once of scripture and of a current philosophy, man is fallen. There is then a need of openness as a gift, as an effect of grace, where grace is taken as *gratia sanans* [healing grace].

Further, the successive enlargements of the actual horizon fall into two classes. There are the enlargements implicit in the very structure of human consciousness, the enlargements that are naturally possible to man. But there is also an ultimate enlargement, beyond the resources of every finite consciousness, where there enters into clear view God as unknown, when the subject knows God face to face, knows as he is known. This ultimate enlargement alone approximates to the possibility of openness defined by the pure desire; as well, it is an openness as a gift, as an effect of grace and, indeed, of grace not as merely *sanans* but as *elevans* [elevating], as *lumen gloriae* [light of glory].

3   Openness and Religious Experience

The three aspects of openness are to be related. Openness as fact is for openness as gift; and openness as achievement rises from the fact, and conditions and, at the same time, is conditioned by the gift.

But openness as fact is the inner self, the self as ground of all higher aspiration.

Openness as achievement is the self in its self-appropriation and self-realization.

Openness as gift is the self entering into personal relationship with God.

Because these three are linked in the historical unfolding of the human spirit, they reveal how religious experience holds a fundamental place primarily in man's making of man but no less in the reflection on that making that is philosophy or, indeed, 'philosophy of...'

Related selections: 1.IX on the notion of being; 1.XV.1 on the immanent source of transcendence; 1.VIII.2 on levels of consciousness; 1.XVII.1 on self-appropriation; 3.IX.2 on religious experience; 3.VIII on theological categories.

III

Cognitional Structure

The article 'Cognitional Structure,' from which the following selection is taken, was Lonergan's contribution to a special issue of *Continuum* honoring him on the occasion of his sixtieth birthday, in 1964. Lonergan's fundamental conception of human knowing as a structured set of related operations, as opposed to the more common conception of knowing as experiential confrontation or as a single act analogous to 'looking,' has been carefully and deliberately worked out in *Insight*. But in that foundational work this basic idea is unfolded gradually, in the course of a wide-ranging and complex argument and in the context of ever-unfolding implications. In his contribution to the *Continuum* volume Lonergan provides a concise account of the basic positions for which he argues at length in *Insight*, beginning with his position that human knowing is a structured set of operations. In the first part of this selection Lonergan distinguishes materially dynamic structures from formally dynamic structures. In the second he provides an account of human knowing as a formally dynamic structure. He turns in the third part to the process of reduplicating that structure in cognitional self-appropriation, or 'knowing knowing.' Here he distinguishes three senses of presence, clarifies the notion of the 'subject as subject,' and draws a basic distinction between mere presence to oneself in cognitional activity and knowledge of oneself as a knower. As knowledge of objects other than the subject can be misconceived, on the model of 'looking,' as experiential confrontation with 'external' objects, so knowledge of the knowing subject can be misconceived as an 'internal' experience of the subject.

This extract is taken from *Collection*, 205–11.

1 Dynamic Structure

A whole, then, has parts. The whole is related to each of the parts, and each of the parts is related to the other parts and to the whole.

Not every whole is a structure. When one thinks of a whole, there may come to mind some conventional quantity or arbitrary collection whose parts are determined by an equally conventional or arbitrary division. In such a case, e.g., a gallon of milk, the closed set of relations between whole and parts will be a no less arbitrary jumble of arithmetic ratios. But it may also happen that the whole one thinks of is some highly organized product of nature or art. Then the set of internal relations is of the greatest significance. Each part is what it is in virtue of its functional relations to other parts; there is no part that is not determined by the exigences of other parts; and the whole possesses a certain inevitability in its unity, so that the removal of any part would destroy the whole, and the addition of any further part would be ludicrous. Such a whole is a structure.

The parts of a whole may be things, bricks, timber, glass, rubber, chrome. But the parts may also be activities, as in a song, a dance, a chorus, a symphony, a drama. Such a whole is dynamic materially. But dynamism may not be restricted to the parts. The whole itself may be self-assembling, self-constituting; then it is formally dynamic. It is a dynamic structure.

2 Human Knowing as Dynamic Structure

Now human knowing involves many distinct and irreducible activities: seeing, hearing, smelling, touching, tasting, inquiring, imagining, understanding, conceiving, reflecting, weighing the evidence, judging.

No one of these activities, alone and by itself, may be named human knowing. An act of ocular vision may be perfect as ocular vision; yet if it occurs without any accompanying glimmer of understanding, it is mere gaping; and mere gaping, so far from being the beau ideal of human knowing, is just stupidity. As merely seeing is not human knowing, so for the same reason merely hearing, merely smelling, merely touching, merely tasting, may be parts, potential components, of human knowing, but they are not human knowing itself.

What is true of sense is no less true of understanding. Without the prior presentations of sense, there is nothing for a man to understand; and when there is nothing to be understood, there is no occurrence of understanding. Moreover, the combination of the operations of sense and of understanding does not suffice for human knowing. There must be added judging. To omit judgment is quite literally silly: it is only by judgment that there emerges a distinction between fact and fiction, logic and sophistry, philosophy and myth, history and legend, astronomy and astrology, chemistry and alchemy.

Nor can one place human knowing in judging to the exclusion of experience and understanding. To pass judgment on what one does not understand is, not human knowing, but human arrogance. To pass judgment independently of all experience is to set fact aside.

Human knowing, then, is not experience alone, not understanding alone, not judgment alone; it is not a combination of only experience and understanding, or of only experience and judgment, or of only understanding and judgment; finally, it is not something totally apart from experience, understanding, and judgment. Inevitably, one has to regard an instance of human knowing, not as this or that operation, but as a whole whose parts are operations. It is a structure and, indeed, a materially dynamic structure.

But human knowing is also formally dynamic. It is self-assembling, self-constituting. It puts itself together, one part summoning forth the next, till the whole is reached. And this occurs, not with the blindness of natural process, but consciously, intelligently, rationally. Experience stimulates inquiry, and inquiry is intelligence bringing itself to act; it leads from experience through imagination to insight, and from insight to the concepts that combine in single objects both what has been grasped by insight and what in experience or imagination is relevant to the insight. In turn, concepts stimulate reflection, and reflection is the conscious exigence of rationality; it marshals the evidence and weighs it either to judge or else to doubt and so renew inquiry.

Such in briefest outline is what is meant by saying that human knowing is a dynamic structure. Let us briefly note its implications.

First, on the verbal level, it implies a distinction between 'knowing' in a loose or generic sense and 'knowing' in a strict and specific sense. Loosely, any cognitional activity may be named knowing; so one may speak of seeing, inquiring, understanding, thinking, weighing the evidence, judging, as each an instance of knowing. Strictly, one will distinguish animal, human, angelic, and divine knowing, and one will investigate what in each case is necessary and sufficient for an instance of knowing.

Secondly, the view that human knowing is a dynamic structure implies that human knowing is not some single operation or activity but, on the contrary, a whole whose parts are cognitional activities.

Thirdly, the parts of a structure are related to one another, not by similarity, but functionally. As in a motorcar the engine is not like the tires and the muffler is not like the differential, so too in human knowing, conceived as a dynamic structure, there is no reason to expect the several cognitional activities to resemble one another. It follows that a study of human knowing cannot safely follow the broad and downhill path of analogy. It will not do, for instance, to scrutinize ocular vision and then assume that other cognitional activities must be the same sort of thing. They may turn out to be quite different and so, if one is to proceed scientifically, each cognitional activity must be examined in and for itself and, no less, in its functional relations to other cognitional activities. This third conclusion brings us to the question of consciousness and self-knowledge, which calls for another section.

3   Consciousness and Self-Knowledge

Where knowing is a structure, knowing knowing must be a reduplication of the structure. Thus if knowing is just looking, then knowing knowing will be looking at looking. But if knowing is a conjunction of experience, understanding, and judging, then knowing knowing has to be a conjunction of (1) experiencing experience, understanding and judging, (2) understanding one's experience of experience, understanding and judging, and (3) judging one's understanding of experience, understanding, and judging to be correct.

On the latter view there follows at once a distinction between consciousness and self-knowledge. Self-knowledge is the reduplicated structure: it is experience, understanding, and judging with respect to experience, understanding, and judging. Consciousness, on the other hand, is not knowing knowing but merely experience of knowing, experience, that is, of experiencing, of understanding, and of judging.

Secondly, it follows that all cognitional activities may be conscious yet none or only some may be known. So it is, in fact, that both acts of seeing and acts of understanding occur consciously, yet most people know what seeing is and most are mystified when asked what understanding is.

Thirdly, it follows that different cognitional activities are not equally accessible. Experience is of the given. Experience of seeing is to be had only when one actually is seeing. Experience of insight is to be had only when one actually is having an insight. But one has only to open one's eyes and one will see; one has only to open and close one's eyes a number of times to alternate the experience of seeing and of not seeing. Insights, on the other hand, cannot be turned on and off in that fashion. To have an insight, one has to be in the process of learning or, at least, one has to reenact in oneself previous processes of learning. While that is not peculiarly difficult, it does require (1) the authenticity that is ready to get down to the elements of a subject, (2) close attention to instances of one's own understanding and, equally, one's failing to understand, and (3) the repeated use of personal experiments in which, at first, one is genuinely puzzled and then catches on.

Fourthly, because human knowing is a structure of different activities, experience of human knowing is qualitatively differentiated. When one is reflecting, weighing the evidence, judging, one is experiencing one's own rationality. When one is inquiring, understanding, conceiving, thinking, one is experiencing one's own intelligence. When one is seeing or hearing, touching or tasting, one is experiencing one's own sensitivity. Just as rationality is quite different from intelligence, so the experience of one's rationality is quite different from the experience of one's intelligence; and just as intelligence is quite different from sensitivity, so the experience of one's intelligence is quite different from the experience of one's sensitivity. Indeed, since consciousness is of the acting subject *qua* acting, the experience of one's rationality is identical with one's rationality bringing itself to act; the experience of one's intelligence is identical with one's bringing one's intelligence to act; and the experiencing of one's sensitivity is identical with one's sensitivity coming to act.

Fifthly, then, experience commonly is divided into external and internal. External experience is of sights and sounds, of odors and tastes, of the hot and cold, hard and soft, rough and smooth, wet and dry. Internal experience is of oneself and one's apprehensive and appetitive activities. Still, if the meaning of the distinction is clear, the usage of the adjectives, internal and external, calls for explanation. Strictly, only spatial objects are internal or external and, while external experience may be of spatial objects, it itself is not a spatial object and, still less, is internal experience. Accordingly, we must ask what is the original datum that has been expressed by a spatial metaphor; and to that end we draw attention to different modes of presence.

There is material presence, in which no knowing is involved, and such is the presence of the statue in the courtyard. There is intentional presence, in which knowing is involved, and it is of two quite distinct kinds. There is the presence of the object to the subject, of the spectacle to the spectator; there is also the presence of the subject to himself, and this is not the presence of another object dividing his attention, of another spectacle distracting the spectator; it is presence in, as it were, another dimension, presence concomitant and correlative and opposite to the presence of the object. Objects are present by being attended to; but subjects are present as subjects, not by being attended to, but by attending. As the parade of objects marches by, spectators do not have to slip into the parade to become present to themselves; they have to be present to themselves for anything to be present to them; and they are present to themselves by the same watching that, as it were, at its other pole makes the parade present to them.

I have been attempting to describe the subject's presence to himself. But the reader, if he tries to find himself as subject, to reach back and, as it were, uncover his subjectivity, cannot succeed. Any such effort is introspecting, attending to the subject; and what is found is, not the subject as subject, but only the subject as object; it is the subject as subject that does the finding. To heighten one's presence to oneself, one does not introspect; one raises the level of one's activity. If one sleeps and dreams, one is present to oneself as the frightened dreamer. If one wakes, one becomes present to oneself, not as moved but as moving, not as felt but as feeling, not as seen but as seeing. If one is puzzled and wonders and inquires, the empirical subject becomes an intellectual subject as well. If one reflects and considers the evidence, the empirical and intellectual subject becomes a rational subject, an incarnate reasonableness. If one deliberates and chooses, one has moved to the level of the rationally conscious, free, responsible subject that by his choices makes himself what he is to be and his world what it is to be.

Sixthly, does this many-leveled subject exist? Each man has to answer that question for himself. But I do not think that the answers are in doubt. Not even behaviorists claim that they are unaware whether or not they see or hear, taste or touch. Not even positivists preface their lectures and their books with the frank avowal that never in their lives did they have the experience of understanding anything whatever. Not even relativists claim that never in their lives did they have the experience of making a rational judgment. Not even determinists claim that never in their lives did they have the experience of making a responsible choice. There exist subjects that are empirically, intellectually, rationally, morally conscious. Not all know themselves as such, for consciousness is not human knowing but only a potential component in the structured whole that is human knowing. But all can know themselves as such, for they have only to attend to what they are already conscious of, and understand what they attend to, and pass judgment on the correctness of their understanding.

Related selections: 1.VIII on consciousness, the structure of human knowing, and self-knowledge; 1.VI.2–3 and 1.XI.1 on the duality in human knowing; 1.IV.2 on biological extroversion and the intellectual pattern of experience; 1.VIII on the structure of cognitional process; 2.VII.1–3 on why study of the subject has been neglected; 3.I.2 for a later discussion of the structure, including its fourth level, as transcendental method; 3V.3 on the use of the structure to ground the division of theological specialties; 3.VII.2 on intellectual conversion as appropriation of the three-level structure; 3.VIII.2 on the dynamic structure as a transcultural base for the derivation of theological categories; 4.I on the dynamic viewpoint grounded by appropriation of the structure; 4.VII for a summary of the degrees of self-transcendence; 1.XVII on self-appropriation.

Dimensions of Meaning

'Dimensions of Meaning' is the text of an address given in 1965 in the Distinguished Lecture Series at Marquette University. It is presented here in its entirety. Lonergan's aim in the address is, first, to convince his audience of the significance of meaning in human living and, second, to bring to light the still greater importance of reflection upon and control of meaning; it was his view that 'changes in the control of meaning mark off the great epochs in human history.'[1] In the course of pursuing these aims Lonergan distinguishes between the world of immediacy, the world mediated by meaning, and the world constituted by meaning; he identifies the various functions of meaning; contrasts classical and modern manners of controlling meaning; and characterizes the contemporary situation as a crisis of meaning brought on by the massive shift from classical to modern controls. In the concluding section of the address, Lonergan expresses the view that this cultural crisis poses the gravest problems for Catholic philosophy and theology.

This selection is taken from *Collection*, 232–45.

1   Meaning and the World of the Subject

My topic is meaning, and at first sight at least it seems to be a very secondary affair. What counts is reality. What is of primary moment is, not the mere meaning, but the reality that is meant.

This contention is quite correct, quite true, as far as it goes. But it is involved, I think, in an oversight. For it overlooks the fact that human

1 *Collection*, 235.

reality, the very stuff of human living, is not merely meant but in large measure constituted through acts of meaning. Thus, if you will bear with me, I now shall endeavor to explain.

Insofar as one is lost in dreamless sleep, or lies helpless in a coma, then meaning is no part of one's being. As long as one is an infant, etymologically a nontalker, one is busy learning to develop, differentiate, combine, group in ever broader syntheses one's capacities for operation in the movements of head and mouth, neck and arms, eyes and hands, in mastering the intricacies of standing on one's feet, then of tottering from one spot to another. When first hearing and speech develop, they are directed to present objects, and so meaning initially is confined to a world of immediacy, to a world no bigger than the nursery, and seemingly no better known because it is not merely experienced but also meant. Then, to all appearances, it is quite correct to say that reality comes first and meaning is quite secondary.

But as the command and use of language develop, there comes a reversal of roles. For words denote not only what is present but also what is absent, not only what is near but also what is far, not only the past but also the future, not only the factual but also the possible, the ideal, the ought-to-be for which we keep striving though we never attain. So we come to live, not as the infant in the world of immediate experience, but in a far vaster world that is brought to us through the memories of other men, through the common sense of the community, through the pages of literature, through the labors of scholars, through the investigations of scientists, through the experience of saints, through the mediations of philosophers and theologians.

This larger world, mediated through meaning, does not lie within anyone's immediate experience. It is not even the sum, the integral, of the totality of all worlds of immediate experience. For meaning is an act that does not merely repeat but goes beyond experiencing. What is meant is not only experienced but also somehow understood and, commonly, also affirmed. It is this addition of understanding and judgment that makes possible the larger world mediated by meaning, that gives it its structure and its unity, that arranges it in an orderly whole of almost endless differences: partly known and familiar, partly in a surrounding penumbra of things we know about but have never examined or explored, partly in an unmeasured region of what we do not know at all. It is this larger world mediated by meaning that we refer to when we speak of the real world, and in it we live out our lives.

It is this larger world mediated by meaning that we know to be insecure, because meaning is insecure, since besides truth there is error, beside fact there is fiction, besides honesty there is deceit, besides science there is myth.

Beyond the world we know about, there is the further world we make. But what we make we first intend. We imagine, we plan, we investigate possibilities, we weigh pros and cons, we enter into contracts, we have countless orders given and executed. From the beginning to the end of the process, we are engaged in acts of meaning; and without them the process would not occur or the end be achieved. The pioneers in this country found shore and heartland, mountains and plains, but they have covered it with cities, laced it with roads, exploited it with their industries, till the world man has made stands between us and a prior world of nature. Yet the whole of that added, manmade, artificial world is the cumulative, now planned, now chaotic product of human acts of meaning.

Man's making is not restricted to the transformation of nature, for there is also the transformation of man himself. It is most conspicuous, perhaps, in the educational process, in the difference between the child beginning kindergarten and the doctoral candidate writing his dissertation. But the difference produced by the education of individuals is only a recapitulation of the longer process of the education of mankind, of the evolution of social institutions, and of the development of cultures. Religions and art forms, languages and literatures, sciences, philosophies, the writing of history, all had their rude beginnings, slowly developed, reached their peak, perhaps went into decline and later underwent a renaissance in another milieu. And what is true of cultural achievements, also, though less conspicuously, is true of social institutions. The family, the state, the law, the economy, are not fixed and immutable entities. They adapt to changing circumstance; they can be reconceived in the light of new ideas; they can be subjected to revolutionary change. Moreover – and this is my present point – all such change is in its essence a change of meaning: a change of idea or concept, a change of judgment or evaluation, a change of the order or the request. The state can be changed by rewriting the constitution; more subtly but no less effectively it can be changed by reinterpreting the constitution or, again, by working on men's minds and hearts to change the objects that command their respect, hold their allegiance, fire their loyalty. Community is a matter of a common field of experience, a common mode of understanding, a common measure of judgment, and a common consent. Such community is the possibility, the source, the ground, of common meaning; and it is this common meaning that is the form and act that finds expression in family and polity, in the legal and economic system, in customary morals and educational arrangements, in language and literature, art and religion, philosophy, science, and the writing of history.

At this point, permit me to resume what I have been trying to say. I have been meeting the objection that meaning is a merely secondary affair, that what counts is the reality that is meant and not the mere meaning that refers to it. My answer has been that the functions of meaning are larger than the objection envisages. I would not dispute that, for the child learning to talk, his little world of immediacy comes first, and that the words he uses are only an added grace. But as the child develops into a man, the world of immediacy shrinks into an inconspicuous and not too important corner of the real world, which is a world we know only through the mediation of meaning. Further, there is man's transformation of his environment, a transformation that is effected through the intentional acts that envisage ends, select means, secure collaborators, direct operations. Finally, besides the transformation of nature, there is man's transformation of man himself; and in this second transformation the role of meaning is not merely directive but also constitutive.

2 Control of Meaning

I might go on to enlarge upon the constitutive functions of meaning, and many profound themes might be touched upon. For it is in the field where meaning is constitutive that man's freedom reaches its highest point. There too his responsibility is greatest. There there occurs the emergence of the existential subject, finding out for himself that he has to decide for himself what he is to make of himself. It is there that individuals become alienated from community, that communities split into factions, that cultures flower and decline, that historical causality exerts its sway.

But I propose to use the little that has been said and the much that I hope has been suggested merely as a springboard. I have been endeavoring to persuade you that meaning is an important part of human living. I wish now to add that reflection on meaning and the consequent control of meaning are still more important. For if social and cultural changes are, at root, changes in the meanings that are grasped and accepted, changes in the control of meaning mark off the great epochs in human history.

2.1 Classical Control: Functioning and Breakdown

The classical expression of the effort to control meaning is found in the early Platonic dialogues. There Socrates is represented as putting very simple questions, listening patiently to answers, and invariably showing that none of the proffered answers was satisfactory. The questions were not abstruse. On the contrary they were of the type that anyone of average common sense, let alone any Athenian, would feel that he could answer. What is courage? What is self-control? What is justice? What is knowledge? After all, no one is going to say that he has no notion of the difference between courage and cowardice, or that he does not know what is meant by self-control, or that he has never been able to figure out what people mean by justice, or that knowledge and ignorance are all one to him. But if everyone naturally felt he could answer Socrates' questions, no one was able to give the kind of answer that Socrates wanted. For Socrates wanted universal definitions, brief and exact statements that fitted every case of courage and, at the same time, fitted nothing except courage; or that fitted every case of self-control and nothing but self-control; that applied to each and every instance of justice and only to justice.

Now, whatever the profundities of Platonism, at least we can all see for ourselves that Socrates carried out on the Athenians an experiment that bears on meaning. The result of the experiment was quite clear. There are at least two levels to meaning. There is the primary, spontaneous level, on which we employ everyday language. There is a secondary, reflexive level, on which we not merely employ but also say what we mean by everyday language. On the primary, spontaneous level, the Athenians were quite at home; they knew perfectly well the difference between courage and cowardice, between self-control and self-indulgence, between justice and injustice, between knowledge and ignorance; they were in no way inclined to confuse one with the other, or to get mixed up in their use of words. But paradoxically this did not enable them to proceed to the secondary, reflexive level, and work out satisfactory definitions of courage and self-control, of justice and knowledge. On the contrary, definition was a new idea; Socrates had to explain repeatedly what a definition was; again and again he would show that a good definition had to be *omni et soli*, had to apply to every instance of the defined and to no instance of something else. The Athenians understood what he meant, but they could not produce the definitions. Socrates himself knew what he meant, but he too could not produce the definitions. He was the wisest of men, according to the Delphic oracle, but the grounds for this accolade were ironical: he was the wisest because at least he knew that he did not know.

No doubt, you will want some better authority than the Delphic oracle before you will be convinced that Socrates was really wise. After all, is there any point to this mediation of meaning, this proceeding from a primary level on which we all know well enough what we mean, to a secondary level on which we discover that we have the greatest difficulty in saying what exactly we do mean? Does it not seem to be an idle waste of time, an excessive effort devoted to useless subtlety? At first sight, one might answer, 'Yes.' But on second thoughts, perhaps, one will say, 'No.' And there are very good grounds for adding second thoughts. Anthropologists will assure you that primitive men are as intelligent and as reasonable as the rest of us in the practical affairs of life, in their hunting and fishing, in their sowing and reaping, in any activity from which there follow ascertainable and palpable results. Yet, despite their intelligence and reasonableness, it remains that all their activities and all their living are penetrated, surrounded, dominated by myth and magic. Moreover, what is true of primitives also is true, though in a modified manner, of the ancient high civilizations, of Babylon, Egypt, and Crete, of the ancient settlements along the Indus and Hoang-ho, of the Incas and Mayas in South and Central America. In those civilizations large-scale enterprises were common: there were great works of irrigation, vast structures of stone or brick, armies and navies, complicated processes of bookkeeping, the beginnings of geometry, arithmetic, astronomy. The poverty and weakness of the primitive had been replaced by the wealth and power of the great state. The area over which man exercised his practical intelligence had been increased enormously. Yet myth and magic remained to penetrate, surround, dominate both the routine activities of daily life and the profound and secret aspirations of the human heart.

Now myth and magic are both instances of meaning. Myth is a

declarative meaning; magic is an imperative meaning. But the declaration of myth is mistaken, and the command of magic is vain. Both have meaning, but the meaning is meaning gone astray. The prevalence, then, of myth and magic among primitives and its survival even in the ancient high civilizations reveal the importance of the Socratic enterprise. The mediation of meaning is not idle talk but a technique that puts an end to idle talk; it is not a vain subtlety but a cure for a malady to which all men are prone. Just as the earth, left to itself, can put forth creepers and shrubs, bushes and trees, with such excessive abundance that there results an impenetrable jungle, so too the human mind, led by imagination and affect and uncontrolled by any reflexive technique, luxuriates in a world of myth with its glories to be achieved and its evils banished by the charms of magic. So it is that in Western culture, for the past twenty-four centuries, the movement associated with the name Socrates and the achievement of fourth-century Athens have been regarded as a high point, as a line of cleavage, as the breaking through of a radically new era in the history of man.

I have been repeating to you, in my own manner, something like the contention put forward by the German existentialist philosopher, Karl Jaspers, in his work, *The Origin and Goal of History*. According to Jaspers, there is an axis on which the whole of human history turns; that axis lies between the years 800 and 200 B.C.; during that period in Greece, in Israel, in Persia, in India, in China, man became of age; he set aside the dreams and fancies of childhood; he began to face the world as perhaps it is.

But if I have been repeating another's view, I have had an ulterior purpose that regards neither primitives nor Greeks but ourselves. For the Greek mediation of meaning resulted in classical culture and, by and large, classical culture has passed away. By and large, its canons of art, its literary forms, its rules of correct speech, its norms of interpretation, its ways of thought, its manner in philosophy, its notion of science, its concept of law, its moral standards, its methods of education, are no longer accepted. What breathed life and form into the civilization of Greece and Rome, what was born again in a European Renaissance, what provided the chrysalis whence issued modern languages and literatures, modern mathematics and science, modern philosophy and history, held its own right into the twentieth century; but today, nearly everywhere, it is dead and almost forgotten. Classical culture has given way to a modern culture, and, I would submit, the crisis of our age is in no small measure the fact that modern culture has not yet reached its maturity. The classical mediation of meaning has broken down; the breakdown has been effected by a whole array of new and more effective techniques; but their very multiplicity and complexity leave us bewildered, disorientated, confused, preyed upon by anxiety, dreading lest we fall victims to the up-to-date myth of ideology and the hypnotic, highly effective magic of thought control.

The clearest and neatest illustration of the breakdown of classical culture lies in the field of science. It is manifest, of course, that modern science understands far more things far more fully than did Greek or medieval science. But the point I would make is not quantitative but qualitative. The significant difference is not more knowledge or more adequate knowledge but the emergence of a quite different conception of science itself. The Greek conception was formulated by Aristotle in his *Posterior Analytics*; it envisaged science as true, certain knowledge of causal necessity. But modern science is not true; it is only on the way towards truth. It is not certain; for its positive affirmations it claims no more than probability. It is not knowledge but hypothesis, theory, system, the best available scientific opinion of the day. Its object is not necessity but verified possibility: bodies fall with a constant acceleration, but they could fall at a different rate; and similarly other natural laws aim at stating, not what cannot possibly be otherwise, but what in fact is so. Finally, while modern science speaks of causes, still it is not concerned with Aristotle's four causes of end, agent, matter, and form; its ultimate objective is to reach a complete explanation of all phenomena, and by such explanation is meant the determination of the terms and intelligible relationships that account for all data. So for each of the five elements constitutive of the Greek ideal of science, for truth, certainty, knowledge, necessity, and causality, the modern ideal substitutes something less arduous, something more accessible, something dynamic, something effective. Modern science works.

Now this shift in the very meaning of the word, science, affects the basic fabric of classical culture. If the object of Greek science was necessary, it also was obvious to the Greeks that in this world of ours there is very much that is not necessary but contingent. The Greek universe, accordingly, was a split universe: partly it was necessary and partly it was contingent. Moreover, this split in the object involved a corresponding split in the development of the human mind. As the universe was partly necessary and partly contingent, so man's mind was divided between science and opinion, theory and practice, wisdom and prudence. Insofar as the universe was necessary, it could be known scientifically; but insofar as it was contingent, it could be known only by opinion. Again, insofar as the universe was necessary, human operation could not change it; it could only contemplate it by theory; but insofar as the universe was contingent, there was a realm in which human operation could be effective; and that was the sphere of practice. Finally, insofar as the universe was necessary, it was possible for man to find ultimate and changeless foundations, and so philosophy was the pursuit of wisdom; but insofar as the universe was contingent, it was a realm of endless differences and variations that could not be subsumed under hard and fast rules; and to navigate on that chartless sea there was needed all the astuteness of prudence.

The modern ideal of science has no such implications. We do not contrast science and opinion; we speak of scientific opinion. We do not put theory and practice in separate compartments; on the contrary, our practice is the fruit of our theory, and our theory is orientated to practical achievement. We distinguish pure science and applied science, applied science and technology, technology and industry; but the distinctions are not separations, and, however great the differences between basic research and industrial activity, the two are linked by intermediate zones of investigation, discovery, invention. Finally, if contemporary philosophic issues are far too complex to be dealt with in the present context, as least we may say that philosophy has invaded the field of the concrete, the particular, and the contingent, of the existential subject's decisions and of the history of peoples, societies, and cultures; and this entry of philosophy into the realm of the existential and the historical not merely extends the role of philosophic wisdom into concrete living but also, by that very extension, curtails the functions formerly attributed to prudence.

Nor is it only from above that prudence is curtailed: its province is also invaded from below. We do not trust the prudent man's memory, but keep files and records and develop systems of information retrieval. We do not trust the prudent man's ingenuity, but call in efficiency experts or set problems for operations research. We do not trust the prudent man's judgment, but employ computers to keep track of inventories and to forecast demand. We do not rely on the prudent man's broad experience, but conduct fact-finding surveys and compile statistics. There is as great a need as ever for memory and ingenuity,

judgment and experience; but they have been supplemented by a host
of devices and techniques, and so they operate on a different level and
in a different mode; while the old-style prudent man, whom some cultural lag sends drifting through the twentieth century, commonly is
known as a stuffed shirt.

2.2   Modern Control: Functioning and Problems

I have been indicating, very summarily, how a new notion of science
has undermined and antiquated certain fundamental elements of classical culture. But besides the new notion itself, there is also its implementation. A new notion of science leads to a new science of man.
Classically orientated science, from its very nature, concentrated on
the essential to ignore the accidental, on the universal to ignore the
particular, on the necessary to ignore the contingent. Man is a rational
animal, composed of body and immortal soul, endowed with vital,
sensitive, and intellectual powers, in need of habits and able to acquire
them, free and responsible in his deliberations and decisions, subject to
a natural law which, in accord with changing circumstances, is to be
supplemented by positive laws enacted by duly constituted authority.
I am very far from having exhausted the content of the classically orientated science of man, but enough has been said to indicate its style. It
is limited to the essential, necessary, universal; it is so phrased as to
hold for all men whether they are awake or asleep, infants or adults,
morons or geniuses; it makes it abundantly plain that you can't change
human nature; the multiplicity and variety, the developments and
achievements, the breakdowns and catastrophes of human living, all
have to be accidental, contingent, particular, and so have to lie outside
the field of scientific interest as classically conceived. But modern science aims at the complete explanation of all phenomena, and so modern studies of man are interested in every human phenomenon. Not
abstract man but, at least in principle, all the men of every time and
place, all their thoughts and words and deeds, the accidental as well as
the essential, the contingent as well as the necessary, the particular as
well as the universal, are to be summoned before the bar of human
understanding. If you object that such knowledge is unattainable, that
the last day of general judgment cannot be anticipated, you will be
answered that modern science is, not a ready-made achievement
stored for all time in a great book, but an ongoing process that no

library, let alone any single mind, is expected to encompass. And even though this ongoing process never can master all human phenomena, still by its complete openness, by its exclusion of every obscurantism, modern study of man can achieve ever so much more than the conventional limitations of classically orientated human studies permitted.

From the modern viewpoint classical culture appears as a somewhat arbitrary standardization of man. It distinguished the literal and the figurative meanings of words and phrases, and it conveyed more than a suggestion that literal meaning is somehow first, while figurative meaning is a dress or ornament that makes the literal meaning more striking, more vivid, more effective. Perhaps it was Giambattista Vico in his *Scienza nuova* that first put forward the contrary view by proclaiming the priority of poetry. In any case his contention is true in the sense already indicated: it is only through uncounted centuries of development that the human mind eventually succeeds in liberating itself from myth and magic, in distinguishing the literal truth from figurative expression, in taking its stand on what literally is so, and in rationalizing figures of speech by reducing them to the categories of classical rhetoric. But this achievement, if a necessary stage in the development of the human mind, easily obscures man's nature, constricts his spontaneity, saps his vitality, limits his freedom. To proclaim with Vico the priority of poetry is to proclaim that the human spirit expresses itself in symbols before it knows, if ever it knows, what its symbols literally mean. It is to open the way to setting aside the classical definition of man as a rational animal and, instead, defining man with the cultural phenomenologists as a symbolic animal or with the personalists as an incarnate spirit.

So the twentieth century has witnessed a rediscovery of myth, and the rediscovery has taken many forms. With Freud one may find in contemporary human living the terrifying figures of family relationships set forth in the Theban cycle of the Greek tragedians. With Jung one may plunge to the primal archetypes and the symbols of transformation attributed to a collective unconscious. With Ludwig Binswanger and Rollo May one may distinguish the dreams of night, occasioned by somatic disturbance, and the dreams of morning when the existential subject, not yet awake and himself, still is already busy with the project that shapes both him himself and his world. With Gilbert Durand one may explore the whole realm of everyday, omnipresent metaphor, and place this vast and complex manifold in a dialectical sequence by relating it to the three dominant reflexes connected with keeping one's balance, swallowing one's food, and mating. One may go on to explore the arts of Madison Avenue in democracies, or of the ministries of culture in totalitarian states. One can join the literary critics that articulate the psychic mechanisms underneath the glossy surface of poetry's immortal lines. One can turn to the liturgists and the historians of religions to search, with Mircea Eliade, for a cross-cultural language that is prior to manmade languages and independent of them. One can read the Old Testament as a reinterpretation of the symbols of Babylon and Canaan and, with Paul Ricoeur, discern the dialectic in which older and less adequate symbols of guilt are complemented, corrected, modified, and still retained in combination with newer ones.

From the affect-laden images within us and from the many interpretations that illuminate them, one may turn outward to the phenomenology of intersubjectivity. Human communication is not the work of a soul hidden in some unlocated recess of a body and emitting signals in some Morse code. Soul and body are not two things but coprinciples in the constitution of a single thing. The bodily presence of another is the presence of the incarnate spirit of the other; and that incarnate spirit reveals itself to me by every shift of eyes, countenance, color, lips, voice, tone, fingers, hands, arms, stance. Such revelation is not an object to be apprehended. Rather it works immediately upon my subjectivity, to make me share the other's seriousness or vivacity, ease or embarrassment, joy or sorrow; and similarly my response affects his subjectivity, leads him on to say more, or quietly and imperceptibly rebuffs him, holds him off, closes the door.

As phenomenology explores the whole drama of our interpersonal relations, so too it takes its stand within us, within that volume (defined by the nude statue) of sensing, feeling, reaching, longing space which is a human body, to make thematic our perceiving, the preconceptual activities of our intellects, the vertical liberty by which we may emerge out of prevoluntary and prepersonal process to become freely and responsibly, resolutely yet precariously, the persons we choose to be.

Still, what are we to choose to be? What are we to choose to make of ourselves? In our lives there still comes the moment of existential crisis when we find out for ourselves that we have to decide for ourselves what we by our own choices and decisions are to make of ourselves, but the psychologists and phenomenologists and existentialists have revealed to us our myriad potentialities without pointing out the tree of life, without unraveling the secret of good and evil. And when we turn from our mysterious interiority to the world about us for instruction, we are confronted with a similar multiplicity, an endless refinement; a great technical exactness, and an ultimate inconclusiveness.

When the educated, or the cultured, or the gentlemanly, or the saintly man was standardized by classical culture, then it was recognized that definitions were to be explained but not disputed. Today terms are still defined, but definitions are not unique: on the contrary, for each term there is a historical sequence of different definitions; there is a learned explanation for each change of definition; and there is no encouragement for the sanguine view that would exclude further developments in this changing series.

What is true of definitions is also true of doctrines. They exist, but they no longer enjoy the splendid isolation that compels their acceptance. We know their histories, the moment of their births, the course of their development, their interweaving, their moments of high synthesis, their periods of stagnation, decline, dissolution. We know the kind of subject to which they appeal and the kind they repel: Tell me what you think and I'll tell you why you think that way. But such endlessly erudite and subtle penetration generates detachment, relativism, scepticism. The spiritual atmosphere becomes too thin to support the life of man.

Shall we turn to authority? But even authorities are historical entities. It is easy enough to repeat what they said. It is a more complex task to say what they meant. There are indeed areas in which problems of interpretation do not occur. Euclid's *Elements* were written some twenty-three centuries ago, and, while one has to study to understand him, still, once one has understood, there exists no problem about his meaning. There is no hermeneutic literature on Euclid. But on Plato and Aristotle, on St Paul and St John, on Augustine and Aquinas, on Kant and Hegel, there are endless works of commentary, interpretation, exegesis, explanation; and there is no expectation that this stream will dry up, that a final word will be spoken.

In brief, the classical mediation of meaning has broken down. It is being replaced by a modern mediation of meaning that interprets our dreams and our symbols, that thematizes our wan smiles and limp gestures, that analyzes our minds and charts our souls, that takes the whole of human history for its kingdom to compare and relate languages and literatures, art forms and religions, family arrangements and customary morals, political, legal, educational, economic systems, sciences, philosophies, theologies, and histories. New books pour forth annually by the thousands; our libraries need ever more space. But the vast modern effort to understand meaning in all its manifestations has not been matched by a comparable effort in judging meaning. The effort to understand is the common task of unnumbered scientists and scholars. But judging and deciding are left to the individual, and he finds his plight desperate. There is far too much to be learnt before he could begin to judge. Yet judge he must and decide he must if he is to exist, if he is to be a man.

3 Conclusion

Many among you will find this picture too bleak. Many, especially, will point out that I have said nothing about the Catholic faith, Catholic philosophy, Catholic theology. On these, then, a word must be added.

The crisis, then, that I have been attempting to depict is a crisis not of faith but of culture. There has been no new revelation from on high to replace the revelation given through Jesus Christ. There has been written no new Bible, and there has been founded no new church, to link us with him. But Catholic philosophy and Catholic theology are matters, not merely of revelation and faith, but also of culture. Both have been fully and deeply involved in classical culture. The breakdown of classical culture and, at last in our day, the manifest comprehensiveness and exclusiveness of modern culture confront Catholic philosophy and Catholic theology with the gravest problems, impose upon them mountainous tasks, invite them to Herculean labors. Indeed, once philosophy becomes existential and historical, once it asks about man, not in the abstract, not as he would be in some state of pure nature, but as in fact he is here and now in all the concreteness of his living and dying, the very possibility of the old distinction between philosophy and theology vanishes. What is true of that distinction is true of others. What is true of distinctions also is true of each of the other techniques that mark the style and fashion the fabric of our cultural heritage. Classical culture cannot be jettisoned without being replaced; and what replaces it cannot but run counter to classical expectations. There is bound to be formed a solid right that is determined to live in a world that no longer exists. There is bound to be formed a scattered left, captivated by now this, now that new development, exploring now this and now that new possibility. But what will count is a perhaps not numerous center, big enough to be at home in both the old and the new, painstaking enough to work out one by one the transitions to be made, strong enough to refuse half measures and insist on complete solutions even though it has to wait.

Related selections: 1.I.1 on the problematic of *Insight*; 1.V on commonsense practicality; 2.V and 2.VIII on classicist and modern control of meaning; 4.V.1 on historicity; 3.III on the commonsense, theoretic, interior, and transcendent modes of conscious intentionality, their corresponding realms of meaning, and the differentiation of consciousness; 3.VIII.2 on differentiation of consciousness as a foundational category in theology; 4.I on the impact on theology and philosophy of the unfolding differentiations of consciousness; 4.II on the dialectic of authority; 4.III.2 on the second enlightenment.

V

The Future of Thomism

Lonergan's doctoral dissertation was a study of Aquinas's theology of grace. In the years immediately prior to writing *Insight*, Lonergan completed a lengthy study of Aquinas's concept of *verbum* or the inner word that is described by him as an effort to bring to the fore the latent cognitional theory underlying Aquinas's metaphysics. These preliminary studies convinced Lonergan of Aquinas's genius. But Lonergan was concerned to meet the demands of the modern situation in which the classical control of meaning has been radically undermined, historical consciousness has come to the fore, and the new human sciences are on the rise. He retained his high regard for Aquinas's genius but came to view him as a thinker meeting the challenges of an earlier age. 'Classical Thomism,' in Lonergan's view, lacks this historically conscious understanding of Aquinas and his thought; it also lacks a clear grasp of the cultural demands of the present time. Even in *Insight*, in which Lonergan's dominant concern is to construct a philosophy capable of accommodating the ongoing developments in modern natural science, he reports that his years 'reaching up to the mind of Aquinas' not only revealed to him what Aquinas's response to the demands of his time actually was, but also made clear to him the new and different challenges of our own time. In 'The Future of Thomism,' a lecture written in 1967 and delivered in 1968, Lonergan distinguishes between Aquinas himself and 'classical Thomism,' and describes five shifts of emphasis or transpositions 'classical Thomism' must undergo if it is to meet the challenges of our time.

The following extract is taken from *A Second Collection*, 47–52.

1 Classical Thomism

Classical Thomism prided itself on its fidelity to St Thomas. It met new questions by extending medieval solutions, and it could do so all the more confidently because of its classicist presuppositions. Truth is immutable. Human nature does not change. God has revealed Himself once and for all in Christ Jesus. It is true enough that times change and that circumstances alter cases. But all that change is incidental. The same eternal principles are equally valid and equally applicable despite the flux of accidental differences.

Along with other Scholastic schools, Thomism cultivated logic. It distinguished different meanings of the same term, and it defined each meaning. It reduced propositions to their presuppositions and worked out their implications. With meanings fixed by definitions, with presuppositions and implications fixed by the laws of logic, there resulted what used to be called eternal verities but today are known as static abstractions.

It derived its notion of science from Aristotle's *Posterior Analytics*. There is science properly so called, and there is science in some weaker, analogous sense. Properly so called, science consists in the conclusions that follow necessarily from self-evident, necessary principles. In some weaker, analogous sense, science consists in conclusions that follow not necessarily but probably; or its principles may be necessary without being evident to us; or they may be not even necessary but only what is fitting, convenient, suitable.

Thomism had much to say on the metaphysics of the soul, but it was little given to psychological introspection to gain knowledge of the subject. Behind this fact there did not lie any neglect of introspection on the part of Aristotle and Aquinas; I believe they hit things off much too accurately for that to be true. The difficulty was, I think, that while Aristotle did practice introspection, his works contain no account of introspective method. In his *De Anima* Aristotle employed one and the same method for the study of plants, animals, and men. One was to know acts by their objects, habits by acts, potencies by habits, and the essences of souls by their potencies. The procedure was purely objective, and made no explicit mention of direct introspection of acts and of their subjects. .

Human nature was studied extensively in a metaphysical psychology, in an enormous and subtle catalogue of virtues and vices, in its native capacities and proneness to evil, in the laws natural, divine, and human to which it was subject, in the great things it could accomplish by God's grace. But such study was not part of some ongoing process; everything essential had been said long ago; the only urgent task was

to find the telling mode of expression and illustration that would communicate to the uneducated of today the wisdom of the great men of
the past. As the study of man was static, so, too, man was conceived in
static fashion. There was no notion that man had existed on earth for
hundreds of thousands of years; or that there had been, and still was
going forward, an ascent from crude primitive cultures, through the
ancient high civilizations, to the effective emergence of critical intelligence in the first millennium B.C., and to the triumph of scientific
intelligence in the last few centuries.

Finally, classical Thomism stressed first principles. It did not undertake to give an exhaustive list of all first principles, each of them
defined with complete accuracy. But its commitment to logic and to
the Aristotelian notion of science was such that to deny first principles
was to involve oneself in scepticism, while to ignore them was to condemn oneself to superficiality.

2 Thomism for Tomorrow

A Thomism for tomorrow will involve, in my opinion, first a shift from
the emphases of classical Thomism and, secondly, a revision of the
results obtained by medieval theology.

To begin from the second point, the technique of the *quaestio* aimed
at a logically coherent reconciliation of conflicting authorities. It met
the demands of human intelligence seeking some understanding of its
faith, and it did so in the grand manner. But its scrutiny of the data
presented by Scripture and tradition was quite insufficient. On the
whole it was unaware of history: of the fact that every act of meaning is
embedded in a context, and that over time contexts change subtly,
slowly, surely. A contemporary theology must take and has taken the
fact of history into account. Inasmuch as it does so, St Thomas ceases to
be the arbiter to whom all can appeal for the solution of contemporary
questions; for, by and large, contemporary questions are not the same
as the questions he treated, and the contemporary context is not the
context in which he treated them. But he remains a magnificent and
venerable figure in the history of Catholic thought. He stands before us
as a model, inviting us to do for our age what he did for his. And, if I
may express a personal opinion of my own, a mature Catholic theology of the twentieth century will not ignore him; it will learn very,
very much from him; and it will be aware of its debt to him, even when

it is effecting its boldest transpositions from the thirteenth century to the twentieth.

What are such transpositions? I have prepared my answer to that question by my list of five emphases of classical Thomism. A Thomism for tomorrow has to move from logic to method; from science as conceived in the *Posterior Analytics* to science as it is conceived today; from the metaphysics of the soul to the self-appropriation of the subject; from an apprehension of man in terms of human nature to an apprehension of man through human history; and from first principles to transcendental method. Before considering these transitions singly, let me remark in general that they are not exclusive; a transition from logic to method does not drop logic, and similarly in most of the other cases.

First, then, from logic to method. Today we frequently hear complaints about metaphysics as static. But what is static is not metaphysics as such but a logically rigorous metaphysics. Indeed, anything that is logically rigorous is static. Defined terms are abstract and abstractions are immobile. Presuppositions and implications, if rigorous, cannot shift a single iota. Logic embodies an ideal of clarity, coherence, and rigor. It is an ideal that we must ever pursue, but the pursuit is a matter not of logic but of method. A method is a normative pattern of related and recurrent operations. There are operations: for instance, to take the simplest example, in natural science there are observing, describing, defining problems, making discoveries, formulating hypotheses, working out their presuppositions and implications, devising experiments, testing hypotheses by experiments, determining whether the hypothesis so far is satisfactory or already is unsatisfactory, and so proceeding to new questions or to a revision of the hypothesis already made. All such operations are related, for each leads to the next. They are recurrent, for they form a circle that is repeated over and over and cumulatively extends the mastery of human intelligence over ever broader fields of data. The pattern of such related and recurrent operations is normative, for that is the right way to do the job. Finally, while this pattern includes all logical operations, it also includes many operations that lie outside a formal logic, such as observing, discovering, experimenting, verifying.

Secondly, from the conception of science in the *Posterior Analytics* to the modern conception of a science. On point after point the two conceptions are opposed. In the Aristotelian notion necessity was a key

category; in modern science it is marginal; it has been replaced by verifiable possibility. For the Aristotelian, science is certain; for the modern, science is no more than probable, the best available scientific
opinion. For the Aristotelian, causality was material, formal, efficient,
exemplary, or final; for the modern, causality is correlation. For the
Aristotelian, a science was a habit in the mind of an individual; for the
modern, science is knowledge divided up among the scientific community; no one knows the whole of modern mathematics, of modern
physics, of modern chemistry, or modern biology, and so on.

Thirdly, from soul to subject. I do not mean that the metaphysical
notion of the soul and of its properties is to be dropped, any more than
I mean that logic is to be dropped. But I urge the necessity of a self-
appropriation of the subject, of coming to know at first hand oneself
and one's own operations both as a believer and as a theologian. It is
there that one will find the foundations of method, there that one will
find the invariants that enable one to steer a steady course, though
theological theories and opinions are subject to revision and change.
Without such a basis systematic theology will remain what it has been
too often in the past, a morass of questions disputed endlessly and
fruitlessly.

Fourthly, from human nature to human history. The point here is that
meaning is constitutive of human living. Just as words without sense
are gibberish, so human living uninformed by human meaning is infantile. Next, not only is meaning constitutive of human living but also it is
subject to change; cultures develop and cultures decline; meaning
flowers and meaning becomes decadent. Finally, Christianity is an historical religion; it is a statement of the meaning of human living; it is a
redeeming statement that cures decadence and fosters growth.

Fifthly, from first principles to transcendental method. First principles, logically first propositions, are the foundations for a mode of
thought that is inspired by logic, by necessity, by objectivity, by nature.
But the contemporary context, the tasks and problems of a theology
that would deal with the issues of today, call for method, verified possibility, full awareness of the subject, and a thorough grasp of man's
historicity. Its foundations lie, not in abstract propositions called first
principles, but in the structural invariants of the concrete human subject. When the natural and the human sciences are on the move, when
the social order is developing, when the everyday dimensions of culture are changing, what is needed is not a dam to block the stream but

control of the river-bed through which the stream must flow. In modern science, what is fixed is not the theory or system but the method that keeps generating, improving, replacing theories and systems. Transcendental method is the assault on the citadel; it is possession of the basic method, and all other methods are just so many extensions and adaptations of it ...

3 Conclusion

You may ask, however, whether after the introduction of the five transpositions just outlined there would be anything left of Thomism. And at once I must grant that the five emphases I attributed to classical Thomism would disappear. One may doubt, however, whether such emphases are essential to the thought of St. Thomas or of the great Thomists.

Related selections: 1.I on the program of *Insight*; 2.VIII.1 on pluralism and classicist culture; 2.IV.2 on classicist and modern controls of meaning; 3.IV.5 on interiorly grounded theology; 2.VI and 3.VIII.1–3 on the foundations required for a contemporary theology; 4.I on static and dynamic viewpoints and the notion of system; 3.VII.3 on the obtrusion in the natural and human sciences of issues that cannot be handled by empirical scientific method; 2.VII.1 on neglect of human subjectivity.

VI

Theology in Its New Context

In 'The New Context of Theology,' a lecture given in 1967, Lonergan outlines the challenges posed for Catholic theology by three centuries of cultural change and proposes a new type of foundation for theological inquiry and practice. While the new foundation has a specifically religious component in religious conversion, Lonergan's reflections on the challenges facing Catholic theology are historical rather than directly theological. The renewal of Catholic theology and its future cultural influence, Lonergan argues, will depend upon its ability to assimilate and adapt to recent and ongoing changes in the cultural context within which theology is practiced. Such a theology must be a methodical theology, one that finds its foundation through reflection on the concrete, dynamic, personal, communal, historical process of religious conversion. The lecture is presented in its entirety.

This extract is taken from *A Second Collection*, 55–67.

Any theology of renewal goes hand in hand with a renewal of theology. For 'renewal' is being used in a novel sense. Usually in Catholic circles 'renewal' has meant a return to the olden times of pristine virtue and deep wisdom. But good Pope John has made 'renewal' mean *'aggiornamento,'* bringing things up to date.

Obviously, if theology is to be brought up to date, it must have fallen behind the times. Again, if we are to know what is to be done to bring theology up to date, we must ascertain when it began to fall behind the times, in what respects it got out of touch, in what respects it failed to meet the issues and effect the developments that long ago were due and now are long overdue.

The answer I wish to suggest takes us back almost three centuries to the end of the seventeenth century and, more precisely, to the year 1680. For that, it seems, was the time of the great beginning. Then it was that Herbert Butterfield placed the origins of modern science, then that Paul Hazard placed the beginning of the Enlightenment, then that Yves Congar placed the beginning of dogmatic theology. When modern science began, when the Enlightenment began, then the theologians began to reassure one another about their certainties. Let me comment briefly on this threefold coincidence.

When Professor Butterfield placed the origins of modern science at the end of the seventeenth century, he by no means meant to deny that from the year 1300 on numerous discoveries were made that since have been included within modern science and integrated with it. But he did make the point that, at the time of their first appearance, these discoveries could not be expressed adequately. For, the dominant cultural context was Aristotelian, and the discoverers themselves had Aristotelian backgrounds. Thus there existed a conflict between the new ideas and the old doctrines, and this conflict existed not merely between an old guard of Aristotelians and a new breed of scientists but, far more gravely, within the very minds of the new scientists. For new ideas are far less than a whole mentality, a whole climate of thought and opinion, a whole mode of approach, and procedure, and judgment. Before these new ideas could be formulated accurately, coherently, cogently, they had to multiply, cumulate, coalesce to bring forth a new system of concepts and a new body of doctrine that was somehow comparable in extent to the Aristotelian and so capable of replacing it.

In brief, Professor Butterfield distinguished between new ideas and the context or horizon within which they were expressed, developed, related. From about the beginning of the fourteenth century the new ideas multiplied. But only towards the close of the seventeenth century did there emerge the context appropriate to these ideas. The origin of this context is for Professor Butterfield the origin of modern science and, in his judgment, 'it outshines everything since the rise of Christianity and reduces the Renaissance and the Reformation to the rank of mere episodes, mere internal displacements, within the system of medieval Christendom.'[1]

---

1 Herbert Butterfield, *The Origins of Modern Science, 1300–1800*, 2nd ed. (New York: Free Press, 1966), 7.

Coincident with the origins of modern science was the beginning of the Enlightenment, of the movement Peter Gay recently named the rise of modern paganism.[2] Moreover, while this movement is commonly located in the eighteenth century, the French academician Paul Hazard has exhibited already in full swing between the years of 1680 and 1715 a far-flung attack on Christianity from almost every quarter and in almost every style.[3] It was a movement revolted by the spectacle of religious persecution and religious war. It was to replace the God of the Christians by the God of the *philosophes* and, eventually, the God of the *philosophes* by agnosticism and atheism. It gloried in the achievements of Newton, criticized social structures, promoted political change, and moved towards a materialist, mechanist, determinist interpretation no less of man than of nature.[4]

It would be unfair to expect the theologians of the end of the seventeenth century to have discerned the good and the evil in the great movements of their time. But at least we may record what in fact they did do. They introduced 'dogmatic' theology. It is true that the word 'dogmatic' had been previously applied to theology. But then it was used to denote a distinction from moral, or ethical, or historical theology. Now it was employed in a new sense, in opposition to scholastic theology. It replaced the inquiry of the *quaestio* by the pedagogy of the thesis. It demoted the quest of faith for understanding to a desirable, but secondary, and indeed, optional goal. It gave basic and central significance to the certitudes of faith, their presuppositions, and their consequences. It owed its mode of proof to Melchior Cano and, as that theologian was also a bishop and inquisitor, so the new dogmatic theology not only proved its theses, but also was supported by the teaching authority and the sanctions of the Church.[5]

Such a conception of theology survived right into the twentieth century, and even today in some circles it is the only conception that is understood. Still, among theologians its limitations and defects have been becoming more and more apparent, especially since the 1890's. During the last seventy years, efforts to find remedies and to imple-

2 Peter Gay, *The Enlightenment: An Interpretation* (New York: Knopf, 1966).

3 *The European Mind* (London: Hollis and Carter, 1953).

4 The lasting influence of such enlightenment right up to the present has been illustrated rather fully by F.W. Matson, *The Broken Image* (New York: Doubleday, 1964).

5 See Yves Congar, 'Théologie,' *Dictionnaire de Théologie Catholique*, vol. 29 (Paris: Letouzey et Ane, 1899–1953), 432 f.

ment them have been going forward steadily, if unobtrusively. The measure of their success is the radically new situation brought to light by the Second Vatican Council.

There is, perhaps, no need for me here to insist that the novelty resides not in a new revelation or a new faith, but in a new cultural context. For a theology is a product not only of the religion it investigates and expounds but also of the cultural ideals and norms that set its problems and direct its solutions. Just as theology in the thirteenth century followed its age by assimilating Aristotle, just as theology in the seventeenth century resisted its age by retiring into a dogmatic corner, so theology today is locked in an encounter with its age. Whether it will grow and triumph, or whether it will wither to insignificance, depends in no small measure on the clarity and the accuracy of its grasp of the external cultural factors that undermine its past achievements and challenge it to new endeavors.

The topics, then, that I am to raise are not directly theological. For that very reason they are all the more apt to be overlooked in an age characterized by specialization. For the same reason it is all the more important to draw attention to them on such an occasion as the present, for the cultural context sets up an undertow that accounts for tendencies and exigences that must be met, yet, if not understood, are too easily neglected or thwarted because they seem superfluous, arbitrary, perplexing, disquieting, or dangerous.

First, then, theology was a deductive, and it has become largely an empirical science. It was a deductive science in the sense that its theses were conclusions to be proven from the premises provided by Scripture and Tradition. It has become an empirical science in the sense that Scripture and Tradition now supply not premises, but data. The data has to be viewed in its historical perspective. It has to be interpreted in the light of contemporary techniques and procedures. Where before the step from premises to conclusions was brief, simple, and certain, today the steps from data to interpretation are long, arduous, and, at best, probable. An empirical science does not demonstrate. It accumulates information, develops understanding, masters ever more of its materials, but it does not preclude the uncovering of further relevant data, the emergence of new insights, the attainment of a more comprehensive view.

Secondly, this shift from a deductivist to an empirical approach has come to stay. One has only to glance at the bibliographies in *Biblica*, in

Altaner's *Patrologie*, in the *Bulletin de théologie ancienne et médiévale*, and in *Ephemerides theologicae lovanienses*, to become aware of the massive commitment of contemporary Catholic thought to an empirical approach. But to understand this movement, to grasp the reasons for it, one must do more than glance at bibliographies; one has to get down to reading the books. Then one gradually discovers that the old dogmatic theology had misconceived history on a classicist model, that it thought not in terms of evolution and development, but of universality and permanence. Vincent of Lérins had proclaimed God's truth to be *quod semper, quod ubique, quod ab omnibus,*[6] and such a view was still quite congenial in the *grand siècle* of French literature.[7] On such assumptions it was quite legitimate to expect the theologian, if only he knew the faith of today, to be equally at home in the Old and New Testaments, in the Greek and Latin Fathers, in the writings of medieval, Renaissance, and more recent theologians. But today such an assumption appears fantastic and preposterous. In almost endless studies the writings of age after age have been examined minutely, and all along the line the notion of fixity has had to give way to the fact of development. Moreover, development is complex, intricate, manifold. Its precise character at any time can be ascertained only through detailed studies of the resources, the problems, the tendencies, and the accidents of the time. Where once the dogmatic theologian was supposed to range over centuries, now Scripture, patristics, medieval and modern studies are divided and subdivided among classes of specialists. Where once the dogmatic theologian could lay down an overall view that echoed the conciliar *tenet atque semper tenuit sancta mater Ecclesia,* now an overall view tends to be either a tentative summary of the present state of research, or a popular simplification of issues that are really not simple at all.

Thirdly, while theology has become largely empirical in its method, it has invoked a new vocabulary, new imagery, new concepts to express its thought. The Aristotelian analyses, concepts, words, that in the Middle Ages became part of the Catholic patrimony to resist both Renaissance scoffing and Protestant condemnation, almost suddenly in the twentieth century have gone out of fashion. With equal rapidity the vacuum is being refilled with biblical words and images, and with

6 *Commonitorium*, II (Cambridge: Cambridge University Press, 1915), 10.
7 See Owen Chadwick, *From Bossuet to Newman: The Idea of Doctrinal Development* (Cambridge: Cambridge University Press, 1957), 17 ff.

ideas worked out by historicist, personalist, phenomenological, and existential reflection. There is so much new in Catholic speculative theology that Karl Rahner felt the need to issue a *Theological Dictionary*[8] and Heinrich Fries organized over one hundred experts to collaborate and produce a two volume *Handbuch theologischer Grundbegriffe*.[9]

As the empirical approach, so too I believe, the new conceptual apparatus has come to stay. Religion is concerned with man's relations to God and to his fellow man, so that any deepening or enriching of our apprehension of man possesses religious significance and relevance. But the new conceptual apparatus does make available such a deepening and enriching. Without denying human nature, it adds the quite distinctive categories of man as an historical being. Without repudiating the analysis of man into body and soul, it adds the richer and more concrete apprehension of man as incarnate subject.

It would be far more than can be attempted within the limits of the present paper to attempt to communicate what precisely is meant by the contrast between nature and history or what is added to the couple, body and soul, by the phrase 'incarnate subject.' Summarily, very summarily, I may perhaps say that such terms refer to a dimension of human reality that has always existed, that has always been lived and experienced, that classicist thought standardized yet tended to overlook, that modern studies have brought to light, thematized, elaborated, illustrated, documented. That dimension is the constitutive role of meaning in human living. It is the fact that acts of meaning inform human living, that such acts proceed from a free and responsible subject incarnate, that meanings differ from nation to nation, from culture to culture, and that, over time, they develop and go astray. Besides the meanings by which man apprehends nature and the meanings by which he transforms it, there are the meanings by which man thinks out the possibilities of his own living and makes his choice among them. In this realm of freedom and creativity, of solidarity and responsibility, of dazzling achievement and pitiable madness, there ever occurs man's making of man.

The wealth, the complexity, the profundity of this modern apprehension of man might be illustrated by pointing to its implications for philosophy, for human science, for art and literature, for education and

8 Karl Rahner, *Theological Dictionary* (New York: Herder and Herder, 1965).
9 *Handbuch theologischer Grundbegriffe*, ed. Heinrich Fries (Munich: Kösel, 1962, 1963).

psychiatry. But what must be mentioned is its significance for the notion of divine revelation. God becomes known to us in two ways: as the ground and end of the material universe; and as the one who speaks to us through Scripture and Tradition. The first manner might found a natural religion. The second adds revealed religion. For the first, one might say that the heavens show forth the glory of God; what can mere words add? But for the second, one must answer that, however trifling the uses to which words may be put, still they are the vehicles of meaning, and meaning is the stuff of man's making of man. So it is that a divine revelation is God's entry and his taking part in man's making of man. It is God's claim to have a say in the aims and purposes, the direction and development of human lives, human societies, human cultures, human history.

From this significance for revealed religion there follows a significance for theology. In the medieval period theology became the queen of the sciences. But in the practice of Aquinas it was also the principle for the molding and transforming of a culture. He was not content to write his systematic works, his commentaries on Scripture and on such Christian writers as the Pseudo-Dionysius and Boethius. At a time when Arabic and Greek thought were penetrating the whole of Western culture, he wrote extensive commentaries on numerous works of Aristotle to fit a pagan's science within a Christian context and to construct a world view that underpinned Dante's *Divine Comedy*. To this paradigm theology today must look if it is to achieve its *aggiornamento*. Its task is not limited to investigating, ordering, expounding, communicating divine revelation. All that is needed, but more must be done. For revelation is God's entry into man's making of man, and so theology not only has to reflect on revelation, but also it has somehow to mediate God's meaning into the whole of human affairs. It is not a small task, but because it is not – in a culture in which God is ignored and there are even theologians to proclaim that God is dead – it is all the more urgent.

My reflections have come full circle. Not only does the cultural context influence theology to undo its past achievements, but theology is also called upon to influence the cultural context, to translate the word of God and so project it into new mentalities and new situations. So a contemporary Catholic theology has to be not only Catholic but also ecumenist. Its concern must reach not only Christians but also non-Christians and atheists. It has to learn to draw not only on the modern philosophies but also on the relatively new sciences of religion, psychology, sociology, and the new techniques of the communication arts.

I have been speaking of our renewed theology and now I must add that a renewed theology needs a renewed foundation. The old foundation will no longer do. But we cannot get along with no foundation at all. So a new foundation and, I should say, a new type of foundation is needed to replace the old.

First, some foundation is needed. If change is to be improvement, if new tasks are to be accomplished fruitfully, discernment is needed and discrimination. If we are to draw on contemporary psychology and sociology, if we are to profit from the modern science of religions, if we are to revise scholastic categories and make our own the concepts worked out in historicist, personalist, phenomenological, or existentialist circles, then we must be able to distinguish tinsel and silver, gilt and gold. No less important than a critique of notions and conclusions is a critique of methods. The new largely empirical approach to theology can too easily be made into a device for reducing doctrines to probable opinions. A hermeneutics can pretend to philosophic neutrality yet force the conclusion that the content of revelation is mostly myth. Scientific history can be so conceived that a study of the narrative of salvation will strip it of matters of fact. If our renewed theology is not to be the dupe of every fashion, it needs a firm basis and a critical stance.

Secondly, the old foundations will no longer do. In saying this I do not mean that they are no longer true, for they are as true now as they ever were. I mean that they are no longer appropriate. I am simply recalling that one must not patch an old cloak with new cloth or put new wine in old wineskins. One type of foundation suits a theology that aims at being deductive, static, abstract, universal, equally applicable to all places and to all times. A quite different foundation is needed when theology turns from deductivism to an empirical approach, from the static to the dynamic, from the abstract to the concrete, from the universal to the historical totality of particulars, from invariable rules to intelligent adjustment and adaptation.

Thirdly, I shall no doubt be asked to give some indication of the nature or character of the new foundation. To this topic I have elsewhere given considerable attention, first, to assure historical continuity, in a study of cognitional theory in the writings of St. Thomas,[10] then in a study of contemporary development entitled *Insight*, to take into account the fact of modern science and the problems of modern philosophy. On the present occasion I may be permitted, perhaps, to offer no more than a few brief approximations.

As a first approximation, to be corrected and complemented shortly by further approximations, let us consider the foundation of a modern science. It does not consist in any part of the science itself, in any of its conclusions, in any of its laws, in any of its principles. All of these are open to revision, and it is in the light of the foundation that the revision would take place. What, then, is the foundation? It is the method that will generate the revision of conclusions, laws, principles that are accepted today. It is the method that will generate the revision of conclusions, laws, principles of tomorrow. What the scientist relies on ultimately is his method.

Now one might be inclined to think of method as a set of verbal propositions enouncing rules to be followed in a scientific investigation and, of course, it is true that there are the hodmen of science who carry out the routines prescribed to them by those who understand the purpose of an investigation and the manner in which it might advance scientific knowledge. But I wish here to use the word 'method' to denote not the prescriptions given the hodmen, but the grounds that governed the prescribing. Such grounds, though perfectly familiar to the director, usually are not objectified or verbalized by him. Indeed, he cannot achieve such objectification with any accuracy, unless he is ready to devote as much time and effort to cognitional theory as he has already devoted to his physics, or chemistry, or biology. This does not happen. But, were it to happen, there would result the account of a normative pattern that related to one another the cognitional operations that recur in scientific investigations. There would be listed, described, illustrated, compared such operations as inquiring, observing, describing, problem defining, discovering, forming hypotheses, working out presuppositions and implications, devising series of experiments, performing them, and verifying. The greatest stress would be placed on the importance of personal experience of the operations, of identifying them within one's experience, and of finding

10 *Verbum.*

within that experience not only the operations, but also the dynamic and normative relations that bind them to one another. In this fashion, you will agree, the subject as scientist would come to know himself as scientist. But the subject as scientist is the reality that is principle and foundation of science, of science as it has been, of science as it is, of science as it will be.

So much for our first approximation. It illustrates by an example what might be meant by a foundation that lies not in a set of verbal propositions named first principles, but in a particular, concrete, dynamic reality generating knowledge of particular, concrete, dynamic realities. It remains that we have to effect the transition from natural science to theology, and so we turn to our second approximation.

Fundamental to religious living is conversion. It is a topic little studied in traditional theology since there remains very little of it when one reaches the universal, the abstract, the static. For conversion occurs in the lives of individuals. It is not merely a change or even a development; rather, it is a radical transformation on which follows, on all levels of living, an interlocked series of changes and developments. What hitherto was unnoticed becomes vivid and present. What had been of no concern becomes a matter of high import. So great a change in one's apprehensions and one's values accompanies no less a change in oneself, in one's relations to other persons, and in one's relations to God.

Not all conversion is as total as the one I have so summarily described. Conversion has many dimensions. A changed relation to God brings or follows changes that are personal, social, moral and intellectual. But there is no fixed rule of antecedence and consequence, no necessity of simultaneity, no prescribed magnitudes of change. Conversion may be compacted into the moment of a blinded Saul falling from his horse on the way to Damascus. It may be extended over the slow maturing process of a lifetime. It may satisfy an intermediate measure.

In a current expression, conversion is ontic. The convert apprehends differently, values differently, relates differently because he has become different. The new apprehension is not so much a new statement or a new set of statements, but rather new meanings that attach to almost any statement. It is not new values so much as a transvaluation of values. In Pauline language, 'When anyone is united to Christ, there is a new world; the old order has gone, and a new order has begun' (2 Cor. 5:17).

Though conversion is intensely personal, utterly intimate, still it is not so private as to be solitary. It can happen to many and they can form a community to sustain one another in their self-transformation, and to help one another in working out the implications, and in fulfilling the promise of their new life. Finally, what can become communal can become historical. It can pass from generation to generation. It can spread from one cultural milieu to another. It can adapt to changing circumstance, confront new situations, survive into a different age, flourish in another period or epoch.

When conversion is viewed as an ongoing process, at once personal, communal, and historical, it coincides with living religion. For religion is conversion in its preparation, in its occurrence, in its development, in its consequents, and also, alas, in its incompleteness, its failures, its breakdowns, its disintegration.

Now theology, and especially the empirical theology of today, is reflection on religion. It follows that theology will be reflection on conversion. But conversion is fundamental to religion. It follows that reflection on conversion can supply theology with its foundation and, indeed, with a foundation that is concrete, dynamic, personal, communal, and historical. Just as reflection on the operations of the scientist brings to light the real foundation of the science, so too reflection on the ongoing process of conversion may bring to light the real foundation of a renewed theology.

I met the question of theological renewal, of its *aggiornamento*, by asking how far we are behind the times. I went back three centuries, for it was then that dogmatic theology had its beginnings, and it has been towards a total transformation of dogmatic theology that the developments of this century have worked. A normative structure that was deductivist has become empirical. A conceptual apparatus that at times clung pathetically to the past is yielding place to historicist, personalist, phenomenological, and existentialist notions.

I have urged that so great a transformation needs a renewed foundation, and that the needed renewal is the introduction of a new type of foundation. It is to consist not in objective statement, but in subjective reality. The objective statements of a *de vera religione, de Christo legato, de ecclesia, de inspiratione scripturae, de locis theologicis,* are as much in need of a foundation as are those of other tracts. But behind all statements is the stating subject. What is normative and foundational for subjects stating theology is to be found, I have suggested, in reflection on conversion, where conversion is taken as an ongoing process, concrete and dynamic, personal, communal, and historical.

Related selections: 3.V.1–3 for Lonergan's proposed method for theology; 3.VII.2 on foundational significance of intellectual, moral, and religious conversion; 3.VIII.1–4 on the bases of the categories for the proposed method; 2.V.2 on renewed Thomism; 2.II and 3.IV.2 on religious experience; 4.I on the transformation of theology demanded by the shift from a static to a dynamic viewpoint; 4.III.1–2 on the outer conditions of the emergence of a new religious consciousness.

The Subject

In 1968 Lonergan gave the Aquinas Lecture at Marquette University. The entire text of that lecture is presented here. In *Insight* Lonergan argues that inadequate or mistaken conceptions of human knowing lie at the root of inadequate or mistaken conceptions of self-knowledge, being, and objectivity. Further, knowing is an essential component of mathematical, scientific, and commonsense activities. In all those endeavors, then, more or less explicit conceptions of knowing, self-knowledge, being, and objectivity are at work. Inasmuch as the chosen involvements of mathematicians, scientists, and men and women of common sense preclude their engagement in serious philosophizing, these fundamental guiding conceptions are adopted from the reigning philosophies of the times. Accordingly, it is the philosopher's basic responsibility to carry out a thorough and accurate analysis of human knowing and to provide for those engaged in other endeavors adequate guiding conceptions of knowing, self-knowledge, being, and objectivity.

Lonergan begins this lecture by drawing our attention to the essential philosophic component of each person's horizon or viewpoint. He then proceeds to ask why serious study of the knowing subject has been neglected. The neglect, he argues, has its cultural source in objectivism, in the persistence of an Aristotelian notion of science, and in the priority traditionally given to metaphysics. The neglect is enforced by behaviorist, logical positivist, and pragmatist philosophies, rationalized by conceptualism, challenged but only partially overcome by idealist philosophies. Finally, existentialism opens the door to a study of the subject in its self-determining freedom, but it does so without having first solved the ancient problems of cognitional theory, epistemology, and metaphysics. In his discussion of the existential subject, Lonergan expands his earlier account of the fourth level of human consciousness, rational self-consciousness, and reflects at length on the continuity of the subject's free and responsible orientation towards value, with its orientation towards knowledge and truth. In 'The Subject,' Lonergan offers a concise clarification of his position by contrasting it with traditional and contemporary philosophical orientations.

This extract is taken from *A Second Collection*, 69–86.

There is a sense in which it may be said that each of us lives in a world of his own. That world usually is a bounded world, and its boundary is fixed by the range of our interests and our knowledge. There are things that exist, that are known to other men, but about them I know nothing at all. There are objects of interest that concern other men, but about them I could not care less. So the extent of our knowledge and the reach of our interests fix a horizon. Within that horizon we are confined.

Such confinement may result from the historical tradition within which we are born, from the limitations of the social milieu in which we were brought up, from our individual psychological aptitudes, efforts, misadventures. But besides specifically historical, social, and psychological determinants of subjects and their horizons, there are also philosophic factors, and to a consideration of such factors the present occasion invites us.

1   The Neglected Subject

In contemporary philosophy there is a great emphasis on the subject, and this emphasis may easily be traced to the influence of Hegel, Kierkegaard, Nietzsche, Heidegger, Buber.[1] This fact, however, points to a previous period of neglect, and it may not be amiss to advert to the causes of such neglect, if only to make sure that they are no longer operative in our own thinking.

---

1 One should, perhaps, start from Kant's Copernican revolution, which brought the subject into technical prominence while making only minimal concessions to its reality. The subsequent movement then appears as a series of attempts to win for the subject acknowledgement of its full reality and its functions. For a careful survey of the movement and its ambiguities, see James Brown, *Subject and Object in Modern Theology* (New York: Macmillan, 1955).

A first cause, then, is the objectivity of truth. The criterion, I believe, by which we arrive at the truth is a virtually unconditioned.[2] But an unconditioned has no conditions. A subject may be needed to arrive at truth, but, once truth is attained, one is beyond the subject and one has reached a realm that is non-spatial, atemporal, impersonal. What is true at any time or place, can be contradicted only by falsity. No one can gainsay it, unless he is mistaken and errs.

Such is the objectivity of truth. But do not be fascinated by it. Intentionally it is independent of the subject, but ontologically it resides only in the subject: *veritas formaliter est in solo iudicio* [truth is formally found only in judgment]. Intentionally it goes completely beyond the subject, yet it does so only because ontologically the subject is capable of an intentional self-transcendence, of going beyond what he feels, what he imagines, what he thinks, what seems to him, to something utterly different, to what is so. Moreover, before the subject can attain the self-transcendence of truth, there is the slow and laborious process of conception, gestation, parturition. But teaching and learning, investigating, coming to understand, marshalling and weighing the evidence, these are not independent of the subject, of times and places, of psychological, social, historical conditions. The fruit of truth must grow and mature on the tree of the subject, before it can be plucked and placed in the absolute realm.

It remains that one can be fascinated by the objectivity of truth, that one can so emphasize objective truth as to disregard or undermine the very conditions of its emergence and existence. In fact, if at the present time among Catholics there is discerned a widespread alienation from the dogmas of faith, this is not unconnected with a previous one-sidedness that so insisted on the objectivity of truth as to leave subjects and their needs out of account.

Symptomatic of such one-sidedness was the difficulty experienced by theologians from the days of Suarez, de Lugo, and Bañez, when confronted with the syllogism: What God has revealed is true. God has revealed the mysteries of faith. Therefore, the mysteries of faith are

---

2 The formally unconditioned has no conditions whatever; it is God. The virtually unconditioned has conditions but they have been fulfilled. Such, I should say, is the cognitional counterpart of contingent being and, as well, a technical formulation of the ordinary criterion of true judgment, namely, sufficient evidence. See my book, *Insight*, chap. 10, for more details [see 1.VII in this reader].

true.[3] There is, perhaps, no need for me to explain why this syllogism was embarrassing, for it implied that the mysteries of faith were demonstrable conclusions. But the point I wish to make is that the syllogism contains an unnoticed fallacy, and the fallacy turns on an exaggerated view of the objectivity of truth. If one recalls that truth exists formally only in judgments and that judgments exist only in the mind, then the fallacy is easily pinned down. What God reveals is a truth in the mind of God and in the minds of believers, but it is not a truth in the minds of nonbelievers; and to conclude that the mysteries of faith, are truths in the mind of God or in the minds of believers in no way suggests that the mysteries are demonstrable. But this simple way out seems to have been missed by the theologians. They seem to have thought of truth as so objective as to get along without minds. Nor does such thinking seem to have been confined to theoretical accounts of the act of faith. The same insistence on objective truth and the same neglect of its subjective conditions informed the old catechetics, which the new catechetics is replacing, and the old censorship, which insisted on true propositions and little understood the need to respect the dynamics of the advance toward truth.

Another source of neglect of the subject is to be found remotely in the Aristotelian notion of science, propounded in the *Posterior Analytics*, and proximately in the rationalist notion of pure reason. When scientific and philosophic conclusions follow necessarily from premises that are self-evident, then the road to science and to philosophy is not straight and narrow but broad and easy. There is no need to be concerned with the subject. No matter who he is, no matter what his interests, almost no matter how cursory his attention, he can hardly fail to grasp what is self-evident and, having grasped it, he can hardly fail to draw conclusions that are necessary. On such assumptions everything is black or white. If one happens to have opinions, one will have to defend them as self-evident or demonstrable. If one begins to doubt, one is likely to end up a complete sceptic. There is no need for concern with the subject, for the maieutic art of a Socrates, for intellectual conversion, for open-mindedness, striving, humility, perseverance.

A third source of neglect of the subject is the metaphysical account

3 See H. Lennerz, *De Virtutibus Theologicis* (Rome: Gregorian University Press, 1947), 98 f., 103, no. 196, 204; L. Billot, *De Virtutibus Infusis* (Rome: Gregorian University Press, 1928), 191 ff., 313.

of the soul. As plants and animals, so men have souls. As in plants and animals, so in men the soul is the first act of an organic body. Still the souls of plants differ essentially from the souls of animals, and the souls of both differ essentially from the souls of men. To discern these differences we must turn from the soul to its potencies, habits, acts, objects. Through the objects we know the acts, through the acts we know the habits, through the habits we know the potencies, and through the potencies we know the essence of soul. The study of the soul, then, is totally objective. One and the same method is applied to study of plants, animals, and men. The results are completely universal. We have souls whether we are awake or asleep, saints or sinners, geniuses or imbeciles.

The study of the subject is quite different, for it is the study of oneself inasmuch as one is conscious. It prescinds from the soul, its essence, its potencies, its habits, for none of these is given in consciousness. It attends to operations and to their center and source which is the self. It discerns the different levels of consciousness, the consciousness of the dream, of the waking subject, of the intelligently inquiring subject, of the rationally reflecting subject, of the responsibly deliberating subject. It examines the different operations on the several levels and their relations to one another.

Subject and soul, then, are two quite different topics. To know one does not exclude the other in any way. But it very easily happens that the study of the soul leaves one with the feeling that one has no need to study the subject and, to that extent, leads to a neglect of the subject.[4]

2   The Truncated Subject

The neglected subject does not know himself. The truncated subject not only does not know himself but also is unaware of his ignorance and so, in one way or another, concludes that what he does not know does not exist. Commonly enough the palpable facts of sensation and speech are admitted. Commonly also there is recognized the difference between sleeping and waking. But if universal, daytime somnambulism is not upheld, behaviorists would pay no attention to the inner workings of the subject; logical positivists would confine meaning to

---

4 For a contrast of Aristotle and Augustine and their relations to Aquinas, see the Introduction in my *Verbum*.

sensible data and the structures of mathematical logic; pragmatists would divert our attention to actions and results.

But there are less gross procedures. One can accept an apparently reasonable rule of acknowledging what is certain and disregarding what is controverted. Almost inevitably this will lead to an oversight of insight. For it is easy enough to be certain about concepts; their existence can be inferred from linguistic usage and from scientific generality. But it is only by close attention to the data of consciousness that one can discover insights, acts of understanding with the triple role of responding to inquiry, grasping intelligible form in sensible representations, and grounding the formation of concepts. So complex a matter will never be noticed as long as the subject is neglected, and so there arises conceptualism: a strong affirmation of concepts, and a sceptical disregard of insights. As insights fulfil three functions, so conceptualism has three basic defects.

A first defect is an anti-historical immobilism. Human understanding develops and, as it develops, it expresses itself in ever more precise and accurate concepts, hypotheses, theories, systems. But conceptualism, as it disregards insight, so it cannot account for the development of concepts. Of themselves, concepts are immobile. They ever remain just what they are defined to mean. They are abstract and so stand outside the spatio-temporal world of change. What does change, is human understanding and, when understanding changes or develops, then defining changes or develops. So it is that, while concepts do not change on their own, still they are changed as the mind that forms them changes.

A second defect of conceptualism is an excessive abstractness. For the generalities of our knowledge are related to concrete reality in two distinct manners. There is the relation of the universal to the particular, of *man* to *this man*, of *circle* to *this circle*. There is also the far more important relation of the intelligible to the sensible, of the unity or pattern grasped by insight to the data in which the unity or pattern is grasped. Now this second relation, which parallels the relation of form to matter, is far more intimate than the first. The universal abstracts from the particular, but the intelligibility, grasped by insight, is immanent in the sensible and, when the sensible datum, image, symbol, is removed, the insight vanishes. But conceptualism ignores human understanding and so it overlooks the concrete mode of understanding that grasps intelligibility in the sensible itself. It is confined to a world of abstract universals, and its only link with the concrete is the relation of universal to particular.

A third defect of conceptualism has to do with the notion of being. Conceptualists have no difficulty in discovering a concept of being, indeed, in finding it implicit in every positive concept. But they think of it as an abstraction, as the most abstract of all abstractions, least in connotation and greatest in denotation. In fact, the notion of being is not abstract but concrete. It intends everything about everything. It prescinds from nothing whatever. But to advert to this clearly and distinctly, one must note not only that concepts express acts of understanding but also that both acts of understanding and concepts respond to questions. The notion of being first appears in questioning. Being is the unknown that questioning intends to know, that answers partially reveal, that further questioning presses on to know more fully. The notion of being, then, is essentially dynamic, proleptic, an anticipation of the entirety, the concreteness, the totality, that we ever intend and since our knowledge is finite never reach.

The neglected subject, then, leads to the truncated subject, to the subject that does not know himself and so unduly impoverishes his account of human knowledge. He condemns himself to an anti-historical immobilism, to an excessively jejune conjunction between abstract concepts and sensible presentations, and to ignorance of the proleptic and utterly concrete character of the notion of being.

3 The Immanentist Subject

The subject is within but he does not remain totally within. His knowing involves an intentional self-transcendence. But while his knowing does so, he has to know his knowing to know that it does so. Such knowledge is denied the neglected and the truncated subject and so we come to the merely immanent subject.

The key to doctrines of immanence is an inadequate notion of objectivity. Human knowing is a compound of many operations of different kinds. It follows that the objectivity of human knowing is not some single uniform property but once more a compound of quite different properties found in quite different kinds of operation.[5] There is an

5 For a fuller statement, *Insight*, chap. 13 [1.x in this reader], and for something more compendious, *Collection* 211–14.

experiential objectivity in the givenness of the data of sense and of the data of consciousness. But such experiential objectivity is not the one and only ingredient in the objectivity of human knowing. The process of inquiry, investigation, reflection, coming to judge is governed throughout by the exigences of human intelligence and human reasonableness; it is these exigences that, in part, are formulated in logics and methodologies; and they are in their own way no less decisive than experiential objectivity in the genesis and progress of human knowing. Finally, there is a third, terminal, or absolute type of objectivity, that comes to the fore when we judge, when we distinguish sharply between what we feel, what we imagine, what we think, what seems to be so and, on the other hand, what is so.

However, though these three components all function in the objectivity of adult human knowing, still it is one thing for them to function and it is quite another to become explicitly aware that they function. Such explicit awareness presupposes that one is not a truncated subject, aware indeed of his sensations and his speech, but aware of little more than that. Then, what is meant by an 'object' and 'objective,' is something to be settled not by any scrutiny of one's operations and their properties, but by picture-thinking. An object, for picture-thinking, has to be something one looks at; knowing it has to be something like looking, peering, seeing, intuiting, perceiving; and objectivity, finally, has to be a matter of seeing all that is there to be seen and nothing that is not there.

Once picture-thinking takes over, immanence is an inevitable consequence.[6] What is intended in questioning, is not seen, intuited, perceived; it is as yet unknown; it is what we do not know but seek to know. It follows that the intention of questioning, the notion of being, is merely immanent, merely subjective. Again, what is grasped in understanding, is not some further datum added on to the data of sense and of consciousness; on the contrary, it is quite unlike all data; it consists in an intelligible unity or pattern that is, not perceived, but understood; and it is understood, not as necessarily relevant to the data, but only as possibly relevant. Now the grasp of something that is possibly relevant is nothing like seeing, intuiting, perceiving, which regard only what is actually there. It follows that, for picture-thinking,

6 Provided, of course, one's account of human intellect is not more picture-thinking, with human intelligence a matter of looking.

understanding too must be merely immanent and merely subjective. What holds for understanding, also holds for concepts, for concepts express what has been grasped by understanding. What holds for concepts, holds no less for judgments, since judgments proceed from a reflective understanding, just as concepts proceed from a direct or inverse understanding.

This conclusion of immanence is inevitable, once picture-thinking is admitted. For picture-thinking means thinking in visual images. Visual images are incapable of representing or suggesting the normative exigences of intelligence and reasonableness, and, much less, their power to effect the intentional self-transcendence of the subject.

The foregoing account, however, though it provides the key to doctrines of immanence, provides no more than a key. It is a general model based on knowledge of the subject. It differs from actual doctrines of immanence, inasmuch as the latter are the work of truncated subjects that have only a partial apprehension of their own reality. But it requires, I think, no great discernment to find a parallel between the foregoing account and, to take but a single example, the Kantian argument for immanence. In this argument the effective distinction is between immediate and mediate relations of cognitional activities to objects. Judgment is only a mediate knowledge of objects, a representation of a representation.[7] Reason is never related right up to objects but only to understanding and, through understanding, to the empirical use of reason itself.[8]

Since our only cognitional activity immediately related to objects is intuition,[9] it follows that the value of our judgments and our reasoning can be no more than the value of our intuitions. But our only intuitions are sensitive; sensitive intuitions reveal not being but phenomena; and so our judgments and reasoning are confined to a merely phenomenal world.[10]

Such, substantially, seems to be the Kantian argument. It is a quite valid argument if one means by 'object' what one can settle by picture-thinking. 'Object' is what one looks at; looking is sensitive intuition; it

---

7 Kant, *Kritik der reinen Vernunft*, A 68, B 93.
8 Ibid., A 643, B 671.
9 Ibid., A 19, B 33.
10 See F. Copleston, *A History of Philosophy* (New York: Doubleday, 1985), vol. 6, chap. 12, nos. 1 and 8. Contrast with discussion of E. Gilson and E. Coreth in *Collection*, 188–204.

alone is immediately related to objects; understanding and reason can be related to objects only mediately, only through sensitive intuition.

Moreover, the neglected and truncated subject is not going to find the answer to Kant, for he does not know himself well enough to break the hold of picture-thinking and to discover that human cognitional activities have as their object being, that the activity immediately related to this object is questioning, that other activities such as sense and consciousness, understanding and judgment, are related mediately to the object, being, inasmuch as they are the means of answering questions, of reaching the goal intended by questioning.

There is a final point to be made. The transition from the neglected and truncated subject to self-appropriation is not a simple matter. It is not just a matter of finding out and assenting to a number of true propositions. More basically, it is a matter of conversion, of a personal philosophic experience, of moving out of a world of sense and of arriving, dazed and disorientated for a while, into a universe of being.

4   The Existential Subject

So far, our reflections on the subject have been concerned with him as a knower, as one that experiences, understands, and judges. We have now to think of him as a doer, as one that deliberates, evaluates, chooses, acts. Such doing, at first sight, affects, modifies, changes the world of objects. But even more it affects the subject himself. For human doing is free and responsible. Within it is contained the reality of morals, of building up or destroying character, of achieving personality or failing in that task. By his own acts the human subject makes himself what he is to be, and he does so freely and responsibly; indeed, he does so precisely because his acts are the free and responsible expressions of himself.

Such is the existential subject. It is a notion that is overlooked on the schematism of older categories that distinguished faculties, such as intellect and will, or different uses of the same faculty, such as speculative and practical intellect, or different types of human activity, such as theoretical inquiry and practical execution. None of these distinctions adverts to the subject as such and, while the reflexive, self-constitutive element in moral living has been known from ancient times, still it was not coupled with the notion of the subject to draw attention to him in his key role of making himself what he is to be.

Because the older schemes are not relevant, it will aid clarity if I indicate the new scheme of distinct but related levels of consciousness, in which the existential subject stands, so to speak, on the top level. For we are subjects, as it were, by degrees. At a lowest level, when unconscious in dreamless sleep or in a coma, we are merely potentially subjects. Next, we have a minimal degree of consciousness and subjectivity when we are the helpless subjects of our dreams. Thirdly, we become experiential subjects when we awake, when we become the subjects of lucid perception, imaginative projects, emotional and conative impulses, and bodily action. Fourthly, the intelligent subject sublates the experiential, i.e., it retains, preserves, goes beyond, completes it, when we inquire about our experience, investigate, grow in understanding, express our inventions and discoveries. Fifthly, the rational subject sublates the intelligent and experiential subject, when we question our own understanding, check our formulations and expressions, ask whether we have got things right, marshal the evidence *pro* and *con*, judge this to be so and that not to be so. Sixthly, finally, rational consciousness is sublated by rational self-consciousness, when we deliberate, evaluate, decide, act. Then there emerges human consciousness at its fullest. Then the existential subject exists and his character, his personal essence, is at stake.

The levels of consciousness are not only distinct but also related, and the relations are best expressed as instances of what Hegel named sublation, of a lower being retained, preserved, yet transcended and completed by a higher.[11] Human intelligence goes beyond human sensitivity yet it cannot get along without sensitivity. Human judgment goes beyond sensitivity and intelligence yet cannot function except in conjunction with them. Human action finally, must in similar fashion both presuppose and complete human sensitivity, intelligence, and judgment.

It is, of course, this fact of successive sublations that is denoted by the metaphor of levels of consciousness. But besides their distinction and their functional interdependence, the levels of consciousness are united by the unfolding of a single transcendental intending of plural, interchangeable objectives.[12] What promotes the subject from experi-

---

11 This omits, however, the Hegelian view that the higher reconciles a contradiction in the lower.

12 These objectives are approximately the Scholastic transcendentals, *ens, unum, verum, bonum,* and they are interchangeable in the sense of mutual predication, of *convertuntur.*

ential to intellectual consciousness is the desire to understand, the intention of intelligibility. What next promotes him from intellectual to rational consciousness, is a fuller unfolding of the same intention: for the desire to understand, once understanding is reached, becomes the desire to understand correctly; in other words, the intention of intelligibility, once an intelligible is reached, becomes the intention of the right intelligible, of the true and, through truth, of reality. Finally, the intention of the intelligible, the true, the real, becomes also the intention of the good, the question of value, of what is worthwhile, when the already acting subject confronts his world and adverts to his own acting in it.

I am suggesting that the transcendental notion of the good regards value. It is distinct from the particular good that satisfies individual appetite, such as the appetite for food and drink, the appetite for union and communion, the appetite for knowledge, or virtue, or pleasure. Again, it is distinct from the good of order, the objective arrangement or institution that ensures for a group of people the regular recurrence of particular goods. As appetite wants breakfast, so an economic system is to ensure breakfast every morning. As appetite wants union, so marriage is to ensure life-long union. As appetite wants knowledge, so an educational system ensures the imparting of knowledge to each successive generation. But beyond the particular good and the good of order, there is the good of value. It is by appealing to value or values that we satisfy some appetites and do not satisfy others, that we approve some systems for achieving the good of order and disapprove of others, that we praise or blame human persons as good or evil and their actions as right or wrong.

What, then, is value? I should say that it is a transcendental notion like the notion of being. Just as the notion of being intends but, of itself, does not know being, so too the notion of value intends but, of itself, does not know value. Again, as the notion of being is a dynamic principle that keeps us moving toward ever fuller knowledge of being, so the notion of value is the fuller flowering of the same dynamic principle that now keeps us moving toward ever fuller realization of the good, of what is worthwhile.

This may seem nebulous, so I beg leave to introduce a parallel. There is to Aristotle's *Ethics* an empiricism that seems almost question-begging. He could write, 'Actions ... are called just and temperate when they are such as the just or the temperate man would do; but it is not the man who does these that is just and temperate, but the man who also does them *as* just and temperate men do them.'[13] Again, he could add, 'Virtue ... is a state of character concerned with choice, lying in a mean, i.e., the mean relative to us, this being determined by a rational principle, and by that principle by which the man of practical wisdom would determine it.'[14] Aristotle, it seems to me, is refusing to speak of ethics apart from the ethical reality of good men, of justice apart from men that are just, of temperance apart from men that are temperate, of the nature of virtue apart from the judgment of the man that possesses practical wisdom.

But, whatever may be the verdict about Aristotle, at least the approach I have just noted fits in admirably with the notion of the good I am outlining. Just as the notion of being functions in one's knowing and it is by reflecting on that functioning that one comes to know what the notion of being is, so also the notion or intention of the good functions within one's human acting and it is by reflection on that functioning that one comes to know what the notion of good is. Again, just as the functioning of the notion of being brings about our limited knowledge of being, so too the functioning of the notion of the good brings about our limited achievement of the good. Finally, as our knowledge of being is, not knowledge of essence, but only knowledge of this and that and other beings, so too the only good to which we have first-hand access is found in instances of the good realized in themselves or produced beyond themselves by good men.

So the paradox of the existential subject extends to the good existential subject. Just as the existential subject freely and responsibly makes himself what he is, so too he makes himself good or evil and his actions right or wrong. The good subject, the good choice, the good action are not found in isolation. For the subject is good by his good choices and good actions. Universally prior to any choice or action there is just the transcendental principle of all appraisal and criticism, the intention of the good. That principle gives rise to instances of the good, but those instances are good choices and actions. However, do not ask me to determine them, for their determination in each case is the work of the free and responsible subject producing the first and only edition of himself.

13 Aristotle, *Nicomachean Ethics*, II, iii, 4; 1105b 5–8.
14 Ibid., II, vi, 15; 1106b 36 f. R. McKeon, *Basic Works of Aristotle*, Trans. W.D. Ross (New York: Random House, 1941), 956, 959.

It is because the determination of the good is the work of freedom that ethical systems can catalogue sins in almost endless genera and species yet always remain rather vague about the good. They urge us to do good as well as to avoid evil, but what it is to do good does not get much beyond the golden rule, the precept of universal charity, and the like. Still the shortcomings of system are not an irremediable defect. We come to know the good from the example of those about us, from the stories people tell of the good and evil men and women of old, from the incessant flow of praise and blame that makes up the great part of human conversation, from the elation and from the shame that fill us when our own choices and deeds are our own determination of ourselves as good or evil, praiseworthy or blameworthy.

I have been affirming a primacy of the existential. I distinguished different levels of human consciousness to place rational self-consciousness at the top. It sublates the three prior levels of experiencing, of understanding, and of judging, where, of course, sublating means not destroying, not interfering, but retaining, preserving, going beyond, perfecting. The experiential, the intelligible, the true, the real, the good are one, so that understanding enlightens experience, truth is the correctness of understanding, and the pursuit of the good, of value, of what is worthwhile in no way conflicts with, in every way promotes and completes, the pursuit of the intelligible, the true, the real.

It is to be noted, however, that we are not speaking of the good in the Aristotelian sense of the object of appetite, *id quod omnia appetunt* [that which all things desire]. Nor are we speaking of the good in the intellectual, and, indeed, Thomist sense of the good of order. Besides these there is a quite distinct meaning of the word 'good'; to it we refer specifically when we speak of value, of what is worthwhile, of what is right as opposed to wrong, of what is good as opposed not to bad but to evil. It is the intention of the good in this sense that prolongs the intention of the intelligible, the true, the real, that founds rational self-consciousness, that constitutes the emergence of the existential subject.

Finally, let me briefly say that the primacy of the existential does not mean the primacy of results, as in pragmatism, or the primacy of will, as a Scotist might urge, or a primacy of practical intellect, or practical reason, as an Aristotelian or Kantian might phrase it. Results proceed from actions, actions from decisions, decisions from evaluations, evaluations from deliberations, and all five from the existential subject, the subject as deliberating, evaluating, deciding, acting, bringing about results. That subject is not just an intellect or just a will. Though concerned with results, he or she more basically is concerned with himself or herself as becoming good or evil and so is to be named, not a practical subject, but an existential subject.

5   The Alienated Subject

Existential reflection is at once enlightening and enriching. Not only does it touch us intimately and speak to us convincingly but also it is the natural starting-point for fuller reflection on the subject as incarnate, as image and feeling as well as mind and will, as moved by symbol and story, as intersubjective, as encountering others and becoming 'I' to 'Thou' to move on to 'We' through acquaintance, companionship, collaboration, friendship, love. Then easily we pass into the whole human world founded on meaning, a world of language, art, literature, science, philosophy, history, of family and mores, society and education, state and law, economy and technology. That human world does not come into being or survive without deliberation, evaluation, decision, action, without the exercise of freedom and responsibility. It is a world of existential subjects and it objectifies the values that they originate in their creativity and their freedom.

But the very wealth of existential reflection can turn out to be a trap. It is indeed the key that opens the doors to a philosophy, not of man in the abstract, but of concrete human living in its historical unfolding. Still, one must not think that such concreteness eliminates the ancient problems of cognitional theory, epistemology, and metaphysics, for if they occur in an abstract context, they recur with all the more force in a concrete context.

Existential reflection, as it reveals what it is for man to be good, so it raises the question whether the world is good. Is this whole process from the nebulae through plants and animals to man, is it good, a true value, something worthwhile? This question can be answered affirmatively, if and only if one acknowledges God's existence, his omnipotence, and his goodness. Granted those three, one can say that created process is good because the creative *fiat* cannot but be good. Doubt or deny any of the three, and then one doubts or denies any intelligent mind and loving will that could justify anyone saying that this world is good, worthwhile, a value worthy of man's approval and consent. For 'good' in the sense we have been using the term is the goodness of the moral agent, his deeds, his works. Unless there is a moral agent responsible for the world's being and becoming, the world cannot be said to be good in that moral sense. If in that sense the world is not good, then goodness in that sense is to be found only in man. If still man would be good, he is alien to the rest of the universe. If on the other hand he renounces authentic living and drifts into the now seductive and now harsh rhythms of his psyche and of nature, then man is alienated from himself.

It is, then, no accident that a theater of the absurd, a literature of the absurd, and philosophies of the absurd flourish in a culture in which there are theologians to proclaim that God is dead. But that absurdity and that death have their roots in a new neglect of the subject, a new truncation, a new immanentism. In the name of phenomenology, of existential self-understanding, of human encounter, of salvation history, there are those that resentfully and disdainfully brush aside the old questions of cognitional theory, epistemology, metaphysics. I have no doubt, I never did doubt, that the old answers were defective. But to reject the questions as well is to refuse to know what one is doing when one is knowing; it is to refuse to know why doing that is knowing; it is to refuse to set up a basic semantics by concluding what one knows when one does it. That threefold refusal is worse than mere neglect of the subject, and it generates a far more radical truncation. It is that truncation that we experience today not only without but within the Church, when we find that the conditions of the possibility of significant dialogue are not grasped, when the distinction between revealed religion and myth is blurred, when the possibility of objective knowledge of God's existence and of his goodness is denied.

These are large and urgent topics. I shall not treat them. Yet I do not think I am neglecting them entirely, for I have pointed throughout this paper to the root difficulty, to neglect of the subject and the vast labor involved in knowing him.

Related selections: 3.VII.3 on philosophic issues in natural and social sciences; 1.VIII for the results of Lonergan's cognitional analysis; 1.IX on being; 1.X on objectivity; 2.III.3 on self-knowledge; 2.V on the transposition of Thomism; 1.XIV.1 on rational self-consciousness; 3.II.1 on judgments of value; 1.XIV.2 on essential and effective freedom; 3.IV.3 on religious development; 1.XVII on self-appropriation and its value.

Pluralism, Classicism, and Relativism

In the 1971 Pere Marquette Theology Lecture at Marquette University, Lonergan undertook to clarify the issue, raised by the shift from classicist to modern culture, of pluralism in church doctrines. The weight of his discussion fell on the nature of the cultural shift rather than on doctrines. In the following selection from that lecture Lonergan characterizes his own position in response to the collapse of classicism as pluralism, and he reflects on the differences separating the pluralist from the classicist and the relativist. In the first part of the selection he presents the theoretic objections to classicist thought. In the second part he sets out the premises of relativism and indicates in what ways they are incomplete and in need of foundations.

This extract is taken from *Doctrinal Pluralism*, 4–12.

1 Pluralism and Classicist Culture

The contemporary notion of culture is empirical. A culture is a set of meanings and values informing a common way of life, and there are as many cultures as there are distinct sets of such meanings and values.

But this manner of conceiving culture is relatively recent. It is a product of empirical human studies. Within less than one hundred years it has replaced an older classicist view that had flourished for over two millennia. On the older view culture was conceived normatively. It was the opposite of barbarism. It was a matter of acquiring and assimilating the tastes and skills, the ideals, virtues and ideas that were pressed upon one in a good home and through a curriculum in the liberal arts. It stressed not facts but values. It could not but claim to be universalist. Its classics were immortal works of art, its philosophy was the perennial philosophy, its laws and structures were the deposit of the prudence and the wisdom of mankind. Classicist education was a matter of models to be imitated, of ideal characters to be emulated, of eternal verities and universally valid laws. It sought to produce not the mere specialist but the *uomo universale* that could turn his hand to anything and do it brilliantly.

The classicist is not a pluralist. He knows that circumstances alter cases but he is far more deeply convinced that circumstances are accidental and that, beyond them, there is some substance or kernel or root that fits in the classicist assumptions of stability, immutability, fixity. Things have their specific natures; these natures, at least in principle, are to be known exhaustively through the properties they possess and the laws they obey; and over and above the specific nature there is only individuation by matter, so that knowledge of one instance of a species automatically is knowledge of any instance. What is true of species in general, also is true of the human species, of the one faith coming through Jesus Christ, of the one charity given through the gift of the Holy Spirit. It follows that the diversities of peoples, cultures, social arrangements can involve only a difference in the dress in which church doctrine is expressed, but cannot involve any diversity in church doctrine itself. That is *semper idem*.

The pluralist begs to differ. He insists that human concepts are products and expressions of human understanding, that human understanding develops over time, and that it develops differently in different places and in different times. Again, he would claim that a human action, determined solely by abstract properties, abstract principles, abstract laws, would be not only abstract but also inhumanly inept on every concrete occasion. For possible courses of action are the discoveries of human intelligence, perhaps remotely guided by principles and laws, but certainly grasped by insight into concrete situations. Moreover, it is by further insight that the probable results of each possible course of action are determined, and that determination, so far from settling the issue, stands in need of a free and hopefully responsible choice before action can ensue. Finally, in so far as a situation or a course of action is intelligible, it can recur; but the less intelligent people are, the less they learn from the defects of previous acts, and the more likely they are to settle into some routine that keeps repeating the same mistakes to make their situation ever worse. On the other hand, the more intelligent they are, the more they can learn from previous mistakes, and the more they will keep changing their situation and so necessitating still further changes in their courses of action.

The pluralist, then, differs from the classicist inasmuch as he acknowledges human historicity both in principle and in fact. Historicity means – very briefly – that human living is informed by meanings, that meanings are the product of intelligence, that human intelligence develops cumulatively over time, and that such cumulative development differs in different histories.

Classicism itself is one very notable and, indeed, very noble instance of such cumulative development. It is not mistaken in its assumption that there is something substantial and common to human nature and human activity. Its oversight is its failure to grasp that that something substantial and common also is something quite open. It may be expressed in the four transcendental precepts: Be attentive, Be intelligent, Be reasonable, Be responsible. But there is an almost endless manifold of situations to which men successively attend. There vary enormously the type and degree of intellectual and moral development brought to deal with situations. The standard both for human reasonableness and for the strength and delicacy of man's conscience is satisfied only by a complete and life-long devotion to human authenticity.

I have been outlining the theoretic objections to classicist thought. Far more massive are the factual objections. For a century and a half there have been developing highly refined methods in hermeneutics and history, and there have been multiplying not only new modes of studying scripture, the Fathers, the Scholastics, the Renaissance and Reformation, and subsequent periods, but also there have emerged numerous historically-minded philosophies. To confine the Catholic Church to a classicist mentality is to keep the Catholic Church out of the modern world and to prolong the already too long prolonged crisis within the Church.

2   Pluralism and Relativism

As the breakdown of Scholasticism has left many Catholics without any philosophy, so the rejection of the classicist outlook leaves many without even a *Weltanschauung*. In this state of almost complete disorientation they feel confronted with an endless relativism when they are told that no one in this life can aspire to a knowledge of all mathematics, or all physics, or all chemistry, or all biology, or the whole of human studies, or of all the philosophies, or even of the whole of theology.

What is worse is that usually they are not equipped to deal effectively and successfully with the premises set forth by relativists. These premises are: (1) the meaning of any statement is relative to its context; (2) every context is subject to change; it stands within a process of development and/or decay; and (3) it is not possible to predict what the future context will be.

The trouble is twofold. On the one hand, these premises, as far as they go, are true. On the other hand, the complement they need does not consist primarily in further propositions; it is to be found only by unveiling the invariant structure of man's conscious and intentional acts; and that unveiling is a long and difficult task. That task cannot be even outlined here, and so we have to be content to indicate briefly the type of qualification that can and should be added to the premises of relativism.

It is true that the meaning of any statement is relative to its context. But it does not follow that the context is unknown or, if it is unknown, that it cannot be discovered.[1] Still less does it follow that the statement understood within its context is mistaken or false. On the contrary, there are many true statements whose context is easily ascertained.

It is true that contexts change, and it can happen that a statement, which was true in its own context, ceases to be adequate in another context. It remains that it was true in its original context, that sound historical and exegetical procedures can reconstitute the original context with greater or less success and, in the same measure, arrive at an apprehension of the original truth.

It is true that one cannot predict in detail what future changes of context will occur. But one can predict, for example, that the contexts of descriptive statements are less subject to change than the contexts of explanatory statements. Again, with regard to explanatory statements, one can predict that a theory that radically revised the periodic table of chemical elements would account not only for all the data accounted for by the periodic table but also for a substantial range of data for which the periodic table does not account.

Finally, as already remarked, if one wishes a more solid and searching treatment of the issue, one has to undertake a thorough exploration

1 On the relativist contention that context is infinite, see *Insight*, 366–71.

of the three basic issues in philosophy, namely, what am I doing when I am knowing (cognitional theory), why is doing that knowing (epistemology), and what do I know when I do it (metaphysics).

Related selections: 2.IV on the shift from classicist to modern controls of meaning; 2.V on the transposition of classical Thomism; 3.III on realms of meaning and differentiations of consciousness; 3.VII on genetically and dialectically related horizons, and the three conversions; 4.I on the implications of the shift for philosophy and theology; 4.VI on natural right and historical mindedness.

PART THREE

Method in Theology

Selections

Introduction

The classicist notion of culture is a normative notion according to which there is just one culture; the modern notion is empirical: a culture is a set of meanings and values that informs and guides a way of life, and many may be identified and distinguished. It is Lonergan's position that the shift from the classicist normative notion of culture to the modern empirical notion requires that theology be conceived, not as a permanent achievement, but as an ongoing process of mediation between an existing cultural matrix and the significance and role of religion in that matrix. A theology for our times must find its foundation in a dynamic method rather than in a set of fixed and unchanging propositions and principles.

Lonergan's *Method in Theology*, the last major work to appear before his death, was sent to the publisher in 1971. The book contains fourteen chapters, in two large divisions. The first part, 'Background,' contains chapters on method, the human good, meaning, and religion, and concludes with a summary account of the eight functional specialties constitutive of his proposed method for theology. The second part, 'Foreground,' consists of separate accounts of each of the eight functional specialties. *Method in Theology* opens with the statement, 'A theology mediates between a cultural matrix and the significance and role of religion in that matrix.'[1] The first part of the book may be regarded as an explication of the terms in this statement. Chapters 1 through 3 are on culture, its ground, and its constituents; Chapter 4 is on religion; Chapter 5 is a summary account of Lonergan's conception of a theology that mediates between a cultural matrix of meanings and values and a religion within that matrix. It is important to note, however, that Lonergan regarded

1 *Method in Theology*, xi.

the method proposed in *Method in Theology* to be a method for any discipline which draws upon the past to move into the future.

In the five selections from the first part of *Method in Theology* Lonergan discusses the meaning of transcendental method and its relevance to the full range of disciplines, including theology; he explores the difference between judgments of fact and judgments of value, and provides an outline of the structure of the human good; he distinguishes the various differentiations of consciousness and their corresponding realms of meaning; he affirms the inevitable emergence of the question of God, identifies religious experience as the fulfillment of human self-transcendence, notes the precariousness of authenticity and the dialectical character of religious development, defines faith as knowledge born of religious love, and reflects on the implications of his overall approach for disputes about the priority of will over intellect or of intellect over will; and he outlines the eight functional specialties of a theology that is to meet the demands of our time.

In the three selections from the second part, 'Foreground,' Lonergan continues to speak primarily as a methodologist. In the first selection, from his discussion of the specialty of history, Lonergan identifies the object of historical investigation, provides a nuanced account of the process of critical historical investigation, and establishes his position on a range of disputed questions surrounding historical method. The second and third selections pertain to Lonergan's conception of the foundations of his proposed method for theology as residing in the horizon of the theologian, as constituted and transformed by intellectual, moral, and religious conversion, and as grounding general and special theological categories.

The positions expressed by Lonergan in *Method in Theology* rest firmly on foundations laid in earlier writings, especially *Insight*. Because Lonergan believed himself to have provided in that work an account of the transcendental structure of human knowing, he regarded his model of eight functionally interdependent specialties to have ecumenical relevance and, indeed, to be relevant to any discipline that looks to the past to move into and transform the future.

Transcendental Method

Method in Theology opens with a summary account of the pattern of operations worked out for the most part in *Insight*. That foundational work exposed the underlying invariant dynamic structure of operations specified by classical, statistical, dialectical, and genetic heuristic structures. In proposing a method for theology Lonergan recalls that dynamic structure. His emphasis here, though, is different. In *Insight* Lonergan speaks of 'cognitional theory' and the 'process of human knowing'; here he speaks more broadly of 'intentionality analysis' and 'transcendental method.' In *Insight*, motivated by the need to resolve basic philosophic problems of knowledge, self-knowledge, objectivity, and being, Lonergan focuses on cognitional operations. But Lonergan's ultimate concern in that work remains the appropriation of rational self-consciousness, of oneself as not only a knower but also as freely and responsibly deciding and acting. After *Insight*, with the philosophic issues resolved to his satisfaction, Lonergan gave additional attention to meaning and its functions, to our apprehension and judgments of value, and to the significance of a fourth level of consciousness for all our endeavors.

In the first part of this selection Lonergan offers a preliminary definition of method and distinguishes it from a mere set of rules to be followed blindly. In the second part he identifies the four levels of conscious intentionality, notes the different quality of awareness on the different levels, and describes the ways in which the various levels make us aware of objects. This basic dynamic structure of conscious intentionality he names transcendental method. This part concludes with his distinction between the categorial and transcendental modes of intentionality. In the third part Lonergan lists six functions of transcendental method and explains its special relevance to theology. All special methods, including theological method, are specifications of precepts derived from the study of the levels of conscious intentionality. These *transcendental precepts* are: Be attentive, Be intelligent, Be reasonable, Be responsible.

These extracts are taken from *Method in Theology*, 4–6, 10–12, 20–4.

1   A Preliminary Notion

A method is a normative pattern of recurrent and related operations yielding cumulative and progressive results. There is a method, then, where there are distinct operations, where each operation is related to the others, where the set of relations forms a pattern, where the pattern is described as the right way of doing the job, where operations in accord with the pattern may be repeated indefinitely, and where the fruits of such repetition are, not repetitious, but cumulative and progressive.

So in the natural sciences method inculcates a spirit of inquiry and inquiries recur. It insists on accurate observation and description: both observations and descriptions recur. Above all, it praises discovery, and discoveries recur. It demands the formulation of discoveries in hypotheses, and hypotheses recur. It requires the deduction of the implications of hypotheses, and deductions recur. It keeps urging that experiments be devised and performed to check the implications of hypotheses against observable fact, and such processes of experimentation recur.

These distinct and recurrent operations are related. Inquiry transforms mere experiencing into the scrutiny of observation. What is observed, is pinned down by description. Contrasting descriptions give rise to problems, and problems are solved by discoveries. What is discovered is expressed in a hypothesis. From the hypothesis are deduced its implications, and these suggest experiments to be performed. So the many operations are related; the relations form a pattern; and the pattern defines the right way of going about scientific investigation.

Finally, the results of investigations are cumulative and progressive. For the process of experimentation yields new data, new observations, new descriptions that may or may not confirm the hypothesis that is being tested. In so far as they are confirmatory, they reveal that the investigation is not altogether on the wrong track. In so far as they are not confirmatory, they lead to a modification of the hypothesis and, in the limit, to new discovery, new hypothesis, new deduction, and new experiments. The wheel of method not only turns but also rolls along. The field of observed data keeps broadening. New discoveries are added to old. New hypotheses and theories express not only the new insights but also all that was valid in the old, to give method its cumulative character and to engender the conviction that, however remote may still be the goal of the complete explanation of all phenomena, at least we now are nearer to it than we were.

Such, very summarily, is method in the natural sciences. The account is far indeed from being sufficiently detailed to guide the natural scientist in his work. At the same time it is too specific to be transposed to other disciplines. But at least it illustrates a preliminary notion of method as *a normative pattern of recurrent and related operations yielding cumulative and progressive results.*

A few observations are in order.

First, method is often conceived as a set of rules that, even when followed blindly by anyone, none the less yield satisfactory results. I should grant that method, so conceived, is possible when the same result is produced over and over, as in the assembly line or 'The New Method Laundry.' But it will not do, if progressive and cumulative results are expected. Results are progressive only if there is a sustained succession of discoveries; they are cumulative only if there is effected a synthesis of each new insight with all previous, valid insights. But neither discovery nor synthesis is at the beck and call of any set of rules. Their occurrence follows statistical laws; they can be made more probable; they cannot be assured by a set of prescriptions.

Next, our preliminary notion conceives method not as a set of rules but as a prior, normative pattern of operations from which the rules may be derived. Further, the operations envisaged are not limited to strictly logical operations, that is, to operations on propositions, terms, relations. It includes such operations, of course, for it speaks of describing, of formulating problems and hypotheses, of deducing implications. But it does not hesitate to move outside this group and to speak of inquiry, observation, discovery, experiment, synthesis, verification ...

2   Four Levels of Conscious Intentionality

Different levels of consciousness and intentionality have to be distinguished. In our dream states consciousness and intentionality commonly are fragmentary and incoherent. When we awake, they take on a different hue to expand on four successive, related, but qualitatively different levels. There is the *empirical* level on which we sense, perceive, imagine, feel, speak, move. There is an *intellectual* level on which we inquire, come to understand, express what we have understood, work out the presuppositions and implications of our expression. There is the *rational* level on which we reflect, marshal the evidence, pass judgment on the truth or falsity, certainty or probability, of a statement. There is the *responsible* level on which we are concerned with ourselves, our own operations, our goals, and so deliberate about possible courses of action, evaluate them, decide, and carry out our decisions.

All the operations on these four levels are intentional and conscious. Still, intentionality and consciousness differ from level to level, and within each level the many operations involve further differences. Our consciousness expands in a new dimension when from mere experiencing we turn to the effort to understand what we have experienced. A third dimension of rationality emerges when the content of our acts of understanding is regarded as, of itself, a mere bright idea and we endeavor to settle what really is so. A fourth dimension comes to the fore when judgment on the facts is followed by deliberation on what we are to do about them. On all four levels, we are aware of ourselves but, as we mount from level to level, it is a fuller self of which we are aware and the awareness itself is different.

As empirically conscious, we do not seem to differ from the higher animals. But in us empirical consciousness and intentionality are only a substratum for further activities. The data of sense provoke inquiry, inquiry leads to understanding, understanding expresses itself in language. Without the data there would be nothing for us to inquire about and nothing to be understood. Yet what is sought by inquiry is never just another datum but the idea or form, the intelligible unity or relatedness, that organizes the data into intelligible wholes. Again, without the effort to understand and its conflicting results, we would have no occasion to judge. But such occasions are recurrent, and then the intelligent center of experiencing reveals his reflective and critical rationality. Once more there is a fuller self of which we become aware, and once more the awareness itself is different. As intelligent, the subject seeks insight and, as insights accumulate, he reveals them in his behavior, his speech, his grasp of situations, his mastery of theoretic domains. But as reflectively and critically conscious, he incarnates detachment and disinterestedness, gives himself over to criteria of truth and certitude, makes his sole concern the determination of what is or is not so; and now, as the self, so also the awareness of self resides in that incarnation, that self-surrender, that single-minded concern for truth. There is a still further dimension to being human, and there we emerge as persons, meet one another in a common concern for values, seek to abolish the organization of human living on the basis of competing egoisms and to replace it by an organization on the basis of man's perceptiveness and intelligence, his reasonableness, and his responsible exercise of freedom ...

[A]s different operations yield qualitatively different modes of being conscious subjects, so too they yield qualitatively different modes of intending. The intending of our senses is an attending; it normally is selective but not creative. The intending of our imaginations may be representative or creative. What is grasped in insight, is neither an actually given datum of sense nor a creation of the imagination but an intelligible organization that may or may not be relevant to data. The intending that is conception puts together both the content of the insight and as much of the image as is essential to the occurrence of the insight; the result is the intending of any concrete being selected by an incompletely determinate (and, in that sense, abstract) content.

However, the most fundamental difference in modes of intending lies between the categorial and the transcendental. Categories are determinations. They have a limited denotation. They vary with cultural variations. They may be illustrated by the type of classification associated with totemism and recently argued to be essentially classification by homology.[1] They may be reflectively known as categories, as were the Aristotelian *substance, quantity, quality, relation, action, passion, place, time, posture, habit.* They need not be called categories, as were the four causes, *end, agent, matter, form,* or the logical distinctions of *genus, difference, species, property, accident.* They may be the fine products of scientific achievement as the concepts of modern physics, the chemist's periodic table, the biologist's evolutionary tree.

In contrast, the transcendentals are comprehensive in connotation, unrestricted in denotation, invariant over cultural change. While cat-

1 Claude Levi-Strauss, *The Savage Mind* (London: Weidenfeld and Nicolson, 1966).

egories are needed to put determinate questions and give determinate answers, the transcendentals are contained in questions prior to the answers. They are the radical intending that moves us from ignorance to knowledge. They are *a priori* because they go beyond what we know to seek what we do not know yet. They are unrestricted because answers are never complete and so only give rise to still further questions. They are comprehensive because they intend the unknown whole or totality of which our answers reveal only part. So intelligence takes us beyond experiencing to ask what and why and how and what for. Reasonableness takes us beyond the answers of intelligence to ask whether the answers are true and whether what they mean really is so. Responsibility goes beyond fact and desire and possibility to discern between what truly is good and what only apparently is good. So if we objectify the content of intelligent intending, we form the transcendental concept of the intelligible. If we objectify the content of reasonable intending, we form the transcendental concepts of the true and the real. If we objectify the content of responsible intending, we get the transcendental concept of value, of the truly good. But quite distinct from such transcendental concepts, which can be misconceived and often are, there are the prior transcendental notions that constitute the very dynamism of our conscious intending, promoting us from mere experiencing towards understanding, from mere understanding towards truth and reality, from factual knowledge to responsible action. That dynamism, so far from being a product of cultural advance, is the condition of its possibility; and any ignorance or error, any negligence or malice, that misrepresents or blocks that dynamism is obscurantism in its most radical form.

3   The Functions of Transcendental Method

We have been inviting the reader to discover in himself the original normative pattern of recurrent and related operations that yield cumulative and progressive results. We have now to consider what uses or functions are served by that basic method.

First, then, there is the normative function. All special methods consist in making specific the transcendental precepts, Be attentive, Be intelligent, Be reasonable, Be responsible. But before they are ever formulated in concepts and expressed in words, those precepts have a prior existence and reality in the spontaneous, structured dynamism of human consciousness. Moreover, just as the transcendental precepts rest simply on a study of the operations themselves, so specific categorial precepts rest on a study of the mind operating in a given field. The ultimate basis of both transcendental and categorial precepts will be advertence to the difference between attention and inattention, intelligence and stupidity, reasonableness and unreasonableness, responsibility and irresponsibility.

Secondly, there is the critical function. The scandal still continues that men, while they tend to agree on scientific questions, tend to disagree in the most outrageous fashion on basic philosophic issues. So they disagree about the activities named knowing, about the relation of those activities to reality, and about reality itself. However, differences on the third, reality, can be reduced to differences about the first and second, knowledge and objectivity. Differences on the second, objectivity, can be reduced to differences on the first, cognitional theory. Finally, differences in cognitional theory can be resolved by bringing to light the contradiction between a mistaken cognitional theory and the actual performance of the mistaken theorist.[2] To take the simplest instance, Hume thought the human mind to be a matter of impressions linked together by custom. But Hume's own mind was quite original. Therefore, Hume's own mind was not what Hume considered the human mind to be.

Thirdly, there is the dialectical function. For the critical use of transcendental method can be applied to every mistaken cognitional theory, whether expressed with philosophic generality or presupposed by a method of hermeneutics, of historical investigation, of theology, or demythologization. Moreover, these applications can be extended to concomitant views on epistemology and metaphysics. In this fashion one can determine the dialectical series of basic positions, which criticism confirms, and of basic counter-positions, which criticism confounds.

Fourthly, there is the systematic function. For in the measure that transcendental method is objectified, there are determined a set of basic terms and relations, namely, the terms that refer to the operations of cognitional process, and the relations that link these operations to one another. Such terms and relations are the substance of cognitional

2 Discussed in greater detail in *Insight*, 412 ff. [1.XI.1–3 in this reader] and in *Collection*, 188 ff.

theory. They reveal the ground for epistemology. They are found to be isomorphic[3] with the terms and relations denoting the ontological structure of any reality proportionate to human cognitional process.

Fifthly, the foregoing systematic function assures continuity without imposing rigidity. Continuity is assured by the source of the basic terms and relations, for that source is human cognitional process in its concrete reality. Rigidity is not imposed, for a fuller and more exact knowledge of human cognitional process is by no means excluded and, in the measure it is attained, there will follow a fuller and more exact determination of basic terms and relations. Finally, the exclusion of rigidity is not a menace to continuity for, as we have seen, the conditions of the possibility of revision set limits to the possibility of revising cognitional theory, and the more elaborate the revision, the stricter and more detailed these limits will be.

Sixthly, there is the heuristic function. Every inquiry aims at transforming some unknown into a known. Inquiry itself, then, is something between ignorance and knowledge. It is less than knowledge, else there would be no need to inquire. It is more than sheer ignorance, for it makes ignorance manifest and strives to replace it with knowledge. This intermediary between ignorance and knowing is an intending, and what is intended is an unknown that is to be known.

Now fundamentally all method is the exploitation of such intending, for it outlines the steps to be taken if one is to proceed from the initial intending of the question to the eventual knowing of what has been intended all along. Moreover, within method the use of heuristic devices is fundamental. They consist in designating and naming the intended unknown, in setting down at once all that can be affirmed about it, and in using this explicit knowledge as a guide, a criterion, and/or a premise in the effort to arrive at a fuller knowledge. Such is the function in algebra of the unknown, x, in the solution of problems. Such is the function in physics of indeterminate or generic functions and of the classes of functions specified by differential equations.

Now transcendental method fulfills a heuristic function. It reveals the very nature of that function by bringing to light the activity of intending and its correlative, the intended that, though unknown, at least is intended. Moreover, inasmuch as the systematic function has

---

3 This isomorphism rests on the fact that one and the same process constructs both elementary acts of knowing into a compound knowing and elementary objects of knowing into the compound object [see 1.XI.2–3 in this reader].

provided sets of basic terms and relations, there are to hand basic determinations that may be set down at once whenever the unknown is a human subject or an object proportionate to human cognitional process, i.e., an object to be known by experiencing, understanding, and judging.

Seventhly, there is the foundational function. Special methods derive their proper norms from the accumulated experience of investigators in their several fields. But besides the proper norms there are also common norms. Besides the tasks in each field there are interdisciplinary problems. Underneath the consent of men as scientists, there is their dissent on matters of ultimate significance and concern. It is in the measure that special methods acknowledge their common core in transcendental method, that norms common to all the sciences will be acknowledged, that a secure basis will be attained for attacking interdisciplinary problems, and that the sciences will be mobilized within a higher unity of vocabulary, thought, and orientation, in which they will be able to make their quite significant contribution to the solution of fundamental problems.

Eighthly, transcendental method is relevant to theology. This relevance, of course, is mediated by the special method proper to theology and developed through the reflection of theologians on the successes and failures of their efforts past and present. But this special method, while it has its own special classes and combinations of operations, none the less is the work of human minds performing the same basic operations in the same basic relations as are found in other special methods. In other words, transcendental method is a constituent part of the special methods proper to the natural and to the human sciences. However true it is that one attends, understands, judges, decides differently in the natural sciences, in the human sciences, and in theology, still these differences in no way imply or suggest a transition from attention to inattention, from intelligence to stupidity, from reasonableness to silliness, from responsibility to irresponsibility.

Ninthly, the objects of theology do not lie outside the transcendental field. For that field is unrestricted, and so outside it there is nothing at all. Moreover, it is not unrestricted in the sense that the transcendental notions are abstract, least in connotation and greatest in denotation; for the transcendental notions are not abstract but comprehensive; they intend everything about everything. So far from being abstract, it is by them that we intend the concrete, i.e., all that is to be known about a thing. Finally, while it is, of course, true that human knowing is limited, still the transcendental notions are not a matter of knowing but of intending; they intended all that each of us has managed to learn, and they now intend all that as yet remains unknown. In other words, the transcendental field is defined not by what man knows, not by what he can know, but by what he can ask about; and it is only because we can ask more questions than we can answer that we know about the limitations of our knowledge.

Tenthly, to assign to transcendental method a role in theology adds no new resource to theology but simply draws attention to a resource that has always been used. For transcendental method is the concrete and dynamic unfolding of human attentiveness, intelligence, reasonableness, and responsibility. That unfolding occurs whenever anyone uses his mind in an appropriate fashion. Hence, to introduce transcendental method introduces no new resource into theology, for theologians always have had minds and always have used them. However, while transcendental method will introduce no new resource, it does add considerable light and precision to the performance of theological tasks, and this, I trust, will become manifest in due course.

Related selections: 1.XVII on self-appropriation; 1.VIII and 2.III on the invariant dynamic structure of knowing; 1.XIV.1 on rational self-consciousness; 4.I on logic and method; 3.V.3 on the use of the four-level structure of consciousness to ground the division of functional specialties in theology; 3.VIII.1 on the relation of transcendental notions to theological categories; 4.VII on degrees of self-transcendence.

The Human Good

In *Method in Theology* theology is conceived as an ongoing process of mediation between religion and its cultural matrix. A notion of the human good is an essential background element of theology conceived as mediating engagement with its own cultural matrix. In the first part of the present selection Lonergan gives an account of the judgment of value, a central operation on the fourth level of conscious intentionality. We are promoted to the level of moral or responsible consciousness by the transcendental notion of value expressed in a good or uneasy conscience. The judgment of value is contrasted here with the judgment of fact, which is analyzed in detail in *Insight*. The issue of the objectivity of judgments of value is raised. The criterion of objectivity in moral judgment, Lonergan claims, is the authenticity of the self-transcending subject. Three elements coalesce in the judgment of value: knowledge of reality; an apprehension of value in feelings; and the act of judgment itself which moves us towards the real, not merely the cognitional, self-transcendence of decision. Lonergan identifies the type of feelings involved in a judgment of value as intentional responses to the truly good. Next he discusses the different contexts within which we make judgments of value, and these contexts are related to stages of development and to deviations from growth. Finally, adopting a distinction drawn by Joseph de Finance, Lonergan distinguishes between a horizontal exercise of liberty within a determinate horizon, and a vertical exercise of liberty by which a horizon is selected. In the second part of the selection Lonergan turns from the subject as morally conscious to the objective side of the human good. He explicates the structure of the human good by employing eighteen heuristic terms. He distinguishes individuals, groups, and ends, individuals in their potentialities and actualities, and kinds of ends corresponding to levels of conscious intentionality, and he relates these elements of the struc-

ture to one another. Lonergan's account of the structure of the human good
emphasizes the 'good of order' and community. The good of order is the concrete functioning of human cooperation to bring about a sustained succession
of particular goods. Lonergan asserts that only in community is the individual
able to advance in authenticity, to develop morally: 'Liberty is exercised within
a matrix of personal relations.'[1]

   These extracts are taken from *Method in Theology*, 36–42; 47–52.

1   Judgments of Value

Judgments of value are simple or comparative. They affirm or deny
that some x is truly or only apparently good. Or they compare distinct
instances of the truly good to affirm or deny that one is better or more
important, or more urgent than the other.

   Such judgments are objective or merely subjective inasmuch as they
proceed or do not proceed from a self-transcending subject. Their truth
or falsity, accordingly, has its criterion in the authenticity or the lack of
authenticity of the subject's being. But the criterion is one thing and the
meaning of the judgment is another. To say that an affirmative judgment of value is true is to say what objectively is or would be good or
better. To say that an affirmative judgment of value is false is to say
what objectively is not or would not be good or better.

   Judgments of value differ in content but not in structure from judgments of fact. They differ in content, for one can approve of what
does not exist, and one can disapprove of what does. They do not differ in structure, inasmuch as in both there is the distinction between
criterion and meaning. In both, the criterion is the self-transcendence
of the subject, which, however, is only cognitive in judgments of fact
but is heading towards moral self-transcendence in judgments of
value. In both, the meaning is or claims to be independent of the subject: judgments of fact state or purport to state what is or is not so;
judgments of value state or purport to state what is or is not truly
good or really better.

   True judgments of value go beyond merely intentional self-transcendence without reaching the fulness of moral self-transcendence. That
fulness is not merely knowing but also doing, and man can know what

---

1 *Method in Theology*, 50.

is right without doing it. Still, if he knows and does not perform, either he must be humble enough to acknowledge himself to be a sinner, or else he will start destroying his moral being by rationalizing, by making out that what truly is good really is not good at all. The judgment of value, then, is itself a reality in the moral order. By it the subject moves beyond pure and simple knowing. By it the subject is constituting himself as proximately capable of moral self-transcendence, of benevolence and beneficence, of true loving.

Intermediate between judgments of fact and judgments of value lie apprehensions of value. Such apprehensions are given in feelings. The feelings in question are not the already described non-intentional states, trends, urges, that are related to efficient and final causes but not to objects. Again, they are not intentional responses to such objects as the agreeable or disagreeable, the pleasant or painful, the satisfying or dissatisfying. For, while these are objects, still they are ambiguous objects that may prove to be truly good or bad or only apparently good or bad. Apprehensions of value occur in a further category of intentional response which greets either the ontic value of a person or the qualitative value of beauty, of understanding, of truth, of noble deeds, of virtuous acts, of great achievements. For we are so endowed that we not only ask questions leading to self-transcendence, not only can recognize correct answers constitutive of intentional self-transcendence, but also respond with the stirring of our very being when we glimpse the possibility or the actuality of moral self-transcendence.

In the judgment of value, then, three components unite. First, there is knowledge of reality and especially of human reality. Secondly, there are intentional responses to values. Thirdly, there is the initial thrust towards moral self-transcendence constituted by the judgment of value itself. The judgment of value presupposes knowledge of human life, of human possibilities proximate and remote, of the probable consequences of projected courses of action. When knowledge is deficient, then fine feelings are apt to be expressed in what is called moral idealism, i.e., lovely proposals that don't work out and often do more harm than good. But knowledge alone is not enough and, while everyone has some measure of moral feeling for, as the saying is, there is honor among thieves, still moral feelings have to be cultivated, enlightened, strengthened, refined, criticized and pruned of oddities. Finally, the development of knowledge and the development of moral feeling head to the existential discovery, the discovery of oneself as a moral being, the realization that one not only chooses between courses of action but also thereby makes oneself an authentic human being or an unauthentic one. With that discovery, there emerges in consciousness the significance of personal value and the meaning of personal responsibility. One's judgments of value are revealed as the door to one's fulfilment or to one's loss. Experience, especially repeated experience, of one's frailty or wickedness raises the question of one's salvation and, on a more fundamental level, there arises the question of God.

The fact of development and the possibility of failure imply that judgments of value occur in different contexts. There is the context of growth, in which one's knowledge of human living and operating is increasing in extent, precision, refinement, and in which one's responses are advancing from the agreeable to vital values, from vital to social, from social to cultural, from cultural to personal, from personal to religious. Then there prevails an openness to ever further achievement.[2] Past gains are organized and consolidated but they are not rounded off into a closed system but remain incomplete and so open to still further discoveries and developments. The free thrust of the subject into new areas is recurrent and, as yet, there is no supreme value that entails all others. But at the summit of the ascent from the initial infantile bundle of needs and clamors and gratifications, there are to be found the deep-set joy and solid peace, the power and the vigor, of being in love with God. In the measure that that summit is reached, then the supreme value is God, and other values are God's expression of his love in this world, in its aspirations, and in its goal. In the measure that one's love of God is complete, then values are whatever one loves, and evils are whatever one hates so that, in Augustine's phrase, if one loves God, one may do as one pleases, *Ama Deum et fac quod vis*. Then affectivity is of a single piece. Further developments only fill out previous achievement. Lapses from grace are rarer and more quickly amended.

But continuous growth seems to be rare.[3] There are the deviations occasioned by neurotic need. There are the refusals to keep on taking

---

2 On growth, growth motivation, and neurotic needs, see A.H. Maslow, *Towards a Psychology of Being* (Princeton, NJ: Van Nostrand, 1962).

3 Ibid., 190. Maslow finds self-actualization in less than 1 percent of the adult population.

the plunge from settled routines to an as yet unexperienced but richer mode of living. There are the mistaken endeavors to quieten an uneasy conscience by ignoring, belittling, denying, rejecting higher values. Preference scales become distorted, feelings soured. Bias creeps into one's outlook, rationalization into one's morals, ideology into one's thought. So one may come to hate the truly good, and love the really evil. Nor is that calamity limited to individuals. It can happen to groups, to nations, to blocks of nations, to mankind.[4] It can take different, opposed, belligerent forms to divide mankind and to menace civilization with destruction. Such is the monster that has stood forth in our day.

In his thorough and penetrating study of human action, Joseph de Finance distinguished between horizontal and vertical liberty.[5] Horizontal liberty is the exercise of liberty within a determinate horizon and from the basis of a corresponding existential stance. Vertical liberty is the exercise of liberty that selects that stance and the corresponding horizon. Such vertical liberty may be implicit: it occurs in responding to the motives that lead one to ever fuller authenticity, or in ignoring such motives and drifting into an ever less authentic selfhood. But it also can be explicit. Then one is responding to the transcendental notion of value, by determining what it would be worthwhile for one to make of oneself, and what it would be worthwhile for one to do for one's fellow men. One works out an ideal of human reality and achievement, and to that ideal one dedicates oneself. As one's knowledge increases, as one's experience is enriched, as one's reach is strengthened or weakened, one's ideal may be revised and the revision may recur many times.

In such vertical liberty, whether implicit or explicit, are to be found the foundations of the judgments of value that occur. Such judgments are felt to be true or false in so far as they generate a peaceful or uneasy conscience. But they attain their proper context, their clarity and refinement, only through man's historical development and the individual's personal appropriation of his social, cultural, and religious heritage. It is by the transcendental notion of value and its expression in a good and an uneasy conscience that man can develop

4 On ressentiment and the distortion of preference scales, see Manfred Frings, *Max Scheler* (Pittsburgh: Duquesne University Press, 1965), chap. 5.
5 J. de Finance, *Essai sur l'agir humain* (Rome: Gregorian University Press, 1962), 287 ff.

morally. But a rounded moral judgment is ever the work of a fully developed self-transcending subject or, as Aristotle would put it, of a virtuous man.[6]

2   The Structure of the Human Good

The human good is at once individual and social, and some account of the way the two aspects combine has now to be attempted. This will be done by selecting some eighteen terms and gradually relating them to one another.

Our eighteen terms regard (1) individuals in their potentialities and actuations, (2) cooperating groups, and (3) ends. A threefold division of ends is allowed to impose a threefold division in the other categories to yield the following scheme.

Individual		Social	Ends
Potentiality	Actuation		
capacity, need	operation	cooperation	particular good
plasticity, perfectibility	development, skill	institution, role, task	good of order
liberty	orientation, conversion	personal relations	terminal value

A first step will relate four terms from the first line: capacity, operation, particular good, and need. Individuals, then, have capacities for operating. By operating they procure themselves instances of the par-

---

6 While Aristotle spoke not of values but of virtues, still his account of virtue presupposes the existence of virtuous men, as my account of value presupposes the existence of self-transcending subjects. See Aristotle, *Nicomachean Ethics*, II, iii, 4; 1105b 5–8: 'Actions, then, are called just and temperate when they are such as the just and temperate man would do; but it is not the man who does these that is just and temperate, but the man who also does them *as* just and temperate men do them.' Similarly, ibid., II, vi, 15; 1106b 36 ff.: 'Virtue, then, is a state of character concerned with choice, lying in a mean, i.e., the mean relative to us, this being determined by a rational principle, and by that principle by which the man of practical wisdom would determine it.' R. McKeon, *The Basic Works of Aristotle*, trans. W.D. Ross (New York: Random House, 1941), 956, 959.

ticular good. By such an instance is meant any entity, whether object or
action, that meets a need of a particular individual at a given place and
time. Needs are to be understood in the broadest sense; they are not to
be restricted to necessities but rather to be stretched to include wants
of every kind.

Next are related four terms from the third column: cooperation,
institution, role, and task. Individuals, then, live in groups. To a notable extent their operating is cooperating. It follows some settled pattern, and this pattern is fixed by a role to be fulfilled or a task to be
performed within an institutional frame-work. Such frame-works are
the family and manners (mores), society and education, the state and
the law, the economy and technology, the church or sect. They constitute the commonly understood and already accepted basis and mode
of cooperation. They tend to change only slowly for change, as distinct
from breakdown, involves a new common understanding and a new
common consent.

Thirdly, there are to be related the remaining terms in the second
row: plasticity, perfectibility, development, skill, and the good of
order. The capacities of individuals, then, for the performance of operations, because they are plastic and perfectible, admit the development
of skills and, indeed, of the very skills demanded by institutional roles
and tasks. But besides the institutional basis of cooperation, there is
also the concrete manner in which cooperation is working out. The
same economic set-up is compatible with prosperity and recession.
The same constitutional and legal arrangements admit wide differences in political life and in the administration of justice. Similar rules
for marriage and the family in one case generate domestic bliss and in
another misery.

This concrete manner, in which cooperation actually is working out,
is what is meant by the good of order. It is distinct from instances of
the particular good but it is not separate from them. It regards them,
however, not singly and as related to the individual they satisfy, but all
together and as recurrent. My dinner today is for me an instance of the
particular good. But dinner every day for all members of the group
that earn it is part of the good of order. Again, my education was for
me a particular good. But education for everyone that wants it is
another part of the good of order.

The good of order, however, is not merely a sustained succession of
recurring instances of types of the particular good. Besides that recur-

rent manifold, there is the order that sustains it. This consists basically (1) in the ordering of operations so that they are cooperations and ensure the recurrence of all effectively desired instances of the particular good, and (2) the interdependence of effective desires or decisions with the appropriate performance by cooperating individuals.[7]

It is to be insisted that the good of order is not some design for utopia, some theoretic ideal, some set of ethical precepts, some code of laws, or some super-institution. It is quite concrete. It is the actually functioning or malfunctioning set of 'if – then' relationships guiding operators and coordinating operations. It is the ground whence recur or fail to recur whatever instances of the particular good are recurring or failing to recur. It has a basis in institutions but it is a product of much more, of all the skill and know-how, all the industry and resourcefulness, all the ambition and fellow-feeling of a whole people, adapting to each change of circumstance, meeting each new emergency, struggling against every tendency to disorder.[8]

There remains the third row of terms: liberty, orientation, conversion, personal relations, and terminal values. Liberty means, of course, not indeterminism but self-determination. Any course of individual or group action is only a finite good and, because only finite, it is open to criticism. It has its alternatives, its limitations, its risks, its drawbacks. Accordingly, the process of deliberation and evaluation is not itself decisive, and so we experience our liberty as the active thrust of the subject terminating the process of deliberation by settling on one of the possible courses of action and proceeding to execute it. Now in so far as that thrust of the self regularly opts, not for the merely apparent good, but for the true good, the self thereby is achieving moral self-transcendence; he is existing authentically; he is constituting himself as an originating value, and he is bringing about terminal values, namely a good of order that is truly good and instances of the particular good that are truly good. On the other hand, in so far as one's decisions have their principal motives, not in the values at stake, but in a calculus of the pleasures and pains involved one is failing in self-transcendence, in authentic human existence, in the origination of value in oneself and in one's society.

7 For the general case of such relationships, see *Insight* on emergent probability, 138–51 [1.III.3–4 in this reader].
8 For a fuller presentation, *Insight* on the good of order, 619; on common sense, 197–204; 232–42; on belief, 725–40; and on bias, 244–67 [1.IV.1, 1.V.1 on common sense; 1.XVI.4 on belief; 1.V.3–5 on bias in this reader].

Liberty is exercised within a matrix of personal relations. In the cooperating community persons are bound together by their needs and by the common good of order that meets their needs. They are related by the commitments that they have freely undertaken and by the expectations aroused in others by the commitments, by the roles they have assumed and by the tasks that they meet to perform. These relationships normally are alive with feeling. There are common or opposed feelings about qualitative values and scales of preference. There are mutual feelings in which one responds to another as an ontic value or as just a source of satisfactions. Beyond feelings there is the substance of community. People are joined by common experience, by common or complementary insights, by similar judgments of fact and of value, by parallel orientations in life. They are separated, estranged, rendered hostile, when they have got out of touch, when they misunderstand one another, when they judge in opposed fashions, opt for contrary social goals. So personal relations vary from intimacy to ignorance, from love to exploitation, from respect to contempt, from friendliness to enmity. They bind a community together, or divide it into factions, or tear it apart.[9]

Terminal values are the values that are chosen: true instances of the particular good, a true good of order, a true scale of preferences regarding values and satisfactions. Correlative to terminal values are the originating values that do the choosing: they are authentic persons achieving self-transcendence by their good choices. Since man can know and choose authenticity and self-transcendence, originating and terminal values can coincide. When each member of the community both wills authenticity in himself and, inasmuch as he can, promotes it in others, then the originating values that choose and the terminal values that are chosen overlap and interlace.

Presently we shall have to speak of the orientation of the community as a whole.[10] But for the moment our concern is with the orientation of

---

9 On interpersonal relations as ongoing processes, there is in Hegel's *Phänomenologie* the dialectic of master and slave, and in Gaston Fessard's *De l'actualité historique* (Paris: Desclée de Brouwer, 1960), vol. 1, a parallel dialectic of Jew and Greek. Far more concrete is Rosemary Haughton's *The Transformation of Man: A Study of Conversion and Community* (London: G. Chapman, and Springfield, IL: Templegate, 1967). Description, technique and some theory in Carl Rogers's *On Becoming a Person* (Boston: Houghton Mifflin, 1961).
10 [See 1.V.5 in this reader on progress and decline.]

the individual within the orientated community. At its root this consists in the transcendental notions that both enable us and require us to advance in understanding, to judge truthfully, to respond to values. Still, this possibility and exigence become effective only through development. One has to acquire the skills and learning of a competent human being in some walk of life. One has to grow in sensitivity and responsiveness to values if one's humanity is to be authentic. But development is not inevitable, and so results vary. There are human failures. There are mediocrities. There are those that keep developing and growing throughout a long life-time, and their achievement varies with their initial background, with their opportunities, with their luck in avoiding pitfalls and setbacks, and with the pace of their advance.[11]

As orientation is, so to speak, the direction of development, so conversion is a change of direction and, indeed, a change for the better. One frees oneself from the unauthentic. One grows in authenticity. Harmful, dangerous, misleading satisfactions are dropped. Fears of discomfort, pain, privation have less power to deflect one from one's course. Values are apprehended where before they were overlooked. Scales of preference shift. Errors, rationalizations, ideologies fall and shatter to leave one open to things as they are and to man as he should be.

The good then is at once individual and social. Individuals do not just operate to meet their needs but cooperate to meet one another's needs. As the community develops its institutions to facilitate cooperation, so individuals develop skills to fulfil the roles and perform the tasks set by the institutional frame-work. Though the roles are fulfilled and the tasks are performed that the needs be met, still all is done not blindly but knowingly, not necessarily but freely. The process is not merely the service of man; it is above all the making of man, his advance in authenticity, the fulfilment of his affectivity, and the direction of his work to the particular goods and a good of order that are worthwhile.

Related selections: 1.VII on judgment; 1. XIV.1 on judgment and decision; 3.I.2 on the levels of conscious intentionality and the transcendental notions; 2.VII.4 on the existential subject and the transcendental notion of value; 1.XII.4 on human development; 3.VII on horizons and conversions; 1.V.5 and 1.XVI.1 on

---

11 On various aspects of growth, see Maslow, *Towards a Psychology of Being*.

progress and decline; 4.VI on natural right in history; 4.II on the dialectic of authority; 4.III.1–2 on social alienation and the second enlightenment; 4.IV on healing and creating in history; 1.V.1 on the dynamic structure of human affairs.

Realms of Meaning

In Chapter 3 of *Method in Theology*, Lonergan approaches the nature of meaning through a discussion of its carriers, its elements, its functions in human living, the various realms of meaning, and the historical development of techniques of meaning. Meaning may be carried or embodied in human intersubjectivity, in art, in symbols, in language, and in the lives and deeds of persons. It has its source in conscious acts and intended contents. It has cognitive, efficient, constitutive, and communicative functions. Different requirements give rise to different modes of conscious and intentional operation, and these modes, in turn, give rise to different realms of meaning. Finally, the distinction between different modes may be employed to formulate ideal constructions or stages of meaning for use in the study of the historical development of meaning. Stages of meaning are ideal-types to be employed when we seek understanding of a given culture at a given moment in its history. With respect to the Western tradition, Lonergan constructs theoretically three stages of meaning: a first stage in which operations follow the mode of common sense; a second in which the common-sense mode is joined by the mode of theory; and a third in which the common-sense and theoretic modes are joined by the critical mode of interiority.

In the present selection on the realms of meaning, which grounds the construction of stages, Lonergan describes four modes of conscious intentionality and the corresponding realms of common sense, theory, interiority, and transcendence. In the course of the discussion Lonergan introduces his more general distinction between undifferentiated and differentiated consciousness.

This extract is taken from *Method in Theology*, 81–5.

Different exigences give rise to different modes of conscious and intentional operation, and different modes of such operation give rise to different realms of meaning.

There is a systematic exigence that separates the realm of common sense from the realm of theory. Both of these realms, by and large, regard the same real objects. But the objects are viewed from such different standpoints that they can be related only by shifting from one standpoint to the other. The realm of common sense is the realm of persons and things in their relations to us. It is the visible universe peopled by relatives, friends, acquaintances, fellow citizens, and the rest of humanity. We come to know it, not by applying some scientific method, but by a self-correcting process of learning, in which insights gradually accumulate, coalesce, qualify and correct one another, until a point is reached where we are able to meet situations as they arise, size them up by adding a few more insights to the acquired store, and so deal with them in an appropriate fashion. Of the objects in this realm we speak in everyday language, in which words have the function, not of naming the intrinsic properties of things, but of completing the focusing of our conscious intentionality on the things, of crystallizing our attitudes, expectations, intentions, of guiding all our actions.

The intrusion of the systematic exigence into the realm of common sense is beautifully illustrated by Plato's early dialogues. Socrates would ask for the definition of this or that virtue. No one could afford to admit that he had no idea of what was meant by courage or temperance or justice. No one could deny that such common names must possess some common meaning found in each instance of courage, or temperance, or justice. And no one, not even Socrates, was able to pin down just what that common meaning was. If from Plato's dialogues one shifts to Aristotle's *Nicomachean Ethics*, one can find definitions worked out both for virtue and vice in general and for a series of virtues each flanked by two opposite vices, one sinning by excess, and the other by defect. But these answers to Socrates' questions have now ceased to be the single objective. The systematic exigence not merely raises questions that common sense cannot answer but also demands a context for its answers, a context that common sense cannot supply or comprehend. This context is theory, and the objects to which it refers are in the realm of theory. To these objects one can ascend from commonsense starting-points, but they are properly known, not by this ascent, but by their internal relations, their congruences and differences, the functions they fulfil in their interactions. As one may approach theoretical objects from a commonsense starting-point, so too one can invoke common sense to correct theory. But the correction will not be effected in commonsense language but in theoretical language, and its implications will be the consequences, not of the commonsense facts that were invoked, but of the theoretical correction that was made.

My illustration was from Plato and Aristotle, but any number of others could be added. Mass, temperature, the electromagnetic field are not objects in the world of common sense. Mass is neither weight nor momentum. A metal object will feel colder than a wooden one beside it, but both will be of the same temperature. Maxwell's equations for the electromagnetic field are magnificent in their abstruseness. If a biologist takes his young son to the zoo and both pause to look at a giraffe, the boy will wonder whether it bites or kicks, but the father will see another manner in which skeletal, locomotive, digestive, vascular, and nervous systems combine and interlock.

There are then a realm of common sense and a realm of theory. We use different languages to speak of them. The difference in the languages involves social differences. ... Finally, what gives rise to these quite different standpoints, methods of coming to know, languages, communities, is the systematic exigence.

However, to meet fully the systematic exigence only reinforces the critical exigence. Is common sense just primitive ignorance to be brushed aside with an acclaim to science as the dawn of intelligence and reason? Or is science of merely pragmatic value, teaching us how to control nature, but failing to reveal what nature is? Or, for that matter, is there any such thing as human knowing? So man is confronted with the three basic questions: What am I doing when I am knowing? Why is doing that knowing? What do I know when I do it? With these questions one turns from the outer realms of common sense and theory to the appropriation of one's own interiority, one's subjectivity, one's operations, their structure, their norms, their potentialities. Such appropriation, in its technical expression, resembles theory. But in itself it is a heightening of intentional consciousness, an attending not merely to objects but also to the intending subject and his acts. And as this heightened consciousness constitutes the evidence for one's account of knowledge, such an account by the proximity of the evidence differs from all other expression.

The withdrawal into interiority is not an end in itself. From it one returns to the realms of common sense and theory with the ability to meet the methodical exigence. For self-appropriation of itself is a grasp of transcendental method, and that grasp provides one with the tools not only for an analysis of commonsense procedures but also for the differentiation of the sciences and the construction of their methods.

Finally, there is the transcendent exigence. There is to human inquiry an unrestricted demand for intelligibility. There is to human judgment a demand for the unconditioned. There is to human deliberation a criterion that criticizes every finite good. So it is ... that man can reach basic fulfilment, peace, joy, only by moving beyond the realms of common sense, theory, and interiority and into the realm in which God is known and loved.

It is, of course, only in a rather highly developed consciousness that the distinction between the realms of meaning is to be carried out. Undifferentiated consciousness uses indiscriminately the procedures of common sense, and so its explanations, its self-knowledge, its religion are rudimentary. Classical consciousness is theoretical as well as common sense, but the theory is not sufficiently advanced for the sharp opposition between the two realms of meaning to be adequately grasped. Troubled consciousness emerges when an Eddington contrasts his two tables: the bulky, solid, colored desk at which he worked, and the manifold of colorless 'wavicles' so minute that the desk was mostly empty space. Differentiated consciousness appears when the critical exigence turns attention upon interiority, when self-appropriation is achieved, when the subject relates his different procedures to the several realms, relates the several realms to one another, and consciously shifts from one realm to another by consciously changing his procedures.

The unity, then, of differentiated consciousness is, not the homogeneity of undifferentiated consciousness, but the self-knowledge that understands the different realms and knows how to shift from any one to any other. It remains, however, that what is easy for differentiated consciousness appears very mysterious to undifferentiated consciousness or to troubled consciousness. Undifferentiated consciousness insists on homogeneity. If the procedures of common sense are correct, then theory must be wrong. If theory is correct, then common sense must be just an antiquated relic from a pre-scientific age. If the transition from the undifferentiated to troubled consciousness cannot be avoided when it is clear that common sense and theory, though disparate, must both be accepted, an entirely different set of procedures has to be learnt before interiority can be revealed and the self-appropriation of differentiated consciousness achieved.

No doubt, we have all to begin from undifferentiated consciousness, from commonsense cognitional procedures, from some one of the multitudinous 'ordinary languages' in which the endless varieties of common sense express themselves. No doubt, it is only by a humble and docile process of learning that anyone can move beyond his original ordinary language and its common sense and come to understand other ordinary languages and their varieties of common sense. It is only by knowledge making its bloody entrance that one can move out of the realm of ordinary languages into the realm of theory and the totally different scientific apprehension of reality. It is only through the long and confused twilight of philosophic initiation that one can find one's way into interiority and achieve through self-appropriation a basis, a foundation, that is distinct from common sense and theory, that acknowledges their disparateness, that accounts for both and critically grounds them both.

Related selections: 2.IV on the functions of meaning and the historical shift from classical to modern controls of meaning; 1.IX.5 on the core of meaning; 4.I on the change in the notion of theory or system brought about by the shift from the second to the third stage of meaning; 3.VIII.2 on modes of meaning as theological categories.

IV

Religion

In the first part of this selection from Chapter 4 of *Method in Theology* Lonergan argues that the many historical and cultural expressions of the question of God, as well as the variety of religious and irreligious answers to that question, are rooted in 'the same transcendental tendency of the human spirit,' in the *pure question of God* that questions questioning itself. The pure question of God is 'our native orientation to the divine,' and its dismissal mutilates or abolishes our transcendental subjectivity. In the second part Lonergan locates the proper fulfillment of the human capacity for self-transcendence, for going beyond ourselves cognitionally and morally, in 'being in love in an unrestricted fashion,' in being in love with God. This love 'takes over the peak of the soul,' it is experienced as the fulfillment of consciousness on the fourth level, of moral consciousness. In the third part Lonergan turns to the dialectical character of religious development: 'Human authenticity is never some pure and serene and secure possession.'[1] Religious development is a struggle between authenticity and unauthenticity. In the fourth part Lonergan defines religious faith as knowledge born of religious love. The final part is a methodological note on the consequences of beginning theological reflection from the standpoint afforded, not by the theoretic mode of consciousness intentionality, but by the mode of interiority described in the preceding selection. Lonergan describes the implications of this new approach for long-standing disputes about the priority of intellect over will or of will over intellect. The conscious and intentional mode of interiority, by which one moves beyond the realm of theoretic meaning, just as theoretic meaning moves beyond commonsense meaning, underpins Lonergan's effort 'to put method in theology.' It supplies the trans-

1 *Method in Theology*, 110.

cultural bases for the future derivation of general and special theological categories.

These extracts are taken from *Method in Theology*, 101–3, 105–7, 110–12, 115–18, 120–3.

1   The Question of God

The facts of good and evil, of progress and decline, raise questions about the character of our universe. Such questions have been put in very many ways, and the answers given have been even more numerous. But behind this multiplicity there is a basic unity that comes to light in the exercise of transcendental method. We can inquire into the possibility of fruitful inquiry. We can reflect on the nature of reflection. We can deliberate whether our deliberating is worthwhile. In each case, there arises the question of God.

The possibility of inquiry on the side of the subject lies in his intelligence, in his drive to know what, why, how, and in his ability to reach intellectualy satisfying answers. But why should the answers that satisfy the intelligence of the subject yield anything more than a subjective satisfaction? Why should they be supposed to possess any relevance to knowledge of the universe? Of course, we assume that they do. We can point to the fact that our assumption is confirmed by its fruits. So implicitly we grant that the universe is intelligible and, once that is granted, there arises the question whether the universe could be intelligible without having an intelligent ground. But that is the question of God.

Again, to reflect on reflection is to ask just what happens when we marshal and weigh the evidence for pronouncing that this probably is so and that probably is not so. To what do these metaphors of marshalling and weighing refer? Elsewhere I have worked out an answer to this question and here I can do no more than summarily repeat my conclusions.[2] Judgment proceeds rationally from a grasp of a virtually unconditioned. By an unconditioned is meant any 'x' that has no conditions. By a virtually unconditioned is meant any 'x' that has no unfulfilled conditions. In other words, a virtually unconditioned is a conditioned whose conditions are all fulfilled. To marshal the evidence

---

2 *Insight*, chaps. 9–11 [see 1.VII and 1.VIII in this reader].

is to ascertain whether all the conditions are fulfilled. To weigh the evidence is to ascertain whether the fulfilment of the conditions certainly or probably involves the existence or occurrence of the conditioned.

Now this account of judgment implicitly contains a further element. If we are to speak of a virtually unconditioned, we must first speak of an unconditioned. The virtually unconditioned has no unfulfilled conditions. The strictly unconditioned has no conditions whatever. In traditional terms, the former is a contingent being, and the latter is a necessary being. In more contemporary terms the former pertains to this world, to the world of possible experience, while the latter transcends this world in the sense that its reality is of a totally different order. But in either case we come to the question of God. Does a necessary being exist? Does there exist a reality that transcends the reality of this world?

To deliberate about 'x' is to ask whether 'x' is worthwhile. To deliberate about deliberating is to ask whether any deliberating is worthwhile. Has 'worthwhile' any ultimate meaning? Is moral enterprise consonant with this world? We praise the developing subject ever more capable of attention, insight, reasonableness, responsibility. We praise progress and denounce every manifestation of decline. But is the universe on our side, or are we just gamblers and, if we are gamblers, are we not perhaps fools, individually struggling for authenticity and collectively endeavoring to snatch progress from the ever mounting welter of decline? The questions arise and, clearly, our attitudes and our resoluteness may be profoundly affected by the answers. Does there or does there not necessarily exist a transcendent, intelligent ground of the universe? Is that ground or are we the primary instance of moral consciousness? Are cosmogenesis, biological evolution, historical process basically cognate to us as moral beings or are they indifferent and so alien to us?

Such is the question of God. It is not a matter of image or feeling, of concept or judgment. They pertain to answers. It is a question. It rises out of our conscious intentionality, out of the *a priori* structured drive that promotes us from experiencing to the effort to understand, from understanding to the effort to judge truly, from judging to the effort to choose rightly. In the measure that we advert to our own questioning and proceed to question it, there arises the question of God.

It is a question that will be manifested differently in the different

stages of man's historical development and in the many varieties of his
culture. But such differences of manifestation and expression are secondary. They may introduce alien elements that overlay, obscure, distort the pure question, the question that questions questioning itself.
None the less, the obscurity and the distortion presuppose what they
obscure and distort. It follows that, however much religious or irreligious answers differ, however much there differ the questions they
explicitly raise, still at their root there is the same transcendental tendency of the human spirit that questions, that questions without
restriction, that questions the significance of its own questioning, and
so comes to the question of God.

The question of God, then, lies within man's horizon. Man's transcendental subjectivity is mutilated or abolished, unless he is stretch-
ing forth towards the intelligible, the unconditioned, the good of value.
The reach, not of his attainment, but of his intending is unrestricted.
There lies within his horizon a region for the divine, a shrine for ultimate holiness. It cannot be ignored. The atheist may pronounce it
empty. The agnostic may urge that he finds his investigation has been
inconclusive. The contemporary humanist will refuse to allow the
question to arise. But their negations presuppose the spark in our clod,
our native orientation to the divine.

2 Religious Experience

As the question of God is implicit in all our questioning, so being in
love with God is the basic fulfilment of our conscious intentionality.
That fulfilment brings a deep-set joy that can remain despite humilia-
tion, failure, privation, pain, betrayal, desertion. That fulfilment brings
a radical peace, the peace that the world cannot give. That fulfilment
bears fruit in a love of one's neighbor that strives mightily to bring
about the kingdom of God on this earth. On the other hand, the
absence of that fulfilment opens the way to the trivialization of human
life in the pursuit of fun, to the harshness of human life arising from
the ruthless exercise of power, to despair about human welfare springing from the conviction that the universe is absurd.

Being in love with God, as experienced, is being in love in an unrestricted fashion. All love is self-surrender, but being in love with God
is being in love without limits or qualifications or conditions or reservations. Just as unrestricted questioning is our capacity for self-

transcendence, so being in love in an unrestricted fashion is the proper fulfilment of that capacity.

That fulfilment is not the product of our knowledge and choice. On the contrary, it dismantles and abolishes the horizon in which our knowing and choosing went on and it sets up a new horizon in which the love of God will transvalue our values and the eyes of that love will transform our knowing.

Though not the product of our knowing and choosing, it is a conscious dynamic state of love, joy, peace, that manifests itself in acts of kindness, goodness, fidelity, gentleness, and self-control (Gal. 5, 22).

To say that this dynamic state is conscious is not to say that it is known. For consciousness is just experience, but knowledge is a compound of experience, understanding, and judging. Because the dynamic state is conscious without being known, it is an experience of mystery. Because it is being in love, the mystery is not merely attractive but fascinating; to it one belongs; by it one is possessed. Because it is an unmeasured love, the mystery evokes awe. Of itself, then, inasmuch as it is conscious without being known, the gift of God's love is an experience of the holy, of Rudolf Otto's *mysterium fascinans et tremendum*.[3] It is what Paul Tillich named being grasped by ultimate concern.[4] It corresponds to St Ignatius Loyola's consolation that has no cause, as expounded by Karl Rahner.[5]

It is conscious on the fourth level of intentional consciousness. It is not the consciousness that accompanies acts of seeing, hearing, smelling, tasting, touching. It is not the consciousness that accompanies acts of inquiry, insight, formulating, speaking. It is not the consciousness that accompanies acts of reflecting, marshalling and weighing the evidence, making judgments of fact or possibility. It is the type of consciousness that deliberates, makes judgments of value, decides, acts responsibly and freely. But it is this consciousness as brought to a fulfilment, as having undergone a conversion, as possessing a basis that may be broadened and deepened and heightened and enriched but not

---

3 Rudolf Otto, *The Idea of the Holy* (London: Oxford: Oxford University Press, 1923). Note that the meaning of *tremendum* varies with the stage of one's religious development.

4 D.M. Brown, *Ultimate Concern: Tillich in Dialogue* (New York: Harper and Row, 1965).

5 Karl Rahner, *The Dynamic Element in the Church, Quaestiones disputatae*, vol. 12 (Montreal: Palm Publishers, 1964), 131 ff. Fr. Rahner takes 'consolation with a cause' to mean 'consolation with a content but without an object.'

superseded, as ready to deliberate and judge and decide and act with the easy freedom of those that do all good because they are in love. So the gift of God's love occupies the ground and root of the fourth and highest level of man's intentional consciousness. It takes over the peak of the soul, the *apex animae* ...

3   The Dialectical Character of Religious Development

Religious development is not simply the unfolding in all its consequences of a dynamic state of being in love in an unrestricted manner. For that love is the utmost in self-transcendence, and man's self-transcendence is ever precarious. Of itself, self-transcendence involves tension between the self as transcending and the self as transcended. So human authenticity is never some pure and serene and secure possession. It is ever a withdrawal from unauthenticity, and every successful withdrawal only brings to light the need for still further withdrawals. Our advance in understanding is also the elimination of oversights and misunderstandings. Our advance in truth is also the correction of mistakes and errors. Our moral development is through repentance for our sins. Genuine religion is discovered and realized by redemption from the many traps of religious aberration. So we are bid to watch and pray, to make our way in fear and trembling. And it is the greatest saints that proclaim themselves the greatest sinners, though their sins seem slight indeed to less holy folk that lack their discernment and their love ...

   I have conceived being in love with God as an ultimate fulfilment of man's capacity for self-transcendence; and this view of religion is sustained when God is conceived as the supreme fulfilment of the transcendental notions, as supreme intelligence, truth, reality, righteousness, goodness. Inversely, when the love of God is not strictly associated with self-transcendence, then easily indeed it is reinforced by the erotic, the sexual, the orgiastic.[6] On the other hand, the love of God also is penetrated with awe. God's thoughts and God's ways are very different from man's and by that difference God is terrifying. Unless religion is totally directed to what is good, to genuine love of one's neighbor and to a self-denial that is subordinated to a fuller goodness in oneself, then the cult of a God that is terrifying can slip

6 A. Vergote, *Psychologie religieuse* (Brussels: Dessart, 1966), 55.

over into the demonic, into an exultant destructiveness of oneself and of others.[7]

Such, then, is what is meant by saying that religious development is dialectical. It is not a struggle between any opposites whatever but the very precise opposition between authenticity and unauthenticity, between the self as transcending and the self as transcended. It is not just an opposition between contrary propositions but an opposition within the human reality of individuals and of groups. It is not to be defined simply by some *a priori* construction of categories but also to be discovered *a posteriori* by a discerning study of history. It is not confined to the oppositions we have sketched but down the ages it ranges through the endless variety of institutional, cultural, personal, and religious development, decline, and recovery ...

4 Faith

Faith is knowledge born of religious love.

First, then, there is a knowledge born of love. Of it Pascal spoke when he remarked that the heart has reasons which reason does not know. Here by reason I would understand the compound of activities on the first three levels of cognitional activity, namely, of experiencing, of understanding, and of judging. By the heart's reasons I would understand feelings that are intentional responses to values; and I would recall the two aspects of such responses, the absolute aspect that is a recognition of value, and the relative aspect that is a preference of one value over another. Finally, by the heart I understand the subject on the fourth, existential level of intentional consciousness and in the dynamic state of being in love. The meaning, then, of Pascal's remark would be that, besides the factual knowledge reached by experiencing, understanding, and verifying, there is another kind of knowledge reached through the discernment of value and the judgments of value of a person in love.

Faith, accordingly, is such further knowledge when the love is God's love flooding our hearts. To our apprehension of vital, social, cultural, and personal values, there is added an apprehension of transcendent value. This apprehension consists in the experienced fulfilment of our unrestricted thrust to self-transcendence, in our actuated orientation

7 Ibid., 57. Cf. Rollo May, *Love and Will* (New York: Norton, 1969), chaps. 5 and 6.

towards the mystery of love and awe. Since that thrust is of intelligence to the intelligible, of reasonableness to the true and real, of freedom and responsibility to the truly good, the experienced fulfilment of that thrust in its unrestrictedness may be objectified as a clouded revelation of absolute intelligence and intelligibility, absolute truth and reality, absolute goodness and holiness. With that objectification there recurs the question of God in a new form. For now it is primarily a question of decision. Will I love him in return, or will I refuse? Will I live out the gift of his love, or will I hold back, turn away, withdraw? Only secondarily do there arise the questions of God's existence and nature, and they are the questions either of the lover seeking to know him or of the unbeliever seeking to escape him. Such is the basic option of the existential subject once called by God.

As other apprehensions of value, so too faith has a relative as well as an absolute aspect. It places all other values in the light and the shadow of transcendent value. In the shadow, for transcendent value is supreme and incomparable. In the light, for transcendent value links itself to all other values to transform, magnify, glorify them. Without faith the originating value is man and the terminal value is the human good man brings about. But in the light of faith, originating value is divine light and love, while terminal value is the whole universe. So the human good becomes absorbed in an all-encompassing good. Where before an account of the human good related men to one another and to nature, now human concern reaches beyond man's world to God and to God's world. Men meet not only to be together and to settle human affairs but also to worship. Human development is not only in skills and virtues but also in holiness. The power of God's love brings forth a new energy and efficacy in all goodness, and the limit of human expectation ceases to be the grave.

To conceive God as originating value and the world as terminal value implies that God too is self-transcending and that the world is the fruit of his self-transcendence, the expression and manifestation of his benevolence and beneficence, his glory. As the excellence of the son is the glory of his father, so too the excellence of mankind is the glory of God. To say that God created the world for his glory is to say that he created it not for his sake but for ours.[8] He made us in his image, for

---

8 'Deus suam gloriam non quaerit propter se sed propter nos.' Aquinas, *Sum. Theol.*, 2–2, q. 132, a. 1 ad 1m.

our authenticity consists in being like him, in self-transcending, in being origins of value, in true love.

Without faith, without the eye of love, the world is too evil for God to be good, for a good God to exist. But faith recognizes that God grants men their freedom, that he wills them to be persons and not just his automata, that he calls them to the higher authenticity that overcomes evil with good. So faith is linked with human progress and it has to meet the challenge of human decline. For faith and progress have a common root in man's cognitional and moral self-transcendence. To promote either is to promote the other indirectly. Faith places human efforts in a friendly universe; it reveals an ultimate significance in human achievement; it strengthens new undertakings with confidence. Inversely, progress realizes the potentialities of man and of nature; it reveals that man exists to bring about an ever fuller achievement in this world; and that achievement because it is man's good also is God's glory. Most of all, faith has the power of undoing decline. Decline disrupts a culture with conflicting ideologies. It inflicts on individuals the social, economic, and psychological pressures that for human frailty amount to determinism. It multiplies and heaps up the abuses and absurdities that breed resentment, hatred, anger, violence. It is not propaganda and it is not argument but religious faith that will liberate human reasonableness from its ideological prisons. It is not the promises of men but religious hope that can enable men to resist the vast pressures of social decay. If passions are to quiet down, if wrongs are to be not exacerbated, not ignored, not merely palliated, but acknowledged and removed, then human possessiveness and human pride have to be replaced by religious charity, by the charity of the suffering servant, by self-sacrificing love. Men are sinners. If human progress is not to be ever distorted and destroyed by the inattention, oversights, irrationality, irresponsibility of decline, men have to be reminded of their sinfulness. They have to acknowledge their real guilt and amend their ways. They have to learn with humility that religious development is dialectical, that the task of repentance and conversion is life-long.

5   A Technical Note

Where we distinguish four realms of meaning, namely, common sense, theory, interiority, and transcendence, an older theology distinguished only two, common sense and theory, under the Aristotelian designation of the *priora quoad nos* [first for us] and *priora quoad se* [first in itself]. Hence, the older theology, when it spoke of inner experience or of God, either did so within the realm of common sense – and then its speech was shot through with figure and symbol – or else it did so in the realm of theory – and then its speech was basically metaphysical. One consequence of this difference has already been noted. The older theology conceived sanctifying grace as an entitative habit, absolutely supernatural, infused into the essence of the soul. On the other hand, because we acknowledge interiority as a distinct realm of meaning, we can begin with a description of religious experience, acknowledge a dynamic state of being in love without restrictions, and later identify this state with the state of sanctifying grace.

But there are other consequences. Because its account of interiority was basically metaphysical, the older theology distinguished sensitive and intellectual, apprehensive and appetitive potencies. There followed complex questions on their mutual interactions. There were disputes about the priority of intellect over will or of will over intellect, of speculative over practical intellect or of practical over speculative. In contrast, we describe interiority in terms of intentional and conscious acts on the four levels of experiencing, understanding, judging, and deciding. The lower levels are presupposed and complemented by the higher. The higher sublate the lower. If one wishes to transpose this analysis into metaphysical terms, then the active potencies are the transcendental notions revealed in questions for intelligence, questions for reflection, questions for deliberation. The passive potencies are the lower levels as presupposed and complemented by the higher. While these relationships are fixed, still they do not settle questions of initiative or precedence. Significant change on any level calls for adjustments on other levels, and the order in which the adjustments take place depends mostly on the readiness with which they can be effected.

The fourth level, which presupposes, complements, and sublates the other three, is the level of freedom and responsibility, of moral self-transcendence and in that sense of existence, of self-direction and self-control. Its failure to function properly is the uneasy or the bad conscience. Its success is marked by the satisfying feeling that one's duty has been done.

As the fourth level is the principle of self-control, it is responsible for proper functioning on the first three levels. It fulfils its responsibility or fails to do so in the measure that we are attentive or inattentive in experiencing, that we are intelligent or unintelligent in our investigations, that we are reasonable or unreasonable in our judgments. Therewith vanish two notions: the notion of pure intellect or pure reason that operates on its own without guidance or control from responsible decision; and the notion of will as an arbitrary power indifferently choosing between good and evil ...

Again, what gives plausibility to the notion of pure intellect or pure reason is the fact that cognitional self-transcendence is much easier than moral self-transcendence. But this does not mean that cognitional self-transcendence is easy. Primitive peoples live under a regime of myth and magic. Only slowly and reluctantly do the young master grammar, logic, method. Only through deliberate decision do people dedicate themselves to lives of scholarship or science, and only through the continuous renewal of that dedication do they achieve the goals they have set themselves. A life of pure intellect or pure reason without the control of deliberation, evaluation, responsible choice is something less than the life of a psychopath.

Let us now turn to a further aspect of the matter. It used to be said, *Nihil amatum nisi praecognitum*, Knowledge precedes love. The truth of this tag is the fact that ordinarily operations on the fourth level of intentional consciousness presuppose and complement corresponding operations on the other three. There is a minor exception to this rule inasmuch as people do fall in love, and that falling in love is something disproportionate to its causes, conditions, occasions, antecedents. For falling in love is a new beginning, an exercise of vertical liberty in which one's world undergoes a new organization. But the major exception to the Latin tag is God's gift of his love flooding our hearts. Then we are in the dynamic state of being in love.[9] But who it is we love, is neither given nor as yet understood. Our capacity for moral self-transcendence has found a fulfilment that brings deep joy and profound peace. Our love reveals to us values we had not appreciated, values of prayer and worship, or repentance and belief. But if we would know what is going on within us, if we would learn to integrate it with the rest of our living, we have to inquire, investigate, seek

9 For equivalent but differing accounts of this being in love, see Alan Richardson, *Religion in Contemporary Debate* (London: SCM, 1966), 113 ff.; Oliver Rabut, *L'expérience religieuse fondamentale* (Tournai: Castermann, 1969), 168.

counsel. So it is that in religious matters love precedes knowledge and, as that love is God's gift, the very beginning of faith is due to God's grace.

Related selections: 1.XV.1–2 on the immanent source of transcendence and the affirmation of God; 2.II on openness and religious experience; 3.VII.2 on religious conversion; 1.XIV.1 on rational self-consciousness, and 2.VII.4 on the existential subject; 2.VI on the new context of theology; 2.IV on classical and modern controls of meaning, and 3.III on realms of meaning; 3.VIII.3 on special theological categories; 4.IV on healing in history; 4.III.1–2 on the outer factors influencing the emergence of a new religious consciousness.

Functional Specialties

In this final selection from Part 1 of *Method in Theology*, Lonergan provides a schematic description of his proposed collaborative method for a theology that mediates between a cultural matrix and the significance and role of religion in that matrix. The proposed theology consists of eight related functional specialties arranged in two phases. In the first part of this selection Lonergan distinguishes functional specialization from more familiar types of specialization. In the second part he describes briefly each of the eight functional specialties. In Part 2 of *Method in Theology* each specialty is discussed at greater length. In the final part of the present selection Lonergan explains the grounds of his division of theological activity into two phases and eight specialties. The division has its grounds both in theological tradition and in the structure of transcendental subjectivity, the four-level structure of the self-transcending subject. As the 'Background' chapters of *Method in Theology* provide a general basis for the methodical and deliberate pursuit of any discipline which looks to the past in order to enlighten the future, so the relevance of the eight functional specialties outlined here extends well beyond the discipline of theology.

This extract is taken from *Method in Theology*, 125–6; 127–33; 133–6.

To put method in theology is to conceive theology as a set of related and recurrent operations cumulatively advancing towards an ideal goal. However, contemporary theology is specialized, and so it is to be conceived, not as a single set of related operations, but as a series of interdependent sets. To formulate this conception of theology, first, we shall distinguish field, subject, and functional specializations. Next, we shall describe the eight functional specializations in theology [and] set forth the grounds for this division ...

1 Three Types of Specialization

Specialities may be distinguished in three manners, namely (1) by dividing and subdividing the field of data, (2) by classifying the results of investigations, and (3) by distinguishing and separating stages of the process from data to results.

Field specialization is the most easily understood. As time passes, as centers of learning increase, as periodicals multiply and monographs follow on one another ever more closely, it becomes increasingly difficult for scholars to keep abreast with the whole movement in their field. For good or ill a division of labor has to be accepted, and this is brought about by dividing and then subdividing the field of relevant data. So scriptural, patristic, medieval, reformation studies become genera to be divided into species and subspecies, to make the specialist one who knows more and more about less and less.

Department and subject specialization is the most familiar type, for everyone has followed courses on subjects in a department. Now what is divided is no longer the field of data to be investigated but the results of investigations to be communicated. Again, where before the division was into material parts, now it is a conceptual classification that distinguishes the departments of a faculty and the subjects taught in a department. Thus, where field specialization would divide the Old Testament into the Law, the Prophets, and the Writings, subject specialization would distinguish semitic languages, Hebrew history, the religions of the ancient Near East, and Christian theology.

Functional specialization distinguishes and separates successive stages in the process from data to results. Thus, textual criticism aims at determining what was written. The interpreter or commentator takes over where the textual critic leaves off; his aim is to determine what was meant. The historian moves in on a third level; he assembles interpreted texts and endeavors to construct a single narrative or view.

Again, to take a quite different instance, experimental physicists alone have the knowledge and skills needed to handle a cyclotron. But only theoretical physicists are able to tell what experiments are worth trying and, when they are tried, what is the significance of the results.

Once more a single process of investigation is divided into successive stages, and each stage becomes a distinct specialty.

It is to be noted that such functional specialties are intrinsically related to one another. They are successive parts of one and the same process. The earlier parts are incomplete without the later. The later presuppose the earlier and complement them. In brief, functional specialties are functionally interdependent.

Such interdependence is of the greatest methodological interest. First, without any prejudice to unity, it divides and clarifies the process from data to results. Secondly, it provides an orderly link between field specialization, based on the division of data, and subject specialization, based on a classification of results. Thirdly, the unity of functional specialties will be found, I think, to overcome or, at least, counter-balance the endless divisions of field specialization.

2   An Eightfold Division

In this section we propose to describe briefly eight functional specialties in theology, namely, (1) research, (2) interpretation, (3) history, (4) dialectic, (5) foundations, (6) doctrines, (7) systematics, and (8) communications. Later we shall attempt to state the grounds for the foregoing division, its precise meaning, and its implications. For the moment, however, we aim at no more than a preliminary indication of the material meaning of functional specialization in theology.

(1) Research makes available the data relevant to theological investigation. It is either general or special. Special research is concerned with assembling the data relevant to some particular question or problem, such as the doctrine of Mr. X on the question Y. Such special research operates all the more rapidly and effectively the more familiar it is with the tools made available by general research. General research locates, excavates, and maps ancient cities. It fills museums and reproduces or copies inscriptions, symbols, pictures, statues. It deciphers unknown scripts and languages. It collects and catalogues manuscripts, and prepares critical editions of texts. It composes indices, tables, repertories, bibliographies, abstracts, bulletins, handbooks, dictionaries, encyclopedias. Some day, perhaps, it will give us a complete information-retrieval system.

(2) While research makes available what was written, interpretation understands what was meant. It grasps that meaning in its proper his-

torical context, in accord with its proper mode and level of thought
and expression, in the light of the circumstances and intention of the
writer. Its product is the commentary or monograph. It is an enterprise
replete with pitfalls and today it is further complicated by the importa-
tion of the problems of cognitional theory, epistemology, and metaphysics ...

(3) History is basic, special, or general.

Basic history tells where (places, territories) and when (dates, periods) who (persons, peoples) did what (public life, external acts) to
enjoy what success, suffer what reverses, exert what influence. So it
makes as specific and precise as possible the more easily recognized
and acknowledged features of human activities in their geographical
distribution and temporal succession.

Special histories tell of movements whether cultural (language, art,
literature, religion), institutional (family, mores, society, education,
state, law, church, sect, economy, technology), or doctrinal (mathematical, natural science, human science, philosophy, history, theology).

General history is, perhaps, just an ideal. It would be basic history
illuminated and completed by the special histories. It would offer the
total view or some approximation to it. It would express the historian's
information, understanding, judgment, and evaluation with regard to
the sum of cultural, institutional, and doctrinal movements in their
concrete setting.

History, as a functional specialty within theology, is concerned in
different degrees and manners with basic, special, and general history.
In the main it has to presuppose basic history. Its substantial concern is
the doctrinal history of Christian theology with its antecedents and
consequents in the cultural and institutional histories of the Christian
religion and the Christian churches and sects. Finally, it cannot remain
aloof from general history, for it is only within the full view that can be
grasped the differences between the Christian churches and sects, the
relations between different religions, and the role of Christianity in
world history.

(4) Our fourth functional specialty is dialectic. While that name has
been employed in many ways, the sense we intend is simple enough.
Dialectic has to do with the concrete, the dynamic, and the contradictory, and so it finds abundant materials in the history of Christian
movements. For all movements are at once concrete and dynamic,
while Christian movements have been marked with external and inter-

nal conflict, whether one considers Christianity as a whole or even this or that larger church or communion.

The materials of dialectic, then, are primarily the conflicts centering in Christian movements. But to these must be added the secondary conflicts in historical accounts and theological interpretations of the movements.

Besides the materials of dialectic, there is its aim. This is high and distant. As empirical science aims at a complete explanation of all phenomena, so dialectic aims at a comprehensive viewpoint. It seeks some single base or some single set of related bases from which it can proceed to an understanding of the character, the oppositions, and the relations of the many viewpoints exhibited in conflicting Christian movements, their conflicting histories, and their conflicting interpretations.

Besides the conflicts of Christians and the distant goal of a comprehensive viewpoint, there is also the past and present fact of the many diverging viewpoints that result in the conflicts. Such viewpoints are manifested in confessions of faith and learned works of apologists. But they also are manifested, often in a more vital manner, in the unnoticed assumptions and oversights, in the predilections and aversions, in the quiet but determined decisions of scholars.

Now the study of these viewpoints takes one beyond the fact to the reasons for conflict. Comparing them will bring to light just where differences are irreducible, where they are complementary and could be brought together within a larger whole, where finally they can be regarded as successive stages in a single process of development.

Besides comparison there is criticism. Not every viewpoint is coherent, and those that are not can be invited to advance to a consistent position. Not every reason is a sound reason, and Christianity has nothing to lose from a purge of unsound reasons, of *ad hoc* explanations, of the stereotypes that body forth suspicions, resentments, hatreds, malice. Not every irreducible difference is a serious difference, and those that are not can be put in second or third or fourth place so that attention, study, analysis can be devoted to differences that are serious and profound.

By dialectic, then, is understood a generalized apologetic conducted in an ecumenical spirit, aiming ultimately at a comprehensive viewpoint, and proceeding towards that goal by acknowledging differences, seeking their grounds real and apparent, and eliminating superfluous oppositions.

(5) As conversion is basic to Christian living, so an objectification of conversion provides theology with its foundations.

By conversion is understood a transformation of the subject and his world. Normally it is a prolonged process though its explicit acknowledgment may be concentrated in a few momentous judgments and decisions. Still it is not just a development or even a series of developments. Rather it is a resultant change of course and direction. It is as if one's eyes were opened and one's former world faded and fell away. There emerges something new that fructifies in interlocking, cumulative sequences of developments on all levels and in all departments of human living.

Conversion is existential, intensely personal, utterly intimate. But it is not so private as to be solitary. It can happen to many, and they can form a community to sustain one another in their self-transformation and to help one another in working out the implications and fulfilling the promise of their new life. Finally, what can become communal, can become historical. It can pass from generation to generation. It can spread from one cultural milieu to another. It can adapt to changing circumstances, confront new situations, survive into a different age, flourish in another period or epoch.

Conversion, as lived, affects all of a man's conscious and intentional operations. It directs his gaze, pervades his imagination, releases the symbols that penetrate to the depths of his psyche. It enriches his understanding, guides his judgments, reinforces his decisions. But as communal and historical, as a movement with its own cultural, institutional, and doctrinal dimensions, conversion calls forth a reflection that makes the movement thematic, that explicitly explores its origins, developments, purposes, achievements, and failures.

Inasmuch as conversion itself is made thematic and explicitly objectified, there emerges the fifth functional specialty, foundations. Such foundations differ from the old fundamental theology in two respects. First, fundamental theology was a theological first; it did not follow on four other specialties named research, interpretation, history, and dialectic. Secondly, fundamental theology was a set of doctrines, *de vera religione, de legato divino, de ecclesia, de inspiratione scripturae, de locis theologicis.* In contrast, foundations present, not doctrines, but the horizon within which the meaning of doctrines can be apprehended. Just as in religious living 'a man who is unspiritual refuses what belongs to the Spirit of God; it is folly to him; he cannot grasp it' (1 Cor. 2, 14), so in theological reflection on religious living there have to be distinguished the horizons within which religious doctrines can or cannot be apprehended; and this distinction is foundational.

In due course we shall have to ask how horizon is to be understood and defined and how one horizon may differ from another. At once, however, we may note that as conversion may be authentic or unauthentic, so there may be many Christian horizons and not all of them need represent authentic conversion. Further, while it may be possible to conceive authentic conversion in more than one manner, still the number of possible manners would seem to be far fewer than the number of possible horizons. It follows that our foundations contain a promise both of an elucidation of the conflicts revealed in dialectic and of a selective principle that will guide the remaining specialties concerned with doctrines, systematics, and communications.

(6) Doctrines express judgments of fact and judgments of value. They are concerned, then, with the affirmations and negations not only of dogmatic theology but also of moral, ascetical, mystical, pastoral, and any similar branch.

Such doctrines stand within the horizon of foundations. They have their precise definition from dialectic, their positive wealth of clarification and development from history, their grounds in the interpretation of the data proper to theology.

(7) The facts and values affirmed in doctrines give rise to further questions. For doctrinal expression may be figurative or symbolic. It may be descriptive and based ultimately on the meaning of words rather than on an understanding of realities. It may, if pressed, quickly become vague and indefinite. It may seem, when examined, to be involved in inconsistency or fallacy.

The functional specialty, systematics, attempts to meet these issues. It is concerned to work out appropriate systems of conceptualization, to remove apparent inconsistencies, to move towards some grasp of spiritual matters both from their own inner coherence and from the analogies offered by more familiar human experience.

(8) Communications is concerned with theology in its external relations. These are of three kinds. There are interdisciplinary relations with art, language, literature, and other religions, with the natural and the human sciences, with philosophy and history. Further, there are the transpositions that theological thought has to develop if religion is to retain its identity and yet at the same time find access into the minds

and hearts of men of all cultures and classes. Finally, there are the adaptations needed to make full and proper use of the diverse media of communication that are available at any place and time.

3 Grounds of the Division

We have indicated in summary fashion eight functional specialties. We have now to explain where this list of eight comes from and what are the principles to be invoked in further clarifications of meaning and delimitations of function.

The first principle of the division is that theological operations occur in two basic phases. If one is to harken to the word, one must also bear witness to it. If one engages in *lectio divina*, there come to mind *questiones*. If one assimilates tradition, one learns that one should pass it on. If one encounters the past, one also has to take one's stand toward the future. In brief, there is a theology *in oratione obliqua* that tells what Paul and John, Augustine and Aquinas, and anyone else had to say about God and the economy of salvation. But there is also a theology *in oratione recta* in which the theologian, enlightened by the past, confronts the problems of his own day.

The second principle of division is derived from the fact that our conscious and intentional operations occur on four distinct levels and that each level has its own proper achievement and end. So the proper achievement and end of the first level, experiencing, is the apprehension of data; that of the second level, understanding, is insight into the apprehended data; that of the third level, judgment, is the acceptance or rejection of the hypotheses and theories put forward by understanding to account for the data; that of the fourth level, decision, the acknowledgment of values and the selection of the methods or other means that lead to their realization.

Now in everyday, commonsense performance, all four levels are employed continuously without any explicit distinction between them. In that case no functional specialization arises, for what is sought is not the end of any particular level but the cumulative, composite resultant of the ends of all four levels. But in a scientific investigation the ends proper to particular levels may become the objective sought by operations on all four levels. So the textual critic will select the method (level of decision) that he feels will lead to the discovery (level of understanding) of what one may reasonably affirm (level of judgment) was written in the original text (level of experience). The textual critic, then, operates on all four levels, but his goal is the end proper to the first level, namely, to ascertain the data. The interpreter, however, pursues a different goal. He wishes to understand the text, and so he selects a different method. Moreover, he cannot confine his operations to the second level, understanding, and to the fourth, a selective decision. He must apprehend the text accurately before he can hope to understand it, and so he has to operate on the first level; and he has to judge whether or not his understanding is correct, for otherwise he will fail to distinguish between understanding and misunderstanding.

Functional specializations arise, then, inasmuch as one operates on all four levels to achieve the end proper to some particular level. But there are four levels and so four proper ends. It follows that the very structure of human inquiry results in four functional specializations and, since in theology there are two distinct phases, we are led to expect eight functional specializations in theology. In the first phase of theology *in oratione obliqua* there are research, interpretation, history, and dialectic. In the second phase of theology *in oratione recta* there are foundations, doctrines, systematics, and communications.

So in assimilating the past, first, there is research that uncovers and makes available the data, secondly, there is interpretation that understands their meaning, thirdly, there is history that judges and narrates what occurred and, fourthly, there is dialectic that endeavors to unravel the conflicts concerning values, facts, meanings, and experiences. The first four functional specialties, then, seek the ends proper respectively to experiencing, understanding, judging, and deciding; and, of course, each one does so by employing not some one but all four of the levels of conscious and intentional operations.

This fourfold specialization corresponds to the four dimensions of the Christian message and the Christian tradition. For that message and tradition, first of all, are a range of data. Secondly, the data purport to convey not the phenomena of things, as in the natural sciences, but the meanings entertained and communicated by minds, as in the human sciences. Thirdly, these meanings were uttered at given times and places and transmitted through determinate channels and under sundry vicissitudes. Fourthly, the utterance and the transmission were the work of persons bearing witness to Christ Jesus and, by their words and deeds, bringing about the present religious situation.

Research, then, interpretation, history, and dialectic reveal the religious situation. They mediate an encounter with persons witnessing to Christ. They challenge to a decision: in what manner or measure am I to carry the burden of continuity or to risk the initiative of change? That decision, however, is primarily not a theological but a religious event; it pertains to the prior more spontaneous level on which theology reflects and which it illuminates and objectifies; it enters explicitly into theology only as reflected on and objectified in the fifth specialty, foundations.

With such a decision, however, there is effected the transition from the first to the second phase. The first phase is mediating theology. It is research, interpretation, history, dialectic that introduce us to knowledge of the Body of Christ. But the second phase is mediated theology. It is knowledge of God and of all things as ordered to God, not indeed as God is known immediately (1 Cor. 13, 12), nor as he is known mediately through created nature, but as he is known mediately through the whole Christ, Head and members.

In the second phase the specialties have been named in inverse order. Like dialectic, foundations is on the level of decision. Like history, doctrines is on the level of judgment. Like interpretation, systematics aims at understanding. Finally, as research tabulates the data from the past, so communications produces data in the present and for the future.

The reason for the inverted order is simple enough. In the first phase one begins from the data and moves through meanings and facts towards personal encounter. In the second phase one begins from reflection on authentic conversion, employs it as the horizon within which doctrines are to be apprehended and an understanding of their content sought, and finally moves to a creative exploration of communications differentiated according to media, according to classes of men, and according to common cultural interests.

Related selections: 3.I on transcendental method and its functions; 2.VI on the new context of theology; 3.1 on method, the four levels of conscious intentionality, and the functions of transcendental method; 4.I on the relativization of logic and emphasis of method resulting from the move into the interior mode of conscious intentionality and the third stage of meaning.

VI

History and Historical Method

The following selections are from the two 'foreground' chapters devoted to the functional specialty, history, in Part 2 of *Method in Theology*. In the first part of the present selection, Lonergan identifies the object of historical inquiry through reflection on the difference between history and natural science. In the second part, from the same chapter, Lonergan describes the procedures that lead historians to affirm the possibility of objective historical knowledge. His description is remarkable for its subtlety and detail. It is informed not only by Lonergan's awareness of others' accounts of historical investigation but also by his personal experience of the process in the production of his two historical studies of the thought of Aquinas. The objectification provided here of the dynamic process of historical inquiry matches in precision and lucidity the descriptions Lonergan gave in *Insight* of intelligence and rationality at work in ordinary living, empirical science, and philosophy. Lonergan notes that the nature of historical investigation has remained obscure because our reflection upon it lacks the guidance of a satisfactory cognitional theory. As the reader will discover, Lonergan's cognitional theory provides the underlying organization for his description of critical history. In the third part, from the second chapter on history, Lonergan raises and answers a series of questions pertaining to the heuristic structure of historical investigation. Already, in *Insight*, he has exposed the heuristic structures of classical, statistical, dialectical, and genetic investigations. Here Lonergan presents succinctly his views on a series of disputed questions surrounding the presuppositions brought to historical investigations by the historian: the historian's connection with philosophy; the employment of analogy in proceeding from the present to the past; the use of ideal-types; the nature of theories of history and their influence on historical inquiry; the nature of historical explanation and what is meant by a 'cause'; the impact of devotion to social and cultural goals and the four biases on historical investigation, and the nature of historical objectivity and detachment; the relation of the historian's value judgments to historical work; and, finally, the place of belief in historical work.

These extracts are taken from *Method in Theology*, 175–80, 185–96, 224–33.

1 Nature and History

The word, history, is employed in two senses. There is history (1) that is written about, and there is history (2) that is written. History (2) aims at expressing knowledge of history (1).

The precise object of historical inquiry and the precise nature of historical investigation are matters of not a little obscurity. This is not because there are no good historians. It is not because good historians have not by and large learnt what to do. It is mainly because historical knowledge is an instance of knowledge, and few people are in possession of a satisfactory cognitional theory.[1]

A first step will be to set forth the basic differences between history and natural science, and we shall begin from a few reflections on time.

One can think of time in connection with such questions as what is the time, what is the date, how soon, how long ago. On that basis one arrives at the Aristotelian definition that time is the number or measure determined by the successive equal stages of a local movement. It is a number when one answers three o'clock or January 26, 1969. It is a measure when one answers three hours or 1969 years. One can push this line of thought further by asking whether there is just one time for the universe or, on the other hand, there are as many distinct times as there are distinct local movements. Now on the Ptolemaic system there

---

1 A similar view has been expressed by Gerhard Ebeling. He considers it unquestionable that modern historical science is still a long way from being able to offer a theoretically unobjectionable account of the critical historical method, and that it needs the cooperation of philosophy to reach that goal. *Word and Faith* (London: SCM, 1963), 49.

A more concrete illustration of the matter may be had by reading the *Epilegomena* in R.G. Collingwood, *The Idea of History* (Oxford: Clarendon, 1946). The first three sections, 'Nature and History,' 'The Historical Imagination,' and 'Historical Evidence,' are right to the point. The fourth 'History as Re-enactment' is complicated by the problems of idealism. See ibid., Editor's Preface, vii–xx. See also Alan Donagon, *The Later Philosophy of R.G. Collingwood* (Oxford: Clarendon, 1962).

did exist a single standard time for the universe, since the outmost of the celestial spheres, the *primum mobile*, contained the material universe and was the first source of all local movement. With the acceptance of the Copernican theory, there vanished the *primum mobile*, but there remained a single standard time, a survival Newton explained by distinguishing true and apparent motion and by conceiving true motion as relative to absolute space and absolute time. Finally, with Einstein, Newton's absolute time vanished, and there emerged as many standard times as there are inertial reference frames that are in relative motion.[2]

Now the foregoing notion of time certainly is of great importance to the historian, for he has to date his events. It is not, however, an adequate account of what time is, for it is limited to counting, measuring, and relating to one another in a comprehensive view all possible instances of such counting and measuring. Moreover, it is this aspect of time that suggests the image of time as a raceway of individual instants, an image that little accords with our experience of time.

Fortunately, besides questions about time that are answered by numbers and measurements, there is a further different set concerned with 'now.' Aristotle asked whether there is a succession of 'now's' or just a single 'now.' He answered with a comparison. Just as 'time' is the measure of the movement, so the 'now' corresponds to the body that is moving. In so far as there is succession, there is difference in the 'now.' But underpinning such differences is the identity of the substratum.[3]

Now this advertence to the identity of the substratum, to the body that is moving, removes from one's notion of time the total extrinsicism of each moment from the next. No doubt, each successive moment is different, but in the difference there is also an identity.

With this clue we may advance to our experience of time. There is succession in the flow of conscious and intentional acts; there is identity in the conscious subject of the acts; there may be either identity or succession in the object intended by the acts. Analysis may reveal that what actually is visible is a succession of different profiles; but experience reveals that what is perceived is the synthesis (*Gestalt*) of the profiles into a single object. Analysis may reveal that the sounds produced

2 More on this topic in *Insight*, 179–83.
3 Aristotle, *Physics*, V, II, 219b 12.

are a succession of notes and chords; but experience reveals that what is heard is their synthesis into a melody. There results what is called the psychological present, which is not an instant, a mathematical point, but a time-span, so that our experience of time is, not of a race-way of instants, but a now leisurely, a now rapid succession of over-lapping time-spans. The time of experience is slow and dull, when the objects of experience change slowly and in expected ways. But time becomes a whirligig, when the objects of experience change rapidly and in novel and unexpected ways.

Whether slow and broad or rapid and short, the psychological present reaches into its past by memories and into its future by antici-pations. Anticipations are not merely of the prospective objects of our fears and our desires but also the shrewd estimate of the man of expe-rience or the rigorously calculated forecast of applied science. Again, besides the memories of each individual, there are the pooled memo-ries of the group, their celebration in song and story, their preservation in written narratives, in coins and monuments and every other trace of the group's words and deeds left to posterity. Such is the field of his-torical investigation.

Now the peculiarity of this field resides in the nature of individual and group action. It has both a conscious and an unconscious side. Apart from neurosis and psychosis the conscious side is in control. But the conscious side consists in the flow of conscious and intentional acts that we have been speaking of since our first chapter. What differenti-ates each of these acts from the others lies in the manifold meanings of meaning ... Meaning, then, is a constitutive element in the conscious flow that is the normally controlling side of human action. It is this constitutive role of meaning in the controlling side of human action that grounds the peculiarity of the historical field of investigation.

Now meaning may regard the general or the universal, but most human thought and speech and action are concerned with the particu-lar and the concrete. Again, there are structural and material invariants to meaning, but there also are changes that affect the manner in which the carriers of meaning are employed, the elements of meaning are combined, the functions of meaning are distinguished and developed, the realms of meaning are extended, the stages of meaning blossom forth, meet resistance, compromise, collapse. Finally, there are the fur-ther vicissitudes of meaning as common meaning. For meaning is com-mon in the measure that community exists and functions, in the measure that there is a common field of experience, common and complementary understanding, common judgments or at least an agreement to disagree, common and complementary commitments. But people can get out of touch, misunderstand one another, hold radically opposed views, commit themselves to conflicting goals. Then common meaning contracts, becomes confined to banalities, moves towards ideological warfare.

It is in this field of meaningful speech and action that the historian is engaged. It is not, of course, the historian's but the exegete's task to determine what was meant. The historian envisages a quite different object. He is not content to understand what people meant. He wants to grasp what was going forward in particular groups at particular places and times. By 'going forward' I mean to exclude the mere repetition of a routine. I mean the change that originated the routine and its dissemination. I mean process and development but, no less, decline and collapse. When things turn out unexpectedly, pious people say, 'Man proposes but God disposes.' The historian is concerned to see how God disposed the matter, not by theological speculation, not by some world-historical dialectic, but through particular human agents. In literary terms history is concerned with the drama of life, with what results through the characters, their decisions, their actions, and not only because of them but also because of their defects, their oversights, their failures to act. In military terms history is concerned, not just with the opposing commanders' plans of the battle, not just with the experiences of the battle had by each soldier and officer, but with the actual course of the battle as the resultant of conflicting plans now successfully and now unsuccessfully executed. In brief, where exegesis is concerned to determine what a particular person meant, history is concerned to determine what, in most cases, contemporaries do not know. For, in most cases, contemporaries do not know what is going forward, first, because experience is individual while the data for history lie in the experiences of many, secondly, because the actual course of events results not only from what people intend but also from their oversights, mistakes, failures to act, thirdly, because history does not predict what will happen but reaches its conclusions from what has happened and, fourthly, because history is not merely a matter of gathering and testing all available evidence but also involves a number of interlocking discoveries that bring to light the significant issues and operative factors.

So the study of history differs from the study of physical, chemical, biological nature. There is a difference in their objects, for the objects of physics, chemistry, biology are not in part constituted by acts of meaning. There is similarity inasmuch as both types of study consist in an ongoing process of cumulative discoveries, that is, of original insights, of original acts of understanding, where by 'insight,' 'act of understanding' is meant a prepropositional, preverbal, preconceptual event, in the sense that propositions, words, concepts express the content of the event and so do not precede it but follow from it. There is, however, a difference in the expression of the respective sets of discoveries. The discoveries of physics, chemistry, biology are expressed in universal systems and are refuted if they are found to be incompatible with a relevant particular instance. But the discoveries of the historian are expressed in narratives and descriptions that regard particular persons, places, and times. They have no claim to universality: they could, of course, be relevant to the understanding of other persons, places, times; but whether in fact they are relevant, and just how relevant they are, can be settled only by a historical investigation of the other persons, places, and times. Finally, because they have no claim to universality, the discoveries of the historians are not verifiable in the fashion proper to the natural sciences; in history verification is parallel to the procedures by which an interpretation is judged correct.

Let us now turn to such human sciences as psychology and sociology. Two cases arise. These sciences may be modelled on the procedures of the natural sciences. In so far as this approach is carried out rigorously, meaning in human speech and action is ignored, and the science regards only the unconscious side of human process. In this case the relations between history and human science are much the same as the relations between history and natural science. However, there is much psychology and sociology that does recognize meaning as a constitutive and normally controlling element in human action. To their study the historian leaves all that is the repetition of routine in human speech and action and all that is universal in the genesis, development, breakdown of routines. Moreover, the more psychology and sociology the historian knows, the more he will increase his interpretative powers. Conversely, the greater the achievements of historians, the broader will be the field of evidence on human speech and action that has been opened up for psychological and sociological investigation.[4]

2 Critical History

A first step towards understanding critical history lies in an account of precritical history. For it, then, the community is the conspicuous community, one's own. Its vehicle is narrative, an ordered recital of events. It recounts who did what, when, where, under what circumstances, from what motives, with what results. Its function is practical: a group can function as a group only by possessing an identity, knowing itself and devoting itself to the cause, at worst of its survival, at best of its betterment. The function of precritical history is to promote such knowledge and devotion. So it is never just a narrative of bald facts. It is *artistic*: it selects, orders, describes; it would awaken the reader's interest and sustain it; it would persuade and convince. Again, it is *ethical*: it not only narrates but also apportions praise and blame. It is *explanatory*: it accounts for existing institutions by telling of their origins and development and by contrasting them with alternative institutions found in other lands. It is *apologetic*, correcting false or tendentious accounts of the people's past, and refuting the calumnies of neighboring peoples. Finally, it is *prophetic*: to hindsight about the past there is joined foresight on the future and there are added the recommendations of a man of wide reading and modest wisdom.

Now such precritical history, ever purged of its defects, though it might well meet very real needs in the functional specialty, communications, at least does not qualify as the functional specialty, history. For that specialty, while it operates on the four levels of experiencing, understanding, judging, and deciding, still operates on the other three with a principal concern for judging, for settling matters of fact. It is not concerned with the highly important educational task of communicating to fellow citizens or fellow churchmen a proper appreciation of their heritage and a proper devotion to its preservation, development, dissemination. It is concerned to set forth what really happened or, in

---

4 For an extensive anthology and a twenty-page bibliography on the foregoing and related topics, see *Theories of History*, ed. Patrick Gardiner (New York: Free Press, 1959). Where authors there diverge from the present approach, I think the reader will find the root difference to lie in cognitional theory.

Ranke's perpetually quoted phrase, *wie es eigentlich gewesen*. Finally, unless this work is done in detachment, quite apart from political or apologetic aims, it is attempting to serve two masters and usually suffers the evangelical consequences.[5]

Next, this work is not just a matter of finding testimonies, checking them for credibility, and stringing together what has been found credible. It is not just that, because historical experience is one thing and historical knowledge is quite another. The string of credible testimonies merely re-edits historical experience. It does not advance to historical knowledge which grasps what was going forward, what, for the most part, contemporaries did not know. Many early Christians may have had a fragmentary experience of the manner in which the elements in the synoptic gospels were formed; but Rudolf Bultmann was concerned to set forth the process as a whole and, while he found his evidence in the synoptic gospels, still that evidence did not presuppose belief in the truth of the evangelists' statements.[6]

Thirdly, only a series of discoveries can advance the historian from the fragmentary experiences, that are the source of his data, to knowledge of a process as a whole. Like a detective confronted with a set of clues that at first leave him baffled, the historian has to discover in the clues, piece by piece, the evidence that will yield a convincing account of what happened.

Since the evidence has to be discovered, a distinction has to be drawn between potential, formal, and actual evidence. Potential evidence is any datum, here and now perceptible. Formal evidence is such a datum in so far as it is used in asking and answering a question for historical intelligence. Actual evidence is a formal evidence invoked in arriving at a historical judgment. In other words, data as perceptible are potential evidence; data as perceptible and understood are formal evidence; data as perceptible, as understood, and as grounding a reasonable judgment are actual evidence.

What starts the process is the question for historical intelligence. With regard to some defined situation in the past one wants to under-

---

5 See, for example, G.P. Gooch, *History and Historians in the Nineteenth Century*, 2nd ed. (London: Longmans, 1952), chap. 8, on the Prussian School.

6 R. Bultmann, *Geschichte der synoptischen Tradition* (Göttingen: Vandenhoeck and Ruprecht, 1958). On the same topic, see *De Jésus aux Evangiles*, ed. I. de la Potterie (Gebloux: Duculot, 1967), in which *Formgeschichte* plays an intermediate role between *Traditionsgeschichte* and *Redaktionsgeschichte*.

stand what was going forward. Clearly, any such question presupposes some historical knowledge. Without it, one would not know of the situation in question, nor would one know what was meant by 'going forward.' History, then, grows out of history. Critical history was a leap forward from precritical history. Precritical history was a leap forward from stories and legends. Inversely, the more history one knows, the more data lie in one's purview, the more questions one can ask, and the more intelligently one can ask them.

The question for historical intelligence is put in the light of previous knowledge and with respect to some particular datum. It may or may not lead to an insight into that datum. If it does not, one moves on to a different question. If it does, the insight is expressed in a surmise, the surmise is represented imaginatively, and the image leads to a further related question. This process may or may not be recurrent. If it is not, one has come to a dead end and must try another approach. If it is recurrent, and all one attains is a series of surmises, then one is following a false trail and once more must try another approach. But if one's surmises are coincident with further data or approximate to them, one is on the right track. The data are ceasing to be merely potential evidence; they are becoming formal evidence; one is discovering what the evidence might be.

Now if one is on the right track long enough, there occurs a shift in the manner of one's questioning for, more and more, the further questions come from the data rather than from images based on surmises. One still has to do the questioning. One still has to be alert. But one has moved out of the assumptions and perspectives one had prior to one's investigation. One has attained sufficient insight into the object of one's inquiry to grasp something of the assumptions and perspectives proper to that object. And this grasp makes one's approach to further data so much more congenial that the further data suggest the further questions to be put. To describe this feature of historical investigation, let us say that the cumulative process of datum, question, insight, surmise, image, formal evidence, is ecstatic. It is not the hot ecstasy of the devotee but the cool one of growing insight. It takes one out of oneself. It sets aside earlier assumptions and perspectives by bringing to light the assumptions and perspectives proper to the object under investigation.

The same process is selective, constructive, and critical. It is selective: not all data are promoted from the status of potential evidence to the status of formal evidence. It is constructive: for the selected data are related to one another through an interconnected set of questions and answers or, expressed alternatively, by a series of insights that complement one another, correct one another, and eventually coalesce into a single view of a whole. Finally, it is critical: for insights not only are direct but also inverse. By direct insight one grasps how things fit together, and one murmurs one's 'Eureka.' By inverse insight one is prompted to exclaim, How could I have been so stupid as to take for granted ... One sees that things are not going to fit and, eventually, by a direct insight one grasps that some item fits not in this context but in some other. So a text is discovered to have been interpolated or mutilated. So the pseudo-Dionysius is extradited from the first century and relocated at the end of the fifth: he quoted Proclus. So an esteemed writer comes under suspicion: the source of his information has been discovered; in whole or in part, without independent confirmation, he is used not as evidence for what he narrates but in the roundabout fashion that rests on his narrating – his intentions, readers, methods, omissions, mistakes.[7]

Now I have been attributing to a single process of developing understanding a whole series of different functions. It is *heuristic*, for it brings to light the relevant data. It is *ecstatic*, for it leads the inquirer out of his original perspectives and into the perspectives proper to his object. It is *selective*, for out of a totality of data it selects those relevant to the understanding achieved. It is *critical*, for it removes from one use or context to another the data that might otherwise be thought relevant to present tasks. It is *constructive*, for the data that are selected are knotted together by the vast and intricate web of interconnecting links that cumulatively came to light as one's understanding progressed.

Now it is the distinguishing mark of critical history that this process occurs twice. In the first instance one is coming to understand one's sources. In the second instance one is using one's understood sources intelligently to come to understand the object to which they are relevant. In both cases the development of understanding is heuristic,

---

7 Note that the word *critical* has two quite different meanings. In precritical history it means that one has tested the credibility of one's authorities before believing them. In critical history it means that one has shifted data from one field of relevance to another. On this topic, R.G. Collingwood is brilliant and convincing. See his two studies, 'The Historical Imagination' and 'Historical Evidence,' in *The Idea of History* (Oxford: Clarendon, 1946), 231–82.

ecstatic, selective, critical, constructive. But in the first case one is identifying authors, locating them and their work in place and time, studying the milieu, ascertaining their purposes in writing and their prospective readers, investigating their sources of information and the use they made of them. In a previous section on *Interpretation* we spoke of understanding the author,[8] but there the ulterior aim was to understand what he meant. In history we also seek to understand the authors of sources, but now the ulterior aim is to understand what they were up to and how they did it. It is this understanding that grounds the critical use of sources, the fine discrimination that distinguishes an author's strength and weaknesses and uses him accordingly. Once this is achieved, one is able to shift one's attention to one's main objective, namely, to understanding the process referred to in one's sources. Where before one's developing understanding was heuristic, ecstatic, selective, critical, constructive in determining what authors were up to, now it is heuristic, ecstatic, selective, critical, and constructive in determining what was going forward in the community.

Needless to say, the two developments are interdependent. Not only does understanding the authors contribute to understanding the historical events, but in coming to understand the events there arise questions that may lead to a revision of one's understanding of the authors and, consequently, to a revision of one's use of them.

Again, while each new insight uncovers evidence, moves one away from previous perspectives, selects or rejects data as relevant or irrelevant, and adds to the picture that is being constructed, still what gains attention is, not each single insight, but the final insight in each cumulative series. It is such final insights that are called discoveries. With them the full force of the cumulative series breaks forth and, as the cumulation has a specific direction and meaning, discoveries now are of the new evidence, now of a new perspective, now of a different selection or critical rejection in the data, now of ever more complicated structures.

So far we have been thinking of structuring as the intelligible pattern grasped in the data and relating the data to one another. But there is a further aspect to the matter. For what is grasped by understanding in data, also is expressed by understanding in concepts and words. So from the intelligible pattern grasped in the data, one moves to the

8 *Method in Theology*, 160–1.

intelligible pattern expressed in the narrative. At first, the narrative is simply the inquirer mumbling his surmises to himself. As surmises less and less are mere surmises, as more and more they lead to the uncovering of further evidence, there begin to emerge trails, linkages, interconnected wholes. As the spirit of inquiry catches every failure to understand, as it brings to attention what is not yet understood and, as a result, is so easily overlooked, one of the interconnected wholes will advance to the role of a dominant theme running through other inter-connected wholes that thereby become subordinate themes. As the investigation progresses and the field of data coming under control broadens, not only will the organization in terms of dominant and sub-ordinate themes keep extending, but also there will emerge ever higher levels of organization. So among dominant themes there will emerge dominant topics to leave other dominant themes just subordi-nate topics; and the fate of dominant themes awaits most of the domi-nant topics, as the process of organization keeps moving, not only over more territory, but up to ever higher levels of organization. It is not to be thought that this process of advancing organization is a single uni-form progress. There occur discoveries that complement and correct previous discoveries and so, as understanding changes, the organiza-tion also must change. Themes and topics become more exactly con-ceived and more happily expressed. The range of their dominance may be extended or curtailed. Items once thought of major interest can slip back to less prominent roles, and, inversely, other items can mount from relative obscurity to notable significance.

The exact conception and happy expression of themes and topics are matters of no small moment. For they shape the further questions that one will ask and it is those further questions that lead to further dis-coveries. Nor is this all. Part by part, historical investigations come to a term. They do so when there have been reached the set of insights that hit all nails squarely on the head. They are known to do so when the stream of further questions on a determinate theme or topic gradually diminishes and finally dries up. The danger of inaccurate or unhappy conception and formulation is that either the stream of questions may dry up prematurely or else that it may keep flowing when really there are no further relevant questions.

It follows that the cumulative process of developing understanding not only is heuristic, ecstatic, selective, critical, and constructive but also is reflective and judicial. The understanding that has been achieved on a determinate point can be complemented, corrected, revised, only if further discoveries on that very point can be made. Such discoveries can be made only if further relevant questions arise. If, in fact, there are no further relevant questions then, in fact, a certain judgment would be true. If, in the light of the historian's knowledge, there are no further relevant questions, then the historian can say that, as far as he knows, the question is closed.

There is, then, a criterion for historical judgment, and so there is a point where formal evidence becomes actual evidence. Such judgments occur repeatedly throughout an investigation, as each minor and then each major portion of the work is completed. But as in natural science, so too in critical history the positive content of judgment aspires to be no more than the best available opinion. This is evident as long as an historical investigation is in process, for later discoveries may force a correction and revision of earlier ones. But what is true of investigations in process, has to be extended to investigations that to all intents and purposes are completed.

For, in the first place, one cannot exclude the possibility that new sources of information will be uncovered and that they will affect subsequent understanding and judgment. So archeological investigations of the ancient Near East complement Old Testament study, the caves of Qumran have yielded documents with a bearing on New Testament studies, while the unpublished writings found at Kenoboskion restrain pronouncements on Gnosticism.

But there is, as well, another source of revision. It is the occurrence of later events that place earlier events in a new perspective. The outcome of a battle fixes the perspective in which the successive stages of the battle are viewed; military victory in a war reveals the significance of the successive battles that were fought; the social and cultural consequences of the victory and the defeat are the measure of the effects of the war. So, in general, history is an ongoing process. As the process advances, the context within which events are to be understood keeps enlarging. As the context enlarges, perspectives shift.

However, neither of these sources of revision will simply invalidate earlier work competently done. New documents fill out the picture; they illuminate what before was obscure; they shift perspectives; they refute what was venturesome or speculative; they do not simply dissolve the whole network of questions and answers that made the original set of data massive evidence for the earlier account. Again, history is an ongoing process, and so the historical context keeps enlarging. But the effects of this enlargement are neither universal nor uniform. For persons and events have their place in history through one or more contexts, and these contexts may be narrow and brief or broad and enduring with any variety of intermediates. Only inasmuch as a context is still open, or can be opened or extended, do later events throw new light on earlier persons, events, processes. As Karl Heussi put it, it is easier to understand Frederick William III of Prussia than to understand Schleiermacher and, while Nero will always be Nero, we cannot as yet say the same for Luther.[9]

Besides the judgments reached by a historian in his investigation, there are the judgments passed upon his work by his peers and his successors. Such judgments constitute critical history at the second degree. For they are not mere wholesale judgments of belief or disbelief. They are based on an understanding of how the work was done. Just as the historian, first, with respect to his sources and, then, with respect to the object of his inquiry, undergoes a development of understanding that at once is heuristic, ecstatic, selective, critical, constructive and, in the limit, judicial, so the critics of a historical work undergo a similar development with respect to the work itself. They do so all the more easily and all the more competently, the more the historian has been at pains not to conceal his tracks but to lay all his cards on the table, and the more the critics already are familiar with the field or, at least, with neighboring fields.

The result of such critical understanding of a critical history is, of course, that one can make an intelligent and discriminating use of the criticized historian. One learns where he has worked well. One has spotted his limitations and his weaknesses. One can say where, to the best of present knowledge, he can be relied on, where he must be revised, where he may have to be revised. Just as historians make an intelligent and discriminating use of their sources, so too the professional historical community makes a discriminating use of the works of its own historians.

Early in this section we noted that asking historical questions presupposed historical knowledge and, the greater that knowledge, the more the data in one's purview, the more questions one could ask, and the more intelligently one could ask them. Our consideration has now

9 Karl Heussi, *Die Krisis des Historismus* (Tubingen: Mohr, 1932), 58.

come full circle, for we have arrived at an account of that presupposed historical knowledge. It is critical history of the second degree. It consists basically in the cumulative works of historians. But it consists actually, not in mere belief in those works, but in a critical appreciation of them. Such critical appreciation is generated by critical book reviews, by the critiques that professors communicate to their students and justify by their explanations and arguments, by informal discussions in common rooms and more formal discussions at congresses.

Critical history of the second degree is a compound. At its base are historical articles and books. On a second level there are critical writings that compare and evaluate the historical writings: these may vary from brief reviews to long studies right up to such a history of the historiography of an issue as Herbert Butterfield's *George III & the Historians*.[10] Finally, there are the considered opinions of professional historians on historians and their critics – opinions that influence their teaching, their remarks in discussions, their procedures in writing on related topics ...

The concern, then, of the present section has been strictly limited. It presupposed the historian knew how to do his research and how to interpret the meaning of documents. It left to later specialties certain aspects of the problem of relativism and the great task of revealing the bearing of historical knowledge on contemporary policy and action. It was confined to formulating the set of procedures that, *caeteris paribus*, yield historical knowledge, to explaining how that knowledge arises, in what it consists, what are its inherent limitations.

If I have been led to adopt the view that the techniques of critical history are unequal to the task of eliminating historical relativism totally, I affirm all the more strongly that they can and do effect a partial elimination. I have contended that critical history is not a matter of believing credible testimonies but of discovering what hitherto had been experienced but not properly known. In that process of discovery I have recognized not only its heuristic, selective, critical, constructive, and judicial aspects, but also an ecstatic aspect that eliminates previously entertained perspectives and opinions to replace them with the perspectives and views that emerge from the cumulative interplay of

10 (London: Collins, 1957). For a variety of views on the history of historiography, see Carl Becker, 'What Is Historiography?' in *Detachment and the Writing of History, Essays and Letters of Carl L. Becker*, ed. Phil. L. Snyder (Ithaca, NY: Cornell University Press, 1958).

data, inquiry, insight, surmise, image, evidence. It is in this manner that critical history of itself moves to objective knowledge of the past, though it may be impeded by such factors as mistaken views on possibility, by mistaken or misleading value-judgments, by an inadequate world-view or standpoint or state of the question.

In brief, this section has been attempting to bring to light the set of procedures that lead historians in various manners to affirm the possibility of objective historical knowledge. Carl Becker, for instance, agreed he was a relativist in the sense that *Weltanschauung* influences the historian's work, but at the same time maintained that a considerable and indeed increasing body of knowledge was objectively ascertainable.[11] Erich Rothacker correlated *Wahrheit* with *Weltanschauung*, granted that they influenced historical thought, but at the same time affirmed the existence of a correctness (*Richtigkeit*) attached to critical procedures and proper influences.[12] In a similar vein Karl Heussi held that philosophic views would not affect critical procedures though they might well have an influence on the way the history was composed;[13] and he advanced that while the relatively simple form, in which the historian organizes his materials, resides not in the enormously complex courses of events but only in the historian's mind, still different historians operating from the same standpoint arrive at the same organization.[14] In like manner, Rudolf Bultmann held that, granted a *Fragestellung*, critical method led to univocal results.[15] These writers are speaking in various manners of the same reality. They mean, I believe, that there exist procedures that, *caeteris paribus*, lead to historical knowledge. Our aim and concern in this section has been to indicate the nature of those procedures.

3   Heuristic Structures in Historical Method

Has the historian philosophic commitments? Does he employ analo-

11 Cited by C.W. Smith, *Carl Becker: On History and the Climate of Opinion* (Ithaca, NY: Cornell University Press, 1956), 97, from Carl Becker, 'Review of Maurice Mendelbaum's *The Problem of Historical Knowledge*,' *Philosophical Review*, 49 (1940), 363.
12 Erich Rothacker, *Logik und Systematik der Geisteswissenschaften* (*Handbuch der Philosophie*) (Bonn: Bouvier, 1947), 144.
13 Ibid., 63.
14 Ibid., 56.
15 Rudolf Bultmann, 'Das Problem der Hermeneutik,' *Zschr. f. Theol. u. Kirche*, 47 (1950), 64; also his *Glauben und Verstehen*, vol. 2 (Tubingen: Mohr, 1961), 229.

gies, use ideal types, follow some theory of history? Does he explain, investigate causes, determine laws? Is he devoted to social and cultural goals, subject to bias, detached from bias? Is history value-free, or is it concerned with values? Do historians know or do they believe?

Such questions are asked. They not merely regard the historian's notion of history but also have a bearing on his practice of historical investigation and historical writing. Different answers, accordingly, would modify this or that heuristic structure,[16] that is, this or that element in historical method.

First, then, the historian need not concern himself at all with philosophy in a common but excessively general sense that denotes the contents of all books and courses purporting to be philosophic. Through that labyrinth there is no reason why a historian should try to find his way.

There is, however, a very real connection between the historian and philosophy, when 'philosophy' is understood in an extremely restricted sense, namely, the set of real conditions of the possibility of historical inquiry. Those real conditions are the human race, remains and traces from its past, the community of historians with their traditions and instruments, their conscious and intentional operations especially in so far as they occur in historical investigation. It is to be noted that the relevant conditions are conditions of possibility and not the far larger and quite determinate set that in each instance condition historical investigation.

In brief, then, history is related to philosophy, as historical method is related to transcendental method or, again, as theological method is related to transcendental method. The historian may or may not know of this relationship. If he does, that is all to the good. If he does not, then, he still can be an excellent historian, just as M. Jourdain might speak excellent French without knowing that his talk was prose. But while he can be an excellent historian, it is not likely that he will be able to speak about the proper procedures in historical investigation without falling into the traps that in this chapter we have been illustrating.

Secondly, it is plain that the historian has to employ something like analogy when he proceeds from the present to the past. The trouble is that the term covers quite different procedures from the extremely reliable to the fallacious. Distinctions accordingly must be drawn.

16 On heuristic structures, see *Insight*. Note that heuristic has the same root as *Eureka*.

In general, the present and the past are said to be analogous when they are partly similar and partly dissimilar. Again, in general, the past is to be assumed similar to the present, except in so far as there is evidence of dissimilarity. Finally, in so far as evidence is produced for dissimilarity, the historian is talking history; but in so far as he asserts that there must be similarity or that there cannot be dissimilarity, then he is drawing upon the climate of opinion in which he lives or else he is representing some philosophic position.

Next, it is not to be assumed that the present is known completely and in its entirety. On the contrary, we have been arguing all along that the rounded view of a historical period is to be expected not from contemporaries but from historians. Moreover, while the historian has to construct his analogies in the first instance by drawing on his knowledge of the present, still he can learn history in this fashion and then construct further history on the analogy of the known past.

Further, nature is uniform, but social arrangements and cultural interpretations are subject to change. There exist at the present time extremely different societies and cultures. There is available evidence for still more differences to be brought to light by historical methods. One hears at times that the past has to conform to present experience, but on that opinion Collingwood commented quite tartly. The ancient Greeks and Romans controlled the size of their populations by exposing new-born infants. The fact is not rendered doubtful because it lies outside current experience of the contributors to the *Cambridge Ancient History*.[17]

Again, while the possibility and the occurrence of miracles are topics, not for the methodologist, but for the theologian, I may remark that the uniformity of nature is conceived differently at different times. In the nineteenth century natural laws were thought to express necessity, and Laplace's view on the possibility in theory of deducing the whole course of events from some given stage of the process was taken seriously. Now laws of the classical type are considered not necessary but just verified possibilities; they are generalized on the principle that similars are similarly understood; they are a basis for prediction or deduction, not by themselves, but only when combined into schemes of recurrence; such schemes function concretely, not absolutely, but only if other things are equal; and whether other things are equal, is a

17 Collingwood, *Idea of History*, 240.

matter of statistical frequencies.[18] Evidently the scientific case concerning miracles has weakened.

Finally, while each historian has to work on the analogy of what he knows of the present and has learnt of the past, still the dialectical confrontation of contradictory histories needs a basis that is generally accessible. The basis we would offer would be transcendental method extended into the methods of theology and history by constructs derived from transcendental method itself. In other words, it would be the sort of thing we have been working out in these chapters. No doubt, those with different philosophic positions would propose alternatives. But such alternatives would only serve to clarify further the dialectic of diverging research, interpretation, and history.

Thirdly, do historians use ideal-types? I may note at once that the notion and use of the ideal-type commonly are associated with the name of the German sociologist, Max Weber, but they have been discussed in a strictly historical context, among others, by M. Marrou.

The ideal-type, then, is not a description of reality or a hypothesis about reality. It is a theoretical construct in which possible events are intelligibly related to constitute an internally coherent system. Its utility is both heuristic and expository, that is, it can be useful inasmuch as it suggests and helps formulate hypotheses and, again, when a concrete situation approximates to the theoretical construct, it can guide an analysis of the situation and promote a clear understanding of it.[19]

M. Marrou took Fustel de Coulanges' *La cité antique* as an ideal-type. The city state is conceived as a confederation of the great patriarchal families, assembled in phratries and then in tribes, consolidated by cults regarding ancestors or heroes and practiced around a common center. Now such a structure is based, not by selecting what is common to all instances of the ancient city, not by taking what is common to most instances, but by concentrating on the most favorable instances, namely, those offering more intelligibility and explanatory power. The use of such an ideal-type is twofold. In so far as the historical situation satisfies the conditions of the ideal-type, the situation is illuminated. In so far as the historical situation does not satisfy the conditions of the ideal-type, it brings to light precise differences that

---

18 For this notion of science, see *Insight*, chaps. 2–4 [see 1.III.4 in this reader].
19 Max Weber, *The Methodology of the Social Sciences* (New York: Free Press, 1949), 89 ff.

otherwise would go unnoticed, and it sets questions that otherwise might not be asked.[20]

M. Marrou approves the use of ideal-types in historical investigation, but he issues two warnings. First, they are just theoretical constructs: one must resist the temptation of the enthusiast that mistakes them for descriptions of reality; even when they do hit off main features of a historical reality, one must not easily be content with them, gloss over inadequacies, reduce history to what essentially is an abstract scheme. Secondly, there is the difficulty of working out appropriate ideal-types: the richer and the more illuminating the construct, the greater the difficulty of applying it; the thinner and looser the construct, the less is it able to contribute much to history.[21]

Finally, I would like to suggest that Arnold Toynbee's *Study of History* might be regarded as a source-book of ideal-types. Toynbee himself has granted that his work was not quite as empirical as he once thought it. At the same time so resolute a critic as Pieter Geyl[22] has found the work immensely stimulating and has confessed that such daring and imaginative spirits as Toynbee have an essential function to fulfil.[23] That function is, I suggest, to provide the materials from which carefully formulated ideal-types might be derived.

Fourthly, does the historian follow some theory of history? By a theory of history I do not mean the application to history of a theory established scientifically, philosophically, or theologically. Such theories have their proper mode of validation; they are to be judged on their own merits; they broaden the historian's knowledge and make his apprehensions more precise; they do not constitute historical knowledge but facilitate its development.

By a theory of history I understand a theory that goes beyond its scientific, philosophic, or theological basis to make statements about the actual course of human events. Such theories are set forth, for instance, by Bruce Mazlish in his discussion of the great speculators from Vico to Freud.[24] They have to be criticized in the light of their scientific, philosophic, or theological basis. In so far as they survive such criti-

20 Marrou, *Meaning of History* (Baltimore, Helicon, 1966), 167 ff.
21 Ibid., 170 ff.
22 See his criticisms in Pieter Geyl, *Debates with Historians* (New York: Meridian Books, 1965).
23 P. Gardiner, *Theories of History* (New York: Free Press, 1959), 319.
24 See B. Mazlish, *The Riddle of History* (New York: Harper and Row), 1966.

cism, they possess the utility of grand-scale ideal-types,[25] and may be employed under the precautions already indicated for the use of ideal-types. But they never grasp the full complexity of historical reality, and consequently they tend to throw in high relief certain aspects and connections and to disregard others that may be of equal or greater importance. In M. Marrou's phrase '... the most ingenious hypothesis ... underlines in red pencil certain lines lost in a diagram whose thousand curves cross one another in every direction.'[26] General hypotheses, though they have their uses, easily become 'big anti-comprehension machines.'[27]

Fifthly, does the historian explain? On the German distinction between *erklaren* and *verstehen*, natural scientists explain but historians only understand. However, this distinction is somewhat artificial. Both scientists and historians understand; both communicate the intelligibility that they grasp. The difference lies in the kind of intelligibility grasped and in the manner in which it develops. Scientific intelligibility aims at being an internally coherent system or structure valid in any of a specified set or series of instances. It is expressed in a technical vocabulary, constantly tested by confronting its every implication with data, and adjusted or superseded when it fails to meet the tests. In contrast, historical intelligibility is like the intelligibility reached by common sense. It is the content of a habitual accumulation of insights that, by themselves, are incomplete; they are never applied in any situation without the pause that grasps how relevant they are and, if need be, adds a few more insights derived from the situation in hand. Such commonsense understanding is like a many purpose adjustable tool, where the number of purposes is enormous, and the adjustment is based on the precise task in hand. Hence, common sense thinks and speaks, proposes and acts, with respect, not to the general, but to the particular and concrete. Its generalities are not principles, relevant to every possible instance, but proverbs saying what may be useful to bear in mind, and commonly rounded out by a contradictory piece of advice. Look before you leap! He who hesitates is lost![28]

Historical explanation is a sophisticated extension of commonsense understanding. Its aim is an intelligent reconstruction of the past, not

25 Ibid., 447.
26 Marrou, *Meaning in History*, 200.
27 Ibid., 201.
28 See *Insight*, 196–204 [see 1.IV.1 in this reader].

in its routines, but in each of its departures from the previous routine, in the interlocked consequences of each departure, in the unfolding of a process that theoretically might but in all probability never will be repeated.

Sixthly, does the historian investigate causes and determine laws? The historian does not determine laws, for the determination of laws is the work of the natural or human scientist. Again, the historian does not investigate causes, where 'cause' is taken in a technical sense developed through the advance of the sciences. However, if 'cause' is understood in the ordinary language meaning of 'because,' then the historian does investigate causes; for ordinary language is just the language of common sense, and historical explanation is the expression of the commonsense type of developing understanding. Finally, the problems concerning historical explanation that currently are discussed seem to arise from a failure to grasp the differences between scientific and commonsense developments of human intelligence.[29]

Seventhly, is the historian devoted to social and cultural goals, is he subject to bias, is he detached from bias?

The historian may well be devoted to social and cultural goals, but in so far as he is practicing the functional specialty, history, his devotion is not proximate but remote. His immediate purpose is to settle what was going forward in the past. If he does his job properly, he will supply the materials which may be employed for promoting social and cultural goals. But he is not likely to do his job properly, if in performing his tasks he is influenced not only by their immanent exigences but also by ulterior motives and purposes.

Accordingly, we are setting up a distinction, parallel in some fashion to Max Weber's distinction between social science and social policy.[30] Social science is an empirical discipline organizing the evidence on group behavior. It has to be pursued in the first instance for its own sake. Only when it has reached its proper term, can it usefully be employed in the construction of effective policies for the attainment of social ends. In somewhat similar fashion our two phases of theology keep apart our encounter with the religious past and, on the other hand, our action in the present on the future.

Next, all men are subject to bias, for a bias is a block or distortion of

29 Mathematical and scientific growth in insight is treated in *Insight*, chaps. 1–5; commonsense growth in chaps. 6 and 7.
30 Weber, *Methodology of the Social Sciences*, 51 ff.

intellectual development, and such blocks or distortions occur in four principal manners. There is the bias of unconscious motivation brought to light by depth psychology. There is the bias of individual egoism, and the more powerful and blinder bias of group egoism. Finally, there is the general bias of common sense, which is a specialization of intelligence in the particular and concrete, but usually considers itself omnicompetent. On all of these I have expanded elsewhere, and I may not repeat myself here.[31]

Further, the historian should be detached from all bias. Indeed, he has greater need of such detachment than the scientist, for scientific work is adequately objectified and publicly controlled, but the historian's discoveries accumulate in the manner of the development of common sense, and the only adequate positive control is to have another historian go over the same evidence.

Just how one conceives the achievement of such detachment depends on one's theory of knowledge and of morals. Our formula is a continuous and ever more exacting application of the transcendental precepts: Be attentive, Be intelligent, Be reasonable, Be responsible. However, nineteenth-century empiricists conceived objectivity as a matter of seeing all that's there to be seen and seeing nothing that's not there. Accordingly, they demanded of the historian a pure receptivity that admitted impressions from phenomena but excluded any subjective activity. This is the view that Becker was attacking in his 'Detachment and the Writing of History' and again in his 'What are Historical Facts?'[32] Later in life, when he had seen relativism at work in its crudest forms, he attacked it and insisted on the pursuit of truth as the primary value.[33] But, as I have noted already, Becker did not work out a complete theory.

Eighthly, is history value-free? History, as a functional specialty, is value-free in the sense already outlined: it is not directly concerned to promote social and cultural goals. It pertains to the first phase of theology which aims at an encounter with the past; the more adequate that encounter, the more fruitful it can prove to be; but one is not pursuing a specialty, when one attempts to do it and something quite different

31 *Insight*, 214–31, 244–69 [see 1.IV.2 and 1.V.3–5 in this reader].
32 Becker, *Detachment, Essays and Letters of Carl Becker*, ed. Phil. L. Snyder (Ithaca, NY: Cornell University Press, 1958), 3–28; 41–64.
33 C.W. Smith, *Carl Becker: On History and the Climate of Opinion* (Ithaca, NY: Cornell University Press, 1956), 117.

at the same time. Further, social and cultural goals are incarnated in values; they are subject to the distortions of bias; and so concern for social and cultural goals can exercise not only a disturbing but even a distorting influence on historical investigation.

Further, history is not value-free in the sense that the historian refrains from all value-judgments. For the functional specialties, while they concentrate on the end proper to one of the four levels of conscious and intentional activity, none the less are the achievement of operations on all four levels. The historian ascertains matters of fact, not by ignoring data, by failing to understand, by omitting judgments of value, but by doing all of these for the purpose of settling matters of fact.[34]

In fact, the historian's value-judgments are precisely the means that make his work a selection of things that are worth knowing, that, in Meinecke's phrase, enables history to be 'the content, the wisdom, and the signposts of our lives.'[35] Nor is this influence of value-judgments an intrusion of subjectivity. There are true and there are false value-judgments. The former are objective in the sense that they result from a moral self-transcendence. The latter are subjective in the sense that they represent a failure to effect moral self-transcendence. False value-judgments are an intrusion of subjectivity. True value-judgments are the achievement of a moral objectivity, of an objectivity that, so far from being opposed to the objectivity of true judgments of fact, presupposes them and completes them by adding to mere cognitional self-transcendence a moral self-transcendence.

However, if the historian makes value-judgments, still that is not his specialty. The task of passing judgments on the values and disvalues offered us by the past pertains to the specialties of dialectic and foundations.

Finally, do historians believe? They do not believe in the sense that critical history is not a compilation of testimonies regarded as credible. But they believe in the sense that they cannot experiment with the past as natural scientists can experiment on natural objects. They believe in the sense that they cannot have before their eyes the realities of which they speak. They believe in the sense that they depend on one another's critically evaluated work and participate in an ongoing collaboration for the advance of knowledge.

34 See Meinecke's essay in Fritz Stern, ed., *The Varieties of History: From Voltaire to the Present* (New York: Meridian Books, 1956), 267–88.
35 Ibid., 272.

Related selections: 1.III.1–3 on classical and statistical method; 1.XI.1–3 on dialectical method; 1.XII.3 on genetic method; 1.XV.3 on critical method; 3.V.2 on the place of history in theological method; 1.IV.2 and 1.V.2–5 on the four biases; 1.X on objectivity; 4.VI.1 on historicity; 1.IV on common sense as intellectual; 3.III.2 on the second enlightenment.

VII

Dialectic

The fourth functional specialty in Lonergan's proposed theological method is dialectic. In the preceding selection on functional specialties Lonergan defined dialectic as 'a generalized apologetic conducted in an ecumenical spirit, aiming ultimately at a comprehensive viewpoint, and proceeding towards that goal by acknowledging differences, seeking their grounds real and apparent, and eliminating superfluous oppositions.'

In the first part of this selection from Chapter 10, Part 2, of *Method in Theology*, Lonergan defines the meaning of horizon in general, and then proceeds to distinguish the three basic ways horizons can differ. A horizon is the limit of the range of one's knowledge and interests. Horizons may be complementary, related genetically as successive stages in a single process of development, or opposed dialectically. Complementary horizons are parts of a single communal world. Genetically related horizons are parts of a single biography or of a single history. Dialectically opposed horizons are mutually repudiating. In the second part of the selection Lonergan, with Joseph de Finance, distinguishes between horizontal and vertical exercises of freedom. The first exercise is a choice that occurs within an established horizon. The second is a set of judgments and decisions by which we move from one horizon to another. This movement may be a development consonant with the previous horizon, or it may involve an about-face and a new beginning. In the latter case, what has occurred is named by Lonergan a conversion. Three conversions are identified, described, and related to one another: intellectual conversion, moral conversion, and religious conversion. Intellectual conversion is 'the elimination of an exceedingly stubborn myth concerning reality, objectivity, and human knowledge.'[1] Moral con-

1 *Method in Theology*, 238.

version 'changes the criterion of one's decisions from satisfactions to values.'[2] Religious conversion is 'other-worldly falling in love.'[3] Considered as modalities of self-transcendence, in a single consciousness religious conversion sublates moral, and moral sublates intellectual. But from a causal viewpoint, religious conversion and God's gift of his love comes first. This part concludes with a discussion of the relations of the three conversions to individual, social, and cultural collapse or breakdown.

In the two concluding parts of the selection, having already exposed the nature and significance of the three conversions, Lonergan identifies the problem to be addressed by the functional specialty, dialectic, and exposes the structure of the method to be employed by the specialist in dialectic. The task of the specialist in dialectic is to develop those statements issued by the preceding specialties that are compatible with the three conversions, and to reverse statements that are incompatible with any of the three conversions.

The extracts in this selection are taken from *Method in Theology*, 235–44, 247–50.

1 Horizons

In its literal sense the word, horizon, denotes the bounding circle, the line at which earth and sky appear to meet. This line is the limit of one's field of vision. As one moves about, it recedes in front and closes in behind so that, for different standpoints, there are different horizons. Moreover, for each different standpoint and horizon, there are different divisions of the totality of visible objects. Beyond the horizon lie the objects that, at least for the moment, cannot be seen. Within the horizon lie the objects that can now be seen.

As our field of vision, so too the scope of our knowledge and the range of our interests are bounded. As fields of vision vary with one's standpoint, so too the scope of one's knowledge and the range of one's interests vary with the period in which one lives, one's social background and milieu, one's education and personal development. So there has arisen a metaphorical or perhaps analogous meaning of the word, horizon. In this sense what lies beyond one's horizon is simply outside the range of one's knowledge and interests: one neither knows

2 Ibid., 240.
3 Ibid.

nor cares. But what lies within one's horizon is in some measure, great or small, an object of interest and of knowledge.

Differences in horizon may be complementary, or genetic, or dialectical. Workers, foremen, supervisors, technicians, engineers, managers, doctors, lawyers, professors have different interests. They live in a sense in different worlds. Each is quite familiar with his own world. But each also knows about the others, and each recognizes the need for the others. So their many horizons in some measure include one another and, for the rest, they complement one another. Singly they are not self-sufficient, and together they represent the motivations and the knowledge needed for the functioning of a communal world. Such horizons are complementary.

Next, horizons may differ genetically. They are related as successive stages in some process of development. Each later stage presupposes earlier stages, partly to include them, and partly to transform them. Precisely because the stages are earlier and later, no two are simultaneous. They are parts, not of a single communal world, but of a single biography or of a single history.

Thirdly, horizons may be opposed dialectically. What in one is found intelligible, in another is unintelligible. What for one is true, for another is false. What for one is good, for another is evil. Each may have some awareness of the other and so each in a manner may include the other. But such inclusion is also negation and rejection. For the other's horizon, at least in part, is attributed to wishful thinking, to an acceptance of myth, to ignorance or fallacy, to blindness or illusion, to backwardness or immaturity, to infidelity, to bad will, to a refusal of God's grace. Such a rejection of the other may be passionate, and then the suggestion that openness is desirable will make one furious. But again rejection may have the firmness of ice without any trace of passion or even any show of feeling, except perhaps a wan smile. Both astrology and genocide are beyond the pale, but the former is ridiculed, the latter is execrated.

Horizons, finally, are the structured resultant of past achievement and, as well, both the condition and the limitation of further development. They are structured. All learning is, not a mere addition to previous learning, but rather an organic growth out of it. So all our intentions, statements, deeds stand within contexts. To such contexts we appeal when we outline the reasons for our goals, when we clarify, amplify, qualify our statements, or when we explain our deeds. Within such contexts must be fitted each new item of knowledge and each new factor in our attitudes. What does not fit, will not be noticed or, if forced on our attention, it will seem irrelevant or unimportant. Horizons then are the sweep of our interests and of our knowledge; they are the fertile source of further knowledge and care; but they also are the boundaries that limit our capacities for assimilating more than we already have attained.

2 Conversions and Breakdowns

Joseph de Finance has drawn a distinction between a horizontal and vertical exercise of freedom.[4] A horizontal exercise is a decision or choice that occurs within an established horizon. A vertical exercise is the set of judgments and decisions by which we move from one horizon to another. Now there may be a sequence of such vertical exercises of freedom, and in each case the new horizon, though notably deeper and broader and richer, none the less is consonant with the old and a development out of its potentialities. But it is also possible that the movement into a new horizon involves an about-face; it comes out of the old by repudiating characteristic features; it begins a new sequence that can keep revealing ever greater depth and breadth and wealth. Such an about-face and new beginning is what is meant by a conversion.

Conversion may be intellectual or moral or religious. While each of the three is connected with the other two, still each is a different type of event and has to be considered in itself before being related to the others.

Intellectual conversion is a radical clarification and, consequently, the elimination of an exceedingly stubborn and misleading myth concerning reality, objectivity, and human knowledge. The myth is that knowing is like looking, that objectivity is seeing what is there to be seen and not seeing what is not there, and that the real is what is out there now to be looked at. Now this myth overlooks the distinction between the world of immediacy, say, the world of the infant and, on the other hand, the world mediated by meaning. The world of immediacy is the sum of what is seen, heard, touched, tasted, smelt, felt. It conforms well enough to the myth's view of reality, objectivity, knowl-

4 J. de Finance, *Essai sur l'agir humain* (Rome: Gregorian University Press, 1962), 287 ff.

edge. But it is but a tiny fragment of the world mediated by meaning. For the world mediated by meaning is a world known not by the sense experience of an individual but by the external and internal experience of a cultural community, and by the continuously checked and rechecked judgments of the community. Knowing, accordingly, is not just seeing; it is experiencing, understanding, judging, and believing. The criteria of objectivity are not just the criteria of ocular vision; they are the compounded criteria of experiencing, of understanding, of judging, and of believing. The reality known is not just looked at; it is given in experience, organized and extrapolated by understanding, posited by judgment and belief.

The consequences of the myth are various. The naive realist knows the world mediated by meaning but thinks he knows it by looking. The empiricist restricts objective knowledge to sense experience; for him, understanding and conceiving, judging and believing are merely subjective activities. The idealist insists that human knowing always includes understanding as well as sense; but he retains the empiricist's notion of reality, and so he thinks of the world mediated by meaning as not real but ideal. Only the critical realist can acknowledge the facts of human knowing and pronounce the world mediated by meaning to be the real world; and he can do so only inasmuch as he shows that the process of experiencing, understanding, and judging is a process of self-transcendence.

Now we are not discussing a merely technical point in philosophy. Empiricism, idealism, and realism name three totally different horizons with no common identical objects. An idealist never means what an empiricist means, and a realist never means what either of them means. An empiricist may argue that quantum theory cannot be about physical reality; it cannot because it deals only with relations between phenomena. An idealist would concur and add that, of course, the same is true of all science and, indeed, of the whole of human knowing. The critical realist will disagree with both: a verified hypothesis is probably true; and what probably is true refers to what in reality probably is so. To change the illustration, What are historical facts? For the empiricist they are what was out there and was capable of being looked at. For the idealist they are mental constructions carefully based on data recorded in documents. For the critical realist they are events in the world mediated by true acts of meaning. To take a third illustration, What is a myth? There are psychological, anthropological, historical, and philosophic answers to the question. But there also are reductionist answers: myth is a narrative about entities not to be found within an empiricist, an idealist, a historicist, an existentialist horizon.

Enough of illustrations. They can be multiplied indefinitely, for philosophic issues are universal in scope, and some form of naive realism seems to appear utterly unquestionable to very many. As soon as they begin to speak of knowing, of objectivity, of reality, there crops up the assumption that all knowing must be something like looking. To be liberated from that blunder, to discover the self-transcendence proper to the human process of coming to know, is to break often long-ingrained habits of thought and speech. It is to acquire the mastery of one's own house that is to be had only when one knows precisely what one is doing when one is knowing. It is a conversion, a new beginning, a fresh start. It opens the way to ever further clarifications and developments.

Moral conversion changes the criterion of one's decisions and choices from satisfactions to values. As children or minors we are persuaded, cajoled, ordered, compelled to do what is right. As our knowledge of human reality increases, as our responses to human values are strengthened and refined, our mentors more and more leave us to ourselves so that our freedom may exercise its ever advancing thrust toward authenticity. So we move to the existential moment when we discover for ourselves that our choosing affects ourselves no less than the chosen or rejected objects, and that it is up to each of us to decide for himself what he is to make of himself. Then is the time for the exercise of vertical freedom and then moral conversion consists in opting for the truly good, even for value against satisfaction when value and satisfaction conflict. Such conversion, of course, falls far short of moral perfection. Deciding is one thing, doing is another. One has yet to uncover and root out one's individual, group, and general bias.[5] One has to keep developing one's knowledge of human reality and potentiality as they are in the existing situation. One has to keep distinct its elements of progress and its elements of decline. One has to keep scrutinizing one's intentional responses to values and their implicit scales of preference. One has to listen to criticism and to protest. One has to remain ready to learn from others. For moral knowledge is the proper possession only of morally good men and, until one has merited that title, one has still to advance and to learn.

5 See *Insight*, 244–69 [see 1.V.3–5 in this reader].

Religious conversion is being grasped by ultimate concern. It is other-worldly falling in love. It is total and permanent self-surrender without conditions, qualifications, reservations. But it is such a surrender, not as an act, but as a dynamic state that is prior to and principle of subsequent acts. It is revealed in retrospect as an undertow of existential consciousness, as a fated acceptance of a vocation to holiness, as perhaps an increasing simplicity and passivity in prayer. It is interpreted differently in the context of different religious traditions. For Christians it is God's love flooding our hearts through the Holy Spirit given to us. It is the gift of grace, and since the days of Augustine, a distinction has been drawn between operative and cooperative grace. Operative grace is the replacement of the heart of stone by a heart of flesh, a replacement beyond the horizon of the heart of stone. Cooperative grace is the heart of flesh becoming effective in good works through human freedom. Operative grace is religious conversion. Cooperative grace is the effectiveness of conversion, the gradual movement towards a full and complete transformation of the whole of one's living and feeling, one's thoughts, words, deeds, and omissions.[6]

As intellectual and moral conversion, so also religious conversion is a modality of self-transcendence. Intellectual conversion is to truth attained by cognitional self-transcendence. Moral conversion is to values apprehended, affirmed, and realized by a real self-transcendence. Religious conversion is to a total being-in-love as the efficacious ground of all self-transcendence, whether in the pursuit of truth, or in the realization of human values, or in the orientation man adopts to the universe, its ground, and its goal.

Because intellectual, moral, and religious conversions all have to do with self-transcendence, it is possible, when all three occur within a single consciousness, to conceive their relations in terms of sublation. I would use this notion in Karl Rahner's sense[7] rather than Hegel's to mean that what sublates goes beyond what is sublated, introduces something new and distinct, puts everything on a new basis, yet so far from interfering with the sublated or destroying it, on the contrary needs it, includes it, preserves all its proper features and properties, and carries them forward to a fuller realization within a richer context.

So moral conversion goes beyond the value, truth, to values gener-

6 On grace as operative and cooperative in St Thomas, see *Grace and Freedom*.
7 K. Rahner, *Hörer des Wortes* (Munich: Kösel, 1963), 40.

ally. It promotes the subject from cognitional to moral self-transcendence. It sets him on a new, existential level of consciousness and establishes him as an originating value. But this in no way interferes with or weakens his devotion to truth. He still needs truth, for he must apprehend reality and real potentiality before he can deliberately respond to value. The truth he needs is still the truth attained in accord with the exigences of rational consciousness. But now his pursuit of it is all the more secure because he has been armed against bias, and it is all the more meaningful and significant because it occurs within, and plays an essential role in, the far richer context of the pursuit of all values.

Similarly, religious conversion goes beyond moral. Questions for intelligence, for reflection, for deliberation reveal the eros of the human spirit, its capacity and its desire for self-transcendence. But that capacity meets fulfilment, that desire turns to joy, when religious conversion transforms the existential subject into a subject in love, a subject held, grasped, possessed, owned through a total and so an other-worldly love. Then there is a new basis for all valuing and all doing good. In no way are fruits of intellectual or moral conversion negated or diminished. On the contrary, all human pursuit of the true and the good is included within and furthered by a cosmic context and purpose and, as well, there now accrues to man the power of love to enable him to accept the suffering involved in undoing the effects of decline.

It is not to be thought, however, that religious conversion means no more than a new and more efficacious ground for the pursuit of intellectual and moral ends. Religious loving is without conditions, qualifications, reservations; it is with all one's heart and all one's soul and all one's mind and all one's strength. This lack of limitation, though it corresponds to the unrestricted character of human questioning, does not pertain to this world. Holiness abounds in truth and moral goodness, but it has a distinct dimension of its own. It is other-worldly fulfilment, joy, peace, bliss. In Christian experience these are the fruits of being in love with a mysterious, uncomprehended God. Sinfulness similarly is distinct from moral evil; it is the privation of total loving; it is a radical dimension of lovelessness. That dimension can be hidden by sustained superficiality, by evading ultimate questions, by absorption in all that the world offers to challenge our resourcefulness, to relax our bodies, to distract our minds. But escape may not be permanent and then the absence of fulfilment reveals itself in unrest, the absence of joy in the pursuit of fun, the absence of peace in disgust – a depressive disgust with oneself or a manic, hostile, even violent disgust with mankind.

Though religious conversion sublates moral, and moral conversion sublates intellectual, one is not to infer that intellectual comes first and then moral and finally religious. On the contrary, from a causal viewpoint, one would say that first there is God's gift of his love. Next, the eye of this love reveals values in their splendor, while the strength of this love brings about their realization, and that is moral conversion. Finally, among the values discerned by the eye of love is the value of believing the truths taught by the religious tradition, and in such tradition and belief are the seeds of intellectual conversion. For the word, spoken and heard, proceeds from and penetrates to all four levels of intentional consciousness. Its content is not just a content of experience but a content of experience and understanding and judging and deciding. The analogy of sight yields the cognitional myth. But fidelity to the word engages the whole man.

Besides conversions there are breakdowns. What has been built up so slowly and so laboriously by the individual, the society, the culture, can collapse. Cognitional self-transcendence is neither an easy notion to grasp nor a readily accessible datum of consciousness to be verified. Values have a certain esoteric imperiousness, but can they keep outweighing carnal pleasure, wealth, power? Religion undoubtedly had its day, but is not that day over? Is it not illusory comfort for weaker souls, an opium distributed by the rich to quiet the poor, a mythical projection of man's own excellence into the sky?

Initially not all but some religion is pronounced illusory, not all but some moral precept is rejected as ineffective and useless, not all truth but some type of metaphysics is dismissed as mere talk. The negations may be true, and then they represent an effort to offset decline. But also they may be false, and then they are the beginning of decline. In the latter case some part of cultural achievement is being destroyed. It will cease being a familiar component in cultural experience. It will recede into a forgotten past for historians, perhaps, to rediscover and reconstruct. Moreover, this elimination of a genuine part of the culture means that a previous whole has been mutilated, that some balance has been upset, that the remainder will become distorted in an effort to compensate. Further, such elimination, mutilation, distortion will, of course, be admired as the forward march of progress, while the evident ills they bring forth are to be remedied, not by a return to a misguided past, but by more elimination, mutilation, distortion. Once a process of dissolution has begun, it is screened by self-deception and it is perpetuated by consistency. But that does not mean that it is confined to some single uniform course. Different nations, different classes of society, different age groups can select different parts of past achievement for elimination, different mutilations to be effected, different distortions to be provoked. Increasing dissolution will then be matched by increasing division, incomprehension, suspicion, distrust, hostility, hatred, violence. The body social is torn apart in many ways, and its cultural soul has been rendered incapable of reasonable convictions and responsible commitments.

For convictions and commitments rest on judgments of fact and judgments of value. Such judgments, in turn, rest largely on beliefs. Few, indeed, are the people that, pressed on almost any point, must not shortly have recourse to what they have believed. Now such recourse can be efficacious only when believers present a solid front, only when intellectual, moral, and religious sceptics are a small and, as yet, uninfluential minority. But their numbers can increase, their influence can mount, their voices can take over the book market, the educational system, the mass media. Then believing begins to work not for but against intellectual, moral, and religious self-transcendence. What had been an uphill but universally respected course collapses into the peculiarity of an outdated minority.

3 Dialectic: The Problem

The presence or absence of intellectual, of moral, of religious conversion gives rise to dialectically opposed horizons. While complementary or genetic differences can be bridged, dialectical differences involve mutual repudiation. Each considers repudiation of its opposites the one and only intelligent, reasonable, and responsible stand and, when sufficient sophistication is attained, each seeks a philosophy or a method that will buttress what are considered appropriate views on the intelligent, the reasonable, the responsible.

There results a babel. All three types of conversion may be lacking; any one may be present, or any two, or all three. Even prescinding from differences in the thoroughness of the conversion, there are eight radically differing types. Moreover, ever investigation is conducted from within some horizon. This remains true even if one does not know one operates from within a horizon, or even if one assumes that one makes no assumptions. Whether they are explicitly acknowledged or not, dialectically opposed horizons lead to opposed value judgments, opposed accounts of historical movements, opposed interpretations of authors, and different selections of relevant data in special research.

To a great extent natural science escapes this trap. It limits itself to questions that can be settled through an appeal to observation and experiment. It draws its theoretical modes from mathematics. It aims at an empirical knowledge in which value judgments have no constitutive role. Still these advantages do not give complete immunity. An account of scientific method stands to cognitional theory as the less to the more general, so that no firm barrier separates science, scientific method, and general cognitional theory. So mechanist determinism used to be part of science; now it is a discarded philosophic opinion. But in its place there is Niels Bohr's doctrine of complementarity, which includes philosophic views on human knowledge and on reality, and any departure from Bohr's position involves still more philosophy.[8] Again, while physics, chemistry, biology do not make value judgments, still the transition from liberal to totalitarian regimes has made scientists reflect on the value of science and their rights as scientists, while military and other uses of scientific discoveries have made them advert to their duties.

In the human sciences the problems are far more acute. Reductionists extend the methods of natural science to the study of man. Their results, accordingly, are valid only in so far as a man resembles a robot or a rat and, while such resemblance does exist, exclusive attention to it gives a grossly mutilated and distorted view.[9] General system theory rejects reductionism in all its forms, but it still is aware of its unsolved problems; for systems engineering involves a progressive mechanization that tends to reduce man's role in the system to that of a robot, while systems generally can be employed for destructive as well as constructive ends.[10] Gibson Winter in his *Elements for a Social Ethic*[11]

8 P.A. Heelan, *Quantum Mechanics and Objectivity* (The Hague: Nijhoff, 1965), chap. 3.
9 F.W. Matson, *The Broken Image* (Garden City: NY: Doubleday, 1966), chap. 2.
10 L. von Bertalanffy, *General System Theory* (New York: Braziller, 1968), 10, 52.
11 Gibson Winter, *Elements for a Social Ethic* (New York: Macmillan, 1966).

has contrasted the diverging styles in sociology associated with the names of Talcott Parsons and C. Wright Mills. After noting that the difference in approach led to different judgments on existing society, he asked whether the opposition was scientific or merely ideological – a question, of course, that transported the discussion from the history of contemporary sociological thought into philosophy and ethics. Prof. Winter worked out a general account of social reality, distinguished physicalist, functionalist, voluntarist, and intentionalist styles in sociology, and assigned to each its sphere of relevance and effectiveness. Where Max Weber distinguished between social science and social policy, Prof. Winter distinguishes between philosophically grounded and graded styles in social science and, on the other hand, social policy grounded not only in social science but also in the value judgments of an ethics.

Both in the natural and in the human sciences, then, there obtrude issues that are not to be solved by empirical methods. These issues can be skirted or evaded with greater success in the natural sciences and less in the human sciences. But a theology can be methodical only if these issues are met head on. To meet them head on is the problem of our fourth functional specialty, dialectic.

4 Dialectic: The Structure

The structure of dialectic has two levels. On an upper level are the operators. On a lower level are assembled the materials to be operated on.

The operators are two precepts: develop positions; reverse counterpositions. Positions are statements compatible with intellectual, moral, and religious conversion; they are developed by being integrated with fresh data and further discovery. Counterpositions are statements incompatible with intellectual, or moral, or religious conversion; they are reversed when the incompatible elements are removed.

Before being operated on, the materials have to be assembled, completed, compared, reduced, classified, selected. *Assembly* includes the researches performed, the interpretations proposed, the histories written, and the events, statements, movements to which they refer. *Completion* adds evaluation interpretation and evaluative history; it picks out the one hundred and one 'good things' and their opposites; it is history in the style of Burckhardt rather than Ranke.[12] *Comparison* examines the completed assembly to seek out affinities and oppositions. *Reduction* finds the same affinity and the same opposition manifested in a number of different manners; from the many manifestations it moves to the underlying root. *Classification* determines which of these sources of affinity or opposition result from dialectically opposed horizons and which have other grounds. *Selection*, finally, picks out the affinities and oppositions grounded in dialectically opposed horizons and dismisses other affinities and oppositions.

Now this work of assembly, completion, comparison, reduction, classification, and selection will be performed by different investigators and they will be operating from within different horizons. The results, accordingly, will not be uniform. But the source of this lack of uniformity will be brought out into the open when each investigator proceeds to distinguish between positions, which are compatible with intellectual, moral, and religious conversion and, on the other hand, counterpositions, which are incompatible either with intellectual, or with moral, or with religious conversion. A further objectification of horizon is obtained when each investigator operates on the materials by indicating the view that would result from developing what he has regarded as positions and by reversing what he has regarded as counterpositions. There is a final objectification of horizon when the results of the foregoing process are themselves regarded as materials, when they are assembled, completed, compared, reduced, classified, selected, when positions and counterpositions are distinguished, when positions are developed and counterpositions are reversed.

Related selections: 3.V on the eight functional specialties; 3.III on realms of meaning; 2.VI on religious conversion and theological foundations; 3.VIII.3 on conversions as theological categories; 1.VI, 1.VIII, and 1.XI.1 on topics related to intellectual conversion; 1.XIV.1, 2.VII.4, and 3.II.1 on moral consciousness; 3.IV.2 on religious experience; 1.V.5 on the longer cycle of decline; 1.V.2 on the notion of dialectic, 1.XI on dialectic as philosophic method, and 4.II on the dialectic of authority; 1.XVI.4 on belief.

---

12 On Burckhardt, see E. Cassirer, *The Problem of Knowledge, Philosophy: Science, and History since Hegel* (New Haven: Yale University Press, 1950), chap. 16; Gooch, *History and Historians in the Nineteenth Century*, 529–33.

VIII

Foundations

In the present selection, from the 'Foreground' chapter on foundations in Part 2 of *Method in Theology*, Lonergan sketches the derivation of theological categories. He proceeds here as a methodologist, rather than as a theologian working in the functional specialty, foundations. His is not the foundational specialist's aim of working out theological categories, but the preliminary task of 'indicating what qualities are desirable in theological categories, what measure of validity is to be demanded of them, and how are the categories with the desired qualities and validity to be obtained.'[1]

In the first part of this selection Lonergan distinguishes general categories which regard objects of other disciplines in addition to theology, and special categories which regard objects proper to theology. He then identifies two bases from which categories 'that in some measure are transcultural' might be derived. Finally, he turns to a consideration of the validity of the categories derived from the transcultural bases. In the second part Lonergan locates the transcultural base of general categories in transcendental subjectivity, that is, in the concrete attending, inquiring, reflecting, deliberating subject, and he proceeds to differentiate the basic nest of terms and relations which results from the analysis and appropriation of transcendental subjectivity. In the third part Lonergan outlines the derivation of five sets of categories proper to a methodical theology that begins, not from a metaphysical psychology in the theoretic mode, but from intentionality analysis in the mode of interiority. The final part of the present selection is on the employment of the categories. They may be used as a basis for methodical control in doing theology and as an *a priori* in theological inquiry.

1 *Method in Theology*, 282.

The extracts in this selection are taken from *Method in Theology*, 281–5; 285–7; 288–93.

1   Categories

It has been pointed out that medieval theology turned to Aristotle for guidance and help in clarifying its thought and making it coherent. On the method we are proposing the source of basic clarification will be interiorly and religiously differentiated consciousness.

The transcendental notions are our capacity for seeking and, when found, for recognizing instances of the intelligible, the true, the real, the good. It follows that they are relevant to every object that we come to know by asking and answering questions.

While the transcendental notions make questions and answers possible, categories make them determinate. Theological categories are either general or special. General categories regard objects that come within the purview of other disciplines as well as theology. Special categories regard the objects proper to theology. The task of working out general and special categories pertains, not to the methodologist, but to the theologian engaged in his fifth functional specialty. The methodologist's task is the preliminary one of indicating what qualities are desirable in theological categories, what measure of validity is to be demanded of them, and how are categories with the desired qualities and validity to be obtained.

First, then, Christianity is a religion that has been developing for over two millennia. Moreover, it has its antecedents in the Old Testament, and it has the mission of preaching to all nations. Plainly, a theology that is to reflect on such a religion and that is to direct its efforts at universal communication must have a transcultural base.

Next, the transcendental method outlined in our first chapter is, in a sense, transcultural.[2] Clearly, it is not transcultural inasmuch as it is explicitly formulated. But it is transcultural in the realities to which the formulation refers, for these realities are not the product of any culture but, on the contrary, the principles that produce cultures, preserve them, develop them. Moreover, since it is to these realities we refer when we speak of *homo sapiens*, it follows that these realities are transcultural with respect to all truly human cultures.

2 [3.I in this reader.]

Similarly, God's gift of his love (Rom. 5, 5) has a transcultural aspect. For if this gift is offered to all men, if it is manifested more or less authentically in the many and diverse religions of mankind, if it is apprehended in as many different manners as there are different cultures, still the gift itself as distinct from its manifestations is transcultural. For of other love it is true enough that it presupposes knowledge – *nihil amatum nisi praecognitum*. But God's gift of his love is free. It is not conditioned by human knowledge; rather it is the cause that leads man to seek knowledge of God. It is not restricted to any stage or section of human culture but rather is the principle that introduces a dimension of other-worldliness into any culture. All the same, it remains true, of course, that God's gift of his love has its proper counterpart in the revelation events in which God discloses to a particular people or to all mankind the completeness of his love for them. For being–in–love is properly itself, not in the isolated individual, but only in a plurality of persons that disclose their love to one another.

There exist, then, bases from which might be derived both general and special categories that in some measure are transcultural. But before attempting to indicate the manner in which such derivation might be achieved, let us first say something about the validity to be expected in the derivation.

First, with regard to the base for general theological categories in transcendental method, we have only to repeat what already has been said. The explicit formulation of that method is historically conditioned and can be expected to be corrected, modified, complemented as the sciences continue to advance and reflection on them to improve. What is transcultural is the reality to which such formulation refers, and that reality is transcultural because it is not the product of any culture but rather the principle that begets and develops cultures that flourish, as it also is the principle that is violated when cultures crumble and decay.

Secondly, with regard to the base of special theological categories, a distinction has to be drawn between being in love in an unrestricted manner (1) as it is defined and (2) as it is achieved. As it is defined, it is the habitual actuation of man's capacity for self-transcendence; it is the religious conversion that grounds both moral and intellectual conversion; it provides the real criterion by which all else is to be judged; and consequently one has only to experience it in oneself or witness it in others, to find in it its own justification. On the other hand, as it actually is achieved in any human being, the achievement is dialectical. It is authenticity as a withdrawal from unauthenticity, and the withdrawal is never complete and always precarious. The greatest of saints have not only their oddities but also their defects, and it is not some but all of us that pray, not out of humility but in truth,[3] to be forgiven our trespasses as we forgive those that trespass against us.

Accordingly, while there is no need to justify critically the charity described by St Paul in the thirteenth chapter of his first epistle to the Corinthians, there is always a great need to eye very critically any religious individual or group and to discern beyond the real charity they may well have been granted the various types of bias that may distort or block their exercise of it.[4]

Thirdly, both with regard to transcendental method and with regard to God's gift of his love we have distinguished between an inner core, which is transcultural, and an outer manifestation, that is subject to variation. Needless to say, theological categories will be transcultural only in so far as they refer to that inner core. In their actual formulation they will be historically conditioned and so subject to correction, modification, complementation. Moreover, the more elaborate they become and the further they are removed from that inner core, the greater will be their precariousness. On what grounds, then, are they to be accepted and employed?

Before answering this question, there must be introduced the notion of a model or ideal-type. Models, then, stand to the human sciences, to philosophies, to theologies, much as mathematics stands to the natural sciences. For models purport to be, not descriptions of reality, not hypotheses about reality, but simply interlocking sets of terms and relations. Such sets, in fact, turn out to be useful in guiding investigations, in framing hypotheses, and in writing descriptions. Thus, a model will direct the attention of an investigator in a determinate direction with either of two results; it may provide him with a basic

3 *Enchiridion Symbolorum, Definitionum et Declarationum de rebus fidei et morum (DS).* ed. H. Denzinger and A. Schönmetzer (Freiburg im Bresgau: Herder, 1963), 230.

4 On bias, see *Insight*, 214–31, 244–69 [see 1.IV.2 and 1.V.3–5 in this reader]. More generally, see the manifold warnings against various forms of illusion in devotional and ascetical writings. While this tradition should be integrated with the findings of depth psychology, it is of great importance to be aware of current corrections of earlier views. See L. von Bertalanffy, *General System Theory* (New York: Braziller, 1968), 106 ff.; 188 ff. A. Maslow, *Toward a Psychology of Being* (Princeton: Van Nostrand, 1962), esp. pp. 19–41; Ernest Becker, *The Structure of Evil* (New York: Braziller, 1968), 154–66; Arthur Janov, *The Primal Scream* (New York: Putnam, 1970).

sketch of what he finds to be the case; or it may prove largely irrelevant, yet the discovery of this irrelevance may be the occasion of uncovering clues that otherwise might be overlooked. Again, when one possesses models, the task of framing an hypothesis is reduced to the simpler matter of tailoring a model to suit a given object or area. Finally, the utility of the model may arise when it comes to describing a known reality. For known realities can be exceedingly complicated, and an adequate language to describe them hard to come by. So the formulation of models and their general acceptance as models can facilitate enormously both description and communication.

Now what has been said about models, is relevant to the question concerning the validity of the general and special theological categories. First, such categories will form a set of interlocking terms and relations and, accordingly, they will possess the utility of models. Further, these models will be built up from basic terms and relations that refer to transcultural components in human living and operation and, accordingly, at their roots they will possess quite exceptional validity. Finally, whether they are to be considered more than models with exceptional foundational validity, is not a methodological but a theological question. In other words, it is up to the theologian to decide whether any model is to become an hypothesis or to be taken as a description.

2   General Theological Categories

If categories are to be derived, there is needed a base from which they are derived. The base of general theological categories is the attending, inquiring, reflecting, deliberating subject along with the operations that result from attending, inquiring, reflecting, deliberating and with the structure within which the operations occur. The subject in question is not any general or abstract or theoretical subject; it is in each case the particular theologian that happens to be doing theology. Similarly, the relevant attending, inquiring, reflecting, deliberating are the attending, inquiring, reflecting, deliberating that he has found to go on in himself; the consequent operations are the operations he has uncovered and identified in his own operating; and the structure within which the operations occur is the pattern of dynamic relations which, as he knows from his own experience, lead from one operation to the next. Finally, the subject is self-transcending. His operations reveal objects: single operations reveal partial objects; a structured compound of operations reveals compounded objects; and as the subject by his operations is conscious of himself operating, he too is revealed though not as object but as subject.

Such is the basic nest of terms and relations. Now there has been for millennia a vast multitude of individuals in whom such basic nests of terms and relations can be verified: for they too attend, understand, judge, decide. Moreover, they do so not in isolation but in social groups, and as such groups develop and progress and also decline, there is not only society but also history.

Further, the basic nest of terms and relations can be differentiated in a number of manners. So one can distinguish and describe: (1) each of the different kinds of conscious operation that occur; (2) the biological, aesthetic, intellectual, dramatic, practical, or worshipful patterns of experience within which the operations occur; (3) the different quality of the consciousness inherent in sensing, in operating intelligently, in operating reasonably, in operating responsibly and freely; (4) the different manners in which operations proceed towards goals: the manner of common sense, of the sciences, of interiority and philosophy, of the life of prayer and theology; (5) the different realms of meaning and the different worlds meant as a result of the various manners of proceeding: the world of immediacy, given in immediate experience and confirmed by successful response; the world of common sense; the world of the sciences; the world of interiority and philosophy; the world of religion and theology; (6) the diverse heuristic structures within which operations accumulate towards the attainment of goals: the classical, statistical, genetic, and dialectical heuristic structures[5] and, embracing them all, the integral heuristic structure which is what I mean by a metaphysics;[6] (7) the contrast between differentiated consciousness that shifts with ease from one manner of operation in one world to another manner of operation in a different world and, on the other hand, undifferentiated consciousness which is at home in its local variety of common sense but finds any message from the worlds of theory, of interiority, of transcendence both alien and incomprehensible; (8) the difference between those that have or have not been converted religiously, or morally, or intellectually; (9) the consequent

---

5 *Insight*, 57–92, 242–69, 476–511, 553–617 [see 1.III.1–3, 1.V.2–5, 1.XII.2–4, and 1.XIII in this reader].

6 *Insight*, 415–21 [1.XI.2 in this reader].

dialectically opposed positions and counter-positions, models, categories.

Such differentiation vastly enriches the initial nest of terms and relations. From such a broadened basis one can go on to a developed account of the human good, values, beliefs, to the carriers, elements, functions, realms, and stages of meaning, to the question of God, of religious experience, its expressions, its dialectical development.

Finally, since the basic nest of terms and relations is a dynamic structure, there are various ways in which models of change can be worked out. Fire, for instance, has been conceived as one of the four elements, as due to phlogiston, and as a process of oxydization. But while the answers have little in common, they are answers to the same question, What will you know when you understand the data on fire? More generally, the nature of any x is what one will know when the data on x are understood. So by turning to the heuristic notions behind common names, one finds the unifying principle of the successive meanings attributed to the name.[7]

Other illustrations mostly from *Insight* follow. Developments can be analyzed as processes from initial global operations of low efficiency, through differentiation and specialization, to the integration of perfected specialties. Revolutionary developments in some departments of thought can be schematized as successive higher viewpoints.[8] A universe in which both classical and statistical laws are verified will be characterized by a process of emergent probability.[9] Authenticity can be shown to generate progress, unauthenticity to bring about decline,[10] while the problem of overcoming decline provides an introduction to religion.[11] The problems of interpretation bring to light the notion of a potential universal viewpoint that moves over different levels and sequences of expression.[12]

3   Special Theological Categories

Let us now turn from deriving general theological categories to deriv-

7 Ibid., 60 ff. [1.III.1 in this reader].
8 Ibid., 37–43 [1.II.3 in this reader].
9 Ibid., 138–51 [1.III.4 in this reader], 284–7.
10 Ibid., 232–69 [1.V in this reader].
11 Ibid., 719–25, 740–51 [see 1.XVI.1–3 in this reader].
12 Ibid., 585–617 [see 1.XIII.3 in this reader].

ing special theological categories. In this task we have a model in the theoretical theology developed in the middle ages. But it is a model that can be imitated only by shifting to a new key. For the categories we want will pertain, not to a theoretical theology, but to a methodical theology.

To illustrate the difference, consider the medieval doctrine of grace. It presupposed a metaphysical psychology in terms of the essence of the soul, its potencies, habits, and acts. This presupposition represented the order of nature. But grace goes beyond nature and perfects it. Grace, accordingly, calls for special theological categories, and these must refer to supernatural entities, for grace is tied up with God's loving gift of himself to us, and that gift is due not to our natures but to God's free initiative. At the same time, these entities have to be prolongations perfecting our nature. Accordingly, they are habits and acts. Supernatural acts ordinarily proceed from supernatural operative habits (virtues) and supernatural operative habits proceed from the supernatural entitative habit (sanctifying grace) which, unlike the operative habits, is radicated not in the potencies but in the essence of the soul.

Now to effect the transition from theoretical to methodical theology one must start, not from a metaphysical psychology, but from intentionality analysis and, indeed, from transcendental method. So in our chapter on religion we noted that the human subject was self-transcendent intellectually by the achievement of knowledge, that he was self-transcendent morally inasmuch as he sought what was worthwhile, what was truly good, and thereby became a principle of benevolence and beneficence, that he was self-transcendent affectively when he fell in love, when the isolation of the individual was broken and he spontaneously functioned not just for himself but for others as well. Further we distinguished different kinds of love: the love of intimacy, of husband and wife, of parents and children; the love of mankind devoted to the pursuit of human welfare locally or nationally or globally; and the love that was other-worldly because it admitted no conditions or qualifications or restrictions or reservations. It is this other-worldly love, not as this or that act, not as a series of acts, but as a dynamic state whence proceed the acts, that constitutes in a methodical theology what in a theoretical theology is named sanctifying grace. Again, it is this dynamic state, manifested in inner and outer acts, that provides the base out of which special theological categories are set up.

Traditionally that dynamic state is manifested in three ways: the purgative way in which one withdraws from sinning and overcomes temptation; the illuminative way in which one's discernment of values is refined and one's commitment to them is strengthened; the unitive way in which the serenity of joy and peace reveal the love that hitherto had been struggling against sin and advancing in virtue.

The data, then, on the dynamic state of other-worldly love are the data on a process of conversion and development. The inner determinants are God's gift of his love and man's consent, but there also are outer determinants in the store of experience and in the accumulated wisdom of the religious tradition. If civil law recognizes adult responsibility at the age of twenty-one years, the professor of religious psychology at Louvain had it that man reaches genuine religious faith and a properly personal assumption of his inherited religion about the age of thirty.[13] But just as one can be a highly successful scientist and yet have very vague notions regarding his own intentional and conscious operations, so too a person can be religiously mature yet have to recall to mind his past life and study it in its religious moments and features before he can discern in it a direction, a pattern, a thrust, a call, to unworldliness. Even then his difficulties may not be at an end: he may be unable to associate any precise meaning with the words I have used; he may be too familiar with the reality of which I speak to connect it with what I say; he may be looking for something with a label on it, when he should simply be heightening his consciousness of the power working within him and adverting to its long-term effects.

But I do not think the matter is in doubt. In the realm of religious experience Oliver Rabut has asked whether there exists any unassailable fact. He found such a fact in the existence of love. It is as though a room were filled with music though one can have no sure knowledge of its source. There is in the world, as it were, a charged field of love and meaning; here and there it reaches a notable intensity; but it is ever unobtrusive, hidden, inviting each of us to join. And join we must if we are to perceive it, for our perceiving is through our own loving.[14]

The functional specialty, foundations, will derive its first set of categories from religious experience. That experience is something exceed-

---

13 A. Vergote, *Psychologie religieuse*, 3rd ed. (Brussels: Dessart, 1969), 319.
14 O. Rabut, *L'expérience religieuse fondamentale* (Tournai: Castermann, 1969), 168.

ingly simple and, in time, also exceedingly simplifying, but it also is
something exceedingly rich and enriching. There are needed studies of
religious interiority: historical, phenomenological, psychological, sociological. There is needed in the theologian the spiritual development
that will enable him both to enter into the experience of others and to
frame the terms and relations that will express that experience.

Secondly, from the subject one moves to subjects, their togetherness
in community, service, and witness, the history of the salvation that is
rooted in a being–in–love, and the function of this history in promoting the kingdom of God amongst men.

The third set of special categories moves from our loving to the loving source of our love. The Christian tradition makes explicit our
implicit intending of God in all our intending by speaking of the Spirit
that is given to us, of the Son who redeemed us, of the Father who sent
the Son and with the Son sends the Spirit, and of our future destiny
when we shall know, not as in a glass darkly, but face to face.

A fourth set of categories results from differentiation. Just as one's
humanity, so too one's Christianity may be authentic or unauthentic or
some blend of the two. What is worse, to the unauthentic man or
Christian, what appears authentic, is the unauthentic. Here, then, is the
root of division, opposition, controversy, denunciation, bitterness,
hatred, violence. Here, too, is the transcendental base for the fourth
functional specialty, dialectic.

A fifth set of categories regards progress, decline, and redemption.
As human authenticity promotes progress, and human unauthenticity
generates decline, so Christian authenticity – which is love of others
that does not shrink from self-sacrifice and suffering – is the sovereign
means for overcoming evil. Christians bring about the kingdom of God
in the world not only by doing good but also by overcoming evil with
good (Rom. 12, 21). Not only is there the progress of mankind but also
there is development and progress within Christianity itself; and as
there is development, so too there is decline; and as there is decline,
there also is the problem of undoing it, of overcoming evil with good
not only in the world but also in the church.

So much for a sketch of general and special theological categories.
As already noted, the task of a methodologist is to sketch the derivation of such categories, but it is up to the theologian working in the
fifth functional specialty to determine in detail what the general and
special categories are to be.

4 Use of the Categories

I have been indicating how general and special categories can be derived from a transcultural base. For general categories the base is the authentic or unauthentic man; attentive or inattentive, intelligent or slow-witted, reasonable or silly, responsible or irresponsible, with the consequent positions and counterpositions. For special categories the base is the authentic or unauthentic Christian, genuinely in love with God, or failing in that love, with a consequent Christian or unchristian outlook and style of living.

The derivation of the categories is a matter of the human and the Christian subject effecting self-appropriation and employing this heightened consciousness both as a basis for methodical control in doing theology and, as well, as an *a priori* whence he can understand other men, their social relations, their history, their religion, their rituals, their destiny.

The purification of the categories – the elimination of the unauthentic – is prepared by the functional specialty, dialectic, and it is effected in the measure that theologians attain authenticity through religious, moral, and intellectual conversion. Nor may one expect the discovery of some 'objective' criterion or test or control. For that meaning of the 'objective' is mere delusion. Genuine objectivity is the fruit of authentic subjectivity. To seek and employ some alternative prop or crutch invariably leads to some measure of reductionism. As Hans-Georg Gadamer has contended at length in his *Wahrheit und Methode*, there are no satisfactory methodical criteria that prescind from the criteria of truth.

The use of the general theological categories occurs in any of the eight functional specialties. The genesis of the special theological categories occurs seminally in dialectic and with explicit commitment in foundations. The commitment, however, is to the categories only as models, as interlocking sets of terms and relations. The use and the acceptance of the categories as hypotheses about reality or description of reality occur in doctrines, systematics, communications.

It is to be stressed that this use of the special categories occurs in interaction with data. They receive further specifications from the data. At the same time, the data set up an exigence for further clarification of the categories and for their correction and development.

In this fashion there is set up a scissors movement with an upper blade in the categories and a lower blade in the data. Just as the principles and laws of physics are neither mathematics nor data but the fruit of an interaction between mathematics and data, so too a theology can be neither purely *a priori* nor purely *a posteriori* but only the fruit of an ongoing process that has one foot in a transcultural base and the other on increasingly organized data.

So, as theology is an ongoing process, as religion and religious doctrine themselves develop, the functional specialty, foundations, will be concerned largely with the origins, the genesis, the present state, the possible developments and adaptations of the categories in which Christians understand themselves, communicate with one another, and preach the gospel to all nations.

Related selections: 3.I on the nature of method, determinate categories and transcultural notions, and the functions of transcendental method; 2.VI on the new context of theology; 4.I on the dynamic viewpoint that emphasizes method, not logic; 3.III on differentiations of consciousness and the distinction between theoretic and interior modes of conscious intentionality; 3.VII.1–2 on horizons and conversion.

PART FOUR

Late Writings

I

Static and Dynamic Viewpoints

In 1973 Lonergan presented a series of lectures on philosophy of God and theology. In the third lecture in the series he took up the question of the relationship of philosophy of God to the seventh functional specialty in his theological method, systematics. From what may be named a 'static viewpoint,' which upholds the ideal of deductivist system, philosophy of God and systematics must remain distinct and separate. One and the same deductivist system 'either does or does not have premises derived from revealed religion.'[1] If the system has such premises, philosophy of God is eliminated; if it is does not, systematics is eliminated. From the static viewpoint, unification of philosophy of God and systematics is impossible. But unification, Lonergan argues, may be possible from a 'dynamic viewpoint': 'They may very well have the unity of a single collaborative process.'[2]

In the present selection Lonergan compares and contrasts a static with a dynamic or 'moving' viewpoint, links the static with logic and the dynamic with method, and distinguishes three notions of system. Finally, he notes the implications of the shift from a static to a dynamic viewpoint – the shift from logical to methodical control of meaning – for the conception of theology and philosophy.

This extract is taken from *Philosophy of God*, 45–6, 47–50, 56–7.

The basic issue is between a static and a dynamic viewpoint. If the viewpoint is static, then from the very start everything really is settled.

1 *Philosophy of God*, 46.
2 Ibid.

Nothing new can be added at any point after one has started. On the other hand, if the viewpoint is dynamic, then there can be added any number of reflections and discoveries that at the start were not included in one's assumptions.

The static viewpoint is the ideal of deductivist logic. One determines one's basic terms and relations. One determines how further terms and relations may be derived from the basic terms and relations. One sets forth one's postulates. One determines rules for valid inference. From this starting point, as a fixed basis, one proceeds. But all that one can discover is what one has already settled implicitly, for any conclusion one reaches must already be implicit in one's premises or else the result of faulty reasoning.

The dynamic viewpoint, on the contrary, is a moving viewpoint. One starts from what one already knows or thinks one knows. One advances by learning what others have discovered and, perhaps occasionally, one may discover something for oneself. One's goal is not settled in advance. One may guess or make predictions, but it is not impossible that the guesses or predictions may prove mistaken ...

Some, no doubt, may feel that to be content with a dynamic viewpoint and unity is to desert the notion of science properly so-called. But while I would grant that it does desert a narrow reading of Aristotle's *Posterior Analytics*, I think many would hesitate to agree that that narrow reading possesses any positive significance in the context of modern science, modern scholarship, or modern philosophy. Indeed, it would seem that only the older generation of contemporary theologians have any acquaintance with Aristotle's *Posterior Analytics* either in a narrow reading or the more intelligent reading that takes into account Aristotle's practice and even theory in his other works.

Indeed, if one accepts the theorem propounded by Kurt Gödel, one will conclude with him that realizations of the deductivist ideal are either trivial or incomplete or incoherent. They are trivial when their content is largely tautologous. They are incomplete when they lead to contradictory alternatives which they cannot resolve. They are incoherent when they demonstrate both the affirmation and the negation of the same proposition.

In brief, like the mortician, the logician achieves a steady state only temporarily. The mortician prevents not the ultimate but only the immediate decomposition of the corpse. In similar fashion the logician brings about, not the clarity, the coherence, and the rigor that will last forever, but only the clarity, the coherence, and the rigor that will bring to light the inadequacy of current views and thereby give rise to the discovery of a more adequate position.

The shift from the static to the dynamic viewpoint relativizes logic and emphasizes method. It relativizes logic. It recognizes to the fullest extent the value of the clarity, coherence, and rigor that logic brings about. But it does not consider logic's achievement to be permanent. On the contrary, it considers it to be recurrent. Human knowledge can be constantly advancing, and the function of logic is to hasten that advance by revealing clearly, coherently, and rigorously the deficiencies of current achievement.

I have said that the shift from the static to the dynamic viewpoint not only relativizes logic but also emphasizes method. For it is method that shows the way from the logically clear, coherent, and rigorous position of today to the quite different but logically clear, coherent, and rigorous position of tomorrow.

Method however can be conceived in quite different manners. Method can be thought of as a set of recipes that can be observed by a blockhead yet lead infallibly to astounding discoveries. Such a notion of method I consider sheer illusion. The function of method is to spell out for each discipline the implications of the transcendental precepts, Be attentive, Be intelligent, Be reasonable, Be responsible. Nor does the explicitness of method make the occurrence of discoveries infallible. The most it can achieve is to make discoveries more probable. The greater the number of investigators following a sound method, the greater the likelihood that someone will attend to the data that are significant. The greater the likelihood of attention focusing on the data that are significant in the solution of current problems, the greater the likelihood that the intelligent hypothesis will be proposed. The greater the likelihood of the intelligent hypothesis being proposed, the greater the likelihood of there being worked out the proper series of experiments to check and verify the hypothesis.

I have been contrasting a static and a dynamic viewpoint and I have been bringing the two together in a higher unity by urging that logic brings to each successive discovery the clarity, coherence, and rigor that will reveal the inadequacy of the discovery, while method shows the way from one discovery to the next. But while logic and method do enter into a higher functional unity, none the less a position that rests solely on the logical deductivist ideal without any awareness of the compensating values of method results in an extremely one-sided position.

For the man that knows his logic and does not think of method, objectivity is apt to be conceived as the fruit of immediate experience, of self-evident and necessary truths, and of rigorous inferences. When method is added to the picture, one may succeed in discovering that objectivity is the fruit of authentic subjectivity, of being attentive, intelligent, reasonable, responsible.

For the man who knows his logic and does not think of method the basic discipline will regard objects generally. It will be a metaphysic. But when method is added to the picture, the basic discipline will regard not objects but subjects: it will be not a metaphysic but a cognitional theory; and the cognitional theory will provide the critical basis both for an epistemology and a metaphysic.

For the man who knows his logic and does not think of method, the relation of the basic discipline to other disciplines will be logical. The basic discipline will provide the basic terms and relations. The other disciplines will add further specifications to the terms and relations provided by the basic discipline. But when method is added to the picture, the relationship between the basic discipline and other disciplines lies in the field not of logic but of method. The basic discipline sets up a transcendental method, a manner of proceeding in any and every cognitional enterprise. The other disciplines add to transcendental method the categorial determinations appropriate to their specific enterprise.

For the man who knows his logic and does not think of method, the term 'system' will have only one meaning. Systems are either true or false. True system is the realization of the deductivist ideal that happens to be true and, in each department of human knowledge, there is only one true system. But when method is added to the picture, three notions of system are distinguished. There is the mistaken notion of system that supposes that it comprehends the eternal verities. There is the empirical notion of system that regards systems as successive expressions of an ever fuller understanding of the relevant data and that considers the currently accepted system as the best available scientific opinion. Finally, there is system in the third sense that results from the appropriation of one's own conscious and intentional operations.

From these differences there arise different conceptions of theology. When the logical view prevails, theology is conceived as the science of

God and of all things in their relation to God. As the methodical view develops, theology is conceived as reflection on the significance and value of a religion within a culture, and culture itself is conceived, not normatively as though *de jure* there was but one human culture, but empirically and so with a full recognition of the many different manners in which sets of meanings and of values have informed human ways of life ...

In brief, the world of the theologian is not some isolated sphere cut off from the affairs of men. But the static viewpoint inevitably leads to such isolation. By rejecting the static viewpoint, by conceiving theology as an ongoing process guided by a method, one puts an end to isolationism. The concern of the theologian is not just a set of propositions but a concrete relation as it has been lived, as it is being lived, and as it is to be lived. So conceived, theology has to draw on the resources not only of scientists and historians but also of philosophers.

It is true, of course, that dropping the static and accepting the dynamic viewpoint imply that one is setting aside the old-time notions of philosophy and theology. Logic ceases to rule the roost. The dominant issue is method. The possibility of method is a multiple differentiation of consciousness: the religious, the linguistic, the literary, the systematic, the scientific, the scholarly, and the self-appropriation of intentionality analysis. When all of these differentiations of consciousness have been achieved, the consequent notions of philosophy and theology are quite different from what they were when only the first four differentiations had occurred ...

Related selections: 1.XV.1 on the immanent source of transcendence; 1.XVI.3 on the continuity of special transcendent knowledge with the universal viewpoint; 2.IV.2 on the shift from classicist to modern controls of meaning; 2.V on the transposition of classical Thomism; 2.VI on the new context of theology; 2.VIII.1 on pluralism and classicist culture; 3.III on differentiations of consciousness and realms of meaning; 3.V.1 on types of specialization; 1.XVII on self-appropriation and the development of the ideal of knowledge.

II

Dialectic of Authority

In a short article written in 1974 and presented here in its entirety, Lonergan defines legitimate authority in terms of the authenticity of the meanings and values that inform a community. Those meanings and values are authentic inasmuch as they result from adherence to the transcendental precepts: Be attentive, Be intelligent, Be reasonable, Be responsible. Lonergan writes: 'Authenticity makes power legitimate. It confers on power the aura and prestige of authority. Unauthenticity leaves power naked. It reveals power as mere power. Similarly, authenticity legitimates authorities, and unauthenticity destroys their authority and reveals them as merely powerful.'[1] Because both authenticity and unauthenticity are found in the community, in authorities in the community, and in individuals that are subject to authority, there is a complex dialectic of authority. It is the complexity of this dialectic that underlies the complexity, length, tediousness, and inconclusiveness of dialectical critiques of the legitimacy of the authority of a community or of the authorities in a community. Lonergan proposes the adoption of a 'more synthetic viewpoint,' expressed in terms of progress, decline, and redemption. The situation that results from disregard of the transcendental precepts, he asserts, is unintelligible. 'It is an objective surd, the realization of the irrational ... But an irrational situation is just stony ground, and to apply intelligence to it yields nothing.'[2] The remedy for the effects of sustained unauthenticity is to be found in redemption and its principle of self-sacrificing love. Grievances are eliminated

---

1 *A Third Collection*, 7–8.
2 Ibid., 9–10.

and objective absurdities corrected 'in the measure that the community becomes a community of love.'[3]

This extract is taken from *A Third Collection*, 5–12.

Authority is legitimate power. The dialectic will emerge from a reflection on power and legitimacy.

The source of power is cooperation. Cooperation is twofold. There is cooperation down the ages. There is cooperation at any given place and time.

Without cooperation down the ages human life today would not differ from that of the most primitive tribe. It would be not merely Preaurignacian, as the celebrated ethologist, Konrad Lorenz, has been repeating to students, but would resemble that of the isolated people recently discovered in the forest rain-country in the Philippines. Power today results from all the achievements of the past that have been accumulated, developed, integrated. Any present is powerful in the measure that past achievement lives on in it.

Besides the cooperation that extends down the ages, there is the cooperation that is going on here and now. The group can do so much that the individual cannot do. The group of groups is so much more efficient than the isolated group. Grouping groups is a device that can be reapplied again and again and, with each reapplication that results in an organic whole, power is multiplied.

As the source of power is cooperation, so the carrier of power is the community. By a community is not meant a number of people within a frontier. Community means people with a common field of experience, with a common or at least complementary way of understanding people and things, with common judgments and common aims. Without a common field of experience people are out of touch. Without a common way of understanding, they will misunderstand one another, grow suspicious, distrustful, hostile, violent. Without common judgments they will live in different worlds, and without common aims they will work at cross-purposes. Such, then, is community, and as it is community that hands on the discoveries and inventions of the past and, as well, cooperates in the present, so it is community that is the carrier of power.

3 Ibid., 10.

The exercise of power is twofold. For men live in two worlds. From infancy they live in a world of immediacy, a world revealed by sense and alive with feeling. Gradually they move into a world mediated by meaning and motivated by values. In this adult world the raw materials are indeed the world of immediacy. But by speech one asks when and where, what and why, what for and how often. Answers cumulatively extrapolate from what is near to what is ever further away, from the present to one's own and to others' memories of the past and anticipations of the future, from what is or was actual to the possible, the probable, the fictitious, the ideal, the normative.

As exercised within the world mediated by meaning and motivated by values, power resides in the word of authority. It is that word that brings the achievements of the past into the present; it is that word that organizes and directs the whole hierarchy of cooperating groups in the present; it is that word that distributes the fruits of cooperation among the cooperating members; it is that word that bans from social intercourse those that would disrupt the cooperating society. In brief, the word of authority is the current actuality of the power generated by past development and contemporary cooperation.

To a great extent the word of authority resides in the sum total of current institutions. By this sum total I mean all ways of cooperating that at any time are commonly understood and commonly accepted. Example defines roles and points to tasks. Custom fixes requisite qualifications and links consequents to antecedents. So in the home and in the educational hierarchy, in the learned professions, in industry and commerce, in politics and finance, in church and state there develops a vast and intricate web of interconnections that set the lines along which cooperation occurs and uncooperativeness is sanctioned.

I have employed the word, institution, in its broadest sense. It is the product of use and wont. It is the sum of the ways of cooperating that commonly are understood and commonly are accepted. It changes slowly, for a new common understanding and a new common consent are not easily developed. Nonetheless, it is within the matrix of use and wont that power comes to be entrusted to individuals within community. There is the spontaneous articulation of the kinship group. There is the need of leaders in times of stress. There is the advantage of arbitrators in disputes. There is the role of judges in settling whether injustice has been done and, if so, what satisfaction is to be made. By way of safeguard rules of due process are devised both with regard to the selection of officials and with regard to the manner in which their office is to be fulfilled. Such rules may remain unwritten. The officials may act only in the name of some subgroup in the community. But eventually there are rules that are enacted as laws, and there are officials that act in the name of the whole community.

So we come to a distinction between authority and authorities. The authorities are the officials to whom certain offices have been entrusted and certain powers delegated. But authority belongs to the community that has a common field of experience, common and complementary ways of understanding, common judgments and common aims. It is the community that is the carrier of a common world mediated by meaning and motivated by values. It is the validity of those meanings and values that gives authority its aura and prestige.

A rhetorical and juridical concept of culture assumed that one and only one set of meanings and values was valid for all mankind. Travel and research have dissipated that illusion. There are many differentiations of human consciousness: linguistic, religious, literary, systematic, scientific, scholarly, introspective. With each differentiation there is a shift of horizon, a transformation of available meanings, a transvaluation of values. So it is that from an empirical point of view culture has come to be conceived as the set of meanings and values that inform a common way of life.

Such meanings and values may be authentic or unauthentic. They are authentic in the measure that cumulatively they are the result of the transcendental precepts, Be attentive, Be intelligent, Be reasonable, Be responsible. They are unauthentic in the measure that they are the product of cumulative inattention, obtuseness, unreasonableness, irresponsibility.

Authenticity makes power legitimate. It confers on power the aura and prestige of authority. Unauthenticity leaves power naked. It reveals power as mere power. Similarly, authenticity legitimates authorities, and unauthenticity destroys their authority and reveals them as merely powerful. Legitimated by authenticity authority and authorities have a hold on the consciences of those subject to authority and authorities. But when they lack the legitimating by authenticity, authority and authorities invite the consciences of subjects to repudiate their claims to rule. However, subjects may be authentic or unauthentic. Insofar as they are authentic, they will accept the claims of legitimate authority and legitimate authorities, and they will resist the claims of illegitimate authority and illegitimate authorities. On the other hand, insofar as they are unauthentic, they will resist legitimate claims, and they will support illegitimate claims.

Dialectic has to do with the concrete, the dynamic, and the contradictory. Cooperation, power, and authority have to do with the concrete and the dynamic. Authenticity and unauthenticity add a pair of contradictories. The resulting dialectic is extremely complicated. Authenticity and unauthenticity are found in three different carriers: (1) in the community, (2) in the individuals that are authorities, and (3) in the individuals that are subject to authority. Again, unauthenticity is realized by any single act of inattention, obtuseness, unreasonableness, irresponsibility. But authenticity is reached only by long and sustained fidelity to the transcendental precepts. It exists only as a cumulative product. Moreover, authenticity in man or woman is ever precarious: our attentiveness is ever apt to be a withdrawal from inattention; our acts of understanding a correction of our oversights; our reasonableness a victory over silliness; our responsibility a repentance for our sins. To be ever attentive, intelligent, reasonable, responsible is to live totally in the world mediated by meaning and motivated by values. But man also lives in a world of immediacy and, while the world of immediacy can be incorporated in the world mediated by meaning and motivated by values, still that incorporation never is secure. Finally, what is authentic for a lesser differentiation of consciousness will be found unauthentic by the standards of a greater differentiation. So there is a sin of backwardness, of the cultures, the authorities, the individuals that fail to live on the level of their times.

The complexity of the dialectic of authority underscores what experience has long made quite plain. Inquiry into the legitimacy of authority or authorities is complex, lengthy, tedious, and often inconclusive.

A more effective approach is to adopt a more synthetic viewpoint. The fruit of authenticity is progress. For authenticity results from a long-sustained exercise of attentiveness, intelligence, reasonableness, responsibility. But long-sustained attentiveness notes just what is going on. Intelligence repeatedly grasps how things can be better. Reasonableness is open to change. Responsibility weighs in the balance short- and long-term advantages and disadvantages, benefits and defects. The longer these four are exercised, the more certain and the greater will be the progress made.

The fruit of unauthenticity is decline. Unauthentic subjects get themselves unauthentic authorities. Unauthentic authorities favor some groups over others. Favoritism breeds suspicion, distrust, dissension, opposition, hatred, violence. Community loses its common aims and begins to operate at cross-purposes. It loses its common judgments so that different groups inhabit different worlds. Common understanding is replaced by mutual incomprehension. The common field of experience is divided into hostile territories.

The breakdown of community entails the breakdown of cooperation. Different groups advocate different policies. Different policies entail different plans, and the different groups deploy all their resources for the implementation of the plans that accord with their policies. There may be a seesaw battle between them with the resultant incoherence and confusion. Or one side may gain the upper hand and then exploitation of the other follows.

Just as sustained authenticity results in increasing responsibility and order, increasing reasonableness and cohesion, increasing intelligence and objective intelligibility, increasing knowledge and mastery of the situation, so sustained unauthenticity has the opposite effects. But the remedy for the opposite effects lies beyond any normal human procedure. There is no use appealing to the sense of responsibility of irresponsible people, to the reasonableness of people that are unreasonable, to the intelligence of people that have chosen to be obtuse, to the attention of people that attend only to their grievances. Again, the objective situation brought about by sustained unauthenticity is not an intelligible situation. It is the product of inattention, obtuseness, unreasonableness, irresponsibility. It is an objective surd, the realization of the irrational. A natural situation yields fruits a hundredfold to the sustained application of intelligence. But an irrational situation is just stony ground, and to apply intelligence to it yields nothing.

However, beyond progress and decline there is redemption. Its principle is self-sacrificing love. To fall in love is to go beyond attention, intelligence, reasonableness, responsibility. It is to set up a new principle that has, indeed, its causes, conditions, occasions, but, as long as it lasts, provides the mainspring of one's desire and fear, hope and despair, joy and sorrow. In the measure that the community becomes a community of love and so capable of making real and great sacrifices, in that measure it can wipe out the grievances and correct the objective absurdities that its unauthenticity has brought about.

I speak of redemption from within the Christian tradition, in which Christ suffering, dying and rising again is at once the motive and the model of self-sacrificing love. But if one is willing to attend to the ideal types propounded by Arnold Toynbee in his *A Study of History*, a more general statement is possible. In that study, of course, Toynbee thought he was contributing to empirical science. Since then, however, he has recanted. But, I believe, his work remains a contribution not to knowledge of reality, not to hypotheses about reality, but to the ideal types that are intelligible sets of concepts and often prove useful to have to hand when it comes to describing reality or to forming hypotheses about it.

Relevant to present purposes would be Toynbee's creative minority, his dominant minority, his internal and external proletariat, and his universal religion within which a new civilization arises from the disorder and conflicts of the old. The creative minority are the representatives of progress. They are the leaders that gain the adhesion of the masses by successfully meeting the challenge of each successive situation. The dominant minority are the representatives of decline. They inherit the power of the creative minority, but they are unable to solve the problems that continuously multiply. The internal proletariat is constituted by the increasingly disaffected and disillusioned masses. The external proletariat are the less developed foreign peoples that are beginning to discover the weaknesses of their envied neighbor. In modern dress the internal and external proletariats would have to be related to John Kenneth Galbraith's multinational corporations. Religion, finally, in an era of crisis has to think less of issuing commands and decrees and more of fostering the self-sacrificing love that alone is capable of providing the solution to the evils of decline and of reinstating the beneficent progress that is entailed by sustained authenticity.

I have placed the legitimacy of authority in its authenticity. But besides the legitimacy of authority, there also is the assertion of that legitimacy, its legitimation. Legitimation is manifold. It occurs on any of the many differentiations of consciousness. In early human society it is a matter of myth and ritual. In the ancient high civilizations it became a matter of law. Among the loquacious and literary Greeks law was reinforced first by rhetoric and later by logic. Historians discovered that different laws obtained at different times and places. Systematizers sought to draw up codes that would express the eternal verities for all times and places. Philosophers sought principles that would underpin this or that system. But if the legitimacy of authority lies in its authenticity, none of these solutions is adequate.

By this I do not mean to deny what already I have affirmed. Besides authority there also are needed authorities. If there are to be authorities, then over and above their authenticity there is needed some external criterion by which their position can be publicly recognized. But while this external criterion is a necessary condition, it is not a sufficient condition. The sufficient condition must include authenticity. The external criterion need not be accompanied by authenticity. For in human beings authenticity always is precarious. Commonly, indeed, it is no more than a withdrawal from unauthenticity.

Such then is the dialectic of authority. It was well expressed by Barbara Barclay Carter in her preface to her translation of Don Luigi Sturzo's *Church and State* when she wrote:

> in every form of social life and in human society as a whole two currents are invariably present, the *'organizational'* and the *'mystical'* or ideal, the one tending to conservation, to practical constructions that perpetuate an established order, the other to renewal, with sharpened awareness of present deficiencies and impellent awareness towards a better future. The distinction between them is never absolute, for they are made up of human individuals and reflect the complexity of human minds; their action is an interweaving, the one eventually consolidating something of what the other conceives, yet they come together only to part anew; the conflict they manifest is the conflict between the ideal and its always only partial realization, between the letter that kills and the spirit that quickens, and while the Church is essentially the expression of the mystical current in the face of the State ... in the Church as in the State the two forces are perennially working.[4]

Related selections: 1.V.1 on the dynamic structure of human affairs; 1.V.2–5 on the dialectic of community, bias, and the social surd; 3.II.2 on the structure of the human good; 1.XVI.1 on the problem of evil; 1.XIV on the problem of liberation; 3.I.2 on the four levels of consciousness; 3.VII.2 on conversions and breakdowns; 4.VI.3 on the dialectic of history.

---

4 Luigi Sturzo, *Church and State*, trans. Barbara Barclay Carter (London: Geoffrey Bles, 1939), ʋ.

Social Alienation and the Second Enlightenment

In 1975 Lonergan presented a paper to the Second International Symposium on Belief, held in Vienna, on factors to be taken into account in an inquiry into the emerging religious consciousness in our time. In the selection presented here Lonergan reflects on the sociocultural factors which constitute in our times the 'common condition or cause or occasion' in the genesis of a new religious consciousness.[1] These outer factors, Lonergan suggests, may combine with inner religious experience to bring about a 'transition from lesser to greater luminousness, intensity, clarity, fulness.'[2] In the first part of the selection Lonergan discusses the social alienation occasioned by large establishments and their bureaucratic administration. In the second part he outlines a 'second enlightenment' marked by the transformation of mathematics, natural science, and philosophy, developments in human studies, and growing dissatisfaction with 'the reductionist postulate of positivist philosophy.'[3] Lonergan suggests that this second enlightenment may have its social mission in 'offering hope and providing leadership to the masses alienated by large establishments under bureaucratic management.'

These extracts are taken from *A Third Collection*, 60–3; 63–5.

1 Social Alienation

Ours is a time of very large establishments. They are conspicuous in

---

1 *A Third Collection*, 56.
2 Ibid., 59.
3 Ibid., 65.

finance, industry, commerce. They have kept growing on all levels of government with its numerous, far-reaching, and intricate depart-ments. They have extended into the intermediate zone in which pri-vate initiative has yielded to public concern for general utilities, for health, for education, for the level of employment, for care of orphans, the sick, the aged. They are found when the adherents of a religion are numerous, their organization elaborate, their transactions extensive.

The numerous tasks to be performed in a large establishment generate the type of organization named bureaucracy. Policies deter-mine goals. Procedures effect the division of labor. Standards settle acceptable performance. To spell out policies calls not only for broad vision but also for the detailed knowledge of the man of experience. An efficient division of labor demands intimate knowledge of the tasks to be performed and of the ability of employees to perform them; and to these must be added the long process of trial and error or, alternatively, the enormous ingenuity that fits the many parts into a smoothly functioning whole. Standards finally have to be set not merely for the end-product but also for each of its distinct stages; nor is it enough to set them without providing suitably exacting controls.

The more precise the policies, the more efficient the procedures, the more exigent the standards and their controls, then the closer will be the approximation to the ideal bureaucracy. The customer will be sup-plied with the very product or service that was intended for him or her or, on a further level of sophistication, with the very variety of prod-ucts or services intended for them. It is the glory of the market system – underlined by the ineptitude of totalitarian bureaucracy – that it strives to meet demand and that it strives to adapt to changes in effec-tive demand.

It remains that the large establishment and its bureaucratic organiza-tion is a fourfold source of that conjunction of dissatisfaction and hope-lessness that is named alienation and foments revolutions.

For policies, procedures, standards are all expressed in general terms. Generalities never reach the full determinateness of concrete reality. But what is good has to be good in every respect, for the pres-ence of any defect makes it bad. My point is very ancient, for over two millennia ago Aristotle pronounced equity to be virtue and defined it as a correction of the law where the law is defective owing to its uni-

versality.[4] Like laws, the policies, procedures, standards of a bureaucracy are universal. But unlike laws, they are not tolerant of equitable
correction.

For such correction would have to be the work of those immediately
concerned, or else it would have to be referred to those higher in
authority. But to grant discretionary power to those immediately concerned would run counter to the purposes of bureaucracy: it would
disperse initiative, interfere with the precise location of responsibility,
cast doubt on the reliability of the product or the quality of the service.
On the other hand, when the chain of command is from above downwards, any flow of information from below upwards tends to be slug-
gish, for it is apt to go unrewarded; unwelcome, for it adds to the work
of those above; ineffective, for those above are unfamiliar with the situation below, less perceptive of the difficulties that are arising, with little insight into the solutions that are possible, and unsure of their own
ability, if need be, to convince those still higher up.

Such rigidity is no great problem in a stationary society. But modern
society is on the move. For the large establishment the line of least
resistance is a judicious combination of apparent change and real stagnation. The product or service remains essentially the same, but the
decor is piquantly novel and the advertising a fresh variation on the
hard or soft sell.

There is a deeper level to the problem. As science advances by a process of trial and error, so too commerce, industry, finance enjoy no
quicker or surer way to greater wisdom. As science can operate and
apparently flourish for long periods despite its mistaken assumptions,
so too can operations in other fields where perceptive attention to data
and openness to fresh viewpoints are less developed. For we readily
perceive what we expect. Conversely, we may sense what we cannot
as yet formulate, but sensation remains mere infrastructure until a relevant suprastructure has been developed.

It is true, of course, that the recondite constructions of theoretical science demand an exactitude that would be out of place in the conduct
of human affairs. But this does not completely invalidate my point. A
new scientific discovery announces, not a change in nature, but a
defect in earlier science. In contrast, a change in human affairs is a
change in the way people feel and think and act. It is apprehended not

4 Aristotle, *Nicomachean Ethics*, V, 10, 1137b 27.

by the natural scientist changing his theories but by the journalist reporting what is occurring and by the psychological or sociological historian noting what had been going forward. Is, for instance, the maximization of profit a socially desirable economic maxim? Some say yes and some say no, but one may also distinguish. What was desirable in individual entrepreneurs at the beginning of the nineteenth century, can be disastrous in the conduct of multinational corporations towards the end of the twentieth.[5] What in nature would be the evolution of a new species, in human affairs is merely the transformation of an institution. My point is simply that as diligent scientists can overlook the evidence calling for a revision of accepted theory, so too men of affairs can overlook the evidence for significantly changed institutions.

There is a further difference between natural process and human affairs. When natural laws are not observed, one concludes, not that nature has gone astray, but that scientists have been mistaken. When the legitimating precepts of a human institution are not observed, matters are more complex, for one has to reckon not only with the adequacy of the precept but also with the honesty of men. If intelligent self-interest has a defensible meaning, it can also be a cloak for bias – for the individual bias of the individual that grabs what he can get away with; for the far more insidious bias of the group insensitive to the rights of outsiders and unaware that its own function has diminished or disappeared; for the general bias of mankind, at best ready to listen to the dictates of common sense, but impatient and even contemptuous of criticism that rests on a theoretical source. And the sundry aspects of this threefold bias, as I have argued elsewhere,[6] can arise not only in the sphere of economics but also in that of government, not only in politics but in any of the areas into which political benevolence may extend, not only in things secular but also in things sacred.

The large establishment and its bureaucratic administration, then, suffer from four defects. Its products and its services are specified by universals, but the good is always more concrete than a set of universals. Its mode of operation is rigid with little tolerance for discretionary adaptation. Its capacity for the more alert observation and the more critical reflection that generate revised ideas and remodeled operations

5 Richard Barnet and Ronald Müller, 'Multinational Corporations,' *New Yorker*, December 2 and 9, 1974.
6 *Insight*, 244–69 [1.V.2–5 in this reader].

seems no greater than that attributed to the scientific community by Thomas Kuhn.[7] Its size, finally, its complexity, and its solidarity with other large establishments and bureaucracies provide a broad field for the ingenuity of egoists, the biases of groups, the disastrous oversights of 'practical' common sense.

I write no more than prolegomena. But if today social alienation exists, the bureaucratic establishment is clearly a candidate for scrutiny. Injustice breeds hatred. A monopoly of power and initiative breeds resentment. The 'black box' of vast and intricate complexity precludes the understanding that might set a limit to criticism.

2   The Second Enlightenment[8]

The Enlightenment – it becomes just the first Enlightenment if a second is recognized – was carried socially and culturally. Socially by the movement that would sweep away the remnants of feudalism and a lingering absolutism by proclaiming liberty, fraternity, equality. Culturally by the triumph of Newton, who did for mechanics what Euclid had done for geometry and whose success led philosophers to desert rationalism and swell the ranks of empiricists.

That movement has lasted into our own day and still enjoys a dominant position. But, as it were, from within it there has developed an antithesis, no less massive though, as yet, it has not crystallized. To it I refer when I speak of a second enlightenment.

Culturally its first underpinnings came with the relativization of Euclidean geometry: from being regarded as the unique deduction of necessary truth from self-evident principles it became just one of many possible geometric systems deduced from freely chosen postulates. Newton's mechanics suffered a similar fate when Einstein's special relativity was accepted: the necessary laws of nature gave way before Heisenberg's uncertainty principle; and the iron laws of economics could be ignored by Lord Keynes in the great depression of the thirties. Moreover, the new significance granted statistics replaced Darwin's

7 T.S. Kuhn, *The Structure of Scientific Revolutions* (Chicago: University of Chicago Press, 1970).
8 For the notion of a second enlightenment I am indebted to Frederick Lawrence, '"The Modern Philosophic Differentiation of Consciousness" or What Is the Enlightenment?' in *Lonergan Workshop*, vol. I, ed. Fred Lawrence (Chico, CA: Scholars Press, 1981), 231–79.

chance variation by the probability of the emergence of new forms, while his survival of the fittest became the higher probabilities of survival. A deductivist world of mechanist determinism was making way for the probability schedules of a world in process from lower to higher species and ecosystems.

By rejecting pure reason yet granting primacy to practical reason Kant had sought a middle ground between empiricism and rationalism. The absolute idealists endeavored to bring about a new rationalist avatar, but the fertility of their suggestiveness was to survive with little acceptance of their abstruse systems. Instead there came Schopenhauer's priority of will and representation, Kierkegaard's surrender to faith, Newman's first toast to conscience, Dilthey's *Lebensphilosophie* and Nietzsche's will to power, Blondel's philosophy of action and Ricoeur's philosophy of will, with similar tendencies found in pragmatists, personalists, phenomenologists, existentialists.

This philosophic assertion of human freedom and autonomy was matched by a counterpart in human studies. Philosophies of history that dispensed with historians were countered by the German Historical School. Its ideal had been formulated by August Boeckh as the interpretative reconstruction of the constructions of mankind. Its deep intuition was that meaning and values have a constitutive and controlling role in human living. Its procedure was empirical without being empiricist. For its basis was the total remains of a culture, whether linguistic, literary, epigraphical, archeological, numismatic; and its background was the whole of previous studies, grammatical, phonetic, chronological, comparative, critical, constructive. Its goal was an understanding that rose out of the data and fitted them in their entirety and particularity as well as was possible at any given time. Its incompletely successful theoretician was Wilhelm Dilthey who grounded the distinction between the *Natur-* and the *Geistes-wissenschaften*.

While the approach to human studies through hermeneutics and history has never become dominant to the west of Germany, pockets are emerging in which reductionist positivism is set aside. Abraham Maslow in psychology belongs to a 'third force' that shuns both the experimental psychologist's concentration on the subhuman and the clinical psychologist's on the abnormal.[9] Freud's mechanist assump-

---

9 On 'third force' see Abraham H. Maslow, *Toward a Psychology of Being* (New York: Van Nostrand, 1968), ix.

tions have been exorcised by various types of hermeneutic.[10] Talcott Parsons has stressed that it was not theologians but sociologists that put out of court the old-style speculations of anthropologists on religion,[11] and assigns, as does Robert Bellah, a notable role to religion in the continuity of a system of social action.[12] Finally ... the correlation between brain waves and various states of consciousness, discovered by Hans Berger in the twenties, has brought to light physiological differences between ordinary consciousness, internally focused states, drowsiness, and deep sleep.[13]

Such in summary fashion is the second enlightenment. It is a profound transformation in mathematics and natural science. It is paralleled by a transformation in philosophy. It is complemented by the vast development in human studies stemming from the initiatives of the German Historical School. It has found allies in sociological and psychological tendencies away from the reductionist postulate of positivist philosophy.

Of itself this second enlightenment is culturally significant. But it may have as well a social mission. Just as the first enlightenment had its carrier in the transition from feudal to bourgeois society, so the second may find a role and task in offering hope and providing leadership to the masses alienated by large establishments under bureaucratic management.

An exploration of this possibility would call for another *Encyclopédie* ...

Related selections: 3.IV.2–3 on religious experience; 3.II.2 on the good of order; 1.V.1 on the fundamental scheme of progress in human affairs; 3.II.2 on the

10 Ernest Becker, *The Denial of Death* (New York: Free Press, 1973); Herbert Fingarette, *The Self in Transformation: Psychoanalysis, Philosophy, and the Life of the Spirit* (New York: Harper Torchbook, 1965); Paul Ricoeur, *Freud and Philosophy: An Essay on Interpretation*, trans. Denis Savage (New Haven: Yale University Press, 1970); and *The Conflict of Interpretations: Essays in Hermeneutics*, ed. Don Ihde, with various translators (Evanston: Northwestern University Press, 1974).
11 Talcott Parsons, 'The Theoretical Development of the Sociology of Religion,' in his *Essays in Sociological Theory* (New York: Free Press, 1966), 197–210.
12 Talcott Parsons, Introduction to Part IV, 'Culture and the Social System,' in *Theories of Society: Foundations of Modern Sociological Theory*, ed. Talcott Parsons et al. (New York: Free Press, 1965), 963–93; see p. 983. R. Bellah, *Beyond Belief* (New York: Harper and Row, 1970), 12.
13 William Johnston, *Silent Music: The Science of Meditation* (New York: Harper and Row, 1974), 32.

structure of the human good; 1.IV.2 and 1.V.3–5 on bias; 2.IV.1–2 on functions of meaning; 2.VII.4–5 on the existential and the alienated subject; 4.VI on natural right and history.

Healing and Creating in History

The present selection is the complete text of a lecture given at the Thomas More Institute in Montreal in 1975. In it Lonergan examines the process of human creativity in history, the malady of breakdown and decline, and the healing by which alone decline and its consequences are to be reversed. By 'history' Lonergan means human affairs, and he takes as his central example the need for creativity in contemporary economics. The application of flawed economic principles, he argues, is having deleterious effects on a global scale. The need for a new economics is revealed and intensified by the threat to our collective survival posed by the operations of multinational corporations. Lonergan outlines here, not the needed economic remedy, but the process of creativity required to bring it about. What is needed is an ongoing accumulation of practical insights that influence policies and programs and eventually give rise to new systems. Lonergan then turns to the breakdown of the creative process characteristic of a civilization in decline, and finds the root of decline in dramatic, individual, group, and general bias. This selection concludes with a brief account of healing in human affairs. While creating can be described as a movement from below upwards, healing can be described as a movement from above downwards. It is the religious falling in love that can dissolve bias. Lonergan notes that healing must be combined with creative process if social decline is to be averted. Finally, as an economic theory ought to address moral principles, so an adequate moral theory cannot do without economic theory.

Lonergan's concern with economic creativity in this selection is not at all a casual one. It reveals an interest that first emerged in his student days, consumed his free time in the 1930s and early 1940s, and reemerged in his final years, after the completion of *Method in Theology*, as a major focus of his intellectual work. His *Essay in Circulation Analysis,* a macroeconomic study of monetary circulation, remained unfinished at the time of his death.

This extract is taken from *A Third Collection,* 100–8.

The topic assigned me reads: Healing and Creating in History.

What precisely it means or even what it might mean, does not seem to be obvious at first glance. An initial clarification appears to be in order.

We have to do with healing and creating *in history.* But no particular kind of history is specified, and so we are not confined to religious or cultural or social or political or economic or technological history. Again no people or country is mentioned, neither Babylonians nor Egyptians, Greeks nor Romans, Asians nor Africans, Europeans nor Americans. It would seem, then, that we have to do with healing and creating in human affairs. For human affairs are the stuff of history, and they merit the attention of the historian when they are taken in a relatively large context and prove their significance by their relatively durable effects.

Now if 'history' may be taken broadly to mean human affairs, it is not too difficult to obtain at least a preliminary notion of what is meant by the other two terms in our title, 'healing' and 'creating.' For there comes to hand a paper by Sir Karl Popper entitled 'The History of Our Time: An Optimist's View.'[1] In it he opposes two different accounts of what is wrong with the world. On the one hand, there is the view he attributes to many quite sincere churchmen and, along with them, to the rationalist philosopher, Bertrand Russell. It is to the effect that our intellectual development has outrun our moral development. He writes:

> We have become very clever, according to Russell, indeed too clever. We can make lots of wonderful gadgets, including television, high-speed rockets, and an atom bomb, or a thermonuclear bomb, if you prefer. But we have not been able to achieve that moral and political growth and maturity which alone could safely direct and control the uses to which we put our tremendous intellectual powers. This is why we now find our-

1 Karl Popper, *Conjectures and Refutations: The Growth of Scientific Knowledge* (New York: Harper Torchbooks, 1968).

selves in mortal danger. Our evil national pride has prevented us from achieving the world-state in time.

To put this view in a nutshell: we are clever, perhaps too clever, but we also are wicked; and this mixture of cleverness and wickedness lies at the root of our troubles.[2]

In contrast, Sir Karl Popper would argue that we are good, perhaps a little too good, but we are also a little stupid; and it is this mixture of goodness and stupidity that lies at the root of our troubles. After avowing that he included himself among those he considered a little stupid, Sir Karl put his point in the following terms:

> The main troubles of our time – and I do not deny that we live in troubled times – are not due to our moral wickedness, but, on the contrary, to our often misguided moral enthusiasm: to our anxiety to better the world we live in. Our wars are fundamentally religious wars; they are wars between competing theories of how to establish a better world. And our moral enthusiasm is often misguided, because we fail to realize that our moral principles, which are sure to be over-simple, are often difficult to apply to the complex human and political situations to which we feel bound to apply them.[3]

In upholding this contention Sir Karl was quite ready to descend to particular instances. He granted the wickedness of Hitler and Stalin. He acknowledged that they appealed to all sorts of hopes and fears, to prejudices and envy, and even to hatred. But he insisted that their main appeal was an appeal to a kind of morality. They had a message; and they demanded sacrifices. He regretted that an appeal to morality could be misused. But he saw it as a fact that the great dictators were always trying to convince their people that they knew a way to a higher morality.

Now one may agree with Lord Russell. One may agree with Sir Karl. Indeed, there is no difficulty in agreeing with both, for the Christian tradition lists among the effects of original sin both a darkening of intellect and a weakening of will. But whatever one's opinion, it remains that there is a profound difference between diagnosing a

2 Ibid., 365.
3 Ibid., 366.

malady and proposing a cure. Whether one stresses with Lord Russell the conjunction of clever but wicked or with Sir Karl the conjunction of good but stupid, one gets no further than diagnosis. On the other hand, when one speaks of healing and creating, one refers to positive courses of action. To this positive aspect of the issue, we now must turn.

The creating in question is not creating out of nothing. Such creating is the divine prerogative. Man's creating is of a different order. Actually, it does not bring something out of nothing, but it may seem to do so. William James, the American psychologist and philosopher, has described three stages in the career of a theory. First, '... it is attacked as absurd; then it is admitted to be true, but obvious and insignificant; finally it is seen to be so important that its adversaries claim that they themselves discovered it.'[4] Such a theory is creative.

Let me illustrate this need for human creating from the contemporary economic situation. Last year there was published a thick volume by Richard Barnet and Ronald Müller with the title, *Global Reach,* and the subtitle, *The Power of the Multinational Corporations.* Its thirteen chapters fell into three parts. The first set forth the aims of the multinational corporations: they propose to run the world, for they can do the job and our little national governments are not equipped to do so. The second set of chapters delineated what the multinational corporations were doing to the underdeveloped countries: they have been making them more hopelessly worse off than otherwise they would be. The third set finally asked what these corporations, which in the main are American, have been doing to the United States; the answer is that they are treating the States in the same way they are treating the underdeveloped countries and, in the long run, the effects will be the same as in the rest of the world.

Now if the multinational corporations are generating worldwide disaster, why are they permitted to do so? The trouble is that there is nothing really new about multinational corporations. They aim at maximizing profit, and that has been the aim of economic enterprise since the mercantile, the industrial, the financial revolutions ever more fully and thoroughly took charge of our affairs. The alternative to making a profit is bankruptcy. The alternative to maximizing profit is

---

4 William James, quoted in Louis Mink, *Mind, History, and Dialectic: The Philosophy of R.G. Collingwood* (Bloomington: Indiana University Press, 1969), 255.

inefficiency.[5] All that the multinational corporation does is maximize profit not in some town or city, not in some region or country, but on the global scale. It buys labor and materials in the countries where they are cheapest. Its credit is unimpeachable and so it can secure all the money it wants from whatever banks or money markets are in a position to create it. Its marketing facilities are a global network and to compete one would have first to build up a global network of one's own. The multinational corporation is a going concern. It is ever growing and expanding. It is built on the very principles that slowly but surely have been molding our technology and our economics, our society and our culture, our ideals and our practice for centuries. It remains that the long-accepted principles are inadequate. They suffer from radical oversights. Their rigorous application on a global scale, according to Barnet and Müller, heads us for disaster. But as the authors also confess: 'The new system needed for our collective survival does not exist.'[6] When survival requires a system that does not exist, then the need for creating is manifest.

While it can take a series of disasters to convince people of the need for creating, still the long, hard, uphill climb is the creative process itself. In retrospect this process may appear as a grand strategy that unfolds in an orderly and cumulative series of steps. But any retrospect has the advantage of knowing the answers. The creative task is to find the answers. It is a matter of insight, not of one insight but of many, not of isolated insights but of insights that coalesce, that complement and correct one another, that influence policies and programs, that reveal their shortcomings in their concrete results, that give rise to further correcting insights, corrected policies, corrected programs, that gradually accumulate into the all-round, balanced, smoothly functioning system that from the start was needed but at the start was not yet known.

This creative process is nothing mysterious. It has been described by Jane Jacobs in her *The Economy of Cities*,[7] as repeatedly finding new uses for existing resources. It has been set forth in the grand style by Arnold Toynbee under the rubric of 'Challenge and Response' in his *A*

5 Where, of course, inefficiency means by definition the failure to maximize profit.
6 Richard J. Barnet and Ronald E. Müller, *Global Reach: The Power of the Multinational Corporations* (New York: Simon and Schuster, 1974), 385.
7 Jane Jacobs, *The Economy of Cities* (New York: Random House, 1970).

Study of History, where the flow of fresh insights takes its rise from a creative minority, and the success of their implementation wins the devoted allegiance of the rank and file.[8]

I have spoken of insights, and I had best add what I do not mean. An insight is not just a slogan, and an ongoing accumulation of insights is not just an advertising campaign. A creative process is a learning process. It is learning what hitherto was not known. It is just the opposite of the mental coma induced by the fables and jingles that unceasingly interrupt television programs in our native land and even in the great republic to the south of us.

Again, insights are one thing, and concepts are quite another. Concepts are ambiguous. They may be heuristic, but then they merely point to unspecified possibilities, as highly desirable as justice, liberty, equality, peace – but still just empty gestures that fail to reveal how the possibilities might be realized and what the realization concretely would entail. Again, concepts may be specific, but then they are definite, rounded off, finished, abstract. Like textbooks on moral theology they can name all the evils to be avoided but get no further than unhelpful platitudes on the good to be achieved. For the good is never an abstraction. Always it is concrete.[9] The whole point to the process of cumulative insight is that each insight regards the concrete while the cumulative process heads towards an ever fuller and more adequate view. Add abstraction to abstraction and one never reaches more than a heap of abstractions. But add insight to insight and one moves to mastery of all the eventualities and complications of a concrete situation.

The creative process culminates in system, but the system is only system on the move. It never reaches static system that comes into existence and remains forever after. So it is that, when the flow of fresh insights dries up, when challenges continue and responses fail to emerge, then the creative minority becomes the merely dominant minority and the eagerness of the rank and file, that exulted in success, turns into the sullenness of an internal proletariat frustrated and disgusted by the discovery that a country in which, more and more,

---

8 For an incomplete list of the critiques of Toynbee's *A Study of History*, see vol. 12 of that work, *Reconsiderations* (London: Oxford University Press, 1961), 680–90. With *Reconsiderations* available, the critics are far less impressive.

9 As the Scholastics put it: *Bonum ex integra causa, malum ex quocumque defectu.*

everything had worked has become a country in which, more and more, nothing works. Such is the disenchantment that, to use Toynbee's terms, brings to an end the genesis of a civilization and introduces first its breakdowns and eventually its disintegration.

But, one may ask, why does the flow of fresh insights dry up? Why, if challenges continue, do responses fail? Why does a minority that was creative cease to be creative and become merely dominant?

There are many intermediate answers that correspond to the many and varied circumstances under which civilizations break down. But there is one ultimate answer that rests on the intrinsic limitations of insight itself. For insights can be implemented only if people have open minds. Problems can be manifest. Insights that solve them may be available. But the insights will not be grasped and implemented by biased minds. There is the bias of the neurotic fertile in evasions of the insight his analyst sees he needs. There is the bias of the individual egoist whose interest is confined to the insights that would enable him to exploit each new situation to his own personal advantage. There is the bias of group egoism blind to the fact that the group no longer fulfils its once useful function and that it is merely clinging to power by all the maneuvers that in one way or another block development and impede progress. There is finally the general bias of all 'good' men of common sense, cherishing the illusion that their single talent, common sense, is omnicompetent, insisting on procedures that no longer work, convinced that the only way to do things is to muddle through, and spurning as idle theorizing and empty verbiage any rational account of what has to be done.[10]

Not only is there this fourfold exclusion of fresh insights by the neurotic, by the bias of individual and, worse, group egoism, and by the illusory omnicompetence of common sense. There also is the distorting effect of all such bias on the whole process of growth. Growth, progress, is a matter of situations yielding insights, insights yielding policies and projects, policies and projects transforming the initial situation, and the transformed situation giving rise to further insights that correct and complement the deficiencies of previous insights. So the wheel of progress moves forward through the succes-

10 I have written at length on bias in *Insight*; see pp. 214–31, 244–69, 650–6, 710–15. In the Hegelian-Marxist tradition bias is obliquely treated under the name of alienation [see 1.IV.2, 1.V.3–5, 1.XIV.2, and 1.XVI.1 in this reader].

sive transformations of an initial situation in which are gathered coherently and cumulatively all the insights that occurred along the way. But this wheel of progress becomes a wheel of decline when the process is distorted by bias. Increasingly the situation becomes, not the cumulative product of coherent and complementary insights, but the dump in which are heaped up the amorphous and incompatible products of all the biases of self-centered and shortsighted individuals and groups. Finally, the more the objective situation becomes a mere dump, the less is there any possibility of human intelligence gathering from the situation anything more than a lengthy catalogue of the aberrations and the follies of the past. As a diagnosis of terminal cancer denies any prospect of health restored, so a social dump is the end of fruitful insight and of the cumulative development it can generate.

I have spoken of creating in history and of its nemesis. But my topic also calls for a few words on healing. In fact, the genesis and breakdown of civilization occupy only the first six of the ten volumes Toynbee devoted to his *A Study of History*. In the last four there emerges a new factor, for out of the frustration and disgust of the internal proletariat there come the world religions and a new style of human development.

For human development is of two quite different kinds. There is development from below upwards, from experience to growing understanding, from growing understanding to balanced judgment, from balanced judgment to fruitful courses of action, and from fruitful courses of action to the new situations that call forth further understanding, profounder judgment, richer courses of action.

But there also is development from above downwards. There is the transformation of falling in love: the domestic love of the family; the human love of one's tribe, one's city, one's country, mankind; the divine love that orientates man in his cosmos and expresses itself in his worship. Where hatred only sees evil, love reveals values. At once it commands commitment and joyfully carries it out, no matter what the sacrifice involved. Where hatred reinforces bias, love dissolves it, whether it be the bias of unconscious motivation, the bias of individual or group egoism, or the bias of omnicompetent, shortsighted common sense. Where hatred plods around in ever narrower vicious circles, love breaks the bonds of psychological and social determinisms with the conviction of faith and the power of hope.

What I have attributed to love and denied to hatred, must also be denied to any ambiguous and so deceptive mixture of love and hatred. If in no other way at least from experience we have learnt that professions of zeal for the eternal salvation of souls do not make the persecution of heretics a means for the reconciliation of heretics. On the contrary, persecution leads to ongoing enmity and in the limit to wars of religion. In like manner wars of religion have not vindicated religion; they have given color to a secularism that in the English-speaking world regards revealed religion as a merely private affair and in continental Europe thinks it an evil.

Again, while secularism has succeeded in making religion a marginal factor in human affairs, it has not succeeded in inventing a vaccine or providing some other antidote for hatred. For secularism is a philosophy and, no less than religion, it may lay claim to absolutes of its own. In their name hatred can shift from the religious group to the social class. So the professions of tolerance of the eighteenth-century Enlightenment did not save from the guillotine the feudal nobility of France, and the Marxist march of history in Russia has attended to the liquidation not merely of the bourgeoisie but also of the Romanovs, the landowners, and the kulaks.[11]

As healing can have no truck with hatred, so too it can have no truck with materialism. For the healer is essentially a reformer: first and foremost he counts on what is best in man. But the materialist is condemned by his own principles to be no more than a manipulator. He will apply to human beings the stick-and-carrot treatment that the Harvard behaviorist, B. F. Skinner, advocates under the name of reinforcement. He will maintain with Marx that cultural attitudes are the by-product of material conditions and so he will bestow upon those subjected to communist power the salutary conditions of a closed frontier, clear and firm indoctrination, controlled media of information, a vigilant secret police, and the terrifying threat of the labor camps. Again, while Christians accord to God's grace the principal role in touching men's hearts and enlightening their minds, it would seem that the true believer in the gospel according to Marx must be immersed in proletarian living conditions, on the ground that only

11 For background see the penetrating analysis by Christopher Dawson, 'Karl Marx and the Dialectic of History,' in *The Dynamics of World History*, ed. John J. Mulloy (London: Sheed and Ward, 1957), 354–65.

such material conditions can confer upon him the right thinking and righteous feeling proper to proletarian class consciousness.[12]

Healing then is not to be confused with the dominating and manipulating to which the reforming materialist is confined by his own principles. It has to be kept apart from religious hatred of heretical sects and from philosophic hatred of social classes.[13] But besides these requirements, intrinsic to the nature of healing, there is the extrinsic requirement of a concomitant creative process. For just as the creative process, when unaccompanied by healing, is distorted and corrupted by bias, so too the healing process, when unaccompanied by creating, is a soul without a body. Christianity developed and spread within the ancient empire of Rome. It possessed the spiritual power to heal what was unsound in that imperial domain. But it was unaccompanied by its natural complement of creating, for a single development has two vectors, one from below upwards, creating, the other from above downwards, healing. So when the Roman empire decayed and disintegrated, the church indeed lived on. But it lived on, not in a civilized world, but in a dark and barbarous age in which, as a contemporary reported, men devoured one another as fishes in the sea.

If we are to escape a similar fate, we must demand that two requirements are met. The first regards economic theorists; the second regards moral theorists. From economic theorists we have to demand, along with as many other types of analysis as they please, a new and specific type that reveals how moral precepts have both a basis in economic process and so an effective application to it. From moral theorists we have to demand, along with their other various forms of wisdom and prudence, specifically economic precepts that arise out of economic process itself and promote its proper functioning.

To put the same points in negative terms, when physicists can think on the basis of indeterminacy, economists can think on the basis of freedom and acknowledge the relevance of morality. Again, when the

---

12 For Marx, morality is relative to social class. As Dawson trenchantly put it: 'Hence it would seem that the only real immorality is to betray the interests of one's own class, and that a man like Karl Marx himself, or F. Engels, who serves the interests of another class even if it be the class of the future, is no social hero, but an apostate and a traitor. He has become a bad bourgeois but he can never become a good proletarian unless he is economically and sociologically absorbed into the proletariat' (ibid., 362–3).

13 Of course, though racism and nationalism are prephilosophic, they can be imagined as absolutes and generate abundant hatred.

system that is needed for our collective survival does not exist, then it is futile to excoriate what does exist while blissfully ignoring the task of constructing a technically viable economic system that can be put in place.[14]

Is my proposal utopian? It asks merely for creativity, for an interdisciplinary theory that at first will be denounced as absurd, then will be admitted to be true but obvious and insignificant, and perhaps finally be regarded as so important that its adversaries will claim that they themselves discovered it.

Related selections: 1.IV.2 on dramatic bias, and 1.V.3–5 on bias and decline; 4.VI.3 on the dialectic of history; 1.XVI.3 on the solution; 1.IV.1 on common sense as intellectual, and 1.V.1 on the dynamic structure of human affairs, and 1.I.2 on the practical import of insight into insight; 1.II on the act of insight; 4.III.1 on social alienation.

14 Moral precepts that are not technically specific turn out to be quite ineffectual, as Christian Duquoc has pointed out in his *Ambiguité des théologies de la sécularisation: Essai critique* (Gembloux: Duculot, 1972). See on p. 67 his remark on *The Secular City* by Harvey Cox; also 103 ff. and 113 ff. on the Pastoral Constitution of the second Vatican council, *Gaudium et Spes*.

V

Praxis

In 1976 Lonergan gave a series of three lectures at Queen's University in Kingston, Ontario, under the general title *Religious Studies and Theology*. In the third lecture in the series, 'The Ongoing Genesis of Methods,' he turns his attention to the historical development, differentiation, and regrouping of methods in response to demands evoked by their advance. He describes the origin of this 'dynamic of methods' in the scientific revolution and confronts the issue of relativism raised by the shift from reliance on basic laws and principles to reliance on a succession of methods that bring forth laws and principles. He argues that increasing specialization actually provokes the emergence of additional, distinct, even disparate methods. With the shift of attention in human studies from abstract universals to concrete human beings, he claims, comes the realization that the 'scientific age of innocence' has come to an end, that human authenticity can no longer be taken for granted. Subsequent to this survey of the emergence of experimental, foundational, historical, and dialectical methods, Lonergan raises the next question evoked by the exigences of the advancing dynamic of methods: Is there any method that can *deal with* the unauthentic as well as the authentic, with the irrational as well as the rational? In the following selection Lonergan offers a brief description of that emerging method which is designated by the Greek name *praxis*.

This extract is taken from *A Third Collection*, 159–61.

Experimental method reveals nature. Historical method reveals man, the self-completing animal, in the manifold variety of his concrete existing. Dialectic confronts us with the problem of the irrational in human life and, as well, provides a technique for distinguishing between authentic and unauthentic evaluations, decisions, actions. Praxis, finally, raises the final issue, What are you to do about it? What use are you to make of your knowledge of nature, of your knowledge of man, of your awareness of the radical conflict between man's aspiration to self-transcendence and, on the other hand, the waywardness that may distort his traditional heritage and even his own personal life.

It is only after the age of innocence that praxis becomes an academic subject. A faculty psychology will give intellect precedence over will and thereby it will liberate the academic world from concern with the irrational in human life. The speculative intellect of the Aristotelians, the pure reason of the rationalists, the automatic progress anticipated by the liberals, all provided shelter for academic serenity. But since the failure of the absolute idealists to encompass human history within the embrace of speculative reason, the issue of praxis has repeatedly come to the fore ...

On an older view contemplative intellect, or speculative reason, or rigorous science was supreme, and practical issues were secondary. But the older view grounded its hegemony on necessity. That claim no longer is made. If we are not simply to flounder, we have to take our stand on authenticity: on the authenticity with which intelligence takes us beyond the experiential infrastructure to enrich it, extend it, organize it, but never to slight it and much less to violate its primordial role; on the authenticity with which rational reflection goes beyond the constructions of intelligence and draws sharply the lines between astrology and astronomy, alchemy and chemistry, legend and history, magic and science, myth and philosophy; on the authenticity with which moral deliberation takes us beyond cognitional process into the realm of freedom and responsibility, evaluation and decision, not in any way to annul or slight experience or understanding or factual judgment, but to add the further and distinct truth of value judgments and the consequent decisions demanded by a situation in which authenticity cannot be taken for granted.

It follows that, while empirical method moves, so to speak, from below upwards, praxis moves from above downwards. Empirical method moves from below upwards, from experience to understanding, and from understanding to factual judgment. It can do so because it can presuppose that the data of experience are intelligible and so are objects that straightforward understanding can master. But praxis acknowledges the end of the age of innocence. It starts from the

assumption that authenticity cannot be taken for granted. Its understanding, accordingly, will follow a hermeneutic of suspicion as well
as a hermeneutic of recovery. Its judgment will discern between products of human authenticity and products of human unauthenticity. But
the basic assumption, the twofold hermeneutic, the discernment
between the authentic and the unauthentic set up a distinct method.
This method is a compound of theoretical and practical judgments of
value. The use of this method follows from a decision, a decision that is
comparable to the claim of Blaise Pascal that the heart has reasons
which reason does not know.

Related selections: 1.III.1–3 on classical and statistic heuristic structures; 3.VI.2–
3 on historical method; 1.V.2 on dialectic, 1.XI.1 on dialectic in philosophy,
3.VII.1–4 on dialectic in theology, 4.II on the dialectic of authority, and 4.VI.3 on
the dialectic of history; 1.I.1 and 1.XIV.1 on rational self-consciousness; 3.II.1 on
judgments of value; 3.IV.2–4 on religious experience and faith; 1.V.2–5 on the
dialectic of community, the social surd, and the longer cycle of decline; 1.XVI.1
on the problem of evil.

VI

Natural Right and Historical Mindedness

In the present selection, an article published in 1977, Lonergan weaves into a single perspective the ancient doctrine of the constancy of human nature and the nineteenth-century recognition of the variability of concrete human history in order to address the question of the possibility of collective responsibility. His aim is 'to so develop the notion of natural right as to make it no less relevant to human historicity than it is to human nature.'[1] He concludes with an identification of natural right with his four transcendental precepts.

In the first part of this selection, after distinguishing human historicity from human nature and inquiry into human nature from inquiry into human historicity, Lonergan suggests that a certain unity may be discerned in the disconcerting multiplicity of human history. The clue to this unity may be found in the ancient doctrine of natural right which arose to counter a view that denied the existence of a permanent and binding force underlying human manners and customs. In the second part Lonergan contrasts the abstract classicist interpretation of natural right, which divorces natural right from human nature, with the concrete and dynamic interpretation, which locates natural right in nature as concretely operating. The second meaning of natural right, he claims, may be employed to 'determine norms in historicity.' Lonergan then proceeds to recast his own account of the levels of human self-transcendence in terms of the Aristotelian account of a nature as an immanent principle of motion and rest. Questions for intelligence, for reflection, and for deliberation are principles of movement; and each is also 'an immanent norm, a criterion, and thereby a principle of rest once the movement is complete.'[2] Natural right in

1 *A Third Collection*, 169
2 Ibid., 174.

historicity, finally, is the movement that begins before consciousness, unfolds through the levels of conscious intentionality, and finds its rest in being-in-love. In the final part Lonergan turns from reflection on the source of natural right to natural right in history and its vindication in the dialectic of history. The development of meaning in human collaboration is technical, social, and cultural. In each of these areas expansion has occurred first in the style of undifferentiated consciousness, then in the style of linguistically and theoretically differentiated consciousness, and finally in the style of interiorly differentiated consciousness. As the second stage of cultural expansion gives way to the third, the dialectic of history evokes a radical analysis of itself and the erection of an ideal of enlightenment and emancipation. The ideal of enlightenment proper to the third plateau of meaning, Lonergan claims, is as always a matter of self-knowledge. But, as the recognition of our historicity implies, the self to be known is a changing, developing, self-making self. Accordingly, to respond adequately today to the ancient precept, Know thyself, is to appropriate the interior foundations of the various realms of meaning and of natural right, and to make one's own an affectivity transformed by love. Emancipation, in the context of the third plateau of meaning, is to be conceived in terms of intellectual, moral, and religious conversion. This selection concludes with a description of the standpoint, principles, division of materials, and categories appropriate to a methodical critique of our historicity.

This extract is taken from *A Third Collection*, 169–82.

The notion of collective responsibility is not without its difficulty. One may claim that, as men individually are responsible for the lives they lead, so collectively they must be responsible for the resultant situation. But that claim is too rapid to be convincing. No doubt, single elements in the resulting situation are identical with the actions or the effects for which individuals are responsible. But the resulting situation as a whole commonly was neither foreseen nor intended or, when it does happen that it was, still such foresight and intention are apt to reside not in the many but in the few and rather in secret schemes and machinations than in public avowal.

It remains that if collective responsibility is not yet an established fact, it may be a possibility. Further, it may be a possibility that we can realize. Finally, it may be a possibility that it is desirable to realize.

Such is my topic. What I have in mind is the conjunction of two elements already existing in our tradition. From the ancient Greeks we have the notion of natural right. From nineteenth-century historical thought we have come to recognize that besides human nature there also is human historicity. What we have to do, I feel, is to bring these two elements together. We have so to develop the notion of natural right as to make it no less relevant to human historicity than it is to human nature.

1 Historicity

A contemporary ontology would distinguish two components in concrete human reality: on the one hand, a constant, human nature; on the other hand, a variable, human historicity. Nature is given man at birth. Historicity is what man makes of man.

This making of man by man is perhaps most conspicuous in the educational process, in the difference between the child beginning kindergarten and the doctoral candidate writing his dissertation. Still this difference produced by the education of individuals is only a recapitulation of the longer process of the education of mankind, of the evolution of social institutions and the development of cultures. Religions and art-forms, languages and literatures, sciences, philosophies, the writing of history, all had their rude beginnings, slowly developed, reached their peak, perhaps went into decline yet later underwent a renaissance in another milieu. And what is true of cultural achievements, also, though less conspicuously, is true of social institutions. The family, the state, the law, the economy, are not fixed and immutable entities. They adapt to changing circumstance: they can be reconceived in the light of new ideas; they can be subjected to revolutionary change.

Moreover, and this is my present point, all such change is in its essence a change of meaning – a change of idea or concept, a change of judgment or evaluation, a change of the order or the request. The state can be changed by rewriting its constitution; more subtly but no less effectively it can be changed by reinterpreting its constitution or, again, by working on men's minds and hearts to change the objects that command their respect, hold their allegiance, fire their loyalty. More generally, human community is a matter of a common field of experience, a common mode of understanding, a common measure of judgment, and a common consent. Such community is the possibility, the source, the ground of common meaning; and it is this common meaning that is the form and act that finds expression in family and polity, in the legal and economic system, in customary morals and educational arrangements, in language and literature, art and religion, philosophy, science, and the writing of history.[3] Still, community itself is not a necessity of nature but an achievement of man. Without a common field of experience people get out of touch. Without a common mode of understanding, there arise misunderstanding, distrust, suspicion, fear, hostility, factions. Without a common measure of judgment people live in different worlds. Without common consent they operate at cross-purposes. Then common meaning is replaced by different and opposed meanings. A cohesion that once seemed automatic has to be bolstered by the pressures, the threats, the force that secure a passing semblance of unity but may prepare a lasting resentment and a smoldering rebellion.

As human nature differs from human historicity, so understanding human nature is one thing and understanding human historicity is another. To understand the constant, nature, one may study any individual. But to understand the variable, historicity, one has to study each instance in its singularity. So we come to what Alan Richardson has named 'historical mindedness.'[4] This means that to understand men and their institutions we have to study their history. For it is in history that man's making of man occurs, that it progresses and regresses, that through such changes there may be discerned a certain unity in an otherwise disconcerting multiplicity.

Indeed, historicity and history are related as object to be known and investigating subject. In a brilliant definition the aim of *Philologie* and later the aim of history was conceived as the interpretative reconstruction of the constructions of the human spirit.[5] The constructions of the human spirit were what we have termed man's making of man, the variable component in human ontology, historicity. The interpretative reconstruction of those constructions was the goal set itself by the German Historical School in its massive, ongoing effort to reveal, not man in the abstract, but mankind in its concrete self-realization.

3 See *Collection*, 233–5 [2.IV.1 in this reader].
4 A. Richardson, *History Sacred and Profane* (London: SCM, 1964), 32.
5 Peter Hünermann, *Der Durchbruch geschichtlichen Denkens im 19. Jahrhundert* (Freiburg: Herder, 1967), 64–5, 106–108.

2 Natural Right in Historicity

It was the sheer multiplicity and diversity of the practices and beliefs of the peoples of the earth that led the ancient Greeks to contrast animals and men. The habits of each species of animal were uniform and so they could be attributed to nature. But the practices and beliefs of men differed from tribe to tribe, from city to city, from region to region: they had to be simply a matter of convention.

From that premise there followed a conclusion. What had been made by human convention, could be unmade by further convention. Underpinning human manners and customs there was no permanent and binding force.

The conclusion was scandalous, and in the notion of natural right was found its rebuttal. Underneath the manifold of human lifestyles, there existed a component or factor that possessed the claims to universality and permanence of nature itself.[6]

However, this component or factor admits two interpretations. It may be placed in universal propositions, self-evident truths, naturally known certitudes. On the other hand, it may be placed in nature itself, in nature not as abstractly conceived, but as concretely operating.[7] It is, I believe, the second alternative that has to be envisaged if we are to determine norms in historicity.

Now Aristotle defined a nature as an immanent principle of movement and of rest.[8] In man such a principle is the human spirit as raising and answering questions. As raising questions, it is an immanent principle of movement. As answering questions and doing so satisfactorily, it is an immanent principle of rest.

Specifically, questions are of three basic kinds: questions for intelligence, questions for reflection, questions for deliberation. In the first kind the immanent principle of movement is human intelligence. It thrusts us above the spontaneous flow of sensible presentations, images, feelings, conations, movements, and it does so by the wonder variously formulated by asking why, or how, or what for. With luck, either at once or eventually, there will follow on the question the satis-

6 Leo Strauss, *Natural Right and History* (Chicago: University of Chicago Press, 1953), 90.
7 Cf. Eric Voegelin, 'Reason: The Classic Experience,' *The Southern Review*, 10 (1974), 237–64.
8 Aristotle, *Physics*, II, 1, 195b 21–2.

faction of having an insight or indeed a series of relevant insights. With the satisfactory answer the principle of movement becomes a principle of rest.

Still, intellectual satisfaction, however welcome, is not all that the human spirit seeks. Beyond satisfaction it is concerned with content and so the attainment of insight leads to the formulation of its content. We express a surmise, suggest a possibility, propose a project. But our surmise may awaken surprise, our suggested possibility give rise to doubts, our project meet with criticism. In this fashion intelligence gives way to reflection. The second type of question has emerged. As intelligence thrust us beyond the flow of sensitive spontaneity, so now reflection thrust us beyond the more elementary concerns of both sense and intelligence. The formulated insight is greeted with such further and different questions as, Is that so? Are you sure? There is a demand for sufficient reason or sufficient evidence; and what is sufficient is nothing less than an unconditioned, though a virtually unconditioned (such as a syllogistic conclusion) will do.[9]

It remains that the successful negotiation of questions for intelligence and questions for reflection is not enough. They do justice to sensitive presentations and representations. But they are strangely dissociated from the feelings that constitute the mass and momentum of our lives. Knowing a world mediated by meaning is only a prelude to man's dealing with nature, to his interpersonal living and working with others, to his existential becoming what he is to make of himself by his own choices and deeds. So there emerge questions for deliberation. Gradually they reveal their scope in their practical, interpersonal, and existential dimensions. Slowly they mount the ladder of burgeoning morality. Asking what's in it for me gives way to asking what's in it for us. And both of these queries become tempered with the more searching, the wrenching question, Is it really worthwhile?

It is a searching question. The mere fact that we ask it points to a distinction between feelings that are self-regarding and feelings that are disinterested. Self-regarding feelings are pleasures and pains, desires and fears. But disinterested feelings recognize excellence: the vital value of health and strength; the communal value of a successfully functioning social order; the cultural value proclaimed as a life to be sustained not by bread alone but also by the word; the personal appro-

9 See *Insight*, chap. 10 [see 1.VII.2–4 in this reader].

priation of these values by individuals; their historical extension in progress; deviation from them in decline; and their recovery by self-sacrificing love.[10]

I have called the question not only searching but also wrenching. Feelings reveal values to us. They dispose us to commitment. But they do not bring commitment about. For commitment is a personal act, a free and responsible act, a very open-eyed act in which we would settle what we are to become. It is open-eyed in the sense that it is consciously a decision about future decisions, aware that the best of plans cannot control the future, even aware that one's present commitment however firm cannot suspend the freedom that will be exercised in its future execution.

Yet all questioning heads into the unknown and all answering contributes to what we are to do. When I ask why or how or what for, I intend intelligibility, but the question would be otiose if already I knew what the intelligibility in question was. When I ask whether this or that is really so, I intend the true and the real, but as yet I do not know what is true or what will be truly meant. When I ask whether this or that project or undertaking really is worthwhile, I intend the good, but as yet I do not know what would be good and in that sense worthwhile.

Questioning heads into the unknown, yet answering has to satisfy the criterion set by the question itself. Otherwise the question returns in the same or in another form. Unless insight hits the bull's-eye, the question for intelligence returns. How about this? How does that fit in? A self-correcting process of learning has begun, and it continues until a complementary and qualifying set of insights have stilled the flow of further relevant questions for intelligence. In like manner questions for reflection require not just evidence but sufficient evidence; until it is forthcoming, we remain in doubt; and once it is had, doubting becomes unreasonable. Finally questions for deliberation have their criterion in what we no longer name consciousness but conscience. The nagging conscience is the recurrence of the original question that has not been met. The good conscience is the peace of mind that confirms the choice of something truly worthwhile.

I have been speaking of nature as a principle of movement and rest, but I have come up with many such principles and so, it would seem,

10 *Insight*, 232–67, 650–6, 718–25, 740–50 [see 1.V, 1.XIV.2, and 1.XVI.3 in this reader].

with many natures. There are different questions: for intelligence, for reflection, for deliberation. Each is a principle of movement. Each also is an immanent norm, a criterion, and thereby a principle of rest once the movement is complete.

It remains that the many form a series, each in turn taking over where its predecessor left off. What is complete under the aspect of intelligibility, is not yet complete under the aspect of factual truth; and what is complete under the aspect of factual truth, has not yet broached the question of the good.[11] Further, if what the several principles attain are only aspects of something richer and fuller, must not the several principles themselves be but aspects of a deeper and more comprehensive principle? And is not that deeper and more comprehensive principle itself a nature, at once a principle of movement and rest, a tidal movement that begins before consciousness, unfolds through sensitivity, intelligence, rational reflection, responsible deliberation, only to find its rest beyond all of these? I think so.[12]

The point beyond is being-in-love, a dynamic state that sublates all that goes before, a principle of movement at once purgative and illuminative, and a principle of rest in which union is fulfilled.

The whole movement is an ongoing process of self-transcendence. There is the not yet conscious self of the dream state. There is the awakened self aware of its environment, exerting its capacities, meeting its needs. There is the intelligent self, serializing and extrapolating and generalizing until by thought it has moved out of the environment of an animal and towards a universe of being. There is the reasonable self, discerning fact from fiction, history from legend, astronomy from astrology, chemistry from alchemy, science from magic, philosophy from myth. There is the moral self, advancing from individual satisfactions to group interests and, beyond these, to the overarching, unrelenting question, What would be really worthwhile?

Yet this great question commonly is more promise than fulfilment, more the fertile ground of an uneasy conscience than the vitality and vigor of achievement. For self-transcendence reaches its term not in righteousness but in love and, when we fall in love, then life begins

---

11 On the human good, see *Method in Theology*, chap. 2 [see 3.II in this reader].
12 On horizontal and vertical finality, see *Collection*, 19–23, 81–91 [see 1.XII.1 on finality and 1.XV.1 on the immanent source of transcendence in this reader]; also Aristotle, *Nicomachean Ethics*, X, 7, 1177a 12–18.

anew. A new principle takes over and, as long as it lasts, we are lifted above ourselves and carried along as parts within an ever more intimate yet ever more liberating dynamic whole.

Such is the love of husband and wife, parents and children. Such again, less conspicuously but no less seriously, is the loyalty constitutive of civil community, where individual advantage yields to the advantage of the group, and individual safety may be sacrificed to the safety of the group. Such finally is God's gift of his own love flooding our hearts through the Holy Spirit he has given us (Rom. 5, 5). For it was by that divine gift that St Paul could proclaim his conviction that '... there is nothing in death or life, in the realm of spirits or superhuman powers, in the world as it is or the world as it shall be, in the forces of the universe, in heights or depths – nothing in all creation that can separate us from the love of God in Christ Jesus our Lord' (Rom. 8: 38–39).

3 The Dialectic of History

I have said that people are responsible individually for the lives they lead and collectively for the world in which they live them. Now the normative source of meaning, of itself, reveals no more than individual responsibility. Only inasmuch as the immanent source becomes revealed in its effects, in the functioning order of society, in cultural vitality and achievement, in the unfolding of human history, does the manifold of isolated responsibilities coalesce into a single object that can gain collective attention.

Further, the normative source of meaning is not the only source, for the norms can be violated. Besides intelligence, there is obtuseness; besides truth there is falsity; besides what is worthwhile, there is what is worthless; besides love there is hatred. So from the total source of meaning we may have to anticipate not only social order but also disorder, not only cultural vitality and achievement but also lassitude and deterioration, not an ongoing and uninterrupted sequence of developments but rather a dialectic of radically opposed tendencies.

It remains that in such a dialectic one finds 'writ large' the very issues that individuals have to deal with in their own minds and hearts. But what before could be dismissed as, in each case, merely an infinitesimal in the total fabric of social and cultural history, now has taken on the dimensions of collective triumph or disaster. Indeed, in the dialectic there is to be discerned the experimental verification or refutation of the validity of a people's way of life, even though it is an experiment devised and conducted not by human choice but by history itself.

Finally, it is in the dialectic of history that one finds the link between natural right and historical mindedness. The source of natural right lies in the norms immanent in human intelligence, human judgment, human evaluation, human affectivity. The vindication of natural right lies in the dialectic of history and awesomely indeed in the experiment of history. Let us set forth briefly its elements under six headings.

First, human meaning develops in human collaboration. There is the expansion of technical meanings as human ingenuity advances from the spears of hunters and the nets of fishers to the industrial complexes of the twentieth century. There is the expansion of social meanings in the evolution of domestic, economic, and political arrangements. There is the expansion of cultural meanings as people reflect on their work, their interpersonal relationships, and the meaning of human life.

Secondly, such expansions occur on a succession of plateaus. The basic forward thrust has to do with doing, and it runs from primitive fruit gatherers to the wealth and power of the ancient high civilizations of Egypt, Mesopotamia, and other lands. Development then is mainly of practical intelligence, and its style is the spontaneous accumulation of insights into the ways of nature and the affairs of men. There also is awareness of the cosmos, of reality being more than nature and man, but this awareness has little more than symbolic expression in the compact style of undifferentiated consciousness.

An intermediate forward thrust has to do mainly with speech. Poets and orators, prophets and wise men, bring about a development of language and a specialization of attention that prepare the way for sophists and philosophers, mathematicians and scientists. There occurs a differentiation of consciousness, as writing makes language an object for the eye as well as the ear; grammarians organize the inflections of words and analyze the construction of sentences; orators learn and teach the art of persuasion; logicians go behind sentences to propositions and behind persuasion to proofs; and philosophers exploit this second-level use of language to the point where they develop technical terms for speaking compendiously about anything that can be spoken about; while the more modest mathematicians confine their technical utterances to relations of identity or equivalence between individuals and sets; and similarly the scientists have their several specialized languages for each of their various fields.

On a third plateau attention shifts beyond developments in doing and in speaking to developments generally. Its central concern is with human understanding where developments originate, with the methods in natural science and in critical history which chart the course of discovery, and more fundamentally with the generalized empirical method that underpins both scientific and historical method to supply philosophy with a basic cognitional theory, an epistemology, and by way of a corollary with a metaphysics of proportionate being.

On this plateau logic loses its key position to become but a modest part within method; and logical concern – with truth, with necessity, with demonstration, with universality – enjoys no more than marginal significance. Science and history become ongoing processes, asserting not necessity but verifiable possibility, claiming not certitude but probability. Where science, as conceived on the second plateau, ambitioned permanent validity but remained content with abstract universality, science and history on the third plateau offer no more than the best available opinion of the time, yet by sundry stratagems and devices endeavor to approximate ever more accurately to the manifold details and nuances of the concrete.

These differences in plateau are not without significance for the very notion of a dialectic of history. The notion of fate or destiny or again of divine providence pertains to the first plateau. It receives a more detailed formulation on the second plateau when an Augustine contrasts the city of God with the earthly city, or when a Hegel or a Marx set forth their idealistic or materialistic systems on what history has been or is to be. A reversal towards the style of the first plateau may be suspected in Spengler's biological analogy, while a preparation for the style of the third plateau may be discerned in Toynbee's *A Study of History*. For that study can be viewed, not as an exercise in empirical method, but as the prolegomena to such an exercise, as a formulation of ideal types that would stand to broad historical investigations as mathematics stands to physics.[13]

In any case the dialectic of history, as we are conceiving it, has its origin in the tensions of adult human consciousness, its unfolding in

---

13 *Method in Theology*, 228 [1.VI in this reader].

the actual course of events, its significance in the radical analysis it provides, its practical utility in the invitation it will present to collective consciousness to understand and repudiate the waywardness of its past and to enlighten its future with the intelligence, the reasonableness, the responsibility, the love demanded by natural right.

Our third topic is the ideal proper to the third plateau. Already in the eighteenth century it was anticipated in terms of enlightenment and emancipation. But then inevitably enough enlightenment was conceived in the well-worn concepts and techniques of the second plateau; and the notion of emancipation was, not a critique of tradition, but rather the project of replacing traditional backwardness by the rule of pure reason.

Subsequent centuries have brought forth the antitheses to the eighteenth-century thesis. The unique geometry of Euclid has yielded to the Riemannian manifold. Newtonian science has been pushed around by Maxwell, Einstein, Heisenberg to modify not merely physics but the very notion of modern science. Concomitant with this transformation has been the even more radical transformation in human studies. Man is to be known not only in his nature but also in his historicity, not only philosophically but also historically, not only abstractly but also concretely.

Such is the context within which we have to conceive enlightenment and emancipation, not indeed as if they were novelties for they have been known all along, but in the specific manner appropriate to what I have named the third plateau. As always enlightenment is a matter of the ancient precept, Know thyself. But in the contemporary context it aims to be such self-awareness, such self-understanding, such self-knowledge, as to grasp the similarities and the differences of common sense, science, and history, to grasp the foundations of these three in interiority which also founds natural right and, beyond all knowledge of knowledge, to give also knowledge of affectivity in its threefold manifestation of love in the family, loyalty in the community, and faith in God.

Again, as always, emancipation has its root in self-transcendence. But in the contemporary context it is such self-transcendence as includes an intellectual, a moral, and an affective conversion. As intellectual, this conversion draws a sharp distinction between the world of immediacy and the world mediated by meaning, between the criteria appropriate to operations in the former and, on the other hand, the criteria appropriate to operations in the latter.[14] Next, as moral, it acknowledges a distinction between satisfactions and values, and it is committed to values even where they conflict with satisfactions. Finally, as affective, it is commitment to love in the home, loyalty in the community, faith in the destiny of man.

We come to our fourth topic. It is the critique of our historicity, of what our past has made us. It will be an ongoing task, for the past is ever the present slipping away from us. It will be an empirical task but one within the orbit of human studies and so concerned with the operative meanings constitutive of our social arrangements and cultural intercourse. Accordingly, it will be a matter of the research that assembles the data, the interpretation that grasps their significance, the history that narrates what has been going forward.[15] It remains that all empirical inquiry that reaches scientific status proceeds within a heuristic structure. Just as mathematics provides the theoretical underpinning of the exact sciences, so there is a generalized empirical method or, if you prefer, a transcendental method that performs a similar role in human studies.[16] It sets forth (1) general critical principles, (2) a basic division of the materials, and (3) categories of analysis. On each of these something must be said.

The general critical principles are dialectical.[17] We have conceived emancipation on the third plateau to consist in a threefold conversion, intellectual, moral, and affective. But we do not postulate that all investigators will be emancipated. If some have been through the threefold conversion, others will have experienced only two, others only one, and some none at all. Hence we must be prepared for the fact that our researchers, our interpreters, our historians may exhibit an eightfold diversity of results, where the diversity does not arise from the data but rather from the horizon, the mind-set, the blik, of those conducting the investigation.

A basic division of the materials is provided by the three plateaus already described. There will be meanings such as prove operative in men of action; further meanings that involve a familiarity with logical techniques; and a still further plateau of meanings that attain their

---

14 *Insight*, 410–15 [1.XI.1 in this reader].
15 *Method in Theology*, chaps. 6–9.
16 Ibid., chap. 1 [see 3.I in this reader].
17 Ibid., chap. 10 [see 3.VII in this reader].

proper significance and status within a methodical approach that has acknowledged its underpinnings in an intentionality analysis. It is to be noted, of course, that all three have their appropriate mode of development, and that their main developments differ chronologically; still, the proper locus of the distinction between the plateaus is not time but meaning.

Categories of analysis, finally, are differentiations of the historian's concern with 'what was going forward.' Now what was going forward may be either (1) development or (2) the handing on of development and each of these may be (3) complete or (4) incomplete. Development may be described, if a spatial metaphor is permitted, as 'from below upwards': it begins from experience, is enriched by full understanding, is accepted by sound judgment, is directed not to satisfactions but to values, and the priority of values is comprehensive, not just of some but of all, to reveal affective conversion as well as moral and intellectual. But development is incomplete when it does not go the whole way upwards: it accepts some values but its evaluations are partial; or it is not concerned with values at all but only with satisfactions; or its understanding may be adequate but its factual judgments faulty; or finally its understanding may be more a compromise than a sound contribution.

Again, the handing on of development may be complete or incomplete. But it works from above downwards: it begins in the affectivity of the infant, the child, the son, the pupil, the follower. On affectivity rests the apprehension of values. On the apprehension of values rests belief. On belief follows the growth in understanding of one who has found a genuine teacher and has been initiated into the study of the masters of the past. Then to confirm one's growth in understanding comes experience made mature and perceptive by one's developed understanding. With experiential confirmation the inverse process may set in. One now is on one's own. One can appropriate all that one has learnt by proceeding as does the original thinker who moved from experience to understanding, to sound judgment, to generous evaluation, to commitment in love, loyalty, faith.

It remains that the process of handing on can be incomplete. There occur socialization, acculturation, education, but education fails to come to life. Or the teacher may at least be a believer. He can transmit enthusiasm. He can teach the accepted formulations. He can persuade. But he never really understood and he is not capable of giving others the understanding that he himself lacks. Then it will be only by accident that his pupils come to appropriate what was sound in their tradition, and it is only by such accidents, or divine graces, that a tradition that has decayed can be renewed.

Our fifth observation has to do with the ambiguity of completeness that arises when first-plateau minds live in a second-plateau context of meaning, or when first- and second-plateau minds find themselves in a third-plateau context. On the first plateau what has meaning is action; lack of completeness is lack of action; and so when the first-plateau mind examines a second- or third-plateau context, he diagnoses a lack of action, and insists on activism as the only meaningful course. On the second plateau there is the further range of meanings accessible to those familiar with classical culture. Second-plateau minds have no doubt that activists are just barbarians, but they criticize a third-plateau context for its neglect of Aristotle or Hegel.

However, such remarks as the foregoing should not be taken to imply that plateaus are uniform. For instance, the third plateau, characterized by method, also is marked by a whole series of methodological blocks. Linguistic analysts and Heideggerian pre-Socratics would confine philosophy to ordinary language. Offspring of the Enlightenment restrict knowledge to the exact sciences. Critical historians may praise human studies provided they are value-free. Humanists are open to values generally yet draw the line at such self-transcendence as is open to God.

Sixthly and finally, beyond dialectic there is dialogue. Dialectic describes concrete process in which intelligence and obtuseness, reasonableness and silliness, responsibility and sin, love and hatred commingle and conflict. But the very people that investigate the dialectic of history also are part of that dialectic and even in their investigating represent its contradictories. To their work too the dialectic is to be applied.

But it can be more helpful, especially when oppositions are less radical, for the investigators to move beyond dialectic to dialogue, to transpose issues from a conflict of statements to an encounter of persons. For every person is an embodiment of natural right. Every person can reveal to any other his natural propensity to seek understanding, to judge reasonably, to evaluate fairly, to be open to friendship. While the dialectic of history coldly relates our conflicts, dialogue adds the principle that prompts us to cure them, the natural right that is the inmost core of our being.

Related selections: 1.I.1 on the crisis of self-knowledge; 1.VIII on self-affirmation of the knower; 3.I.2–3 on the four levels of consciousness and transcendental precepts; 4.VII on degrees of self-transcendence; 2.IV on the constitutive
function of meaning, and 3.III on realms of meaning; 4.III.2 on the second
enlightenment; 2.VIII on classicist and modern culture, and 4.I on static and
dynamic viewpoints; 3.VII.2 on the three conversions; 1.V.2 on dialectic, and
3.VII.4 on the structure of dialectical method; 3.VI.2–3 on historical method; 4.V
on praxis; 4.II on dialectic of authority.

VII

The Degrees of
Self-Transcendence

This summary account of five successive degrees of self-transcendence is offered by Lonergan in a 1980 article, 'A Post-Hegelian Philosophy of Religion.' Throughout his writings Lonergan issues the invitation he first extended to his readers in the prefaces and introduction to *Insight* – to appropriate, to make their own, the normative dynamism of their own concrete subjectivity. In the original 1954 preface to *Insight* Lonergan wrote: 'For it is the paradox of man that what he is by nature is so much less than what he can become; and it is the tragedy of man that the truth, which portrays him as actually he is, can descend like an iron curtain to frustrate what he would and might be.'[1] Lonergan proposed self-appropriation then as the strategy whereby the stubborn facts about man are to be outflanked and tragedy averted. But the invitation to self-appropriation in *Insight* was primarily to self-possession in the second, third, and fourth degrees of one's self-transcendence. That invitation was steadily broadened after *Insight* until eventually it became an invitation to full self-possession in the fifth degree of one's self-transcendence and to the fulfillment of the thrust of self-transcendence in unrestricted being-in-love.

This extract is taken from *A Third Collection*, 208.

The *first* is the emergence of consciousness in the fragmentary form of the dream, where human substance yields place to the human subject. The *second* is waking when our senses and feelings come to life, where our memories recall pleasures and our imaginations anticipate fears, but our vitality envisages courses of action. The *third* is inquiry which

---

1 'The Original Preface of *Insight*,' 3.

enables us to move out of the mere habitat of an animal and into our
human world of relatives, friends, acquaintances, associates, projects,
accomplishments, ambitions, fears. The *fourth* is the discovery of a
truth, which is not the idle repetition of a 'good look' but the grasp in a
manifold of data of the sufficiency of the evidence for our affirmation
or negation. The *fifth* is the successive negotiation of the stages of
morality and/or identity till we reach the point where we discover that
it is up to ourselves to decide for ourselves what we are to make of
ourselves, where we decisively meet the challenge of that discovery,
where we set ourselves apart from the drifters. For drifters have not
yet found themselves. They have not yet found their own deed and so
are content to do what everyone else is doing. They have not yet found
a will of their own, and so they are content to choose what everyone
else is choosing. They have not yet developed minds of their own, and
so they are content to think and say what everyone else is thinking and
saying. And everyone else, it happens, can be doing and choosing and
thinking and saying what others are doing and choosing and thinking
and saying.

But this fifth stage in self-transcendence becomes a successful way of
life only when we really are pulled out of ourselves as, for example,
when we fall in love, whether our love be the domestic love that unites
husband and wife and children, or the love of our fellows whose well-
being we promote and defend, or the love of God above all in whom
we love our neighbor as ourselves.

Related selections: 2.VII on neglect of the subject; 1.I.1 on the program of
Insight; 1.VIII on self-affirmation of the knower; 3.I on transcendental method;
1.IX on the notion of being; 1.XII.1 on finality; 1.XIV.2 on the problem of liberation; 4.VI.3 on enlightenment and emancipation; 1.XVII on self-appropriation.

Chronology

Date	Biographical Information
1904	17 December: Lonergan's birth in Buckingham, Quebec
1918–22	Student at Loyola College, Montreal
1922	29 July: enters the Jesuit novitiate at Guelph, Ontario
1922–6	Spiritual training and study of classics at Guelph
1926–9	Philosophical studies at Heythrop College, England; pursuit of degree at the University of London
1930	Awarded BA in Greek, Latin, French, and mathematics by the University of London
1930–3	Teaching and other duties at Loyola College, Montreal
1933–7	Theological studies at the Gregorian University, Rome
1936	25 July: ordination to the priesthood in Rome
1937–8	Tertianship in Amiens, France
1938–40	Doctoral studies at the Gregorian University, Rome
1940–6	Professor of Theology at the Collège de l'Immaculée Conception, Montreal
1941–2	Publication of doctoral dissertation in *Theological Studies*
1944	Writes Initial version of 'An Essay in Circulation Analysis'
1945	Teaches course entitled 'Thought and Reality,' Thomas More Institute, Montreal
1946–9	Publication of 'The Concept of *Verbum* in the Writings of St Thomas Aquinas' in five articles in *Theological Studies*
1947–53	Professor of Theology, Regis College, Toronto
1949–53	Preparation of the manuscript of *Insight: A Study of Human Understanding*
1953–65	Professor of Theology at the Gregorian University, Rome

1957	Publication of *Insight*; lectures on existentialism and lectures on mathematical logic at Boston College
1958	Lectures on *Insight* at Saint Mary's University, Halifax
1959	Lectures on the philosophy of education at Xavier University, Cincinnati
1960	Publication of *De Verbo Incarnato*
1961	Publication of *De Deo Trino*
1965	Returns to Toronto on sabbatical; major surgery for cancer
1965–75	Research professor at Regis College, Toronto
1965–71	Preparation of *Method in Theology*
1971–2	Stillman Professor, Harvard University
1971	Holds institute on *Method in Theology*, Milltown Park, Dublin
1972	Publication of *Method in Theology*
1975–83	Visiting Distinguished Professor of Theology at Boston College; resumption of work on economics
1983	Retirement to the Jesuit infirmary in Pickering, Ontario
1984	26 November: death of Lonergan in Pickering

Bibliography

CWL refers to Collected Works of Bernard Lonergan. Where appropriate the actual or anticipated volume numbers in the series are indicated in parentheses.

Works by Lonergan

'Analytic Concept of History.' *Method: Journal of Lonergan Studies* 11:1 (1993) 1–35 (CWL 21).

'Bernard Lonergan Responds.' In *Foundations of Theology: Papers from the International Lonergan Congress, 1970*. Ed. Philip McShane, 223–34. Notre Dame: Notre Dame University Press, 1972.

Caring about Meaning: Patterns in the Life of Bernard Lonergan. Ed. P. Lambert, C. Tansey, and C. Going. Montreal: Thomas More Institute, 1982.

Collection. 2nd ed. Ed. Frederick E. Crowe and Robert M. Doran. Toronto: University of Toronto Press, 1988 (CWL 4).

De Constitutione Christi Ontologica et Psychologica. Rome: Gregorian University Press, 1956 (CWL 7).

De Deo trino. Vol. 1: *Pars dogmatica*; vol. 2: *Pars systematica* (2nd ed.), (3rd ed.). Rome: Gregorian University Press, 1964 (CWL 9).

De Verbo incarnato. 3rd ed. Rome: Gregorian University Press, 1964 (CWL 8).

Doctrinal Pluralism. Milwaukee: Marquette University Press, 1971.

Grace and Freedom: Operative Grace in the Thought of St. Thomas Aquinas. Ed. J. Patout Burns. London: Darton, Longman & Todd, 1974 (CWL 1).

'The *Gratia Operans* Dissertation: Preface and Introduction.' *Method: Journal of Lonergan Studies* 3:2 (1985) 9–46.

Insight: A Study of Human Understanding. 5th ed. Ed. Frederick E. Crowe and Robert M. Doran. Toronto: University of Toronto Press, 1992 (CWL 3).

Lecturas historiográficas: Antología de textos de Bernard Lonergan. Trans. X. Cacho. Mexico City: Universidad Iberoamericana, 1985.

'Merging Horizons: System, Common Sense, Scholarship.' *Cultural Hermeneutics* 1 (1973) 87–99.

Method in Theology. London: Darton, Longman & Todd, 1972 (CWL 12).

'The Original Preface of *Insight.*' *Method: Journal of Lonergan Studies* 3:1 (1985) 3–7 (CWL 21).

'*Pantôn Anakephalaiôsis* [The Restoration of All Things].' *Method: Journal of Lonergan Studies* 9:2 (1991) 134–72.

Philosophical and Theological Papers, 1958–1964. Ed. Robert C. Croken, Frederick E. Crowe, and Robert M. Doran. Toronto: University of Toronto Press, 1996 (CWL 6).

'Philosophy and the Religious Phenomenon.' *Method: Journal of Lonergan Studies* 12:2 (1994) 121–46.

Philosophy of God, and Theology: The Relationship between Philosophy of God and the Functional Specialty, Systematics. London: Darton, Longman & Todd, 1973.

Pour une méthodologie philosophique: Ecrits philosophiques choisis. Trans. B. Allard, E. Dumas, and P. Lambert. Montreal: Editions Bellarmin, 1991.

'Questionnaire on Philosophy.' *Method: Journal of Lonergan Studies* 2:2 (1984) 1–35 (CWL 14).

'Reality, Myth, Symbol.' In *Myth, Symbol, and Reality.* Ed. Alan M. Olson, 31–37. Notre Dame: University of Notre Dame Press, 1980.

A Second Collection: Papers by Bernard J.F. Lonergan. 2nd ed. Ed. William F.J. Ryan and Bernard J. Tyrrell. Toronto: University of Toronto Press, 1996 (CWL 11).

Theologie im Pluralismus heutiger Kulturen. Ed. Giovanni Sala. Freiburg: Herder, 1975.

A Third Collection: Papers by Bernard J.F. Lonergan, S.J. Ed. Frederick E. Crowe. New York: Paulist, 1985 (CWL 13).

Topics in Education: The Cincinnati Lectures of 1959 on the Philosophy of Education. Ed. Robert M. Doran and Frederick E. Crowe. Toronto: University of Toronto Press, 1993 (CWL 10).

Understanding and Being: The Halifax Lectures on Insight. 2nd ed. Ed. Elizabeth A. Morelli, Mark D. Morelli, Frederick E. Crowe, Robert M. Doran, Thomas V. Daly. Toronto: University of Toronto Press, 1990 (CWL 5).

Verbum: Word and Idea in Aquinas. Ed. David B. Burrell. Notre Dame: University of Notre Dame Press, 1967 (CWL 2).

The Way to Nicea: The Dialectical Development of Trinitarian Theology. London: Darton, Longman & Todd, 1976 (CWL 9).

Selected Other Works

Barden, G. *After Principles.* Notre Dame, IN: University of Notre Dame Press, 1990.

Braio. F. *Lonergan's Retrieval of the Notion of Human Being: Clarifications of and Reflections on the Argument of Insight*. Lanham, MD: University Press of America, 1988.

Byrne, P., Hefling, C., Morelli, M., eds. *Method: Journal of Lonergan Studies* (1983–).

Carmody, J. *Ecology and Religion: Toward a New Christian Theology of Nature*. New York: Paulist Press, 1983.

Conn. W. E. *Conscience: Development and Self-Transcendence*. Birmingham, AL: Religious Education Press, 1981.

Corcoran, P., ed. *Looking at Lonergan's Method*. Dublin: The Talbot Press, 1975.

Crowe, F.E. *Appropriating the Lonergan Idea*. Ed. Michael Vertin. Washington, DC: Catholic University of America Press, 1989.

– *Lonergan*. Collegeville, MN: Liturgical Press, 1992.

– *The Lonergan Enterprise*. Cambridge, MA: Cowley Publications, 1980.

– *Method in Theology: An Organon for Our Time*. Milwaukee, WI: Marquette University Press, 1980.

– *Old Things and New: A Strategy for Education*. Atlanta, GA: Scholars Press, 1985.

– ed. *Spirit as Inquiry: Studies in Honor of Bernard Lonergan*. Chicago: St Xavier College, 1964.

– *Three Thomist Studies*. Atlanta, GA: Scholars Press, 1996.

Crysdale, C., ed. *Lonergan and Feminism*. Toronto: University of Toronto Press, 1994.

Doran, R.M. *Psychic Conversion and Theological Foundations: Toward a Reorientation of the Human Sciences*. Chico, CA: Scholars Press, 1981.

– *Subject and Psyche: Ricoeur, Jung and the Search for Foundations*. Washington, DC: University Press of America, 1977.

– *Theology and the Dialectics of History*. Toronto: University of Toronto Press, 1990.

Dunne, T. *Lonergan and Spirituality: Towards a Spiritual Integration*. Chicago: Loyola University Press, 1985.

Eidle, W. R. *The Self-Appropriation of Interiority: A Foundation for Psychology*. New York: Lang, 1990.

Fallon, T.P., and Riley, P.B., eds. *Religion and Culture: Essays in Honor of Bernard Lonergan, S.J.* Albany, NY: SUNY Press, 1987.

– eds. *Religion in Context: Recent Studies in Lonergan*. Lanham, MD: University Press of America, 1988.

Farrell. T.J., and Soukup, P.A., eds. *Communication and Lonergan: Common Ground for Forging the New Age*. Kansas City, MO: Sheed and Ward, 1993.

Flanagan, J. *The Quest for Self-Knowledge*. Toronto: University of Toronto Press, 1996.

Fluri, P. *Einsicht in Insight: Bernard J.F. Lonergans kritische-realistische Wissenschafts- und Erkenntnistheorie*. Frankfurt am Main: Haag and Herchen, 1988.

Granfield, D. *Heightened Consciousness: The Mystical Difference*. New York:
Paulist Press, 1991.
- *The Inner Experience of Law: A Jurisprudence of Subjectivity*. Washington, DC:
Catholic University Press of America, 1989.
Gregson, V. *Lonergan, Spirituality, and the Meeting of Religions*. Lanham, MD:
University Press of America, 1985.
- ed. *The Desires of the Human Heart: An Introduction to the Theology of Bernard
Lonergan*. New York: Paulist Press, 1988.
Haught, J. *Religion and Self-Acceptance: A Study of the Relationship between Belief
in God and the Desire to Know*. Washington, DC: University Press of America,
1980.
Hefling, C. *Why Doctrines?* Cambridge, MA: Cowley Publications, 1984.
Helminiak, D.A. *Spiritual Development: An Interdisciplinary Study*. Chicago:
Loyola University Press, 1987.
Kelly, J. *A Philosophy of Communication*. London: Centre for the Study of Com-
munication and Culture, 1981.
LaCentra, W. *The Authentic Self: Toward a Philosophy of Personality*. New York:
Lang, 1988.
Lamb, M.L. *History, Method, and Theology: A Dialectical Comparison of Wilhelm
Dilthey's Critique of Historical Reason and Bernard Lonergan's Meta-
Methodology*. Missoula, MT: Scholars Press, 1978.
- *Solidarity with Victims: Toward a Theology of Social Transformation*. New York:
Crossroad, 1982.
- ed. *Creativity and Method: Essays in Honor of Bernard Lonergan, S.J.* Milwau-
kee: Marquette University Press, 1981.
Lawrence, F., ed. *Lonergan Workshop* (1978–).
- ed. *The Beginning and the Beyond: Papers from the Gadamer and Voegelin
Conferences*. Chico, CA: Scholars Press, 1984.
Liddy, R. *Transforming Light: Intellectual Conversion in the Early Lonergan*.
Collegeville, MN: Liturgical Press, 1993.
Lonergan Research Institute. *Lonergan Studies Newsletter*. Toronto, 1980–.
Lonergan Review: A Multidisciplinary Journal (1992–).
McCarthy, M.H. *The Crisis of Philosophy*. Albany, NY: SUNY Press, 1989.
McEvenue, S.E., and Meyer, B.F., eds. *Lonergan's Hermeneutics: Its Development
and Application*. Washington, DC: Catholic University of America Press,
1989.
McShane, P., ed. *Foundations of Theology: Papers from the International Lonergan
Congress 1970*. Notre Dame, IN: University of Notre Dame Press, 1971.
- ed. *Language, Truth and Meaning: Papers from the International Lonergan
Congress 1970*. Notre Dame, IN: University of Notre Dame Press, 1972.
- *Lonergan's Challenge to the University and the Economy*. Washington, DC:
University Press of America, 1980.

– *Randomness, Statistics and Emergence*. Notre Dame, IN: University of Notre Dame Press, 1970.
– ed. *Searching for Cultural Foundations*. Lanham, MD: University Press of America, 1988.
– *The Shaping of the Foundations: Being at Home in the Transcendental Method*. Washington, DC: University Press of America, 1977.
– *Wealth of Self and Wealth of Nations: Self-Axis of the Great Ascent*. Hicksville, NY: Exposition Press, 1975.
Marsh, J. *Critique, Action, and Liberation*. Albany, NY: SUNY Press, 1995.
Mascall, E.L. *Nature and Supernature*. London: Darton, Longman and Todd, 1976.
Matustik, M.J. *Mediation of Deconstruction: Bernard Lonergan's Method in Philosophy*. Lanham, MD: University Press of America, 1988.
Melchin, K.F. *History, Ethics, and Emergent Probability: Ethics, Society and History in the Work of Bernard Lonergan*. Lanham, MD: University Press of America, 1987.
Meyer, B.F. *Critical Realism and the New Testament*. Alison Park, PA: Pickwick Publications, 1989.
– *Reality and Illusion in New Testament Scholarship: A Primer in Critical Realist Hermeneutics*. Collegeville, MN: Liturgical Press, 1994.
Meynell, H. *An Introduction to the Philosophy of Bernard Lonergan*. Toronto: University of Toronto Press, 1991.
– *The Theology of Bernard Lonergan*. Atlanta, GA: Scholars Press, 1986.
Miller, J. *In the Throe of Wonder: Intimations of the Sacred in a Post-Modern World*. Albany: SUNY Press, 1992.
Morelli, E.A. *Anxiety: A Study of the Affectivity of Moral Consciousness*. Lanham, MD: University Press of America, 1985.
Morelli, M.D. *Philosophy's Place in Culture: A Model*. Lanham, MD: University Press of America, 1984.
O'Callaghan, M. *Unity in Theology: Lonergan's Framework for Theology in Its New Context*. Washington, DC: University Press of America, 1980.
Rende, M. *Lonergan on Conversion: Development of a Notion*. Lanham, MD: University Press of America, 1991.
Sala, G.B. *Das Apriori in der menschlichen Erkenntnis*. Meisenheim am Glan: Verlag Anton Hain, 1971.
– *Lonergan and Kant: Five Essays on Human Knowledge*. Toronto: University of Toronto Press, 1994.
Shute, M. *The Origin of Lonergan's Notion of the Dialectic of History: A Study of His Early Writings on History*. Lanham, MD: University Press of America, 1993.
Tracy, D. *The Achievement of Bernard Lonergan*. New York: Herder and Herder, 1970.

Tyrrell, B. *Bernard Lonergan's Philosophy of God*. Notre Dame, IN: University of
    Notre Dame Press, 1974.
Webb, E. *Philosophers of Consciousness: Polanyi, Lonergan, Voegelin, Ricoeur,
    Girard, Kierkegaard*. Seattle, WA: University of Washington Press, 1988.

Index

Aberration: of censorship, 117; in cognitional process, 203; of conduct, 310; religious, 476; of scientific and philosophical thought, 160, 306

Abstraction, 70–2, 206, 405; and alienation, 349–51; and art, 371; being as, 426; and eternal verities, 403; and good, 571; modes of, 85; realm of, 155; Scotist theory of, 243

Absurd, 15, 16, 147, 312, 435, 474, 479, 551, 555

Act(s): and content, 181–2; in human knowing, 381–6; of insight, 37–9, 42, 46–75; of meaning, 208–10, 219; sense and sensible in, 368–9; of understanding, unrestricted, 296–311. *See also* Operation

Action, 22, 105, 175, 205, 253–4, 311, 353, 430, 437–8, 457–9, 462, 592, 594; and affects, 326; courses of, 38–8, 114, 133–6; and decision, 276–8; individual and group, 496; and progress, 123, 569, 573

Activism, 594

Actuality, 276, 279–81, 315; of God, 297

Adaptation: biological, 251; and bureaucracy, 561; and intersubjec-

tivity, 148; of practical common sense, 126–7; of sensitivity, 127, 132–3, 267, 270, 309, 311; of theory to practice, 142; of theology, 415, 542; of transcendental method, 407

Advertence, 20, 118, 236, 260, 357, 451

Affectivity, 25, 113–14, 118–21, 127, 142, 250, 256, 260, 283, 326–7, 329, 366–7, 393, 398, 458, 464, 538, 556, 591–3

Affirmation, 168, 171, 187, 190, 192, 215, 218, 244–5, 268, 295

Aggiornamento, 408, 414, 418

Agnosticism, 301, 410, 474

Alienation, 16, 349–50, 390, 422, 434–5

Already-out-there-now-real, 160–1, 178, 223, 226–7, 242–5, 263, 268–9, 272; defined, 158–9

Altaner, B., 412

Altruism, 128–9

Analogy: argument from, 100–1; and historian, 508–10; psychological, 346; of sight, 526

Analysis, and synthesis, 345–9, 356

Anima, 119–21

Mechanist determinism, 3, 86, 146, 335, 528, 563

Meinecke, F., 516

Memory, 107–9, 111, 113, 157, 164, 364, 388, 395, 596; and cognitional process, 211, 269; and insight, 33, 37; and judgment, 157, 164, 173, 334; and psychological present, 496

Metaphysics, 223–38; dismissal of, 526; explicit, 230–5; logically rigorous, 405; of the soul, 403; three stages of, 229

Method: of Aristotelian and Thomist thought, 238; of Aristotle's *De Anima*, 403; of Aquinas, 32; basic, 35, 407, 450; classical, 77–81, 252–3; classical and statistical compared, 85–6; of common sense, 236, 242; critical, 306–7; dialectical, 222–45, 321, 529–30, 577; and discovery, 547; of eliminating mistaken beliefs, 336–9; empirical, 74, 86, 96, 165, 172, 194–5, 218, 279, 306, 578; of empiricism, 242–5; of ethics, 275; experimental, 577; foundations of, 406; function of, 547; general definition of, 21, 233, 416–17; generalized empirical, 590, 592; genetic, 248, 252–3; in German context, 13; and heuristic structures, 79, 452–3, 508–11; historical, 12, 508–11, 577, 590; of human mind, 21; of human sciences, 140–1; of *Insight*, 341; and intelligibility of the universe, 320–1; introspective, 403; and linguistic analysis, 13; and logic, 21, 217, 405, 547–9, 590; and manipulative procedure, 14; in metaphysics, 222–38, 306; and methodological blocks, 594; of natural sciences, 92, 236; and objectivity, 548; in philosophy, 225, 242; of praxis, 577–9; pre-liminary notion of, 446–7; of pure reason, 348; questions of, 341, 356; and recipe, 13–14, 547; scientific, 84, 103–4, 145, 242, 306–7, 342, 407, 416–17, 528, 590; of self-criticism, 45; statistical, 81–5; study of, 7; of study of the soul and of the subject, 424; and system, 548; and technique, 21; for theology, 2, 8, 12, 13, 23, 31, 406, 412, 453–4, 483–92, 532–4, 538, 549; transcendental, 22–3, 405–6, 407, 445–54, 469, 509, 511, 532, 534, 538, 548, 592; of universal doubt, 238–42

Methodologist, 219, 510, 532, 540; Lonergan as, 14; Plato as, 6

Methodology, 14, 21, 48–9, 86, 427

Mills, C. Wright, 529

Minkowski, H., 67

Miracles, 510–11

Modernism, 33

Moral idealism, 11, 457

Moral impotence, 22, 283–7

Mozart, W.A., 370

Music, 112, 343, 364, 369

Mystery, 311, 314, 326–7, 331, 422–3, 475, 478, 525

Mystical, 224, 254, 557; theology, 489

Myth: cognitional, 526; and consciousness, 303–4, 306, 333; and magic, 392–3; and mystery, 270, 327, 331; and philosophy, 382, 578, 587; political, 150; and religion, 526; and ritual, 556; and science, 389; totalitarian, 141–2, 144.

Naive realism, 522–3

Narrative, 415, 484, 499, 504

Natural right, 580–95

'Nature,' 77–9, 304, 537

Neural demand functions, 114–22

Neurosis, 140, 144, 282, 458, 496, 572

Newman, J.H., 5, 6, 563

Newton, I., 62, 65, 66, 80, 145, 192, 232, 244, 334, 345, 348, 356, 410, 495, 562, 591

Nietzsche, F., 421, 565

Nihilism, 144

Notion(s): active potencies, 480; of being, 198–209, 233, 304, 426, 431–2; defined, 205; of God, 295, 301, 304; of the grounded, 206; heuristic, 207, 230–2, 246, 247, 252, 537; of the intelligible, 206; mistaken, 267–8; of nature, 304; transcendental, 431, 450, 453–4, 464, 476, 486, 532; of value, 431–2, 459

Objectification: in art, 370–2; of conversion, 488; of horizon, 530; of method, 416; of orientation towards mystery, 477–8

Objectivity, 211–21, 224–6, 242–3, 264, 366, 422–3, 548; fruit of authentic subjectivity, 541; and immanence, 426–7; moral, 516

Obligation, 277–8

Obscurantism, 39, 45, 217, 294, 301–2, 304, 397, 450; total vs. partial, 294

Ontic, 352, 368, 417, 457, 463

Ontological argument, 296–8

Openness, 283, 331, 367, 379, 397, 458, 520, 560

Operations: attending, inquiring, reflecting, deliberating, 535; cognitional, 416–17; and cooperation, 461–2; deliberating, evaluating, deciding, acting, bringing about results, 433; deliberation, evaluation, decision, action, 434; deliberation, evaluation, responsible choice, 481; and development, 252, 537; logical and prelogical, 405, 447; and materially dynamic structures,

382, 535–6; and method, 405, 446–7; and rules, 59–63; sensation, perception, imagination, inquiry, insight, formulation, reflection, grasp of the unconditioned, and judgment, 192; sensitivity, intelligence, rational reflection, responsible deliberation, 587; and skills, 461; symbolic, 74–5. *See also* Experiencing, understanding, and judging

Operator(s), 22, 253, 260, 262, 270, 282, 292, 300, 307, 367, 462, 529

Ortega y Gasset, J., 34

'Other things being equal,' 89

Otto, Rudolf, 475

Parsons, Talcott, 529, 564

Pascal, B., 477, 579

Paul, St, 372, 373, 399, 417, 490, 534, 588

Perception, 74, 115, 365, 375, 430

Person(s), 320, 398, 449, 463, 479, 594; divine, 346–7

Phenomenology, 8, 36, 398, 435

Philologie, 583

Philoponus, John, 65

Philosophy: basis and expansion of, 226–7; Catholic, 400; classical vs. historical, 395, 400; conflict in, 225; and the historian, 509; and ideals of knowledge, 348–50; and liberation, 287–8, 378; modern, 243–4; of philosophies, 161, 313; 'philosophy of ...,' 376–7, 379; and the polymorphism of consciousness, 223–8, 312–13; and the subject, 421–4; task of, 224–5; and theology, 400; on third plateau of meaning, 590; three basic questions in, 440

Picture-thinking, 427–9

Plato, 6, 70, 126, 224, 231, 243, 391, 399, 467–8

bility, 479; inattention, stupidity, unreasonableness, irresponsibility, 451, 453; inattentive, slow-witted, silly, irresponsible, 541
Unconditioned: formally and virtually, 170–1, 473. *See also* Judgment
Understanding. *See* Insight

Value, 332, 449; aesthetic, 113; apprehensions of, 457, 477–8, 593; human, 330; intentional responses to, 477; judgments of, 456–60, 475, 516; and moral conversion, 523–4, 593; ontic and qualitative, 457, 463; originating and terminal, 462–3; possible object of choice, 317; transcendental concept of, 450; transcendental notion of, 431–3, 459; transvaluation of, 417, 475, 478, 533; vital, social, cultural, personal, and religious, 458, 477, 585–6
Verstehen, 513
Vico, G., 143, 397, 512
Viewpoint(s): higher, 57–61, 74–5, 294; potential totality of all, 270–4; spiral of, 111; static and dynamic, 545–9; succession of lower, 138–42; successive higher, 61–3, 247, 294, 537
Vincent of Lérins, 412
Violence, 15, 39, 125, 135, 221, 240, 313, 331, 479, 526–7, 540, 551, 555
Virtue, 129, 403, 408, 431–2, 436, 478,

538–9; and equity, 559; of tolerance, 141
Voluntarism, 529

Way(s): purgative, illuminative, unitive, 539; the way up and the way down, 593
'We,' 434
Weber, Max, 511, 514, 529
Weltanschauung, 438, 508
Whitehead, A.N., 347
'Why': primordial, 53
Will: act of, 276–9; dialectical attitude of, 321; good, 286–7, 310–11, 314, 318, 320, 331; and willingness and willing, 282–3
Winter, Gibson, 528–9
Withdrawal and return, 369, 468–9
Wolff, C., 348, 357, 359
Wonder, 22, 54, 98, 110, 191, 198, 201, 207, 342, 367, 377, 584
Wordsworth, W., 370
Work of art, 364, 370, 372
World: of immediacy, 388, 390, 521, 536, 552, 554, 591; mediated by meaning, 388–9, 521–2, 585, 591; mediated by meaning and motivated by values, 552–4
World process: properties of, 93–6
'Worthwhile': ultimate meaning of, 473

Zeno, 66–7, 216